Baltic States

written and researched by

Jonathan Bousfield

ROUGH
GUIDES

NEW YORK • LONDON • DELHI

www.roughguides.com

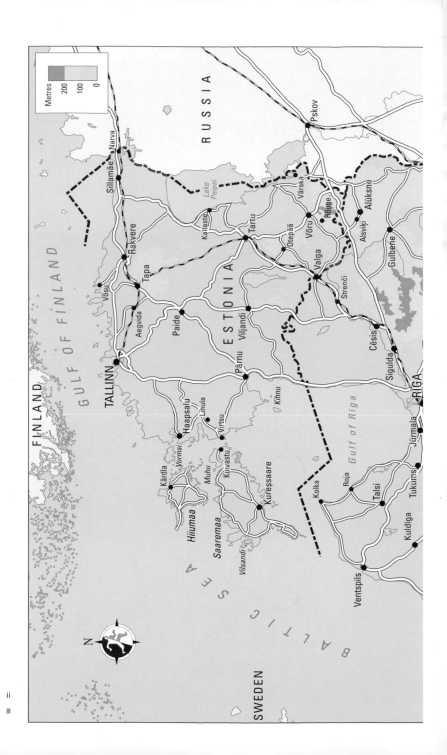

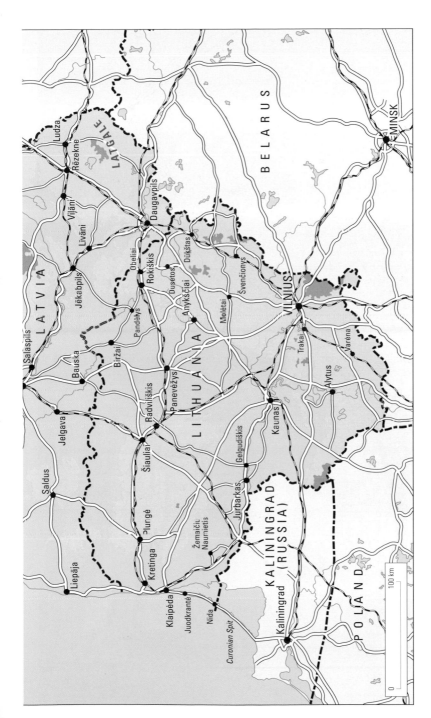

iii

Introduction to

the
Baltic States

The Baltic States – Lithuania, Latvia and Estonia – are far from being the grey, Soviet-scarred republics that many people imagine them to be. For a start, they're graced by three of the most enthralling national capitals in Eastern Europe, each highly individual in character and boasting an extraordinary wealth of historic buildings, as well as an expanding and energetic nightlife and cultural scene. Outside the cities lie great swathes of unspoiled countryside, with deep, dark pine forests punctuated by stands of silver birch, calm blue lakes, and a wealth of bogs and wetlands, all bordered by literally hundreds of kilometres of silvery beach. Peppering the landscape are villages that look like something out of the paintings of Marc Chagall, their dainty churches and wonky timber houses leaning over narrow, rutted streets. As you'd expect from a region periodically battered by outside invaders, there are dramatic historical remains aplenty, from the grizzled ruins of the fortresses thrown up by land-hungry Teutonic Knights in the thirteenth century, to the crumbling military installations bequeathed by Soviet occupiers some 700 years later.

Although the half century spent under Soviet rule has left Lithuanians, Latvians and Estonians with a great deal in common, they're each fiercely proud of their separate status, and tend to regard the "Baltic States" label as a matter of geographical convenience rather than a real indicator of shared culture. The Latvians and Lithuanians do at least have similar **origins**, having emerged from the Indo-European tribes who settled the area some two thousand years before Christ, and they still speak closely related languages. The Estonians, on the other hand, have lived here at least three millen-

nia longer and speak a Finno-Ugric tongue that has more in common with Finnish than with the languages of their next-door neighbours. In historical and religious terms, it's the Lithuanians that are a nation apart – having carved out a huge, independent empire in medieval times, they then converted to the Catholic faith in order to cement an alliance with Poland. In contrast, the Latvians and Estonians were conquered by Teutonic Knights in the thirteenth century and subjected to a German-speaking feudal culture that had become solidly Protestant by the mid-1500s. From the eighteenth-century onwards, the destinies of the three Baltic peoples began to converge, with most Latvians and Estonians being swallowed up by the **Tsarist Empire** during the reign of Peter the Great and the Lithuanians following several decades later. Despite

Song festivals

Each of the Baltic States holds a truly massive national Song Festival once every four or five years, when choirs from all over the country assemble to sing traditional songs on huge, outdoor stages. These festivals have played a crucial role in Baltic life ever since the nineteenth century, when the rediscovery of folk songs was an important step in rejuvenating indigenous cultures weakened by centuries of foreign domination. During the Soviet period, song festivals nurtured feelings of national solidarity at a time when any other expression of patriotic sentiment was severely frowned upon. In June 1988, the Song Festival Grounds in Tallinn became the focus of mass demonstrations against the Soviet regime, and the phrase "Singing Revolution" was coined to describe the independence movements in all three Baltic States. These struggles may be over, but the sight and sound of thousands of performers singing in unison still carries unique emotional power.

their common predicament, no great tradition of Baltic cooperation emerged, and when the three Baltic States became independent democracies in 1918–1920 – only to lose their independence to the USSR and Nazi Germany two decades later – they did so as isolated units rather than as allies.

The one occasion on which the Baltic nations truly came together was in the 1988–1991 period, when a shared sense of injustice at what the Soviet Union had done to them produced an outpouring of **inter-Baltic solidarity**. At no time was this more evident than when an estimated two million people joined hands to form a human chain stretching from Tallinn to Vilnius on 23 August, 1989, the fiftieth anniversary of the 1939 Molotov-Ribbentrop pact – the cynical Soviet-Nazi carve-up that had brought the curtain down on inter-war Baltic independence. Baltic fellow feeling became less pronounced in the post-Soviet period when each country began to focus on its own problems, and it's now the differences – rather than the similarities – between the Baltic peoples that most locals seem eager to impress upon visitors.

Storks

If there's one thing that characterizes the Baltic countryside in spring and early summer it's the sight of large numbers of white storks, nesting atop telegraph poles and farmyard buildings, or poking around in recently tilled land looking for tasty insects. Arriving in late March or early April, the birds hatch their young in May, then spend a couple of months filling up on bugs and frogs before returning to their wintering grounds towards the end of August. While the twentieth century saw a dramatic decrease in the stork population in Western Europe, their numbers are actually on the rise in the Baltics – the unspoiled expanses of food-rich wetlands combined with the comparatively low use of pesticides in Baltic agriculture having made the region into something of a haven for the creatures. With folk wisdom maintaining that the presence of a stork's nest promises good fortune and protection from fire and lightning, their presence is much appreciated by the locals.

How different they actually are remains open to question, with both locals and outsiders resorting to a convenient collection of clichés whenever the question of **national identity** comes under discussion: the Lithuanians are thought to be warm and spontaneous, the Estonians distant and difficult to know, while the Latvians belong somewhere in between. In truth there are plenty of ethnographic similarities linking the three nationalities. A century ago the majority of Lithuanians, Latvians and Estonians lived on isolated farmsteads or small villages, and a **love for the countryside**, coupled with a contemplative, almost mystical feeling for nature, still runs in the blood. Shared historical experiences – especially the years of Soviet occupation and the sudden re-imposition of capitalism that followed it – have produced people with broadly similar outlooks and, wherever you are in the Baltic States, you'll come across older people marked by fatalism and lack of initiative and younger generations characterized by ambition, impatience and adaptability to change.

The Baltic peoples today are also united by gnawing concerns about whether such relatively small countries can preserve their distinct identities in a rapidly globalizing world.

A love for the countryside, coupled with a contemplative,
almost mystical feeling for nature, still runs in the blood.

The rush to join NATO and the EU has been broadly welcomed in all three countries, not least because membership of both organizations promises protection against any future resurgence of Russian power. However, locals remain keenly aware that they can only be bit-part players in any future Europe. Lithuania has a **population** of 3.8 million, Latvia 2.3 million, and Estonia only 1.4 million – hardly the stuff of economic or cultural superpowers. Combined with this is a looming fear of population decline in countries that share some of the lowest birth rates in the world.

Midsummer's Eve

Given the shortness of the Baltic summer, it's no great surprise that the arrival of the longest day of the year is celebrated with much enthusiasm in all three Baltic States. Although the festival is known by the Christian name of St John's Day (Jaanipäev in Estonian, Jāņi in Latvian, Joninės in Lithuanian), it's an unashamedly pagan affair, with families or groups of friends lighting a bonfire on the night of June 23 and waiting up to see the sunrise, often fortified by large quantities of alcohol. As well as being the last chance for a booze-up before the hard work of the harvest season began, Midsummer's Eve was traditionally a fertility festival in which the bounty of nature was celebrated in all its forms. Folk wisdom still maintains that herbs, grasses and even morning dew collected early on the 24th can have magical medicinal powers. Above all it was – and still is – a great opportunity for young members of the community to get together and do what comes naturally, with couples setting off into the forest supposedly in search of the mythical fern flower (which, rather like the four-leafed clover, will bring untold good fortune to whoever succeeds in actually finding it).

Such anxieties are particularly strong in Estonia and Latvia, where the indigenous populations are in many towns and cities outnumbered by other **ethnic groups** – particularly Russians – who were encouraged to move here during the Soviet period. Only 55 percent of Latvia's inhabitants are ethnic Latvians, and the figure in Estonia, at 65 percent, isn't much better. Eager to immerse themselves in the new Europe and yet profoundly concerned with the need to preserve their national uniqueness, the Baltic States find themselves at a challenging crossroads.

   Transport in the Baltic States presents no real hardships, providing you're prepared to put up with badly sur-faced roads or don't mind travelling in rural buses that look as if they belong in a transport museum. Gloomy, Soviet-era hotels are everywhere outnumbered by spanking-new establishments offering high standards of **accommodation** at slightly less than Western-standard prices. Even though the three national capitals are beginning to take off as popular city-break destinations, the volume of visitors remains low by Western European standards, leaving you with the feeling that there's still much to be discovered.

When to go

L
ate spring and summer are the best times to visit the Baltic States, when there's usually enough fine weather to allow you to stroll around the cities and make significant forays into the great out-doors. On the whole though, the only thing that's predictable about the Baltic climate is the deep, dark winters – in all other seasons the weather can be changeable in the extreme.

Summers are relatively short (roughly mid-June to late August), and although you may well experience a string of hot, dry days during this period, showers and chilly nights are equally likely. Remember to pack a waterproof jacket and warm sweater alongside your favourite T-shirts.

Temperatures cool down rapidly from mid-September onwards, although **autumn** can be an extraordinarily beautiful season in which to travel, with the golden-brown leaves of deciduous trees contrasting with the dark-green pines.

The first snowfalls can come as early as mid-November, and by early to mid-December **winter** sets in with a vengeance. Average daytime temper-

In spring a sudden explosion of colour transforms the landscape.

atures can remain below zero right through until March, plummeting to minus 15–20°C in particularly cold spells. Winter can of course be a magical time, with lakes, rivers and large expanses of the Baltic Sea freezing over, and crunchy snow cover adding an air of enchantment to medieval city centres. However, rural areas can be difficult to get to without a 4WD vehicle (only the main highways are ploughed), and you'll have to be well togged up in order to endure anything but the shortest of walks. Wherever you are in winter, some form of hat or head covering is absolutely essential.

Even when the **spring** thaw sets in, the countryside can remain grey and barren until well into April (or even May in northern Estonia), when a sudden explosion of colour transforms the landscape. The countryside takes on a green lushness, drawing cattle and horses out from their winter barns, while city dwellers indulge in a frenzied stampede for the pavement cafés.

Average daily maximum temperatures in degrees centigrade

	Jan	Feb	Mar	Apr	May	June
Vilnius	-5	-3	1	12	18	21
Rīga	-4	-3	2	10	16	21
Tallinn	-4	-4	0	7	14	19
	July	Aug	Sept	Oct	Nov	Dec
Vilnius	23	22	17	11	4	-3
Rīga	22	21	17	11	4	-2
Tallinn	20	19	15	10	3	-1

30

things not to miss

It's not possible to see everything the Baltic States have to offer in one trip – and we don't suggest you try. What follows is a selective taste of the region's highlights – outstanding buildings, natural wonders and colourful festivals. Arranged in five colour-coded categories, you can browse through to find the very best things to see, do and experience. All highlights have a page reference to take you straight into the guide, where you can find out more.

01 Trakai Page **101** • This wonderfully restored island fortress recalls the grandeur of Lithuania's medieval empire, which once stretched from the Baltic to the Black Sea.

02 Pažaislis monastery, Kaunas Page **128** • A stately example of Lithuanian Baroque, perched near the shores of the Kauno marijos reservoir.

03 Piusa sand caves Page **399** • These eerie man-made caverns make for one of the more off-beat attractions of southeast Estonia.

04 Gauja National Park Page **261** • A slow-moving raft or gently gliding kayak provides the best vantage point from which to enjoy the sandstone cliffs and virgin forests of Latvia's most beautiful valley.

05 **Nida** Page **158** • Silky-smooth beaches and towering dunes add an air of Saharan grandeur to this popular summer resort on the Curonian Spit.

06 **Skamba skamba kankliai** Page **97** • The most intimate and accessible of Baltic folk festivals, with performances in the streets and courtyards of Vilnius's Old Town.

07 **Bogs** Page **34** • The Baltic region is especially rich in these bewitchingly barren landscapes of squelchy mosses and stunted trees.

08 **Āraiši lake village** Page **272** • This quietly impressive replica of a ninth-century log-built settlement evokes the simplicity and harshness of life in ancient Latvia.

09 **Grūto parkas** Page **142** • Rescued from the scrap merchant and replanted in rural parkland, this collection of Soviet-era statues provides a walk-round history lesson you're unlikely to forget.

10 **Cepelinai** Page **50** • Lithuania's national dish, these zeppelin-shaped potato dumplings stuffed with meat are enough to take the edge off anyone's hunger.

12 Vilsandi National Park
Page **350** • Pebble-strewn shores, juniper thickets and lonely lighthouses on Saaremaa's northwestern coast.

11 Jewish heritage Pages **84, 127 & 217** • Both Lithuania and Latvia were home to a glittering Jewish civilization before World War II. The Holocaust memorial in Rīga's Biķernieki forest is a fitting and eloquent monument to its disappearance.

13 Rīga Page **187–227** • The Baltic States' one true metropolis, Rīga can muster the kind of architectural monuments that any capital city would be proud of – including one of the biggest collections of Art Nouveau buildings in Europe.

14 **Pedvāle Open-air Art Museum** Page **246** • An exuberant collection of plein-air sculptures scattered over 2km of farmland, forests and stream-carved hills.

16 **Yule log** Page **184** • Dragging the *bĺuks* (yule log) through the snow before putting it to the torch is a time-honoured means of blowing away the winter blues – one of many archaic folk practices still enacted in Latvia's towns and cities.

15 **The Madonna of the Gate of Dawn** Page **80** • This mysterious and much-revered image has watched more than the people of Vilnius for over three centuries.

17 **Vilnius Old Town** Page **69** • Each of Vilnius's crooked alleys seems to have a magnificent church at the end of it, and the Gothic masterpiece that is St Anne's is no exception.

18 **Pape** Page **259** • A magnificently unspoiled stretch of coastal heath in southern Latvia, famous for its free-roaming herd of wild horses.

19 Rīga Open-air Ethnographic Museum

Page **218** • For an insight into how nineteenth-century Latvians used to live, visit this vast ensemble of timber-built farmhouses gathered from all over the country.

20 Tallinn pub crawl

Page **327** • There's something to suit hedonists of all persuasions in northeastern Europe's prime venue for going out. And staying out.

21 Tallinn

Page **300** • Tallinn's Old Town is an addictive warren of maze-like alleys and medieval squares.

23 **Mushroom picking** Page **34** • Combing the woods for fresh fungi is pretty much a Baltic obsession – especially after wet summers, when the forest floor is covered with the things.

22 **Rīgas melnais balzams** Page **182** • Many locals swear by the elixir-like qualities of the gloppy, herb-flavoured spirit that is Rīga Black Balsam – just don't be surprised if it turns out to be something of an acquired taste.

24 **Aglona basilica, Latgale** Page **281** • The spiritual centre of Latvia's Catholic minority, located amid the rolling hills and tranquil lakes of the far southeast.

25 **Erratic boulders** Page **366** • Enigmatic lumps of rock left behind long ago by retreating glaciers lie scattered along the shores of the Lahemaa National Park.

26 **Hill of Crosses** Page **146** • Bristling with crosses, statues and wood-carved shrines, this otherworldly pilgrimage site packs a powerful spiritual punch.

27 **Old Town, Rīga** Page **196** • Narrow alleys, ancient houses and red-brick churches provide an absorbing contrast to the bustling boulevards elsewhere in the city.

28 **Pärnu beach**

Page **351** • Estonia's premier bucket-and-spade resort is also a big hit with free-spending, fun-seeking youngsters.

29 **Saaremaa** Page **341** • Enjoy weather-beaten coastal wilderness, castles and windmills on Estonia's most enchanting island.

30 **Tartu** Page **375** • An invitingly easy-going university town with an attractive jumble of historic buildings and plenty of student-filled pubs.

Contents

Using the Rough Guide

We've tried to make this Rough Guide a good read and easy to use. The book is divided into six main sections, and you should be able to find whatever you want in one of them.

Colour section

The front colour section offers a quick tour of the Baltic States. The **introduction** aims to give you a feel for the place, with suggestions on where to go. We also tell you what the weather is like. Next, our author rounds up his favourite aspects of the Baltic States in the **things not to miss** section – whether it's great food, amazing sights or a special hotel. Right after this comes a full **contents** list.

Basics

The Basics section covers all the **pre-departure** nitty-gritty to help you plan your trip. This is where to find out which airlines fly to your destination, what paperwork you'll need, what to do about money and insurance, about Internet access, food, security, public transport, car rental – in fact just about every piece of **general practical information** you might need.

Guide

This is the heart of the Rough Guide, divided into user-friendly chapters, each of which covers a specific region. Every country section starts with a list of **highlights** and an **introduction** that helps you to decide where to go, depending on your time and budget. Likewise, introductions to the various towns and smaller regions within each chapter should help you plan your itinerary. We start most town accounts

with information on arrival and accommodation, followed by a tour of the sights, and finally reviews of places to eat and drink, and details of nightlife. Longer accounts also have a directory of practical listings. Each chapter concludes with **public transport** details for that region.

Contexts

Read Contexts to get a deeper understanding of what makes the Baltic States tick. We include a brief history, an article about **folk music** and, and a detailed further reading section that reviews dozens of **books** relating to each country.

Language

The **language** section gives useful guidance for speaking Lithuanian, Latvian and Estonian and pulls together all the vocabulary you might need on your trip, including a comprehensive menu reader. Here you'll also find a glossary of words and terms peculiar to the Baltic States.

Index + small print

Apart from a **full index**, which includes maps as well as places, this section covers publishing information, credits and acknowledgements, and also has our contact details in case you want to send in updates and corrections to the book – or suggestions as to how we might improve it.

Map and chapter list

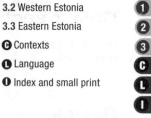

Contents

Colour section   i–xxiv

Basics   7–38

Guide   39–400

Contexts

401–439

Language

441–455

Index and small print

457–466

map symbols

maps are listed in the full index using coloured text

Motorway		ⓘ	Information office
Road		✉	Post office
Railway		@	Internet access
Steps		▣	Restaurant
Unpaved/gravel road		⊙	Statue/memorial
Track		🏛	Monument
Pedestrianized street		♟	Museum
Footpath		⚘	Viewpoint
Funicular railway		⍑	Public gardens
Ferry route		⚕	Campsite
Waterway		⊠-⊠	Gate
Chapter boundary		⊞	Hospital
International border		♜	Mosque
Provincial boundary		⊛	Swimming pool
Point of interest		▬▬▬	Wall
Bridge/tunnel		▬	Building
Airport		☐	Market
Mountain range		◯	Stadium
Mountain peak		⊞ ⚑	Church
Border post		⌐⌐ ⚐	Christian cemetery
Castle		✡	Synagogue
Lighthouse		☐	Jewish cemetery
Cave		▨	Park/national park
Spring		▧	Forest
Waterfall		▨	Marshland/bog
Concentration camp		▨	Beach

Basics

Basics

Getting there

From the UK and Ireland the most convenient way of getting to the Baltic States is to fly – there's a reasonable choice of direct and non-direct flights taking from three to five hours respectively, whereas the overland journey by car, train or coach can easily run to two or three days. While there are no direct flights to the Baltic capitals from North America or Australasia, plenty of airlines offer one- or two-stop connections. Budget deals from either continent are often hard to find however – it may work out cheaper to get a bargain flight to a Western European destination and continue your journey by land. It's relatively easy to combine a visit to the Baltic States with a more general trip around northeastern Europe, with Poland to the west and Scandinavia to the north providing plenty in the way of bus and ferry links respectively.

When it comes to buying **flights**, it's worth bearing in mind that while some airlines have fixed return fares which don't change from one month to the next, others depend very much on the **season**, with high season being from early June to mid-September, when the weather is best; fares drop during the "shoulder" seasons – mid-September to the end of October and mid-April to early June – and you'll get the best prices during the low season, November to mid-April (excluding Christmas and New Year when prices are hiked up and seats are at a premium). Note also that flying on weekends is generally more expensive; price ranges quoted below assume midweek travel, unless otherwise stated.

You can often cut costs by going through a specialist flight agent – either a **consolidator**, who buys up blocks of tickets from the airlines and sells them at a discount, or a **discount agent**, who in addition to dealing with discounted flights may also offer special student and youth fares and a range of other travel-related services such as travel insurance, rail passes, car rentals, tours and the like. Some agents specialize in **charter flights**, which may be cheaper than anything available on a scheduled flight, but again departure dates are fixed and withdrawal penalties are high.

If you're travelling to the Baltic States as part of a longer trip, consider buying a **Round-the-World (RTW) ticket**, although since the Baltic States are not typical stop-offs for round-the-world travellers, you'll probably have to ask your travel agent to custom-design a ticket for you, which will work out more expensive than an off-the-shelf RTW ticket.

Finally, it's worth noting that an increasing number of international travel companies are offering **city breaks** in the three Baltic capitals of Tallinn, Rīga and Vilnius – taking advantage of their flight-plus-accommodation deals may work out cheaper than organizing your trip independently. Specialist travel agencies are listed on the following pages.

Note that all airline fares quoted on the following pages are inclusive of airport taxes.

Booking flights online

Many airlines and discount travel websites offer you the opportunity to book your tickets online, cutting out the costs of agents and middlemen. Good deals can often be found through discount or auction sites, as well as through the airlines' own websites.

Online booking agents and general travel sites

ⓦ **www.travel.yahoo.com** Incorporates a lot of Rough Guide material in its coverage of destination countries and cities across the world, with information about places to eat, sleep etc.
ⓦ **www.cheapflights.co.uk** Bookings from the UK and Ireland only (for US,
ⓦ www.cheapflights.com; for Canada,
ⓦ www.cheapflights.ca; for Australia,
ⓦ www.cheapflights.com.au). Flight deals, travel

agents, plus links to other travel sites.

⊛**www.cheaptickets.com** Discount flight specialists (US only).

⊛**www.etn.nl/discount.htm** A hub of consolidator and discount agent Web links, maintained by the non-profit European Travel Network.

⊛**www.expedia.com** Discount airfares, all-airline search engine and daily deals (US only; for the UK, ⊛ www.expedia.co.uk; for Canada, ⊛ www.expedia.ca).

⊛**www.flyaow.com** Online air travel info and reservations site.

⊛**www.hotwire.com** Bookings from the US only. Last-minute savings of up to forty percent on regular published fares. Travellers must be at least 18 and there are no refunds, transfers or changes allowed. Log-in required.

⊛**www.lastminute.com** Offers good last-minute holiday package and flight-only deals (UK only; for Australia, ⊛ www.lastminute.com.au).

⊛**www.priceline.com** Name-your-own-price website that has deals at around forty percent off standard fares. You cannot specify flight times (although you do specify dates) and the tickets are non-refundable, non-transferable and non-changeable (US only; for the UK, ⊛ www.priceline.co.uk).

⊛**www.skyauction.com** Bookings from the US only. Auctions tickets and travel packages using a "second bid" scheme. The best strategy is to bid the maximum you're willing to pay, since if you win you'll pay just enough to beat the runner-up regardless of your maximum bid.

⊛**www.smilinjack.com/airlines.htm** Lists an up-to-date compilation of airline website addresses.

⊛**www.travelocity.com** Destination guides, hot Web fares and best deals for car rental, accommodation and lodging as well as fares. Provides access to the travel agent system SABRE, the most comprehensive central reservations system in the US.

⊛**www.travelshop.com.au** Australian website offering discounted flights, packages, insurance and online bookings.

Flights from the UK and Ireland

The Baltic capitals of Vilnius, Rīga and Tallinn are served by daily **direct flights from London**. In each case the routes are monopolized by one airline only, and the lack of competition means cheap deals are few and far between – you'll rarely get a seat on

London–Vilnius or London–Tallinn services for less than £250 return, for instance. The London–Rīga route is cheaper, with fares averaging at £205.

You might save money by shopping around for **indirect flights**, which involve changing planes at a European hub such as Copenhagen, Frankfurt, Warsaw or Prague. If you're setting off to the Baltics from northern England, Scotland or Ireland, it's usually cheaper and quicker to fly via Europe from one of your local airports rather than attempting to travel via London. Flights to the Baltics are rarely advertised in the travel pages of newspapers and magazines, so your best sources of information will be discount flight agents (see p.12) or the airlines themselves (see p.11).

Another option that might work out cheaper than flying direct is to fly to a **nearby country** and continue your journey overland or by ferry. The Finnish capital Helsinki is the obvious choice, being only a couple of hours away from Tallinn by boat, although you might also consider Stockholm (with an overnight ferry to Rīga) or Warsaw (an eight-hour bus ride from Vilnius); see pp.20–21 for further details.

To Lithuania

Lithuanian Airlines operates daily services **from London Gatwick** to Vilnius (2hr 55min), with tickets currently priced at £270 return. You'll occasionally pick up cheaper fares travelling non-direct, for example London–Helsinki–Vilnius with Finnair, London–Amsterdam–Vilnius with KLM (Lithuanian Airlines operates the Amsterdam–Vilnius leg), or even London–Prague–Vilnius with Czech Airlines.

From outside London, both SAS and Czech airlines offer indirect flights from Birmingham and Manchester for about £330 return, while Finnair does similar deals on flights from Manchester and Dublin. KLM operates flights from a wide range of British airports (Leeds–Bradford and Glasgow included) to Amsterdam, from where you can pick up a flight to Vilnius, although their prices are slightly higher.

You can also approach Lithuania by flying to neighbouring capitals like **Rīga** (see "To

Latvia" below) or **Warsaw**, then continuing your journey by land. Both British Airways and LOT fly from London Heathrow to Warsaw several times a day, and LOT also flies there direct from Manchester. Fares to Warsaw begin at £150 return on low-season weekends, rising to £270 return in summer – although you might get cheaper fares from specialist flight agents such as the Polish Travel Centre (see p.12).

To Latvia

British Airways operates daily flights **from London Heathrow** to Rīga (2hr 50min), with scheduled fares starting at £180 in the low season, rising to £230 in July and August. Travelling with BA from regional airports such as Manchester or Glasgow and changing at Heathrow will add £70–90 to this figure, though one of the European carriers may be able to undercut this: Lufthansa operates from a range of UK and Irish airports (via Frankfurt); Finnair flies from Manchester (and London) via Helsinki; and SAS goes from Birmingham and Manchester via Copenhagen, with Latvia's national carrier Air Baltic doing the second leg. Flights **from Dublin** with Finnair via Helsinki currently come in at €320–350.

You can also get to Rīga by taking one of the numerous flights to **Stockholm** and catching a ferry (from £43 return), although this will add 24 hours to your journey. BA, SAS and Finnair fly direct from London and Manchester, SAS flies direct from Dublin, and Ryanair flies direct from Stansted, Glasgow and Shannon. Expect to pay upwards of £130 return, unless you're travelling with Ryanair, which might work out significantly cheaper. For ferry details see p.21.

To Estonia

Estonian Airlines offers direct flights **from London Gatwick** to Tallinn (2hr 55min), with fares hovering in the £220–250 range. There's a reasonable choice of indirect flights, with Finnair offering return fares via Helsinki from London Heathrow and Manchester for around £250, and from Dublin for around €350. You can also fly from Belfast, Dublin, Manchester or

Birmingham with SAS via Copenhagen, although their scheduled fares are more expensive at around £360 return.

A cheaper alternative may be to fly to Helsinki and catch a **ferry to Tallinn** – the sea crossing takes between 1hr 40min and 3hr 30min and can cost as little as £22/$30 return. Flying Finn operates daily flights from London Stansted **to Helsinki**, with returns costing anywhere between £100 and £200, depending on availability. There are also direct flights to Helsinki from London Heathrow, Manchester and Dublin with Finnair, and from London with British Airways. Standard return fares cost around £220, although you'll often pick up seasonal specials for around £150. Ryanair operates a daily service to the Finnish city of Tampere (a 2hr train ride from Helsinki) from Stansted, Glasgow or Shannon – prices vary considerably, but are sometimes as low as £70 return. For more on the Helsinki–Tallinn ferry see p.21.

Airlines in the UK and Ireland

Aer Lingus UK ☎0845/084 4444, Republic of Ireland ☎0818/365 000; ⊛www.aerlingus.ie. Flights from Dublin and Cork to London Heathrow, where you can pick up connecting flights to the Baltics.
Aeroflot UK ☎020/7355 2233, ⊛www.aeroflot.co.uk. Flights to Vilnius and Rīga via Moscow.
Air Baltic UK ☎0845/607 2772, Republic of Ireland ☎01/844 5440; ⊛www.airbaltic.com. Flights to Riga from Copenhagen and Stockholm, with incoming connections from the UK and Ireland handled by SAS (see p.12).
Austrian Airlines UK ☎0845/601 0948 or 020/7434 7350, ⊛www.aua.com. London to Vilnius, changing planes in Vienna.
British Airways UK ☎0845/773 3377, Republic of Ireland ☎1800/626 747; ⊛www.ba.com. Direct flights to Rīga from London Heathrow, with connecting flights from most British airports.
British Midland UK ☎0870/607 0555, Republic of Ireland ☎01/407 3036; ⊛www.flybmi.com. Flights from British regional airports to London, with onward connections to the Baltics.
CSA Czech Airlines UK ☎0870/4443 747, Republic of Ireland ☎01/814 4626; ⊛www.csa.cz/en. Flights to Rīga and Vilnius from Birmingham, London and Manchester, changing in Prague.

Estonian Airlines UK ☎020/7333 0196, @www.estonian-air.ee. Direct fights from London Gatwick to Tallinn, with onward connections to Riga and Vilnius.

Finnair UK ☎0870/241 4411, Republic of Ireland ☎01/844 6565; @www.finnair.com. Direct flights from Dublin, Heathrow and Manchester to Helsinki, from where there are connecting flights to Vilnius, Riga and Tallinn.

Flying Finn UK ☎0870/744 7315, @www.flyingfinn.fi. Budget flights from London Stansted to Helsinki.

KLM UK ☎0870/243 0541, @www.klmuk.com. Flights from a range of UK and Irish airports to Amsterdam, connections to Vilnius.

Lithuanian Airlines UK ☎01293/579900, @www.lal.lt. Direct flights from London Gatwick to Vilnius, with onward connections to Tallinn.

LOT Polish Airlines UK ☎020/7580 5037, @www.lot.com. Direct flights from London and Manchester to Warsaw, connecting flights to Vilnius, Riga and Tallinn.

Lufthansa UK ☎0845/773 7747, Republic of Ireland ☎01/844 5544; @www.lufthansa.co.uk. Flights from various UK and Irish airports to Frankfurt, with onward connections to all three Baltic capitals.

Ryanair UK ☎0871/246 0000, Republic of Ireland ☎0818/303 030; @www.ryanair.com. Low-cost flights from Stansted to Tampere (Finland), with connecting flights from Glasgow and Shannon.

SAS Scandinavian Airlines UK ☎0845/607 2772, Republic of Ireland ☎01/844 5440; @www.scandinavian.net. Flights to Riga from London, Belfast, Dublin and Manchester, changing at either Copenhagen or Stockholm.

Swiss UK ☎0845/601 0956, @www.swiss.com. Flights to Warsaw and Stockholm via Zürich, with departures from London, Birmingham, Manchester and Dublin.

Flight and travel agents in the UK and Ireland

Aran Travel International Republic of Ireland ☎091/562 595, @homepages.iol.ie/~arantvl/aranmain.htm. Good-value flights to all parts of the world.

Bridge the World UK ☎0870/444 7474, @www.bridgetheworld.com. Specializing in Round-the-World tickets, with good deals aimed at the backpacker market.

CIE Tours International Republic of Ireland ☎01/703 1888, @www.cietours.ie. General flight and tour agent.

Co-op Travel Care UK ☎0870/112 0099, @www.travelcareonline.com. Flights and holidays around the world.

Destination Group UK ☎020/7400 7045, @www.destination-group.com. Good discount airfares.

Flightbookers UK ☎0870/010 7000, @www.ebookers.com. Low fares on an extensive selection of scheduled flights.

Joe Walsh Tours Republic of Ireland ☎01/676 0991, @www.joewalshtours.ie. General budget fares agent.

Lee Travel Republic of Ireland ☎021/277 111, @www.leetravel.ie. Flights and holidays worldwide.

McCarthy's Travel Republic of Ireland ☎021/427 0127, @www.mccarthystravel.ie. General flight agent.

Neenan Travel Republic of Ireland ☎01/607 9900, @www.neenantrav.ie. Specialists in European city breaks.

North South Travel UK ☎01245/608 291, @www.northsouthtravel.co.uk. Friendly, competitive travel agency, offering discounted fares worldwide – profits are used to support projects in the developing world, especially the promotion of sustainable tourism.

Polish Travel Centre UK ☎020/8741 5541. Specialists in discounted flights to Poland.

Premier Travel Northern Ireland ☎028/7126 3333, @www.premiertravel.uk.com. Discount flight specialists.

Rosetta Travel Northern Ireland ☎028/9064 4996, @www.rosettatravel.com. Flight and holiday agent.

STA Travel UK ☎0870/1600 599, @www.statravel.co.uk. Worldwide specialists in low-cost flights and tours for students and under-26s, though other customers welcome.

Student & Group Travel Republic of Ireland ☎01/677 7834. Student and group specialists, mostly to Europe.

Top Deck UK ☎020/7244 8000, @www.topdecktravel.co.uk. Long-established agent dealing in discount flights.

Trailfinders UK ☎020/7628 7628, @www.trailfinders.co.uk; Republic of Ireland ☎01/677 7888, @www.trailfinders.ie. One of the best-informed and most efficient agents for independent travellers.

Travel Cuts UK ☎020/7255 2082 or 7255 1944, @www.travelcuts.co.uk. Canadian company specializing in budget, student and youth travel and Round-the-World tickets.

usit NOW Republic of Ireland ☎01/602 1600, Northern Ireland ☎028/9032 7111; @www.usitnow.ie. Student and youth specialists for flights and trains.

Organized tours

An increasing number of tour operators are including Vilnius, Rīga and Tallinn in their city-break brochures. This is an excellent way of getting a flight-plus-accommodation **package** at a reasonable price – the comfortable 3- to 4-star hotels used by tour operators would probably work out more expensive if you tried to book them independently. A **three-night city break** in one of the Baltic capitals costs somewhere in the region of £300–350 in the low season (Nov & Dec), rising to £380–450 in high season (July–Sept), with additional nights costing £35–55 depending on the hotel. Prices assume that you're departing from London – add-on fares for Birmingham, Manchester and elsewhere can be pretty hefty.

In addition, several specialist companies offer **general Baltic tours** taking in all three capitals and a few outlying attractions. Prices vary according to group size and hotel quality, but expect to pay upwards of £850 for a week-long tour taking in a little of all three states, and from £1200 for a two-week trip. Baltic specialists like Regent Holidays and Lithuanian Holidays are the best places to enquire about tailor-made itineraries and specialist interest tours.

Several companies offer **Baltic Sea cruises** including St Petersburg, a couple of Scandinavian ports, Tallinn and/or Rīga, although you won't get much more than a day to look round each place en route.

Specialist tour operators in the UK and Ireland

Bridge Travel UK ☎0870/191 7277, ⓦwww.bridgetravel.co.uk. City breaks to Tallinn and Rīga.

Crystal UK ☎0970/160 9030, ⓦwww.lunnpoly.com. City breaks in Tallinn.

Dovetail Birding ⓦwww.dovetailbirding.com. US-based Web resource that lists birdwatching holidays in the Baltics, most of which depart from London.

Estonia Holidays UK ☎01773/850222, ⓦwww.estoniaholidays.com. City breaks to Tallinn.

Explore Worldwide UK ☎01252/760 000, ⓦwww.explore.co.uk. Two-week tour of Baltic cities and national parks.

Lithuanian Holidays UK ☎0870/757 9233, ⓦwww.lithuanianholidays.com. City breaks to Vilnius, stag weekends, ten-day tours of Lithuania, and Jewish Heritage tours based in Vilnius and Kaunas.

Martin Randall Travel UK ☎020/8742 3355, ⓦwww.martinrandall.com. Seven- and twelve-day cultural tours, taking in the main urban sights of all three Baltic states.

Norwegian Cruise Line/Freestyle Cruising UK ☎0845/658 8030, ⓦwww.uk.ncl.com. Twelve-night sea cruises taking in Scandinavian capitals, St Petersburg and Tallinn.

P&O Cruises UK ☎0845/355 5333, ⓦwww.pocruises.co.uk. Two-week Baltic Sea cruises including the chance to potter around Tallinn.

Railway Touring Company UK ☎01553/661500, ⓦwww.railwaytouring.co.uk. Twelve-day railway odyssey (for around £2000) from the Black Sea to the Baltic, calling at Odessa, Kiev, Vilnius and Rīga en route.

Regent Holidays UK ☎0117/921 1711, ⓦwww.regent-holidays.co.uk. City breaks to Tallinn, Rīga and Vilnius. Accompanied ten- and fifteen-day tours through the Baltics, and nine-day cycling holidays on the Estonian island of Saaremaa.

Russian Travel Company UK ☎0870/366 5454, ⓦwww.russiantravel.co.uk. City breaks in Tallinn, Rīga and Vilnius.

Scan Tours UK ☎020/7839 2927, ⓦwww.scantoursuk.com. Pan-Baltic tours and tailor-made holidays based in Vilnius, Rīga and Tallinn.

Travel Editions UK ☎020/7251 0045, ⓦwww.traveleditions.co.uk. City breaks to Tallinn.

Travellers Cities UK ☎01959/540700, ⓦwww.travellerscities.co.uk. City breaks to Tallinn.

Travelscene UK ☎0870/777 4445, ⓦwww.travelscene.co.uk. City breaks in Rīga and Tallinn. Multi-centre combinations featuring Stockholm, Helsinki, Tallinn and Rīga.

Flights from the US and Canada

Although there are no direct flights **from North America** to the Baltic States, there are plenty of indirect routings to choose from. If you're departing from one of North America's gateway cities you'll probably only have to change planes once – otherwise, a two-stop flight seems more likely. Fares vary widely according to which Baltic capital you're flying to and which city you're setting out from, and it might make sense to fly to whichever Baltic destination offers the cheapest return fares, then continue your trip by land. Another option is to fly to a neighbouring country, such as Poland, Finland or Sweden, and continue your journey from there (see "Flights from the UK and Ireland", p.10, for details).

The **best fares** tend to be with north European airlines with frequent Baltic connections: flying from New York to Tallinn with Finnair, for example, currently costs around US$600 in low season, US$800 high. Return fares from Chicago to Tallinn or Vilnius with SAS cost around US$800 and US$1000 respectively. From elsewhere in North America, the cheapest scheduled fares to the Baltic capitals fluctuate between US$1200 and US$1500 return – although it's always worth looking out for special seasonal fares.

Airlines in North America

Aeroflot US ☎1-888/340-6400, Canada ☎416/642-1653; ⓦwww.aeroflot.com. Flights from New York, Washington, Seattle, San Francisco and Los Angeles to Moscow, with onward connections to Rīga and Vilnius.
Air Canada ☎1-888/247-2262, ⓦwww.aircanada.ca. Flights to various European hubs with connecting flights to Tallinn, Rīga and Vilnius.
Air France US ☎1-800/237-2747, ⓦwww.airfrance.com; Canada ☎1-800/667-2747, ⓦwww.airfrance.ca. Flights from numerous North American cities to Paris with onward connections to Vilnius.
American Airlines ☎1-800/433-7300, ⓦwww.aa.com. Flights to London and Frankfurt with onward connections to Tallinn, Rīga and Vilnius.
Austrian Airlines ☎1-800/843-0002, ⓦwww.aua.com. Flights from Toronto, Montreal, New York and Washington to Vilnius, changing planes in Vienna.
British Airways ☎1-800/247-9297, ⓦwww.ba.com. Flights to Rīga from a number of North American cities, via London.
British Midland ☎1-800/788-0555, ⓦwww.flybmi.com. Flights from Washington and Chicago to Manchester, with onward connections to the Baltic capitals.
Continental Airlines domestic ☎1-800/523-3273, international ☎1-800/231-0856, ⓦwww.continental.com. Daily flights from various North American cities to most major European hubs, with onward connections to Baltic capitals.
Czech Airlines US ☎1-877/359-6629 or 212/765-6022, Canada ☎416/363-3174;

ⓦwww.czechairlines.com. Flights to Rīga and Vilnius from New York, Washington and Toronto, changing planes in Prague.
Delta Air Lines domestic ☎1-800/221-1212, international ☎1-800/241-4141; ⓦwww.delta.com. Flights to Stockholm, London and other European hubs with onward connections to Tallinn, Rīga and Vilnius.
Finnair ☎1-800/950-5000, ⓦwww.finnair.com. Flights from New York and Toronto to Tallinn, Rīga and Vilnius, changing at Helsinki.
LOT Polish Airlines US ☎1-800/223-0593 or 718/264-6480, Canada ☎1-800/668-5928; ⓦwww.lot.com. Direct flights from New York, Chicago and Toronto to Warsaw, with onward connections to Vilnius, Rīga and Tallinn.
Lufthansa US ☎1-800/645-3880, Canada ☎1-800/563-5954; ⓦwww.lufthansa-usa.com. Flights from Toronto, Montreal and various American cities to Frankfurt, with onward connections to Vilnius and and Rīga.
Northwest/KLM Airlines domestic ☎1-800/225-2525, international ☎1-800/447-4747; ⓦwww.nwa.com, ⓦww.klm.com. Flights from various North American cities to Vilnius, via Amsterdam.
Scandinavian Airlines ☎1-800/221-2350, ⓦwww.scandinavian.net. Flights from New York, Washington, Chicago and Seattle to Tallinn, Rīga and Vilnius, changing planes in Copenhagen or Stockholm.
US Airways domestic ☎1-800/428-4322, international ☎1-800/622-1015; ⓦwww.usair.com. Flights to London, Frankfurt and Amsterdam, with onward connections to the Baltic capitals.
Virgin Atlantic Airways ☎1-800/862-8621, ⓦwww.virgin-atlantic.com. Flights to London, with onward connections to Vilnius, Tallinn and Rīga.

Discount travel companies in North America

Airtech ☎212/219-7000, ⓦwww.airtech.com. Standby seat broker; also deals in consolidator fares and courier flights.
Airtreks.com ☎1-877-AIRTREKS or 415/912-5600, ⓦwww.airtreks.com. Round-the-world tickets. The website features an interactive database that lets you build and price your own round-the-world itinerary.
Council Travel ☎1-800/2COUNCIL, ⓦwww.counciltravel.com. Nationwide organization that mostly specializes in student/budget travel. Flights from the US only. Owned by STA Travel.

Educational Travel Center ☎1-800/747-5551 or 608/256-5551, ⊕www.edtrav.com. Student/youth discount agent.

New Frontiers ☎1-800/677-0720 or 310/670-7318, ⊕www.newfrontiers.com. French discount-travel firm based in Los Angeles.

Pekao ☎416/588 1414, ⊕www.pekao.canada.com. Toronto-based agent specializing in budget flights to Warsaw, from where you can continue your journey overland.

SkyLink US ☎1-800/AIR-ONLY or 212/573-8980, Canada ☎1-800/SKY-LINK; ⊕www.skylinkus.com. Consolidator.

STA Travel US ☎1-800/781-4040, Canada 1-888/427-5639; ⊕www.sta-travel.com. Worldwide specialists in independent travel; also student IDs, travel insurance, car rental, rail passes, etc.

Student Flights ☎1-800/255-8000 or 480/951-1177, ⊕www.isecard.com. Student/youth fares, student IDs.

TFI Tours ☎1-800/745-8000 or 212/736-1140, ⊕www.lowestairprice.com. Consolidator.

Travac ☎1-800/TRAV-800, ⊕www.thetravelsite.com. Consolidator and charter broker with offices in New York City and Orlando.

Travel Avenue ☎1-800/333-3335, ⊕www.travelavenue.com. Full-service travel agent that offers discounts in the form of rebates.

Travel Cuts Canada ☎1-800/667-2887, US ☎1-866/246-9762; ⊕www.travelcuts.com. Canadian student-travel organization.

Travelers Advantage ☎1-877/259-2691, ⊕www.travelersadvantage.com. Discount travel club; annual membership fee required (currently $1 for three months' trial).

Worldtek Travel ☎1-800/243-1723, ⊕www.worldtek.com. Discount travel agency for worldwide travel.

Packages and organized tours

A small but growing number of companies operate **organized tours** to the Baltic States, ranging from city breaks to two-week cultural tours of the whole region. Booking a flights-plus-accommodation deal through a specialist travel agent can often work out cheaper than organizing things yourself. Group tours tend to be more expensive, ranging in price from US$1200 for seven days to US$2000 for a fortnight, not including flights from North America.

Tour operators in North America

Adventure Center ☎1-800/228-8747 or 510/654-1879, ⊕www.adventurecenter.com. Four-

day trips to Tallinn and wider-ranging two-week Baltic tours.

Adventures Abroad ☎1-800/665-3998 or 360/775-9926, ⊕www.adventures-abroad.com. A range of seven- to twenty-day tours of the Baltic capitals, with optional visits to St Petersburg and Warsaw thrown in.

Cross-Culture ☎1-800/491-1148 or 413/256-6303, ⊕www.crosscultureinc.com. General Baltic tours incorporating the three capital cities.

Dovetail Birding US ☎1-877/881-1145, ⊕www.dovetailbirding.com. Web resource that lists birdwatching holidays in the Baltics, most of which depart from London in the UK.

Go To Russia Travel ☎1-888/263-0023, ⊕www.gotorussia.com. City breaks in Tallinn, Rīga and Vilnius, and tailor-made arrangements.

Isram World of Travel ☎1-800/223-7460, ⊕www.isram.com. City breaks in the Baltic capitals.

Riga Ven Travel ☎631/665-4455, ⊕http://rigaven.homestead.com. Latvian and general Baltics specialist offering organized tours as well as flight-plus-accommodation deals.

Scantours ☎1-800/223-7226, ⊕www.scantours.com. City breaks in Vilnius, Rīga and Tallinn, general Baltic tours, plus bicycle tours in Lithuania. Also agents for European rail passes.

Travcoa ☎1-800/922-2003, ⊕www.travcoa.com. General two- to-three-week Baltic tours.

Vytis Tours ☎1-718/423-6161, ⊕www.vytistours.com. Baltic specialist offering tailor-made accommodation plus flights packages, tours and car rental.

Flights from Australia and New Zealand

Although one-stop flights **from Australia** to the Baltics do exist (typical routings involve European hubs such as London, Frankfurt or Vienna), they tend to be expensive, with the average return fare from Sydney/Melbourne/Perth to Tallinn, Rīga or Vilnius hovering around the AUS$4000 mark. Cheaper deals involve a combination of airlines and two stops en route. Australia–Kuala Lumpur–Amsterdam–Vilnius, or Australia–Bangkok–Helsinki–Tallinn are two typical routings. Fares on these routes range from AUS$2200 in low season to AUS$2700 in high season.

From **New Zealand**, Air New Zealand operates daily flights from Auckland to London and Frankfurt, where you can pick up connecting flights to the Baltic capitals.

All other flights from New Zealand involve at least two stops. Return fares start at around NZ$4000 in low season, rising to NZ$4900 in high season.

You might save money by picking up a budget flight to a Western European city and continuing overland to the Baltic States (see "Flights from the UK and Ireland", p.10, for some suggestions); if you want to see the country as part of a wider trip across Europe, it might be worth your while considering a European rail pass (see p.17).

There's a small number of **package-tour operators** offering holidays in the Baltic States from Australia and New Zealand, including accommodation, sightseeing packages and rail passes.

Airlines in Australia and New Zealand

Air New Zealand Australia ☎ 13 24 76, ⊛ www.airnz.com.au; New Zealand ☎ 0800/737 000, ⊛ www.airnz.co.nz. Daily flights from Auckland to London via Los Angeles, then onward connections to Riga, Tallinn and Vilnius.
Austrian Airlines Australia ☎ 1800/642 438 ⊛ www.aua.com. From Melbourne and Sydney to Vilnius via Vienna.
British Airways Australia ☎ 1300/767 177, New Zealand ☎ 0800/274 847 or 09/356 8690; ⊛ www.ba.com. Daily to London from Sydney, Melbourne or Perth with onward connections to the Baltic capitals.
Cathay Pacific Australia ☎ 13 17 47, ⊛ www.cathaypacific.com/au; New Zealand ☎ 09/379 0861 or 0508/800 454, ⊛ www.cathaypacific.com/nz. Flights from Australia and New Zealand to Hong Kong, with onward connections to major European hubs then the Baltic States.
Finnair Australia ☎ 02/9244 2299, New Zealand ☎ 09/308 3365; ⊛ www.finnair.com. Flights via Bangkok or Singapore to Helsinki, with onward connections to Tallinn, Riga and Vilnius.
KLM/Northwest Airlines Australia ☎ 1300/303 747, ⊛ www.klm.com/au_en; New Zealand ☎ 09/309 1782, ⊛ www.klm.com/nz_en. Flights from Australia and New Zealand to Vilnius, via Kuala Lumpur and Amsterdam.
Lufthansa Australia ☎ 1300/655 727, ⊛ www.lufthansa-australia.com; New Zealand ☎ 09/303 1529, ⊛ www.lufthansa.com/index_en.html. Flights from Australia to Frankfurt with onward connections to Vilnius and Riga.

Malaysia Airlines Australia ☎ 13 26 27, New Zealand ☎ 0800/777 747; ⊛ www.malaysiaairlines.com.my. Flights from Melbourne to Vienna via Kuala Lumpur, with onward connections to Vilnius.
Qantas Australia ☎ 13 13 13, ⊛ www.qantas.com.au; New Zealand ☎ 0800/808 767, ⊛ www.qantas.co.nz. Flights from Sydney to Frankfurt with onward connections to Vilnius and Riga.
Scandinavian Airlines (SAS) Australia ☎ 1300/727 707, New Zealand agent: Air New Zealand ☎ 09/357 3000; ⊛ www.scandinavian.net. Flights to Tallinn, Riga and Vilnius via Singapore and Copenhagen.
Singapore Airlines Australia ☎ 13 10 11, New Zealand ☎ 0800/808 909; ⊛ www.singaporeair.com. Flights from Auckland to major European hubs via Singapore, with onward connections to Baltic capitals.
Thai Airlines ⊛ www.thaiair.com. Flights from Auckland to Bangkok with onward connections to Baltic cities via Copenhagen, London, Frankurt or Amsterdam.

Flight and travel agents in Australia and New Zealand

Flight Centre Australia ☎ 13 31 33 or 02/9235 3522, ⊛ www.flightcentre.com.au; New Zealand ☎ 0800 243 544 or 09/358 4310, ⊛ www.flightcentre.co.nz.
Holiday Shoppe New Zealand ☎ 0800/808 480, ⊛ www.holidayshoppe.co.nz.
STA Travel Australia ☎ 1300/733 035, ⊛ www.statravel.com.au; New Zealand ☎ 0508/782 872, ⊛ www.statravel.co.nz.
Student Uni Travel Australia ☎ 02/9232 8444, ⊛ www.sut.com.au; New Zealand ☎ 09/379 4224, ⊛ www.sut.co.nz.
Trailfinders Australia ☎ 02/9247 7666, ⊛ www.trailfinders.com.au.

Specialist agents and tour operators in Australia and New Zealand

Bentours Australia ☎ 02/9241 1353, ⊛ www.bentours.com.au. Seven-day tours incorporating the Baltic capitals, with an optional extra seven days in Sandinavia. Also flights to the Baltics and Scandinavia.
Eastern European Travel Bureau Australia ☎ 02/9262 1144, ⊛ www.eetb.citysearch.com.au. Concentrates on Russia and the Baltic States.
Eastern Eurotours Australia ☎ 07/5526 2855 or 1800/242 353, ⊛ www.easterneurotours.com.au.

Flights, hotel accommodation and city breaks in the Baltic States.

Gateway Travel Australia ☎02/9745 3333, ⓦwww.russian-gateway.com.au. Eastern European and Russian specialists.

Passport Travel Australia ☎03/9867 3888, ⓦwww.travelcentre.com.au. City breaks and Baltic tours.

By rail from the UK

Travelling to the Baltic States **by train** from the UK is more expensive than flying, but it gives you the option of stopping off in other parts of Europe on the way. From Western Europe there's only one route into the Baltics – the line from Warsaw in Poland to Vilnius in Lithuania, and beyond Vilnius the Baltic rail network itself is pretty limited, with a single overnight train to Rīga, but nothing from there to Tallinn.

The main **London–Vilnius** itinerary runs via Brussels, Cologne, Berlin and Warsaw, and takes about 45 hours if you're lucky with connections – somewhat longer if you cross the Channel by ferry rather than taking Eurostar. Buying a through ticket for this route isn't easy: most major UK train stations can sell tickets as far as Brussels, but are rarely equipped to deal with destinations beyond. The agents who specialize in international train journeys (see "Rail Contacts" p.18) may be able to book your passage as far as Warsaw, but are unlikely to sell tickets further east. The price of a return ticket from London to Warsaw using Eurostar hovers around the £290 mark – to this you'll need to add a further £30–40 to cover the Warsaw–Vilnius leg. The trip will work out slightly cheaper if you cross the Channel by ferry, but as none of the ticket agents sells

through tickets on continental journeys not using Eurostar, you'll have to buy tickets as you go.

Rail passes

If you're travelling across Europe by train, it's worth considering one of the many **rail passes** available, covering regions as well as individual countries. None of them actually extend to the Baltic States themselves, but they're a useful way of getting across most of the other countries on the way. Some passes have to be bought before leaving home, while others can only be bought in the country for which they're valid.

Inter-Rail passes

Inter-Rail passes are only available to European residents, and you'll be asked to provide proof of residency before being allowed to purchase one. They come in over-26 and (cheaper) under-26 versions, and cover 28 European countries (including Turkey and Morocco) grouped together in zones:

A Republic of Ireland/Britain

B Norway, Sweden, Finland

C Germany, Austria, Switzerland, Denmark

D Czech & Slovak Republics, Poland, Hungary, Croatia

E France, Belgium, Netherlands, Luxembourg

F Spain, Portugal, Morocco

G Italy, Greece, Turkey, Slovenia plus some ferry services between Italy and Greece

H Bulgaria, Romania, Yugoslavia, Macedonia

Useful publications

The red-covered *Thomas Cook European Timetables* details schedules of over 50,000 trains in Europe, as well as timings of over 200 ferry routes and rail-connecting bus services. It's updated and issued every month; the main changes are in the June edition (published end of May), which has details of the summer European schedules, and the October one, (published end of Sept), which includes winter schedules; some have advance summer/winter timings also. The book can be purchased online (which gets you a ten-percent discount) at ⓦwww.thomascookpublishing.com or from branches of Thomas Cook (see ⓦwww.thomascook.co.uk for your nearest branch), and costs £9.50. Their useful Rail Map of Europe can be purchased online for £6.95.

The passes are available for 12 or 22 days (one zone only) or one month, and you can purchase up to three zones or a global pass covering all zones. Assuming you're heading for the Baltic States via Belgium, Germany and Poland, you'll need a pass covering zones C, D and E (£320; £225 for under-26s) to get there from the UK or Ireland. Inter-Rail passes do not include travel between Britain and the Continent, although Inter-Rail pass holders are eligible for discounts on rail travel in the UK and cross-Channel ferries.

Eurail passes

Non-European residents qualify for the **Eurail pass**, which must be purchased before arrival in Europe (or from Rail Europe in London by non-residents who were unable to get it at home). The pass allows unlimited free first-class train travel in seventeen European countries, including Belgium and Germany but not Poland or the Baltic States – so you'll have to buy a regular ticket to cover the last leg of the journey. The pass is available in increments of 15 days ($588), 21 days ($762), 1 month ($946), 2 months ($1338) and 3 months ($1654). If you're under 26, you can save money with a **Eurail Youthpass** (from $414), which is valid for second-class travel only, or, if you're travelling with up to four other companions, a joint **Eurail Saverpass** (from $498), both of which are available in the same increments as the Eurail pass. Also good value is the **Eurail Flexipass**, which is good for 10 or 15 days' travel within a two-month period. This, too, comes in first-class, under-26/second-class (prices from $488). Further details of these passes and other Eurail permutations, as well as prices, can be found on ⓦwww.raileurope.com.

Rail contacts

In the UK and Ireland

Belgian Railways UK ☎020/7593 2332, ⓦwww.b-rail.be. Timetable information and through ticketing on European routes.
Eurostar UK ☎0870/160 6600, ⓦwww.eurostar.com. Passenger train which goes from Waterloo International in London to Paris (2hr 35min) or Brussels (2hr 20min). You can get through tickets – including the tube journey to Waterloo International – from Eurostar itself, from most travel agents or from mainline train stations in Britain. Inter-Rail passes give discounts on the Eurostar service.
German Rail UK ☎0870/243 5363, ⓦwww.bahn.de. Timetable information and through ticketing on European routes.
International Rail UK ☎0870/120 1606 or 01962/773 646, ⓦwww.international-rail.com. Through tickets from the UK as far as Warsaw, and Inter-Rail passes.
Northern Ireland Railways UK ☎028/9089 9411, ⓦwww.nirailways.co.uk. Sells Inter-Rail passes.
Rail Europe UK ☎0870/584 8848, ⓦwww.raileurope.co.uk. Discounted rail fares for under-26s on a variety of European routes; also agents for Inter-Rail and Eurostar.
Trainseurope UK ☎0900/195 0101, ⓦwww.trainseurope.co.uk. Tickets from the UK to Poland. Inter-Rail and other individual country passes.

In North America

CIT Rail US ☎1-800/CIT-RAIL or 212/730-2400, Canada ☎1-800/361-7799; ⓦwww.cit-rail.com. Eurail, Europass, German and Italian passes.
DER Travel US ☎1-888/337-7350, ⓦwww.dertravel.com/rail. Eurail, Europass and many individual country passes.
Europrail International Canada ☎1-888/667-9734, ⓦwww.europrail.net. Eurail, Europass and individual country passes.
Rail Europe US ☎1-877/257-2887, Canada ☎1-800/361-RAIL; ⓦwww.raileurope.com/us. Official North American Eurail pass agent; also sells Europass, multinational passes and most single-country passes.
ScanTours US ☎1-800/223-7226 or 310/636-4656, ⓦwww.scantours.com. Eurail, Scandinavian and many other European country passes.

In Australia and New Zealand

CIT World Travel Australia ☎02/9267 1255 or 03/9650 5510, ⓦwww.cittravel.com.au. Eurail and Europass rail passes.
Rail Plus Australia ☎1300/555 003 or 03/9642 8644, ⓦwww.railplus.com.au. Sells Eurail, Europass, Britrail and Amtrak passes.
Trailfinders Australia ☎02/9247 7666, ⓦwww.trailfinder.com.au. All Europe passes.

By bus from the UK and Ireland

One of the cheapest ways of getting to the Baltic States from the UK is by bus. **Eurolines** operates services four times a week to Rīga via Vilnius, taking something in the order of 38 and 43 hours respectively. It's not as gruelling an experience as you might think, with drivers making refreshment stops at regular intervals, although the experience of spending the best part of two days in the same seat will not be to everyone's taste. Tickets to Rīga cost £86 one-way, £160 return (slightly less if you're only going as far as Vilnius), with a ten-percent reduction for under-26s and seniors.

Eurolines offers a **pass** for Europe-wide travel, valid for either 15, 30, or 60 days, between 46 European cities (starting from £113) – no Baltic destination is featured among these, but you could get as far as Warsaw on this pass and pay for an onward bus or train ticket to Vilnius or Rīga once you get there.

Bus contacts

Eurolines UK ☎0870/514 3219, Republic of Ireland ☎01/836 6111; ✆www.eurolines.co.uk. Tickets can also be purchased from any Eurolines or National Express agent (☎0870/580 8080, ✆www .nationalexpress.co.uk or wwww.gobycoach.com). If you're starting your journey in Ireland, there are Eurolines services to London from Dublin, Cork, Killarney, Limerick, Tralee and Belfast.
Ulsterbus Northern Ireland ☎028/9033 7003, ✆www.ulsterbus.co.uk. Runs services from Belfast to London.

By car and ferry from the UK and Ireland

Driving to the Baltic States involves a long haul of 1800km from Calais or Ostend to the Lithuanian border, followed by a further 170km, 360km or 660km to Vilnius, Rīga or Tallinn respectively. Using the motorways of Belgium, Holland and northern Germany, you'll find the first 1000km of the journey are reasonably straightforward and might easily be covered in a couple of days' hard driving. From the Polish border onwards however, roads are mostly single carriageway and are not always in the best state of repair – you'll

have to adopt a leisurely approach to the Polish leg of the journey if you want to arrive with your nerves intact.

The most convenient **Channel crossings** are on the P&O Stena services from Dover/Folkestone to Calais, Hoverspeed to Ostend, or Eurotunnel's Le Shuttle Channel Tunnel option from Folkestone to Calais (£180–299 for two adults and a car depending on season, although there are frequent special offers). Once in Calais or Ostend, you can pick up the main motorway route east through Belgium and beyond, bypassing Brussels, Düsseldorf, Hannover and Berlin on the way.

You can cut down the driving distance by taking one of the thrice-weekly Scandinavian Seaways **sailings from Harwich to Hamburg** (19hr), costing £240–300 per passenger, depending on season, and £100 per car. The most convenient ferry route from the north of England is the nightly North Sea Ferries service **from Hull to Rotterdam** (14hr; from around £300 return for two passengers, including car).

If you don't fancy driving across Poland, you could consider a handful of **ferry options from northern Europe** that would cut the country out of your itinerary. Scandline's weekly sailing **from Arhus** in Denmark to Klaipėda in Lithuania (45hr) costs €136 one-way for a place in a two-bed cabin, €315 with a car. There are also daily sailings operated by either Scandlines or Lisco **from Kiel** to Klaipėda (23hr) and a thrice-weekly Lisco service **from Sassnitz** (a small port northeast of Rostock) to Klaipėda (21hr). Whichever port you depart from, the Klaipėda trip costs €80–200 per person one-way, depending on size of cabin, and €120–180 per car. Finally, **Rostock** is the departure point for twice-weekly Scandlines services to Liepāja in Latvia (19hr) and summer-only, thrice-weekly Silja Line services to Tallinn in Estonia (23hr).

A more time-consuming but undoubtedly rewarding way of getting to the Baltic States is to cross the North Sea to Scandinavia, before catching a Baltic-bound ferry from the Swedish ports of Stockholm or Karlshamn. **Fjord Line** operates a thrice-weekly service from **Newcastle to Stavanger** (20hr) and **Bergen** (27hr) in Norway, with a minimum fare of £62 each way in winter, £96 in summer, plus £60–70 for a vehicle. From Bergen it's a 700-kilometre drive to Stockholm. Alternatively, DFDS Seaways sails twice weekly from **Newcastle to Gothenburg** in Sweden (26hr), priced at £132 per person return, or there's an "all in one car" family fare of £374 return. From Gothenburg, it's a four-hour drive to Stockholm. For details of ferries from Stockholm and Karlshamn to the Baltic States, see p.21.

Ferry contacts

Ferry operators in the UK and Ireland

DFDS Seaways UK ☎0870/5333 000, 🖰www.dfdsseaways.co.uk. Harwich to Cuxhaven (Germany), Esbjerg (Denmark); Newcastle to Amsterdam, and seasonally to Gothenburg (Sweden) and Kristiansand (Norway).

Eurotunnel UK ☎0870/535 3535, 🖰www.eurotunnel.com. Shuttle train via the Channel Tunnel for vehicles and their passengers only. The service runs continuously between Folkestone and Coquelles, near Calais, with up to four departures per hour (only one per hour midnight–6am) and takes 35min (45min for some night departure times), though you must arrive at least 30min before departure. It is possible to turn up and buy your ticket at the toll booths (after exiting the M20 at junction 11a), though at busy times booking is advisable. Rates depend on the time of year, time of day and length of stay; it's cheaper to travel between 10pm and 6am, while the highest fares are reserved for weekend departures and returns in July and August.

Fjord Line UK ☎0191/296 1313, 🖰www.fjordline.com. Newcastle to Norway: principally Stavanger, Bergen and Haugesund.

Hoverspeed UK ☎0870/240 8070, 🖰www.hoverspeed.co.uk. 24 daily departures. Dover to Calais and Ostend; Newhaven to Dieppe.

Irish Ferries UK ☎0870/517 1717, Northern Ireland ☎0800/0182 211, Republic of Ireland ☎1890/313 131; 🖰www.irishferries.com. Dublin to Holyhead; Rosslare to Pembroke.

Norse Merchant Ferries UK ☎0870/600 4321, Republic of Ireland ☎01/819 2999; 🖰www.norsemerchant.com. Belfast and Dublin to Liverpool.

P&O Irish Sea UK ☎0870/242 4777, Republic of Ireland ☎1800/409 049; 🖰www.poirishsea.com. Larne to Cairnryan and to Fleetwood; Dublin to Liverpool.

P&O North Sea Ferries UK ☎0870/129 6002, 🖰www.ponorthseaferries.com. Hull to Rotterdam and Zeebrugge.

P&O Stena Line UK ☎0870/600 0600 or 01304/864 003, 🖰www.posl.com. Dover to Calais.

Sea Cat UK ☎0870/5523 523, Republic of Ireland ☎1800/805055; 🖰www.seacat.co.uk. Belfast to Stranraer, Heysham and Troon; Dublin to Liverpool.

Sea France UK ☎0870/571 1711, 🖰www.seafrance.com. Dover to Calais.

Stena Line UK ☎0870/570 7070, Northern Ireland ☎028/9074 7747, Republic of Ireland ☎01/204 7777; 🖰www.stenaline.co.uk. Harwich to the Hook of Holland.

Swansea Cork Ferries UK ☎01792/456 116, Republic of Ireland ☎021/427 1166; 🖰www.swansea-cork.ie. Cork to Swansea (no sailings Nov 7 to March 11).

Ferry operators in Germany and Denmark

Lisco Lithuania ☎8-46/393 616, 🖰www.lisco.lt. Six weekly sailings from Kiel to Klaipėda; and three weekly sailings from Sassnitz to Klaipėda.

Scandlines Denmark ☎33 15 15 15, 🖰www.scandlines.dk; Germany ☎0431/2097 6480, 🖰www.scandlines.de. Arhus to Klaipėda in Lithuania once a week; Kiel to Klaipėda three times weekly; Rostock to Liepāja in Latvia twice weekly.

Silja Line Germany ☎0451/589 9222, 🖰www.silja.com. From Rostock to Tallinn June–Sept; three times weekly.

From Poland

Travelling overland from Poland to the Baltics is very cheap, with train and bus tickets from Warsaw to the Lithuanian capital Vilnius rarely exceeding £17/US$25 each way. Daily **bus services** operate from Warsaw's Warszawa Zachodnia terminal to Vilnius (8–10hr). There are also services from Gdańsk to Vilnius daily (12hr; overnight); Olsztyn to Vilnius five days a week (8hr; overnight) and Kraków to Vilnius four times a week (16hr; overnight). There's also a daily bus from Warsaw to Rīga, travelling via Białystok (18hr).

A direct **train** runs **from Warsaw to Vilnius** three times a week; otherwise head for the near-border town of Suwałki, from where there are two trains a day to Šeštokai on the Lithuanian side of the frontier, each of which is met by a connecting service to Kaunas and Vilnius.

There are **flights** too, though at around £140/US$210, they're not much of a bargain. The Polish national carrier LOT flies from Warsaw to Rīga and Tallinn five-to-six times weekly, and Lithuanian Airlines flies from Warsaw to Vilnius daily.

From Finland

One of the most popular jumping-off points for travel into the Baltic States is the Finnish capital **Helsinki**, with five **ferry** companies – Eckerö Line, Lindaline, Tallink, Silja Line and Nordic Jet Line – offering daily services to the Estonian capital **Tallinn**. The 85-kilometre crossing takes three and a half hours in the older, larger ferries operated by Eckerö and Tallink, and about half that time in the more modern catamarans.

One-way passenger **fares** range from £11/$16 to £15/$23 on the slower services to £15/$23 to £30/$45 on the catamarans, with prices depending on the day of travel – weekend crossings work out the most expensive. Expect to add £11/$16–£22/$35 for a car, £7/$11–£11/$16 for a motorbike, and £3.50/$5.50 for a bicycle. Note that catamarans only run when the sea is free of ice (usually mid-March to late Dec).

All services depart from Helsinki's South Harbour, an easy ten-minute walk from central train and bus stations. The terminals for Eckerö Line, Lindaline, Tallink and Silja Line are located on the western side of the harbour; Nordic Jet Line is on the east.

Finland ferry contacts

Eckerö Line ☎09/228 8544, 🌐www.eckeroline.ee. One daily Helsinki–Tallinn ferry (3hr 30min).
Lindaline ☎09/668 9700, 🌐www.lindaline.fi. Six daily services from Helsinki to Tallinn (1hr 30min).
Nordic Jet Line ☎09/681770, 🌐www.njl.info. Helsinki–Tallinn three times daily (1hr 40min).
Silja Line ☎09/180 4422, 🌐www.silja.fi. Three catamaran services daily (1hr 45min).

Tallink ☎09/228311, 🌐www.tallink.fi. Three daily car ferries (3hr 30min) and three daily catamarans (1hr 40min) from Helsinki to Tallinn.

From Sweden

Sweden enjoys ferry links with all three Baltic States and, although crossings involve spending one night on the boat, fares are reasonable enough to make this a good budget alternative to flying.

From Stockholm Tallink operates a daily ferry to Tallinn, while Rigasealine runs three times a week to Rīga. On both routes simple deck passage costs around £45/US$68 return – a cabin berth can add anything from £10/US$15 to £35/US$52 to this price, depending on how much luxury you're accustomed to. Taking a car will cost £70/US$105 return, a motorbike £30/US$45.

The port of **Karlshamn**, 350km southwest of Stockholm, is the departure point for both Lisco's thrice-weekly ferry to Liepāja in Latvia and Scandlines' six-times-a-week service to Klaipéda in Lithuania. Prices for both destinations are roughly comparable, with deck passage costing £40/US$60 return, a cabin berth £40/US$60 extra, £48/US$70 for a car, £20–30/US$30–45 for a motorbike. Note that Karlshamn ferry terminal is 4km west of town, and there's no public transport – so foot passengers should budget for the cost of a taxi.

Sweden ferry contacts

Lisco Lithuania ☎8-46/393 616, 🌐www.lisco.lt. Six weekly services from Karlshamm in Sweden to Klaipéda in Lithuania (16hr).
Rigasealine ☎08/5100 1500, 🌐www.rigasealine.lv. Three sailings a week from Stockholm to the Latvian capital Rīga (18hr).
Scandlines ☎0454/19080, 🌐www.scandlines.se. Thrice-weekly ferry from Karlshamm in Sweden to Liepāja in Latvia (16hr).
Tallink ☎08/666 6001, 🌐www.tallink.se. One daily ferry from Stockholm to Tallinn (15hr).

Red tape and visas

Citizens of the USA and EU-member states require only a valid passport to enter Estonia, Latvia and Lithuania. Australians, New Zealanders and Canadians are allowed visa-free entry into Estonia and Lithuania, but need a visa (US$15) to enter Latvia – this is available from embassies and consulates in your home country, at Rīga airport on arrival, but not at land borders. Nationals of other countries should check on visa regulations at the relevant embassy or consulate before setting out.

Visitors are allowed to stay in each Baltic state for a total of ninety days in any given calendar year. If you wish to stay longer than this you'll need to apply for a residence or work permit – simply crossing the border and re-entering again every ninety days won't work. Up-to-date information on entrance regulations and visa costs can be found on the websites of the relevant foreign ministry: ⓦwww.vm.ee for Estonia, ⓦwww.mfa.gov.lv or ⓦwww.am.gov.lv for Latvia, and ⓦwww.urm.lt for Lithuania.

Embassies and consulates

Australia and New Zealand
Estonia 86 Louisa Rd, Birchgrove, NSW 2041 ☏02/9810 7468, ✉eestikon@ozemail.com.au.
Latvia 32 Parnell St, Strathfield, NSW 2135 ☏02/9745 5981.
Lithuania 40B Fiddlers Wharf Rd, Killara, Sydney, NSW 2071 ☏02/9498 2571.

Canada
Estonia 202-958 Broadview Ave, Toronto, Ontario M4K 2R6 ☏416/461 0764, ✉estconsu@inforamp.net.
Latvia 280 Albert St, Suite 300, Ottawa, Ontario K1P 5G8 ☏613/238 6014, ✉embassy.canada@mfa.gov.lv.

Lithuania 130 Albert St, Suite 204, Ottawa, Ontario K1P 5G4 ☏613/567 5458, ⓦwww.lithuanianembassy.ca.

Ireland
Estonia 24 Merlyn Park, Ballsbridge, Dublin 4 ☏01/269 1552, ✉asjur@gofree.indigo.ie.
Latvia contact UK embassy.
Lithuania contact UK embassy.

UK
Estonia 6 Hyde Park Gate, London SW7 5DG ☏020/7589 3428, ⓦwww.estonia.gov.uk.
Latvia 45 Nottingham Place, London W1U 5LR ☏020/7312 0040, ✉embassy@embassyoflatvia.co.uk.
Lithuania 84 Gloucester Place, London W1H 3HN ☏020/7486 6401, ✉amb.uk@urm.lt.

US
Estonia 2131 Massachusetts Ave, NW, Washington DC 20008 ☏202/588-0101, ⓦwww.estemb.org.
Latvia 4325 17th St NW, Washington DC 20011 ☏202/726-8213, ⓦwww.latvia.usa.org.
Lithuania 2622 16th St NW, Washington, DC 20009 ☏202/234 5860, ⓦwww.ltembassyus.org; 211 E Ontario, suite 1500, Chicago, IL 60611 ☏312/397-0382, ✉kons.cikaga@urm.lt; 420 Fifth Ave, 3rd floor, New York, NY10018 ☏212/354-7840, ✉kons.niujorkas@urm.lt.

Information and maps

Although each of the Baltic States has a national tourist board, none of them as yet has an international network of tourist information offices. However, most embassies keep a modest stock of free maps and brochures and will do their best to supply you with information on specific destinations. You can also examine the national tourist boards' websites and make enquiries by email.

Almost every major city and resort in the Baltic States has a **tourist office** where you can pick up information on sights, public transport and accommodation; most can also book hotels and B&Bs on your behalf. Tourist offices are much less common in smaller provincial centres and countryside areas, although many national parks maintain "visitors' centres" which essentially do the same job. Staff usually have a working knowledge of English, German and Russian are the other most frequently spoken languages. The quantity and quality of available maps and brochures varies from one place to the next, and they're often for sale rather than given away free. **Opening hours** are usually Mon–Fri 9am–5pm, although tourist offices in more popular areas may open for a few hours at weekends, especially during the summer. You'll find details of individual offices throughout the guide.

National tourist boards

Estonian National Tourist Association
ⓦ www.visitestonia.com.
Latvian Tourism Development Agency
ⓦ www.latviatourism.lv.
Lithuanian State Department of Tourism
ⓣ +370 5 210 8753, ⓦ www.tourism.lt or
ⓦ www.travel.lt.

Maps

The **maps** in this book should be adequate for most purposes, but drivers, cyclists and hikers will require something more detailed. The city plans and regional maps stocked by local tourist offices tend towards the rudimentary and are rarely given away free.

Latvian publishers **Jāna Sēta**, who themselves run a lovely travel bookshop in Rīga,

provide the most comprehensive coverage of the Baltics with regularly updated maps. The three countries are available separately at 1:500,000, or combined into a handy pocket-size atlas at the same scale, with 72 street plans in addition. Jāna Sēta also produces the best individual fold-out maps of the three Baltic capitals, as well as most other cities and provincial towns in Latvia and Lithuania.

Cartographers of the highly regarded **World Mapping Project** have prepared excellent clear maps of Lithuania at 1:325,000 and the Baltic States at 1:600,000, both printed on waterproof and tear-resistant plastic by the German company Reise Know-How. Their map of Estonia at 1:275,000 is due out in early 2004.

If you intend to do some **serious hiking** you'll need to get hold of more detailed maps. **In Latvia**, Jāna Sēta produces indispensable maps of the national parks, while other areas are covered by the 1:50,000 maps in the Latvijas republikas satelitkarte series, though they're hard to get hold of – the Jāna Sēta bookshop (see p.24) is the most likely outlet.

In Lithuania, local firm Briedis publishes a series of 1:130,000 regional road maps that cover just about every country lane and farmstead. Lithuania's national park areas are badly served by cartographers, and you might have to rely on the rough-and-ready maps provided by local tourist offices.

In Estonia the highly detailed 1:50,000 Eesti baaskart series, based on satellite photographs, are useful for walking, although not all shops stock them. Also handy are the Regio 1:100,000 maps of national parks and islands.

23

Map outlets

In the Baltics
Jāņa Sēta Elizabetes 83/85, Rīga, Latvia ☎709 2288, ⓦwww.kartes.lv. The only dedicated travel and map bookshop in the Baltics.

In the UK and Ireland
Blackwell's Map and Travel Shop 50 Broad St, Oxford OX1 3BQ ☎01865/793 550, ⓦmaps.blackwell.co.uk.
Easons Bookshop 40 O'Connell St, Dublin 1 ☎01/858 3881, ⓦwww.eason.ie.
Heffers Map and Travel 20 Trinity St, Cambridge CB2 1TJ ☎01865/333 536, ⓦwww.heffers.co.uk.
Hodges Figgis Bookshop 56–58 Dawson St, Dublin 2 ☎01/677 4754.
The Map Shop 30A Belvoir St, Leicester LE1 6QH ☎0116/247 1400, ⓦwww.mapshopleicester.co.uk.
National Map Centre 22–24 Caxton St, London SW1H 0QU ☎020/7222 2466, ⓦwww.mapsnmc.co.uk.
Newcastle Map Centre 55 Grey St, Newcastle upon Tyne, NE1 6EF ☎0191/261 5622.
Stanfords 12–14 Long Acre, WC2E 9LP ☎020/7836 1321; 29 Corn St, Bristol BS1 1HT ☎0117/929 9966; 39 Spring Gardens, Manchester M2 2BG ☎0161/831 0250; ⓦwww.stanfords.co.uk.
The Travel Bookshop 13–15 Blenheim Crescent, W11 2EE ☎020/7229 5260, ⓦwww.thetravelbookshop.co.uk.

In the US and Canada
Adventurous Traveler.com US ☎1-800/282-3963, ⓦadventuroustraveler.com.

Book Passage 51 Tamal Vista Blvd, Corte Madera, CA 94925 ☎1-800/999-7909, ⓦwww.bookpassage.com.
Distant Lands 56 S Raymond Ave, Pasadena, CA 91105 ☎1-800/310-3220, ⓦwww.distantlands.com.
Elliot Bay Book Company 101 S Main St, Seattle, WA 98104 ☎1-800/962-5311, ⓦwww.elliotbaybook.com.
Globe Corner Bookstore 28 Church St, Cambridge, MA 02138 ☎1-800/358-6013, ⓦwww.globercorner.com.
Map Link 30 S La Patera Lane, Unit 5, Santa Barbara, CA 93117 ☎1-800/962-1394, ⓦwww.maplink.com.
Rand McNally US ☎1-800/333-0136, ⓦwww.randmcnally.com. Around thirty stores across the US; dial ext ☎2111 or check the website for the nearest location.
The Travel Bug Bookstore 2667 W Broadway, Vancouver V6K 2G2 ☎604/737-1122, ⓦwww.swifty.com/tbug.
World of Maps 1235 Wellington St, Ottawa, Ontario K1Y 3A3 ☎1-800/214-8524, ⓦwww.worldofmaps.com.

In Australia and New Zealand
The Map Shop 6–10 Peel St, Adelaide, SA 5000 ☎08/8231 2033, ⓦwww.mapshop.net.au.
Mapland 372 Little Bourke St, Melbourne, Victoria 3000 ☎03/9670 4383, ⓦwww.mapland.com.au.
MapWorld 173 Gloucester St, Christchurch ☎0800/627 967 or 03/374 5399, ⓦwww.mapworld.co.nz.
Perth Map Centre 900 Hay St, Perth, WA 6000 ☎08/9322 5733, ⓦwww.perthmap.com.au.
Specialty Maps 46 Albert St, Auckland 1001 ☎09/307 2217, ⓦwww.specialtymaps.co.nz.

Health

The health risks of travelling in the Baltic States are minimal, and no immunizations are required before you visit. If you plan to do a lot of walking in woodland areas between March and October, it's worth considering getting vaccinated against tick-borne encephalitis, though the chance of contracting the disease from a single tick-bite is very low.

The local **tap water** is safe, despite frequently being somewhat less than palatable – stick to bottled mineral water if you're bothered by the taste.

Minor complaints can be treated at a **pharmacy** (*apteek* in Estonia, *aptieka* in Latvia, *vaistinė* in Lithuania), most of which stock a wide range of international drugs. Pharmacy **opening hours** vary widely, but generally they're Mon–Fri 8am–8pm, Sat 8/10am–3pm, and some city-centre establishments open on Sundays as well. Big cities will have at least one pharmacy with a night counter; details of where to find the nearest one are posted in the windows of most other pharmacies.

For serious complaints, head for the nearest **hospital** (*haigla* in Estonia, *slimnīca* in Latvia, *ligoninė* in Lithuania) or call an ambulance (☎112 in Estonia, ☎03 in Latvia and Lithuania). Emergency treatment is free in all three Baltic States, but in the event of your being admitted to hospital, you'll be charged a small fee for your bed space and for drugs. Although the standard of medical training in the region is high, public hospitals are under-funded and staff are unlikely to speak much English. **Private clinics** with English-speaking doctors exist in the major cities – and are a much better bet if you have a decent travel insurance policy (see "Insurance" below). Always check what the fee covers when booking an appointment with a private practitioner – many of them assume that all Westerners are insured to the hilt and will happily pay through the nose for unnecessary treatment.

Insurance

Even though EU health care privileges apply in Estonia, Latvia and Lithuania, you'd do well to take out an insurance policy before travelling to cover against theft, loss and illness or injury. Before paying for a new policy, however, it's worth checking whether you are already covered: some all-risks home insurance policies may cover your possessions when overseas, and many private medical schemes include cover when abroad. In Canada, provincial health plans usually provide partial cover for medical mishaps overseas, while holders of official student/teacher/youth cards in Canada and the US are entitled to meagre accident coverage and hospital in-patient benefits. Students will often find that their student health coverage extends during the vacations and for one term beyond the date of last enrolment.

After exhausting the possibilities above, you might want to contact a specialist travel insurance company, or consider the travel insurance deal we offer (see box). A typical travel insurance policy usually provides cover for the loss of baggage, tickets and – up to a certain limit – cash or cheques, as well as cancellation or curtailment of your journey. Most of them exclude so-called dangerous sports unless an extra premium is paid: in the Baltic States this can mean skiing, though probably not kayaking. Many policies can be chopped and changed to exclude coverage you don't need – for example, sickness and accident benefits can often be excluded or included at will. If you do take medical coverage, ascertain whether benefits will be paid as treatment proceeds or only after return home, and whether there is a 24-hour medical emergency number.

Rough Guides travel insurance

Rough Guides offers its own travel insurance, customized for our readers by a leading UK broker and backed by a Lloyd's underwriter. It's available for anyone, of any nationality and any age, travelling anywhere in the world.

There are two main Rough Guide insurance plans: **Essential**, for basic, no-frills cover; and **Premier** – with more generous and extensive benefits. Alternatively, you can take out **annual multi-trip** insurance, which covers you for any number of trips throughout the year (with a maximum of sixty days for any one trip). Unlike many policies, the Rough Guides schemes are calculated by the day, so if you're travelling for 27 days rather than a month, that's all you pay for. If you intend to be away for the whole year, the **Adventurer policy** will cover you for 365 days. Each plan can be supplemented with a "Hazardous Activities Premium" if you plan to indulge in sports considered dangerous, such as skiing.

For a policy **quote**, call the Rough Guide Insurance Line on UK freefone ☎0800/015 0906; US toll-free ☎1-866/220-5588, or, if you're calling from elsewhere ☎+44 1243/621046. Alternatively, get an online quote or buy online at ⓦwww.roughguidesinsurance.com.

When securing baggage cover, make sure that the per-article limit – typically under £500 – will cover your most valuable possession. If you need to make a claim, you should keep receipts for medicines and medical treatment, and in the event you have anything stolen, you must obtain an official statement from the police.

Money and banks

The national currencies of Estonia, Latvia and Lithuania are all pegged to the euro, ensuring fairly stable exchange rates for the foreseeable future. The Estonian kroon (EEK) works out at about 22EEK to £1, 14.5EEK to US$1; the Latvian lats (Ls) at about 0.90Ls to £1, 0.60Ls to US$1; and the Lithuanian litas (Lt) at about 5Lt to £1, 3.40Lt to $1.

Traveller's cheques

The safest way to carry money is in the form of **traveller's cheques**, in either dollars, euros or pounds sterling; they're insured, and in the event of theft or loss are reimbursed in full. They're relatively easy to cash in city-centre banks in the Baltic States, though the transaction can take an inordinately long time in provincial towns, where banking staff may be unsure of the correct procedure. Cheques are available from any bank and some building societies. The usual fee for traveller's cheque sales is one or two percent, though this fee may be waived if you buy the cheques through a bank where you have an account. It pays to get a selection of denominations. Make sure you keep the purchase agreement and a record of cheque serial numbers safe and separate from the cheques themselves. In the event that cheques are lost or stolen, the issuing company will expect you to report the loss forthwith to their local office; most companies claim to replace lost or stolen cheques within 24 hours.

Credit, charge and debit cards

The major **credit and charge cards** – Visa, MasterCard, American Express and Diners Club – are accepted in the bigger hotels, restaurants and shops throughout the Baltic States, although most medium- and small-sized businesses only take cash. You can also use your credit card to withdraw money from cash machines (**ATMs**), providing you have a PIN number, though remember that all cash advances are treated as loans, with interest accruing daily from the date of withdrawal; there may be a transaction fee on top of this. Most major **debit cards** can also be used to withdraw cash from an ATM (check with your bank). You'll pay a flat transaction fee for these withdrawals – your bank will be able to advise you on this.

Getting around

The public transport network in the Baltic States is fairly comprehensive, although some of the vehicles used by bus and train companies may be rather more decrepit than their Western European counterparts. In general, buses are both more frequent and quicker than trains; trains are restricted to commuter lines around the major cities and a meagre handful of inter-city routes. International rail and bus passes (see pp.17–19) are not valid for the Baltic States, but regular ticket prices are reasonably cheap. A one-way bus ticket from Tallinn to Vilnius costs around £18/$27; Rīga–Vilnius or Rīga–Tallinn comes to around £7/$11; inter-city routes within each country are considerably cheaper.

Buses are your best means of getting from one Baltic state to another, with express services taking about five hours to travel from Tallinn to Rīga and the same again from Rīga to Vilnius. **Flights** between the capitals take only 45 minutes, but are ten times more expensive than buses. For further information about public transport see each country's "Getting around" section and the "Travel details" at the end of every chapter.

Car rental in the Baltic States works out at about £50–70/US$75–105 a day and £330/US$495 a week for a small car with unlimited mileage if you go through one of the big firms, slightly less if you go through a smaller local operator. Bear in mind, however, that the cheaper deals invariably involve scruffier, less well-maintained cars. You may well find it more convenient to arrange car rental before setting off. The big international operators have agents throughout the Baltic States, so this is fairly easy to do.

Car rental agencies

In Britain

Avis ☎ 0870/606 0100, ⊛ www.avis.co.uk.
Budget ☎ 0800/181181, ⊛ www.budget.co.uk.
Europcar ☎ 0845/722 2525, ⊛ www.europcar.co.uk.
Hertz ☎ 0870/844 8844, ⊛ www.hertz.co.uk.
Holiday Autos ☎ 0870/400 0099, ⊛ www.holidayautos.co.uk.

In Ireland

Avis Northern Ireland ☎ 028/9024 0404, Republic of Ireland ☎ 01/605 7500; ⊛ www.avis.ie.
Budget Republic of Ireland ☎ 0903/277 11, ⊛ www.budget.ie.
Europcar Northern Ireland ☎ 028/9442 3444, Republic of Ireland ☎ 01/614 2888; ⊛ www.europcar.ie.
Hertz Republic of Ireland ☎ 01/676 7476, ⊛ www.hertz.ie.

Holiday Autos Republic of Ireland ☏ 01/872 9366, ⓦ www.holidayautos.ie.

In North America
Avis US ☏ 1-800/331-1084, Canada ☏ 1-800/272-5871; ⓦ www.avis.com.
Budget US ☏ 1-800/527-0700, ⓦ www.budgetrentacar.com.
Europcar US & Canada ☏ 1-877/940 6900, ⓦ www.europcar.com.
Hertz US ☏ 1-800/654-3001, Canada ☏ 1-800/263-0600; ⓦ www.hertz.com.
Holiday Autos US ☏ 1-800/422-7737, ⓦ www.holidayautos.com.

In Australia
Avis ☏ 13 63 33 or 02/9353 9000, ⓦ www.avis.com.au
Budget ☏ 1300/362 848, ⓦ www.budget.com.au.
Europcar ☏ 1300/131 390, ⓦ www.deltaeuropcar.com.au.
Hertz ☏ 13 30 39 or 03/9698 2555, ⓦ www.hertz.com.au.

In New Zealand
Avis ☏ 09/526 2847 or 0800/655 111, ⓦ www.avis.co.nz.
Budget ☏ 09/976 2222, ⓦ www.budget.co.nz.
Hertz ☏ 0800/654 321, ⓦ www.hertz.co.nz.

Mail and communications

Post office opening hours and more information on mail, telephone and Internet facilities are given under each individual country's section on "Communications".

Mail

You can have letters sent **poste restante** to any post office in the Baltic States: simply mark them "Poste Restante", followed by the name of the town and country. When picking up mail you'll need to take your passport; make sure you check under middle names and initials, as letters often get misfiled.

Telephones

Phone boxes offering international direct dialling are plentiful and almost always work; English instructions are often posted inside. Phone cards are most commonly available from newspaper and tobacco kiosks, although post offices and supermarket checkouts often sell them as well.

Calling home from abroad

One of the most convenient ways of phoning home from abroad is via a **telephone charge card** from your phone company back home. Using a PIN number, you can make calls from most hotel, public and private phones and the calls are charged to your account. Since most major charge cards are free to obtain, it's certainly worth getting one at least for emergencies; enquire first though whether your destination is covered, and bear in mind that rates aren't necessarily cheaper than calling from a public phone.

In the **UK and Ireland**, British Telecom (☏ 0800/345 144, ⓦ www.chargecard.bt.com) will issue free to all BT customers the BT Charge Card, which can be used in 116 countries. AT&T has the Global Calling Card (dial ☏ 0800/890 011, then 888/641-6123 when you hear the AT&T prompt to be transferred to the Florida Call Centre, free 24 hours), while NTL (☏ 0500/100 505) issues its own Global Calling Card, which can be used in more than sixty countries abroad, though the fees cannot be charged to a normal phone bill.

In the **US and Canada**, AT&T, MCI, Sprint, Canada Direct and other North American long-distance companies all enable their customers to make credit-card calls while overseas, billed to your home number. Call your company's customer service line to find out if they provide a service from the Baltic States, and if so, what the toll-free access code is.

To call **Australia and New Zealand** from overseas, telephone charge cards such as Telstra Telecard or Optus Calling Card in Australia, and Telecom NZ's Calling Card can be used to make calls abroad, which are charged back to a domestic account or credit card. Apply to Telstra (☎1800/038 000), Optus (☎1300/300 937), or Telecom NZ (☎04/801 9000).

Mobile phones

GSM mobile phone networks enjoy almost blanket coverage in the Baltic States – and the absence of high mountains helps ensure that there are very few blind spots. If you want to use your mobile phone in the Baltics, you'll need to check with your phone provider whether it will work abroad, and what the call charges are. Getting your international access switched on may depend upon payment of a hefty deposit. Bear in mind that you're likely to be charged extra for incoming calls when abroad, as the people calling you will be paying the usual rate. If you want to retrieve messages while you're away, you'll have to ask your provider for a new access code, as your home one is unlikely to work abroad.

One way of avoiding hefty call charges while you're away is to buy a pre-paid SIM card from one of the local telecom companies on your arrival in the Baltics, and insert it into your phone. You'll then be charged for local calls at the local rate, and won't pay extra for incoming calls.

International dialling codes

Phoning the Baltic States
Dial your country's international access code, then:
Estonia ☎372
Latvia ☎371
Lithuania ☎370

From Estonia and Latvia to:
Australia ☎0061
Britain ☎0044
Ireland ☎00353
New Zealand ☎0064
US & Canada ☎001

From Lithuania to:
Australia ☎8-10-61
Britain ☎8-10-44
Ireland ☎8-10-353
New Zealand ☎8-10-64
US & Canada ☎8-10-1

Email

One of the best ways to keep in touch while travelling is to sign up for a free **Internet email address** that can be accessed from anywhere, for example YahooMail or Hotmail – accessible through ⓦwww.yahoo.com and ⓦwww.hotmail.com. Once you've set up an account, you can use these sites to pick up and send mail from any Internet café, or hotel with Internet access.

ⓦwww.kropla.com is a useful website giving details of how to plug your laptop in when abroad, phone country codes around the world and information about electrical systems in different countries.

The media

Specific information on Estonian, Latvian and Lithuanian newspapers, magazines and TV can be found under each individual country's section on "Media".

A small number of useful English-language publications are available Baltic-wide. Prime among these is the *Baltic Times* (☞www.baltictimes.com), a pan-Baltic weekly newspaper based in Rīga. Published every Thursday, it carries a mixture of local news, features and business info and also contains entertainment listings for the coming weekend. It's sold in newspaper kiosks in all three Baltic capitals and in a few provincial cities like Kaunas in Lithuania and Tartu in Estonia, but is hard to get hold of elsewhere.

Also good for news-based features and informed analysis is *City Paper* (☞www.balticsworldwide.com), a bi-monthly magazine which contains hotel, restaurant and café listings for Tallinn, Rīga and Vilnius. Published in Estonia, *City Paper* is relatively easy to find in Tallinn and Rīga, though only sporadically available in Vilnius.

Other handy publications are the small-format city guides produced by *In Your Pocket*

(☞www.inyourpocket.com). Largely concentrating on sleeping, eating and drinking rather than sightseeing, their separate publications on Tallinn, Rīga and Vilnius (each updated every two to three months), are lively, opinionated and up-to-date – and are also an invaluable source of Yellow-Pages-style information. The same company produces a guide to Pärnu in Estonia and a single-volume guide to Kaunas and Klaipėda in Lithuania, both of which are updated annually. The guides are on sale in big bookshops in the three Baltic capitals, but can be hard to find in the provinces.

The main international English-language **radio** broadcasters can be picked up on long wave throughout the region, but frequencies change from one time of day to the next: BBC (☞www.bbc.co.uk/worldservice), Radio Canada (☞www.rcinet.ca) and Voice of America (☞www.voa.gov) will have further information.

Accommodation

Accommodation will probably account for most of your essential expenditure in the Baltic States. The hotel market has witnessed a considerable shake-up in recent years, with the construction of new business-oriented hotels and the arrival of international franchises, alongside the privatization and refurbishment of old state-run establishments. Budget options boil down to private rooms rented out by local families, a handful of hostels and some rough-and-ready campsites.

Hotels

These days, the standard and range of **hotel accommodation** in the major cities and resorts of the Baltic States approaches that

of Western Europe. With Vilnius, Rīga and Tallinn becoming popular city-break destinations, hotels often offer special weekend deals, while establishments in coastal areas drop their prices dramatically outside the peak summer season – it always pays to ask.

In provincial towns the quality of accommodation is much more unpredictable, with smart hotels aimed at the modern business traveller rubbing shoulder with Soviet-era establishments that rejoice in gloomy furnishings and mildewed shower curtains. Many of the best deals are in family-run **guesthouses and B&Bs**, especially in rural areas, where down-on-the-farm **homestays** are increasingly being promoted by local tourist authorities. More details, together with a guide to prices, are given under each country's "Accommodation" section.

Hostels and camping

In general, **youth hostels** are fairly thin on the ground in the Baltics and are mostly concentrated in Vilnius and Tallinn. Several others are scattered around the provinces, especially in Estonia. Most of these establishments are affiliated to the **Hostelling International (HI)** organization, membership of which will get you a discount of ten percent or more on the price of accommodation.

You can join Hostelling International before leaving home (for addresses, see below) or when you get to the Baltic States; the addresses of the relevant national hostelling organizations are given in each country's "Accommodation" section.

There are only a handful of **campsites** in the Baltic States equipped with washing facilities, toilet blocks and other amenities. Others have primitive earth toilets and – if you're lucky – a tap for drinking water, while many are simply fields with tent space and clearings for lighting fires, but no other facilities.

Youth hostel associations

In England and Wales
Youth Hostel Association (YHA) ☏0870/770 8868, ⊛www.yha.org.uk. Annual membership £13; under-18s £6.50; lifetime £190 (or five annual payments of £40).

In Scotland
Scottish Youth Hostel Association ☏0870/155 3255, ⊛www.syha.org.uk. Annual membership £6, under-18s £2.50.

In Ireland
Irish Youth Hostel Association ☏01/830 4555, ⊛www.irelandyha.org. Annual membership €15; under-18s €7.50; family €31.50; lifetime €75.
Hostelling International Northern Ireland ☏028/9032 4733, ⊛www.hini.org.uk. Adult membership £10; under-18s £6; family £20; lifetime £75.

In the US
Hostelling International-American Youth Hostels ☏202/783-6161, ⊛www.hiayh.org. Annual membership for adults (18–55) is $25, for seniors (55 or over) is $15, and for under-18s and groups of ten or more, is free. Lifetime memberships are $250.

In Canada
Hostelling International Canada ☏1-800/663 5777 or 613/237 7884, ⊛www.hostellingintl.ca. Rather than sell the traditional one- or two-year memberships, the association now sells one Individual Adult membership with a 28- to 16-month term. The length of the term depends on when the membership is sold, but a member can receive up to 28 months of membership for just $35. Membership is free for under-18s and you can become a lifetime member for $175.

In Australia
Australia Youth Hostels Association ☏02/9261 1111, ⊛www.yha.com.au. Adult membership rate AUS$52 (under-18s, AUS$16) for the first twelve months and then AUS$32 each year after.

In New Zealand
Youth Hostelling Association New Zealand ☏0800/278 299 or 03/379 9970, ⊛www.yha.co.nz. Adult membership NZ$40 for one year, NZ$60 for two and NZ$80 for three; under-18s free; lifetime NZ$300.

Crime and personal safety

Despite an increase in theft, corruption and mafia-style organized crime in the years following the collapse of communism, the three Baltic States are relatively unthreatening countries in which to travel, and most tourists will have little or no contact with the local police. Technically, everyone is required to carry ID at all times, so it's a good idea to have your passport (or other form of photo ID) handy in order to satisfy any policeman making a random check.

The principal crimes to which visitors are likely to be exposed are **petty theft** and **mugging**. Your main defence against these is to exercise common sense and refrain from flaunting luxury items, expensive cameras and snazzy mobile phones. Beware of sneak-thieves and pickpockets in markets, bus stations and areas popular with tourists – especially the historic quarters of the three captial cities and busy beach resorts like Palanga and Jūrmala. In urban areas, it's best to avoid going to late-night bars on your own – it has been known for muggers to stake out popular bars and clubs ready to pounce on lone travellers stumbling out onto the street in the early hours of the morning.

Take out an insurance policy before you leave home (see p.25) and always stow a photocopy of the last page of your passport in a safe place – this will enable your consulate to issue you with new travel documents in the event of your passport being stolen.

Car theft (either its contents, or the whole vehicle) is an ever-present danger. It's worth paying to leave your car in a guarded car park (hotels will either have one of their own or tell you where the nearest one is), and avoid leaving your car on the street unless it's equipped with immobilizers. Never leave anything of value in your car if you park it in unguarded car parks, near isolated beaches, or in rural beauty spots (especially national parks) – these are all high-risk areas for theft.

Although younger policemen are likely to understand at least some English, Russian is more common among their older colleagues. **Police** are usually courteous and businesslike in their dealings with foreigners, but may be slow to fill out reports should you be unlucky enough to have anything stolen. A mixture of patience and persistence should be enough to resolve most problems.

Travellers with disabilities

Many public places in the Baltic States are wheelchair-accessible, especially in larger cities, though in general, access to public transport and tourist sites still leaves a lot to be desired.

Spa visits, rest-cures and mud baths have been an important aspect of Baltic tourism ever since the mid-nineteenth century, and it's in the **spa resorts** that you're most likely to find hotels used to receiving guests with disabilities. In Estonia, Haapsalu, Kuressaare and Pärnu have a particularly good range of facilities. Forest-fringed Druskininkai, Lithuania's oldest health resort, also caters well to disabled visitors.

Elsewhere, especially in the capital cities, there's a growing number of **wheelchair-accessible hotels**, though these tend to be in the more expensive price brackets. Tourist offices throughout the Baltics will usually find out whether there are any suitable accommodation facilities in their region if you ring in advance, but be sure to double-check the information they give you – some hotels advertise disabled facilities, but haven't got round to building them yet.

Planning a holiday

There are as yet no organized tours for people with disabilities in the Baltic States, so you're pretty much on your own. It's important to become an authority on where you must be self-reliant and where you may expect help, especially regarding transport and accommodation. It's also vital to be honest – with travel agencies, insurance companies and travel companions. Know your limitations and make sure others know them. If you don't use a wheelchair all the time but your walking capabilities are limited, remember that you are likely to need to cover greater distances while travelling than you are used to. If you use a wheelchair, have it serviced before you go and carry a repair kit.

Read your travel insurance small print carefully to make sure that people with a pre-existing medical condition are not excluded, and use your travel agent to make your journey simpler: airline or bus companies can cope better if they are expecting you, with a wheelchair provided at airports and staff primed to help. A medical certificate of your fitness to travel, provided by your doctor, is also extremely useful; some airlines or insurance companies may insist on it. Make sure that you have extra supplies of drugs – carried with you if you fly – and a prescription including the generic name in case of emergency. Carry spares of any clothing or equipment that might be hard to find; if there's an association representing people with your disability, contact them early in the planning process.

Contacts for travellers with disabilities

In the UK and Ireland
Irish Wheelchair Association Blackheath Drive, Clontarf, Dublin 3 ☎01/818 6400, ⊛www.iwa.ie. Useful information provided about travelling abroad with a wheelchair.
Tripscope Alexandra House, Albany Road, Brentford, Middlesex TW8 0NE ☎0845/758 5641, ⊛www.tripscope.org.uk. This registered charity provides a national telephone information service offering free advice on UK and international transport for those with a mobility problem.

In the US and Canada
Access-Able ⊛www.access-able.com. Online resource for travellers with disabilities.
Society for the Advancement of Travelers with Handicaps (SATH) 347 5th Ave, New York, NY 10016 ☎212/447-7284, ⊛www.sath.org. Non-profit educational organization that has actively represented travellers with disabilities since 1976.
Wheels Up! ☎1-888/38-WHEELS, ⊛www.wheelsup.com. Provides discounted airfare, tour and cruise prices for disabled travellers; also publishes a free monthly newsletter and has a comprehensive website.

In Australia and New Zealand
ACROD (Australian Council for Rehabilitation of the Disabled) PO Box 60, Curtin ACT 2605; Suite 103, 1st floor, 1–5 Commercial Rd, Kings Grove 2208; ☎02/6282 4333, TTY ☎02/6282 4333, ⊛www.acrod.org.au. Provides lists of travel agencies and tour operators for people with disabilities.
Disabled Persons Assembly 4/173–175 Victoria St, Wellington ☎04/801 9100 (also TTY), ⊛www.dpa.org.nz. Resource centre with lists of travel agencies and tour operators for people with disabilities.

Outdoor activities

For many visitors, the wide range of outdoor pursuits that the Baltic States have to offer constitutes the region's chief allure. Indeed, if you like the outdoors it's a truly wonderful place, abounding in dense forests, secluded lakes, long, sandy beaches and large tracts of wilderness rich in wildlife. Best of all, you won't find the countryside overcrowded – there's plenty of space to get away from it all.

Hiking

Despite the absence of anything remotely resembling a mountain, the low-lying Baltic States offer a rich menu of hiking possibilities. If you like forests, then you'll love the **woodland trails** on offer in Estonia's Lahemaa National Park or the Dzūkija National Park in Lithuania (p.134), where it's possible to walk for miles without seeing another soul. The Gauja National Park in Latvia (p.261) probably offers the most exciting terrain, with lush woodland, knobbly hills and twisting riverbanks overlooked by ruddy sandstone cliffs.

Everywhere the forests support a wide variety of **fauna** – you're almost certain to catch sight of roe deer during your stay, and if you're lucky you might also see wild boar, moose, elk or even bears. Beavers abound wherever there are streams – although the creatures themselves are much less visible than their handiwork – in the shape of dams and felled trees.

It's easy to combine a forest hike with traditional activities like **berry picking** in summer and **mushrooming** in autumn – although for the latter activity you really need to know what you're looking for. You're usually banned from picking the cranberries that cover the region's **peat bogs**, a number of which have become important nature conservation areas. Many of these regions of mosses, stunted conifers and marshy pools can be explored via specially constructed wooden walkways – most notably in the Soomaa National Park in Estonia (see p.358), the Ķemeri National Park in Latvia (p.242) and the Čepkeliu Nature Reserve in Lithuania (p.137).

If a short, non-strenuous nature walk is what you're after, there are plenty of well-maintained paths through areas of natural beauty, with signboards along the route detailing the local flora and fauna – good examples are the Slītere Nature Trail near Cape Kolka in Latvia (see p.238), Tervete Nature Park in southern Latvia (see p.237) and the Šeirė Nature Trail in western Lithuania (p.168).

If you do want to climb a hill, then consider **Suur Munamägi** in southern Estonia, which at 318m above sea level is the highest point in the Baltic States and the vicinity offers plenty of other wooded heights to explore.

Finally, the glorious **expanses of sand** that run almost uninterruptedly along the Baltic coast provide any number of opportunities for beach walking. While the Sahara-esque dunescapes around Nida in Lithunia can't be matched in terms of spectacle, the wild beauty of Cape Kolka in Latvia shouldn't be overlooked. Beach walkers can try their luck hunting for amber, especially after storms, when tiny nuggets of the stuff are washed up along the coast – especially the stretch between Liepāja and Ventspils in Latvia.

Canoeing

Large stretches of the Baltic landscape are dotted with lakes, and it's relatively easy to rent a variety of watercraft. Most people content themselves with a day or two on the water, although the number of navigable waterways ensures that there's a host of lengthy **canoeing and kayaking** itineraries to choose from, often involving overnight stops at campsites en route. The most popular routes involve the Gauja and Abava rivers in Latvia, the lakes of the Aukštaitija National Park in northeastern Lithuania, and the Ūla and Merkys rivers in southern Lithuania. In Estonia's Soomaa National

Park, you can try your hand at paddling a *haabja*, a traditional canoe hewn from a single trunk of aspen.

Cycling

Although few places in the Baltic States are equipped with cycle paths or cycle lanes, the flat, quiet country roads of many rural areas are ideally suited to exploration by bike. Unfortunately, the business of **bike rental** has yet to be developed in many areas, but it shouldn't be too difficult to pick up a bicycle from agencies in the major national parks and in specific regions where cycling is beginning to take off – notably the islands of Saaremaa and Hiiumaa in Estonia and the Curonian Spit in Lithuania.

Birdwatching

Occupying a key position on north–south migration routes, the Baltic States are visited by **hundreds of bird species** every year. Most visible of these are white storks, which arrive in their thousands every spring and proceed to set up home on roofs and telegraph poles all over the region – with many birds returning to the same nesting spot year after year. Fish-rich wetland areas bordering the Baltic coast attract many migrating birds that have been all but squeezed out of Western Europe by intensive farming – bitterns, corncrakes, black storks, cranes, mute swans, and all manner of geese among them. Many wetland areas have been declared protected zones, some of which are totally off-limits to visitors, although you'll usually be able to make use of observation towers on the edges of these reserves.

Key areas for birdwatching **in Estonia** include the Lahemaa National Park (🌐www.lahemaa.ee), Vilsandi National Park on the island of Saaremaa (🌐www.saaremaa.ee) and the Matsalu Nature Reserve (🌐www.matsalu.ee) south of Haapsalu. **In Latvia**, reed-shrouded lakes at Engure and Pape (🌐www.wwf.lv) are well worth visiting; the website 🌐www.putni.lv is a useful source of information on other locations. **In Lithuania**, wading birds can be observed all along the coast – the Curonian Spit National Park and the Nemunas Delta Regional Park are the best places to see them.

Skiing

Despite the largely flat landscape, the Baltic States can boast a handful of **downhill skiing** opportunities, although pistes tend to be short in length. The Baltic climate does at least ensure that snow cover is guaranteed for a good four months of the year. The most versatile of all the Baltic winter resorts is **Õtepää** in southern Estonia: it has a wide range of downhill slopes and endless opportunities for **cross-country skiing**, as well as a lively nightlife. If an undemanding day out on the slopes is all you're after, you could do worse than head for the Gauja Valley in Latvia, where resorts like Sigulda (see p.263) and Cīrulīši (just outside Cēsis; p.269) are within easy day-trip range of the capital, Rīga. It's pretty easy to rent gear on arrival; a day's use of skis and boots rarely costs over £10/$15.

Work and study

Casual work in the Baltic States is hard to find unless you know one of the local languages, and wages are in any case low – anything above £285/$400 a month is generous, and many of the locals have to make do on much less. The back pages of the *Baltic Times* (see p.30) occasionally advertise vacancies for English-speaking job seekers, but opportunities are thin on the ground.

Teaching English is probably your best bet: there's a growing demand for native-language English teachers in the private language schools that have sprung up all over the region recently. However, you'll need a CELTA (Certificate in English Language Teaching to Adults) qualification in order to secure a job at any but the most fly-by-night organizations. Vacancies are sometimes advertised in the education supplements of Western newspapers; otherwise it's a question of touting your CV around the language schools and making use of local contacts once you arrive.

A handful of organizations run volunteer work camps in the Baltic States, most of which are concerned with environmental or social issues – Earthwatch and Volunteers for Peace (see below) might provide some pointers.

Study

There are several language-learning opportunities in the Baltic States. In Lithuania, Vilnius University organizes two- and four-week intensive Lithuanian courses in winter and summer, as well as a one-year programme spanning two university semesters. Expect to pay around 1100–1400Lt for two weeks, 8200Lt for a whole year. The university can organize accommodation – either in student dorms or with a Lithuanian family – for an extra charge. Full details are available from the Department of Lithuanian Studies, Vilnius University, Universiteto 5, 2734 Vilnius (☎+370 5/268 7214, ⊛www.flf.vu.lt/lsk).

Lithuania is also a good place to learn Yiddish: the local Jewish community, in association with Vilnius University, organizes intensive four-week language courses in August ($1200 not including accommoda-tion; fifty percent discount for full-time students) and year-long university courses. Contact the Program in Yiddish, Pylimo 4, Vilnius 2001 (☎+370 5/261 3003, ⊛www.yiddishvilnius.com).

In Latvia, the Valodu Mācību Centrs ("Language Study Centre"), Smilšu iela 1/3 1050 Rīga (☎721 2251; Ⓔpslc@com.latnet.lv), offers tuition in Latvian for individuals (from 16.50Ls per lesson), or in groups if enough people turn up (from around 2.40Ls per lesson). Rīga Technical University runs beginners' Latvian language courses throughout the academic year. They're primarily intended for foreign exchange students, although other interested parties can take part – for details contact the university's International Relations office (☎+371 708 9313, ⊛www.rtu.lv).

In Estonia, Tartu University runs a year-long Estonian language course for foreign students and has been known to organize short-term intensive courses in the past – consult ⊛www.ut.ee/english for current details. The same university also organizes a two-semester Baltic Studies programme (⊛www.baltic.ut.ee), taught in the English language, and featuring a pick-and-mix menu of politics-, history- and culture-related courses. Again, it's intended for full-time exchange students, although others are admitted for a fee – currently about $1200 per semester.

Useful work and study contacts

In the UK and Ireland
British Council ☎020/7930 8466. Produces a free leaflet which details study opportunities abroad. The Council's Central Management Direct Teaching (t020/7389 4931) recruits TEFL teachers

for posts worldwide (check www.britishcouncil.org/work/jobs.htm for a current list of vacancies), and its Central Bureau for International Educational and Training (t020/7389 4004, wwww.centralbureau.org.uk) enables those who already work as teachers to find out about teacher development programmes abroad.

Erasmus EU-run student exchange programme enabling students at participating universities in Britain and Ireland to study in one of 26 European countries (including Estonia, Latvia and Lithuania). Mobility grants available for three months to a full academic year. Anyone interested should contact their university's international relations office, or check the Erasmus website weuropa.eu.int/comm/education/erasmus.html.

International House ☎020/7518 6999, ⊛www.ihlondon.com. Head office for reputable English-teaching organization which offers TEFL training leading to the award of a Certificate in English Language Teaching to Adults (CELTA), and recruits for teaching positions in Britain and abroad.

In the US

Note: most universities have semester- or year-abroad programmes to certain countries; the following are independent organizations that run programmes in lots of countries.

AFS Intercultural Programs ☎800 AFS-INFO, ⊛www.afs.org. Student exchange organization offering a semester in Latvia studying Latvian or Russian.

Bernan Associates ☎1-800/274-4888, ⊛www.bernan.com. Distributes UNESCO's encyclopedic Study Abroad.

Earthwatch Institute ☎1-800/776-0188 or 978/461-0081, ⊛www.earthwatch.org. International non-profit organization with offices in Boston; Oxford, England; Melbourne, Australia and Tokyo, Japan. 50,000 members and supporters are spread across the US, Europe, Africa, Asia and Australia and volunteer their time and skills to work with 120 research scientists each year on Earthwatch field research projects in over 50 countries all around the world, including one in Estonia.

Volunteers for Peace ☎802/259-2759, ⊛www.vfp.org. Non-profit organization with links to a huge international network of "workcamps", two- to four-week programmes that bring volunteers together from many countries to carry out needed community projects. Most workcamps are in summer, with registration in April–May. Annual membership including directory costs $20. Programmes worldwide, including Lithuania, Latvia and Estonia.

Directory

Bring Even at the height of summer, a raincoat and/or foldaway umbrella are more or less essential. Mosquito repellent comes in handy if you're staying in lakeland or seaside areas.

Electricity 220 volts. Round, two-pin plugs are used, so it's best to get hold of an adaptor before leaving home.

Gay and lesbian travellers Although homosexuality is legal in the Baltic States, social attitudes remain conservative. Generally speaking, young, educated urban-dwellers are increasingly open-minded on questions of sexual preference, but few other sections of society can muster much in the way of tolerance. The Estonian capital Tallinn boasts a broad range of openly gay bars and clubs, whereas Lithuania's main city Vilnius has only a couple. The Latvian capital Rīga is somewhere in between. Outside the capital cities, the scene is either non-existent or so far underground that you won't be able to find it without local knowledge. Good general sources of information are ⊛www.gay.lv in Latvia; ⊛www.gayline.lt; and ⊛www.gay.lt in Lithuania.

Nude bathing Some beaches in the Baltic – notably at Palanga in Lithuania and Jūrmala in Latvia – have designated areas for nude bathing, usually segregated by sex (fairly obvious signboards at the approaches to the dunes will let you know which section is which). Elsewhere, stripping off is much frowned upon, unless you find a secluded lake in the forest.

Photographic film Major brands of colour print film are widely available in all three Baltic States, as well as instant developing facilities. Film for black-and-white prints or colour transparencies is hard to get hold of outside a handful of specialist shops and you won't be offered the range you're used to at home – it's best to stock up before you leave.

Saunas Most Baltic hotels will have a sauna on site – usually it costs money to use them, although they're often free to guests at certain times of day. Many people have saunas built into their homes and it's common for visitors to be invited to share one – it's a sure sign that they value your friendship and should not be refused lightly. In the countryside, look out for old-style, log-fired saunas – smokey, pungent and usually followed by a dip in an ice-cold lake.

Smoking Smoking is forbidden on all forms of public transport and in train and bus stations. It is also prohibited in some of the more old-fashioned cafés, but no-smoking sections in other eating and drinking establishments are rare – going out in the Baltic States can be an oppressively fuggy business. Note that even hardened smokers don't always light up in their own homes, preferring to stand outside (even in the depths of winter) to do so.

Most international brands of cigarettes are sold in the Baltic States – many of them are made under licence at one of northeastern Europe's biggest tobacco factories in Klaipėda, Lithuania.

Student discounts Full-time students in possession of an International Student ID Card (ISIC, ⓦwww.isiccard.com), qualify for 30–50 percent discounts in museums and galleries in all three Baltic States, and occasionally get 10–20 percent off accommodation prices and bus tickets as well. The card costs $22 in the USA; Can$16 in Canada; AUS$16.50 in Australia; NZ$21 in New Zealand; £6 in the UK; and €12.70 in the Republic of Ireland.

Time Estonia and Latvia are two hours ahead of the UK, and seven hours ahead of New York, with clocks going backwards and forwards in March and October respectively. In Lithuania, however the time stays the same all year round – which means that in summer Lithuania is one hour ahead of the UK (and six hours ahead of New York), and in winter two hours ahead of the UK (and seven hours ahead of New York).

Guide

Guide

Lithuania

Lithuania highlights

✳ **Vilnius Old Town** An inviting warren of alleyways overlooked by a handsome collection of Baroque and neoclassical churches. See p.69-86

✳ **St Casimir's Fair, Vilnius** A colourful craft fair attracting just about every woodcarver, ironmonger and basket-weaver in the country. See p.67

✳ **Trakai** This beautifully restored fourteenth-century fortress, set in serene lakeland, is one of the finest in the Baltics. See p.101

✳ **Dzūkija National Park** Rural Lithuania at its most unspoiled, with tumbledown villages, and sandy-soiled pine forests teeming with mushrooms and berries. See p.134

✳ **M.K. Čiurlionis Art Museum, Kaunas** A huge collection of haunting, hallucinatory pictures by Lithuania's finest artist. See p.123

✳ **Rumšiškės Open-air Museum** A rambling, enormously enjoyable collection of nineteenth-century wooden homes from all over the country. See p.132

✳ **Hill of Crosses** A compelling memorial to faith, national suffering and hope, set amid the green pasturelands of the northwest. See p.146

✳ **Nida** A relaxing village of fishermen's cottages set at the foot of towering, tawny dunes. See p.158

✳ **Palanga** A something-for-all-family beach resort with bucket-and-spade beach culture and dance-till-dawn nightlife. See p.161

Introduction and basics

Unlike its Baltic neighbours, Lithuania once enjoyed a period of sustained independence. Having driven off the German Knights of the Sword in 1236 at Šiauliai, the Lithuanians emerged as a unified state under Grand Duke Gediminas (1316–1341). The 1569 Union of Lublin established a combined Polish-Lithuanian state that reached its zenith under King Stefan Bathory, but the Great Northern War of 1700–1721, in which Poland-Lithuania, Russia and Sweden battled for control of the Baltics, left the country devastated, and by the end of the eighteenth century most of Lithuania had fallen into Russian hands. Uprisings in 1830 and 1863 presaged a rise in nationalist feeling, and Russia's collapse in World War I enabled the Lithuanians to re-establish their independence. In July 1940, however, the country was effectively annexed by the USSR. German occupation from 1941 to 1944 wiped out Lithuania's Jewish population and wrecked the country, and things scarcely improved with the return of the Soviets. When Moscow eventually relaxed its hard line in the late 1980s, demands for greater autonomy led to the declaration of independence on March 11, 1990, way ahead of the other Baltic States. A prolonged stand-off came to a head on January 11, 1991 when Soviet forces killed fourteen people at Vilnius TV Tower, but as the anti-Gorbachev coup foundered in August 1991, the world recognized Lithuanian independence.

Where to go

The Lithuanian capital **Vilnius**, with its cobbled alleys and Baroque churches, is arguably the most architecturally beautiful of the Baltic capitals, with an easy-going charm all of its own. Easily reached from the capital is the imposing island fortress of **Trakai**, perhaps the country's best-known landmark and something of a national symbol. The rest of eastern Lithuania is characterized by deep forest, sandy-soiled pine woods and lakes, the most scenic stretches of which fall within the **Aukštaitija National Park** and **Dzūkija National Park**.

Set amid the green farmland of central Lithuania is the second city **Kaunas**, boasting an attractive old town and several set-piece museums. The main city in the northwest is **Šiauliai**, a rather workaday place, but a convenient base from which to visit the **Hill of Crosses**, a remarkable monument to Catholic piety and mysticism.

On the coast, the busy port city of **Klaipėda** has something of an old quarter and a lively handful of bars and clubs. It's also the gateway to the **Curonian Spit**, a uniquely beautiful offshore strip of sand dunes and forest that shields Lithuania from the open Baltic Sea.

Up the coast from Klaipėda, **Palanga** is an inviting cross between family beach resort and bar crawler's paradise, while the **Žemaitija National Park**, just inland, offers an engaging mixture of pretty rural villages and forested wilderness.

Costs, money and banks

Most of life's **essentials** – including food, drink and travel – are relatively cheap in Lithuania, and even if you're on a strict budget you shouldn't have too much trouble enjoying yourself here. The only real exception is the price of **accommodation**, which is slowly creeping up towards Western European levels. Prices vary considerably, though, depending on which parts of Lithuania you stay in. In Vilnius, Kaunas and Klaipėda, a bed in a hostel will cost £6/$9, while private rooms and the cheapest hotels work out at around £28/$42 for a double, with the price of the same in a comfy, medium-range hotel

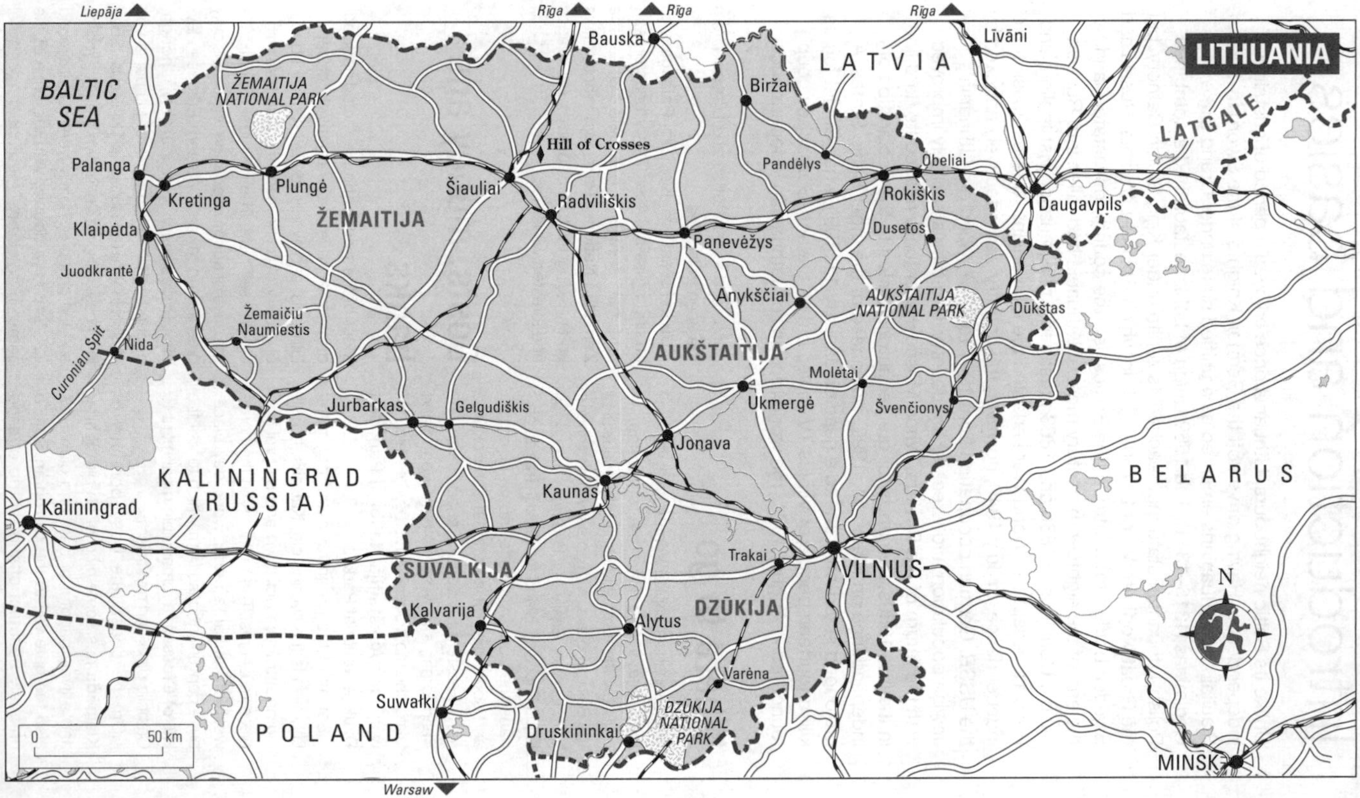

LITHUANIA

BALTIC SEA

ŽEMAITIJA

AUKŠTAITIJA

DZŪKIJA

SUVALKIJA

LATGALE

BELARUS

LATVIA

POLAND

KALININGRAD (RUSSIA)

N

ŽEMAITIJA NATIONAL PARK

AUKŠTAITIJA NATIONAL PARK

DZŪKIJA NATIONAL PARK

Curonian Spit

Hill of Crosses

Palanga
Kretinga
Klaipėda
Juodkrantė
Nida
Plungė
Žemaičiu Naumiestis
Jurbarkas
Kalvarija
Suwałki
Druskininkai
Alytus
Varėna
Trakai
VILNIUS
Švenčionys
Molėtai
Ukmergė
Jonava
Kaunas
Gelgudiškis
Radviliškis
Šiauliai
Panevėžys
Anykščiai
Pandėlys
Biržai
Bauska
Dusetos
Rokiškis
Obeliai
Livāni
Daugavpils
Dūkštas

Kaliningrad

MINSK

Liepāja
Rīga
Rīga
Rīga
Warsaw

50 km
0

rising to £60/$90. Out in the provinces you won't find much in the way of hostels or private rooms, but you can stay in a cheap hotel for as little as £16.50/$25 per double room.

Once you've got accommodation out of the way, things are pretty cheap: short journeys by **bus** (say from Vilnius to Trakai) are unlikely to even dent your budget, falling under the £0.70/$1 mark, while moving across country from Vilnius to Klaipėda costs in the region of £4/$6.

About £5/$7.50 per person per day will suffice for **food and drink** if you're shopping in markets for picnic ingredients, maybe allowing yourself a meal out in a cheap café or restaurant and limiting yourself to a couple of drinks; £15/$22 a day should be enough for a sit-down lunch and a decent dinner followed by a couple of night-time drinks.

Currency

Lithuania's unit of currency is the **litas** (usually abbreviated to Lt), which is divided into 100 centai. Coins come in denominations of 0.01, 0.02, 0.05, 0.10, 0.20, 0.50, 1, 2 and 5Lt and bank notes in 1, 10, 20, 50, 100 and 200Lt denominations.

Currently the **exchange rate** is 5Lt to the pound sterling, 3.4Lt to the euro and 3Lt to the dollar, and looks set to remain reasonably stable.

Banks and exchange

The main high-street **banks** (*bankas*) are Vilniaus bankas, Lietuvos taupomasis bankas,

Lietuvos žemes ukio bankas, Hansabankas and Snoras bankas – this last, despite operating out of a chain of pre-fabricated blue pavilions, is a perfectly respectable outfit. Branches of all the above can change money, give cash advances on Visa, MasterCard or American Express cards, and cash traveller's cheques (for a commission of 2–3 percent). **Opening hours** vary, with most branches operating Monday to Friday 8am to 5/7pm. Big-city branches may well open on Saturday (typically 8am–3pm or 10am–5pm), and in rare cases for a few hours on Sunday too. **ATM cash dispensers** are scattered liberally throughout central Vilnius, Kaunas and Klaipėda, and you'll find one or two in most other town centres.

If you want to exchange cash outside banking hours, head for an **exchange office** (*valutos keitykla*), often just a counter in a corner of a high-street department store. They only deal in cash transactions, but they're usually open in the evenings and at weekends.

Credit cards are widely accepted by hotels, restaurants, big shops and petrol stations in Vilnius and other major urban centres. In small towns and villages, you're unlikely to have much luck.

Communications

Lithuanian postal and telephone services are in general well organized and easy to use. There's a good choice of **Internet cafés** in

Vilnius, Kaunas and Klaipėda, but they're still pretty rare elsewhere; expect to pay around 5–6Lt for an hour of surfing time.

Post offices and mail

In major towns, **post offices** (*paštas*) are usually open Monday to Friday 8am–6/7pm, Saturday 8am–3pm; in smaller places hours are more restricted. Larger post offices often have a confusing array of counters: if you just want to buy a stamp, head for the counter marked *laiškai* ("letters"). Airmail takes about four days to reach Britain, eight to reach North America; surface mail takes twice as long.

Phones

Virtually all **public telephones** now operate on cards (*telefono kortelė*; 9Lt, 13Lt, 16Lt and 30Lt) available from post offices and newspaper kiosks – a 9Lt card will suffice for a handful of local calls; a 13Lt card should cover a medium-duration international call.

For all local calls from land lines you just dial the subscriber number. To make a long-distance call within Lithuania, first dial 8, before dialling the area code and phone number. If you're using a mobile phone inside Lithuania, all numbers have to be preceded by 8 and the area code, even if you're in the same city as the recipient. When calling Lithuania from abroad on any phone, the initial 8 is omitted. For international calls from Lithuania, dial 8, wait for the tone, followed by 10, then the country code, area code and subscriber number.

Mobile phones

For general information on using mobile phones in the Baltic States, see p.29. Lithuania's three **mobile phone operators**, Bitė, Omnitel and Tele2, run schemes that allow you to make calls within the country at local rates and receive calls without the caller incurring international charges. To get on the scheme you need to buy a local SIM card for your GSM phone – this costs as little as 13Lt – after which you can purchase pre-payment top-ups from newspaper kiosks in increments of 10Lt and upwards. Tele2 allows you to go roaming in Latvia and Estonia, too, where your calls will cost only slightly more than the local Lithuanian rate.

Getting around

Lithuania's comprehensive and cheap **public transport system** somehow continues to function efficiently, despite being reliant on clapped-out vehicles and decaying station buildings. Buses provide the most convenient way of getting around: there are frequent services between the main cities and departures to the remotest of villages at least once or twice a day. Trains are slightly cheaper, but although they connect the major towns, departures are infrequent and journey times painfully slow. For details of travel from one Baltic State to another, see p.27.

Buses

Lithuania's **bus network** is run by an at times confusing array of local companies – Toks (ⓦ www.toks.lt) in Vilnius and Kautra (ⓦ www.kautra.lt) in Kaunas being two of the biggest – but services are well integrated and bus stations (*autobusų stotis*) are generally well organized, with clearly marked departure boards and ticket counters allowing you to book your seats in advance. Smaller towns and villages will have a simple bus stop (*stotelė*) with no timetable information, so it's best to enquire about timings at one of the bigger bus stations before heading out into rural areas.

On inter-city routes you might have a choice between **regular buses**, which stop at innumerable halts en route, and **expresses** (*ekspresas*, usually marked on timetables by the letter E), which travel more or less directly to their destination and cost a few litai extra. An express bus from Vilnius to Klaipėda, for example, will cost around 60Lt. Short routes (such as Vilnius to Kaunas, Klaipėda to Nida, and Klaipėda to Palanga) are often operated by **minibuses** (*mikroautobusas*) – timetable information for these services is usually displayed in bus stations.

At big city bus stations, you usually buy your **ticket** from ticket windows before boarding the bus. Tickets show the departure time (*laikas*), platform number (*aikštė*) and seat number (*vieta*). It will also probably carry the name of the bus company you're travelling with – useful to know if two companies are running services to the same destination at round about the same time. If you're catching a bus from some intermediate point on the route, it's often impossible to buy tickets in advance – pay the driver or conductor instead. Small items of luggage are taken on board – large bags are stowed in the luggage compartment, for which you might have to pay an extra 3–5Lt.

Buses on the major intercity routes can get busy on summer weekends, so it's well worth **reserving seats** a day or two in advance.

Trains

Services run by **Lithuanian Railways** have been cut back considerably since the fall of communism. Commuter lines running in and out of Vilnius and to Kaunas are still served by frequent trains, but longer routes (Vilnius to Šiauliai, or Vilnius to Klaipėda, for example) only see a couple of departures a day – they're also slower than the much more frequent buses.

Tickets (*bilietas*) have to be bought before you board. Train stations (*geležinkelio stotis*) often have separate windows for long-distance (*priemiestinis*) and suburban (*vietinis*) trains. **Long-distance services** are divided into two categories: passenger (*keleivinis traukinys*) and fast (*greitas*). Both are in fact painfully slow, but the latter won't stop at every second village at least. Most international trains (*tarptautinis*) travel overnight and offer couchette or sleeping-car accommodation.

Printed **timetables** (*tvarkaraštis*) are few and far between, so you'll have to rely on train-station departure boards for information, or consult the Lithuanian railway's website ⊛www.litrail.lt, though information is currently in Lithuanian only. "Departure" is written *išvyksta*, *išvykimas* or *išvykimo laikas*; and "arrival" *atvyksta*, *atvykimas* or *atvykimo laikas*. Trains that operate on working days (ie Mon–Sat) are marked with the words *darbų dienomis*; those running on Sundays and public holidays are marked *švenčių dienomis*. Otherwise, numbers 1–7 are used to denote the days of the week on which a particular service operates (1 is Monday, 2 is Tuesday, and so on), often accompanied by the word *kursuoja* ("it is running") or *nekursuoja* ("it isn't running").

Driving

Driving in Lithuania throws up a number of hazards. Besides a number of high-powered Western cars and four-wheel drives, you'll also see some spectacularly decrepit cars on the roads, and in country areas you may have to contend with slow-moving tractors, horses and carts, stray farm animals and the odd drunk wandering onto the road.

The **roads** from Vilnius to Panevėžys, and Vilnius to Klaipėda via Kaunas, are fairly respectable two-lane highways for much of their length. Most other main roads are in reasonable repair, but many minor roads are little more than dirt tracks.

How much of the road network is passable depends very much on the time of year. From April through to November you can go pretty much where you like, but in winter you may well need a four-wheel drive to access country areas. **Snow** is the main problem here – although the main routes are regularly ploughed and only become impassable during the heaviest blizzards, secondary roads are often left with a snow covering throughout the winter season.

Petrol (*degalinė*) is reasonably cheap by European standards, costing roughly 35p/$0.60/litre for a gallon. Though most towns and highways are well provided with 24hr petrol stations, there are few in rural areas – so carry a spare can if you're spending time in the sticks.

The use of **seatbelts** is compulsory, and it's against the law to drive after drinking any alcohol – even the tiniest drop. **Speed limits** are 60kph in built-up areas and 90kph on the open road. The limit on two-lane highways is 130kph (April–Sept) and 100kph (Oct–March). The police are extremely vigilant, and will spot-fine you for any transgressions.

Car rental costs around £50–57/$75–85 per day from one of the big companies, slightly less from some local firms – bear in mind though that with the latter, contracts can be dubious, insurance coverage sketchy and the cars may not be well maintained. Addresses of major car rental firms are given on p.27.

Accommodation

There's a growing range and diversity of accommodation in Lithuania, especially at the top end of the scale, with new, business-oriented hotels opening up and international franchises moving in; in addition, many old state-run establishments are being privatized and refurbished. The overall effect of these developments has been to push prices up. That said, however, bargains are still easy to come by – especially if you're staying in hotels and guesthouses on the coast or in the provinces. If you don't mind a bit less privacy, there's also plenty of inexpensive, good-value accommodation in the form of rooms in private houses and on rural farmstays. At the budget end of the scale, a handful of basic but friendly hostels exist in Vilnius, though they're few and far between in the rest of the country. Campsites tend to be rather basic, but on the plus side, are usually set in idyllic, rural surroundings.

Hotels

There's a good variety of hotel accommodation in Lithuania, although standards of service and value for money vary widely from place to place. The international five-star grading system has yet to be applied with any consistency, so for the time being, a hotel's price is your only real guide to its quality – or pretensions.

Many towns and cities still retain one or two **budget hotels** dating from the Soviet period, offering dowdy but perfectly habitable rooms with shared bathrooms – often for under 100Lt for a double room (breakfast not included). However, there's a natural tendency to modernize and upgrade these establishments (or simply sell them off and put them to some other use), so these bargain deals may be disappearing soon.

You'll find plenty of competitively priced **mid-range hotels** offering en-suite showers, TV and breakfast – establishments that would fit comfortably into the international two- and three-star brackets. Prices and quality vary considerably in this category: the majority are of post-1991 vintage, often occupying renovated town houses and featuring new furniture. However, Soviet-era resorts such as Druskininkai and Nida still have a large stock of hotel rooms with brown colour schemes, though they're perfectly comfortable in all other respects. Expect to pay 250–300Lt for a mid-range double in Vilnius, slightly less in Kaunas. Elsewhere, doubles are more likely to fall somewhere in the 100–160Lt range.

International business-class hotels are sprouting up all over Vilnius and are increasingly common in other cities as well. For 400–500Lt you'll get a standard range of familiar comforts: satellite TV, air conditioning, minibar and a lavish buffet breakfast.

Private rooms

Private rooms (*kambariai*) with local families are available in Vilnius, Kaunas, Klaipėda, Palanga and in the resorts of the Curonian Spit. Conditions vary widely from place to place: some hosts have refurbished their flats and installed new furniture with guests in mind; others will plonk you in a bedroom recently vacated by their grown-up offspring. In most cases you'll be sharing your host's bathroom and whether or not you'll be allowed access to tea/coffee-making facilities is a matter of pot luck. Staying in private rooms doesn't necessarily constitute a great way of meeting the locals: some hosts will

Accommodation price codes

The hotels and guesthouses listed in the Lithuanian chapters of this guide have been graded according to the following price bands, based on the cost of the least expensive double room in summer.

- ❶ Under 90Lt
- ❷ 90–120Lt
- ❸ 120–160Lt
- ❹ 160–220Lt
- ❺ 220–300Lt
- ❻ 300–400Lt
- ❼ 400–600Lt
- ❽ Over 600Lt

brew you a welcome glass of tea and show a willingness to talk; others will simply give you a set of house keys and leave you to get on with it.

Local tourist offices can sometimes help you secure a room, but the only nationwide booking agency is **Litinterp**, with offices in Vilnius, Kaunas and Klaipėda (the latter also deals with Palanga and Nida) – see the relevant sections of the guide for contact details. Rooms arranged through Litinterp cost 70–90Lt per person and an additional 10–15Lt gets you breakfast. Cheaper rooms are available in Palanga and Nida if you're prepared to tramp the streets looking for vacancies – signs advertising *kambarių nuoma* ("rooms for rent") and *laisvos vietos* ("vacancies") are posted outside individual houses.

Rural homestays

In an attempt to stimulate the provincial economy, authorities are encouraging the development of **rural homestays** (*poilsis kaime*), where you have the chance to stay on working farms or in village houses and eat locally produced food and drink.

Room quality varies from place to place, although most are neat little en-suites, often with a rustic feel. Some hosts offer self-contained apartments with catering facilities.

Prices start from as little as 40Lt per person, rising to about 80Lt if the property has been swankily modernized. Half- or full-board featuring tasty home-cooked food is often available for an extra cost (20–30Lt per person). While offering a wonderful taste of rural life, bear in mind that most of these homestays are a long way from regular bus routes – so you'll really need your own transport to get around.

Local tourist offices are extremely keen to push this form of tourism and will always help you secure a room in their region, although it pays to contact them a few days in advance. The **Lithuanian Rural Tourism Association** (Lietuvos kaimo turizmo asociacija; Lietuvos respublikos žemės ūkio rūmai, Donelaičio 2, LT-3000 Kaunas, ☏37/400 354, ⓦwww.sala.lt, ⓦwww.atostogos.lt) publishes a catalogue of properties throughout the country and also handles advance reservations.

Hostels and camping

There are few genuine **hostels** in Lithuania. A couple exist in Vilnius and Klaipėda, offering dorm accommodation for as little as 30Lt a night, although they're oversubscribed in summer, so it's a good idea to reserve in advance. Vilnius also has a couple of students' and teachers' hostels that rent out rooms throughout the year when there's space – expect to pay around 40Lt for a bed in a double or triple room.

The Lithuanian Youth Hostelling Association doesn't have a permanent office, but their website, ⓦwww.lithuanianhostels.org, provides contact details for individual hostels in Vilnius, Šiauliai, Klaipėda and Zverynos (in the Dzūkija National Park).

Staying in a Lithuanian **campsite** (*kempingas*) can be a wonderfully idyllic experience if you're prepared to rough it. Sites equipped with toilet blocks and washing facilities are the exception rather than the rule; in most cases campsites are nothing more than grassy areas supplied with picnic benches and (if you're lucky) simple outhouse toilets, which will probably just be a hole in the ground. Most sites are concentrated in national park areas and charge 5–10Lt for a tent space.

Eating and drinking

Lithuanian cuisine is based around a traditional repertoire of hearty peasant dishes, in which potatoes and pork play the starring roles. **Main meals** tend to be heavy and calorie-laden – perfect for the long winters. International and ethnic cuisine is beginning to appear in the cities, and pizzerias are popping up almost everywhere. Although vegetarianism has yet to establish itself, it's possible to find meat-free options on most menus – mushroom- or cheese-filled pancakes being the most common.

Lithuanian **restaurants** (*restoranas*) range from swanky city-centre places, with starched napkins and pan-European menus, to unpretentious eateries offering a cheap range of Lithuanian standards and not much else – a quick glance through the window will tell you which market they're aiming for. Most Lithuanians like to combine eating and drinking in the same venue. Many **cafés** (*kavinė*), for example, are restaurants in all but name, serving up inexpensive and simple Lithuanian standards at prices alongside the usual coffee and cakes, and most places that describe themselves as **bars and pubs** (see "Drinking", p.51) also offer a full menu of hot food. In addition, there's a growing number of homely establishments featuring folksy wooden furnishings and a big choice of drinks and local specialities at mid-range prices – these places often go under names such as **užeiga** ("inn") or **smuklė** ("tavern"), underlining the cosy, bucolic theme.

Even in a fairly upmarket restaurant a meal shouldn't work out much more expensive than in a mid-range establishment in Western Europe, and it's possible to eat really well for much less if you head for the inns and cafés, where a main course usually costs less than 10Lt. Wherever you eat, though, be prepared for **slow service**. You'll find a **glossary** of food and drink terms on p.445.

What to eat

Most Lithuanians tuck straight into a main course (usually listed under *karšti patiekalai* or "hot meals"), although menus invariably include a short list of **starters** that would also do as light snacks (*šalti užkandžiai* are cold starters; *karšti užkandžiai* are hot starters) – typical choices are marinated mushrooms (*marinuoti grybai*), herring (*silkė*) and smoked sausage (*rūkyta dešra*). Soup (*sriuba*) is sometimes offered as a starter, although it's more commonly treated as a quick and cheap lunchtime meal in its own right. Cold beetroot soup (*šaltibarščiai*) is a Lithuanian speciality, and can be deliciously refreshing in summer.

Typical Lithuanian staples

The mainstay of the nation's cuisine is the **potato**, which not only serves as the staple accompaniment to most main courses, but also forms the central ingredient in a series of typical Lithuanian specialities. Raw potatoes are passed through the fine end of a grater, mixed with egg and then dropped in hot oil to form *bulviniai blynai* (potato pancakes) – they're delicious on their own, or

are sometimes filled with meat. The same grated-potato mixture forms the basis of *cepelinai*, Zeppelin-shaped parcels stuffed with minced meat, mushrooms or cheese and then cooked in boiling water, while *kugelis* (also known as *bulvių plokštainis* or "potato slab") is a brick-shaped helping of grated or mashed potato baked in the oven. Another favourite is *žemaičių blynai* (Žemaitija pancakes), mashed potato moulded into heart shapes, stuffed with minced meat and then fried. One dish that is definitely tastier than it sounds is *vedarai*: sausage made from pig intestine and filled with potato pieces.

Common, potato-free dishes include *koldūnai* (ravioli-like pasta stuffed with minced pork), *balandeliai* (cabbage leaves stuffed with meat and rice) and all manner of pancakes (for which *blynai*, *blyneliai* or *lietiniai* are synonyms for more or less the same thing), containing ham, cheese, mushrooms or other savoury fillings.

All of the above are usually served without accompanying vegetables or bread, but can be enormously filling in their own right – not least because they're invariably garnished with pieces of fried bacon fat, lashings of sour cream (*grietinė*), or a tasty mixture of both.

Meat and fish dishes

Meat (*mėsa*) in Lithuanian restaurants usually comes in the form of *kepsnys*, a chop or cutlet which is either roasted or pan-fried (menus find it difficult to specify which, because the expressions "to fry" and "to roast" are covered by the same verb: *kepti*). A *kepsnys* traditionally consists of a fat slice of pork (*kiauliena*), although cuts of beef (*jautiena*), veal (*veršiena*), chicken (*vištiena*) and turkey (*kalakutiena*) are increasingly common. A *kepsnys* might come garnished with a sauce (*su padažu*), mushroom sauce (*grybų padažas*) being the most common.

Other common meat dishes include **sausages** (*dešrelės*), usually made from spicy, heavily seasoned pork rather than the bland, boiled variety. **Stew** (*troškinys*) may come in the form of a satisfying meat-and-vegetable meal, but might equally be a thin soup with a few bits of beef floating around in it. **Lamb** (*aviena*) rarely figures on menus, except in recipes borrowed from other republics of the former Soviet Union – notably *šašlykai* (grilled kebabs) from the Caucasus.

Fish (*žuvis*) is much less common than meat; it usually crops up in the better city-centre establishments, rustic restaurants in freshwater-fishing areas and in all kinds of eateries on the coast. The commonest kinds of fish are trout (*upėtakis*), cod (*menkė*) and salmon (*lašiša*) – all are usually pan-fried or baked, although salmon steaks are sometimes prepared *ant grotelių* ("grilled"). A speciality of the Nida region is smoked eel (*rukytas unguris*), sliced and eaten cold.

Meat and fish main courses are usually accompanied by (often quite small) portions of potatoes and seasonal **vegetables**, alongside generous amounts of bread.

Desserts and cakes

Typical restaurant desserts include ice cream (*ledai*), cakes (*pyragai*), stewed fruit (*kompotas*) and innumerable fruit-filled varieties of pancake (*blyneliai* or *lietiniai*). One of the most popular pastries you'll come across in cafés and bakeries are Lithuanian doughnuts (*spurgos*), which look like deep-fried tennis balls and have neither a hole nor jam in the middle – but they're delightfully fluffy when fresh. More spectacular are *šakotis*, a large, honey-coloured cake in the shape of a spiky fir tree; and *skruzdėlynas* (literally "ant-hill"), a pyramid of pastry pieces covered in syrup. These two creations are usually consumed at family feasts and birthday parties and hardly ever appear on café or restaurant menus – though you can always buy a small one from a supermarket or a bakery and scoff it in your room.

Breakfasts and snacks

Unless you're staying in a budget hotel, hostel or private room, **breakfast** will almost always be included in the cost of your accommodation. At its simplest, it will consist of bread, cheese, ham and a choice of tea or coffee. Mid- and top-range hotels will offer a buffet breakfast, complete with a range of cereals, scrambled eggs and bacon. Pastries (*bandelės*) can be picked up from bakeries, cafés and street kiosks.

Basic self-catering and **picnic ingredients** like cheese, vegetables and fruit can be bought at a food store (*maisto prekės*), supermarket (*prekybos centras*) or an open-air market (*turgus*). **Bread** (*duona*) can be bought from any of the above places or from a bakery (*kepykla*). Most Lithuanian bread is of the brown, rye-flour variety found across the Baltics. It's often baked in big square blocks, and you're more likely to buy a quarter (*ketvirtas*) or half (*pusė*) than a whole loaf (*kepalas*). White bread is much less common, and is usually produced in French-style, baton form (*batonas*).

Lithuanian **street-food** culture revolves around kiosks (often located near markets or bus stations), selling *čeburekai* or *kibinai* (pies stuffed with spicy minced meat).

Drinking

Cafés (*kavinė*) come in all shapes and sizes: some are trendy and modern in style and have a varied food menu, others are chintzy places serving pastries and cakes. Most serve a full range of alcoholic as well as soft drinks. **Coffee** (*kava*) and **tea** (*arbata*) are usually served black, unless you specify *su grietinele* ("with cream") or *su pienu* ("with milk"). *Su cukrumi* is with sugar, *be cukraus* is without.

Vilnius, Kaunas and Klaipėda can all muster a growing range of lively **bars** – many aping American or Irish models, although there are also plenty of folksy Lithuanian places featuring wooden bench seating and rustic decor.

Beer (*alus*) is the most popular alcoholic drink. The biggest local brewers – Utenos, Švylurys and Kalnapilis – all produce eminently drinkable, light, lager-type beer (*šviesus alus*), as well as a dark porter (*tamsus alus*). It's common to nibble beer-snacks (*užkandžiai prie alaus*) alongside your drinks – *kepta duona* (fingers of brown bread fried with garlic) being the standard order.

An increasingly impressive range of imported **wines** (*vynas*) are available in bars and shops. Alita, the locally produced brand of sparkling, champagne-style wine (*šampanas*) is both extremely palatable and very cheap – a bottle of the stuff costs around $3 in supermarkets.

Vodka (*degtinė*) is widely consumed, alongside more traditional firewaters like Starka, Trejos devynerios and Medžiotojų – invigorating, amber-coloured **spirits** flavoured with a variety of herbs and leaves. Strongest of them all is *samanė*, a clear, grain-based spirit which is often brewed illicitly in the countryside and speedily incapacitates the brains of those who drink it – a weaker version is available in shops.

Opening hours and public holidays

Typical **opening times of shops** are Monday to Friday from 10/11pm to 6/7pm, and Saturdays from 10/11pm to 3/4pm. Food stores and supermarkets in the cities usually keep longer hours, opening as early as 7am and working right through to 8 or 10pm, even at weekends. In rural areas, shops may take a break for lunch and close earlier in the evenings.

The opening times of **museums**, galleries and other tourist attractions vary widely from one place to the next. Generally speaking, they're open from Tuesday to Sunday (and in some cases Wednesday to Sunday) from around 11am to 5/6pm – although be warned that some museums work on a Monday-to-Friday basis.

Public holidays

Most shops, museums and all banks are closed on the following public holidays:

Jan 1 New Year's Day
Feb 16 Independence Day
March 11 Restoration of Independence Day
Easter Sunday
Easter Monday
May 1 May Day
July 6 Statehood Day
August 15 Assumption
Nov 1 All Saints' Day
Dec 25 and 26 Christmas

Churches in city centres may well be open seven days a week from 7am until around 7pm, but in most other cases they only open their doors for holy Mass (times of which are posted outside).

Festivals

The Lithuanian year is peppered with traditional events and celebrations that mix ancient pagan tradition, Catholic ritual and the simple pragmatic need for a knees-up. Falling into the last category are the **Sartai horse races** on the first weekend of February, a contest of nineteenth-century origins involving horse-and-trap teams racing each other on the frozen surface of Lake Sartai, 150km north of Vilnius. It's one of the most important social events of the winter, attracting top politicians from Vilnius. If the ice isn't thick enough, the races are moved to the hippodrome in the nearby village of Dusetos.

The promise of approaching spring brings people out onto the streets of Vilnius on March 4, St Casimir's Day, to take part in **Kaziuko Mugė** (St Casimir's Fair), an enormous handicrafts market at which artisans from all over Lithuania come to display and sell their wares. Soon afterwards, **Užgavėnės** or Shrove Tuesday marks the beginning of the Lenten fast – as in the rest of Europe, it's celebrated by the over-consumption of pancakes. However, Užgavėnės in Lithuania bears characteristics that are clearly pre-Christian in origin – children in animal masks pass from house to house bringing good luck for the coming agricultural year (they're given sweets or small gifts in return), and the symbolic ending of winter is marked by burning an effigy of the Morė – an archetypal scapegoat figure – on a bonfire. Užgavėnės celebrations are organized in Vilnius on Shrove Tuesday, and the Lithuanian Open Air Museum at Rumšiškės (see p.132) also organizes a full day of Užgavėnės-related events, but these usually fall on the nearest Sunday rather than on the Tuesday itself.

Most Lithuanians mark the coming of spring by purchasing a sprig of catkins (*kačiukai*) with which to decorate the home.

This practice is closely related to **Palm Sunday** (Verbų sekmadienis), when *verbos* (colourful wands bound from dried grasses, corn stalks and flowers) are bought from street vendors – they're usually on sale from St Casimir's Day onwards – and are proudly displayed in the home for the remainder of the year. *Verbos* would make the perfect Lithuanian souvenir were it not for the fact that the dried flowers disintegrate as soon as you put them in your luggage. **Easter Day** itself is marked by eating a large family meal – usually ham accompanied by a sharp-tasting purée made from horseradish (*krienas*).

The biggest event of the year for many is the night of June 23–24, which in origin is a pagan summer solstice celebration, despite being known by it's Christian name of **Joninės** – after St John's Day, June 24. The festival is also known in some quarters as Rasos ("Dew") on account of the magical healing properties attached to the dew collected at sunrise on June 24. Most people celebrate Joninės by heading for the countryside, where they either sing songs around a bonfire until dawn or head off into the woods with a loved one – deities attached to fertility are supposedly particularly powerful on this night.

As in the rest of Catholic Europe, November 1 and 2 (**All Saints' and All Souls' days** respectively) are marked by mass visits to cemeteries to honour the dead – full of flowers and lit up by innumerable candles, they can be atmospheric places to visit at dusk.

The central event of **Christmas** (Kalėdos) is the Christmas Eve meal (*kučios*), when the whole family gathers to eat twelve courses (symbolizing the twelve apostles), none of which should contain meat or dairy products – pies stuffed with mushrooms, and top-quality fish (notably carp) feature heavily. Also gracing the Christmas table are *kučiukai*, tiny, hard biscuits which are sold in shops in the weeks before Christmas, and dipped into poppy-seed milk before eating.

Cultural festivals

Kino Pavasaris Film Festival Vilnius, late March.

Kaunas Jazz Kaunas, late April.

City Festival Kaunas, third weekend in May.

Skamba Skamba Kankliai Vilnius, late May. *Folk music festival.*

Kunigunda Lunaria Goth festival Vilnius, late May; ⓦwww.dangus.net. *Music festival (metal and goth) with strong neo-pagan undertones.*

LIFE International Theatre Festival Vilnius, late May to early June.

Klaipėda Jazz Klaipėda, early June.

Vilnius Festival Vilnius, late May to early July. *Classical music festival.*

St Christopher Summer Music Festival Vilnius, July. *Chamber music performed in St Casimir's Church and in Old Town courtyards.*

Experimental Archeology Festival Vilnius and Kernavė, early July. *Enthusiasts in Iron Age dress demonstrate ancient Lithuanian music, dancing and traditional crafts.*

Thomas Mann Festival Nida, second half of July. *Chamber music festival.*

Sea Festival Klaipėda, late July. *Carnival floats, folk dancing and pop music.*

Pažaislis Music Festival Pažaislis and other venues in and around Kaunas, July and August. *Classical music festival.*

Trakai Festival Trakai, August. *Orchestral music and opera.*

Mėnuo Juodaragis Late August. ⓦwww.dangus.net. *Weekend-long neo-pagan festival of folk, metal and electronica, held in a different countryside location each year.*

Modern Dance Festival Kaunas, early October.

Gaida Festival of Contemporary Classical Music Vilnius, October.

Autumn Poetry Festival Druskininkai, October.

Entertainment and the arts

Lithuania offers a broad spectrum of entertainment, including a lot of serious music and drama. It's all very accessible too: tickets for even the most prestigious events are rarely impossible to come by, and ticket prices are cheap by European standards. Almost every branch of culture is marked by at least one major festival – see the box on "Cultural festivals" on p.53 and the "Nightlife and entertainment" section of the Vilnius chapter (see p.96) for a thorough run-down.

Classical music and opera

Between them, Vilnius and Kaunas ensure a rich programme of year-round music. Vilnius boasts two symphony orchestras, an opera and a ballet company, while Kaunas has a chamber orchestra and highly rated choir. The capital attracts a large number of top international conductors and soloists during the regular concert season, while the **Vilnius Festival** in June and **Trakai Festival** in August take the top performers out into the open air.

The one "national" composer who features regularly in the repertoire is **Mikalojus Konstantinis Čiurlionis** (1875–1911), whose tone poems *Jūra* ("The Sea") and *Miške* ("In the Forest") were the first full-length symphonic pieces to be composed by a Lithuanian and the first to attempt a symbolic evocation of the country's unspoiled landscapes.

Less regularly performed, but creating big waves internationally, are works by an impressive stable of **contemporary composers** led by Bronius Kutavičius, Mindaugas Urbaitis and Ona Narbutienė, who mix the mystical sounds of Lithuanian folklore with minimalism and contemporary instrumentation. The **Gaida Festival of Contemporary Classical Music** (see p.98) is one occasion when you can bank on hearing a wide selection of their music.

Popular music and clubbing

Lithuanians love dancing and are much less self-conscious about what they strut their stuff to than their modish north European counterparts. Mainstream **discos** are hugely enjoyable affairs featuring everything from Eminem to Boney-M – but you're unlikely to chance upon niche styles of dance music outside a handful of specialist clubs in Vilnius.

Plenty of bars host **live bands** who play rock-pop covers in order to keep people moving and grooving, but there's little in the way of a serious gig circuit, and many local groups restrict themselves to ad-hoc performances in unofficial spaces. Unsurprisingly then, there's little in the way of a local rock scene (and any scene that does exist will be so far underground that you probably won't find it), although several semi-legendary names still mean a great deal to local fans. In the late 1980s and early 1990s, the angular, experimental band **Bix** seemed to personify Lithuania's break-out from the Soviet cultural straitjacket – their CDs are still available even though the band no longer perform. At around the same time, **Fojė** imported a stylish new-wave sensibility to Lithuanian pop – since going solo, their lead singer **Andrijus Mamantovas** has proved to be the country's most enduring rock-pop performer.

Jazz

A handful of venues stage regular **jazz** gigs in Vilnius and Klaipėda, and there are worthwhile festivals involving international guests in Vilnius and Kaunas (see p.53). In the 1970s and 80s, Vilnius was home to the **Ganelin-Chekasin-Tarasov Trio**, the greatest – perhaps the only – avant-garde jazz ensemble in the Soviet Union, and still enjoying legendary status in the world at large. Keyboardist Ganelin and saxophone-bellower Chekasin emigrated years ago, but drummer **Vladimir Tarasov** is still around, playing occasional (and highly recommended) percussion performances in Vilnius, and organizing sound installations in art galleries abroad. Other contemporary performers to look out for are sax-player **Petras**

Vyšniauskas, a pioneer in the field of jazz-folk crossover, and younger-generation vocalist **Neda**, a far more stirring live performer than her bland coffee-table albums would suggest.

Drama

The Lithuanian capital is currently home to some of the most critically acclaimed directors in Europe – their works are regularly staged in Vilnius and if you're at all interested in theatre it's well worth making the effort to find out what's on in the city during your stay. English-language earphone commentary is sometimes provided in the bigger theatres, although there's usually enough happening on stage to make a visit worthwhile whether there's a translation or not.

Godfather of the Vilnius drama scene is **Eimuntas Nekrošius**, who spent most of the 1980s as director of the Vilnius Youth Theatre (see p.99) and now heads a production company of his own, Meno Fortas ("Art Fortress"). His lengthy performances (4–5 hours being typical) feature minimal stage props and repetitive, ritualistic movement. Between 1997 and 2001 his *Hamlet*, *Macbeth* and *Othello* garnered an enthusiastic international response, although his slow-moving 2003 production *Seasons*, based on the works of eighteenth-century Lithuanian poet Kristijonas Donelaitis, pushed the boundaries of what the average theatre audience could be expected to sit through.

A generation younger, **Oskaras Koršunovas** is something of an antidote to this, combining an experimental approach (strongly influenced by Russian avant-gardists Daniil Kharms and Aleksandar Vvedensky) with a thoroughly contemporary taste for bright lights, big noises and visual jokes – he's probably one of the few directors who could stage a version of *Oedipus Rex* in which the inclusion of a giant talking teddy bear fails to detract from the tragic sense of the original. Koršunovas has turned his hand to everything, from intense studio performances to musicals, and has latterly become something of a one-man national industry, with numerous productions on the go at any one time.

One other name worth looking out for is **Rimas Tuminas**, founder of Vilnius Little Theatre (see p.99); his understated but innovative productions of contemporary pieces and Shakespearean classics have earned him Europe-wide critical acclaim.

Cinema

Lithuanian cinemas show English-language movies soon after their release in Western Europe – in the original language with Lithuanian subtitles. During the Soviet period, Lithuania's film studios churned out a respectable handful of local-language movies a year, and their facilities are currently very much in demand with Western production companies seeking to employ skilled technicians on the cheap; domestic film production, meanwhile, has shrivelled to nothing.

One hugely popular Lithuanian cinema classic which you'll see in video stores – and might be tempted to buy if you have a taste for the bizarre – is Arūnas Žebriūnas's 1973 film *Velnio Nuotaka* ("Devil's Bride"), a lavish musical based on Lithuanian folk tales and featuring the cream of theatrical and artistic talent of the time. Featuring an overblown screenplay by poet Sigitas Geda (see "Books", p.435) and a prog-rock-meets-Europop score courtesy of keyboard-bashing groovster Vyacheslav Ganelin (see "Jazz", p.54), it's a one-of-its-kind experience.

Media

The biggest-selling and most influential of Lithuania's daily **newspapers** is *Lietuvos Rytas* ("Lithuanian Morning"; www.lrytas .lt), a self-consciously serious publication famous for stodgy reporting and tortuously long sentences. The lifestyle supplements that come with the weekend editions provide light relief, and Friday's entertainment listings are pretty thorough if you can understand the language. Tabloid-sized *Respublika* is a bright and breezy alternative, while evening paper *Vakaro Žinios* is an entertainingly downmarket scandal rag.

News **magazines** and special-interest periodicals are pretty uninspiring, and it's in the women's market that you'll find most in the way of good design and visual style: avoid the Lithuanian-language versions of well-known international titles like *Cosmopolitan* and take a look instead at home-grown monthlies like *Laima* ("Fortune") and *Moterys* ("Woman") to get an idea of how contemporary Lithuanians really see themselves. Interior-design magazines like *Naujas Namas* and *Namas ir Aš* convey a Scandinavian sense of contemporary cool and may well provide you with a few makeover ideas into the bargain. Finally, Lithuanian Airlines' English-language inflight magazine *Lithuania in the World* is sometimes available from bookshops in Vilnius – it's great to look at, but a bit of a bore to read. For details of English-language publications common to all three Baltic States, see p.30.

Most hotel-room **televisions** will probably offer a handful of German- and English-language channels in addition to national networks like state-owned LRT and private stations LNK and TV3. All the national TV channels feature a surfeit of quiz programmes and reality shows, and almost all of their drama output is imported from North or South America. The schedules include lots of English-language films invariably dubbed into Lithuanian, usually with a single actor reading all the parts.

Spectator sports

The country's most popular spectator sport by far is **basketball** (*krepšinis*). Lithuania has been a basketball superpower ever since the 1930s, when the national team won the first-ever European championships in Rīga in 1937, and retained the title on their home turf two years later. During the communist period, Lithuania's leading club team Žalgiris Kaunas were a major force in the Soviet league and served as an important symbol of national pride at a time when outright manifestations of Lithuanian patriotism were officially discouraged. With the restoration of independence in 1991, Lithuania bounced back onto the international basketball scene, winning the Olympic bronze in 1992, 1996 and 2000. On the last occasion, the Lithuanians came within two points of defeating the superstar-studded American team in the semi-final – a result so close that it was greeted as a moral victory by a nation gone basketball-bonkers. Victory in the European championships in Sweden in 2003 confirmed Lithuania's international standing.

In domestic competition, Žalgiris Kaunas remain the top side, although Lietuvos Rytas Vilnius have offered stiff competition in recent years – matches between the two can be intensely heated affairs. The season runs from October through to April, with a regular diet of Lithuanian league matches (on Saturdays or Sundays) augmented by midweek games featuring Lithuanian representatives in one of two international leagues – the Euroleague, which is the continent's premier club competition, and the North European Basketball League (NEBL), which features teams from the Ukraine to the UK.

No other team sports can compete with basketball in terms of popularity. Lithuanian **football** (*futbolas*) is in a comparatively sorry state, with top league matches frequently attracting crowds of under a hundred and most fans contenting themselves instead with TV broadcasts of top European games. Individual **sporting heroes** whose faces you're likely to see adorning magazine covers or advertising billboards include Rasa Polikevičiūtė and Edita Pučinskaitė (2001 women's world cycling champion and vicechampion respectively), and Olympic discusthrowing champs Romas Ubartas (1992) and Virgilius Aleksna (2000).

Directory

Addresses In Lithuania the street name always comes before the number, and the word for "street" (*gatvė*) is often omitted, eg Pilies 28 would be 28 Pilies Street. A street number comprising two figures separated by slash (7/2 or 9/25 for example) means that the building is on a corner or intersection – the first number denotes its position in the main street, while the second number refers to its position in the street being intersected.

Contraceptives Supermarkets and street kiosks are the best places to look for condoms (*prezervatyvai*); reliable international brands are widely available.

Emergencies Police ☎02; ambulance ☎03; fire ☎01.

Laundry Dry-cleaners (*cheminis valymas*) are reasonably common, but self-service launderettes are almost non-existent in Lithuania – you may have to resort to washing your smalls in the hotel sink.

Left luggage Most train and bus stations have a left-luggage office (*bagažinė*). The daily charge per item deposited is rarely more than 3–4Lt.

Tipping Tipping is not always expected in Lithuania, especially if you've only had a cup of coffee or a snack. After a round of drinks or a full meal, however, it's polite to leave roughly ten percent or to round up the bill to a convenient figure.

Toilets Public toilets (*tualetas*) are rare outside bus and train stations (where a small fee, normally no more than 1Lt, is charged), although almost every café, restaurant and bar will have one. Gents are marked with a letter V or a ▼ symbol; ladies with an M or a ▲ symbol.

1.1

Vilnius and around

"**N**arrow cobblestone streets and an orgy of Baroque: almost like a Jesuit city somewhere in the middle of Latin America," wrote the author Czesław Miłosz of prewar **VILNIUS** – a description that in many ways still holds true. Laid out in a bowl carved by the winding River Neris and surrounded by pine-covered hills, central Vilnius remains largely untainted by the high-rise development that characterizes the post-war suburbs and boasts perhaps the most impressive concentration of Baroque architecture in northern Europe, its skyline of domes and belfries making a lasting impression on visitors to the city. At ground level, the centre is a maze of atmospheric alleyways lined with solid eighteenth-century town houses, punctuated by archways leading through to cobbled backyards.

Despite the impression of continuity given by its well-preserved architecture, Vilnius's history is as fragmented as any in Eastern Europe. Since the town's emergence as capital of the Lithuanian Dukes in the Middle Ages, Russians, Belarussians, Jews and Poles have all left their mark, and Vilnius has been an important cultural centre to each in turn. The city's place in Polish hearts is particularly cherished: as well as Nobel prize-winner Miłosz, literary figures as diverse as Adam Mickiewicz, Juliusz Słowacki and Tadeusz Konwicki all spent their formative years here, and the city belonged to Poland from 1920 to 1939. Now firmly part of Lithuania, Vilnius is still a cosmopolitan place – around twenty percent of its population is Polish and another twenty percent is Russian – though with just under 600,000 inhabitants it has an almost village-like atmosphere, making it an easy place to get to know.

A little too far east to be included in most European grand tours, Vilnius is rather neglected and underrated. True, it has few set-piece sights, and its museums tend to be dutifully didactic rather than spectacular, but it's the atmosphere that draws the visitor in – the **Old Town** in particular, with its winding, narrow streets and stately churches. Vilnius is also a good base from which to explore much of eastern Lithuania. The medieval fortress at lake-bound **Trakai**, the Iron Age hill-forts of **Kernavė** and the grandly named **Centre of Europe sculpture park**, are easy day-trips from here, and Lithuania's second city Kaunas (see Chapter 1.2) can also be reached in a couple of hours.

Some history

The city of Vilnius was born some time in the eleventh century when the sandy hills overlooking the confluence of the Vilija and Neris rivers became key strongholds for Lithuanian chieftains seeking to secure a rapidly expanding tribal state. Mindaugas, the thirteenth-century chieftain who first united the Lithuanian tribes into a centralized state, probably based his court here for a time, although it was his grandson, Gediminas, who made it a permanent power base. Although still a pagan, Gediminas encouraged the settlement of Christian peoples – notably German traders from Rīga and Russian-speaking nobles from the east – and many of Vilnius's churches pre-date the Lithuanian state's official acceptance of Christianity in 1386.

After the dynastic union between Lithuania and Poland in 1387, real power shifted towards Kraków (and subsequently Warsaw), where the kings of the new

Polish-Lithuanian state spent most of their time – although Vilnius remained the capital of the Grand Duchy of Lithuania. However, the nobility of the Grand Duchy increasingly adopted the language and manners of their more sophisticated Polish neighbours, turning Vilnius into a culturally (if not necessarily ethnically) Polish city.

The close relationship with Poland ensured that Vilnius remained in touch with many of the key developments in central European culture. Sigismund August (Grand Duke of Lithuania 1544–1572 and King of Poland 1548–1572) maintained a magnificent court in the city, encouraging learned minds from the rest of Europe to settle here. In addition, his successor-but-one, Stefan Bathory, presided over the creation of Vilnius University in 1579, and it's been one of the most prestigious seats of learning in northeastern Europe ever since.

When the creation of the Polish-Lithuanian Commonwealth at the Union of Lublin in 1569 effectively ended the autonomy of the Grand Duchy, Vilnius lost some of its pre-eminence and increasingly became a peripheral provincial city. Nevertheless, the Grand Duchy's leading magnates – drawn from powerful families such as the Radvilas, Sapiehas and Pacs – continued to build palaces in Vilnius and

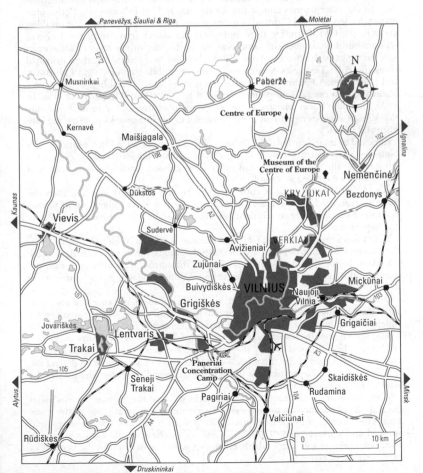

fund the building of churches, often in the exuberant Baroque style that soon became the town's architectural trademark.

The incorporation of Vilnius into the Russian Empire in 1795 led to an influx of Russians, a renewed wave of Orthodox-church building and the expansion of the city beyond its Old Town boundaries. The key Russian legacy was the construction of Gedimino prospektas, the showpiece boulevard around which the principal administrative and business districts subsequently developed. If anything, Tsarist rule only reinforced Vilnius's role as a centre of Polish patriotism and culture, however, and the university was closed down in 1831 (and remained closed for over eighty years) in order to prevent the nurturing of a seditious anti-Russian elite.

By the end of the nineteenth century, Vilnius was an amazingly diverse city, with the Jews making up 40 percent of the population, followed by Poles at 31 percent and the Russians at 20 percent – Lithuanians had been reduced to a tiny minority. Notwithstanding their numerically weak position in the city, the Lithuanians still regarded Vilnius as their historical capital, and accordingly based most of their social and cultural institutions here. The opportunity for the Lithuanians to flex their political muscle came with the withdrawal of the Russian authorities in World War I. Vilnius's new German masters encouraged Lithuanian sentiment as a counterbalance to the other nations competing for the city, and on February 16, 1918, community leaders declared Lithuania's independence from a second-floor flat on Pilies gatvė in the Old Town. De facto independence didn't arrive until the German withdrawal in November the same year, the authorities of the nascent Lithuanian state racing to establish control over Vilnius before it was claimed by their principal rivals, the Poles. Two years of confused three-way fighting ensued, with Lithuanian and Polish armies fighting both against each other and the Bolsheviks, who were advancing into central Europe in an attempt to export the Russian revolution. In 1920, the Polish leader Marshal Piłsudski – himself a native of the countryside outside Vilnius – encouraged maverick General Lucjan Żeligowski to seize the city once and for all.

Annexed to inter-war Poland, Vilnius declined in importance. Poor relations with both the newly independent Lithuanian state and the Soviet Republic of Belarus ensured that the Vilnius region had no near neighbours with which to trade, and the economy stagnated as a result.

World War II saw Vilnius occupied by the Soviets, the Germans, and then the Soviets again: the Polish resistance played a major part in the liberation of Vilnius from the Germans, only to see their leaders arrested by the victorious Red Army and deported to Siberia.

With Vilnius becoming the capital of the Soviet Republic of Lithuania after 1945, the majority of Vilnius's Poles left for Poland, although in many cases their place was taken by immigrant Polish-speakers from the surrounding villages – with the paradoxical result that the Polish population of Vilnius today is just as numerous as it was in 1939.

Despite the straitjacket of Soviet rule, Vilnius soon became the focus of Lithuanian political and cultural activity, and it was inevitable that the struggle for independence from the Soviet Union was concentrated here at the close of the 1980s. The attempt by Soviet forces to gain control of strategic buildings in the city on January 13, 1991, was met by mass unarmed resistance from Vilnius's citizens – twelve of them died under the wheels of Soviet tanks in an attempt to defend the TV Tower (see p.92), provoking a flood of international sympathy and paving the way for full Lithuanian independence.

While many of the outlying high-rise suburbs still bear the imprint of post-Soviet decay, parts of the city centre can easily bear comparison with some of the more prosperous central European capitals. Filled with banks and snazzy shops, and spruced up by a succession of ambitious mayors, the heart of old Vilnius is now an island of wealth in a country which, taken as a whole, is still to reap the benefits of post-communist change.

Arrival, information and city transport

Vilnius **airport** (Oro Uostas) is around 5km south of the city centre on Rodūnės kelias and is connected by regular buses. From outside the main entrance, bus #2 runs a couple of times an hour to Lukiškių aikštė, handy for the downtown area around Gedimino prospektas, while bus #1 will take you to the train and bus station area, from where you can walk into the Old Town. Both journeys take approximately 25 minutes and **tickets** cost 1Lt from the driver. **Taxis** should cost no more than 10–15Lt for the journey to the Old Town, though some will try to get away with charging more.

The main **train station** (Geležinkelio stotis) is at Geležinkelio 16, just south of the Old Town, and the main **bus station** (Autobusų stotis) is just across the road. You could walk into the Old Town from here or catch trolleybus #2 from the square in front of the train station to Katedros aikštė, the main square. Station-based taxi drivers don't like picking up short-distance fares and may overcharge as a result.

Information

The municipal **tourist office** has two branches, one in the Town Hall on Rotušės aikštė (Mon–Fri 10am–6pm; ☎8-5/262 6470), the other at Vilniaus 22 (May–Sept Mon–Fri 9am–7pm, Sat noon–6pm; Oct–April Mon–Fri 9am–6pm; ☎8-5/262 9660, ✉turizm.info@vilnius.lt). Both offer information on hotels and museums and sell maps, guidebooks and city tours. It's also worth buying a copy of the *Vilnius in Your Pocket* city guide (8Lt from newspaper kiosks and bookshops; ⊕www .inyourpocket.com), which gives critical coverage of hotel, restaurant and bar listings as well as addresses of all kinds of useful services. A worthy alternative is the Tallinn-based *City Paper* (10Lt), which has listings for Tallinn, Rīga and Vilnius in a single magazine-style publication, but it appears only sporadically in Vilnius newspaper kiosks.

The best **maps** of Vilnius (sold in the two tourist offices and bigger bookstores) are produced by the Rīga-based cartographers Jāņa Sēta; their 1:25 000 plan includes public transport routes and a street index, and is available either as a fold-out map or a spiral-bound street atlas. Local firm Briedis's 1:18 000 fold-out map of the city is also pretty serviceable.

City transport

Central Vilnius is easily explored on foot, while the more far-flung sights can be reached by **bus or trolleybus**. **Tickets**, costing a flat fare of 0.80Lt, are best bought in advance from newspaper kiosks (*kioskas*), or you can get them from the driver – for a little extra (1Lt) – unless there's a sign reading *bilietai neparduodami* ("tickets not for sale") posted in the window. Whether you've bought your ticket in advance or from the driver, you'll need to validate it by punching it in the machine on board. Ticketless travellers face a spot-fine of 20Lt if caught by an inspector.

Moving on from Vilnius

There are several **bus** departures a day from Vilnius to Rīga, Tallinn, Warsaw, Minsk and Kaliningrad, as well as a fair number of buses to Western Europe, including direct services to Berlin, London, Paris and Amsterdam. Numerous other destinations can be reached by changing in Warsaw – tickets covering the whole journey can be purchased in Vilnius from either the Eurolines or Toks counters in the bus station. See Travel details on p.105 for frequency of departures and journey times.

There's less in the way of international trains, and services are usually slower than buses. Trains to Rīga and Warsaw run only once every two days, and tend to be overnight services, arriving at their destinations uncomfortably early in the morning.

Some routes are also served by minibuses (*maršrutinis taxi*), which halt at the same stops as buses, but tend to be faster; there's a flat fare of 2Lt and you pay the driver.

Taxi prices are very reasonable providing you stick to companies using newer cars and functioning meters (see "Listings" on p.101 for reputable taxi firms), and fares should cost no more than around 1Lt per kilometre in the daytime, double that at night.

Accommodation

Vilnius is reasonably well served with **hotels**, although budget choices are relatively thin on the ground and should be booked well in advance, especially in summer. Other inexpensive options include an increasing number of **hostels** and **bed-and-**

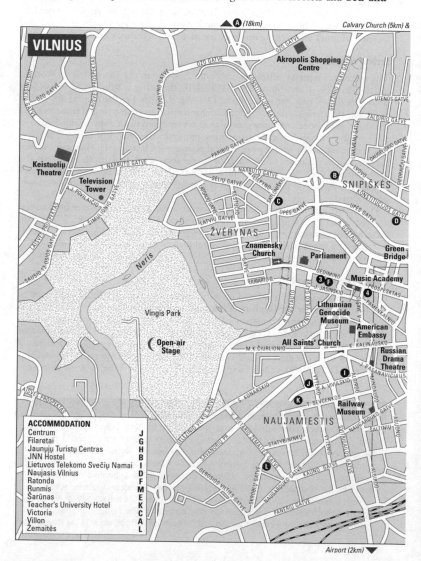

▲**Ⓐ** (18km)　　　　Calvary Church (5km) &

VILNIUS

Akropolis Shopping Centre

SNIPIŠKĖS

Keistuolių Theatre

Television Tower

ŽVĖRYNAS

Znamensky Church

Parliament

Green Bridge

Music Academy

Neris

Lithuanian Genocide Museum

American Embassy

Vingis Park

All Saints' Church

Russian Drama Theatre

Open-air Stage

Railway Museum

NAUJAMIESTIS

ACCOMMODATION	
Centrum	J
Filaretai	G
Jaunųjų Turistų Centras	H
JNN Hostel	B
Lietuvos Telekomo Svečių Namai	I
Naujasis Vilnius	D
Ratonda	F
Runmis	M
Šarūnas	E
Teacher's University Hotel	K
Victoria	C
Villon	A
Žemaitės	L

Airport (2km) ▼

62

breakfast accommodation with local families – the cheapest way of staying in or close to the Old Town. The best bed-and-breakfast agency is Litinterp, Bernardinų 7-2 (Mon–Fri 8.30am–5.30pm, Sat 9am–3pm; ☎8-5/212 3850, ℻212 3559, ⊕www.litinterp.lt), which charges from 80Lt for a single room, 140Lt for a double. Similarly priced accommodation is available in Litinterp's own guesthouse (see p.65 under "Hotels"), just above the office. The two Vilnius tourist offices (see "Information", p.61) also have lists of local families offering homestays at similar prices.

The nearest **campsite**, *Rytų kempingas* (☎8-5/265 1195), is 25km east of the city on the main road to Minsk – hardly a convenient base for sightseeing. It has toilets and four-person cabins (25Lt per person), but you'll need your own transport to get there.

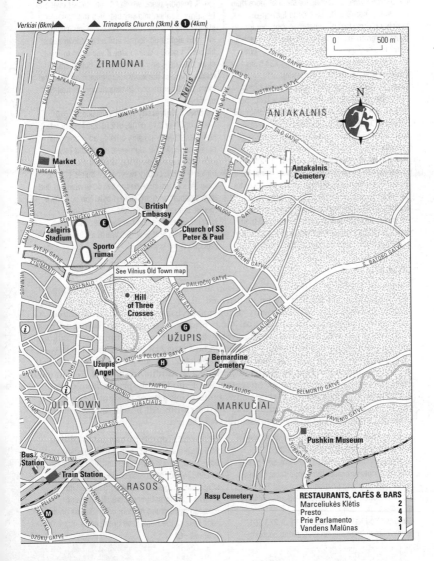

RESTAURANTS, CAFÉS & BARS

Marceliukės Klėtis	2
Presto	4
Prie Parlamento	3
Vandens Malūnas	1

Hostels

Hostels in Vilnius are basic compared to their counterparts in Western Europe: rooms are often cramped and very simply furnished, though invariably clean, and the staff usually enthusiastic and friendly.

Filaretai (HI) Filaretų 17 ☎8-5/215 4627, ✉filaretai@post.omnitel.net. A basic, cramped but well-run hostel about fifteen minutes' walk from the Old Town in the atmospherically shabby Užupis district. Accommodation ranges from two-bed rooms (37Lt per person) to eight-bed dorms (29Lt per person), with reductions for stays of more than one night. There's a 2Lt surcharge for non-HI members. Breakfast is sometimes available in summer for an extra charge, and there's a kitchen. Other facilities include a big common room with TV, and washing machines. Take bus #34 from bus/train stations to the Filaretų stop.

Jaunųjų Turistų Centras Polocko 7 ☎8-5/261 3576. Cheap, spartan triples and quads (20Lt per person) in a friendly place, a ten-minute walk east of the Old Town in the Užupis district. Breakfast costs a few litas extra; cooking facilities are also available.

JNN Hostel Konstitucijos 25 ☎8-5/272 2270, ✉jnn@lvjc.lt. Clean and cosy en-suite rooms in the lower floors of a hulking concrete youth centre on the north side of the river. Most rooms are doubles (120Lt; single occupancy possible for 80Lt), although there are some triples (150Lt) and quads (190Lt). Breakfast is included, and there's a twenty-percent discount for ISIC card holders.

From the airport, take bus #2 to the Šnipiškės stop; from the train and bus stations, take trolleybus #5 to Žaliasis Tiltas, then bus #2 or #46 to Šnipiškės.

Old Town Hostel (HI) Aušros Vartų 20-15A ☎8-5/262 5357, ⊛www.balticbackpackers.com. A small, friendly place which fills up quickly owing to its prime location midway between the train station and the Old Town. Functional, but clean, six- and eight-bed dorms, and a cosy downstairs kitchen. A good place to stay if you want to meet other travellers and don't mind co-hostellers rolling home in the early hours after a night on the town. 32Lt per person, 2Lt surcharge for non-HI members.

Teacher's University Hotel Vivulskio 36 ☎8-5/213 0509 or 213 0704, ℗216 2291. Concrete high-rise (there's no sign outside advertising its presence) just over 1km west of the Old Town, with plentiful singles (65Lt), doubles (66Lt) and triples (100Lt). Luxury two-person suites (130Lt) have TV and en-suite bathroom: otherwise WC and showers/bathtubs are shared between every two rooms. Some of the interiors look as if they haven't changed since the early 1960s, but the place is clean and well run. Worth asking about reductions for students.

Hotels

There are plenty of $100-a-night hotels in Vilnius, with new ones opening up all the time. Many are modern, business-oriented affairs, but there's also a good choice of characterful, cosy establishments occupying stylishly restored old buildings. A number of budget and mid-range hotels are concentrated **near the train and bus stations**, a generally safe area despite grubby appearances and within easy walking distance of the sights. There's an increasingly good range of places immediately west of the Old Town around **Gedimino prospektas**, the city's main commercial boulevard, and in the **Naujamiestis**, the nineteenth-century residential area on the high ground above it. Another concentration of moderately priced hotels can be found **north of the River Neris**, a fairly uninspiring area of residential blocks and offices, but still within walking distance of the centre. All hotels reviewed below include **breakfast** in the price unless otherwise stated.

Near the train and bus stations

City Gate Bazilijonų 3 ☎8-5/210 7306, ✉citygate@mail.lt. A newish, medium-size place offering simply furnished but comfortable rooms with TV, minibar and pristine bathrooms. The cosy top-floor doubles come with sloping attic ceilings. ❻

Gintaras Sodų 14 ☎8-5/273 8011 or 273 8012, ⊛www.hotelgintaras.lt. An uninspiring concrete lump directly opposite the train and bus stations with plain but acceptable en-suites boasting Soviet-era, colour-clash interiors. All rooms have satellite TV, but otherwise come in various stages of renovation: gloomy standard doubles with ancient-looking bathrooms are slowly being replaced by brighter, modern ones. Rooms on the north side of the hotel have great views of the Old Town. ❷–❺

Mikotel Pylimo 63 ☎8-5/260 9626, 🖷260 9627. A small hotel, with pristine modern interior and quirky paintings in the hallways. Rooms are simple but neat with TV, WC and shower. ❺

Runmis Panevežio 8A ☎8-5/265 6816, 🖳biuro@runmis.com. A medium-sized cheapie in a residential street immediately south of the station (cross the footbridge and bear right up Panevežio gatvė). Small, simple en-suites with slightly dowdy furnishings, plus a pair of plusher rooms with TV on the top floor. ❷

The Old Town

Grybas House Aušros Vartų 3A ☎8-5/261 9695, 🖳www.grybashouse.com. A congenial, family-run place offering cosy en-suites with TV, in an attractive house bang in the heart of the Old Town. Only ten rooms, so reservations essential. ❻

Litinterp Guest House Bernardinų 7-2 ☎8-5/212 3850, 🖷212 3559, 🖳vilnius@litinterp.lt. Neat little rooms with simple pine furnishings in the apartment block just above the Litinterp Bed-and-Breakfast agency (see p.63). Rooms are either en-suite or have WC/shower (shared between two rooms) in the hall. Kitchen facilities are available for making your own tea, coffee etc. No smoking throughout. The place is deservedly popular, and reservations are essential in summer. If you're going to be arriving outside Litinterp office hours, you'll have to ring or email in advance. ❸

Mabre Residence Maironio 13 ☎8-5/212 2087, 🖳www.mabre.lt. Fine courtyard and elegant quarters in a converted Orthodox monastery, just round the corner from St Anne's Church. Breakfast costs an extra 30Lt. ❼

Radisson SAS Astoria Didžioji 35/2 ☎8-5/212 0110, 🖷212 1762, 🖳www.radissonsas.com. A big place popular with businessmen, large tour groups and visiting dignitaries, occupying a commanding position on the Old Town's main thoroughfare. Rooms are spacious and plush, and those on the north-facing side of the hotel come with excellent views of Old Town roofs and church domes. Hallways in the west wing boast replicas of the Art Deco wall paintings that decorated the place when it was a Jewish community savings bank in the 1920s and 30s. ❽

Rūdninkų Vartai Rūdninkų 15/46 ☎8-5/261 3916, 🖷212 0507, 🖳rudvar@takas.lt. A newish, medium-sized place on the fringes of the Old Town, occupying a couple of town houses knocked together. Rooms are neat, tasteful and relatively spacious – some have baths, others showers. Gym and sauna on site. ❻–❼

Rinno Vingrių 25 ☎8-5/262 2828, 🖳www.rinno.lt. A clean and cosy place in a quiet side street, offering a mixture of "standard" rooms with TV and en-suite shower, and more spacious "superior" rooms equipped with minibars and bathtubs. Strictly speaking this isn't really in the Old Town, but it's close enough – just across the road – not to make much difference. ❺–❻

Shakespeare Bernardinų 8 ☎8-5/231 4521, 🖷231 4522, 🖳www.shakespeare.lt. On a narrow Old Town alley, this is a superbly renovated town house with fifteen rooms – each named after a famous writer and decked out with pictures related to the author and his books. Rooms feature original timber beams, simple oriental rugs, spacious bathrooms and tea-and-coffee making facilities. The smaller *Shakespeare Too*, round the corner at Pilies 34 ☎5/266 1626, has rooms themed on famous painters. ❼

Vilniaus Narutis Pilies 24 ☎8-5/212 2894, 🖳www.narutis.lt. A central, intimate hotel housed in a much-modernized sixteenth-century building, with rooms grouped around a glass-roofed courtyard. Rooms are plain but classy, and those on the top floor have low attic ceilings. Breakfast is served in an atmospheric medieval cellar. ❼

Gedimino prospektas and Naujamiestis

Centrum Vytenio 9/25 ☎8-5/268 3300, 🖳www.centrum.lt. A newish building on a quiet intersection in the Naujamiestis area, within walking distance of both Gedimino prospektas and the Old Town. Rooms are simple, but stylish, with large bathtubs. Kooky ceramics and minimalist furniture in the hallways lend a chic modernist feel. There's a small swimming pool and fitness room on the ground floor. ❼

Lietuvos Telekomo Svečių Namai Vivulskio 13A ☎8-5/260 3715, 🖳www.telecomguesthouse.lt. A small guesthouse, with mostly single rooms, run by Lithuanian Telecom and located in a quiet off-street courtyard, ten minutes' walk uphill from the Old Town. Comfortable en-suite rooms with TV and minibar. Advance booking recommended. ❻

Ratonda Gedimino 52/1 ☎8-5/212 0670, 🖳www.centrum.lt. A modern business hotel a few steps away from the Parliament building, offering plush, smallish but undeniably snug rooms with bathroom, TV and minibar. ❼

Scandic Hotel Neringa Gedimino 23 ☎8-5/268 1910, 🖳www.scandic-hotels.com. A business hotel, with top-quality rooms decked out in pastel colours and pale wooden furniture. The hotel restaurant – long famous for its chicken Kiev – was the birthplace of Soviet jazz in the late Sixties (see p.86), although the polo-neck-wearing crowd moved on years ago. ❼–❽

Žemaitės Žemaitės 15 ☎8-5/213 5453, ⓦwww.hotelzemaites.lt. A modern block in an uninspiring area 2km west of the Old Town, but fairly handy for the stations. You'll be steered towards the comfy modernized doubles with TV and bath, although the simpler, unrenovated rooms with TV, fridge and shared shower/WC (one for every two rooms) are eminently habitable. Trolleybus #15, #16 and bus #23 or #54 from the train and bus stations. ❷–❺

North of the River Neris

Naujasis Vilnius Konstitucijos14 ☎8-5/273 9595, ⓦwww.hotelnv.lt. Probably the best of the business-class places in this part of town, with friendly service and comfortable rooms. Facilities include on-site gym, sauna and a dinky swimming pool. Handily placed for the Baltasis Tiltas footbridge, which leads across the Neris towards Gedimino prospektas. ❼

Šarūnas Raitininku 4 ☎8-5/272 3888, ⓦwww.hotelsarunas.lt. A modern hotel on the north bank of the river, owned by former Sacramento Kings basketball player Šarūnas Marčiulionis. Far enough from the main road to be peaceful, and set around a quiet courtyard, the hotel offers comfy, pastel-hued rooms, some with shower, others with bathtub. There's a fully equipped gym and a bar stuffed with NBA memorabilia. ❼

Victoria Saltoniškių 56 ☎8-5/272 4013, ⓦwww.victoria.lt. An unprepossessing block-house exterior, but friendly service and pleasant en-suites with TV and fridge inside. In the largely residential district of Žvėrynas, within walking distance of Gedimino prospektas and 2km away from the Old Town. From the train and bus stations, trolleybus #5 to Žaliasis Tiltas followed by trolleybus #8, #9 or #19 to Pedagoginis universitetas. ❺

Villon 19km out of town on the A2 motorway to Panevėžys and Rīga ☎8-5/273 9700, ⓦwww.lemeridien.com. A gargantuan hotel complex with swish rooms, set in a landscaped park with its own lake. A popular venue for business conferences, it's also the perfect spot for a luxury out-of-town break (weekend discounts available). Courtesy bus service to the town centre. ❽

The City

Most of Vilnius's sights are concentrated in a reasonably compact area on the south bank of the River Neris. At the centre of the city is the main square, **Katedros aikštė**, site of the **cathedral**. South of here extends the atmospheric **Old Town**, with its impressive collection of Baroque churches and venerable university, while to the west stretches the long, straight boulevard of **Gedimino prospektas**, the focus of the city's commercial and administrative life. On the high ground above it lies the nineteenth-century residential area of **Naujamiestis** (New Town). Running towards Gedimino prospektas along the eastern side of the Old Town is **Pylimo gatvė**, bearing just a few traces of the sizeable Jewish community that once lived here. Beyond the centre, there's only a handful of sights – mostly in the western, southern and eastern suburbs – for which you'll need recourse to public transport or taxi.

Katedros aikštė and around

Lording it over the broad, flagstoned expanse of **Cathedral Square** (Katedros aikštė) is the off-white, colonnaded **Cathedral** (Arkikatedros bazilika; daily 7am–7pm), rather accurately described as "a cross between a Greek temple and a Polish civic theatre" by the German Expressionist writer Alfred Döblin, who passed through town in the early 1920s. The site was originally a shrine to Perkūnas, the Lithuanian god of thunder, and Mindaugas the Great chose to build a simple brick church here in the thirteenth century – this did not go down well though with the resolutely pagan Lithuanian nobles who had him murdered in 1263, and the spot wasn't associated with Christianity again until the conversion of Lithuania to Catholicism under Grand Duke Jogaila after 1387. The church Jogaila built was constantly added to and reconstructed over the next four hundred years, and the building you see today is largely the result of a late-eighteenth century facelift carried out by Laurynas Stuoka-Gucevičius. Turned into a museum by the Soviets, it

St Casimir and the Kaziukas Fair

St Casimir, the patron saint of Lithuania, was born in 1458, the second son of Casimir IV, King of Poland and Grand Duke of Lithuania. Intensely spiritual, he devoted himself to study and prayer and seemed singularly ill-suited to the dynastic role marked out for him. His reputation for purity and holiness blossomed into a full-blown popular cult after his death from illness at the age of 26. Fuelled by court propagandists eager to ensure local support for the ruling dynasty, the cult grew quickly in the Grand Duchy of Lithuania (Casimir had been designated viceroy of Lithuania just before his death), and he was worshipped as a saint here long before his official canonization by Pope Clement VIII in 1602.

It was in the second half of the nineteenth-century that St Casimir's Day (March 4), traditionally the occasion of ceremonial masses and processions, began metamorphosing into the **Kaziukas Fair** ("Kaziukas" being the diminutive form of Casimir in Lithuanian). Peasants from the surrounding villages would throng the square, selling handicrafts – particularly wicker boxes and baskets. The tradition continued under the communists, although it was shorn of its religious significance, and the basket-sellers were shifted north of the River Neris to the Kalvarijų market. The fair moved back to the centre in the 1990s, and every year since then craft stalls have taken over Pilies gatvė and Rotušės aikštė on the days leading up to and including St Casimir's Day itself.

was restored to the Catholic Church by a reform-minded local communist leadership in 1988, and reconsecrated the following year. As the symbolic heart of Lithuanian Christianity, the cathedral was the natural focus of mass rallies in the run-up to independence. The most moving of these took place in January 1991, when the coffins of those killed by Soviet troops at the TV Tower (see p.92) were laid on the flagstones of the square, draped in Lithuanian tricolors, for an outdoor memorial service that united tens of thousands in grief and defiance.

The pediment of the cathedral's main **facade** is crowned by a trio of monumental statues, with St Helena brandishing a huge cross at the apex, accompanied by Casimir, patron saint of Lithuania, on the right, and Stanislas, patron saint of Poland, on the left. All are modern replicas of early nineteenth-century originals, destroyed by the Soviets after World War II. Running round the sides of the building are statues of past rulers of Poland-Lithuania, caught in stiff mid-gesture, often to unintentionally comic effect. To the right of the main entrance looms the free-standing, three-tiered **belfry** (Arkikatedros varpinė), a coffee and cream coloured cylinder which looks like a stranded Baroque lighthouse.

Inside (head for the side door on the northern side if the main doors are shut), devotional paintings crowd the walls and pillars, and locals kneel deep in prayer, reinforcing the aura of devotion and spirituality – found in so many Lithuanian churches. The most dramatic of the canvases on display are the scenes of the life of Christ running right round the ambulatory, a cycle painted by Franciszek Smugliewicz (see p.77), Vilnius's leading neoclassicist and professor at the local art academy in the early nineteenth century.

A constant stream of pilgrims heads down the right-hand ambulatory towards the cathedral's main attraction, the **Chapel of St Casimir** (Kazimiero koplyčia), commissioned by King Sigismund Wasa III in 1623 in a propagandistic attempt to associate the Wasas (a dynasty which was relatively new to the throne of Poland-Lithuania) with their rather more illustrious Jagiellonian predecessors – the family to which fifteenth-century royal prince Casimir (see box above) belonged. A riot of marble, stucco and silver statuary, the chapel is Vilnius's most complete Baroque statement – and was one of the few parts of the cathedral untouched by Stuoka-Gucevičius's refurbishments. Designed by Italian architect Constante Tencalla, the chapel consists of a black, marble-lined square chamber, with a second octagonal tier on top supporting a richly decorated cupola. On the south-facing wall is the ornate, silver-plated casket containing the bones of St Casimir, a relic that was returned to the cathedral with much pomp in 1989 after being exiled to the Church of SS Peter and Paul (see p.90) during the Soviet period. The icon-like image of the saint directly below is remarkable because it depicts Casimir with three hands (nobody really knows why), and because it was painted in around 1520, a full eighty years before Casimir was officially declared a saint – evidence of the strength of Casimir's cult. Occupying niches in the walls of the chapel are eight silver-plated statues of Jagiellonian and Wasa rulers, while frescoes on the ceilings and side walls show episodes from the saint's life. Two of the larger scenes, painted by Michelangelo Palloni in 1692, portray the miracle cures experienced by those praying at St Casimir's grave.

Behind the cathedral's main altar, a doorway leads down to the **crypt**, where chunks of masonry survive from both the original pagan temple and Mindaugas's short-lived church. It's not possible to visit the crypt without joining a guided tour, arranged on an ad-hoc basis: enquire at the souvenir shop at the northern entrance to the cathedral about times and prices. If you do manage to make it down here, you'll see some reverentially displayed modern caskets bearing aristocratic remains, notably that of Barbora Radvilaitė (Barbara Radziwiłłówna), the local noblewoman whose marriage to Sigismund August in 1547 made her Queen of Poland and Grand Duchess of Lithuania. The marriage was greeted with horror by the Polish nobility, who feared that too close an alliance between Sigismund and the Lithuanian aristocracy would upset plans for the final absorption of Lithuania by the Polish state. Barbora in any case died childless six months later, and Sigismund August failed to produce an heir despite remarrying twice, thus bringing an end to the dynasty which had ruled over Poland and Lithuania since the days of Jogaila.

Leaving the cathedral and moving round towards the square's eastern end, you'll come across a tall, grey plinth bearing a statue of Grand Duke of Lithuania and legendary founder of Vilnius, **Gediminas** (1271–1341), depicted here as a lean, martial figure gesturing towards the city with an outstretched sword. Below the duke and his horse crouches a wolf – a reference to the popular folk tale which seeks to explain Vilnius's origins. Gediminas, so the story goes, was taking a rest while hunting in the hills above the Vilnia River when he dreamt of an iron wolf howling in the night. Asked to explain this dream, the duke's head priest suggested that the wolf's howling represented the fame which would one day reverberate around the world of a great city built on this site. Suitably impressed, Gediminas ordered the construction of a new capital here without delay.

The Lower and Upper Castles

Immediately behind the cathedral, a stretch of open ground that looks like – indeed is – a cross between an archeological dig and a building site marks the erstwhile position of the so-called **Lower Castle** (Žemutinės pilis; Wed–Sun 10am–5pm; 4Lt). It was here that Sigismund Augustus (1520–1572), King of Poland and Grand Duke of Lithuania, maintained a glittering ducal court complete with an orchestra, art collection and a library of over four thousand books, enhancing Vilnius's reputation as an important cultural centre. The palace had fallen into disuse by the late eighteenth century, when the Tsarist authorities had it pulled down, and there's now little to see save for a grid of ruined palace walls. In 1998, the Lithuanian government resolved to build a replica of the palace on this very site, even though archeological experts are far from sure what the original looked like. With an eighteenth-century engraving (copies of which adorn signboards around the site) providing the inspiration, the project is now well under way.

The tree-clad hill immediately behind the Lower Castle was originally crowned by the **Upper Castle** (Aukštutinės pilis), a tenth-century stockade fort subsequently strengthened in stone by Gediminas and his successors. The only bit of the castle left standing – and one of the city's best-known landmarks – is the **Gediminas Tower** (Gedimino bokštas), an appealing, red-brick octagon that rises sand-castle-like from the brow of the hill. It retains little original stonework from Gediminas's time, having been rebuilt in the nineteenth century to provide recreational strollers with a viewing platform. You can get an idea, though, of what the castle looked like in medieval times by examining the impressive array of scale models in the **Upper Castle Museum** (Aukštutinės pilies muziejus; Wed–Sun 11am–5pm; 4Lt; free on Wed in winter) inside the tower. There's a superb panorama of the Old Town's church spires and towers from the top.

The Lithuanian National Museum and the Applied Art Museum

A hundred metres or so north of the cathedral lie the arsenal buildings, a pair of creamy-yellow barrack blocks built in the sixteenth century and given a touch of neoclassical grandeur by the Russians some three hundred years later. The first of these, at Arsenalo 1, is now home to the **Lithuanian National Museum** (Lietuvos Nacionalinis muziejus; Wed–Sun: May–Sept 11am–6pm; Oct–April 11am–5pm; 4Lt; free Wed in winter), containing a jumble of artefacts ranging from old prints of Vilnius to re-created farmhouse interiors from the eighteenth and nineteenth centuries. Traditional Lithuanian crafts are represented with an assortment of wicker baskets, chequered bedspreads and the wood-carved figures of saints used to decorate wayside shrines in the countryside.

A separate annexe of the museum (entrance a little further north on Arsenalo) houses the **Prehistoric Lithuania exhibition** (same times; 4Lt), an extremely well-mounted display, with explanations in English, on the history of Lithuania up to the twelfth century. It begins with the flint and bone tools and distinctive boat-shaped battle axes used by the Baltic region's earliest inhabitants – the ancestors of today's Lithuanians and Latvians arrived in the area sometime on the cusp of the second and third millennia BC. In the museum's upstairs gallery, you can see models of the stockaded hill forts, dating from the tenth to twelfth centuries, in which tribal leaders held sway. Isolated from the rest of Europe by thick forests, the Lithuanians were slow to develop unified state structures, and lived in loosely bound tribal units until well into the Middle Ages. Also on display are reproductions of sumptuous Iron Age Lithuanian costumes and some delicate silver jewellery.

A few hundred metres further along Arsenalo at no. 3 is the **Applied Art Museum** (Taikomosios Dailės muziejus; Tues–Sun noon–5/6pm; 4Lt, free Wed in winter), displaying chalices, reliquaries and Baroque paintings – including a fleshy *Lot and his Daughters* by the Austrian master Johann-Michael Rottmayr – taken from the region's churches. There's also a modest display of folk art, with several examples of the wooden wayside crosses (still a common feature of rural Lithuania) that typically combine Christian imagery with much older pagan sun motifs, as well as bunches of colourful *verbos* – the bundles of dried grasses and flowers traditionally prepared in the run-up to Palm Sunday.

The Old Town

Just south of Cathedral Square lies the **Old Town** (Senamiestis), a dense network of narrow, largely pedestrianized streets that forms the heart of Vilnius and invites aimless wandering. The following account starts in the north and proceeds roughly southwards, although any tour of the area will inevitably involve numerous detours down side streets or into inviting corners. The main reference points are **Pilies gatvė** (Castle Street), which ascends gently from Cathedral Square, and its extensions **Didžioji** and **Aušros Vartų** which cut south through the heart of historic Vilnius. Almost everything you'll want to see in the Old Town lies on or just off this artery.

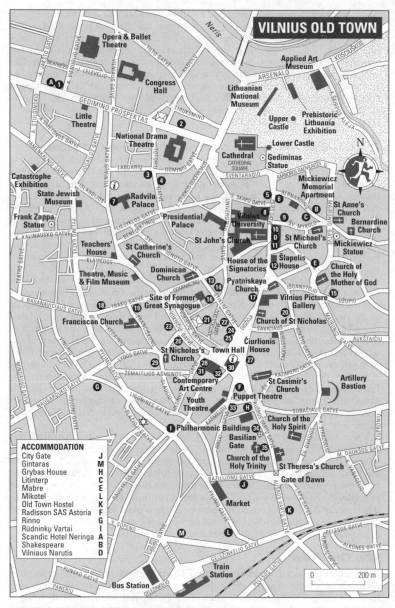

VILNIUS OLD TOWN

Opera & Ballet Theatre
Congress Hall
Applied Art Museum
Lithuanian National Museum
Little Theatre
National Drama Theatre
Upper Castle
Prehistoric Lithuania Exhibition
Lower Castle
Cathedral
CATHEDRAL SQUARE
Gediminas Statue
Catastrophe Exhibition
State Jewish Museum
Frank Zappa Statue
Radvila Palace
Mickiewicz Memorial Apartment
St Anne's Church
Bernardine Church
Presidential Palace
Vilnius University
Teachers' House
St Catherine's Church
St John's Church
St Michael's Church
Mickiewicz Statue
Theatre, Music & Film Museum
Dominican Church
House of the Signatories
Šlapelis House
Church of the Holy Mother of God
Pyatniskaya Church
Site of Former Great Synagogue
Vilnius Picture Gallery
Franciscan Church
Church of St Nicholas
St Nicholas's Church
Town Hall
Čiurlionis House
Contemporary Art Centre
Youth Theatre
St Casimir's Church
Artillery Bastion
Puppet Theatre
Philharmonic Building
Church of the Holy Spirit
Basilian Gate
Church of the Holy Trinity
St Theresa's Church
Gate of Dawn
Market
Train Station
Bus Station

ACCOMMODATION

City Gate	J
Gintaras	H
Grybas House	C
Litinterp	E
Mabre	L
Mikotel	K
Old Town Hostel	F
Radisson SAS Astoria	G
Rinno	I
Rūdninkų Vartai	A
Scandic Hotel Neringa	B
Shakespeare	D
Vilniaus Narutis	

0   200 m

RESTAURANTS & CAFÉS

Afrika	11	Freskos	30	
Aqua	27	Gabi	9	
Arka	34	Kaukazo Belaisvė	19	
Čili	1	Kebab House	35	
Café de Paris	17	Lokys	22	
Da Antonio	10	Mano kavinė	20	
Finjan	26	Markus ir Ko	21	

Pieno Baras	25
Pilies Kepyklė	5
Pilies Menė	6
Po Saule	3
Skonis ir Kvapas	18
Stikliai Café	16
Stikliai Restaurant	14
Žemaičių Smuklė	23

BARS & PUBS

Amatininkų Užeiga	24	Jazz & Rock Café	29
Avylis	2	Prie Universiteto	13
Bix	33	Savas Kampas	28
Brodvėjus	31	Šuolaikinio	
Būsi Trečias	4	Meno Centras	32
Džiazo Klubas	7	Užupio kavinė	15
Gero Viskio Baras	12	Žaltvykslė	8

Bernardinų gatvė

Leading off Pilies to the east is **Bernardinų gatvė**, one of the Old Town's most appealing back streets, a narrow lane lined with seventeenth- and eighteenth-century houses. Occupying no. 11 is the **Adam Mickiewicz Memorial Apartment** (Adomo Mickevičiaus Memorialinis butas; Tues–Fri 10am–5pm, Sat & Sun 10am–2pm; free), where the Polish poet lived for a few short months in 1822. The rather paltry collection of exhibits includes a couple of period chairs, a desk once owned by Mickiewicz and a number of Polish and Lithuanian first editions of his works.

St Michael's Church

At the far end of Bernardinų, the stately ochre bulk of **St Michael's Church** (Šv Mykolo bažnyčia) peeks out from its walled enclosure. The twin towers of its seventeenth-century facade are complemented by a free-standing belfry, the main gateway into the church courtyard. Closed down by the Soviets in 1948 and never reconsecrated, the church now provides a home for the **Architecture Museum** (Architektūros muziejus; Mon 10am–5pm, Wed–Sat 11am–5.30pm; 1Lt), an exhaustive collection of photographs detailing every major building project to have taken place in Lithuania since the end of the nineteenth century. The transformation of inter-war Kaunas into a European capital full of government buildings, banks and offices gets full coverage, while projects documented in and around Vilnius range from the construction of high-rise suburbs like Lazdynai and Žirmūnai in the 1960s to the functional concrete bays of Vilnius bus station.

Most of the church's interior furnishings have survived, notably the funerary monuments belonging to the brood of church founder **Leo Sapieha** (1557–1633), who envisaged St Michael's as his own family mausoleum. A typical product of the Grand Duchy of Lithuania's cosmopolitan elite, Sapieha was a nobleman of Belarussian origin who converted from the Orthodox faith to Protestantism and then to Catholicism in an attempt to retain his political influence in the shifting religious landscape of sixteenth-century Europe. Sapieha's own granite-coloured memorial is located in the southeastern corner of the church: his reclining figure is clad in impressively voluminous pantaloons and ruff, while his two wives lie obediently on either side. Sapieha's body is entombed in the **crypt**, keeping him company are the coffins containing sundry family members – their bodies mummified by the cool, dry air of the vault. To visit the crypt (and its coffins) you'll need to book a tour in advance (10Lt per person; apply at the museum ticket desk in person).

St Anne's Church

Opposite St Michael's Church soar the fairytale, pinnacle-encrusted towers of **St Anne's** (Šv Onos bažnyčia; daily 10am–3pm), the church that so impressed Napoleon Bonaparte that he's said to have wanted to take it back to Paris in the palm of his hand. Intricate, red-brick traceries weave like intertwined thorn branches across its tall, narrow facade. The most outstanding Gothic building in Lithuania, it's nevertheless a relatively late example of the style: the facade is thought to have been completed only in 1582, by which time the Baroque was already beginning to make its presence felt in Vilnius. Inside, spindly lines of red-brick rib vaulting extend across a white ceiling, sheltering a relatively undistinguished ensemble of altars bunched up at the end of the small nave.

The Bernardine Church

Rising directly behind St Anne's is the considerably more restrained facade of the much larger **Bernardine Church** (Bernardinų vienuolyno bažnyčia), built at around the same time as its neighbour, together with the adjoining Bernardine **monastery** (now occupied by the Vilnius Art Academy). According to communist folklore, the church cellar was where Vilnius high-school student and future

Adam Mickiewicz (1798–1855)

Litwo! Ojczyzno moja! ty jesteś jak zdrowie;
Ile cię trzeba cenić, ten tylko się dowie,
Kto się stracił

(O Lithuania, my homeland, thou art like health itself;
I never knew till now, how precious,
Till I lost thee)

The opening lines of Adam Mickiewicz's *Pan Tadeusz* (1834)

It's paradoxical that the most famous lines ever written about Lithuania were the work of a Polish poet, yet **Adam Mickiewicz** (or Adomas Mickevičius, as he is known in Lithuania) is one of the few literary figures whose words have been adopted as rallying cries by both nations. Above all, Mickiewicz embodies the nostalgia shared by both Lithuanians and Poles for the **Grand Duchy of Lithuania**, the multi-ethnic and multilingual territory carved out by Lithuanian rulers in the Middle Ages, and subsequently a key component (some would say equal partner) in the Polish-Lithuanian Commonwealth.

Mickiewicz himself was a typical product of the Grand Duchy, born to an impoverished Polish gentry family in the countryside near Novogrudok (now in Belarus). In 1815, Mickiewicz went to study at **Vilnius University**, and was a founder member of the Philomaths, a pseudo-masonic organization dedicated to fighting Tsarist rule through the promotion of local culture. In November 1823, he was arrested along with fellow members on suspicion of "spreading Polish nationalism", and imprisoned in the Basilian monastery (see p.79) before being deported to Russia where he remained, mostly in **Moscow**, for the rest of the decade.

Mickiewicz already had a local literary reputation, but it was in Russia that his talents blossomed, and his fame began to spread. Notable works of this period include *Konrad Wallenrod*, a popular epic poem depicting the medieval struggle between the Teutonic Knights and the Grand Duchy of Lithuania, in reality a thinly disguised allegory of the age-old Polish-German conflict.

Following the failure of the **November 1830 Polish Uprising**, Mickiewicz went into exile in **Paris** like many Polish intellectuals and quickly immersed himself in émigré

founder of the KGB Felix Dzerzhinsky (see p.89) established an underground printing press, confident that the Tsarist police would never think of looking for it here. The church's **interior**, rich in Baroque furnishings and medieval frescoes, was neglected during the Soviet era and is currently undergoing restoration. Among the few things that have escaped damage are the two fine seventeenth-century funerary monuments (that of Stanislaus Radziwiłł on the northern side, Petras Veselovskis on the south) that face each other across the nave – their incumbents are depicted in relief form, reclining contentedly as if on a country picnic.

The Mickiewicz statue and the Church of the Holy Mother of God

Just south of the Bernardine Church is a modern **statue** of Adam Mickiewicz (see box above), leaning authoritatively on a lectern as if about to launch into a reading of his verse. The statue was the site of one of the first Glasnost-era demonstrations against Soviet power in Lithuania, when on August 23, 1987, a few hundred people gathered to demand the publication of the **Molotov–Ribbentrop Pact**, the secret agreement in which the Soviets and Germans carved out spheres of influence in the Baltics and Poland in 1939.

South of here, Mairono gatvė swings around the **Church of the Holy Mother of God** (Skaisčiausios dievo motinos cerkvė; daily 8am–6pm), Vilnius's largest politics. It was here too that Mickiewicz wrote *Pan Tadeusz* (1834), his greatest epic poem; modelled on the novels of Walter Scott, it is a masterful, richly lyrical depiction of traditional gentry life in the multi-ethnic borderlands east of Vilnius. As in all of Mickiewicz's works, Lithuania is represented as a wild, mythic land of dark forests – a seductive contrast to the ordered, urban world of Warsaw or Kraków.

Banned from re-entering the Tsarist Empire, Mickiewicz never returned to either Poland or Lithuania. For the next two decades he taught Slavonic literature at both Lausanne and Paris, at the same time canvassing the courts of Europe for support in Poland's struggle against the Russians. The writer's life came abruptly to an end in 1855 when Prince Adam Czartoryski, a leader of the Paris exile community, sent Mickiewicz on a mission to Turkey to organize Polish volunteer forces in the approaching Crimean War: having contracted typhus soon after his arrival, Mickiewicz died in November 1855 in **Istanbul**. Already a national hero of almost mythic proportions, his remains were eventually brought back to Poland and placed, along with other Polish "greats", in the crypt of Kraków's Wawel Cathedral.

Although Mickiewicz was never a Lithuanian patriot in the modern sense (he believed that the country's destiny was inextricably bound up with that of Poland), his heritage was readily appropriated by the Lithuanian national movement. His fascination with the history and traditions of the Grand Duchy helped to provide Lithuanians with a sense of their own past greatness, and his lyrical descriptions of the Lithuanian countryside inspired hordes of local imitators. When priest and poet Antanas Baranauskas wrote the seminal *Forest of Anykščiai* in 1861, he was essentially trying to prove that the Lithuanian language was versatile enough to evoke the Lithuanian landscape in the manner of Mickiewicz. Translations of Mickiewicz's works were very popular in late nineteenth-century Lithuania, and nationalist ideologue Vincas Kudirka adapted the opening words of *Pan Tadeusz* to form the first line of a patriotic hymn – which is still in use as the Lithuanian National Anthem. However his keynote work, *Pan Tadeusz*, was largely ignored by a Lithuanian elite who felt that it over-romanticized the Polish-speaking gentry. When it was finally translated in 1927, most of the references to "Poland" were left out – sparking the inevitable protests from Warsaw.

Orthodox place of worship, an off-white nineteenth-century cube topped by a fat central cupola and four fortress-like towers. Beside the church a small bridge leads across the River Vilnia to the inner-city suburb of Užupis (see p.89). West of Mairono, the network of crooked alleys made up of Rusų, Volano, Literatų and Šv Mykolo provides numerous opportunities for zipping back towards Pilies.

The House of Signatories

The middle reaches of Pilies boast a handsome ensemble of balconied town houses, most dating from the eighteenth and nineteenth centuries, and now occupied by a brash collection of cafés and upmarket jewellery and shoe shops. One of the most impressive edifices along this stretch is the lovingly restored **House of Signatories** (Signatarų namai; Mon–Fri noon–4pm; 2Lt) at no. 26, where the Lithuanian National Council declared the country's independence on February 16, 1918. The Germans, whose army was in control of Vilnius at the time, initially encouraged the National Council to make such a move, hoping that a puppet Lithuanian government could be established under German auspices, but soon withdrew their support when it became clear that the declaration could be used against them. Lithuania had to wait until Germany's defeat in November the same year before it could begin setting up state institutions of its own, yet February 16 is still considered a hallowed date in the country's history, officially celebrated as one of Lithuania's two independence days. The second-floor suite of apartments occupied by the National Council in 1918 is today the site of a small **museum**, worth visiting for its beautifully restored belle époque interiors. The room where the declaration was signed has been left bare save for a baize-topped writing desk, although the council and its members – sober men in stiff collars and with even stiffer beards – are celebrated in a modest display of photographs in the adjoining halls.

Rearing up immediately opposite the house is the back end of St John's Church (entered via the main entrance to the university; see p.75), beside which Šv Jono gatvė veers west towards the university district.

The University

Occupying a jumble of buildings constructed between the sixteenth and eighteenth centuries around nine linked courtyards, **Vilnius University** (Vilniaus Universitetas; access to the courtyards Mon–Fri 9am–5pm, Sat 9am–noon) squeezes into a neat quadrant of land between Pilies and Universiteto gatvė. In response to the spread of Calvinism in Vilnius, a college was established here by Bishop Walerijan Protasewicz in 1569 to serve as a Jesuit-run vehicle for the propagation of Catholic, Counter-Reformation ideals. Despite resistance from Protestant nobles, the King of Poland and Lithuania **Stefan Bathory** upgraded the college to university status ten years later. Tuition was initially in Latin, but by the early nineteenth century the university enjoyed a growing reputation as the leading educational institution in the Polish-speaking world. It also became a hotbed of Polish resistance to Tsarist rule: students formed conspiratorial societies such as the Philomaths (Towarzystwie Filomatów), dedicated to raising the anti-Russian consciousness of the locals through the promotion of Polish and Lithuanian culture. However, it was broken up by the authorities in November 1823 and its leading lights – including young poet **Adam Mickiewicz** (see p.72) – exiled from the city. The Russians closed the university down altogether in 1832 in the wake of the failed anti-Tsarist rebellion of 1830–31, and it wasn't reopened until after World War I when it once more resumed its position as one of Poland's top universities. Before long it was back in the political fray: right-wing students periodically mounted anti-semitic raids on the nearby Jewish districts of town, while nonconformists gravitated towards left-of-centre groupings such as the Vagabonds' Club (Akademicky klub Włóczęgów), whose members, among them future Nobel laureate **Czesław Miłosz**, advertised their bohemian leanings by wearing floppy black berets. Thoroughly "Lithuanianized" after World War II, the university survived the Soviet era with its academic reputation intact, and is now the country's undisputed centre of learning, with over fourteen thousand students.

The university's **main entrance** is on Universiteto gatvė, where a small office beside the main gate sells tickets (4Lt) and hands out plans. You're then free to wander around the courtyards and visit St John's Church (see opposite), but you're not supposed to peek inside any of the university interiors unless you've pre-booked a place on a guided tour (☎8-5/268 7298 or 268 7009; prices depend on numbers). If you do opt for the tour – and it's definitely worth doing – make sure you ask to see the barrel-vaulted **Smugliewicz Hall** (originally the refectory, now the university library's rare books department), decorated with Smugliewicz frescoes depicting Jesuit theologians sheltering under the Virgin Mary's cape; and the neo-classical **White Hall** of the **observatory**, crammed with old telescopes and celestial globes, and featuring an ornate portal by Carlo Sampari straddled by figures of Diana and Urania.

Assuming you're going it alone, the first courtyard you come to is the Sarbievijus courtyard (Sarbijevijaus kiemas), named after Jesuit theologian and university lecturer **Mattheus Sarbiewski** (1595–1640), who was widely admired throughout Europe for his Latin-language verse. From here you can move off to the left in search of some of the smaller courtyards, or head right through an archway to the

Grand Courtyard (Didysis kiemas), an arcaded quadrangle dominated by the scrumptious wedding-cake facade of **St John's Church** (Šv Jono bažnyčia), its three custard-coloured tiers seemingly held aloft by slender Corinthian pilasters arranged in clusters of two or three. Although of fourteenth-century origin, the church's outer appearance is due to a mid-eighteenth-century face-lift by Jan Krzysztof Glaubitz, architect of more than a few of Vilnius's Baroque buildings. Placed in the care of first the Jesuits, and then the university authorities, the church was closed in 1948 and pressed into service as a warehouse for the newpaper *Tiesa* ("Truth"), the Lithuanian Communist Party's answer to *Pravda*. Vilnius University managed to get the church back in 1963, and turned it into a science museum. It wasn't reconsecrated until 1991.

Inside, a group of altars in no-holds-barred Baroque clusters at the far end of the church. The high altar resembles a vast gateway, guarded by statues of St John Chrysostom, St Gregory the Great, St Anselm and St Augustine, and through which a small statue of the Virgin is barely visible on the far side. Archways on either side of the nave lead off to richly decorated chapels – often locked – some of which still hold books and manuscripts left over from the church's days as a science museum. Over to the left as you face the altar is the **Guild of Musicians' Chapel**, with a fresco of robed academic figures in the cupola, and a richly-gilded Madonna, credited with miracle-working powers, on the altar. Cherubs wrestling with pointy-eared demons frame the doorway to the adjacent **St Anne's Chapel**, which houses a brightly painted, eighteenth-century wooden altar showing Christ on the Cross, with the disciples represented as bunches of grapes.

Turning to leave the church, you'll see the slender pipes of the organ high above the main door, topped by trumpeting angels and fronted by a bust of Stanisław Moniuszko (1819–1872), the Polish composer who worked as the organist here before becoming a big-time conductor in Warsaw, and penning *Halka*, Poland's first important national opera. Standing apart from the main body of the church is the bell tower, a stout structure capped with a collection of tiny urns that look like sporting trophies. At 68m, it's the tallest belfry in the Old Town. Next to the tower is a stately, barrel-roofed structure that looks as if it ought to be a chapel or an oratory; actually it's a rather swish daytime café for university students.

The Presidential Palace

Stretching west of Universiteto gatvė, the neat, flagstoned triangle of **Daukanto aikštė** is overlooked by the regal facade of the **Presidential Palace** (Prezidentūra), a former merchant's house remodelled in its present neoclassical form at the end of the eighteenth century, when it served as the comfy downtown residence of the Bishop of Vilnius. It became the home of the Russian governor general soon afterwards, and it's likely that Adam Mickiewicz was interrogated here prior to his imprisonment in the Basilian monastery (see p.79). The building's most despised denizen was Governor General Muravyev, nicknamed "the hangman" for his brutal suppresssion of the anti-Tsarist revolt of 1863–64. Salt was rubbed into local wounds by establishing a Muravyev Museum in the palace after his departure. There was also a statue of the man in front of the palace, but this was dismantled – along with a bombastic Catherine the Great memorial which graced Cathedral Square – and evacuated to safety by retreating Russian troops in 1915, never to return. Despite being right at the heart of the Lithuanian state, the square is a restrained, sober place free of ideological or national symbols – save for the orange, red and green Lithuanian tricolors fluttering gamely from a trio of flagpoles.

The Pyatnitskaya Church and Šlapelis House

From the university you can cut back east along the broad, park-like space of Syrvido skveras to the northern end of Pilies, which culminates in a triangular piazza occupied by a year-round craft market selling paintings, amber jewellery and wicker baskets. Hidden behind the street stalls is the Orthodox **Pyatnitskaya**

The Cathedral △

Church (Pjatnickajos cerkvė), a modest piece of mid-nineteenth-century architecture, rather like a domed brick shed. A Russian-language inscription on the outside wall relates the (admittedly apocryphal) tale that the poet Alexander Pushkin's grandfather Hannibal – an African slave presented to Tsar Peter the Great by the Turkish Sultan – was baptized here in 1704. Hugging the eastern side of the street at no. 40 is **Šlapelis House** (Šlapelių namai; Wed–Sun 11am–4pm; free), the former home of Jurgis and Marija Šlapelis, the husband-and-wife team who energetically promoted Lithuanian literature throughout the first half of the twentieth century – a time when Lithuanians were a small minority in a largely Polish- and Yiddish-speaking city. The pair were galvanized into action by the sudden lifting of the ban on printing Lithuanian in the Latin script in 1904: Jurgis threw himself enthusiastically into publishing, while Marija opened Vilnius's first Lithuanian bookshop. Upstairs, there's a display of old photographs evoking life in Vilnius in the early twentieth century, while downstairs is a re-creation of the bookshop (the original was at Dominikonų 13), where self-help pamphlets like *How to Live Without Vodka* and *Health for Mothers and Children* can be found alongside Lithuanian editions of Shakespeare.

Vilnius Picture Gallery

Further south, Pilies gives way to **Didžioji gatvė** or "Main Street". Kicking off the sights along here is the Chodkiewicz palace at no. 4, an opulent pied-a-terre built three centuries ago for one of the Grand Duchy's most prominent families and now occupied by the **Vilnius Picture Gallery**, home to the permanent collection of the Lithuanian Art Museum (Tues–Sat noon–6pm, Sun noon–5pm; 4Lt; free on Wed in winter). Second Empire furnishings and creaky parquet floors provide an elegant backdrop to the somewhat patchy overview of local painters through the ages. **Franciszek Smugliewicz** (1745–1807), the doyen of Vilnius's neoclassicists, is particularly well represented, with numerous overblown canvases depicting biblical and historical subjects – look out for the pseudo-oriental pantomime costumes worn by the protagonists of his *Scythian Messengers with Darius, King of Persia*. Most of the other nineteenth- and twentieth-century artists featured here are pretty second-rate, save perhaps for **Ferdynand Ruszczycz**, whose dreamy, post-impressionist *Golden Room* (1913) is the most modernist work in a largely conservative display.

South of the gallery, it would be difficult to miss the eye-catching jumble of architectural styles that makes up the Orthodox **Church of St Nicholas** (Šv Mikalojaus cerkvė), remodelled in the wake of the brutal suppression of the 1863–64 rebellion by the Tsar's governor general in Vilnius, General Muravyev, to serve as a propagandist statement of the virtues of Russian culture. Framed by a squat, Byzantine-style chapel on one side and a tapering Muscovite spire on the other, the church's facade is resplendently decked out in bright ochre with brick-red trimmings.

Rotušės aikštė

Immediately beyond the Church of St Nicholas, Didžioji opens out into **Rotušės aikštė**, or "Town Hall Square", very much the hub around which life in the Old Town revolves and it's crammed with craft stalls during the annual Kaziukas Fair (see p.67). Little changed since the late eighteenth century, the square is a pretty assemblage of two- and three-storey town houses colour-washed in blue, orange and burgundy. Standing at its southern end is the old **Town Hall** (Rotušė) itself, an imposing, off-white pile fronted by a dignified colonnade, built in 1799 by Laurynas Stuoka Gucevičius, the architect of Vilnius Cathedral. Nowadays, the erstwhile council chamber is reserved for occasional concerts and civic receptions.

On the western side of the square, **Stiklių gatvė** ("Glassmakers' Street" – a reference to the glassmaking workshops established here in the mid-sixteenth century) winds its way back towards the university area, passing craft shops stocked with upmarket linen souvenirs. On the eastern side of the square, a short detour up Savičiaus gatvė brings you to **Čiurlionis House** (Čiurliono namai; Mon–Fri 10am–4pm; donation requested) at no. 11. It's here that Lithuania's most celebrated artist and composer, Mikalojus Konstantinis Čiurlionis (see box on p.124), spent the winter of 1907–8 trying to promote Lithuanian culture in the city. He helped to organize the first-ever group exhibitions by Lithuanian artists and was disheartened by the low cultural horizons of the people who came to the shows, but failed to buy any of his paintings: "As far as art is concerned," he notoriously grumbled, "Vilnius is still in nappies!" There's not a great deal to see here, though, apart from a few prints, family photographs and coffee-table books showing reproductions of his artwork.

A few paces beyond the Čiurlionis House at Savičiaus 5, the five-storey, rocket-like belfry of the eighteenth-century **Augustine Church** (Augustijonų bažnyčia; currently closed for restoration) is one of the most exhilarating architectural sights in the city.

The Contemporary Art Centre

The pale, concrete building marking the southwest corner of Rotušės aikštė, just behind the Town Hall, is the **Contemporary Art Centre** (Šiuolaikinio Meno Centras; ⊚www.cac.lt; Tues–Sun 11am–7pm; 4Lt, free Wed in winter), which hosts high-profile exhibitions featuring artists from Lithuania and elsewhere. The building initially served as the main exhibition space for the Soviet-era Artists' Union, many members of which were accustomed to having their works displayed here whatever the quality, and found themselves excluded after the centre's post-1991 transformation into a showcase for challenging contemporary work.

The only permanent exhibit is the small but undeniably arresting **George Maciunas Fluxus Cabinet** (ask for it to be opened up when you buy your ticket), a room commemorating the Kaunas-born, New York-based artist George Maciunas (1931–1978), who in the early 1960s inspired the Fluxus movement – a playfully iconoclastic group of avant-garde nonconformists. Figures as diverse as Joseph Beuys and Yoko Ono were attracted to a Maciunas-penned Fluxus manifesto (reproduced here) which aimed to "purge the world of bourgeois sickness", and "promote a revolutionary flood and tide in art, promote living art, anti-art, promote non-art reality to be grasped by all peoples, not only critics, dilettantes and professionals." There are Maciunas-designed posters, photographs of happenings, and the "scores" of Maciunas's twelve compositions for pianist Nam June Paik – one of which consists of an exhortation to "place a dog or cat (or both) inside the piano and play Chopin". The art centre's ground-floor café (see "Bars and pubs", p.96) is the main city-centre gathering point for Vilnius bohemians.

St Casimir's Church

Hogging the eastern shoulder of Rotušes aikštė, **St Casimir's Church** (Šv Kazimiero bažnyčia; Mon–Fri 4–6.30pm, Sun 8am–2pm) boasts an arresting facade of homely pink broken up by vertical cream stripes. Built for the Jesuits in the early seventeenth century, the church was turned into a grain store by the Napoleonic French, transformed into an Orthodox church by Tsarist Russia, handed over to the Lutheran congregation by the Germans in World War I and used to house a museum of atheism by the Soviets after World War II, before being finally returned to the Catholic Church in 1987. The church's most striking exterior feature is the elaborate crown and cross on top of the central dome. Representing the ducal crown of the Grand Duchy of Lithuania, it was placed here in 1942 to symbolize Lithuanian sovereignty over the city of Vilnius – which was under Nazi occupation at the time. The towers flanking the building house a series of bells which chime gently whenever the striking mechanism is stirred by the wind – a sound sculpture designed by erstwhile giant of the Soviet jazz scene Vladimir Tarasov. Unsurprisingly, given the church's chequered history, the interior is largely bare, save for a trio of lovingly restored eighteenth-century altars, their gilded capitals appearing to drip down the sombre, grey pillars. The recently restored **organ** is one of the city's finest – and frequently features in weekend concerts (see posters at the church entrance for dates and times).

Along Didžioji and Aušros Vartų

Continuing south along Didžioji, you come to the **Philharmonic building**, whose sober, grey-green neoclassical front hides a charmingly old-fashioned, chandelier-studded interior. It was here in 1909 that Jascha Heifetz gave his famous performance of Mendelssohn's Violin Concerto in E minor at the age of 8, before leaving his native Vilnius for St Petersburg, then the West, where he became one of the most celebrated virtuosi of the twentieth century – a musician so perfect that George Bernard Shaw once advised him to play "one wrong note every night before you go to bed". Now the home of the Lithuanian National Philharmonic Orchestra, the building has hosted an impressive number of top international soloists and conductors since 1990 – before this all visting artists had to be approved by the stiflingly bureaucratic ministry of culture in Moscow.

The Basilian Gate and the Church of the Holy Trinity

Didžioji gives way to **Aušros Vartų gatvė**, which curves gently southwards past **Basilian Gate**, an ornate coffee-and-cream archway which leads through to the courtyard of the long-defunct Basilian monastery. The monastery was a major centre of learning in the sixteenth and seventeenth centuries, when it served as the headquarters of the Uniate (also known as Greek-Catholic) community. Created by the Union of Brest in 1596 to accommodate those Orthodox believers prepared to accept the primacy of the pope, the Uniate Church was conceived as a handy way of allowing the Grand Duchy's many Russian and Belarussian nobles access to the country's Catholic-dominated elite. The hulking grey form of the monastery's **Church of the Holy Trinity** (Šv Trejybės cerkvė) still serves the city's small community of Ukranian Greek-Catholics, although it's currently undergoing long-term restoration and only one of its chapels is open for prayer. The surrounding monastery buildings (some of which are still occupied by monks, although most belong to a technical college) were used as a prison during the Tsarist period – the poet Adam Mickiewicz (see box on p.72) was one of the many Polish intellectuals incarcerated here following the round-ups of October 1823.

The Church of the Holy Spirit

A short distance further south, a gateway on the left-hand side of the street leads through to the **Church of the Holy Spirit** (Šv Dvasios cerkvė), one of the oldest Orthodox churches in Lithuania and the most popular city-centre place of worship for Vilnius Russians. Inside the church's lofty, light-filled interior, rich with the smell of incense and candles, you're immediately drawn to the Baroque iconostasis in three stunning tiers of frivolous bright greens, blues and pinks, designed by the city's oustanding architect of the time, Jan Krzystof Glaubitz. In front of the iconostasis, the bodies of three fourteenth-century martyrs, Anthony, Ioan and Eustachius, are displayed in a glass casket, dressed in red velvet robes (white at Christmas, and black during Lent). According to tradition, the trio were hung from an oak tree on the orders of the rigidly pagan Grand Duke Algirdas in 1347, although the latter subsequently married an Orthodox Russian princess, converted to Christianity, and ordered the construction of a chapel (the forerunner of today's church) on the execution site before retiring to become a monk.

St Theresa's Church

A little further along Aušros Vartų gatvė on the left, rises the stately orange-and-grey **St Theresa's Church** (Šv Teresės bažnyčia), another soaring testament to the city's dominant architectural style. Founded in the mid-1600s by the Grand Duchy's treasurer, Stephen Christopher Pac, the church didn't receive its vibrant, salmon-pink rococo interior until over a century later, when local painter Mateusz Śuśzczański provided the exuberant ceiling frescoes depicting scenes from the life of St Theresa.

The Gate of Dawn

The end of Aušros Vartų is marked by the **Gate of Dawn** (Aušros Vartai), the sole survivor of nine city gates that once studded the walls of Vilnius. In 1671, Carmelite monks from nearby St Theresa's Church built a **chapel** inside the gate to house the most revered of the city's many sacred images, the **Madonna of the Gate of Dawn** (Aušros vartų Marija), and the gate has been a place of pilgrimage for both Lithuanians and Poles ever since. The Madonna is just about visible through a trio of arched windows directly above the gate, and it's rare to see locals who don't look up to the image and cross themselves as they pass underneath it.

Entrance to the chapel is via a doorway at the rear end of St Theresa's, from where a narrow staircase leads up to the chamber where the image is kept. It's a small and intimate space, filled with kneeling supplicants whispering prayers, the aura of sanctity strangely undisturbed by the steady shuffle of visitors' footsteps. Her slender fingers splayed in a stylized gesture of grace, the Madonna herself is all but hidden by an extravagant silver-plated covering that emits a beckoning sparkle to those approaching the gate along the street below. The air of glittering opulence is enhanced by the panels on either side of the image, covered with the heart-shaped plaques left by grateful pilgrims.

The southern side of the gate is surprisingly plain, save for a relief depicting a horse-borne knight known as the **Vytis**, which served as the symbol of the Grand Duchy of Lithuania from the times of Vytautas the Great onwards, and was resurrected after 1991 to feature on the newly independent republic's coat of arms.

The Artillery Bastion

Two minutes' walk east of Aušros Vartų gatvė at Boksto 20/18 is the **Artillery Bastion** (Artilerijos Bastėja; Tues–Sun 10am–7pm; 4Lt), a semicircular, red-brick cannon battery built in the seventeenth century to defend the (no longer standing) Subāaius gate nearby. There's a modest display of weapons and armour inside, although the museum is more interesting for its setting than its contents: visitors descend via a long brick passageway into the bowels of the building, where cannons similar to those used to defend the city have been placed in the embrasures. A door at the top of the passageway leads outside to a viewing terrace, from where you can gaze across towards the crowd of Old Town belfries to the northwest and the narrow streets of the hilly Užupis district to the northeast.

The Old Town's western fringes: the old Jewish quarter, Pylimo gatvė and Vilniaus gatvė

Before World War II, Vilnius was one of the most important centres of Jewish life and culture in Eastern Europe and was known as the "Jerusalem of the North" – a name allegedly bestowed on it by Napoleon Bonaparte when he paused in the city in 1812. First invited to settle in 1410 by Grand Duke Vytautas, the Jews made up a third of the city's population by the nineteenth century, inhabiting a sizeable chunk of the Old Town. The **Jewish quarter** was concentrated in the warren of alleyways either side of **Vokiečių gatvė**, an area vividly remembered by Czesław Miłosz in his book *Beginning with my Streets* (see "Books", p.435) as "a labyrinth of absolutely medieval, narrow little streets, the houses connected by arcades, the uneven pavements two or three metres wide". Little of this world now survives: the 70,000-strong community that once lived here was almost totally wiped out during the Nazi occupation, and few survivors chose to move back after 1945. A handful of the Jewish quarter's streets still retain something of their pre-World War II appearance, although most were reduced to rubble during the war and overlaid with parking lots and office blocks in the years that followed.

The Jewish quarter was carved into two separate **ghettos** by the Germans in 1941, with the streets north of Vokiečių becoming the so-called **Ghetto no. 1** (which was cleared in September 1941), and those to the south becoming **Ghetto no. 2** (cleared in September 1943). The ghettos were rebuilt and repopulated with Lithuanians from the countryside after the war's end, and the area's past was quietly forgotten. The Soviet regime drew a discreet veil over the true extent of Jewish suffering, preferring to present the "Soviet people" as the sole victim of Nazi terror. Vilnius's Jews remained without monuments or memorials until the 1990s, when a scattering of inconspicuous plaques were put up to help fill the yawning gap in the city's collective memory.

Vokiečių and around

Vokiečių gatvė curves northwestwards from Rotušės aikštė, its name (literally "German Street") a relic of the medieval period when merchants from various countries were allowed to settle in different quarters of the city. A broad, tree-lined boulevard with a slim ribbon of park running down the middle, it's busy on summer evenings, when young Vilniusites congregate round the tables of open-air cafés or sprawl on park benches to swig their take-out beers. The Vokiečių of today, however, has little in common with its pre-World War II incarnation, when it served as the main commercial artery of Vilnius's Jewish community and would have been a chaotic jumble of carts, stalls and bilingual Yiddish and Polish shop signs.

Something of the Jewish quarter's original warren-like street plan has been preserved off the southwestern side of Vokiečių, where Mėsinių ("Butchers' Street") leads into the heart of the **former site of Ghetto no. 2**. About 150m up the street lies a small, scruffy square at the junction with Ašmenos, where a modest, easy-to-miss granite memorial bears a Hebrew and Lithuanian text reading "In remembrance of those who suffered and struggled in the Vilnius ghetto". Across a grassy park to the east lies Rūdninkų gatvė, where the main gate to Ghetto no. 2 was located – it was through here that work details left in the morning, and were locked back in at night. A wall plaque bearing a map of the ghetto marks the spot.

West of Mėsinių, take Ašmenos gatvė and its extension, Žemaitijos gatvė, and you'll see a plaque at no. 12 marking the location where the armed Jewish underground put up barricades on September 1, 1943, in a desperate attempt to prevent German troops from clearing the ghetto. From here, Šv Mikalojaus gatvė spins back north to rejoin Vokiečių, on the way passing **St Nicholas's Church** (Šv Mikalojaus bažnyčia), whose red-brick, stepped gable peers over a white courtyard wall. During the inter-war period this was the only Lithuanian-speaking church in Vilnius – services in all the other Catholic establishments were conducted in Polish. The interior is currently being restored, although it's usually open around Mass times.

Immediately opposite St Nicholas's, Pranciškonų darts north towards the eighteenth-century **Franciscan Church** (Pranciškonų bažnyčia), whose impressively lofty interior is once more open for worship after serving as a storehouse during the communist period. Harbouring little else besides a marble statue of the Madonna, this draughty, semi-devastated space packs a spiritual punch more powerful than many of the better preserved places of worship.

Žydų gatvė and around

The historical heart of Jewish Vilnius lay on the northeastern side of Vokiečių around **Žydų gatvė** or "Jews' Street" ("Yidishe gas" to its pre-World War II inhabitants), site of the **Great Synagogue** and the labyrinth of courtyards and alleyways that once surrounded it. Seriously damaged in World War II, the synagogue was levelled by the Soviets, and its place is now occupied by a kindergarten tucked between post-war apartment blocks. Outwardly unassuming, the synagogue was built slightly underground, possibly as a ruse to prevent its grandeur from inviting the envy of local Christians. "It took my breath away, for I had never expected it to be so grand," wrote Lucy Dawidowicz, whose book *At that Time and Place* (see "Books", p.436) describes the year she spent as an American student in pre-World War II Vilnius. "Outside, the synagogue looked to be about three stories tall, but inside it soared to over five stories." It's said that the synagogue's cavernous, domed interior crammed in congregations of five thousand people on major religious holidays.

There's no plaque marking the location of the synagogue, but squeezed between the kindergarten and a neighbouring house is a bust of the **Gaon of Vilnius**, Elijah ben Solomon (1720–1797), the renowned Talmudic scholar who lived and taught here. The Gaon was one of the main opponents of Hasidism (the ecstatic, mystical sect which spread throughout the Jewish communities of Eastern Europe in the mid-eighteenth century), and his reputation as an authority on all aspects of doctrine added to Vilnius's prestige as a centre of Jewish learning.

Between Žydų and Antokolskio to the east once existed a warren of courtyards and tiny alleys (now it's just a car park), home to the poorest of Vilnius's Jewish poor, who would eke out a living by selling old clothes and flea-market junk from makeshift stalls. It was here that Lucy Dawidowicz came across the "Durkhoyf" or "Through-Yard", which she called "the most dismal place of poverty I knew in Vilna", where the air "was close, musty and fetid with the odor of old clothes, the stink of refuse, and the rank odor emanating from the buildings' moldering walls".

The Dominican Church
At the northern end of Vokiečių, Dominikonų heads back east into the heart of the Old Town, passing after 100m or so the **Dominican Church** (Dominikonų bažnyčia), yet another medieval edifice rebuilt in Baroque style by the ubiquitous Jan Krzystof Glaubitz in the 1770s. Given the narrowness of the street, it's difficult to get a good look at the church's most arresting external feature – the broad cupola squatting atop a hefty octagonal drum – without viewing it from some distance away. Approaching or leaving along Stiklių gatvė, just to the southeast, should do the trick.

The macabre *Last Judgement* scenes covering the walls of the porch provide little advance warning of the show-off pink and mauve tones of the church's effervescent interior. Beyond a pulpit decked with sprightly angels and cherubs lies a vivacious cluster of altars, from which gesticulating saints appear poised to leap into the congregation. Up above, a dizzying swirl of frescoes depicting the *Apotheosis of the Holy Spirit* run around the cupola in celestial comic-strip style.

The church's congregation is largely drawn from the city's Polish community, many of whom come to linger in the side chapels dedicated to a generous assortment of supposedly miracle-working Virgins and saints. Most, however, gravitate towards an unremarkable-looking painting, roughly halfway down the nave, which portrays a robed Christ with divine rays emanating from his chest – a work inspired by the visions experienced by one Sister Faustyna Helena Kowalska, a celebrated Catholic mystic of the inter-war period. A local rector encouraged Sister Faustyna to describe what she'd seen to the painter Eugeniusz Kazimirowski in 1934, and the resulting canvas has been the focus of a cult ever since. Sister Faustyna herself was beatified in April 1993 on the occasion of Pope John Paul II's visit to Vilnius.

Along Pylimo gatvė
Running parallel to Vokiečių to the southwest, **Pylimo gatvė** follows the line of the former town walls, and still acts as an unofficial boundary between the Old Town and the nineteenth-century Naujamiestis (see p.87) beyond. A slightly scruffy thoroughfare traversed by lumbering trolleybuses, it's nevertheless rich in memories of Jewish Vilnius, not least because of the two Jewish museum sites towards its northern end.

Nearer the southern end at Pylimo 39 is the city's one surviving **synagogue** (Mon–Thurs 8am–10am, Sun 7pm–9pm), a Moorish-style structure put up in 1903 to serve a congregation that belonged to the Haskalah ("Enlightenment") tradition – a nineteenth-century movement which aimed to bring Judaism into line with modern secularism. Originally known as the Choral Synagogue, owing to the (then innovative) use of a boys' choir during services, it was a popular place of worship for wealthier Westernized Jews in pre-World War II days, and now serves the whole of Vilnius's remaining Jewish community.

Continuing north along Pylimo and making the briefest of detours up Kalinausko brings you to one of the city's more unexpected cultural monuments. Tucked away in the carpark of an ear, nose and throat hospital, and mounted on a soaring pillar, is a bust of the American rock avant-gardist **Frank Zappa**, erected in 1995 on the initiative of local jazz musician Saulius Paukstys. The choice of Zappa – a widely understood symbol of nonconformity perhaps, but hardly a Lithuanian icon – seemed to be a wryly ironic gesture in a country that had seen enough of ideologically charged public monuments, and the project was supported by many people who had never even heard a note of the man's music.

The State Jewish Museum

A little further north at Pylimo 4, a labyrinthine building occupied by numerous Jewish cultural organizations houses the **Lithuanian State Jewish Museum** (Lietuvos valstybnis Žydų muziejus; Mon–Thurs 9.30am–5.30pm, Fri 9.30am–4.30pm; 1Lt, free on Wed in winter), where the main display, on the first floor, shows items salvaged from the Great Synagogue, including puppets used during the Purim festival, as well as pictures of wooden synagogues from small towns in Lithuania, none of which survived World War II. Upstairs is the Gallery of the Righteous (Teisuolių galerija), a small room containing photographs of Lithuanians who were honoured by post-war Israel for their help in sheltering Jews from the Germans. An adjacent room remembers the anti-Nazi resistance groups in the wartime ghettos of Vilnius and Kaunas and the smuggling operations that allowed a small number of Jews to escape to the forests where they could link up with the partisans.

Located at another site two minutes' northwest of here at Pamėnkalnio 12 is the **Catastrophe Exhibition** (ekspozicija "Katastrofa"; Mon–Thurs 9am–5pm, Fri 9am–4pm; donation requested), housed in a building colloquially known as the **"Green House"** on account of its colourful timber construction. This is by far the most compelling branch of the museum, containing a harrowing display about the fate of Lithuania's Jews during the war. An English-language leaflet will guide you round the collection of photographs and documents – most chilling of the latter are the matter-of-fact reports submitted by Einsatzkommando leaders in December 1941, detailing how the killing of Jews had been organized and the numbers involved. Most of Lithuania's Jews were murdered within months of the Nazi takeover, although a few exhibits hint at the remarkable tales of the few who survived: there are scale models of the underground hideaways into which people retreated in order to avoid Nazi round-ups and diagrams of the sewer system used by resistance fighters to make their way in and out of the Vilnius ghettos.

Vilniaus gatvė

If you don't fancy the idea of trudging down Pylimo, an alternative route through the western fringes of the Old Town is offered by Vilniaus gatvė, a sinuous street which starts at the northwestern end of Vokiečių and works its way up towards the bustling shops of Gedimino prospektas. There's a smattering of sights along its length, beginning with the gorgeous strawberries-and-cream exterior of **St Catherine's Church** (Šv Kotrynos bažnyčia), an elegant twin-towered structure, the interior of which still awaits renovation. Opposite the church, the two-storey

Jewish Vilnius

On the eve of World War II the Jewish community constituted the biggest single ethnic group in Vilnius, making the city one of the most important centres of Jewish culture in northeastern Europe. Although they had been present in the city since at least the time of Vytautas the Great, their numbers rose significantly after 1795, when the western territories of the Tsarist Empire (of which Lithuania was now a part) were specifically earmarked for Jewish colonization – a ruse designed to keep them out of the Russian heartlands of the east.

As the main urban centre for Jews living in the territories of present-day Lithuania and northern Belarus, Vilnius became a hot-house of intellectual activity towards the end of the nineteenth century. In 1897, the city saw the birth of the **Bund**, the international Jewish socialist movement which had a major influence on the development of left-wing ideas in the Tsarist Empire and beyond. The city also enjoyed a rich artistic life: both the painter **Chaim Soutine** and the sculptor **Jacques Lipchitz** passed through Vilnius Art School in the years before World War I, while violin virtuoso **Jascha Heifetz** was groomed by the city's Music Academy.

The inter-war period saw an upsurge in Yiddish culture, Yiddish being the first language of the majority of Vilnius Jews. In the 1930s, the literary periodical **Yung Vilne** ("Young Vilnius") provided an outlet for a new generation of Jewish poetry and prose writers, of whom Chaim Grade (best known for the autobiographical short-story collection *My Mother's Sabbath Days*; see "Books" p.436) is the most famous representative. The idea of Yiddish as a national Jewish language equal in importance to Hebrew was promoted by the **YIVO** (Yidisher Visnshaflekher Institut or Yiddish Scientific Institute), founded here in 1925 to conduct research into the ethnology and folklore of Yiddish-speaking communities throughout Eastern Europe.

However, Vilnius was not immune from the waves of **anti-semitism** that swept across central Europe in the wake of World War I. Already in 1919, units of the Polish Legion – in Vilnius to defend the region against the Bolsheviks – had run amok in the Jewish-inhabited parts of the Old Town, leaving many dead. In the late-1930s, Jewish students at Vilnius University were made to sit on special benches at the back of the lecture hall, in order to prevent them from "contaminating the morals" of their Catholic classmates.

None of this, however, prepared Vilnius's Jews for the fate that lay ahead under the **Nazi occupation**, which began with the German army's arrival in the city on June 24, 1941. Within weeks of taking control of the city, the Nazi authorities were joined by special units known as the Einsatzkommandos, who were specifically charged with the job of ridding the German-controlled areas of Eastern Europe of their Jewish inhabitants. From July 8 onwards, the Einsatzkommando responsible for the Vilnius region – aided by Lithuanian auxiliaries – started taking an average of five hundred Jews a day to the Paneriai forest on the outskirts of Vilnius (see p.93), where they were shot and thrown into pits. On September 6, 1941, the Jewish quarter of Vilnius's Old Town was divided into two **ghettos**, in which the city's surviving Jews were confined. The smaller of the two ("Ghetto no. 1"), comprising the narrow streets on the northeastern side of Vokiečių gatvė, contained about 11,000 people, most of whom were killed over the next two weeks. The larger ghetto ("Ghetto no.

town house at Vilniaus 41 provides a suitably refined home for the **Lithuanian Theatre, Music and Film Museum** (Lietuvos teatro, muzikos ir kino muziejus; Tues–Fri noon–6pm, Sat 11am–4pm; 4Lt), which harbours an alluring jumble of posters, costumes and antiquated cameras. Many of Lithuania's leading artists found work designing costumes and sets for the theatre, and the selection of their sketches on show here – including the work of mid-twentieth-century modernists such as Adomas Varnas and Stasys Ušinskas – beats anything in the city's picture galleries.

2"), which occupied the streets southwest of Vokiečių, initially held 29,000 inhabitants (mostly able-bodied Jews considered fit for work, together with their families), although this number was gradually reduced over the next two years as more and more people were taken away – either to provide slave labour elsewhere, or to be killed at Paneriai.

Despite the constant lack of food and the spirit-sapping fear of Nazi round-ups, Ghetto no. 2 continued to function as an urban community with a semblance of normality, boasting a hospital (jammed between Ligoninės and Pylimo), a public library and sports club (both located at Žemaitijos 4) and even a theatre (at Arklių 3), where a drama troupe, choir and symphony orchestra performed. The ghetto also had a **resistance movement** in the shape of the United Partisan Organization (Fareinikte Partisaner Organizatsie or **FPO**), formed in January 1942 with the aim of smuggling Jews out of the ghetto and into the forests outside Vilnius, where partisan groups were active throughout the war. After an escape attempt in summer 1943, in which twelve made it out of the ghetto (another nine were caught and shot), the Germans announced that they would execute all family members of anyone who tried to flee. The FPO henceforth concentrated on arming itself, which it did by bringing in weapons through the sewer system. In July 1943, the Germans declared that they would liquidate the ghetto forthwith unless the FPO leader, Iztak Witenberg, was handed over to the Gestapo. He gave himself up immediately in order to save the rest of the community.

On September 1, increased military activity around the ghetto persuaded the remaining FPO leaders that the ghetto was about to be cleared and its inhabitants relocated to concentration camps. Barricades were set up at either end of Žemaitijos gatvė in an attempt to protect the FPO headquarters (at Žemaitijos 4) and buy time. Approaching German troops were fired on from a building at the eastern end of Žemaitijos and forced to retreat before returning to blow the building up. This act of resistance was no more than a minor inconvenience to the Germans, but it did persuade them to postpone the full clearing of the ghetto for a couple of weeks, allowing several FPO members and other young Jews to escape (either through the sewers, or via gates in the ghetto wall which were supervised by slack Lithuanian police). One of those who got away was Abraham Sutskever, a member of the pre-war Yung Vilne literary set who went on to become one of the major post-war writers in the Yiddish language.

However, the vast majority of the ghetto's remaining 10,000 inhabitants were rounded up on September 23 and despatched to a variety of destinations: able-bodied adults were sent to labour camps in Estonia and Latvia; most of the women and children were delivered to the death camps. Those too sick to be transported were taken straight to the Paneriai forest to be shot.

Today, Vilnius has a Jewish population of around 3000, although most of these belong to families who moved to the city from other parts of Lithuania after 1945. Many of the Vilnius-born Jews who survived the Holocaust simply couldn't bear the pain of living here after 1945 and left for North America or Israel – consigning the cosmopolitan world of pre-war Vilnius to the realm of history books and reminiscences.

A little further along at no. 39, the **Teachers' House** (Mokytojų namai), overlooking the junction of Vilniaus and Klaipėdos, is occupied by a multitude of cultural organizations – including the **Vartai Art Gallery** on the second floor (Mon–Fri 1–6pm; free), which quite apart from putting on some of the best contemporary art shows in the capital, retains some spectacular Art Nouveau stucco work in its high-ceilinged rooms. Five minutes' further north, a squat ochre-plastered block at no. 22 is the one surviving wing of the seventeenth-century **Radvila**

Palace (Radvilų rūmai; Tues–Sat 11am–6pm; 4Lt), the downtown pad of one of the Grand Duchy of Lithuania's leading aristocratic families. Rising to prominence in the fifteenth century, the Radvilas (more widely known by their Polonized name of Radziwiłł) went on to provide the duchy with many of its most outstanding military commanders, diplomats and bishops. Their palace now contains a rather mundane collection of paintings and furniture, enlivened only by occasional visiting exhibitions, and a downstairs room plastered with 165 oddly compelling prints from the Radvila family album. Commissioned by Mykolas Radvila, "the Small Fish" (depicted in portrait no. 157, he doesn't look nearly as fish-like as the majority of his ancestors), the series portrays all the prominent family members through the ages, starting with mysterious, semi-mythical founder of the dynasty Vaišunda, and culminating with Karol Stanisław Radvila (1734–1790), who – despite being pictured here as a foppish aristocrat – was a shaven-headed drunkard and hooligan accused by contemporary chroniclers of shooting his own servants for sport.

Gedimino prospektas

Gedimino prospektas, running west from Cathedral Square, was the main thoroughfare of nineteenth-century Vilnius, and remains the city's most important commercial street. A broad, cobbled boulevard, overlooked by trolleybus wires and spruced-up, stuccoed buildings, it has been named after St George, Mickiewicz, Stalin and Lenin in the past, reflecting the succession of different regimes. It's a place to come and shop or do business rather than sightsee, although few of its buildings are without deep historical associations.

Around 600m west of Cathedral Square is the **Hotel Neringa**, whose restaurant was the favoured haunt of the city's artistic elite during the brief golden age of relative cultural freedom in the late 1960s and early 1970s. The Russian dissident poet and Nobel prize winner, Jozef Brodsky, whiled away the evenings here when visiting Lithuanian literary colleague Tomas Venclova, and the avant-garde Ganelin-Tarasov-Chekasin jazz trio (which went on to achieve world renown) played four-hour sets to appreciative crowds of coffee-swilling intellectuals. Perhaps inevitably, the *Neringa* was also a stronghold of the local KGB: foreign visitors to the restaurant were invariably ushered towards private booths fitted with listening devices. The trend-setting crowd moved away from the *Neringa* decades ago, and the restaurant nowadays caters to fat cats rather than hep cats, but it still preserves much of its original decor, notably the famous murals featuring idealized scenes of fisherfolk from Neringa, the sandy peninsula after which the hotel is named.

Another 400m brings you to the broad open space of **Lukiškių aikštė**, a square which has long played an infamous role in the city's history. After the 1863–64 uprising against the Tsarist regime, a number of rebels were publicly hanged here by the hardline Russian governor Muravyev. From 1952 to 1991 it was graced by a monumental **statue of Lenin**, unceremoniously carted away in August 1991 as the collapse of the Moscow coup signalled the final break-up of the Soviet Union. Preserved as a warning to future generations, the statue can still be seen in the Grūtas sculpture park outside Druskininkai (see p.142).

On the southern side of the square, the forbiddingly grey, neoclassical building at no. 40 is the former site of Lithuania's KGB headquarters and now the educative and moving **Lithuanian Genocide Museum** (Lietuvos genocido aukų muziejus; entrance on Aukų 2A; mid-May to mid-Sept Tues–Sun 10am–6pm; mid-Sept to mid-May Tues–Sun 10am–4pm; donation expected; English-language leaflet 2Lt, tape commentary 8Lt). Originally built in 1899 to serve as the city court house, the building was taken over by the NKVD (as the KGB was initially known) during the first Soviet occupation of Lithuania in 1940. It then served as the HQ of the Gestapo when the Germans took over in July the following year, and reverted to the Soviets in 1944. The dank, green cells in the basement, where the KGB incarcerated and tortured political prisoners, have been preserved in their pre-1991 state. There are texts and photographs relating to some of the more famous prisoners to have passed through here – notably the Catholic Bishop Borisevičius, shot in the basement in 1946; and partisan leaders Jonas Žemaitis and Adolfas Ramanauskas, who survived for years in the forests of Soviet Lithuania before being captured – and executed – in the mid-1950s. Particularly chilling are the water isolation cells, in which prisoners had to stand on precarious concrete perches for hours on end – or risk falling into a dirty pool of freezing water below.

Next door to the Genocide Museum at no. 42 looms the neoclassical bulk of the **Lithuanian Music Academy** (Lietuvos muzikos akademija), where vast pictures of Lenin were hung on Soviet state holidays such as May Day and November 11 (the anniversary of the Bolshevik revolution), and terracing erected so that party leaders could observe the bombastic parades with which such occasions were marked.

At the extreme western end of Gedimino prospektas stands Lithuania's **Parliament Building** (Seimas), a graceless, modern structure built in the 1980s to serve as the home of the Lithuanian republic's Supreme Soviet – a toothless assembly of party appointees. The first free elections to the Soviet in February 1990 transformed this bastion of communist authority into a focus of Lithuanian patriotism overnight, and it was here that the restoration of Lithuanian independence was declared on March 11 of the same year – to the intense annoyance of Mikhail Gorbachev, who was on an official visit to Vilnius at the time. When the Kremlin moved to crush the Lithuanian independence movement on January 13 1991, thousands of ordinary citizens descended on the parliament to prevent its capture by Soviet forces, who had already killed twelve unarmed civilians while storming Vilnius's TV Tower (see p.92). On the side of the parliament facing the river some of the barricades built to defend the building have been preserved, complete with anti-Soviet graffiti; there's also a moving memorial of traditional wooden crosses commemorating those who died at the TV Tower, and the seven border guards killed at Medeninkai by Soviet special forces six months later.

On the opposite bank of the river, the glimmering gunmetal domes of the Orthodox **Znamensky Church** (Znamenskio cerkvė) provide the Gedimino strip with one final architectural flourish, although the bare interior is hardly worth venturing across the bridge for.

Naujamiestis

Extending over the hilly terrain which overlooks the Old Town from the west, the **Naujamiestis** or "New Town" began life in the mid- to late nineteenth century, when a grid-pattern of broad boulevards and sturdy apartment blocks was laid out in order to accommodate the city's growing middle class. The few real attractions here begin with the modest display at the **Lithuanian Railway Museum** (Lietuvos Geležinkelių muziejus; 2.50Lt), just uphill to the west of Pylimo gatvė at Mindaugo 15. It contains models of old locomotives, photographs of the building of the Warsaw–St Petersburg line (which connected Vilnius to the Tsarist train network in 1862), and a model train layout with no noticeable Lithuanian connection. It's a short walk north from here to Basanavičiaus, the main artery of the Naujamiestis and home to the Orthodox **All Saints' Church**, one of the city's prettiest. Shaming the street's drab office blocks with its sparkling array of green onion domes, the church was built in 1913 to celebrate the three-hundredth anniversary of the Romanov dynasty's accession to the Russian throne. It's pretty bare and gloomy inside, though, save for an intricate, filigree-effect brass iconostasis.

Marking the western border of the Naujamiestis is **Vingis Park** (Vingio parkas), the city's largest, a gently undulating area of pine forest traversed by asphalt paths. A popular strolling area all year round, it's also the site of a large open-air stage where pop concerts are held in the summer. A full 2km from the Old Town, it's best accessed by walking west along M.K. Čiurlionio gatvė, which runs roughly parallel to Basanavičiaus to the north.

Romain Gary (1914–1980)

Lists of famous Vilniusites often fail to include the French war hero, novelist and diplomat **Romain Gary**, who spent the early 1920s living at Basanavičiaus 16, just to the west of Pylimo gatvė. The nineteenth-century apartment block is still standing and has probably changed little since his time, save for the unobtrusive plaque attached to the wall in his honour.

Gary was a complex character who frequently hid behind aliases and fabricated biographical details, and much about his early life remains obscure. The way he tells it, he arrived in Vilnius in 1921 – the first stage in what his Russian Jewish mother hoped would be a passage to a better life in France. In the meantime she eked out a living making women's hats, which she then passed off as expensive imports from Paris. She even went as far as to organize a promotional party at which a failed actor from Warsaw was drafted in to impersonate a top French couturier. The ladies of Vilnius fell for the ruse, and the business prospered for a time, leaving Gary's ambitious mother free to invest in her son's education by hiring a whole roster of private teachers. When he wasn't being tutored in etiquette or horsemanship, Romain spent his days playing in the communal yard behind Basanavičiaus 16, or hovering beside a nearby alley where he frequently caught the local baker indulging in adventurous al-fresco sex with a serving girl – an experience wistfully recounted in the 1960 account of his childhood, *La Promesse de l'Aube*.

After a year in Vilnius, the hat business collapsed and the family moved on, first to Warsaw, and then to France, where Gary passed through the Foreign Legion and the French Air Force before joining up with General de Gaulle's Free French. While in London he met and married the writer, journalist and Vogue editor, Lesley Blanch.

Just after the war, Gary burst onto the French literary scene with his first novel, *Education Européene* (a story of World War II Polish partisans in the forests near Vilnius), received with critical acclaim. At around the same time, he entered the French diplomatic service and was immediately posted to Sofia, where the Bulgarian secret service set him up with a local girl and secretly filmed the results. Not surprisingly, his next foreign posting was in politically uneventful Switzerland, from where Gary mischievously filed reports on snow conditions to unamused superiors in Paris.

In 1956, Gary won France's most prestigious literary prize, the Prix Goncourt, for his macho tale of elephant hunters in Africa, *Les Racines du Ciel* (subsequently filmed by John Huston and starring Errol Flynn, Juliet Greco and Trevor Howard). The same year he became Consul General in Los Angeles and entertained the Hollywood elite at lavish receptions. A reputation for paying more attention to film starlets than to French economic interests led one newspaper to dub him the "French sexual attaché". It was in LA that he met his second wife, Jean Seberg, a young film star 25 years his junior.

Gary quit the diplomatic service in 1961 in order to concentrate on writing, churning out film scripts for big studio producers like Daryll Zanuck and David Selznick. He even directed features himself, few of which made it into the annals of cinema history – although 1972's *Kill* earned notoriety by being banned in the UK for its excessive use of violence.

In 1975, writing under the pseudonym Emile Ajar, Gary again won the Prix Goncourt – the only person to win it twice – for *La Vie Devant Soi*. The Académie Goncourt decided to award the prize without knowing the real identity behind the pseudonym. Gary's cousin, Paul Pavlowitch, posed as the author for a while, and it was only in his posthumous work, *Vie et mort d'Emile Ajar*, that Gary revealed the truth.

Although they divorced, Gary and Jean Seberg remained close, and some months after Seberg committed suicide, on December 2, 1980, Gary, too, took his own life.

East of the Old Town

From Mairono gatvė, which marks the eastern boundary of the Old Town, a narrow bridge leads over the fast-flowing Vilnia River towards the district of **UŽUPIS** (literally "beyond the river"), a shabby hillside heap of crumbling nineteenth-century houses that seems a world away from the Vilnius of the tourist brochures. However, this former urban backwater is changing fast, not least because the faded charms of its alleyways and courtyards have recently attracted two very different groups of incomers: nouveaux-riches eager to buy and renovate houses on the cheap, and impoverished bohemians on the lookout for low-rent accommodation and squats. It's the latter who are largely responsible for the creation of the so-called **Užupis Republic** (Užupio respublika), which declared its independence from the rest of Vilnius on April Fool's Day 2000. Intended as a wry comment on the very notion of independence in the era of globalization, the "republic" also represents a serious attempt to build a sense of community in the district and to stimulate the activities of the numerous artists and nonconformists who have gathered here. Annual fashion shows, art exhibitions and chaotic summer regattas on the River Vilnia have all been organized here in recent years, alongside a whole host of more impromptu happenings. Unfortunately for the outsider, events tend to be publicized on a word-of-mouth basis, and it's difficult to find out about them unless you have local contacts. The best place to start is probably the *Užupio kavinė* (see "Bars and pubs" p.96), just over the bridge from the Old Town, where many of the republic's leading lights are wont to congregate. Beyond here, a short walk along the gently ascending Užupio gatvė should be enough to give you a flavour of the district; after some 200m it passes a small triangular piazza, dominated by a tall pillar topped by a trumpet-blowing bronze angel – unveiled in April 2001 to mark the first birthday of the republic.

One of the more famous former residents of this part of town was **"Iron" Felix Dzerzhinsky**, the Lithuanian-born Pole who went on to become a committed Bolshevik and one of Lenin's closest collaborators. Dzerzhinsky lived at Užupio 14 (roughly level with the angel) while a high-school student, before moving on to become a socialist agitator in Kaunas. After the Russian revolution Dzerzhinsky was charged with setting up the Cheka, the much-feared state security service which later metamorphozed into the KGB – hardly an organization remembered with great affection by the majority of Lithuanians. Unsurprisingly, there's no commemorative plaque.

Continuing your ascent and bearing left along Polocko gatvė brings you after about ten minutes to the **Bernardine cemetery** (Bernardinų kapinės), one of the city's most attractive graveyards – a dense cluster of predominantly nineteenth-century memorials atmospherically situated on a hillside overlooking a curve in the River Vilnia.

The Hill of Three Crosses

Pathways on the northern side of the Užupis district lead up onto a group of sandy, pine-covered knolls known by the collective name of Kalnų parkas ("Hill Park"), a peaceful area which seems light years away from the bustle of the city below. The most prominent – and most visited – of the heights here is the **Hill of Three Crosses** (Trijų kryžių kalnas), reached more conveniently from its northern side, where an asphalted road climbs up from Kosciuškos gatvė, near to the Applied Art Museum (see p.69). According to popular tradition, it's here that Jogaila erected three crosses in memory of the seven Franciscan monks executed on this spot by his grandfather, Grand Duke Algirdas. Whatever their origins, a trio of crosses did exist here until Russian Governor General Muravyev's decision to remove them – a reprisal for the 1863–4 uprising. Vilnius town council celebrated the departure of the Russians in 1915 by building three new crosses in gleaming white stone, a much-loved landmark on the city's eastern skyline until the Soviets dynamited them in 1950. The replicas erected after 1990 have quickly re-established themselves as popular targets for weekend strollers. Those who make it up here are rewarded with excellent views of the city, with the Old Town laid out in the foreground and more distant landmarks, such as the bright-green cupolas of All Saints' Church (see p.87) and the spear-like form of the TV Tower (p.92), further away to the east.

The Church of St Peter and Paul and Antakalnis cemetery

Past the Hill of Three Crosses, Kosciuškos continues 800m northeast towards the **Church of SS Peter and Paul** (Šv Petro ir Povilo bažnyčia), its twin-towered facade presiding over a busy traffic roundabout. Of fifteenth-century origin, the church was rebuilt as a three-aisled basilica in 1668 on the initiative of Lithuania's Grand Hetman (military commander-in-chief and second only to the Grand Duke in times of war), Michael Casimir Pac. Pac intended the church to be a celebration of Vilnius's deliverance from the Russians, who had just vacated the city after a thirteen-year occupation. The interior looks cold and grey at first sight, but on closer inspection comes alive with gloriously over-the-top stucco work, featuring cavorting cherubs, rich foliage and exotic plants laden with fruit. The whole ensemble was conceived by Italian craftsmen Pietro Perti and Giovanni Maria Galli, who spent eleven years cramming every available centimetre of the upper walls and ceiling with over two thousand mouldings. Some of the most complex work is around the dome, where angels twang away on musical instruments and contorted human forms appear to be holding up the central lantern. Of the several richly decorated chapels on either side of the nave, the most famous is the altar of the Madonna of Misericord in the left-hand transept, where an image of the Virgin supposedly protects parishioners from ill health and disease. Donated to the church by Bishop Jerzy Tyszkiewicz in 1647, it became the focus of a serious cult during the plague epidemic of 1708–10, when Bishop Brzostowski began holding forty-hour Masses at the altar in an attempt to soothe the anxieties of his flock. As you leave, look out for the stucco figure of death prancing mischeviously on one side of the main doorway – a memento mori said to mark the grave of Pac himself.

Northeast of the church lies the low-key suburb of **Antakalnis**, worth venturing into if only to explore the peaceful, park-like terrain of **Antakalnis cemetery** (Antakalnio kapinės) about 800m beyond – follow Antakalnio gatvė past the church and then bear right along Sapiegos, from where the cemetery is well signed. Ranged across pine-covered hills, the cemetery bears the mark of all the regimes to have ruled over Vilnius during the last two centuries. The tombs of wealthy Tsarist families dot the area near the entrance, while over to the left lies a vale of neatly laid-out crosses honouring the Poles who died defending the Vilnius region from the Red Army in 1919–20. The eastern end of the cemetery is overlooked by an angular Soviet-era war memorial and a terraced hillside occupied by the graves of Lithuania's post-1945 communist elite – a uniformly poker-faced bunch if the accompanying busts and reliefs are to be taken seriously. Finally, providing a focus for contemporary patriotism in the central part of the cemetery, a semicircular memorial remembers the thirteen Lithuanian victims of Soviet aggression in January 1991, twelve of whom died defending the Vilnius TV Tower (see p.92).

Antakalnis cemetery has recently been earmarked as the site of a new memorial to the French war dead of winter 1812, when the Grande Armée (deserted by Napoleon himself) retreated in disarray through Vilnius – a city Napoleon had entered in triumph only five months earlier. Renewed interest in the period arose in 2001, when a building site northeast of the city centre yielded the remains of over two thousand soldiers, most of whom had succumbed to a lethal mixture of hunger, typhus and cold weather. Many of the dead were not French nationals, but volunteers picked up in Poland and Lithuania during Napoleon's march westwards. Once they've been fully examined by archeologists, their remains will be laid to rest here.

The outskirts

Outside central Vilnius, there's a handful of isolated attractions, each of which could be seen in a morning or an afternoon. The city north of the River Neris presents a particularly unexciting jumble of modern office blocks and housing projects – until you get to the park-like open spaces of the Jeruzalė suburb, where paths in the vicinity of the **Calvary Church** and the **Verkiai Palace** make for some excellent walks. On the eastern margins of the city, both the **Alexander Pushkin Museum** in Markučiai and the **cemetery** in the suburb of **Rasos** are reasonably short hops from the centre and provide a glimpse of the semi-rustic, forest-fringed outskirts which girdle the city centre. Further afield to the west, the **Television Tower** is an engaging tourist attraction in its own right, as well as a powerful reminder of Lithuania's resistance to the Soviet agression of January 1990. Historical memories of an altogether more harrowing kind are attached to the forest of **Paneriai**, 10km southwest of town, where the bulk of Vilnius's pre-war Jewish population were brutally murdered by the Nazis.

The Calvary Church and Verkiai Palace

Beginning at the northern end of the Green Bridge (Žaliasis tiltas), the main crossing point over the River Neris, Kalvarijų gatvė spears northwards through suburbs for some 6km before arriving at the **Calvary Church of the Holy Cross** (Kalvarijų Šv kryžaus bažnyčia; bus #26 from Savivaldybės aikštė), an eighteenth-century structure built to provide the focus for a group of nineteen calvary chapels arranged in the nearby woods. The Soviets wrecked all but four of the chapels, but the others are being rebuilt, and all are linked by paths winding pleasantly over undulating, pine-covered terrain – a signboard bearing a map of the area helpfully leads the way. Following the circuit southeast and continuing downhill brings you out at the **Trinapolis Church** (Trinapolio bažnyčia), a pleasing, twin-towered Baroque affair in a lovely location overlooking the grassy banks of the River Neris. Follow paths northeast from the Calvary Church and you'll emerge on Verkių gatvė (also reached by walking due north from Trinapolis), which hugs the west bank of the Neris for a while before arriving at a densely wooded hillock occupied by the **Verkiai Palace** (Verkių rūmai; also accessible by bus #35 and #36 from the southern end of Kalvarijų gatvė). Originally built as the summer retreat of the bishop of Vilnius, the two surviving wings of this neoclassical pile now belong to the Lithuanian Botanical Institute. One wing of the palace is used for art exhibitions, allowing you a glimpse of some wonderfully restored early-nineteenth-century interiors complete with cake-icing ceilings. There's not much in the way of a botanical garden to look around save for a few trees and shrubs in the palace park, but it's a soothing place in which to wander – a balustraded area at the southern end of the park offers an excellent view of the twisting River Neris, with the twin domes of Trinapolis in the background.

The Alexander Pushkin Museum

Situated in the suburb of Markučiai, 2km east of the Old Town, the **Alexander Pushkin Museum** (Aleksandro Puškino muziejus; Wed–Sun 10am–5pm; 4Lt) is a bit of a fake, bearing in mind that it was the home of Pushkin's son rather than that of the great Russian poet himself. Such details shouldn't put you off, however – the timber building in which the museum is housed harbours the best-preserved nineteenth-century interior in the city, and the surrounding woods make it a lovely place for a short stroll. Built for the Russian General Melnikov in 1867, the house was inherited by his daughter, Varvara, who subsequently married Pushkin's youngest son Grigorii. Chunky period furniture and reproduction wallpaper provide the backdrop to a words-and-pictures display (texts in Lithuanian and Russian only) about the poet's life and work, including several references to Adam Mickiewicz (see p.72) – the poets knew each other in Moscow, and Pushkin's enthusiasm for his colleague's writings contributed greatly to Mickiewicz's growing international reputation. Outside the house, pathways lead through deciduous forest to the small onion-domed chapel beside which Grigorii and Varvara lie buried. To get to the museum, take bus #10 from the Užupio stop on Maironio gatvė to the Markučiai terminus – the house is on a knoll straight ahead.

Rasų cemetery

A forest of predominantly nineteenth-century funerary monuments ranged across tree-shaded hillocks, **Rasų cemetery** is an important place of pilgrimage for Lithuanians and Poles alike, owing to the unusually large number of historical figures buried here. It lies in otherwise undistinguished suburbs about 1600m southeast of the Old Town: from Rotušės aikštė, walk east along Subačiaus then south along Rasų gatvė; otherwise take bus #31 from the train station. Prime among the remains laid to rest here is the **heart of Marshal Józef Piłsudski**, leader of the Polish independence movement at the beginning of the twentieth century and the country's first president after 1918. Born into an impoverished gentry family in the Polish–Lithuanian borderlands, Piłsudski went to school in Vilnius, and owned land outside the town in the 1920s. He long entertained the romantic notion that the Polish–Lithuanian Commonwealth of old could be restored (a Commonwealth in which the Poles, of course, would play the leading role), and was genuinely disappointed that the strength of Lithuanian national sentiment after World War I rendered such a dream impossible. He gave tacit support to the Żeligowski coup that restored Vilnius to Poland in 1920, and remained sentimentally attached to the Vilnius region throughout his life – hence the desire to have at least one portion of himself laid to rest here. Buried with much pomp on May 12, 1936, the marshal's heart lies underneath a black granite slab just to the left of the cemetery's main entrance, surrounded by the graves of Polish soldiers who defended Vilnius against Bolshevik forces in 1919. Piłsudski's remaining body parts can be found in the crypt of Kraków's Wawel Cathedral.

One of the few prominent Lithuanians who chose to stay in Vilnius during the Piłsudski era was **Jonas Basanavičius** (1851–1927), the publicist and patriot who had become the leader of the Lithuanian national movement at the close of the nineteenth century. A simple obelisk marks his final resting place opposite the cemetery's main chapel, which is uphill and to the right of the Piłsudski memorial. Basanavičius was one of the prime movers behind the Lithuanian Declaration of Independence on February 16, 1918, and wreaths are laid here on the anniversary. A Lithuanian cultural icon of equal stature – the painter and composer **Mikalojus Konstantinis Čiurlionis** (see p.124) – lies a short distance away in the northern part of the cemetery, marked by an angular grey tombstone.

The Television Tower

Perched on high ground 3km west of the centre in the suburb of Karoliniškės, the slender form of the 326-metre **Television Tower** (Televizijos bokštas; daily 10am–9pm; 12Lt) soars gracefully above the surrounding pines. On January 13, 1991, the Kremlin ordered its troops to sieze control of the TV Tower and other key public buildings in a ham-fisted attempt to reassert authority over the wayward republic. When unarmed civilians gathered to defend the tower, twelve of them died under the wheels of Soviet tanks. Once in control of the tower, the Soviets closed down the Lithuanian TV service – which simply continued broadcasting from its studios in Kaunas. Fearful of causing further casualties, the Soviets backed off from their plans to storm the Seimas (see p.87), where many thousands more civilians had gathered. The events of January 13 provoked international outrage (irredeemably tarnishing the image of Soviet leader Mikhail Gorbachev) and only served to boost the prestige of the Lithuanian independence movement.

Today, the dead are commemorated by a group of wooden crosses at the tower's base, while a photographic exhibition on the ground floor inside vividly captures the drama and heroism of the time. Lifts convey visitors to the rather drab café-restaurant near the tower's summit, although the trip is rewarded with the chance to savour a superb panorama of the city from the slowly revolving viewing deck.

To **get to** the tower take trolleybus #16 or bus #54 from the train station, or trolleybus #11 from Lukiškių aikštė; alight at the Televizijos bokštas stop on Sausio 13-Osios gatvė.

Paneriai

PANERIAI, the forested site where the Nazis and their Lithuanian accomplices murdered one hundred thousand people during World War II, lies among nondescript suburbs 10km southwest of the centre. The site was initially used by the Soviet army, who dug oil storage pits here in 1941. The Nazis, who arrived in July the same year, found the pits especially convenient. Political undesirables from all over Europe were among those killed and buried here, although the vast majority (an estimated 70,000) were the Jews of Vilnius, who were systematically exterminated from July 8, 1941, onwards, the biggest waves of killing taking place in September 1941 and September 1943.

The killing grounds are about 1km into the woods due west of Paneriai train station and marshalling yards. The entrance to the site is marked by two stone slabs dating from the communist period, whose Russian and Lithuanian inscriptions refer to murdered "Soviet citizens" rather than Jews – a typical example of how the Soviet authorities exploited the Holocaust for their own political ends, failing to spell out who its real victims were. A central slab with an inscription in Hebrew commemorating "seventy thousand Jewish men, women and children" was only added in 1990. From the memorial a path leads to the **Paneriai Memorial Museum** (Panerių memorialinis muziejus, Agrastų 15; official times are Mon & Wed–Fri noon–6pm, Sat & Sun 11am–6pm, but ring ☏8-5/260 2001 to check that it's open) with a small display detailing what happened here. From the museum, paths lead to the pits into which the Nazis initially threw their victims; the bodies of many were later exhumed and burned when the advance of Soviet armies prompted the Germans to start hiding the evidence of their crimes. This latter task was carried out by an eighty-man, corpse-burning team composed of Jews and Russian POWs. They were kept chained at all times and slept in a heavily-defended bunker served by a ladder which was removed at night. After spending three months digging a tunnel with spoons and bare hands, forty of the corpse burners escaped on April 15, 1944. Twenty-five of them were caught and killed straight away, while the rest broke through to join partisan groups in the forest. The forty corpse burners who had stayed behind were executed five days later.

To **get to Paneriai** take a southwest-bound suburban train from Vilnius station and alight at Paneriai. From the station platform descend onto Agrastų gatvė, turn right and follow the road through the woods for about 1km.

Eating and drinking

Vilnius has a rapidly growing choice of **restaurants**, offering everything from Lithuanian to Lebanese cuisine, with prices to suit all budgets. There's not much in the way of **café culture** in the city, but plenty of smallish places offer snacks and cheap meals, as well as the full range of alcoholic and non-alcoholic drinks. Such cafés may stay open until late evening, although most night-time drinking takes place in the ever-growing range of **bars**, many of which keep going until the early hours. Most bars and restaurants are concentrated around Gedimino or in the Old Town, and there's little point in straying outside this area unless you're looking for one of the few characterful suburban establishments listed below.

Picnic supplies and other **foodstuffs** can be purchased from big stores like Rimi, opposite the town hall at Didžioji 28 (daily 8am–10pm); Iki, in the same building as the bus station (daily 8am–10pm); Minima, on the corner of Gedimino and Vilniaus (daily 8am–10pm); or from the mega-supermarket Maxima, just west of the Old Town at Mindaugo 11 (daily 8am–midnight).

Restaurants

Many Vilnius **restaurants** serve the kind of cuisine you come across in most north European countries: solid meat-and-potato fare, schnitzels and chops. An increasing number of establishments, however, are starting to serve up traditional Lithuanian food, such as *cepelinai*, *koldūnai* and *blynai*, in folksy, wood-furnished surroundings. In addition, there's no end of pizzerias and a handful of other ethnic restaurants around the centre.

Apart from a few upscale, starched-napkin restaurants in the pricier hotels, most places cultivate an air of relaxed informality. **Prices** for main courses usually fall into the 20–35Lt bracket, although speciality dishes, especially in the posher places, often cost more. In some restaurants it's a good idea to book a table in advance at weekends; we've included telephone numbers where necessary.

Old Town

Aqua Didžioji 28. A bright, breezy and popular café-restaurant opposite the Town Hall, offering a good-value, self-service buffet during the day and waitress service in the evening. A wide range of excellently prepared and attractively priced fish dishes. Daily 10am–midnight.

Da Antonio Pilies 20. Decent thin-crust pizzas, some pasta choices, and a small number of more expensive classic Italian dishes. There are other branches at Vilniaus 23 and Vilniaus 47. Daily 8.30am–11pm.

Finjan Vokiečių 18. A Middle Eastern place that looks like a fast-food café but charges restaurant prices. The kebabs, shawarma and felafel on offer taste good and the portions are reasonable. Daily 11am–midnight.

Freskos Didžioji 31 ☎8-5/261 8133. Imaginative, well-presented modern European cuisine in a barrel-vaulted chamber occupying the rear end of the Town Hall. Good-value lunchtime salad buffet. Daily 11am–midnight.

Kaukazo Belaisvė Trakų 7. A smart, comfortable Georgian restaurant, with decor themed around the Soviet-era comedy film *Prisoner of the Caucasus*. Superb range of *shashlyks* (Caucasian kebabs) and stews, garnished with *lavash* (flat bread) and spicy traditional sauces. Daily 11am–11pm.

Kebab House Aušros vartų 11. A cosy, Turkish-carpeted hideaway serving up the classic repertoire of Middle Eastern meat-on-a-stick treats – although portions are small, so you may need more than one dish per person to make a full meal.

Lokys Stiklių 8/10. A reasonably priced and highly recommended Lithuanian cellar restaurant serving boar, elk and a wide range of pork and beef standards. Daily noon–midnight.

Markus ir Ko Antokolskio 11 ☎8-5/262 3185. Cosily plush Old Town restaurant drawing an upmarket clientele of eager carnivores with its superb steaks. Live jazz at weekends, when it's a good idea to reserve. Daily noon–midnight.

Po Saule Labdarių 7/11. French bistro with superb food at very resonable prices. Great place for a quick *tarte à l'oignon* or a more leisurely three-course meal. Daily 10am–10pm.

Stikliai Gaono 7 ☎8-5/262 4501. French food in the posh restaurant upstairs, homely Lithuanian fare in the beer-cellar-style restaurant downstairs. The latter hosts live Lithuanian folk music every evening bar Sunday. Daily noon–midnight.

Žemaičių Smuklė Vokiečių 24. A restaurant specializing in Žemaitijan (ie west Lithuanian) cuisine. An excellent place to try *cepelinai* or *Žemaičių blynai* (potato pancakes stuffed with mincemeat), as well as some tasty pork and beef dishes. Head for the folksy downstairs labyrinth of dining rooms in winter, or the two tiers of seating in the rustic courtyard in summer. Daily 1pm–midnight.

Gedimino and around

Čili Gedimino 23. A popular place for a quick, inexpensive bite, offering a wide choice of thin-crust and deep-pan pizzas in bright and breezy surroundings. There's another branch at Didžioji 5. Home delivery available on ☎8-5/233 3555. Daily 10am–midnight.

North of the river

Marceliukės Klėtis Tuskulėnų 35. Traditional Lithuanian favourites in a folksy tavern-style pavilion jammed between tower blocks north of the River Neris. Food is top quality and not too expensive. Live folk music most nights. Daily 11am–midnight.

Vandens Malūnas Verkių 100. Traditional Lithuanian meaty fare in an old mill 6km north of the centre, a short walk from Verkiai Palace (see p.91). Three storeys of wooden-beamed rooms, with antiquated milling machines dotted around the place and dried herbs hanging from the rafters. Daily 11am–midnight.

Cafés

Many of Vilnius's **cafés** offer much the same fare as those establishments that class themselves as restaurants, but in more informal surroundings and at sometimes significantly cheaper prices.

Afrika Pilies 28. A conveniently located spot, good for a quick lunch, offering soups, salads and Lithuanian standards such as *cepelinai* and *blynai*, as well as a decent chili-con-carne. Often colonized by a studeny crowd of drinkers in the evenings. Order your food at the counter. Daily 9am–11pm.

Arka Aušros vartų 7. A good place for a quick bite, with a reasonable choice of inexpensive eats ranging from salads and omelettes to more substantial chicken and pork dishes. Occasional live jazz or blues at weekends. Daily 10.30am–midnight.

Café de Paris Didžioji 1. Decent coffee and crepes and an ideal Old Town location make this a perfect pit-stop. Daily 10am–11pm.

Gabi Šv Mykolo 6. Inexpensive drinks and solid home cooking in a relaxed, no-smoking atmosphere. Daily 11am–10pm.

Mano kavinė Bokšto 7. Located on a quiet Old Town street, this café with chic modernist decor serves an extensive range of speciality teas, generously served by the potful. Range of cakes, snacks and full meals, including decent pancakes (*blynai*) and salads. Daily 10am–11pm.

Pieno Baras Didžioji 21. An old-fashioned milk bar bang on Town Hall square, offering dirt-cheap pastries and non-alcoholic drinks. Best place in the Old Town for an early-morning breakfast. Mon–Sat 8am–8pm, Sun 9am–7pm.

Pilies Kepyklė Pilies 19. Homely main-street stop-off for coffee, pastries, cakes and more substantial meals. Daily 9am–10pm.

Pilies Menė Pilies 8. Flash, modern café-bar with extensive menu of pancakes. Good place for a daytime coffee or night-time drink. Daily 10am–midnight.

Presto Gedimino 32A. A bright, modern coffe bar with an impressive range of brews, as well as salads and sumptuous cakes. Mon–Thurs 7am–10pm, Fri 7am–midnight, Sat 11am–midnight, Sun 11am–10pm.

Skonis ir Kvapas Trakų 8. A relaxing café occupying an elegant suite of barrel-vaulted rooms, and offering big pots of tea, excellent coffee, and an affordable range of hot meals. Daily 8am–midnight.

Drinking

There are innumerable watering-holes in central Vilnius, especially in the Old Town, ranging in style from faux-rustic taverns with wooden-bench seating, to swish, modern, designer bars with minimalist decor. Several of them call themselves "pubs", although few really try to ape British or Irish styles directly, preferring instead to cultivate a cosmopolitan, fun, drinking atmosphere that wouldn't be out of place in any large, hedonism-driven city. Most drinking venues serve a wide range of food, and the locals are as likely to visit them for lunch or dinner as for a session of serious imbibing. A few hostelries close at 11pm or midnight, although the majority are now open into the early hours of the morning, especially at weekends.

Bars and pubs

Amatininkų Užeiga Didžioji 19/2. Right on the main Old Town square, this comfy café-pub has been a popular meeting point ever since the 1980s, when it was central Vilnius's trendiest, most modern bar. Several dimly lit rooms with homely rustic touches, and an extensive range of Lithuanian food. Till 5am.

Avylis Gedimino 5. A smartish but atmospheric brick-clad basement with beer brewed on site and a big menu of Lithuanian food. Till 1am.

Bix Etmonų 6. A great bar founded by legendary 1990s alternative rock band Bix, with industrial-chic decor on the ground floor and a cave-like basement bar which turns into a disco after midnight. Serves full meals too. Sun–Thurs till

2am, Fri & Sat till 5am.

Brodvėjus (aka "Broadway") Mėsinių 4. A deservedly popular drinking-and-dancing venue built around a long, galleried space packed with tables – with a stage at one end for live bands (Thurs–Sun) and bopping. Full menu of snacks and hot meals; lunchtime specials are chalked up on a board outside. Mon–Thurs till 2am, Fri & Sat till 5am.

Būsi Trečias Totorių 18. A comfy, unpretentious ground-floor bar with a neighbourhood-pub feel and a folksy upstairs bar with wooden tables under a slanting attic roof. Full food menu. Till 11pm.

Džiazo Klubas Vilniaus 22. Atmospheric but animated brick cellar underneath the Radvila Palace (see p.85) with full range of food, drinks and often live jazz. On weekend gig nights you should arrive early to grab a table. Sun–Thurs till midnight, Fri & Sat till 2am.

Gero Viskio Baras Pilies 34. A ground-floor café-bar with upmarket cocktail lounge upstairs, cattle-market disco in the tight-packed cellar downstairs. Sun–Thurs till 2am, Fri & Sat till 5am.

Jazz & Rock Café Šv Mikalojaus 15. Roomy but bland café-bar with decent food and live music at the weekends – mostly cover bands but decent jazz or rock outfits might occasionally show up. Discos in the basement bar. Sun–Wed till midnight, Thurs–Sat till 3am.

Prie Parlamento Gedimino 46. A large drinking, snacking and dining venue with smart café-bar downstairs, and a pair of pub-like rooms upstairs. The menu includes toasted sandwiches, good pizzas, a satisfying lasagne and a decent

shepherd's pie. Popular with expats. Sun–Thurs till 3am, Fri & Sat till 5am.

Prie Universiteto (aka "The Pub") Dominikonų 9. A popular bar with dark, wooden interior and extensive pub-grub food menu similar to that of its sister pub, *Prie Parlamento* (see above). The covered courtyard frequently hosts live music, discos and big-screen basketball. Sun–Thurs till 2am, Fri & Sat till 5am.

Savas Kampas Vokiečių 4. The dark interior and homely pine furniture set a good mood in which to peruse the extensive list of alcohol available. Decent pizzas and a small range of other food. Till 2am.

Šuolaikinio Meno Centras (ŠMC) In the Contemporary Art Centre at Vokiečių 2. Dark, minimally decorated café-bar which has long been a prime meeting point for arty types and nonconformists of all ages. Ranges in atmosphere from cosy coffee bar to human zoo, depending on who's around. Till midnight.

Užupio kavinė Užupio 2. A comfortable café-bar just over the Užupio bridge from the Old Town, catering for a mixed crowd of youngish professionals and the arty denizens of the bohemian Užupis district (see p.89). Full range of drinks and snacks. Deservedly popular in summer, with tree-shaded outdoor terrace overlooking the Vilnia River. Till 11pm.

Žaltvykslė Pilies 11. An enjoyable mixture of the medieval and the modern, with arched ceilings and stiff-backed chairs accommodating crowds of students from the nearby university. It has a substantial food menu, and a wonderful cellar bar that occasionally hosts DJ events or live bands. Till 11pm.

Nightlife and entertainment

Vilnius is a major centre for high culture, with three full-size **orchestras**, two chamber orchestras and a clutch of quartets pulling in appreciative crowds all year round. Ground-breaking contemporary **drama** is also a regular feature of the cultural calendar, alongside a regular diet of classical theatre. More sybaritic tastes are catered for by the city's ever-changing roster of **clubs** and discos, where mainstream commercial techno is the order of the day. There are always a few local bars or restaurants hosting gigs by local **jazz** musicians; decent live rock on the other hand is hard to find.

The tourist office will have upcoming programme details for the main classical music and drama venues. Otherwise, the *Baltic Times* is your most likely source of cinema, theatre and concert **listings**, unless you can read Lithuanian, in which case the back pages of local daily *Lietuvos Rytas* or cerebral arts weekly *Septyni Meno Dienos* carry more detailed information.

Clubbing and live music

Vilnius has several large **mainstream clubs** attracting a friendly, relaxed crowd with an unsophisticated mixture of Western, commercial dance tunes and

Lithuanian and Russian techno. In addition, many of the establishments listed under "Bars and pubs" (see p.95) feature DJs and dancing as the evening wears on. Be warned, though, that nightlife venues come and go with alarming regularity.

Alternative dance music has its devotees, but no regular venues. Both the hip, local monthly magazine *Ore* (⊕www.ore.lt) and DJ collective, Boogaloo, organize irregular, but usually excellent, rave parties in a variety of spots around town, although you'll have to rely on street posters or local knowledge to find out where they are.

There's not much of a **rock** scene in Vilnius, although international touring bands (often rock behemoths whose best days are over) sometimes appear at the Sporto rūmai ("Palace of Sports") just north of the River Neris at Rinktinės 1 (⊕8-5/272 8942). Local cover bands and pop-rock acts play at *Broadway* and *Jazz & Rock Café* (see "Bars and pubs" opposite; details of upcoming events are posted on the door). Alternative bands occasionally appear in unlicensed, unofficial spaces, but you'll need local knowledge to find out what's on (checking out the excellent punk/alternative site ⊕www.hardcore.lt will help). Goth and pagan-metal bands have their own festival in the shape of **Kunigunda Lunaria**, in late April or early May (⊕www.dangus.net).

Fans of **jazz** are much better served, with regular gigs at *Jazz & Rock Café*, *Džiazo Klubas*, *Broadway* and occasionally *Užupio kavinė* (see "Bars and pubs" opposite). Traditional **folk** music is conspicuous by its absence in Vilnius unless you head for one of the more touristy eateries (see "Restaurants"; p.94), although there's one annual festival in the shape of **Skamba Skamba Kankliai**, when bands from all over Lithuania play in old-town courtyards and parks in late May.

Clubs

The venues listed below are open Thursday to Saturday, unless stated otherwise. Expect to pay anything between 10 and 25Lt, depending on who is spinning the discs.

Galaxy Konstitucijos 26. A huge, hangar-sized venue for mainstream fun on the northern side of the Neris. Special weekend party events and frequent live bands – look out for posters before setting out.

Gravity Jasinskio 16 ⊕www.clubgravity.lt. Self-consciously stylish and slightly more expensive than the rest, but cutting-edge DJs from Europe sometimes turn up at weekends – look out for posters.

Helios Didžioji 28 ⊕www.heliosclub.lt. A reliably enjoyable place, in the centre of the Old Town, catering for a good-natured, dressed-up crowd. Face control keeps the hoi polloi outside.

Intro Maironio 3 ⊕www.intro.lt. A minimally decorated, warehouse-style club with a wide-ranging menu of specialist DJ-nights – anything from dancehall reggae to hip-hop.

Ministerija Gedimino 46. A good-natured, sweaty cellar club below *Prie Parlamento*. Newish dance stuff as well as popular classics. Favoured gathering point for expats, as well as local beautiful young things. Open daily.

Neringa Gedimino 23. An elegant and intimate dance-bar beneath the *Neringa* hotel attracting a stylish twenty-something crowd. Broad range of danceable pop classics and occasional cover bands.

Classical music, opera and ballet

Vilnius can boast two symphony orchestras, of which the **Lithuanian National Philharmonic Orchestra** (Lietuvos nacionalinis simfoninis orkestras) is marginally the more prestigious, receiving the lion's share of visiting soloists and also embarking on major international tours in its own right. The **Lithuanian State Symphony Orchestra** (Lietuvos valstybinis simfoninis orkestras) is a newer outfit that doesn't have quite the same pedigree, but it is also of the highest quality, as is the other jewel in Vilnius's musical crown, the **Lithuanian National Opera and Ballet Theatre** (Nacionalinis operos ir baleto teatras). All three perform concerts throughout the year, except for short periods (notably in July and/or August) when they are either touring abroad or on holiday. In addition, look out for the numerous chamber concerts and solo recitals which round out the programmes of the main venues listed below.

A wide range of national and international musicians pack the programme of the **Vilnius Festival** (late May to early July), and the **St Christopher Summer Music Festival** (July) features local and international chamber ensembles, with most performances taking place in St Ignatius's Church on Šv Ignoto gatvė. In August, city folk head out to the summer festival in the nearby town of **Trakai** (see p.101) to enjoy concerts, opera and ballet in the romantic setting of the castle courtyard. The biggest event in autumn is the **Gaida Festival of Contemporary Classical Music**, to which composers come from far and wide to hear their music performed in a variety of venues across town.

Concert halls

Music Academy (Muzikos akademija) Gedimino 42 ☎8-5/261 2691. Venue for recitals by local music students. Tickets available on the night of the performance.

National Philharmonic (Nacionalinė filharmonija) Aušros Vartų 5 ☎8-5/212 2290, ⓦwww.filharmonija.lt. The elegant but not over-formal home of the country's premier orchestra, the Lithuanian National Philharmonic. Symphonic concerts on most Saturdays throughout the year, frequently featuring guest appearances by international soloists and conductors. Also "family" concerts of popular classics Sunday lunchtimes, and a regular programme of chamber music. Box office Tues–Sat 11am–7pm, Sun 11am–1pm.

Opera and Ballet Theatre (Operos ir baleto teatras) Vienuolio 1 ☎8-5/262 0727,

ⓦwww.opera.lt. A modern auditorium with a busy programme of top-notch productions. Performances take place four or five times a week and are hugely popular, so book well in advance. Box office Tues–Sat 11am–6pm, Sun 11am–3pm.

St John's Church (Šv Jono Bažnyčia) Vilnius University main courtyard. Organ and choral concerts every Sunday: check posters in and around the university, or ask at the tourist office for details.

Vilnius Congress Hall (Vilniaus kongresų rūmai) Vilniaus 6/14 ☎8-5/618828. A modern venue hosting performances by the Lithuanian State Symphony Orchestra (ⓦwww.lvso.lt) about once a fortnight, as well as chamber concerts, and occasional musicals. Box office Tues–Fri 1am–7pm, Sat 11am–3pm, Sun 11am–2pm.

Theatre

Vilnius's theatre scene is interesting and varied, although performances are invariably in Lithuanian (or Russian) except on the rare occasions when visiting companies are in town. However, the language barrier shouldn't prevent you from enjoying shows by the best of the contemporary drama companies, for whom movement and stagecraft are often just as important as the text. Three Lithuanian directors of world-wide renown whose performances should not be missed are Eimundas Nekrošius, Rimas Tuminas and Oskaras Koršunovas – new productions by all of them are often staged at the nation's most prestigious venue, the National Drama Theatre.

The **Lithuanian International Theatre Festival**, or LIFE (advance information from LIFE, Basanavičiaus 5; ☎8-5/262 5158), brings a number of foreign drama companies to town for a fortnight between late May and early June. With the emphasis on young and experimental directors, it offers a good mix of avantgarde craziness and more mainstream drama, with performances taking place at outdoor locations or at some of the venues listed below.

Lėlė Puppet Theatre (Lėlių teatras) Arklių 5 ☎8-5/262 8678. Top-quality children's entertainment featuring superbly designed puppets and enchanting stage sets. Performances take place lunchtime or mid-afternoon. Box office Tues–Sun 10am–4pm.

Lithuanian National Drama Theatre (Lietuvos nacionalinis dramos teatras) Gedimino 4 ☎8-5/262 9771, ⓦwww.teatras.lt. Flagship of Lithuanian theatre with a comfortable modern auditorium. As well as being home to the state drama company, it also hosts productions by

prestigious independent drama troupes and high-profile performances from abroad. Some performances take place in the Small Hall (Mažoji salė), entered via Odminių gatvė round the back. Box office Tues–Sun 10am–6pm.
Keistuolių Teatras Laisvės 60 ☎8-5/2424585. Cabaret, comedy and child-oriented lunchtime shows in the Spaudos rūmai ("House of the Press"), 3.5km northwest of the centre – take trolleybus #8 from Gedimino to the Spaudos rūmai stop. Tickets available one hour before performance.
Russian Drama Theatre (Rusų dramos teatras) Basanavičiaus ☎8-5/262 7133. Mixed programme of Russian-language classics and modern experimental work in a lovely 150-year-old building in sore need of renovation. An atmospheric place with good acoustics, but the glitzy theatre crowd tends to hang out elsewhere. Tues–Sun 1–7pm.
Vilnius Little Theatre (Vilniaus mažasis teatras) Gedimino 22. Serious contemporary work in a small studio theatre.
Youth Theatre (Jaunimo teatras) Arklių 5 ☎8-5/261 6126. A mixture of classical and experimental productions performed by youth companies. Box office Tues–Sun 11am–2pm & 3.30–7.30pm.

Cinema

Films are usually shown in the original language with Lithuanian subtitles. Tickets cost around 12–20Lt except on Mondays, when most cinemas drop their prices. The only **film festival** of real note is Kino Pavasaris (Cinema Spring), which falls in the last week of March and screens the odd new Lithuanian film alongside recent international releases.

Akropolis Akropolis shopping centre, Ozo 25. A state-of-the-art multiplex 2.5km northwest of the centre, in a retail complex packed with restaurants and bars. Minibus #2 from Pylimo.
Coca Cola Plaza Savanorių 7 ✆www.multiplex.lt. A modern multiscreen showing mainstream first run movies. The only drawback is that it's about 2km west of the centre in an area with few other nightlife amenities. Buses #4, #6, #11, #12, #14, #21 and #22.
Lietuva Pylimo 17 ✆www.ktlietuva.lt. A good mixture of commercial and arty movies in a large auditorium with comfy seats and good sound. There's a smaller screen, Sale 88, in the basement – the last two rows have double seats for canoodling couples.
Ozo Kino salė Ozo 4. A repertory cinema showing movie classics, stranded in a residential area 2.5km north of the centre.
Skalvija Goštauto 2/15. A good place to catch international art-house movies, if you can put up with the hard seats, muggy sound and general lack of atmosphere.

Shopping

Retail culture has wrought major changes on central Vilnius over the last decade, and streets like Gedimino prospektas, Pilies gatvė and Vokiečių gatvė are lined with the kind of clothes, footwear and other high-street stores that you'd expect to find in any European city. However, many locals still buy foodstuffs and household essentials from vast, bustling **markets**, where regular stallholders sell top-quality farm produce alongside small-time traders dealing in all manner of contraband. The most central of these are on Bazilionų gatvė, just north of the train and bus stations, and on Kalvarijų gatvė, north of the River Neris but still within walking distance of the centre. The biggest of the lot, however, attracting bargain-hunters from all over the Baltic States, is at Gariūnai, 4km west of the centre (Mon–Sat mornings only; bus #29 from Savanorių), where you'll find everything from cooking pots to car parts.

For souvenirs, you should head first to the outdoor **crafts market** at the junction of Didžioji and Pilies, where a gaggle of stalls sell traditional items like wicker baskets, wooden handicrafts and amber jewellery. The goods on display here are of variable quality, but may well be cheaper than those in souvenir shops, of which there are a growing number in the more tourist-trodden streets of the Old Town. Typical **opening times of shops** are Monday to Friday from 10/11pm to 6/7pm, and Saturdays from 10/11pm to 3/4pm.

Souvenir shops

Dailė Žydų 2/2. A good choice of linen, wooden toys and pottery.
Linas Stiklių 3. Linen shirts, dresses, bed sheets and tablecloths, alongside other traditional textiles.
Sauluva Šv Mykolo 4. Sells a range of gifts,

including a wide selection of *verbos* or "palms", the wand-like bundles of dried flowers and grasses which are used to decorate homes in the run-up to Palm Sunday.

Bookstores

Akademinė Knyga Universiteto 4. An academic bookstore with English-language books about Lithuania on the ground floor and English-language fiction in the basement.
Littera Šv Jono 12. In the main courtyard of Vilnius University. Worth checking out for the neo-Baroque ceiling paintings as well as the books.

Masiulio knygynas Corner of Pylimo and Sodų. Good choice of guidebooks and large-format art titles.
Vaga Gedimino 50. One of the bigger downtown bookstores, with a small selection of English-language fiction and tourist-oriented titles.

Music shops

Muzikos Bomba Corner of Jakšto and Goštauto. A wide selection of Lithuanian classical CDs, as well as international rock and pop.

Thelonious Second Hand Music Stiklių 12 ⊛ www.omnitel.net/thelonious. A good place to browse for secondhand jazz and folk.

Listings

Airlines Aeroflot, Pylimo 8/2 ☏ 8-5/222 4189 and at the airport ☏ 8-5/226 0357, ⊛ www.aeroflot.org; Austrian Airlines, Basanavičiaus 11 ☏ 8-5/222 6063, ⊛ www.aua.com; Estonian Air, at the airport ☏ 8-5/273 9022, ⊛ www.estonian-air.ee; Finnair Rūdninkų 18/2 ☏ 8-5/261 9339 and at the airport ☏ 8-5/233 0810, ⊛ www.finnair.fi; Lithuanian Airlines, Ukmergės 12 ☏ 8-5/275 2585 and at the airport ☏ 8-5/223 3345, ⊛ www.lal.lt; LOT, in the *Hotel Skrydis* right by the airport, Rodūnios kelias 2 ☏ 8-5/273 9020, ⊛ www.lot.com; Lufthansa, at the airport ☏ 8-5/226 2222, ⊛ www.lufthansa.com; SAS, at the airport ☏ 8-5/239 5500, ⊛ www.scandinavian.net.
Airport 4km south of the centre at Rodūnios kelias 2. Bus #1 from the train station or bus #2 from Lukiškių Square. Information ☏ 8-5/230 6666.
American Express Traveller's cheques can be cashed at Lietuvos Taupomasis Bankas, Gedimino 10/1; and Vilniaus Bankas, Gedimino 12.
Car rental A & A Litinterp, Bernardinų 7-2 ☏ 8-5/212 3850, ⊛ www.litinterp.lt; Aunela, Vytenio 6-110 ☏ 8-5/233 0318, ⊛ www.aunela.lt; Avis, at the airport ☏ 8-5/232 9316, ⊛ www.avis.lt; Budget, at the airport ☏ 8-5/230 6708, ⊛ www.budget.lt; Europcar, Stuokos-Gucevičiaus 9-1 ☏ 8-5/212 0207 and at the airport ☏ 8-5/216

3442, ⊛ www.europcar.lt; Hertz, Kalvarijų 14 ☏ 8-5/272 6940 and at the airport ☏ 8-5/232 9301, ⊛ www.hertz.lt.
Embassies and consulates Australia, Vilniaus 23 ☏ 8-5/212 3369; Belarus embassy: Mindaugo 13 ☏ 8-5/266 2200, consulate: Muitinės 41 ☏ 8-5/223 3322; Canada, Gedimino 64 ☏ 8-5/249 6853, ⊛ www.canada.lt; Estonia, Mickevičiaus 4A ☏ 8-5/278 0200, ℮ sekretar@estemb.lt; Latvia, Čiurlionio 76 ☏ 8-5/213 1260; Poland, Smėlio 20A ☏ 8-5/270 9001; Russia, Latvių 53/54 ☏ 8-5/272 1763, ⊛ www.lithuania.mid.ru (visas Mon–Fri 8.30am–noon); UK, Antakalnio 2 ☏ 8-5/212 2070, ⊛ www.britain.lt; USA, Akmenų 6 ☏ 8-5/266 5500, ⊛ www.usembassy.lt. Irish citizens should contact their consulate in Rīga (see p.226). The nearest New Zealand embassy is at ul. Migdałowa 4, Warsaw, Poland ☏ +48 22/645 1407.
Exchange Of the high-street banks, Lietuvos Žemės Ukio Bankas, Didžioji 25 (Mon–Fri 8am–7pm, Sat & Sun 10am–5pm) has the longest opening hours. The Parex Bankas exchange office outside the train station at Geležinkelio 8 is open 24hr.
Hospitals Baltic-American Medical & Surgical Clinic, inside Vilnius University Hospital at Antakalnio 124 ☏ 8-5/234 2020.
Internet access Bazė Gedimino 50/2 (open 24hr); Collegium, Pilies 22 (daily 8am–midnight);

Spausk.lt, Basanavičiaus 18 (daily 1am–10pm).
Laundry Joglė, in the Maxima supermarket at
Mindaugo 11, for service washes and dry-cleaning
(Mon–Sat 10am–10pm, Sun 10am–6pm).
Left luggage At the bus station (Mon–Sat
5.30am–9pm, Sun 7am–9pm).
Libraries American Center Library, Pranciškonų
3/6 (Tues–Thurs 2–5pm); British Council Library,
Vilniaus 39-6 (Tues & Thurs noon–6pm, Wed & Fri
11am–5pm, Sat 10am–3pm).
Newspapers Lietuvos Spauda, Gedimino 7, has a
few English-language titles.
Pharmacies Gedimino Vaistinė, Gedimino 27
(open 24hr); Gulbė, Didžioji 39 (Mon–Fri
8am–8pm, Sat & Sun 9am–4pm).
Phones Public telephones are located throughout
the city. Buy cards from kiosks or from the Central
Phone and Telegraph Office, Vilniaus 33.
Photographic developing and supplies Fuji
image service, Gedimino 38/2; and Fotoservisas,

Pilies 23, process holiday snaps, sell all kinds of
film and offer professional developing services.
Police Jogailos 3 ☎8-5/261 6208.
Post office The main post office is at Gedimino 7
(Mon–Fri 7am–7pm, Sat 9am–4pm).
Taxis Taxi ranks are located on Rotūšės aikštė,
although be warned that overcharging of
foreigners is rife. You stand a better chance of
securing a fair price by ringing for a taxi in
advance – try Vilniaus taxi (☎8-5/212 8888) or
Denvila (☎8-5/244 4444).
Travel agents AAA Wrislit, Rūdininkų 18 (☎8-
5/212 2081, ⊛www.wrislit.lt), deals in tickets for
international airlines and ferries from Klaipėda to
Scandinavia; Gintarinė Sala, Vokiečių 8 (☎8-5/212
3116, ⊛www.gintarinesala.lt), sells plane tickets;
and Lithuanian Student and Youth Travel Bureau,
Basanavičiaus 30 (☎8-5/239 7397,
⊛www.jaunimas.lt) offers student cheapies.

Around Vilnius

An appealing mixture of gently rolling agricultural land, pine forests and lakes, the
countryside **around Vilnius** is fairly typical of much of Lithuania and makes a
good introduction to the country as a whole. Within easy day-trip distance of the
capital are **Trakai**, the much-visited site of a major medieval fortress; the Iron Age
site of **Kernavė**; and the open-air sculpture park which goes under the modest
name of the **Museum of the Centre of Europe**, just under 20km north. Trakai
and Kernavė are easily accessible by bus; to get to the Museum of the Centre of
Europe however, you will need your own transport.

Trakai

Twenty-five kilometres west of the capital, lakeside **TRAKAI** once rivalled Vilnius
as a key centre of political and military power. The town's imposing island castle,
completed during the reign of Vytautas the Great, is arguably the single best-known
monument in the country – an instantly recognizable national symbol that receives
a year-round stream of visitors. The lakes and forests surrounding the settlement
further enhance Trakai's status as a beauty spot, and it's an ideal place for a lazy day
of swimming, boating or water's-edge strolling.

Served by regular **buses** and minibuses from Vilnius, Trakai is an easy day-trip
from the capital, though the soothing beauty of the surrounding countryside –
coupled with a decent range of accommodation choices – makes it a good spot for
a longer rural break.

Some history

Together with Vilnius and Kernavė, Trakai was one of the earliest military strongholds in Lithuania, and occupied a crucial position in the ring of castles that protected the heartland of the Grand Duchy from the expansionist forays of the
Teutons. The first fortified settlement here was located 3km southeast of the current
town, where the village of Senieji Trakai ("Old Trakai") now stands. Senieji Trakai
was the ruling stronghold of **Grand Duke Gediminas** before he moved his capital to Vilnius, and it is also thought to be the birthplace of Gediminas's grandson,
Vytautas the Great, under whom Lithuanian power reached its apogee in the
early fifteenth century. It was Vytautas's father, Kęstutis, who founded modern-day

The Karaim

A Turkic-speaking group practising a branch of Judaism, the **Karaim** are thought to be descended from the **Khazars**, a central Asian people who held sway over a steppe empire stretching between the Black and Caspian seas in the seventh and eighth centuries AD. It's thought that the Khazar rulers invited Christian, Islamic and Hebrew missionaries to their court, and eventually chose the latter as the religion of the Khazarian elite. Although the Khazar empire was swallowed up by rivals some time in the ninth century, the Khazar language and culture was preserved by individual groups, one of which is believed to be the Karaim.

Whatever their origins, Karaim had by the eleventh century settled in the **Crimea**, which was then ruled by the Tatars – another central Asian group who spoke a similar language. It was here that they came into contact with the Lithuanian ruler **Vytautas**, who after campaigning here in 1397 invited several Karaim and Tatar families to **Trakai** in order to form an elite guard loyal only to the Grand Duke. Karaim migration to the Grand Duchy of Lithuania continued over the next few centuries, with families often coming to Trakai first before moving on to new centres. One such place was **Lutsk** (now in the Ukraine), which became an important centre of Karaim learning and book publishing.

At the beginning of the twentieth century there were thought to be over 5000 Karaim in the Crimea and about 800 in Lithuania. Since then numbers have steadily declined, largely owing to intermarriage and assimilation. The preservation of Karaim culture in Trakai was given some encouragement during the inter-war period, when the Vilnius region found itself in Poland, and any non-Lithuanian minorities were given support, but under the Soviets the community's religious and cultural activities were discouraged. Karaim tended to assimilate into larger ethnic groups, abandoning their language in favour of the more dominant Lithuanian and Russian tongues. Only with the weakening of communist control was there a gradual reawakening of Karaim consciousness, with a Karaim conference in Lithuania in 1989 and a further conference in the Crimea in 1995. There are now an estimated 300 Karaim in Lithuania, just over 100 of whom are in Trakai – numbers so small that any real Karaim cultural renaissance must remain outside the realms of possibility.

Trakai, choosing an island in Lake Galvė to build his impressive **castle**. Vytautas the Great resided here when not on campaign, and invited the **Karaim** (a Judaic sect from the Crimea; see box above) to settle here and serve as his personal bodyguards. A couple of hundred Karaim still live in Trakai, their distinctive wooden cottages lining the town's main street. After the reign of Vytautas, Trakai continued to be second only to Vilnius in political importance: the whole of south-central Lithuania was governed from here, and whoever controlled Trakai castle was effectively the vice-ruler of the Lithuanian state. The town's significance declined in the sixteenth century, and the castle itself was abandoned after being sacked by the Russians in the war of 1654–67 – to be rediscovered in the twentieth century as a potent symbol of the country's medieval greatness.

The Town

Trakai extends over a long, narrow peninsula which touches on three lakes: Bernardinų to the east, Totoriškų to the west and the biggest, Galvė, to the north. From the **train** and **bus stations** follow Vytauto gatvė north to reach the main sights, which kick off after about 1000m with the Orthodox **Church of the Holy Mother of God** (Skaisčiausios Dievo Motinos gimimo cerkvė), a creamy-brown building topped with a Russian spire. Squatting on high ground a couple of hundred metres further on is the twin-towered **Church of the Visitation** (Šv Mergelės Marijos apsilankymo bažnyčia), a fairly unprepossessing place rebuilt many times since its original foundation by Grand Duke Vytautas in 1407. Inside, the garish pulpit and side altars look as if they've been given an over-generous coat of glossy house paint. The main altar, bearing a neo-Gothic representation of the Virgin, is surrounded by the small votive plaques (in the shape of hearts, legs and other body parts presumably healed with the Virgin's intervention) donated to the church by grateful pilgrims.

After another 500m, turn right down Kęstučio gatvė to find the remains of the **Peninsula Castle** (Pusiašalio pilis), thought to have been built by Duke Kęstutis, son of Gediminas and father of Vytautas. These days only the walls, rebuilt to a height of about 1–2m, remain, penning in an inner courtyard given over to wild grasses.

From here the main street changes its name to Karaimų gatvė and continues north through the part of town traditionally inhabited by the Karaim, their bright-yellow and -green, timber-clad houses laid end-on to the road, each sporting three ground-floor windows – "one for God, one for oneself, and one for Grand Duke Vytautas", as the local saying has it. Down the street at no. 22 is the **Karaim Ethnographic Exhibition** (Karaimu etnografinė paroda; Wed–Sun 10am–6pm; 2Lt), a modern pavillion with sepia photographs of nineteenth-century Karaim families, the men in their dark caftans and black-and-white felt hats, the women in embroidered velvet jackets and ornate clogs with two-inch heels. Filigree jugs and coffee cups add further to the oriental flavour, aided somewhat incongruously by some medieval Persian swords and a suit of samurai armour. Further on at no. 30 is the nineteenth-century **Kenessa** (Kenesa), or Karaim prayer house, a simple ochre cube with a greening roof.

The Island Castle

A hundred metres or so beyond the Kenessa, Karaimų descends to the shores of Lake Galvė, where stalls selling amber jewellery and hawkers renting out rowing boats and pedaloes vie for your attention. Forming a wondrous backdrop to the waterfront scene is the **Island Castle** (Šalos pilis), about 500m offshore, a satisfyingly romantic cluster of red-brick watchtowers and squat round turrets topped with spindly weather cocks, grouped around a central, sky-scraping keep. The whole place was a ruin intil 1962, when the Lithuanian government decided to rebuild the castle as it must have looked in Vytautas the Great's time. It was a display of national pride to which Moscow chose to turn a blind eye, although Nikita Khruschev was said to be infuriated by the project.

Two wooden footbridges lead across the water to the castle, now home to a **museum** (Tues–Sun: May–Sept 10am–7pm; Oct–April 10am–5pm; 7Lt), which interweaves the castle's history with local ethnography. The most important exhibits are displayed in the warren of halls within the central **keep**, separated from the rest of the castle by an inner moat, and holding within its sturdy frame a surprisingly delicate galleried courtyard. Inside are scale models of the castle at different stages of its development, medieval weaponry, and the colourful garments traditionally worn by the local Karaim. There's also a crowd of mannequins dressed in the traditional dress of the local Lithuanian population – white smocks and straw hats for the men, full skirts with black aprons, embroidered with flower designs for the women. Exhibits in the outer buildings evoke medieval castle life: there are wild-boar skins, drinking horns and a jumble of furniture, including a bizarre table-and-chair set fashioned from stag antlers in the "Hunters' Room". The museum winds up with an eminently missable history of pipe smoking throughout the ages, where you'll chance upon Meerschaum pipes carved into whimsical shapes such as reclining female nudes and horses' heads.

In summer, a **lake steamer** (10Lt return) runs from the castle to the northern end of Lake Galvė (also accessible by road), where the Tyszkiewicz family built the summer residence of **Užtrakis Palace**, and called in French landscape gardener Edouard André (who also worked for the family in Palanga; see p.163) to lay out a wooded park. The half-derelict palace is not open to the public, but the leafy park is a pleasant place to wander and a good place for savouring the views back towards Trakai.

Practicalities

Trakai's friendly **tourist office** (Mon–Fri 8am–noon & 1–5pm, Sat 10am–3pm; ☎8-38/51934, ⓦwww.trakai.lt) is about 800m north of the train and bus stations at Vytauto 69, although there are plans to move to a site nearer the Island Castle. The office sells local maps and can organize **bed and breakfast** accommodation (❶) with local families, although vacancies disappear fast in summer. An acceptable budget hotel is the lakeside *Trakų Sporto Bazė*, Karaimų 73 (☎8-38/55501, ⓕ55387; ❶–❺), a largish concrete **hotel** and sporting complex offering utilitarian doubles (with one toilet and shower shared between every two rooms; ❶), or renovated doubles with TV and minibar. A comfier choice is the *Trakų viešbutis*, just west of the main strip at Ežero 7 (☎8-38/55505; ⓔhotel.traku@takas.lt; ❺; breakfast 20Lt extra), a cosy, nine-room hotel with homely, wooden-ceilinged en-suites, a small beach and boating pier, and even a tiny indoor pool.

Ask the tourist office about accommodation in **nearby villages**: one of the best local hosts is Antanas Gedvilas (☎8-38/74494 or 74416; English spoken), 5km northwest of town in the village of Jovariškes, who has four two- or three-person self-catering apartments (❶) in a house overlooking Lake Akmena (Akmenos ežeras), complete with sailing dinghies, rowing boats and windsurfing boards that guests can use. The *Kempingas Slėnyje* **campsite**, 7km by road from Trakai on the far side of Lake Galvė, has a small guesthouse with lovely pine-furnished en-suites (❸), simple bungalows with toilets shared between two rooms (❶), plenty of camping space, and access to lovely lakeside walks.

Trakai's main culinary claim to fame is the *kibinas*, a Cornish-pasty-like creation filled with meat that unleashes a deadly drip of hot fat after a few bites. Buy it from the open-air cafés near the footbridge leading to the Island Castle, or from *Kibininė*, a seemingly tumbledown shack about 1km further on along Karaimų, which turns out to house a rather cosy split-level café. For a wider choice of sit-down **food**, *Karališkas Sodas*, immediately to the north of the footbridge, has an inexpensive range of substantial main courses, as well as being a good place for a daytime coffee or evening drink. Right by the footbridge, *Prie Pilies* is a more formal **restaurant** with attentive service, good views of the castle and tasty local fish – there's a self-service hatch if you just want a drink and a snack.

In August, the **Trakai Festival** sees outdoor orchestral and opera performances in the courtyards of both the Island and Peninsula castles – contact the tourist office for details.

Kernavė

Just outside the village of **KERNAVĖ**, 30km northwest of Vilnius, a cluster of five flat-topped hills overlooking the River Neris once made up the military and administrative centre of the pre-Christian Lithuanian state. Originally crowned with wooden stockade forts, the hills almost certainly served as the main power base of Mindaugas, the thirteenth-century strongman who welded the Lithuanian tribes into a unified and expansionist state. The site was abandoned at the end of the fourteenth century after repeated sackings by the Teutonic Knights – the last of which, in 1390, probably included volunteer crusader Henry Bolingbroke, future King Henry IV of England. Now protected as an **archeological reserve** (archeologinis rezervatas; Wed–Sun 10am–5pm; 3Lt), the hills can be scaled by wooden stairways for sweeping views of the surrounding terrain.

The site's combination of historical pedigree and natural beauty have ensured its popularity with present-day neo-pagans, who congregate here for summer solstice bonfires on the night of June 23/24. Another good time to visit is the first or second weekend in July, when the **Kernavė Festival of Experimental Archeology**

(Eksperimentinės archeologijos festivalis; ring the archeological reserve administration for details; ☎8-382/47385 & 47371) provides enthusiasts with the chance to dress up as medieval Lithuanian warriors and peasants and give demonstrations of pottery and metalwork.

Kernavė is a well-signed, twelve-kilometre journey west of the main Vilnius–Panevėžys highway. There are four to six daily **buses** to Kernavė from Vilnius, but many of these leave uncomfortably early in the morning; catching the 1.30pm bus from Vilnius and returning at 6pm (5pm on Saturdays and Sundays) is currently your best option.

The Museum of the Centre of Europe

According to a study made by the French National Geographical Institute in 1989, the official centre of Europe is located at 25 degrees 19' longitude, 54 degrees 54' latitude – in other words 25km north of Vilnius just beside the main road to Utena. The exact spot is marked by a sundial about 400m west of the road, accessible via a (signed) track. A handful of passers-by stop off here to take a look, though there's little to detain you.

However, the institute's findings do serve as a handy raison d'être for the grandly titled **Museum of the Centre of Europe** (Europos parkas; ⓦ www .europosparkas.lt; 9am–dusk; 10Lt), a significantly more worthwhile destination, located – somewhat confusingly – 17km to the southeast (it's 19km out of Vilnius: leave town via Kalvarių gatvė and it's well signed from there). Set amidst forested hills, the museum is basically an open-air **sculpture park**, established on the initiative of local artist Gintaras Karosas in 1991, and featuring an ever-growing display of over 65 works by sculptors from all over the world. There's something to please everyone in a collection that ranges from the impenetrably abstract to the facile: falling into the latter category is Karosas's *Infotree* right by the entrance, where a maze constructed from over three thousand old television sets comments on the role of the media as the bearers of state propaganda – a statue of Lenin is buried inside. The main body of sculptures is 1km further on, conveniently grouped around a café-restaurant (where you can pick up an English-language plan of the park to aid your wanderings; 1Lt). Karosas's set-piece *Monument of the Centre of Europe*, a small pyramid with the names (and distances in kilometres) of various world capitals arranged around it, is probably less captivating than the title would suggest. Genuine highlights elsewhere include Magdalena Abakanowicz's *Space of Unknown Growth*, a family of giant concrete eggs lurking in a small dell; Dennis Oppenheim's *Drinking Structure with Exposed Kidney Pool*, a strange and rather unnerving cross between a caravan and an elephant; and Aleš Vesely's rather jolly *Sculpture idea – structure*, a metal temple-like chamber on a spring-mounted floor, which starts to slowly bounce up and down when you enter.

Travel details

Buses

Vilnius to: Alytus (5 daily; 2hr); Anykščiai (3 daily weekends only; 2hr); Biržai (4 daily; 3hr 40min–4hr 20min); Druskininkai (6 daily; 2hr 5min–3hr 30min); Jurbarkas (3 daily; 3hr 50min); Kaunas (every 15–30min; 1hr 30min–1hr 55min); Klaipėda (7 daily; 4hr); Molėtai (5 daily; 2hr 10min–2hr 30min); Palanga (7 daily; 4hr 15min); Panevėžys (10 daily; 1hr 50min–3hr); Raseiniai (7 daily; 3hr 40min); Rokiškis (4 daily; 3–4hr); Šiauliai (8 daily; 3hr 15min); Tauragė (4 daily; 5hr); Telšiai (1 daily; 6hr 15min); Trakai (Mon–Fri 30 daily, Sat & Sun 20 daily; 40–50min); Ukmergė (4 daily; 1hr 30min); Utena (4 daily; 2hr).

Trains

Vilnius to: Ignalina (6 daily; 2hr); Kaunas (Mon–Fri 11 daily; Sat & Sun 8 daily; 1hr 40min–2hr); Klaipėda (3 daily; 5hr); Marcinkonys (Mon–Fri 5 daily; Sat & Sun 3 daily; 2hr); Mažeikiai (1 daily; 5hr 50min); Paneriai (Mon–Fri 24 daily; Sat & Sun 17 daily; 10min); Šiauliai (1 daily; 3hr 50min); Šeštokai (1 daily; 3hr 30min); Trakai (Mon–Fri 7 daily, Sat & Sun 4 daily; 40min).

International trains

Vilnius to: Daugavpils (3 weekly; 3hr); Kaliningrad (2 daily; 6hr 30min); Lvov (2 weekly; 16hr 10min); Minsk (2 daily; 4hr 10min); Moscow (2 daily; 16hr); Rīga (3 weekly; 6hr 30min); St Petersburg (3 weekly; 12hr); Warsaw (3 weekly; 9hr).

International buses

Vilnius to Amsterdam (5 weekly; 26hr); Berlin (5 weekly; 18hr); Brussels (5 weekly; 30hr); Gdańsk (1 daily; 11hr); Hamburg (3 weekly; 24hr); Kaliningrad (2 daily; 8hr); Minsk (3 daily; 4–6hr); Olsztyn (4 weekly; 8hr 30min); Rīga (4 daily; 5hr); Rotterdam (3 weekly; 27hr); Tallinn (2 daily; 10hr 15min); Warsaw (3 daily; 9hr).

Flights

Vilnius to: Amsterdam (1 daily; 2hr 35min); Berlin (1 daily; 1hr 45min); Copenhagen (3 daily; 1hr 40min); Frankfurt (2 daily; 2hr 15min); Helsinki 2 daily; 1hr 25min); Kiev (3 weekly; 1hr 40min); London (1 daily; 3hr); Moscow (2 daily; 1hr 55min); Paris (3 weekly; 3hr 20min); Prague (1 daily; 2hr 20min); Rīga (3 weekly; 55min); Stockholm (1 daily; 1hr 10min); Tallinn (2 daily; 1hr 35min); Vienna (1 daily; 1hr 45min); Warsaw (1 daily; 1hr 10min).

1.2

Eastern and central Lithuania

A vast, rolling expanse of grazing land and cereal crops broken up by deep swathes of forest, eastern and central Lithuania are the heartland of what is still a predominantly agricultural country. There's a modest scattering of fair-sized, industrial cities, each filled with the energies one would expect from a fast-changing, post-communist country, but even these lie only kilometres away from bucolic market towns and isolated villages – the kind of communities that

Lithuanian-born Polish novelist Tadeusz Konwicki described as "the desert islands of Central Europe".

Eastern and central Lithuania are traditionally made up of three distinct ethnographic areas, Aukštaitija in the northern and central parts of the country, Dzūkija in the south, and Suvalkija in the southwest. **Aukštaitija** (which literally means "Uplands", although it's not particularly higher than any other part of the country) is such a big, amorphous region that it no longer serves as a common badge of identity to the people who live there – they're more likely to see themselves as inhabitants of a particular city or district. There's more in the way of local patriotism in **Dzūkija**, a densely forested region famous for its wild mushrooms, wood-carving traditions and folk music – especially the unaccompanied narrative songs performed by women. The hard-working farming folk of **Suvalkija** (named after the regional centre of Suwałki, which is now just over the border in Poland) are said to speak the purest form of Lithuanian in the country – their dialect was chosen to form the basis of the official literary language by nineteenth-century reformers.

The region sees far fewer tourists than either Vilnius or the Baltic coast, but there's a great deal to discover. With an absorbing Old Town and an impressive clutch of museums, Lithuania's second city of **Kaunas** is as rewarding as any of the big urban centres of the Baltics, and also offers easy access to the Baroque monastery at **Pažaislis** and the unmissable open-air ethnographic museum at **Rumšiškes**. The region's remaining cities are largely modern, concrete affairs: **Panevėžys** is a useful transport hub for northern Lithuania, but offers far less in the way of attractions than **Šiauliai**, a youthful, energetic place that's also the main jumping-off point for the pilgrim-tramped route to the mysterious **Hill of Crosses**. There's much more in the way of atmosphere in the small towns of central Lithuania, with both **Biržai** and **Kėdainiai** boasting a wealth of historic monuments bequeathed by the aristocratic Radvila clan, and sleepy **Anykščiai** offering lazy woodland walks and a brace of quirky museums. For a taste of wild, unspoiled nature, the **Aukštaitija National Park** covers the most accessible chunk of northwestern Lithuania's extensive lakeland region, while the **Dzūkija National Park** presents a superb opportunity to sample the enticing woodland environments of the south – the laid-back spa town of **Druskininkai** is the best base from which to explore it.

Getting around the region **by car** is relatively swift if you're travelling via the two main highways, which serve the Vilnius–Kaunas–Klaipėda and Vilnius–Panevėžys–Rīga routes respectively. Main roads elsewhere are mostly single-lane affairs and can be slow-going, although given the unspoiled beauty of the countryside this is no great hardship. Vilnius, Kaunas and Panevėžys are the main nodal points of an extensive **bus** network that covers all the places mentioned in this chapter – again, bear in mind that services on country roads can take an age to get anywhere. If Vilnius is your starting point then a number of places can be accessed **by train**, with routes fanning out towards Kaunas, the Aukštaitija National Park, the Dzūkija National Park and Šiauliai.

Aukštaitija National Park

Northeast of Vilnius extends a rippling, green landscape scattered with a glittering archipelago of lakes, occupying the troughs and hollows gouged out of the Baltic plain by glaciers during the last ice age. Among the most attractive and easily visited of the lakeland regions is the **Aukštaitija National Park**, 100km north of Vilnius, where the River Žeimena and its tributaries feed over one hundred lakes of various shapes and sizes. It's an understandably popular area with canoeists, who use the network of lakes and rivers as an aquatic highway traversing one of Lithuania's most unspoiled regions. It's prime walking territory, too, with waterside trails leading up into the low, rounded hills that cluster around the lake shores. Some seventy percent of the park is made up of forest – predominantly pine, spruce and birch. The dens-

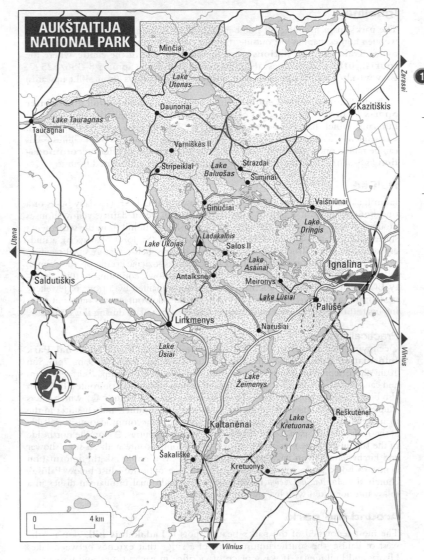

est woodland is concentrated in the sparsely populated northern parts of the park, and it's here that you're most likely to come across roe deer, red deer and wild boar, and more rarely elk, martens and beaver.

Entry tickets (2Lt) to the park are available from the **information centre** in the park's main settlement, **Palūšė** (see p.110). Both the information centre in Palūšė and the tourist office in nearby **Ignalina** can provide details of the handful of small hotels and rural homestays in and around Palūšė, as well as the park's rough-and-ready campsites, most of which are just lakeside patches of grass with no running water or toilet facilities.

Ignalina

The park's main jumping-off point is **IGNALINA**, a small town of pastel-hued wooden houses that lies just outside the park, on the Vilnius–Visaginas road and rail routes. **Train** and **bus stations** stand together just east of the centre, where the **tourist office** at Laisvės alėja 70 (Mon–Fri 9am–5pm; ☎8-386/52597, ⓦwww.lsa.lt/ignalina) can book you into **rural homestays** (from 40Lt upwards) all over the park.

About 2km east of the centre, pushed up against a wooded hill, the **Winter Sports Centre** (Žiemo sporto centras) at Sporto 3 is about the only place in Lithuania which has a slope long enough (at 300m) to be worth skiing down. Consequently, it's a popular day-trip venue for winter sports fans from Vilnius – skis can be rented once you arrive for 30Lt a day. The centre also offers **accommodation** (☎8-386/54193; ❶) in the form of simple doubles with shared facilities.

Palūšė

From Ignalina a minor road runs 5km west towards **PALŪŠĖ** (10 daily buses or a one-hour walk from Ignalina train station), a village of dainty, yellow houses grouped around the eastern end of Lake Lūšiai. Slightly uphill from the settlement's single street lies the wooden **Church of St Joseph** (Šv Jozefo bažnyčia), a mid-eighteenth-century structure with a squat two-storey bell tower. A small pavilion nearby holds the **Pilkapis Exhibition** (Pilkapio ekspozicija; erratic opening times; ask at the National Park Information Centre; see below), consisting of fifth-century-BC burial finds, namely a female skeleton accompanied by a trove of jewellery made from stones and animal bones. Down by the lakefront, a shed rents out rowing boats (6Lt/hr; 25Lt/day) and canoes (12Lt/hr; 35Lt/day) during the summer.

Practicalities

Occupying the former priest's house beside the church, the **National Park Information Centre** (June–Aug Mon–Thurs 9am–5pm, Fri & Sat 9am–7pm, Sun 10am–2pm; Sept–May Mon–Fri 9am–5pm; ☎8-386/52891, ⓔanp@is.lt) sells maps and can provide information on renting out canoes and advice on routes. They can also book you into the next-door *Tourism Centre* (Turismo centras; ❶), which offers simple rooms with shared facilities in cabins over the summer, and en-suites in the main building all year round. Slightly more salubrious accommodation is available at the *Ecological Education Centre* (Ekologinio švietimo centras; ❷), on the north side of the lake just off the road to Meironys, where rooms come with en-suite shower and kitchenette. If you have your own transport, you could ask the information centre to book you a room in Ginučiai mill (see opposite). Just below Palūšė's church, the *Aukštaičių Užeiga* **restaurant** offers traditional Lithuanian dishes in a folksy interior, often with live music in summer.

Around the park

The most renowned of the park's beauty spots is **Ladakalnis hill**, 9km north-west of Palūšė, the southernmost point of a ridge that extends between lakes Ūkojas and Linkmenas. It was a place of sacrifice in pagan times, and it's easy to see why it might have appealed, with its commanding views of six surrounding lakes, their waters bisected by green fingers of forested land. Follow the ridge north to find **Ginučiai castle mound** (Ginučių piliakalnis), a tenth-century hill fort whose summit is accessible via a wooden stairway. The forest cover is thicker here, but sweeping views occasionally open up between the trees. The easiest way to get to Ladakalnis is by car, heading northeast from Palūšė along the Tauragnai road and turning north onto a dirt road. Alternatively, you can walk from Palūšė (3–4hr), following a trail along the northern shores of Lake Lūšiai which takes you through a pair of wonderfully preserved villages full of timber houses, **Salos-I** and **Salos-II**.

Five kilometres north of Ladakalnis, **GINUČIAI** is a picturesque village of pea-green houses squeezed between lakes Alnajos and Sravinaitis. The nineteenth-century water mill in the centre of the village is now a national park-operated guesthouse (booked through the information centre in Palūšė; ❶), offering tasteful, wooden-floored rooms with shared facilities – there's no breakfast but you do get use of a kitchen. The former mill pond is a popular bathing spot in summer, and you can rent boats at the bridge where the two lakes meet. Ginučiai also boasts the one **campsite** in the park which comes with a water supply and hole-in-the-ground toilets.

Ten kilometres east of Ginučiai, on the shores of Lake Dringis, **VAIŠNIŪNAI** is another lovely village of timber houses and granaries, watched over by a huge road-side Rupintojėlis figure sculpted by a local craftsman. Heading west from Ginučiai along dirt roads will bring you after 5km to **STRIPEIKAI**, where the **Ancient Beekeeping Museum** (Senovinės bitininkystės muziejus; May to mid-Oct daily 10am–7pm; 3Lt), displays an oddly riveting collection of traditional beehives, carved out of tree trunks into various shapes and spread across a grassy meadow like timber tombstones.

Anykščiai and around

One hundred and ten kilometres northwest of Vilnius, **ANYKŠČIAI** (pronounced "A-*neeksh*-chey") is one of the most attractive towns in the Lithuanian northeast, nestling in a rolling patchwork of forest and green pasture either side of the River Šventoji. The beauty of the region occupies a treasured place in the Lithuanian psyche, thanks largely to local-born priest Antanas Baranauskas (1835–1902) and his poem *Forest of Anykščiai* (*Anykščių Šilelis*) – a lyrical evocation of nature, regarded as one of the nation's most sacred texts. The town has an absorbing museum devoted to Baranauskas and makes a good base-camp for woodland walks, while horse-lovers will be intrigued by nearby **Niūronys** – where there's a museum devoted to the creatures. With four to five **buses** a day from Vilnius, Anykščiai is an easy day-trip from the capital – if you miss one of these services, head for Ukmergė and change there.

The Town

Perched on a hill just above the town's bus station, the **Baranauskas and Vienuolis-Žukauskas Memorial Museum** at Vienuolio 4 (Baranausko ir Vienuolio-Žukausko memorialinis muziejus; daily 8am–5pm; 3Lt) pays homage to both the author of the *Forest of Anykščiai* and the self-appointed keeper of the Baranauskas flame, Antanas Žukauskas (1882–1957), who wrote short stories under the pen-name of Vienuolis ("the monk"). The museum was originally the site of the Baranauskas family farmstead, and Vienuolis bought it in 1922 with the express intention of turning its one surviving building – a log-built granary – into a national shrine. Now enclosed in a concrete-and-glass shell to protect it from the elements, the granary contains a chair and table belonging to Baranauskas, a few facsimile manuscripts, but little to convey the scale of his achievements – as well as being a prolific author, he was one of nineteenth-century Lithuania's leading ecclesiastics, rising to become Bishop of Seinai (now Sejny in Poland) in 1897. You can also look around the house Vienuolis built for himself next door to the granary; its mid-twentieth-century interior of floral wallpaper and ticking grandfather clocks has been lovingly preserved.

Across the river from the museum, Anykščiai's unassuming town centre is dominated by the neo-Gothic **Church of St Matthew** (Šv Mato bažnyčia), whose twin towers – at 79m each – are the tallest in the country. The impressively cavernous interior features some lovely nineteenth-century, floral-motif wall coverings and brightly coloured stained glass by contemporary artist Anortė Mackelaitė.

To reach what remains of the **forest** Baranauskas waxed so lyrically about, head southwest from the church along Vilniaus gatvė and keep on going past the town cemetery. The road soon turns into an asphalted path surrounded on both sides by dense woodland rich in pine, birch, oak and elm. Following the trail for 5km leads eventually to the **Puntukas boulder** (Puntuko akmuo), a six-metre-high lump of rock deposited by a retreating glacier some 12,000 years ago and nowadays a much-loved landmark – no self-respecting local newlyweds would dream of having their photograph taken anywhere else. One side of the boulder is decorated with an Assyrian-style bas-relief of pointy-helmeted pilots Darius and Girėnas, who plummeted to their deaths while attempting to fly from New York to Kaunas in 1933 (see p.122).

Anykščiai has one other attraction: the **narrow-gauge railway** (siaurukas; ⓦwww.ngr.lt) that runs northwest to Panevėžys (see opposite) and east to Lake Rubikiai (Rubikių ežeras). Sadly, regular passenger services were discontinued in 2001 and the line is now only used by occasional excursion trains, which normally have to be booked in advance by groups, although individuals can sometimes hitch a ride – contact the Anykščiai tourist office for details. The railway station, ten minutes' walk north of the Baranauskas museum along Gegužės, is a handsome wooden building that hasn't changed much since the inter-war years, and there's usually some old rolling stock parked outside.

Practicalities

Anykščiai's **tourist office**, just below the Baranauskas museum at Gegužės 1 (daily 9am–5pm; ☏8-381/59177, ⓦwww.anyksciai.lt), can book you into a clutch of rural homestays (❶–❷) in the region, including several around Lake Rubikiai, 10km east of town – few of these are anywhere near public transport routes so you'll need a car. The best **hotel** is the *Mindaugo Karūna*, just east of the centre at Liudiskių 18 (☏8-381/58520, ⓔmindaugo.karuna@takas.lt; ❹), a sports and conference centre with cosy en-suites, and indoor and outdoor swimming pools on the premises. Cheaper options include the *Puntukas*, in the centre at Baranausko 8 (☏8-381/51345; ❶), offering frumpy rooms with shared facilities and a handful of more expensive en-suites with new furniture and TV, while *Anykščių Šilelis* (☏8-381/51672; ❶), on the forested southern outskirts of town at Vilniaus 80, is basically a sanatorium offering sparsely furnished rooms on the side. The cosiest of the **cafés** is *Erdvė*, on the main square, offering a full menu of meat and fish dishes and bench seating in the yard. *Bangelė*, occupying a weir-side building above the River Šventoji, is a good place for a drink.

Niūronys

Six kilometres north of Anykščiai, just off the Rokiškis road, the village of **NIŪRONYS** is the site of the rather delightful **Museum of the Horse** (Arklio muziejus; daily 10am–6pm; 3Lt), occupying an ensemble of five traditional, timber-built buildings arranged farmstead-style beside the village's main crossroads. Lithuania's relationship with the beast is explored through a series of displays, including photographs of working horses through the ages, a re-created village

---

Bėk, bėk, žirgelį

Only a horse-mad nation like the Lithuanians could come up with a festival entitled Bėk, bėk, žirgelį ("Run, ye little horse!"), a celebration of all things equine which takes place in the field below the Museum of the Horse on the second or third weekend in June – the tourist office in Anykščiai will have full details. Farmers from all over the region descend on the village with their horses and traps, and large crowds assemble to watch a day-long programme of races involving everything from donkeys to thoroughbreds. There's also plenty in the way of craft stalls, beer tents and grilled food. Extra buses from Anykščiai are laid on for the occasion.

smithy, and a barn full of horse-drawn ploughs, rakes and traps. The museum is far from being a tribute to a disappearing culture: in fact the use of horses on Lithuanian farms has increased over the last decade and a half – the break-up of Soviet-era collective farms has led to fewer working tractors in circulation. Between spring and autumn, you'll see plenty of characteristically stocky, Lithuanian farm horses grazing in the fields outside, and there's a paddock where kids can ride ponies. Horse-and-carriage excursions (horse-and-sledge in winter) are a great way to take in the local countryside, but should be booked in advance (☎8-381/51722; if you can't get through to an English-speaker, Anykščiai tourist office might help).

Three **buses** a day run to the village from Anykščiai, and walking back to town through the gently undulating landscape of forest and pastureland (1hr 20min) is no great hardship. The *Pasagelė* **café** next to the museum doles out scrumptious potato pancakes, as well as soup of the day and more substantial pork dishes.

Panevėžys

The fifth-largest city in Lithuania, **PANEVĖŽYS** is an unenticing, grey sprawl which owes its place on tourist itineraries to its position on the Vilnius–Rīga highway rather than any particular attractions. It's a very useful transport hub if you're shuttling around by bus between north-Lithuanian towns like Anykščiai, Biržai and Šiauliai – and with fast connections to and from both Kaunas and Vilnius, you'll rarely end up having to stay here overnight.

If you do have time to kill, head uphill from the bus station to the main square, then follow the west-bound Vasario 16-os gatvė to find the **Panevėžys Regional Museum** at no. 23 (Panevėžio kraštotyros muziejus; Tues–Sat 10am–5pm; 1.50Lt), a small, but entertaining, collection comprising exhibits as diverse as mammoth tusks and milk churns. Its main focus is rural life in the nineteenth century, illustrated through a reconstructed, peasant living room. Upstairs, glass cases are crammed with butterflies and bugs, while a bunker-like basement holds exhibitions of contemporary art. The nearby **Photography Gallery**, Vasario 16-os 31 (Tues–Sat 10am–5pm; 2Lt), has a regular programme of quality exhibitions; somewhat less predictable are the shows sporadically held at the **Panevėžys Art Gallery**, a block south of here at Respublikos 3.

The helpful **tourist office** is on the main square at Laisės 11 (Mon–Fri 9am–5pm; ☎8-45/508080, ✉pantic@takas.lt). If you do end up **staying** the night, try the fairly comfortable *Romantic*, in a lakeside park north of the centre at Kranto 24 (☎8-45/584860, ⊛www.hotel.romantic.lt; ❹), or *Panevėžys* at Laisės 26 (☎8-45/435428; ❸), an uninspiring, if habitable, concrete box in the centre. The best place for a drink or snack is *Galerija XX*, Laisės 7, a lively **café** decked out in old clocks and sepia photographs of pre-World War I Panevėžys.

Biržai

Two hundred kilometres north of Vilnius and 20km east of the main Vilnius–Rīga highway lies the border town of **BIRŽAI**. It was put on the map by the Radvila family, who owned the town from the fifteenth to the nineteenth centuries, turning it into a flourishing trade centre and key military stronghold in the process. Nowadays, Biržai is a pretty uneventful place, but it's worth visiting for its **fortress**, lapped by the waters of Lake Širvėna.

The Town

Attractively set in a leafy park (called the "Biržai Castle Cultural Reserve") at the northern end of the town's main artery, Vytauto gatvė, Biržai's **fortress** is actually a twentieth-century reconstruction of the much-modified original dating from 1586, built by Kristupas Radvila, "the Thunderer" (1547–1603). Surrounded by grassy ramparts and reached via a dainty drawbridge, it's a creamy, elegantly arcaded,

Renaissance-style building, looking more like a stately home than a castle. The Radvilas, who had plenty of estates elsewhere in Lithuania, abandoned the fortress when it was blown up by the Swedes in 1704. What remained of it was put to the torch seven decades later as part of a lavish theatrical entertainment put on by the hooligan-aristocrat Karol Stanisław Radvila.

The fortress now houses the **Biržai District Museum** (Biržų krašto muziejus; Wed–Sun 9am–5pm; 2Lt), which starts off with a rather daunting collection of rows of ancient swords and axe heads labelled in Lithuanian only. Things pick up with a scale model of the fortress as it looked in the time of "the Thunderer", overlooked by striking portraits of Augustus II "the Strong" of Poland-Lithuania and Peter the Great of Russia – the pair met here in 1701 to agree on a common front against the invading Swedes. Upstairs, wooden sculptures of Catholic saints throng a room dedicated to folk art.

A short stroll southeast through the park will bring you to the gleaming-white **Church of St John the Baptist**, its twin nineteenth-century towers piled wedding-cake style in three tiers. Immediately to the east lies a broad, flagstoned square dominated by a monument to Lithuanian Bolshevik poet, Julius Janonis (1896–1917). Squatting on top of an enormous concrete pole, he looks more like a pillar-dwelling saint of old than a rabble-rousing bard.

From the square, head east along Basanavičiaus, cross the Apaščia River and turn left up Malūno gatvė to reach the most picturesque part of reed-shrouded **Lake Širvėna**. A rickety footbridge leads over the heads of inquisitive swans to the lake's northern shore, where a wooded park surrounds the stately **Astravas Palace** (Astravo dvaras) – a summer retreat built by the Tyszkiewicz family after the Radvilas sold them the town of Biržai in 1812. You can't visit the interior, but it's a lovely sight nonetheless, its mock-Renaissance lookout tower giving it the appearance of a grandiose village fire station.

Practicalities

Biržai is served by a handful of direct **buses** from Vilnius and by regular services from Panevėžys and Pašvalys. Biržai's bus station is at the northern end of Vytauto gatvė, near the castle park. Once you've done the rounds of the sights there's not much reason to stay, but if you do decide to stop over, the **tourist office** at Vytauto 27 (Mon–Fri 9am–5pm; ☎8-220/33496) has details of a few rural homestays (❶) in outlying villages; otherwise the *Tyla* **hotel**, 2km north of the centre at Tylos 2 (☎8-220/31191, ✆www.tyla.lt; ❹), is the only sure-fire source of accommodation in town. There are a couple of serviceable **cafés** on the main strip and a handful of gloomy beer bars serving up the local tipple, Biržų alus (Biržai beer).

Kaunas and around

With a population of 420,000, **KAUNAS** is the third-biggest city in the Baltic States, a bustling, metropolitan place and a major commercial and industrial centre. It served as the temporary capital of Lithuania for twenty years following World War I, and contains museums and galleries of national importance, yet still seems overwhelmingly provincial and self-absorbed in relation to Vilnius.

Although not as extensive as that of the capital, Kaunas's medieval **Old Town** still boasts an enjoyable ensemble of red-brick buildings and ice-cream-coloured churches, gathered around a handsome main square. Extending east of here along the shop- and café-lined Laisvės alėja, the **New Town** is characterized by the (now peeling) modernist and Art Deco buildings hastily thrown up during the inter-war period to make Kaunas look worthy of its capital-city status. Strewn along the way are some highly individual museums, offering everything from fine art to folk sculpture and carnival masks. Easily accessible, out-of-town attractions include the Baroque monastery of **Pažaislis** and the superb open-air ethnography museum at **Rumšiškės**. Traces of the Jewish community that once thrived in Kaunas are thin on the ground; many were executed by the Nazis at **Ninth Fort**, located northwest of the city and preserved as a grimly moving memorial.

Only 100km west of Vilnius and easily reached by **bus or rail**, Kaunas can be treated as a day-trip from the capital – although you'll need a few days to get the most out of it and explore some of the outlying attractions as well. Its good transport links also make it an ideal base from which to roam the whole of central Lithuania.

Some history

Kaunas started out as one of Lithuania's key border strongholds, defending the south of the realm from frequent incursions from the Teutonic Knights. After the Battle of Žalgiris in 1410, the Teutonic danger receded, leaving Kaunas free to grow rich from commerce – its position on the Nemunas River providing access to a network of trade routes. Several centuries of prosperity followed, marred only briefly by the sacking of the town by the Russians in 1655. Kaunas also became an important ecclesiastical centre, the city's Catholic seminary producing many of the nation's spiritual leaders.

A major turning point in Kaunas's development was the Tsarist Empire's decision to make it the lynchpin of their western defences in the 1880s. The Russians thoroughly redeveloped the place, constructing a new city centre around a long straight boulevard (now Laisvės alėja; see p.121) and a ring of nine forts. Kaunas flourished, although its forts were in such a state of disrepair by 1914 that commander-in-chief Grand Duke Nikolai suggested that the city's name be changed from Kovno (Russian for "Kaunas") to Govno (an informal Russian word for "excrement"). The fortifications were in any case never put to the test: scared witless by the German offensive of summer 1915, Kaunas's commander General Grigoriev ran away to Vilnius rather than lead the city's defence, for which he was sentenced to eight years' hard labour.

After World War I, Vilnius was occupied by the Poles, and Kaunas had to step into the breach. Declared the "provisional" capital, Kaunas seemed an unlikely seat of power, not least because it lacked the set-piece administrative buildings that a national capital needed. Visiting in the early 1920s, British traveller Owen Rutter found Kaunas to be "not worthy of the name city and, quite frankly, it is filthy. Moreover, its hotels are the worst in the Baltic States". By the 1930s, however, Kaunas had been transformed, with a rash of construction turning the city into a showroom for modern architecture – the Resurrection Church (see p.125), Vytautas the Great War Museum (p.122) and main Post Office being the principal surviving monuments from this go-ahead era.

In the wake of World War II, Kaunas lost its political role, but gained an important place in the national psyche. Taking in fewer Russian immigrants than other big centres, Kaunas remained a Lithuanian-speaking city, proudly aware of its status as a repository of national values. It was here that art student Romas Kalanta burnt himself to death in 1972 to protest against Soviet power, sparking days of rioting. During the pro-independence upsurge of the late 1980s, Kaunas was the kind of place where Russian-speaking visitors would be met with blank stares or given wrong directions by locals who claimed to know no other language than their own.

Initially slow to reap the benefits of post-independence economic change, Kaunas is now beginning to transform itself into a modern European city. Quirky souvenir shops in the Old Town and chic, glass-fronted cafés along Laisvės alėja lend the place a welcoming and animated air. One thing that hasn't changed is the city's deep-seated feeling of inferiority vis-a-vis near-neighbour Vilnius – comments about the culture and sophistication of the capital are usually met here with silence and a grinding of teeth.

Arrival and information

The **bus** and **train stations** are within 400m of each other on Vytauto prospektas on the eastern edges of the city centre. It takes the best part of forty minutes to

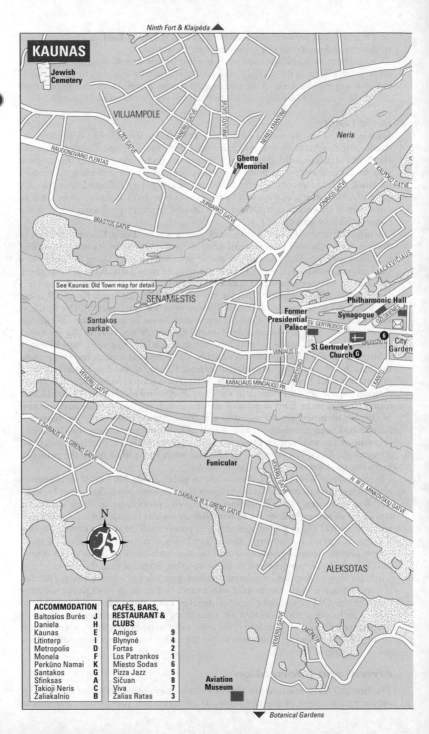

Ninth Fort & Klaipėda ▲

KAUNAS

Jewish Cemetery

VILIJAMPOLE

Neris

PANERIŲ GATVĖ
LINKUVOS GATVĖ
TILŽĖS GATVĖ
NERIES KRANTINE
P. KALPOKO GATVĖ

RAUDONDVARIO PLENTAS

Ghetto Memorial

JURBARKO GATVĖ

BRASTOS GATVĖ

JONAVOS GATVĖ

A. MACKEVIČIAUS

See Kaunas: Old Town map for detail

SENAMIESTIS

Philharmonic Hall

Santakos parkas

Former Presidential Palace

Synagogue

SV. GERTRUDOS G.
E. OŽEŠKIENĖS

St Gertrude's Church **G**

VIINIAUS G.

GRUODŽIO G.

6

City Garden

VEVERIŲ GATVĖ

KARALIAUS MINDAUGO PR.

BIRŠTONO

KANTO

S. DARIAUS IR S. GIRENO GATVĖ

Funicular

VEVERIŲ GATVĖ

H. IR O. MINKOVSKIŲ GATVĖ

S. DARIAUS IR S. GIRENO GATVĖ

N

ALEKSOTAS

VEVERIŲ GATVĖ

LAKŪNŲ PL.

ACCOMMODATION	
Baltosios Burės	J
Daniela	H
Kaunas	E
Litinterp	I
Metropolis	D
Monela	F
Perkūno Namai	K
Santakos	G
Sfinksas	A
Takioji Neris	C
Žaliakalnio	B

CAFÉS, BARS, RESTAURANT & CLUBS	
Amigos	9
Blynynė	4
Fortas	2
Los Patrankos	1
Miesto Sodas	6
Pizza Jazz	5
Sičuan	8
Viva	7
Žalias Ratas	3

Aviation Museum

Botanical Gardens ▼

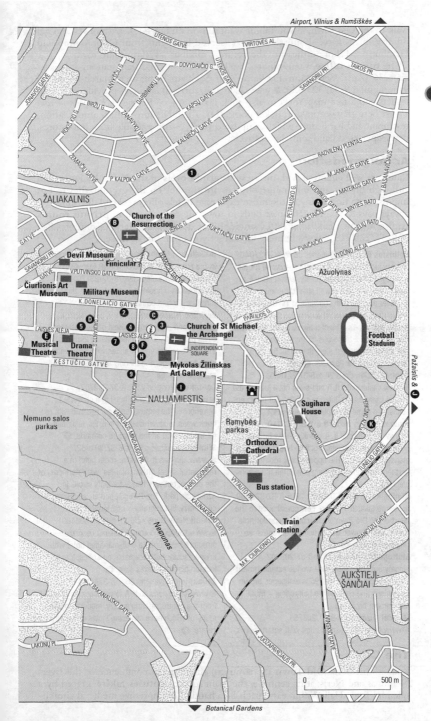

Airport, Vilnius & Rumšiškės ▲

UTENOS GATVĖ

TVIRTOVĖS AL.

P. DOVYDAIČIO G

TAIKOS PR.

JONAVOS GATVĖ

ANYKŠČIŲ G

DARBININKŲ G

UTENOS GATVĖ

SAVANORIŲ PR.

BIRŽŲ G

KAPSŲ GATVĖ

ROKIŠ KIO G

ŽANAVYKŲ GATVĖ

KALNIEČIŲ GATVĖ

RADVILĖNŲ PLENTAS

ŽEMAIČIŲ GATVĖ

M.JANKAUS GATVĖ

P. KALPOKO GATVĖ

AUŠROS G.

J. MATEIKOS GATVĖ

BASANAVIČIAUS

ŽALIAKALNIS

K. PETRAUSKO G

KUDIRKOS GATVĖ

AUKŠTAIČIŲ

A

MINTIES RATO

B **Church of the Resurrection**

AUŠROS G.

AUKŠTAIČIŲ GATVĖ

ŠELIŲ RATO

PVAIČIČIO

VYDŪNO ALĖJA

GATVĖ

Devil Museum

Funicular

V.PUTVINSKIO GATVĖ

Ažuolynas

SAVANORIŲ PR

GATVĖ

Čiurlionis Art Museum

Military Museum

K. DONELAIČIO GATVĖ

PARNIDOS G.

2

C

3

Church of St Michael the Archangel

Football Staduim

LAISVĖS ALĖJA

D

5

DAUKANTO

4

i

LAISVĖS ALĖJA

E

Musical Theatre

Drama Theatre

7

8

F

H

G

INDEPENDENCE SQUARE

KĘSTUČIO GATVĖ

Mykolas Žilinskas Art Gallery

Pažaislis & **J** ▶

9

MICKEVIČIAUS

VYTAUTO PR

NAUJAMIESTIS

I

DAUKANTO

Nemuno salos parkas

Ramybės parkas

Sugihara House

ALEKSANTO G

K

KARALIAUS MINDAUGO PR

Orthodox Cathedral

PERKŪNO AL.

TUNELIO GATVĖ

Nemunas

KARO LIGONINĖS

VYTAUTO PR

Bus station

KAUNAKIEMIO GATVĖ

Train station

PRANCŪZŲ GATVĖ

J. BAKANAUSKO GATVĖ

AUKŠTIEJI-ŠANČIAI

M.K. ČIURLIONIO PR

A. JUOZAPAVIČIAUS PR

LIUVINSKIO GATVĖ

LAKŪNŲ PL

0   500 m

117

Botanical Gardens ▼

walk to the Old Town, so you might want to hop on bus #1, #3, #5 or #7 and get off at Vilniaus gatvė. Kaunas's **airport** (served by flights from Oslo, Mälmo and Hamburg) is 12km northeast of the centre – minibus #120 runs into town.

The **tourist office** is ten minutes' walk from the bus and train stations at Laisvės alėja 36 (April–Sept Mon–Fri 9am–7pm, Sat 9am–3pm; Oct–March Mon–Fri 9am–6pm; ☎8-37/323 436, ⊛www.kaunas.lt/turistui), and can provide you with leaflets and a free map. You can also pick up a copy of *Kaunas & Klaipėda in Your Pocket* here (⊛www.inyourpocket.com; 8Lt), a handy source of accommodation, restaurant and bar listings which is updated yearly – also available from bookstores, newspaper kiosks and some hotel foyers.

Accommodation

Kaunas is well endowed with business-standard **hotels** in the $100-plus range, and although budget and mid-range choices are thinner on the ground, they're not impossible to find. Many of the more expensive hotels offer weekend discounts – it always pays to ask. The cheapest beds in town are to be found in **private rooms** with downtown landladies (80Lt single, 140Lt double); Litinterp, Gedimino 28-7 (☎8-37/228 718, ⊛www.litinterp.lt), can set you up in one of these.

Baltosios Burės Gimbutienės 35 ☎8-37/370467, ⊛www.jachtklubas.lt. A yacht-club-owned motel just beyond Pažaislis monastery, with a choice of simple box-like rooms with shared facilities, or chintzier doubles with shower and TV. Boasting a wonderful pine-shrouded position on the shores of Kauno marios, it's a bit of a hike without your own transport – take trolleybus #5 from opposite the bus station to the last stop, then walk for 2km following signs for Pažaislis. **①**–**③**

Daniela Mickevičiaus 28 ☎8-37/321505, ⊛www.danielahotel.lt. A mid-sized hotel just off the central Laisvės alėja, offering smallish but plush en-suites, and some nice split-level suites. **❼**

Kaunas Laisvės alėja 79 ☎8-37/323110, ⊛www.kaunashotel.lt. A spanking-new business hotel on the main boulevard, with bright business-standard en-suites. The upper-storey rooms on the northern side offer a striking panorama of Laisvės alėja. **❻**

Kunigaikščio menė Daukšos 28 ☎8-37/320800, ✉mene@takas.lt. A smart, new guesthouse in the heart of the Old Town offering bright, comfortable rooms with shower. Only a handful of rooms, so ring well in advance. **❻**

Metropolis Daukanto 21 ☎8-37/205992. A gloomy but charmingly olde-worlde establishment whose rooms come with 1950s wallpaper, brown furnishings and chipped-tile bathrooms – most have proper baths. **❸**

Minotel Kuzmos 8 ☎8-37/203759, ⊛www.minotel.lt. A small hotel with smart rooms

decked out in warm colours. Tea-making facilities in the rooms add to the cosy B&B feel. **❻**

Monela Laisvės alėja 35 ☎8-37/221791. Unrenovated but tolerable doubles with thrift-store furniture, TV and bathtub. **❷**

Perkūno Namai Perkūno 61 ☎8-37/320230, ⊛www.perkuno-namai.lt. Best of the business-class places if you don't mind being 2km east of the Old Town. Roomy en-suites with Scandinavian-style furnishings, and friendly attention-to-detail management. **❼**

Santakos Gruodžio 21 ☎8-37/302702, ⊛www.santaka.lt. Swish hotel in a converted warehouse. The atmospheric rooms come with red-brick walls, wooden-beamed ceilings, luxurious furnishings and all the creature comforts. **❼**

Sfinksas Aukštaičių 55 ☎8-37/301982, ⊛www.sfinksas.lt. A twelve-room hotel in a residential street fifteen minutes' walk northeast of the centre, but very handy for leafy strolls in Ąžuolynas park. The TV-equipped en-suites are a bit chintzy, but supremely comfortable. **❻**

Takioji Neris Donelaičio 27 ☎8-37/306100, ⊛www.takiojineris.com. A hulking concrete structure harbouring a well-managed hotel with unspectacular but acceptable en-suites. Ideally located just off Laisvės alėja. **❻**

Žaliakalnio Savanorių 66 ☎8-37/321412, ⊛www.takiojineris.com. A tower-block hotel uphill from the centre, offering snazzy, modern doubles, many of which have sweeping views of the city centre. **❻**

The City

Kaunas's medieval **Old Town** (Senamiestis) sits near the confluence of the rivers Nemunas and Neris; at its centre is the main square, **Rotušės aikštė**, graced by a splendid Town Hall. Within easy reach lie a handful of impressive medieval church-

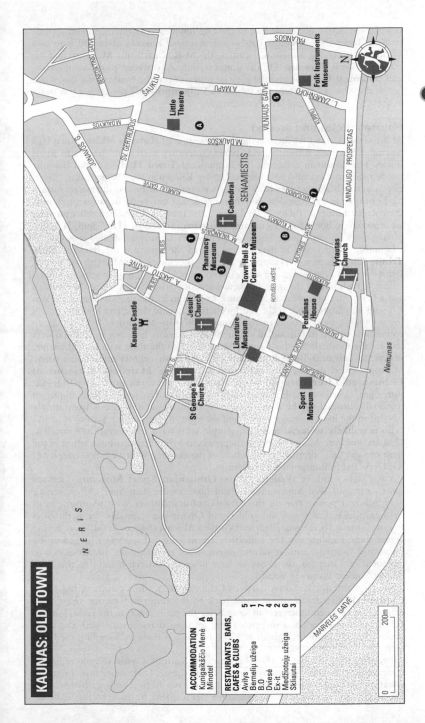

KAUNAS: OLD TOWN

Little Theatre

Folk Instruments Museum

Cathedral

SENAMIESTIS

Pharmacy Museum

Town Hall & Ceramics Museum

Jesuit Church

Kaunas Castle

Vytautas Church

ROTUŠĖS AIKŠTĖ

Literature Museum

Perkūnas House

St George's Church

Sport Museum

NERIS

Nemunas

N

ŠAUKLIŲ

BENEDIKTINŲ GATVĖ

M.DAUKŠOS

JONAVOS G.

SV. GERTRŪDOS

KUMELIŲ GATVĖ

PILIES

PILIES GATVĖ

A.JAKŠTO GATVĖ

PAPILO G.

M.VALANČIAUS

SANTAKOS GATVĖ

MUZIEJAUS

A.MAPŲ

VILNIAUS GATVĖ

L.ZAMENHOFO

PALANGOS

KARILL

MINDAUGO PROSPEKTAS

NAUGARDO

V.KUZMOS

MUITINĖS GATVĖ

ALEKSOTO

T.DAUKŠOS

MARVELĖS GATVĖ

ACCOMMODATION
Kunigaikščio Menė   A
Minotel   B

RESTAURANTS, BARS, CAFÉS & CLUBS
Avilys   5
Bernelių užeiga   1
B.O.   7
Dviese   4
Ex-it   2
Medžiotojų užeiga   6
Skliautai   3

200m

0

119

es and some quirky museums. East of the Old Town extends the nineteenth-century **New Town** (Naujamiestis), cut by pedestrianized **Laisvės alėja**. Off here lie a number of rewarding museums, including the **M.K. Čiurlionis Museum** and the eccentric **Devil Museum**. On the outskirts, leafy **Ąžuolynas park** and the tranquil **Botanical Gardens** provide pleasant retreats from the bustle of the city, while just to the west of the centre, the suburb of **Vilijampolė** still preserves a few traces of the city's once-thriving Jewish community.

Rotušės aikštė and around

At the centre of the Old Town is the broad expanse of **Rotušės aikštė** (Town Hall Square), lined with fifteenth- and sixteenth-century merchants' houses in pastel shades. The dominant feature is the magnificent **Town Hall**, its tiered Baroque facade rising to a graceful 53-metre-tall tower. Known as the "White Swan" for its elegance, this building dates back to the sixteenth century and during its history has been used as an Orthodox church, a theatre and university department, though these days it houses a "Palace of Weddings". The Town Hall's vaulted cellar provides an atmospheric home for a **Ceramics Museum** (Tues–Sun 11am–5pm; 3Lt), displaying work by some of the best of contemporary Lithuania's applied artists.

Looming towards you at the western end of the square is the Baroque **Holy Trinity Church**, its towers topped with cast-iron crosses adorned with sun motifs. Behind it lies a dignified group of creamy-coloured buildings belonging to Kaunas seminary, traditionally the most important seat of Catholic learning in the country, and a key centre of intellectual resistance to Tsarism in the years before World War I. A smooth granite statue at the southwestern corner of the square honours one of the seminary's most famous rectors, **Jonas Mačiulis–Maironis** (1862–1932), an enthusiastic patron of Lithuanian culture who also wrote lyric poetry suffused with love for the motherland – his *Voices of Spring* (1895) is the most widely-read volume of verse in Lithuania. Behind the statue, the eighteenth-century town house where Maironis lived during his rectorship is now the **Maironis Museum of Lithuanian Literature** (Maironio lietuvių literatūros muziejus; Tues–Sat 9am–5pm; closed on last Friday of each month; 3Lt). The ground-floor display of materials chronicling the development of Lithuanian literature is frustratingly labelled in the local language only – and the sight of exhibits like Šatrijos Ragana's cello is unlikely to mean much to people who have never read her novellas. Upstairs, however, Maironis's perfectly preserved living quarters boast some of the most eye-catching interiors in the whole of the country, with a fabulous display of Art Deco and folk-inspired wall coverings.

A few steps south at Muziejaus 7, the **Lithuanian Sport Museum** (Lietuvos sporto muziejus; Wed–Sun: summer 10am–6pm; winter 9am–5pm; 2Lt) presents a very different perspective on the nation's cultural history, with photographs of champion basketball teams and gold-medal Olympians – notably discus throwers Romas Ubartas (Barcelona 1992) and Virgilius Aleksna (Sydney 2000) – occupying centre stage. Padding out the collection are all kinds of souvenirs picked up by Lithuanian sporting teams at various international competitions: a hideous doll in the form of a marmot turns out to have been the official mascot of the 1992 Winter Student Games in Poland.

Hogging the northeastern corner of the square, Kaunas's austere, red-brick **Cathedral** (Katedra Basilika) dates back to the reign of Vytautas the Great, although it has been much rebuilt since. After the plain exterior, the lavish gilt and marble interior comes as a surprise. There are nine altars in total, with the large, statue-adorned, Baroque high altar (1775) by Tomasz Podhayski stealing the limelight.

Predating the cathedral by several centuries is **Kaunas Castle** (Kauno pilis), the scant remains of which lie just northwest of the square. Little more than a restored tower and a couple of sections of wall are left, the rest having been washed away by the Neris, but in its day the fortification was a major obstacle to the Teutonic

Knights. The fifteenth-century **St George's Church** (Šv Jurgio bažnyčia), next door, is an impressive Gothic pile in crumbling red brick, where restoration has so far done little to arrest fifty years of decay. West of here, foot- and cycle-paths converge on the spit of land where the river Neris flows into the Nemunas. It was here that a crowd of over 50,000 gathered to salute the returning Lithuanian basketball team after their victory in the 2003 European Championships in Sweden.

There's better-preserved Gothic finery south of the main square. The **Perkūnas House** (Perkūno namas) at Aleksoto 6 is an elaborately gabled red-brick structure, thought to have been built as a merchants' meeting hall or possibly a Jesuit chapel, standing on the reputed site of a temple to Perkūnas, the pagan god of thunder (a statue of the god was found on the site in the nineteenth century). From here Aleksoto descends to the banks of the Nemunas and the glowering **Vytautas Church** (Vytauto bažnyčia), built by Vytautas the Great in around 1399 to give thanks for his deliverance from the armies of the Tatars. During its long existence it has suffered various indignities, including use as a munitions magazine and potato store, and, like many other Lithuanian churches, it also had a stint as an Orthodox place of worship.

Three blocks east of the church at Zamenhofo 12B, the **Lithuanian Folk Instruments Museum** (Wed–Sun 10am–5pm; 4Lt) contains a fascinating array of archaic-looking instruments, including *kanklės* (traditional Baltic zithers) of all sizes, and sonorous wooden horns wrapped in birch bark.

Laisvės alėja and around

Running east from the Old Town through Kaunas's **Naujamiestis** (New Town) is **Laisvės alėja** (Freedom Avenue), a broad, pedestrianized shopping street. The whole street was, bizarrely, a no-smoking zone between 1990 and 2000, when the city council finally gave up trying to enforce it. At the western end of Laisvės, near the junction with Vilniaus, an elegant, ochre mansion in a well-tended park served as the **Presidential Palace** during Kaunas's period as the provisional capital and is currently being redeveloped as a history museum. Opposite the palace, a passageway leads off Laisvės into a yard containing **St Gertrude's Church** (Šv Gertrudos bažnyčia; Mon–Sat 10am–7pm, Sun 7.30am–noon), a fourteenth-century, red-brick structure so dwarfed by the surrounding apartment blocks that it looks more like a clay-house lantern souvenir than a church. Inside there's an especially ornate Baroque pulpit topped by a gesticulating statue of St John Nepomuk, and a much-venerated crucifix on the high altar – you'll see the devout crawling round it on their knees.

At the junction with L. Sapiegos the street is enlivened by a bronze **statue of Vytautas the Great**, which faces the **City Garden** (Miesto sodas), where, on May 14, 1972, the 19-year-old art student Romas Kalanta immolated himself in protest against Soviet rule. The act sparked several days of anti-Soviet rioting, and an estimated five hundred people were arrested. Kalanta's act is commemorated by local sculptor Robertas Antinis's memorial sculpture *Field of Sacrifice*, a rust-coloured assemblage of horizontal shards. The southern end of the park is marked by the **Musical Theatre**, the country's prime venue for operetta and the site – in May 1929 – of an attempt on the life of Prime Minister Augustinas Voldemaras. The assassin missed, killing the PM's grand-nephew instead.

Making a brief detour north from the City Garden up Sapiegos brings you to the **Kaunas Philharmonic Hall** at no. 9, where the Lithuanian Seima (Parliament) held its deliberations from 1919 until 1926, when President Smetona's imposition of authoritarian rule rendered it superfluous to requirements. Just round the corner at Ožeškienės 17, the nineteenth-century **Choral Synagogue** (Choralinė sinagoga; Sat 10am–noon & 6–6.30pm, Sun–Fri 6–6.30pm) is the sole Jewish place of worship left in a city that used to boast them by the handful. The sky-blue, balustraded interior contains an intricately carved Aron ha Kodesh, or high altar, which somehow survived the Nazi occupation. In the yard behind the synagogue is another striking monument by Robertas Antinis, this time honouring the child victims of the Holocaust with a slab of metal studded with tiny stars.

Vienybės aikštė and the Military Museum

Kaunas celebrates its role in sustaining Lithuanian national identity on **Unity Square** (Vienybės aikštė), at the junction of S. Daukanto and K. Donelaičio, a block north of Laisvės. Here a **monument** depicting Liberty as a female figure faces an eternal flame flanked by traditional wooden crosses, with busts of prominent Lithuanians from the nineteenth century between the two. Overlooking all this is the **Military Museum of Vytautas the Great** (Vytauto Didžiojo karo muziejus; summer Wed–Sun 10am–6pm; winter Wed–Sun 9am–5pm; closed last Thurs of every month; 3Lt), an angular, grey symbol of inter-war modernity which was intended to put Kaunas on the architectural map when it was completed in 1937. Swords, pikes, and scale models of stockade forts conjure up the martial vigour of the medieval Lithuanian state, while the independence struggles of 1918–20 are remembered in an impressive display of uniforms and weaponry. The museum also functions as a shrine to the Lithuanian pilots Darius and Girėnas (see box below), whose death in a plane crash during a transatlantic flight provided the inter-war Lithuanian state with its defining moment of heroism and sacrifice. One room displays poignant pictures of the pair being feted at farewell dinners before their departure from New York, while the ripped and blood-spattered shirts they were wearing when they crashed are kept in a case nearby. Preserved in an enormous glass box upstairs, the wreckage of their bright-orange plane, the *Lituanica*, looks more like a contemporary art installation than a tragic relic.

Darius and Girėnas

Most European nations had aviator heroes in the inter-war years, and in Darius and Girėnas Lithuania was not to be left out. Born in western Lithuania and taken to live in the USA at an early age, Steponas "Stephen" Darius (1896–1933) and Stasys "Stanley" Girėnas (1893–1933) both fought with US forces in World War I, learning to fly towards the war's end. Darius was the more flamboyant of the two, winning a Purple Heart for bravery in 1918, and turning up in Lithuania to take part in the seizure of Klaipėda in 1923 (see p.150). A sports nut who excelled at just about every activity that involved kicking, throwing or hitting a ball, Darius was also influential in turning basketball into inter-war Lithuania's most popular team game.

Darius had long dreamed of flying non-stop from New York to Kaunas and enlisted Girėnas as his co-pilot. Money raised by the Lithuanian community in North America helped fund the purchase of a secondhand plane, which they named the *Lituanica*. They took off on July 15, 1933, only to crash two days later in an East Prussian forest, tantalizingly short of their target. The cause of the accident remains unknown. The vast crowds who had assembled at Kaunas airport to greet their arrival were shattered by the news, and a deep sense of national loss spread across the country. As the first famous dead Lithuanians of the modern media age, Darius and Girėnas were quickly enshrined as national martyrs. Their embalmed bodies were on permanent display until 1944, when they were banished to a storeroom by a Soviet regime that disapproved of patriotic cults. In 1964 they were finally laid to rest at Aukštieji Šančiai cemetery in the southeast of the city, but public remembrance of their exploits was broadly discouraged.

Post-independence Lithuania has been quick to restore Darius and Girėnas to the national pantheon: the pair are featured on the 10Lt banknote, and have been honoured with a monument next to the Kaunas sports stadium that bears their name. A scale model of the *Lituanica* hangs from the ceiling of the departure lounge of Vilnius airport, although it's not clear whether this is intended to inspire travellers or scare them witless.

The M.K. Čiurlionis Art Museum

Part of the same building as the Military Museum, the **M.K. Čiurlionis Art Museum** (M. K. Čiurlionio dailės muziejus; summer Tues–Sun noon–6pm; winter Tues–Sun 11am–5pm; closed last Tues of every month; 3Lt), houses an exhaustive collection of pictures by Lithuania's greatest artist. During his short career (he died of pneumonia at the age of 36 in 1911), Čiurlionis created a unique body of work, producing enigmatic paintings influenced by the French Symbolists, many of them suffused with religious imagery. A composer as well as a painter, Čiurlionis believed that the feelings aroused by symphonic music could also be expressed in two-dimensional art – the dreamy, pulsating and often hypnotic results of his labours are on show by the cartload here. He produced small-format watercolours and pastels for the most part, rendering them in hazy greens, yellows and blues, and giving them contemplative titles like "Sorrow", "Truth" or "Thought". Castles, mountains and rivers feature prominently in his works, but they're often lost in wavy washes of colour – leading some to claim him as a precursor of abstract art.

If you've had enough Čiurlionis, there's a solid collection of Lithuanian art from the inter-war years, when Kaunas was the site of the country's only art school. Particularly striking are the expressionist landscapes of bendy trees and collapsing skies produced by Antanas Samuolis (1899–1942), and the Gaugin-esque portraits of Viktoras Vizgirda (1904–1993). There's also a good deal of Lithuanian folk art, notably the wooden statuettes of saints that traditionally decorate wayside shrines.

The Devil Museum

Kaunas has a second unique art collection nearby in the shape of the **A. Žmuidzinavičius Art Museum**, at Putvinskio 64 (A. Žmuidzinavičiaus kūrinių ir rinkinių muziejus; summer Tues–Sun noon–6pm; winter Tues–Sun 11am–5pm; closed last Tues of every month; 4Lt). Better known as the **Devil's Museum** (Velnių muziejus), this houses a vast collection of figures put together by the artist Antanas Žmuidzinavičius (1876–1966), who devoted his life to the collection of all kinds of folk art, specializing in the demonic masks worn by Lithuanian revellers at shrovetide – when the spirit of winter is driven away by donning Halloween-like disguises. There's an extensive display of the masks here, sporting fearsome horns, yellow teeth and lolling red tongues. Ranged elsewhere are all manner of devil-related objects donated to the museum by artists both domestic and foreign, including some rather desirable Latvian crockery decorated with cavorting impish forms. Although there's a lot of disappointing junk, too (think pitch-fork-wielding garden gnomes), some exhibits will stick in the memory – look out for Kazys Derškevičius's sinister representation of Hitler and Stalin as devils dancing on a Lithuania composed of skulls. The museum also has an impressive collection of more mainstream wooden folk sculpture, with several representations of the Rupintojėlis or Sorrowful Christ, a popular subject in Lithuanian folk art, in which Christ is traditionally depicted seated with his head in his hands. Other sculptures include a squadron of dragon-spearing St Georges and a typically Lithuanian semi-pagan symbol of fertility in the shape of The Sower – a mysterious figure in a black pork pie hat who scatters seed from a flaxen bag.

Church of St Michael the Archangel and the Mykolas Žilinskas Art Gallery

Marking the eastern end of Laisvės alėja, the silver-domed **Church of St Michael the Archangel** (Igulos bažnyčia) stands imperiously over Nepriklausomybes aikštė ("Independence Square"). Originally an Orthodox church built for the Tsarist garrison in the 1890s, this neo-Byzantine structure has preserved its military associations despite several changes of regime and denomination, serving as the (Protestant) German army church in World War I, and becoming the (Catholic) Lithuanian army church immediately afterwards. Its bare interior is a reflection of

Mikalojus Konstantinis Čiurlionis (1875–1911)

Born in the southeastern town of Varėna and raised in the nearby spa resort of Druskininkai from the age of 3, Lithuania's most famous painter and composer was introduced to music by his father, who was the organist at Liškiava church (see p.143). The talented youth soon caught the attention of Count Michał Ogiński, who installed Čiurlionis in his private music school in Plungė, and went on to finance further study abroad. Čiurlionis graduated from the Warsaw Conservatoire in 1899, and was set to continue his studies in Leipzig when Ogiński died and the money dried up. Equipped with a sound grasp of musical theory however, Čiurlionis set about composing lengthy symphonic pieces, the best known of which are the tone poems *In the Forest* (Miške; 1900) and *The Sea* (Jūra; 1907). At the same time Čiurlionis was pursuing his career as an artist, enrolling in the newly opened Warsaw School of Fine Arts in 1904.

Čiurlionis believed that both music and art could be used to tap the raw emotive power of the human spirit. This dovetailed rather nicely with his belief in the Lithuanians themselves as a uniquely spiritual nation, who were closer to their Indo-European origins than many of their neighbours and therefore represented a bridge between European religions and eastern mysticism. He believed that Lithuanian spirituality was expressed in its folk art, and – even though he didn't always use folk imagery in his own paintings – he strongly advocated a return to folk traditions in order to develop a true Lithuanian culture.

Like many urbanized Lithuanians of his generation however, Čiurlionis grew up speaking Polish, and only mastered Lithuanian after 1907 on the promptings of his fiancée, the essayist and critic Sofia Kymanautė. In 1907, the couple helped to organize the first Lithuanian Art Exhibition in Vilnius, hoping to raise public perception of the arts in general and Čiurlionis's own paintings in particular. The response was disappointingly lukewarm. Unable to make a living from painting or composing in Vilnius, Čiurlionis headed for St Petersburg in 1909 in the hope of breaking into the flourishing art scene there. His work made a big impression on critics and fellow painters, but none of the local dealers offered him an exhibition. Back in Vilnius, lack of both money and an appreciative audience drove Čiurlionis into apathy, depression and, ultimately, serious mental illness. Thus weakened, he was unable to withstand the onslaught of pneumonia, and died at a sanatorium outside Warsaw on April 10, 1911.

Čiurlionis died in obscurity because he was a Lithuanian artist working at a time when there was no Lithuanian art establishment capable of promoting his works. Within a decade of his demise, however, Lithuania was an independent state desperately in need of cultural icons, and Čiurlionis fitted the bill perfectly. An art museum bearing his name was established in 1925, and proceeded to buy all Čiurlionis's paintings from his widow. The symphonic poems, hardly ever peformed during his composer's lifetime, became regular fixtures in the repertoire of the Lithuanian Philharmonic.

In the early years of the Soviet occupation, Čiurlionis's taste for mysticism was considered decadent and reactionary, and it wasn't until the late 1960s that the local communist party began to curry intellectual favour by readmitting Čiurlionis to the national pantheon. Nowadays, Čiurlionis's soulful, contemplative art is considered to be one of the most eloquent expressions of the Lithuanian national character.

In general, Čiurlionis's reputation has failed to travel beyond Lithuania's borders, and despite the inclusion of a couple of his paintings in Roger Fry's influential Post-Impressionism exhibition in London in 1912, his work has rarely been seen abroad. He's never been short of enthusiasts, though: Russian critics have always considered him to be a big name in the development of Symbolism, and in 1930 French writer Romain Rolland – never one to be bashful about his enthusiasms – told Čiurlionis's widow that "this is a continent for the spirit and Čiurlionis is its Christopher Columbus!"

the fact that it was an art gallery for most of the Soviet period. A rather garish modern altar painting of the Archangel adds a dash of colour to the place, and a side altar to the right harbours a superb example of a Rupintojėlis or "Sorrowful Christ" sculpture (see p.123).

Occupying a contemporary building in the northeast corner of the square, the **Mykolas Žilinskas Art Gallery** (Mykolo Žilinsko dailės galerija; summer Tues–Sun noon–6pm; winter 11am–5pm, closed last Tues of every month; 4Lt) is a hugely rewarding collection of fine and applied art from around the globe. Dominating a room of Egyptian amulets, Roman glassware and Ming vases is a show-stopping eighteenth-century set of over fifty ceramic figures representing the Apotheosis of Catherine the Great – as well as the Empress herself, there are Greek gods, and figures in Turkish and Tatar garb representing the grateful subject nations of the Russian Empire. Less ostentatious, but still too good to eat your dinner off, are Art Deco plates from the 1920s and propagandist porcelain from Soviet Russia decorated with cubist workers waving hammers and sickles. Among the paintings are Lithuania's only Rubens, a sombrely effective *Crucifixion,* and Gustave Courbet's *Portrait of a Girl* – the subject of which sizes up the viewer with quietly confident gaze. Right outside the gallery, Petras Mozūras's towering statue of an unabashedly naked man is something of a local talking point.

Žaliakalnis

Ten minutes' walk northeast of Nepriklausomybės, on the northern side of Putvinskio, lies the lower station of a 1930s **funicular railway** (funikulierius; Mon–Fri 7.30am–6pm, Sat & Sun 9am–6pm; 0.50Lt), which climbs up to **Žaliakalnis** (Green Hill), a leafy residential area favoured by the Kaunas middle classes during the inter-war years. Near the upper terminal is the **Church of the Resurrection** (Prisikėlimo bažnyčia), a masterpiece of 1930s architecture whose soaring tower is topped by a slender cross. Having been a radio factory during Soviet times, the church is currently under restoration, its bright-white paint job adding a touch of futuristic glamour to the Kaunas skyline.

East of the centre: the Sugihara House and Ąžuolynas

Just east of the bus and train stations paths lead up to another prosperous area of quiet, residential streets – the kind of place where foreign diplomats set up home during the period when Kaunas was the provisional capital. One of these was Chiune Sugihara (see box overleaf), the unassuming consul who has been dubbed "Japan's Schindler" for his action in supplying thousands of Jewish refugees with Japanese visas – allowing them to escape a city threatened by Nazi invasion. The **Sugihara House** (May–Sept Mon–Fri 10am–5pm, Sat & Sun 11am–4pm; Oct–April Mon–Fri noon–4pm; donation requested), occupying the consul's former home at Vaizganto 30, displays fascinating photographic evidence of Sugihara's activities – one picture shows him still issuing visas from the window of a train compartment moments before his final departure from the city.

From the Sugihara House it's a short walk northeast to the Darius and Girėnas Sports Stadium, which, as the best equipped in the country, is where the Lithuanian football team play most of their matches. Immediately behind it lies **Ąžuolynas** ("oakwood"), a wonderfully leafy square-kilometre of park filled with ash, elm, lime and oak. Follow paths to its eastern end and you'll emerge opposite Lithuania's only **zoo** (Zoologijos sodas; daily: April–Sept 9am–7pm; Oct–March 9am–5pm; 5Lt), which brings together a wide variety of bored and listless animals from around the world.

South of the centre: the Botanical Garden

A further swathe of residential suburbs runs along the hillside on the south bank of the River Nemunas. The one destination of real interest here is the **Botanical**

Chiune Sugihara (1900–1986)

A career diplomat and Russian specialist in the Japanese foreign ministry, Chiune Sugihara was posted to Kaunas as Japanese consul in March 1939 in order to report on Soviet intentions in the region. When Soviet forces occupied Lithuania in July 1940, most foreign diplomats were ordered to leave without delay, but Sugihara, and the Dutch consul, Jan Zwartendijk, where allowed to stay for one more month.

At the time thousands of Jewish refugees from Nazi-occupied western Poland were arriving in Kaunas, only to discover that the Soviet authorities refused to give them transit visas unless they first obtained valid visas for their next destination. As the only representative of a country bordering the Soviet Union left in the city, Sugihara was besieged with requests for help. However, he couldn't give the refugees normal Japanese entry visas because of objections from his ministry in Tokyo, so he opted instead to hand out Japanese transit visas – under the pretence that the refugees were ultimately bound for Dutch colonies in the east. Local Soviet officials turned a blind eye to Sugihara's scheme, but approval from Tokyo was slow in coming – so Sugihara simply went ahead on his own initiative, writing out the relevant documents by hand, thereby providing an estimated 6000 people with passage out of the country. When he finally left Kaunas on September 1, he presented his consular stamp to a refugee so that more visas could be issued on his behalf. Sugihara went on to serve in the Japanese embassy in Prague, but was sacked by the foreign ministry in 1945 – a belated punishment for his refusal to do things by the book in Kaunas.

Sugihara built a career as a businessman after the war and remained ignorant about the fate of those he had helped escape until a survivor sought him out in 1969. Enthused by the renewal of old contacts, Sugihara visited Israel the same year. However, he remained largely unrecognized until 1984, when the Vad Yashem Institute declared him one of the "Righteous Among the Nations" – the title given to gentiles who took personal risks to save Jewish lives. Hillel Levine's biography of Sugihara, published in 1996 (see "Books"; p.436), was the first attempt to tell the whole story – although it outraged Sugihara's family with its warts-and-all treatment of a subject who had visited brothels as a young diplomat and been married to a White Russian emigré before settling down with his second (still living) spouse.

Garden (Botanikos sodas; daily: June–Aug 9am–6.30pm; Sept–May 8.30am–5.30pm; 4Lt), a relaxing stretch of rose gardens, flowerbeds and shrubberies that lies at the end of minibus route #49 (from Birštono in the Old Town). Highlights include a lily-choked serpentine and a central Orangery (Oranžerija; daily June–Aug 11am–6.30pm, Sept–May 10am–5pm) containing banana palms, bengal fig trees and a goldfish-stocked pond.

West of the centre: Vilijampolė

Before World War II, Kaunas, like Vilnius, had a large **Jewish population**. Nearly all were killed during the war and little remains of their presence. The main area of Jewish settlement was **Vilijampolė** (known for much of its history by the Russian name of Slobodka), a suburb just across the Neris from the Old Town, and it was here that the Nazis created a closed ghetto in July 1941. An attractive grid of timber houses, today's Vilijampolė contains little in the way of memorials to the people who once lived and died here. A granite obelisk at the junction of Linkuvos and Kriščiukaičio bears an inscription in Lithuanian and Hebrew stating simply that "on this spot stood the gates of the Kaunas ghetto 1941–44". From here you'll have to zigzag your way north through residential streets to find a small (and easily missed) plaque at Goštautų 4 that marks the former location of the ghetto hospital, burned down by the Nazis on October 4, 1941, with staff and patients still inside. Finally,

Jewish Kaunas

Jews first came to Kaunas in the early fifteenth century at the invitation of Grand Duke Vytautas the Great, and were settled in Vilijampolė in order to keep them separate from the Lithuanian population of the city centre. The Jews soon established a trading settlement in the centre, although outbreaks of anti-Semitism resulted in their periodic expulsion (notably in 1495, 1753 and 1761), adding to the importance of Vilijampolė as their natural refuge. The Jews had re-established themselves in the centre of Kaunas by the late nineteenth century, and by the time of World War I they made up the majority of the population in the Old Town. On the eve of World War II, there were approximately 35,000 Jews in Kaunas (of which 6000 lived in Vilijampolė), about forty percent of the city's total.

Although there was little social integration betwen the Jewish and Lithuanian populations of pre-war Kaunas, outbreaks of explicit anti-Semitism were rare. However, the arrival of the German troops on June 23, 1941 unleashed an unexpectedly ferocious wave of popular violence. On June 25, Lithuanian gangs ran riot in Vilijampolė, killing an estimated 1000 civilians and decapitating chief rabbi Zalman Ossovsky. Two days later in central Kaunas, a group of over fifty Jews was driven onto the forecourt of the Lietūkis garage and clubbed to death by the locals, with German soldiers looking on. Gruesome footage of the incident has subsequently been used in several Holocaust-related documentaries.

On July 10, all the city's Jews were herded into the newly established ghetto in Vilijampolė. Many were relieved by the move, thinking that this would protect them from the violence of Lithuanian hooligans. However, regular "actions", in which arbitrarily chosen groups of Jews were rounded up and shot by the Germans, became commonplace as the autumn of 1941 wore on. The enthusiasm of the local Lithuanian population for anti-Semitic excesses continued to astound even the Germans. Colonel Jäger of Einsatzgruppe A, the organization charged with organizing mass killings throughout northeastern Europe, notoriously reported that Kaunas, "where trained Lithuanian volunteers are available in sufficient numbers, is comparatively speaking a shooting paradise."

Right from the start it was clear that those members of the community required by the Germans for work duty stood a good chance of surviving (for the time being), while the others were likely to be murdered. This placed Jewish leaders – who controlled the distribution of work permits – in the unenviable position of deciding who lived and who died. Some argued that a refusal to issue any work permits at all would be the only morally correct action to take, until the new chief rabbi Abraham Dov Shapiro decreed that an attempt to save some Jewish lives was better than no attempt at all. On October 28, the Jews of Vilijampolė were assembled by their community leaders so that several thousand of them could be selected for work duties by the SS. Of the 20,000-plus that were surplus to requirements, approximately 10,000 of them were taken away and shot within weeks – most were murdered in the notorious Ninth Fort (see p.128) just outside the city.

Despite frequent actions and arbitrary shootings, Vilijampolė's surviving Jews attempted to preserve a semblance of normal life in the years that followed. The able-bodied continued to work in factories inside and outside the ghetto, squares were ploughed up and used to grow vegetables, and a 35-piece ghetto orchestra gave regular concerts. In April 1944, the Germans decided to clear the ghetto of its remaining 8000 inhabitants. The women were sent to Stutthof, the men to Dachau, where 75 percent of them perished. By the time the Red Army arrived in August there were no Jews left in Kaunas – save for the fortunate handful who had found hiding places in the city or had escaped to join partisans in the surrounding forests.

After the war, most survivors moved to Vilnius or emigrated entirely, and the local Jewish population currently stands at just over 1000 – the wonderfully restored synagogue on Ožeškienės gatvė (see p.121) functions as their social and spiritual centre.

there's an overgrown, barely accessible **Jewish cemetery** (Senosios žydų kapinės) clinging to a hillside in the northwest of the suburb, just off Kalnų.

The Ninth Fort

Many of Kaunas's Jews ended their lives at the **Ninth Fort** (Devintasis fortas) on the northwestern fringes of the city, one of several forts built around Kaunas by the Russians in the nineteenth century, and known by their numbers ever since. The Ninth Fort was used as a camp for political prisoners by the Lithuanians during the inter-war years, was subsequently used by the Soviet NKVD in 1940, and then transformed into a holding prison and killing ground by the Nazis from June 1941 onwards. It's thought that as many as 50,000 people lost their lives over the next four years – at least 30,000 of them were Jews from Kaunas or the surrounding region: the others came from locations as diverse as Munich and Marseilles.

Surrounded by banked-up earthworks, the fort forms the centrepiece of an extensive park criss-crossed by paths and planted with saplings. A flagstoned avenue leads to a huge Soviet-era memorial, a jagged concrete outcrop pitted with the shapes of human faces and fists. Like all such monuments of the period, it's dedicated to the "victims of Fascism" and fails to mention the Jews by name – Soviet ideology always denied the true nature of the Holocaust in an attempt to portray Marxism-Leninism as the sole target of Nazi hatred. Nearby are smaller post-1991 memorials, honouring particular communities of Jews who ended up here, and a sign indicating one of the trenches where many of them were shot.

A modern pavilion nearby sells tickets to the **Ninth Fort Museum** (daily except Tues 10am–4pm; 4Lt), which occupies a series of cells in the fort's barbed-wire-topped blockhouses. Among the poignant reminders of those incarcerated here is a section of glass-covered wall covered in graffiti by those about to be murdered – "we are 500 Frenchmen," wrote Abraham Wechsler of Limoges.

The Ninth Fort is 4km out of central Kaunas, right beside the main highway to Klaipėda. **To get there**, catch any west-bound inter-city service from the main bus station and get off when you see the memorial looming up on your left.

Pažaislis monastery

Some 7km east of the city centre, the Baroque **Pažaislis monastery** (Pažaislio vienuolynas) is worth visiting for its location as much as its fine architecture, situated as it is in a belt of forest beside the shores of the so-called Kaunas Sea, or Kauno marios, an artificial lake created to feed a hydroelectric power station in the late 1950s. Surrounded by sandy shores shaded by pines, it's a popular recreation spot in summer and an invigorating place for a stroll whatever the season. It's easy to get to – take **trolleybus #5** from opposite the bus station to the end of the line and carry on walking in the same direction, bearing left and under the railway tracks after about five minutes.

The monastery was built for the Camaldolese Order in 1667 by one of the Grand Duchy of Lithuania's leading aristocrats, Krzysztof Zygmunt Pac. Looted by Napoleon's troops in 1812 and closed down by the Tsarist authorities in 1832, it was subsequently used as an Orthodox church until its resettlement by Lithuanian-American nuns in the 1920s. The Soviets used it as a psychiatric hospital, and it wasn't until 1992 that the nuns returned. Presiding magisterially over a grassy courtyard, the monastery church is one of the most striking examples of the Baroque style in the country, with a twin-towered facade thrusting forward from a huge octagonal drum topped by a bulbous cupola. The interior (officially open Tues–Sun 11am–5pm, but often closed without explanation) is vibrantly decorated with frescoes, with Giuseppe Rossi's *Coronation of the Virgin* filling the central dome, and Michelangelo Palloni's scenes from the lives of Christ and St Benedict covering the walls. The church's period as an Orthodox foundation is recalled by the tombstone of Aleksii Fedorovich Lvov (1798–1870), outside the main door and to the

Užgavėnės mask △

right – he penned the music to the Tsarist Empire's national anthem, "God Save the Tsar". The monastery grounds are used for **concerts** in summer, when the Lithuanian Philharmonic Orchestra frequently guests.

Eating, drinking and nightlife

You can eat and imbibe very well and very reasonably in Kaunas, and you shouldn't have to stray far from the central strip formed by Laisvės alėja, Vilniaus gatvė and Rotušės aikštė in order to find a convivial place to settle. Innumerable establishments along the way cater for a café-crowd during the daytime, serious diners in the evening and even more serious drinkers as the night draws on. As usual in Lithuania, there's not always a clear boundary separating cafés, restaurants and bars, and the categories below are only intended as a general guide. Many of the hipper establishments along Laisvės feature live music and dancing at week-ends – otherwise late drinkers move on to the clubs, for which there's a small entrance charge.

Cafés

Blynynė Laisvės 56. An order-at-the-counter café serving all manner of sweet and savoury pancakes, alongside a simple repertoire of potato-based dishes – a good place to tuck into a slice of *bulvių plokštainis*. Till 7pm.

Dviesė Vilniaus 8. Cheap and filling savoury pies and *spurgos*, in a place decked out with the kind of pop-art furnishings that would make Austin Powers feel at home. Till 10pm.

Viva Laisvės 53. Snazzy self-service offering a cheap and quick selection of pancakes, *koldūnai*, fresh salads and cakes. Mon–Thurs till 9pm, Fri & Sat till 10pm, Sun till 8pm.

Restaurants

Amigos Mickevičiaus 22. There's a vaguely Mexican flavour to the menu in this plush, dark-red basement restaurant, but a lot more besides, with indigenous porky main courses vying for attention with pasta dishes and healthy salads. A good sweet selection ensures that this is an agreeable place for a daytime coffee-and-cake stop.

Bernelių Užeiga Valančiaus 9. Lively Old Town restaurant where you can dine on traditional Lithuanian staples like *cepelinai* and *vedarai*, as well as grill-steaks and fish, all in an attractive rustic interior on two levels.

Medžiotojų užeiga Rotušės aikštė 10. Elegant, upscale restaurant with a gamey theme that's reflected in the hunting trophies dotted around the walls. Meat-gluttons will be satisfied with whatever they order here, although venison and wild boar are the specialities.

Miesto Sodas Laisvės alėja. Bright, roomy café-restaurant on the main strip with everything from T-bone steaks to weight-watching salads. Big menu of cocktails, and jazzy piano tinkling in the evenings.

Pizza Jazz Laisvės alėja 68. Dependable source of thin-crust pies in a bright and breezy atmosphere. Lasagne and other pasta dishes round out the menu.

Sičuan Mickevičiaus 30. Simply furnished basement offering some of the best Chinese food in Lithuania. A good choice of authentically spiced dishes and inexpensive, too.

Žalias Ratas Laisvės 36B. A building that looks like a country cottage, tucked incongruously in a yard behind the tourist office. Homely trad cooking, wooden benches, and an open fire in winter.

Bars

Avilys Vilniaus gatvė. Upmarket pub in a tastefully renovated brick cellar that brews its own beer – including the strong, honey-flavoured and strangely addictive *medaus alus*. Full range of beer snacks and meaty main courses.

Blue Orange ("B.O." for short) Muitinės 9. Home-from-home drinking den drawing a wide cross-section of arty nonconformists and mainstream boozers eager to enjoy the laid-back vibe and vaguely alternative sounds on the CD player.

Fortas Donelaičio 65. Irish pub on three levels, with quiet alcove seating downstairs, standing-room-only bar with live music upstairs. Full food menu.

Skliautai Rotušės aikštė 26. A cosy, barrel-vaulted chamber in an alleyway just off the Old Town's main square, decked out in sepia photos of pre-war Kaunas. A good place for a cheap, filling lunch or a relaxing evening drink.

Clubs

Ex-it Jakšto 4. Minimally decorated, youth-oriented bastion of DJ-culture in the Old Town.

Los Patrankos Savanorių 124. Enjoyably cavernous place which has more in the way of lighting effects, dry ice and podium dancers than the other places in town. A long trudge uphill from the centre – taxis might come in useful. **Siena** Laisvės alėja 93. Basement club beneath

the *Miesto sodas* restaurant serving up a selection of mainstream sounds to a relaxed, fun-seeking crowd. Good place for a late-night drink as well a bop.

Entertainment and annual events

There's a lot of serious culture on offer in Kaunas, although visitors are often caught out by the seriously early performance times – 5 or 6pm being the norm. The city's musical flagship is the **Kaunas Philharmonic** (Kauno Filharmonija), Sapiegos 5 (☎8-37/200478; box office daily 2–6pm), site of regular performances by the Kaunas Chamber Orchestra and the Kaunas State Choir (probably the top choral group in the country), as well as Friday-evening visits from the Vilnius-based Lithuanian National Symphony Orchestra. The **Musical Theatre** (Muzikinis teatras), Laisvės alėja 91 (☎8-37/200933; box office Tues–Sat 10am–1pm & 3–6pm, Sun 10am–3pm) is the venue for light opera and musicals.

Lithuanian-language **drama** – including major touring productions from Vilnius – can be seen at the Drama Theatre (Dramos teatras), Laisvės 71 (☎8-37/224064; box office Tues–Sat 11am–2pm & 3–6.30pm, Sun 1hr before performance). Kaunas Little Theatre (Kauno Mažasis teatras), Daukšos 34 (☎8-37/206546; box office Wed–Fri 3–7pm, Sat 11am–6pm, Sun 1hr before performance), is the place to see contemporary drama in a smallish, intimate space.

Cinemas showing mainstream international films include Laisvė, Laisvės 46A; Planeta, Vytauto 6; Romuva, Laisvės 54; and Senasis Trestas, Mickevičiaus 8A. The Mykolas Žilinskas Art Gallery (see p.125) sometimes screens art movies.

Annual festivals and events

The most prestigious of the year's culture-fests is the **Pažaislis Music Festival** in July and August, when concerts featuring top classical performers from Lithuania and abroad are held in churches throughout the city centre and in the grounds of Pažaislis monastery – concerts held here are definitely worth attending if you have the chance. Information and tickets are available from Kaunas Philharmonic (see above).

The tourist office can provide details of other annual events: the **Kaunas Jazz Festival** brings together the best Lithuanian musicians and several international guests during the last week in April, while the **Kaunas Modern Dance Festival** attracts a broad spectrum of innovative groups from the Baltic region in early October. The **Days of Kaunas**, a city festival, held on a Saturday in mid-to-late May, culminates with a massive open-air pop concert on the Old Town's main square.

Listings

Airlines Air Lithuania, Kęstučio 69 ☎8-37/229706, ⊛www.airlithuania.lt. Flights from Kaunas to Oslo, Mälmo and Hamburg.
Car rental Budget, Savanorių 443A ☎8-37/490440, ⊛www.budget.lt; Litinterp, Gedimino 28-7 ☎8-37/228718, ⊛www.litinterp.lt.
Internet Kavinė Internetas, Vilniaus 26 ⊛www.cafenet.ot.lt.
Left luggage In the train station (daily 7am–7pm with a break for lunch).
Pharmacy Corner of Vytauto and Čiurlionio (open 24hr).
Post Office Laisvės alėja 102 (Mon–Fri 7am–7pm, Sat 7am–5pm).

Taxis Einesa ☎331 011 or Milvasa ☎1400.
Travel agents Baltic Clipper, Laisvės 61-1 (☎8-37/320300), sells international plane tickets; Mūsų Odisėja, M.K. Čiurliono 15 (☎8-37/408 410, ⊛www.tourinfo.lt), organizes coach trips and hotel reservations throughout Lithuania; Studentų kelionės, Kęstučio 57-4 (☎8-37/220552, ⊛www.studentukeliones.lt) deals in youth and student discount travel. Kautra, Laisvės 36 (☎8-37/209836, ⊛www.kautra.lt) and at the bus station (☎8-37/322222) sells long-distance and international bus tickets.

Outside Kaunas: Rumšiškės

Twenty kilometres east of Kaunas, just off the main Vilnius-bound highway, **RUM-ŠIŠKĖS** is an unremarkable modern village built to accomodate locals whose homes were submerged by the creation of the Kaunas Sea (see p.128). However, the rolling green countryside just outside provides a perfect setting for the open-air **Museum of Lithuanian Life** (Lietuvos liaudies buities muziejus; Easter–Oct Wed–Sun 10am–6pm; 6Lt), where approximately 150 original buildings – mostly from the nineteenth century – from all over Lithuania have been gathered together. Covering 175 hectares, it's a big site, and you'll need a couple of hours to do it justice – an English-language map (5Lt from the ticket office) will help you find your way around.

The buildings are arranged in four groups, each representing Lithuania's principal ethnographic areas, with – roughly at any rate – Aukštaitija to the north, Žemaitija to the south, Suvalkija to the west and Dzūkija somewhere in the middle. Each group of buildings is separated from the next by a couple of hundred metres of farmland or forest, making the whole ensemble perfect for a countryside stroll. Many of the farmhouse interiors reveal how self-sufficient rustic households had to be, with furniture and farm tools crafted by the man of the house during the long winters, and bedspreads – very often the only sign of colour in the wood-floored, wood-panelled rooms – woven or embroidered by the womenfolk. Despite the obvious harshness of nineteenth-century farming life, its re-creation here comes across as invitingly idyllic, with long Žemaitijan farmhouses groaning under vast overhanging thatched roofs, and horses grazing in the fields nearby. At the northern end of the museum, an octagonal wooden church, resembling a sail-less windmill, marks the approaches to an Aukštaitijan grid-plan village, its neat cottage gardens, porched houses and picket fences looking like an ideal piece of rural suburbia. Occupying a hill brow at the centre of the museum is the main street of a typical late-nineteenth-century town, its parallel rows of wooden buildings full of craft workshops where you can watch woodcarvers, ceramicists and weavers at work – they'll have some of their handicraft for sale here, too. You can pick up snacks and soft drinks at the town's *arbatinė* or "tea room".

The museum is closed throughout the winter except on the Sunday preceding **Shrove Tuesday** (Užgavėnės), when folklore enthusiasts dress up in mummers' costumes and burn an effigy known as the *morė* to mark the death of winter.

Practicalities

Rumšiškės is served by Kaunas–Vilnius **buses** (but not express minibuses), which pick up and drop off at the bus shelter on the main highway; from here it's a straightforward 25-minute walk south to the museum entrance. On the way you'll pass a small **tourist office** at S. Nėries 4-6 (June–Aug Mon–Fri 9am–5pm; ℡8-346/47247, ✉turinfo@takas.lt), which can organize **B&B accommodation** (❷) in Rumšiškės and surrounding villages. There's also a couple of family-run hotels at the western end of Rumšiškės: *Pas Poną*, Rumšos 33 (℡8-346/47631; ❸) is a café-bar and food store with simply furnished rooms above, while *Jolė*, Maironio 12 (℡8-346/47379; ❹) is slightly grander, with Sat-TV in the rooms and a dinky swimming pool on site.

Kėdainiai and around

An easy day-trip from Kaunas, or a pleasant stop-off en route to Panevėžys or Šiauliai, **KĖDAINIAI** is a 35,000-strong, semi-industrialized provincial centre. With its well-preserved churches of every denomination, a brace of surviving synagogues and an elegantly proportioned main square, Kėdainiai exudes the sense of cultural tolerance and taste for fine architecture that characterized the courtly culture of early-sixteenth-century Lithuania. It was then that this minor market town on the River Nevėžis became the property of the Calvinist branch of the Radvila family, who sought to utilize its money-earning potential as a stop-off on the Vilnius–Baltic Sea trade routes, while simultaneously turning it into an important focus of Protestant culture. It was hero of campaigns against the Swedes, Kristupas Radvila (son of Kristupas "the Thunderer" of Biržai; see p.113), who set the ball rolling, endowing Calvinist churches and encouraging merchants of various faiths to settle in the town, while his German-educated son Jonušas (who took first a Catholic, then an Orthodox wife in order to preserve his alliances with non-Protestant sections of the aristocracy) set up a printing press in the hope of weaning intellectuals away from Vilnius. However, this economic and cultural flowering was short-lived – Kėdainiai was repeatedly sacked during the Swedish-Russian wars of the 1650s, and didn't really recover until the late nineteenth century, by which time its importance as a processing point for the locally grown cucumber harvest had made it the pickled gherkin capital of the Baltics – a status it still enjoys. Kėdainiai is served by hourly **buses** from Kaunas and Panevėžys, and a handful from Vilnius and Šiauliai.

The Town

Kėdainiai's train station is at the northern end of town, but as this is only served by two Vilnius–Šiauliai services a day, you're more likely to arrive at the bus station, 2km to the southwest, on the town's main through road, **Basanavičiaus gatvė**. Head up Basanavičiaus and turn left into Didžioji to find the historic heart of town, a neat chequerboard of pre-twentieth-century buildings and post-war concrete cubes. You'll gain some idea of the town's past glories by visiting the **Kėdainiai District Museum**, an attractively arranged collection occupying a former Carmelite convent at Didžioji 19 (Tues–Sat 9am–5pm; 2Lt). Alongside portraits of sundry Radvilas and a case containing Kristupas Radvila's ceremonial sash, there's a model of Kėdainiai's main market square as it looked in its seventeenth-century heyday, made out of colourful clay houses that look like gaudily iced cakes. In the next room there's a pre-World War I photograph of the same square – so packed with horses and carts that it looks as if every peasant from central Lithuania came to trade here. Elsewhere there's a display of beautifully carved wooden crosses and a room full of nineteenth-century furniture made from antlers that has to be seen to be believed. Photographs crowding the walls of former convent cells include a snap of Nobel prize-winning author **Czesław Miłosz**, who was born to a Polish-speaking minor gentry family in Šeteniai, 15km northeast of town, on June 30, 1911 – he lived there for ten years before heading for High School in Vilnius. Winding lazily past his childhood home is the Nevėžis River, which, disguised by the name of Issa, was to crop up in his autobiographical fiction some fifty years later (see "Books"; p.434).

A couple of blocks east of the museum, the seventeenth-century **Reformed Church** (Reformatų bažnyčia; ask at the museum if it can be opened up for you; 2Lt) is the town's trademark edifice, a high-sided oblong with a pair of ice-cream-cone towers either side of the main portal. Begun under Kristupas Radvila and finished under Jonušas, it's a wonderful exercise in ascetic religious architecture, its light, lofty and only minimally decorated interior clearly designed to induce feelings of spiritual contemplation. The communists were so impressed by its spaciousness they turned the building into a basketball court. Now used for occasional services attended by a dwindling congregation of local Protestants, the church is mainly visited for the Radvila family vault which lies beneath the main altar. The grandest of the sarcophagi are a richly ornamented Baroque affair containing the remains of Jonušas Radvila and the next-door casket of his grandfather Kristupas "the Thunderer", embossed with suitably fearsome lions' heads. The smaller coffins, each mounted on balled feet as if intended to be periodically rearranged by a macabre interior designer, belong to Jonušas's four siblings, all of whom died in infancy.

Immediately east of the church lies the **Didžioji Rinka**, or Great Market, a broad, open space bordered by a sprinkling of old-ish buildings. Most eye-catching are the merchants' houses at the square's northern end, their brightly painted curvy gables looking like jellies at a childrens' party. Moving north from the Didžioji Rinka along Senoji gatvė brings you out onto another large square, **Senoji Rinka** or Old Market, once monopolized by the town's Jewish stall-holders. Encouraged to settle in the area by the Radvilas in the seventeenth century, Kėdainiai's Jewish community played a prominent role in the town's social and economic life until August 28, 1941, when the Nazis shot an estimated 2076 victims in one day. Two synagogues survive, standing end-to-end at the far side of the square. The larger of the two is now an arts school, while its smaller neighbour serves as the **Kėdainiai Multicultural Centre** (Daugiakultūris centras; Tues–Sat 10am–5pm; 2Lt), hosting seasonal exhibitions by contemporary artists and photographers. Whatever's on show, it's definitely worth having a peek at the spirit-soothing, light-blue interior, its ceiling held up by a quartet of spindly columns.

Returning to Basanavičiaus and heading north towards the train station brings you after fifteen minutes' walk or so to a leafy park sprawling along both banks of the Dotnuvėlė, a tributary of the Nevėžis. Spearing skywards on the north side of the river is the rather incongruous-looking **Kėdainiai Minaret**, a folly built by General Totleben, who lived in a manor house that stood nearby until its destruction in World War II. A veteran of the Russo-Turkish War of 1877–1878, when he commanded Tsarist armies in Bulgaria, Totleben considered it Russia's destiny to save the Near East from Ottoman misrule – and built this minaret in celebration of his big idea.

Practicalities

The **tourist office** at Didžioji 1 (Mon–Fri 9am–5pm; ☎8-347/60363, ⓦwww.kedainiai.ten.lt) can book you into a small number of rural **B&Bs** in the region. Nearest at hand is the *Lifosa*, 2km northeast of the centre just off the Panevėžys road at Šėtos 112 (☎8-347/68348; ④), a six-room guesthouse with showers and TVs in the rooms. Of the handful of **cafés** in the town centre, *Skaitykla*, Didžioji Rinka 11, offers a formidable choice of potato pancakes and riverside seating out the back, while *Ritmas*, Didžioji 44, offers a full range of tasty food and is also a relaxing place to drink – the pictures of Lithuanian rock bands plastered across the walls make you wish you knew more about the local music scene.

Dzūkija National Park

With its deep swathes of sandy-soiled pine forest punctuated by the occasional one-street village, the **Dzūkija National Park** (Dzūkijos nacionalinis parkas; ⓦwww.atostogos.lt/dzukijanp) is about as far away from urban Lithuania as you can get. This 56,000-hectare stretch of rolling terrain on the east bank of the River Nemunas has never been a major agricultural area, most of the population making a living from forestry, beekeeping, or gathering the berries, nuts and mushrooms for which the Dzūkijan woodland is famous. The local villages, sparsely inhabited by an ageing population, have preserved traditional features that elsewhere in the country can only be seen in ethnographic museums: timber houses adorned with intricate, filigree-effect window frames and gardens sporting boldly carved, wooden crosses topped with shrines or sun symbols. The forest itself is teeming with animal life: eagles, buzzards and woodpeckers inhabit the canopy, while elk, deer and wild boar root around among the lichens and ferns below.

There are two main routes into the region: the main Vilnius–Druskininkai road runs along the park's northern boundaries, passing through **Merkinė** en route, while the Vilnius–**Marcinkonys** rail line cuts through the more densely forested

southern section of the park. There are national park visitors' centres at both Merkinė and Marcinkonys – the latter is marginally better as a base for woodland walks and is also within striking distance of the **Čepkelių marshes**, a protected bog on the park's southern border.

One of the best ways to enjoy Dzūkija's woodland scenery is to **canoe** down the Nemunas tributaries, Merkys and Ūla, athough permits (available from the visitors' centre in Marcinkonys for a nominal fee) are required for the Ūla. You can only travel along national park-authorized itineraries, which are as follows: the half-day trip down the Merkys from Puvočiai to Merkinė, the one-day trip down the Ūla from Zervynos to Žiūrai, and the two-day trip down the Ūla from Zervynos to Puvočiai. Canoe rental (40Lt/day) and their transport to (and from) the river can be organized by the visitors' centre in Marcinkonys or the youth hostel in Zervynos.

A few village homestays and tent-pitching sites aside, the park doesn't offer a great deal in the way of **accommodation**, and most visitors end up staying just outside the park in Druskininkai (see p.138).

Approaching the park along the main Vilnius–Druskininkai highway, you'll notice a series of exquisitely carved roadside **shrine-poles** topped with all manner of faces and figures, which start just after Varėna, 82km out from the capital, and continue until well past Merkinė. They're based on themes contained in the Symbolist paintings and symphonic compositions of Mikalojus Konstantinis Čiurlionis (see p.124), who was born in Varėna and grew up in Druskininkai – the poles, sculpted by contemporary folk artists, were erected in 1976 to commemorate the centenary of his birth.

Merkinė and around

Twenty-five kilometres beyond Varėna, Vilnius–Druskininkai buses pick up and drop off at a dusty road junction at the eastern end of **MERKINĖ** – hardly the best of introductions to what turns out to be a neat country town of one-storey wooden dwellings and cottage gardens. There's a handful of incongruous concrete buildings on the main square, one of which houses the **National Park Vistors' Centre**, Vilniaus 3 (Mon–Fri 8am–noon & 1–5pm; ☏8-310/57245); it has a few basic maps for sale and also holds a display of handicrafts – notably the locally made, dark-earthenware pottery, traditionally fired in a log-fuelled hole in the ground rather than a conventional kiln. The craft is still practised in the villages north of Merkinė and most potters are eager to show visitors around their workshops providing that you arrange things through the visitors' centre first (best to give them a day or two's notice).

Opposite the information centre, a former Orthodox church now serves as the **Museum of Local Lore** (Merkinės kraštotyros muziejus; June–Sept Wed–Sun 11am–7pm; 2Lt), with wooden looms, spinning wheels and agricultural implements crammed into a junk-shop interior. Heading downhill along J. Bakšio, past the lipstick-bright Baroque facade of the Church of the Assumption soon brings you to the River Nemunas. Overlooking the north bank, a grassy **castle mound** (piliakalnis) was the site of a wooden stockade fort in the fourteenth century, an important link in a chain of fortifications protecting southern Lithuania from frequent incursions by the Teutonic Knights. Climbable via a wooden stairway, it's a great spot from which to contemplate the curve of the river and the grey-green forests beyond.

Practicalities

Accommodation around Merkinė is pretty meagre. The visitors' centre can organize B&B accommodation in a few local farmhouses, and there are tent-pitching sites without facilities on the far bank of the River Nemunas (cross the road bridge and turn right), and beside a pair of small lakes called Mergelės akelės ("little girls' eyes"), 2km east of town just off the Vilnius road. You can get **food and drink** from the supermarket on Merkinė's main square.

North of Merkinė

For a taste of the countryside around Merkinė your best bet is to head for the area of rolling pastureland and mixed coniferous and oak forest north of town. Despite a healthy sprinkling of farmsteads, the only real village is **SUBARTONYS**, 5km north, where an attractive collection of wooden houses lies scattered along a single street. One wooden-shuttered cottage in the centre of the village was the birthplace of writer **Vincas Krėvė Mickevičius** in 1882, and now houses an engaging **museum** (Vinco Krėvės Mickevičiaus muziejus; Wed–Sun 11am–4pm; 3Lt) packed with the wooden furnishings and simple household utensils that would have filled a house like this at the time of his childhood. The countryside around Subartonys featured strongly in Krėvė's verse epics and novels, which, full of sympathy for the historic sufferings of Lithuania and its toiling peasant population, were suffused with a sense of national mission. A towering cultural presence in the inter-war years, Krėvė became Lithuanian prime minister in the wake of Stalin's occupation of the country in June 1940 – after failing to extract any concessions from the Soviets, Krėvė fled to the USA, where he died in 1954.

The best way to get to Subartonys **by car** is to take the main Alytus road from Merkinė and turn left after 4km. **By foot** or bike, it's better to head up Kauno gatvė from Merkinė's main square and continue due north by dirt road.

Marcinkonys and around

If you want to get a flavour of life in Dzūkija's backwoods, then the mellow village of **MARCINKONYS** is on balance the best base for exploration, and with three trains a day from Vilnius, it makes an easy day-trip. If you're approaching by car, take the Vilnius–Druskininkai highway and turn off at either Varėna or Merkinė.

Marcinkonys is a narrow, two-kilometre-long village, built around a single street, Miškininkų gatvė, heading off north from the train station. After 100m or so it passes the **Ethnographic Museum** (Etnografinės muziejus; June–Sept Tues–Sat 9am–5pm; Oct–May Mon–Fri 11am–4pm; 2Lt), a wonderfully restored old farmhouse, packed with domestic utensils, hand-woven textiles and the kind of practical pine furniture that would command a high price in today's interior design stores. A barn on the opposite side of the farmyard displays craft items made by present-day Dzūkijans, including a cluster of traditional wooden distaffs carved with wheel-like sun motifs.

Another 800m up the main street, the **National Park Visitors' Centre** at Miškininkų 61 (Mon–Fri 9am–5pm; ☎8-310/44466) has a few Lithuanian-language leaflets and basic maps for sale, and can point you in the direction of worthwhile local walks. Continuing north along the main street brings you after another 1km to one of the most appealing wooden **parish churches** in the country, a twin-towered, canary-yellow building, overlooking a pine-shaded graveyard. About 400m east of the church lies **Gaidzų kopa**, one of the most impressive of the local dunes.

The easiest walk in the area – which can be done in full or in part – is the **Zackagiris Nature Path** (Zackagirio gamtinis takas), a thirteen-kilometre-long circuit that starts at the visitors' centre and loops through the forest on either side of the village. For a short fifty-minute walk, head west along the trail to enjoy a quiet waterside trek along the Grūda River, where several hives carved by beekeepers from living tree trunks can be seen. The eastern part of the circuit passes through thick pine forest growing on an undulating bed of sand dunes.

The visitors' centre can book you into a handful of rural homestays (❶–❷), although they're mostly well outside the village and you'll need your own transport to get around. **Accommodation** in Marcinkonys itself is provided by the *Eglė* just behind the visitors' centre, offering prim en-suites with TV and breakfast (☎8-310/44469; ❸). There's a tent-pitching site, with no facilities, beside Lake Kastionis (Kastinio ežeras), 1km northeast of the train station. *Kavinė po liepa* **café**, midway between the visitors' centre and the ethnographic museum, sells simple snacks and locally brewed Perloja beer.

Čepkelių bog

Five kilometres southeast of Marcinkonys, the area's trademark sandy-floored pine forest suddenly gives way to the soggy terrain and stunted plants of **Čepkelių bog** (Čepkelių raistas). Although lying just outside the boundaries of the Dzūkija National Park, the bog is a state-protected area into which you are strictly forbidden to wander. However, you can get as far as the reserve's northwestern corner, where paths bordering the bog afford good views of the Čepkelių landscape along the way. Bristling with heath plants, lichens and coniferous shrubs, it's a memorably stark spectacle. Keep still and you may catch sight of capercaillie strutting their way through the Čepkelių heather.

To get to the marshes, pick up the lane behind Marcinkonys train station and follow it southwest (ignoring a sign to the left reading "Čepkelių" after 800m – this simply leads to the reserve's administration office), a lovely walk through blissfully quiet forest. After 4km you arrive at a picnic spot and signboard that directs you to the edge of the bog.

The Ūla Valley

Running along the northeastern boundaries of the park, the **Ūla** is one of the park's most beautiful rivers, winding its way between sandy, tree-covered banks before emptying into the Merkys (which in turn joins the Nemunas at Merkinė). The most picturesque of the half-forgotten villages along its banks is

ZERVYNOS, 10km northeast of Marcinkonys and only one stop away on the train. As well as a wonderful collection of traditional timber buildings and a number of nearby forest trails, the village can boast a friendly **youth hostel** (mid-May to mid-Sept; ☎8-620/52720, ✆svirnelis@hotmail.com; 10Lt), offering dorm beds in a rustic, facility-free cabin. Meals are available for a few extra litai and the staff can arrange canoeing on the Ūla River.

Six kilometres northwest of Zervynos and 2km beyond the river's-edge village of Mančiagirė, a wooden stairway leads down from the main Merkinė-bound road to a lovely wood-shrouded stretch of riverbank. A signed path leads off from here to the tiny lake known as **Ūlos akis** ("Eye of the Ūla"), where hot springwater agitates the dark sand on the lake floor to create a bubbling-cauldron effect.

A further 3km down the road from Ūlos akis lies the invitingly sleepy village of **ŽIŪRAI**, full of traditional wooden houses, their window frames carved into swirls and arabesques. The walk between Žiūrai and Marcinkonys, a two-hour trot along logging roads, is as atmospheric a woodland trek as you'll find. Whether you attempt the whole trail or not, be sure to make a short detour to forest-engulfed **BIŽAI**, a tiny village, 1.5km due south of Žiūrai; it's only accessible by dirt track and has a compelling end-of-the-world feel.

Margionys and Musteika

Heading southwest from Marcinkonys along the Druskininkai road brings you after 10km to **MARGIONYS**, a pretty village famous for the funeral laments sung by the villagers around a bonfire on All Soul's Day. More importantly for the casual visitor, it stands at the southern end of the disarmingly beautiful valley of the Skroblus, a stream which S-bends its way through wildflower-laden meadows. The downstream stretches of the Skroblus are in an off-limits nature reserve and therefore not accessible, but the banks of the stream around Margionys and the hamlet of **KAPINIŠKĖS**, 1.5km north, are well worth a wander.

In the woods 9km south of the Marcinkonys–Druskininkai road, **MUSTEIKA** is one of the more traditional villages in the area, a nest of timber houses lurking behind grey-brown picket fences. Trails lead south of the village into a captivating landscape of forest and marshland, where you stand a good chance of seeing cranes, grouse and even elk.

Druskininkai

Lying just beyond the western boundaries of the Dzūkija National Park, the spa resort of **DRUSKININKAI** is a strange mixture of modern town and rural getaway, its concrete buildings set incongruously in thick pine forest. The name of the town comes from the Lithuanian for salt (*druska*), a reference to the mineral-rich spring waters to which the town owes its health-retreat reputation. As well as being used in all kinds of physiotherapy, the waters are used to treat ailments ranging from arthritis, to heart disease, bronchitis and asthma. Although the curative powers of the local waters had been well known to the locals for centuries (and King Stanisław August Poniatowski of Poland-Lithuania issued a decree recognizing this in 1794), Druskininkai's history as a spa really begins with the nineteenth-century craze for rest-cures. The first sanatorium was built here in 1838, and Druskininkai soon became the favoured summer retreat of Vilnius society – a status which to a large extent it still enjoys. During the Soviet period, when spa treatment was free to anyone who could talk a doctor into giving them the requisite sick-note, Druskininkai's sanatoria were receiving over 100,000 guests a year from all over the USSR. These numbers went into steep decline after the Soviet Union's collapse, but Druskininkai is still the health resort of choice for ailing Lithuanians, with tourists from nearby Poland forming the biggest foreign contingent.

Served by five daily **buses** and four express minibuses from Vilnius, Druskininkai is just about do-able as a day-trip from the capital, although you'll need a night or two

RESTAURANTS, CAFÉS & BARS

Alka	7
Dangaus Skliautas	2
Naminukas	6
Nostalgija	4
Šašlykinė pas Armenus	8
Sicilija	3
Širdelė	1
Švežios Bandelės	5

ACCOMMODATION

Dainava	A
Draugystė	F
Druspolis	G
Eglė	E
Galia	B
Galia II	C
Regina	D

DRUSKININKAI

to allow its uniquely soothing, forest-shrouded ambience to take effect. There's plenty to see in the immediate surroundings, with the collection of Soviet-era sculptures at **Gruto parkas** and the Baroque church at **Liškiava** both a short trip away.

Arrival, information and accommodation

Druskininkai's **bus station** lies a ten-minute walk south of the town centre at Gardino 1. The train station just beyond it is currently unused because the Vilnius–Druskininkai line – very popular in Soviet times – now runs through a corner of Belarus. The main **tourist office** is on the upstairs floor of the bus station building (℡8-313/51777, ⊛www.druskonis.lt), and they also operate an information booth on the corner of Dineikos and Čiurlionio. Both places can give you a free copy of the useful *Exploring Druskininkai* listings booklet and book you into B&B **accommodation** (**①**–**③**) in Druskininkai and outlying villages. There's a wide choice of hotels in Druskininkai, including plenty of sanatoria that cater for patients referred to the resort by Lithuania's health system, as well as tourists pure and simple – rooms are generally comfy and good value so don't be put off by the institutionalized air of some of these places. You can pitch a **tent** in the gardens of the Dainava and Eglė sanatoria (see overleaf).

There are plenty of marked bike trails leading out of town and into the forest: you can **rent bikes** at the Dainava and Eglė sanatoria or at a number of ad-hoc outlets around town – check the tourist office for latest details. Some of the sanatoria have fun indoor swimming pools: one of the best is at the *Belarus*, Maironio 5 (8Lt/hr for non-residents).

Hotels and guesthouses

Dainava Maironio 22 ☎8-313/59090, ⓦwww.centrasdainava.lt. Combined sanatorium, hotel and conference centre perfectly placed for the town centre. Standard en-suites come with old-style brown colour schemes but a few brighter, renovated doubles are available for a few extra litai. ❶–❷

Draugystė V. Krėvės 7 ☎8-313/52378, ⓦwww.is.lt/draugyste. Old-fashioned sanatorium ten minutes' walk east of the centre, with a grandiose colonnaded facade and lovingly tended flowerbeds out front. The seemingly endless corridors patrolled by white-coated staff can be quite atmospheric, and there's the usual mixture of simply furnished regular en-suites or smarter ones with TV. Big range of spa treatments and mud baths on site. ❶–❷

Druspolis Dineikos 9 ☎8-313/52886, ⓔdruspolis@email.lt. A small place occupying a historic wooden villa, with romantic, pointy-roofed exterior and lots of creaky floorboards inside.

Choice of simple rooms with WC/shower in the hallway, or cosy en-suites. ❶–❷

Eglė Eglės 11 ☎8-313/60222, ⓦwww.sanegle.lt. A huge ziggurat-shaped sanatorium on the eastern outskirts of town with plenty of wooded parkland on its doorstep. There's a choice of simple en-suites with Soviet-era furnishings, or modernized ones with TV. ❶–❸

Galia I Maironio 3 ☎8-313/60511, ⓦwww.is.lt/galia. Modernized rooms, good standards of service and an intimate feel in a centrally located villa. There's more of the same at *Galia II* and *Galia III*, round the corner at Dabintos 3 and 4 respectively. ❸

Regina T. Kosčiuškos 3 ☎8-313/59060, ⓦwww.regina.lt. The hotel of choice if you want top-quality accommodation in a central location. Rooms are decked out in warm colours, each featuring sizeable bathrooms with tubs. Snazzy suites ❼, regular doubles ❺

The Town

Although mostly made up of straight boulevards lined with modern buildings, Druskininkai can still muster some elegant reminders of the Tsarist era. There's a cluster of attractive wooden villas on or near **Laisvės aikštė**, a central roundabout where traffic trundles around the nineteenth-century **Orthodox Church** (Stačiatikių cerkvė) in the middle of the central reservation. Sprouting a forest of blue spires capped with purple-coloured domes, it's arguably the most extrovert building in the country. The interior, covered in what looks like Victorian wallpaper, conveys a strong sense of period.

Just south of here, at Šv Jokūbo 17, a one-storey house with intricately carved verandah screens now serves as the **Jacques Lipchitz Museum** (Žako Lipšico muziejus; Tues–Fri noon–5pm; 2Lt), honouring the Druskininkai-born Lithuanian-Jewish artist with a modest display of mementos and period furnishings, as well as photographs of Druskininkai's once-thriving Jewish community. Born in 1891 to a family of architects, Lipchitz attended art school in Vilnius before heading for Paris, where he lived in the so-called "Beehive" – a famously buzzing artists' colony that also included fellow emigrés from Russia's western provinces, Chaim Soutine and Marc Chagall. Lipchitz (1891–1973) made his name during World War I with a series of what he called "abstract architectural sculptures" – thrusting geometric forms which look like scale models of yet-to-be-built skyscrapers.

East of Laisvės aikštė, the pedestrianized Laisvės gatvė leads eastwards to the historical centre of the resort, where a frumpy collection of vaguely neoclassical spa buildings have been brightened up with the recent addition of an all-new **Pump Room** (gydykla; daily 8am–8pm). Its minimalist, marble-effect interior provides a suitably clinical ambience in which to sample one of two local spa waters, Dzūkija and Druskininkai – the latter has a higher mineral content and is especially effective in treating the digestive system (and also goes down a treat as a hangover cure). North of here lies a futuristic grey tangle of concrete buildings built in the 1970s to serve as a state-of-the-art spa treatment centre. A conspicuous casualty of the decline of Soviet health tourism after 1991, it's currently standing empty, though there are plans to transform it into a swimming pool and casino complex.

Heading south from the Pump Room along the flowerbed-lined **Vilniaus gatvė**, you come to the red-brick neo-Gothic **Church of the Virgin Mary of the Scapular** (Šv Mergelės Marijos Škaplierinės bažnyčia), before meeting up with Čiurlionio gatvė, which borders the kidney-shaped **Lake Druskonis**. Occupying a turreted belle époque holiday home known as the Villa Linksma ("Happy Villa"), the **Town Museum** (Miesto muziejus; Tues–Sun 11am–5pm; 2Lt) at Čiurlionio 78, displays a marvellous collection of engravings showing nineteenth-century spa-town life, alongside views of Druskininkai in old postcards.

A few doors down at Čiurlionio 35, the **M.K. Čiurlionis Memorial Museum** (M.K. Čiurlionis Memorialininis muziejus; Tues–Sun 11am–5pm; 3Lt) provides a fascinating insight into the life of the painter and composer (see box p.124) who spent his early years in Druskininkai, and returned every summer in adulthood to brainstorm and brood. These seasonal visits certainly made an impression on a young Jacques Lipchitz (see p.140), who recalled later that he would watch Čiurlionis "passing like a shadow, always in deep thoughts... and I would dream to be like him." The exhibition begins with a modern pavilion filled with sepia photographs of Čiurlionis and family; behind it, the pastel-painted wooden house purchased by Čiurlionis's piano-teacher father in 1896 is crammed with nineteenth-century domestic nick-nacks. The focus of attention in the parlour is the piano presented to Čiurlionis by his patron, the Count Ogiński, on the occasion of the former's graduation from the Warsaw Conservatoire in 1899. A second house immediately next door was purchased by the family so they could rent holiday flats to tourists, although one room was kept aside as Čiurlionis's summer studio, preserved pretty much as he left it, complete with easel, writing desk and a couple of his paintings – devotional works intended for the family home, they reveal nothing of the Symbolist style for which he's famous.

A few steps further west, the **Vytautas Kazimieras Jonynas Gallery** (Vytauto Kazimiero Jonyno galerija; Tues–Sun 11am–5pm) remembers the work of Vytautas Kazimieras Jonynas (1907–1997), another locally raised artist, who taught at Kaunas art school prior to World War II, designed stamps for the West German postal services in the late 1940s, and went on to create stained glass and devotional sculptures for Catholic churches throughout the USA. The gallery displays a broad cross-section of Jonynas's work in a succession of chic, light-filled spaces. From here you can descend to Lake Druskonis, where there are **rowing boats and pedaloes for rent**. On the far side of the lake, asphalted foot- and cycle-paths present plenty of opportunities for exploring the forest.

About 1.5km east of the town centre, the **Echo of the Forest** natural history museum (Girios Aidas) at Čiurlionio 102 (Wed–Sun 10am–6pm; 3Lt) occupies a purpose-built wooden house of almost fairy-tale appearance, with door posts in the form of giants and spindly balustrades carved into fir-branch shapes. It was constructed to replace an even odder original construction, which was suspended in the fork of a huge tree – both house and tree burned down in 1992. The museum is divided into sections, each devoted to a particular tree typical of the region, with a display of the tools and furnishings traditionally made from it and information on its animal and bird life – unsurprisingly there's a lot of stuffed pine martens. There are some live ponies and deer out the back.

Eating and drinking

Outside the hotels – most of which have dining halls serving up perfunctory meat-and-potatoes stodge – Druskininkai offers no more than a handful of dedicated restaurants. There's an increasing number of cafés and bars in the city centre, though, all of which serve food of some description. The following places are open daily till 11pm unless otherwise stated.

Alka Veisiejų 13B. A restaurant in a characterful wooden hut on the edge of the forest: a perfect place to combine lunch with a woodland walk. Traditional Lithuanian pork-chop fare, augmented with plenty of dishes based on the local mushrooms – delicious whether used as fillings for pancakes or served on their own.

Dangaus Skliautas Kurorto 6. A kooky café-bar with a wonderful terrace overlooking the River Nemunas, and late-night disco upstairs. Sun–Wed till midnight, Thurs–Sat till 2am.

Naminukas Druskininkų 3. An unassuming hut with a cosy wooden-furnished bar inside and dancing in the evenings. Till 1am.

Nostalgija Čiurlionio 55. A smart and roomy bar-restaurant with a full menu of hearty meat-based dishes and tempting salads. The terrace overlooking Lake Druskonis makes it a popular place for a daytime coffee or evening drink.

Šašlykine pas Armenus Čiurlionio 128. An

Armenian-run kebab house 2km out of town on the Vilnius road, offering grilled lamb by the skewer-load, accompanied by *lavaš* (Caucasian flat bread) in homely, unpretentious surroundings. Handily placed for Grūtas Park.

Sicilija Taikos 9. A café-restaurant in a chic modern pavilion serving up tasty thin-crust pizzas, as well as traditional Lithuanian stomach fillers – including some divine potato pancakes drenched in sour cream.

Širdelė Maironio 22. A rather old-fashioned café in a delightful wooden villa attatched to the Dainava sanatorium. Simple pork and chicken dishes, cheap prices, and a home-from-home atmosphere. Till 9pm.

Svežios bandelės Čiurlionio 63. A bakery-cum-café churning out fresh pastries with either savoury or sweet fillings. The perfect place for breakfast or a take-away snack. Till 7.30pm.

Entertainment

Piano recitals are given at the Čiurlionis Museum every Sunday in summer, with performers tinkling away indoors while the audience sit on benches in the garden, watching and listening through a large open window. There's also a **Violin Festival** (Smuiko muzikos festivalis), held at various venues in town, in late July/early August – contact the tourist office for details. The **Druskininkai Autumn Poetry Festival** (Poetinis Druskininkų ruduo) is a must for literati from all over the country – English-language writers are occasionally included in the programme.

Grūto parkas

Three kilometres northeast of Druskininkai on the Vilnius road, just outside the village of Grūtas, **Grūto parkas** ("Grūtas Park"; daily: May–Sept 9am–7pm; Oct–April 9am–5pm; 5Lt) is the last resting place for many of the Soviet-era statues which were uprooted from town squares all over the land in the days and weeks following the collapse of the Moscow Coup in August 1991. The park is the private initiative of mushroom magnate Viliumas Malinauskas, who has earned a fortune from exporting the local fungus since setting up shop here in the late 1980s. Malinauskas began buying up discarded Soviet-era statues in the mid-1990s, hoping to establish a park that would tell the story of Lithuania in the second half of the twentieth century. The fact that he also saw the collection as a commercial tourist attraction was, however, regarded as a sign of insensitivity to Lithuanian sufferings by many observers. Malinauskas's plan to include a train ride in cattle trucks similar to those used in the deportations of Lithuanians to Siberia in 1941 and 1949 had to be dropped when critics complained that he was creating a "Soviet disneyland". Officially opened in spring 2001, the park has swiftly become the number-one tourist draw in southern Lithuania – a status particularly valued by the hoteliers and restaurateurs of nearby Druskininkai, a town of which Malinauskas's son is currently mayor.

The park

Grūto parkas is an extensive site that takes a good hour to walk around, with the statues themselves scattered throughout a superbly laid-out park landscaped with shrubs and streams. Each statue is accompanied by a plaque in both Lithuanian and English explaining its significance, ensuring that the park functions both as enjoyable history lesson and plein-air sculpture gallery – not all Soviet-era statuary was as bad as you might think. Among the instantly recognizeable pieces on display here are a Stalin that once stood outside Vilnius railway station, and numerous Lenins in all shapes and sizes – including the one which dominated the capital's Lukiškių aikštė until ceremonially hauled away by crane in August 1991 (note the join just below the knee – the lower legs were sliced off by demonstrators unable to detach the statue from its pedestal). Look out, too, for the stern visage of Felix Dzerzhinsky, the Vilnius-educated Polish communist who founded the Cheka (forerunner of the KGB) in 1918, and has been something of a pin-up for secret policemen the world over ever since. There are also plenty of statues honouring specifically Lithuanian revolutionary heroes, including one of Vincas Mickevičius-Kapsukas, who led the short-lived Lithuanian Bolshevik dictatorship of 1919, and an ensemble piece depicting Požela, Greifendingeris, Giedrys and Čarna – the underground communist leaders who were shot in Kaunas in 1926 and commemorated with this angular monument some fifty years later. In the middle of the park stands a projection hall where you can watch boy-meets-tractor propaganda films and examine a range of old photographs, newspapers and agit-prop posters – including one with a primary-school slogan that reads "Love the Party, child, as you love your own mother!"

Liškiava

Perched on a bluff overlooking the River Nemunas, **LIŠKIAVA** occupies the extreme western corner of the Dzūkija National Park. Its main draw is the eighteenth-century **Church of the Holy Trinity** (Šv trejybės bažnyčia), a pastel-pink structure crowned by a stately grey-green dome, built to serve a now defunct Dominican monastery. The interior is one of the few examples of the florid rococo style in Lithuania, with swirling ceiling frescoes overlooking a show-stopping line-up of seven gilded altars, each decorated with expressive statues. Once you've seen this you can tour the remains of a nearby fourteenth-century hill fort, commanding views of the majestic sweep of the river.

Liškiava is usually approached from the Druskininkai direction – from where it's an easy nine-kilometre bus or cycle ride along the riverbank. It's also the target of popular river cruises, which set off from a jetty just east of Druskininkai town centre every afternoon in season (June–Sept; timings and tickets from the tourist office).

Šiauliai and around

Although **ŠIAULIAI** (pronounced "Shyow-ley") is Lithuania's fourth-largest city and the administrative centre of the northwest, its historical origins remain something of a mystery. It's thought to have taken its name from a battle fought hereabouts in 1236 and known in German chronicles as the Battle of the Sun ("Saulės mūšis" in Lithuanian), when a Lithuanian-Žemaitijan army inflicted such a crushing blow on the Knights of The Sword that the Germanic crusaders thought twice about ever invading Lithuania again. Certainly by the mid-sixteenth century, Šiauliai had established itself as an important market town mid-way along the Königsberg–Rīga road – a position which also facilitated the arrival of successive waves of Swedish and Russian invaders. Emerging as a handsome and prosperous provincial centre under the Tsarist Empire, Šiauliai was so pummelled by Soviet artillery in World War II that it had to be almost completely rebuilt in the aftermath, and today's grid-iron of concrete buildings is the result. However, there's an enjoyable clutch of **off-beat museums** to explore, and one of Lithuania's most important cult sights, the **Hill of Crosses**, lies just beyond the northern outskirts. The city also serves as a convenient stepping-stone if you're journeying west towards the Žemaitija National Park (see p.166) and the Baltic coast. **Trains** on the Vilnius–Klaipėda line pass through Šiauliai twice a day, and there are plenty of **buses** from Vilnius, Kaunas, Panevėžys and Rīga.

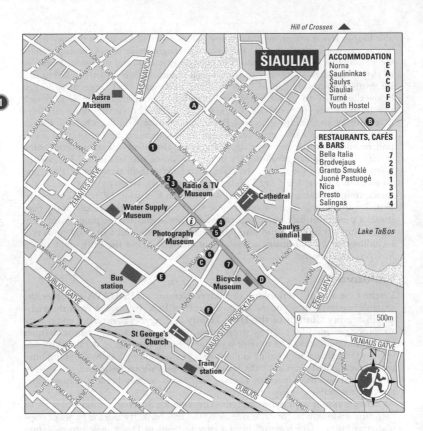

Hill of Crosses

ŠIAULIAI

ACCOMMODATION	
Norna	E
Šaulininkas	A
Šaulys	C
Šiauliai	D
Turnė	F
Youth Hostel	B

RESTAURANTS, CAFÉS & BARS	
Bella Italia	7
Brodvejaus	2
Granto Smuklė	6
Juonė Pastuogė	1
Nica	3
Presto	5
Salingas	4

Aušra Museum

Radio & TV Museum

Cathedral

Water Supply Museum

Photography Museum

Šaulys sundial

Lake Talšos

Bus station

Bicycle Museum

St George's Church

Train station

0 — 500m

N

Arrival, information and accommodation

Šiauliai's main points of reference are the dead-straight Tilžės gatvė, which slices through the town on a northeast–southwest axis, and the pedestrianized Vilniaus gatvė, which cuts across Tilžeš at right angles. The bus station is on Tilžės, about 500m southwest of Vilniaus, while the train station is slightly further out in the same direction, at the southwestern end of Draugystės prospektas. The **tourist office**, Vilniaus 213 (Tues–Fri 9am–6pm, Sat 10am–5pm, Sun 10am–4pm; ☎8-41/521105, ⊛www.siauliai.lt), can sell you a town map and reserve accommodation on your behalf. The town has a **youth hostel** (☎8-41/523992; 18Lt per person), located at Rygos 36; it's clean, though basic and there are no English-speaking staff.

Norna Tilžės 126C ☎8-41/429326. A handful of smartish en-suites above a parade of downtown shops. Handy for the bus station. ❸

Šaulininkas Lukausko 5A ☎8-41/436555, ⓔsaulinink@splius.lt. A medium-sized place on a quiet residential street opposite a park, offering a mixed bag of rooms with Sat-TV and shower. ❸

Šaulys Vasario 16-osios 40 ☎8-41/520812, ⊛www.saulys.lt. The swankiest place to stay in

town by a long chalk, with plush carpets and bathtubs in every room – although the slime-green colour scheme might be a bit much to take after a night on the tiles. Luxury apartments ❼, regular doubles ❺

Šiauliai Draugystės 25 ☎8-41/437333. Grey, multistorey monument to Soviet-era tourism, currently undergoing a slow process of renovation. Drab en-suites on the lower floors, pricier, thick-carpeted rooms with TV further up. Great views of the city from the west-facing side of the building.

①–**②**

Turnė Rūdės 9 ☎ 8-41/500150, ⓦ www.turne.lt.
Central, but on a reasonably quiet street, this is a

modern hotel with an intimate feel and attentive
staff. Simply furnished en-suites in muted greens
and pinks. **④**

The City

Explorations of Šiauliai inevitably start with flagstoned **Vilniaus gatvė**, the prime
venue for daytime shopping and the place where everyone wants to see and be seen
in the evening. There's an unusual array of museums along its length, starting at its
southeastern end with the **Bicycle Museum** at no. 139 (Dviračių muziejus;
Tues–Fri 9am–5pm, Sat 11am–4pm; 3Lt), which offers an entertaining round-up of
two-wheeled transport throughout the ages, including just about every model ever
produced by the local Vairas factory. Formed in 1948, Vairas was the USSR's leading
manufacturer of trendy chopper-style bikes for kids in the 1970s, and nowadays
churns out thousands of mountain and racing bikes a year, the bulk of which are
bound for export.

At Vilniaus 140, the **Photography Museum**, (Fotografijos muziejus; Tues–Fri
10am–6pm, Sat 11am–4pm; 3Lt), has an impressive collection of cameras through
the ages and a thorough round-up of the work of famous Lithuanian-based photographers, beginning with Józef Czechowitz's pioneering pictures of Vilnius in
the 1870s. The seasonal exhibitions of contemporary work hosted by the museum's first-floor gallery are usually of the highest quality. A few doors down, the
Radio and Television Museum at no. 174 (Radijo ir televizijos muziejus;
Tues–Fri 10am–6pm, Sat 11am–4pm; 3Lt) was inaugurated to celebrate the output
of local TV firm Tauras, although there's a lot else here besides, from old record
players with enormous horns, to Art Deco radiograms from the inter-war years,
and – if you needed proof that consumer-oriented gimmickry wasn't entirely a
Western invention – a portable radio in the form of a toy robot, made by a Rīga
firm in 1980.

A block away to the northeast, the gloomy corridors of the **Aušra Museum**,
Aušros 47 (Aušros muziejus; Tues–Fri 9am–5pm, Sat 11am–4pm; 3Lt), are enlivened
by a colourful display of folk costume from all over the country and a powerful collection of traditional sculpture, including a crowd of stern-faced saints and a riveting pietà. Down at the southeastern end of Aušros, the junction with Tilžės gatvė is
dominated by the **Cathedral of SS Peter and Paul**. Built in 1625, it burned
down along with just about everything else in the city in 1944. The current edifice
dates from 1954, but is a faithful replica of the original, with a single white belfry
(Lithuania's highest) rising up beside a supporting cast of tiny turrets – suggesting
that it was originally intended as a fortified church capable of withstanding attacks
by Swedes or Russians. Inside, all is light and purity, with a balustraded gallery overlooking a white-painted interior.

A short eastbound stroll along Aušros takas will bring you face to face with the
Archer (Šaulys), a gilded, bow-wielding statue on top of a twenty-metre-high concrete pillar. Built in 1986 to celebrate the 750th anniversary of the Battle of Saulė,
the monument also functions as a huge sundial – the flagstoned expanse beneath it
is marked out with lines denoting the hours of the day.

The sight that stands out in the streets southwest of Vilniaus is the elegantly
tapering, red-brick cylinder of the **Water Supply Museum** at Vytauto 103
(Mon–Fri 8am–noon & 1–5pm; 2Lt). A former storage tower dating from the
early twentieth century, when a public water supply was first plumbed in, the
building contains photographs of Šiauliai, old and new. A couple of blocks northwest, the **Venclauskis House** at Vytauto 89 (Venclauskių namai; Tues–Fri
9am–5pm, Sat 11am–4pm; 3Lt) was the home of a prominent nineteenth-century
lawyer and art collector, and now houses a huge collection of furniture and
porcelain.

Eating and drinking

Vilniaus gatvė and the streets abutting it hold most of the eating and drinking places. The establishments along this strip have a tendency to go in and out of fashion at an alarming speed, but at least there are plenty of places to choose from.

Bella Italia Vilniaus 167. A bright, roomy café-pizzeria, with a palatable range of thin-crust pies, sizeable salads and a full range of drinks.

Brodvėjaus Vilniaus 146. A comfortable bar-restaurant on the ground level, serving up a reliable spread of mainstream meat-and-potato dishes, and a funkier, cushion-strewn bar in the basement.

Granto Smuklė Višinskio 41. A roomy basement pub with traditional Lithuanian food on the menu, attracting a wide cross-section of locals.

Juonė Pastuogė Aušros 31A. A big, wooden-benched, beer-swilling and pork-chop-munching venue, with live bands purveying Lithuanian pop-folk and country-and-western covers.

Nica Vilniaus 146. Ideal for a daytime breather, with good coffee, pastries and ice cream.

Presto Cnr of Vilniaus and Vasario 16-osios. Fancy teas, superb cakes, and soups-of-the-day chalked up on a board at lunchtime.

Salingas Tilžės 168. Passable Chinese food in an intimate basement restaurant.

Hill of Crosses

Twelve kilometres north of Šiauliai, just off the main road to Rīga, the **Hill of Crosses** (Kryžų kalnas) sums up the Lithuanian character more than any other single sight in the country. Combining evidence of profound Catholic piety, a deep appreciation for the simple forms of folk art and a fondness for contemplating the mysterious, it's a genuinely unique and strange attraction, and one that you should on no account leave out of your itinerary.

Like many similar mounds dotting the Lithuanian countryside, the hill may have been associated with various forms of ancestor worship in the pre-Christian era, evolving naturally (with pagan totems replaced by crosses) as the centuries wore on. Tradition maintains that the rebellions of 1831 and 1863 – and the need to commemorate the fallen in some way – was what turned the hill into a major focus of remembrance, with locals planting crosses out here in the countryside because the Tsarist authorities wouldn't have tolerated such an open display of national sentiment in an urban setting. It was certainly known as a focus of patriotic pilgrimage by the 1950s, when another round of cross-planting was undertaken by Lithuanians keen to preserve the memory of those who had died or disappeared as a result of the mass deportations to Siberia. Determined to discourage any further manifestations of religious or patriotic sentiment, the Soviet authorities had the site bulldozed repeatedly in the 1960s – each time, the locals responded by planting new crosses. A visit by Pope John Paul II in September 1993 helped to propel the hill into the premier league of pilgrimage destinations, with the construction of a brand-new Fransiscan monastery just north of the site in 2001 serving to underline the place's growing spiritual stature.

Getting to the hill is fairly easy. If you're driving, head out of town on the Rīga road and turn right when you see the sign for Kryžų kalnas about 6km beyond the city limits. By bus, seven daily Šiauliai–Joniškis services and four daily Šiauliai–Rīga services drop off and pick up right beside the Kryžų kalnas turn-off, from where it's a two-kilometre walk to the hill itself – Šiauliai tourist office might be a more reliable source of English language timetable information than the bus station.

The hill

Approaching the hill along an avenue of lime trees, it's initially difficult to work out what the bristling brown mass rising out of the flat green landscape actually is. It's only when you hit the coach-packed car park that you begin to pick out individual pilgrims and the strange collection of monuments they've come to visit. A cross presented by the Pope stands at the foot of the hill, its base inscribed with the words "Thank you Lithuanians for this Hill of Crosses, which testifies to the nations of Europe and the whole world the faith of the people of this land." Behind it, a towering wooden statue of Jesus, arms outstretched, seems to be ushering pilgrims onto the hill itself. More of a mound than a hill, it's an undeniably impressive site, with every inch of ground planted with crosses of every conceivable size. There are even tiny crosses hanging by metal chains around the crosspieces of the larger ones – the jangling sound they all make when the wind gets up is unearthly indeed. Among the crosses are some marvellous examples of Lithuanian woodcarving, with totem-like pillars adorned with images of various saints, and numerous examples of the Rupintojėlis, or Sorrowful Christ.

Travel details

Buses

Anykščiai to: Biržai (1 daily; 2hr); Kaunas (10 daily; 2hr 30min), Panevėžys (8 daily; 1hr); Vilnius (Mon–Thurs & Sat 4 daily; Fri & Sun 5 daily; 2hr 30min).

Kaunas to: Anykščiai (10 daily; 2hr 30min); Biržai (3 daily; 3hr 30min); Klaipėda (12 daily; 3hr 30min); Kėdainiai (hourly; 1hr); Panevėžys (13 daily; 2hr 30min); Šiauliai (7 daily; 2hr 30min); Vilnius (every 15–30min; 1hr 30min).

Kėdainiai to: Biržai (4 daily; 3hr 30min); Kaunas (hourly; 1hr); Panevėžys (12 daily; 1hr 20min); Šiauliai (8 daily; 1hr 30min); Vilnius (3 daily; 2hr 20min).

Panevėžys to: Anykščiai (8 daily; 1hr); Biržai (16; 1hr 20min); Kaunas (13 daily; 2hr 30min); Kėdainiai (13 daily; 1hr 20min); Šiauliai (11 daily; 2hr).

Šiauliai to: Panevėžys (11 daily; 2hr)

Trains

Kaunas to: Klaipėda (2 daily; 6hr); Vilnius (12 daily; 1hr 30min).

Vilnius to: Ignalina (6 daily; 2hr); Marcinkonys (3 daily; 2hr); Šiauliai (2 daily; 4hr); Zervynos (3 daily; 1hr 50min).

International buses

Kaunas to: Rīga (3 daily; 5hr 20min).

Šiauliai to: Rīga (4 daily; 3hr 15min).

1.3
Western Lithuania

The undulating landscape of forests and lakes that characterizes much of western Lithuania rolls all the way to the Baltic Sea, where it culminates in a golden ribbon of sand backed by fragrant pines. With its seemingly limitless stretches of beach, towering dunes and church-topped hills, this part of Lithuania incorporates many of the country's most characteristic holiday-postcard images and is one of its most visited areas. The presence of a thriving resort culture along the seaboard ensures that there's plenty in the way of accommodation and entertainment, although you're never too far away from semi-abandoned beaches and tranquil, woodland paths. Strong folk art traditions survive in the villages: wooden farmsteads and fishermen's cottages sport intricately carved gables (the twin horse-head motif known as the *žirgelis* being one of the most typical designs), while totemic shrine-poles topped with statues of saints are commonly seen in gardens.

The region's unofficial capital is **Klaipėda**, a work-hard-play-hard port city with a medieval, German-flavoured Old Town at its heart. A short ferry ride away lies the **Curonian Spit** (also known as Neringa), an offshore bar of sand boasting dense pine forests, rippling sand dunes and picturesque fishing villages, of which **Nida** is the most celebrated. Completely different in atmosphere is **Palanga**, just north of Klaipėda, a candyfloss-and-cocktails beach resort popular with families and fun-seeking youngsters in equal measure. The main attraction inland is the **Žemaitija National Park**, where you can enjoy boating on tranquil Lake Plateliai or walking and cycling around the region's pretty villages.

Getting to the coast **by road** involves a less than inspiring 275-kilometre journey (4–5hr by bus) along the Vilnius–Kaunas–Klaipėda highway, a dual carriageway that passes through an unchanging landscape of arable fields and pasture. The Vilnius–Klaipėda **rail line** loops northwards via Šiauliai and takes marginally longer; it also passes through **Plungė**, the main gateway to the Žemaitija National Park.

Some history: Žemaitijans, Curonians and Prussians

Western Lithuania is made up of two distinct areas: **Žemaitija** (sometimes called Samogitia in western sources), which covers the rolling terrain in the northwestern corner of the country, and **Lithuania Minor** (Mažoji Lietuva), comprising the lowlands around the Nemunas estuary in the southwest and the whole of the coastal strip. Žemaitija is named after the Žemaitijans, one of the original tribes that came to the Baltic around four thousand years ago, providing the ethnic bedrock from which the Lithuanian nation emerged. The Žemaitijans held on to their tribal identity much longer than other Lithuanians, however, remaining independent of the medieval Lithuanian state that came into being in the thirteenth century. They joined Lithuanian ruler Mindaugas in defeating the Teutonic Knights at Šiauliai in 1236, but remained only loosely allied to Lithuania until the fifteenth century, when they were formally absorbed into the Grand Duchy. They missed out on Lithuania's conversion to Christianity in 1389, remaining pagan for a further half century – as a result, Žemaitija is still regarded as a repository of ancient, pre-Christian, Lithuanian traditions.

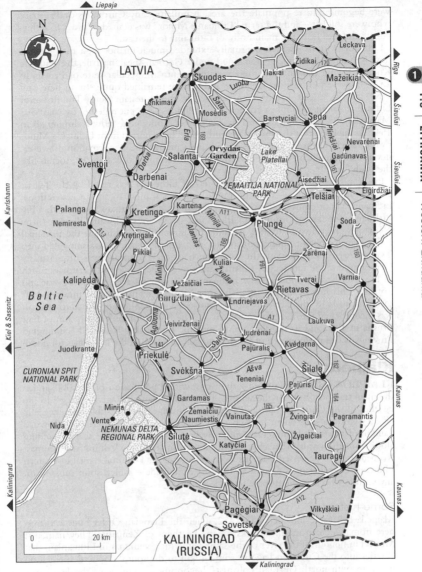

In the southwest were two other Baltic tribes: the Curonians (Kurši) on the coast and Prussians (Prusai) on the banks of the Nemunas River. Both of these peoples were conquered by the Teutonic Knights in the thirteenth century and were either exterminated or driven into exile (the name "Prussia" survived though as a geographical label). The Teutons deliberately turned the whole of the seaboard into a wasteland, believing that this would deter attacks by the Žemaitijans and Lithuanians. By the fifteenth century, however, peasants from all over Lithuania were beginning to re-populate the area, assimilating any Curonians or Prussians who were still left – and the term "Lithuania Minor" was coined in order to differentiate this area from the main body of Lithuania to the east.

Lithuania Minor – which originally extended much further west into what is now Kaliningrad Province – remained under German-speaking rule, the Teutonic Knights having transformed their territories into the secular state of Prussia in 1525. However, Lithuanian language and culture remained quite strong here, and was – initially at least – actively encouraged by the Protestant clergy. The first-ever Lithuanian-language book, a collection of religious texts put together by Martynas Mažvydas, was published in the Prussian city of Königsberg (now Kaliningrad) in 1547, in the hope that the Protestant faith could be exported from Lithuania Minor to the largely Catholic populace of Lithuania proper; the Reformation, however, never really caught on here, despite the Calvinist leanings of leading aristocrats like the Radvilas.

In the nineteenth century, when the rest of Lithuania was ruled by the Tsarist Empire and Lithuanian-language publishing was subject to severe restrictions, Lithuania Minor enjoyed comparative cultural freedom. Prussian towns with a big Lithuanian-speaking population like Tilsit (now Sovyetsk) and Ragnit (now Neman) were a hive of literary activity, and it was from Tilsit that the principal Lithuanian nationalist publication of the era, *Aušra* ("Dawn"), was smuggled into Tsarist territory. However, the area south of the Nemunas was increasingly Germanized as the nineteenth century drew to a close, while the territories north of the river became more solidly Lithuanian – a process accentuated by war and politics. This northern half of Lithuania Minor became part of independent Lithuania in 1918 (the city of Klaipėda was added in 1923), while the southern half was incorporated into German East Prussia. The Soviet Union's absorption of East Prussia in 1945 and its transformation into the thoroughly Russified Kaliningrad Province ended the presence of Lithuanian culture south of the Nemunas for good.

Klaipėda

KLAIPĖDA is Lithuania's third-largest city, with a population of 200,000, and is the main transport hub for the whole of the Lithuanian coast, giving access to the beaches of the Curonian Spit and Palanga. A small, easily digestible, yet energetic city, it's worth a stop-off in its own right, thanks to an atmospheric Old Town, a handful of worthwhile museums and a lively year-round nightlife scene. Standing aloof from the rivalry that characterizes relations between Vilnius and Kaunas, Klaipėda is a self-possessed place, its role as economic and cultural capital of western Lithuania engendering a certain amount of civic pride – which soon rubs off on any visitors who take the trouble to stick around.

Some history

Klaipėda first came into being in 1252, when the Livonian Order built a fortress here from which to mount attacks on the heathens of Žemaitija. They named it **Memel** in honour of the river of the same name (the Nemunas in Lithuanian) that empties into the Curonian Lagoon some 40km to the south. The settlement soon filled up with north German colonists, becoming a member of the Hanseatic League and an important centre for the export of Lithuanian timber. Despite a brief spell as the capital of Prussia in 1806, when the court of Frederick Wilhelm III was penned in here by Napoleon's armies, Memel's real period in the political limelight didn't come until the end of World War I when, evacuated by German troops, it was claimed by the newly independent state of Lithuania. Although surrounded by Lithuanian-speaking villages, the city itself was predominantly German, and the Great Powers assembled at the Paris Peace Conference didn't really know what to do with it. The French troops sent to garrison it turned a blind eye when the Lithuanians took matters into their own hands, seizing Memel by force in January,

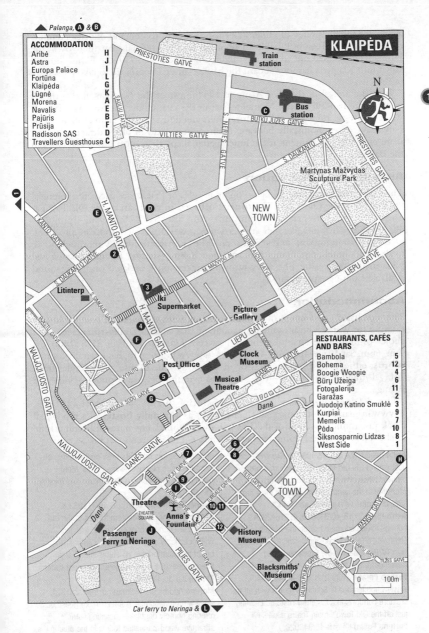

Palanga, **A** & **B**

KLAIPĖDA

Train station

Bus station

Martynas Mažvydas
Sculpture Park

NEW TOWN

Litinterp

Iki Supermarket

Picture Gallery

Clock Museum

Post Office

Musical Theatre

OLD TOWN

Theatre

Anna's Fountain

History Museum

Passenger Ferry to Neringa

Blacksmiths' Museum

0   100m

Car ferry to Neringa & **L**

1923. The Lithuanians had already lost Vilnius to the Poles, and many in the international community saw their smash-and-grab raid on Memel as some form of compensation.

Renamed Klaipėda, the city retained its German population, and both German and Lithuanian were the official languages in local government. The two communities got on reasonably well until the 1930s, when local Nazis – emboldened by the aggressive foreign policy of Hitler's Germany – began to demand the city's reunification with the Reich. Unable to stand up to the Germans on their own, the Lithuanians decided not to put up a fight. On March 23, 1939, the Führer himself sailed into Klaipėda harbour aboard the battle cruiser *Deutschland* to take possession of the city.

With the arrival of the Red Army in 1944, most of the Germans fled – there's now a mere handful of true Memelites left in the city. Under the Soviets, Klaipėda was a strategic port city which foreigners needed special permission to visit. Nowadays, an economically buoyant, cosmopolitan kind of place attracting its fair share of foreign investment, it's in much better shape than most provincial cities in the Baltics.

Arrival and information

The **train and bus stations** lie on opposite sides of Priestoties gatvė, ten minutes' walk north of the Old Town. The **tourist office** is in the heart of the Old Town at Turgaus 5/7 (Mon–Fri 9am–6pm; June–Aug also Sat & Sun 9am–3pm; ☎8-46/412186, ✆tic@one.lt); staff are particularly well informed and can also book accommodation for you. *In Your Pocket* publishes a characteristically thorough guide to the city's hotels, restaurants, bars and shops (also including Kaunas, Palanga and Nida in the same issue; 8Lt; ⚈www.inyourpocket.com), updated once a year and available from newspaper kiosks.

Accommodation

The city has a good range of accommodation, with a couple of swanky **hotels** catering for Western businessmen, a handful of characterful, family-run places and a choice of mid-range establishments in between. *Litinterp*, Šimkaus 21/8 (Mon–Fri 9am–6pm, Sat 10am–4pm; ☎8-46/411814, ⚈www.litinterp.lt), has centrally located **rooms**, either with local families or in their own guesthouse, with singles from 70Lt, doubles from 100Lt – they can also arrange private rooms in Nida and Palanga.

The *Klaipėda Travellers' Guesthouse*, Butkų Juzės 7-4 (☎8-46/211879, ⚈www.lithuanianhostels.org; 32Lt per person), is a friendly **hostel** in a residential block just round the back of the bus station. Cramped, but neat, and with a little kitchen, it's a bit like sleeping over at a friend's flat. It also rents out bikes.

Aribė Bangų 17A ☎8-46/490940, ⚈www.aribe.lt. Just east of the Old Town, this medium-sized, modern place offers both affordability and proximity to the centre. Rooms are on the simple side, but come with shower and TV. ❹

Astra Pilies 2 ☎8-46/313849, ✆216420. A boring-looking concrete box on the fringes of the Old Town, offering surprisingly swanky en-suites with TV. Right next to the Smyltinė-bound passenger ferry. ❺

Europa Palace Žvejų 21/1 ☎8-46/404444, ⚈www.hoteleuropa.lt. Spacious rooms with all the creature comforts in a tastefully restored building just off the Old Town's main Teatro aikštė. ❼

Fortųna Poilsio 64 ☎8-46/348028, ⚈www.fortuna.lt. A small pension 4km south of the centre, with cosy en-suite rooms and friendly, attentive staff. Best booked in advance. Suites ❺, regular doubles ❸

Klaipėda Naujoji Sodo 1 ☎8-46/404372, ⚈www.klaipedahotel.lt. Another hotel that shouldn't be judged by its exterior, this red-brick lump harbours classy en-suite rooms. More expensive rooms come with bathtubs and minibar. ❹–❺

Lūgnė Galinio pylimo 16 ☎8-46/411883 & 411884. On the southeastern fringes of the Old Town, the *Lūgnė* is grey on the outside, but unimpeachably chic on the inside, with smart, bright and comfortable en-suites aimed at an international business clientele. Two-room suites ❺, regular doubles ❸

Morena Audros 8A, Melnragė ☎8-46/351314, ⚈www.morenahotel.lt. A fifteen-room guesthouse, offering homely doubles – including some attractive wood-pannelled rooms in the attic in the beachside suburb of Melnragė 4km northwest of town. Minibus #4 or #6 from the centre. ❹

Navalis Manto 23 ☎8-46/404200, ⚈www.navalis.lt. Business-class comforts in a medium-sized, charmingly intimate place, housed in a handsome, nineteenth-century building.

Handily located midway between train/bus stations and the Old Town. **⑥**
Pajūris Šlaito 18A, Giruliai ☎8-46/490154, ⓦwww.pajuris.lt. A nicely refurbished Soviet-era place within easy reach of sandy beaches, 8km north of town. Unfussy en-suites with TV, and a small indoor pool. **❸**
Prūsija Šimkaus 6 ☎8-46/412081. A family-run pension offering cosy little en-suites with colour-clash decor, most of which come with a simple TV. Only eight rooms, so arrive early or ring in advance. **❹**
Radisson SAS Šiaulių 28 ☎8-46/490800, ⓦwww.radissonsas.com. Ten minutes' walk north of the centre, with comfortable, modern, well-equipped rooms decorated in a vaguely nautical theme. **❼**

The City

Tucked into the right angle formed by the River Danė and the Curonian Lagoon, Klaipėda's **Old Town** (Senamiestis) boasts the kind of cobbled streets and half-timbered houses reminiscent of a provincial German town – which is essentially what Klaipėda was until 1944. Many of the buildings, however, were damaged in World War II and rebuilt in not-quite-authentic style, giving the centre a rather untidy, fragmented air. The medieval, grid-iron street plan still survives though, and reminders of the trades once practised here live on in street names such as Kalvių (Blacksmiths'), Kurpių (Cobblers') and Vežėjų (Carters').

At the heart of the Old Town is cobbled **Theatre Square** (Teatro aikštė) named after the ornate neoclassical theatre on its northern side. Hitler spoke from the balcony in March 1939 after Germany annexed Klaipėda in its last act of territorial aggrandizement before the outbreak of war. In front of the theatre is **Anna's Fountain** (Anikės fontanas), a replica of a famous prewar monument to the German poet Simon Dach (1605–1659), depicting the heroine of his folksong, *Ännchen von Tharau.*

Southeast of the square, at Didžioji vandens 6, the **History Museum of Lithuania Minor** (Mažosios Lietuvos istorijos muziejus; Wed–Sun 11am–7pm; 3Lt) presents a comprehensive chronological account of the region's history, including plenty of archeological interest, notably a scale model of a Lithuanian pagan sanctuary which once occupied Birutė's hill, a well-known landmark in nearby Palanga (see p.163). The arrangement of the sanctuary reveals a high degree of astronomical knowledge, with the placing of totem-like poles dictated by the positions of the planets throughout the year, and the main axis of the ensemble aligned with the rays of the setting sun on April 23. The later, Christianized inhabitants of Lithuania Minor were obviously a sober, serious-minded bunch if the costumes on display here are anything to go by – greys and blacks predominate, with delicately embroidered belt-purses providing the only splash of colour. Finally, look out for photographs of Lithuania's seizure of Klaipėda in 1923, and a 1939 snap of Adolf Hitler riding down Manto gatvė in a motorcade, greeted by ranks of local brown-shirts.

Nearby at Šaltakalvių 2 is the **Blacksmiths' Museum of Lithuania Minor** (Mažosios Lietuvos kalvystės muziejus; Wed–Sun 11am–7pm; 3Lt), the main attraction of which is a functioning forge where you can observe the smiths at work. There's also a substantial display of wrought-iron work, a traditional Lithuanian folk art form, including some ornate weathercocks and graveyard crosses.

The principal artery of the **New Town** (Naujamiestis), on the northern side of the Danė, is the shop- and café-lined **Manto gatvė**, which heads north in the general direction of Palanga. More interesting, though, is **Liepų gatvė**, which runs parallel to the river and on which stands Klaipėda's splendid, red-brick, Gothic-revival **Post Office** (no. 16). Built between 1883 and 1893, it's a vivid reminder of German civic pride, not least because of the 48-bell carillon that rings out from the clock tower at noon every Saturday and Sunday. The post office is also famous for being the workplace of telephonist Erika Rostel, awarded the Iron Cross for staying at her post (and giving a running commentary on events to the German General

Staff) when the Russian army raided the city in March, 1915 – most of the other civilians had taken to the Curonian Lagoon in boats.

A few doors along at Liepų 12, the **Clock Museum** (Laikrodžių muziejus; Tues–Sun: March–Oct noon–6pm; Nov–Feb noon–5pm; 4Lt) is stuffed with time-pieces from the earliest candle clocks onwards. As much as anything else the display provides a fascinating overview of changing fashions in interior design, with some magnificently over-the-top seventeenth- and eighteenth-century creations, and the odd Art Nouveau grandfather clock bringing up the rear. The nearby **Klaipėda Picture Gallery** at Liepų 33 (same times as Clock Museum; 3Lt) has a small collection of twentieth-century Lithuanian paintings and mounts challenging seasonal exhibitions by contemporary artists. More contemporary art is on display northeast of here at the **Martynas Mažvydas Sculpture Park** (Martyno Mažvydo skulptūrų parkas), peppered with all manner of abstract creations. Sixteenth-century priest and publicist Mažvydas provides the inspiration for several of the works here – although local sculptor Algirdas Bosas's characteristically angular portrayal of the man looks more like a football star seen through the eyes of Pablo Picasso than a distinguished literary figure. Standing at the park's northern end is a megalithic memorial honouring the Soviet war dead.

Eating and drinking

There's a decent selection of eating and drinking places in Klaipėda, many of which are concentrated on or around the city's main thoroughfare, Manto gatvė, and its Old Town continuation, Tiltų gatvė. You can pick up food supplies from the Iki supermarket, on the corner of Mažvydo and Šiaulių (daily 8am–10pm).

Bambola Manto 1. A bright pizzeria on the main strip serving up cheap and fast thin-crust pies, some salads and the full range of alcoholic drinks.

Bohema Aukštoji 3/3. A friendly drinking den with stools arranged round a semi-circular bar in the (no-smoking) interior, and outdoor seating in an animated courtyard.

Boogie Woogie Manto 5. This over-designed fun pub with ghastly chintz decor still attracts a classy crowd of enthusiastic drinkers at weekends. Full menu of food including pizza, salads and steaks.

Būrų užeiga Kepėjų 17. One of the best restaurants in the Old Town, with cosy wooden interior, a full menu of trusty Lithuanian pork-and-potato favourites, plus an array of steak and veal dishes with an international slant. None too expensive either, with mains starting at 18Lt.

Fotogalerija Tomo 7. Old Town photography gallery with pokily atmospheric café, a popular venue for caffeine-fuelled, arty discussions. Also serves up some of the cheapest lunches in the city.

Garažas Manto 33. Bright, glass-fronted café with automotive theme (bike parts used as furniture), some excellent, affordable food in the shape of soups, salads and omelettes, and the full range of alcoholic drinks.

Juodojo Katino Smuklė Mažvydo 1. The "Black Cat Pub" isn't great shakes as a bar, but is one of the best places in town to tuck into *Žemaičių blynai*, *cepelinai*, and other potato-based stomach-fillers.

Kurpiai Kurpių 1A. Something of a Klaipėda legend: a cosy brick-and-timber pub with good food, and some of the best live jazz in the Baltics. Check the schedule at the door.

Memelis Žvejų 4. A beautifully restored red-brick warehouse on the banks of the Danė River with hearty meat and fish fare, beer brewed on the premises, and late-night drinking and dancing in the top-floor club.

Pėda Turgaus 10. A civilized gallery-cum-café serving the full range of drinks and food, with contemporary paintings and sculpture for company.

Šiksnosparnio Lizdas Tiltų 5 (entrance round the corner on Jono gatvė). A popular subterranean eating and drinking venue offering Lithuanian meaty favourites. Live pop-rock bands on occasion.

West Side Kanto 44. A roomy bar some way northwest of the Old Town, worth investigating for its broad choice of international beers and lengthy steaks-and-ribs-dominated menu. Decked out in all manner of Americana: you'll either love it or hate it.

Entertainment

Klaipėda's main cultural flagship is the **Drama Theatre**, Teatro 2 (Dramos teatras; box office Tues–Sun 10am–2pm & 4–6pm; ⊛www.kldteatras.lt), although you'll encounter less of a language barrier at the **Musical Theatre** (Muzikinis teatras; box

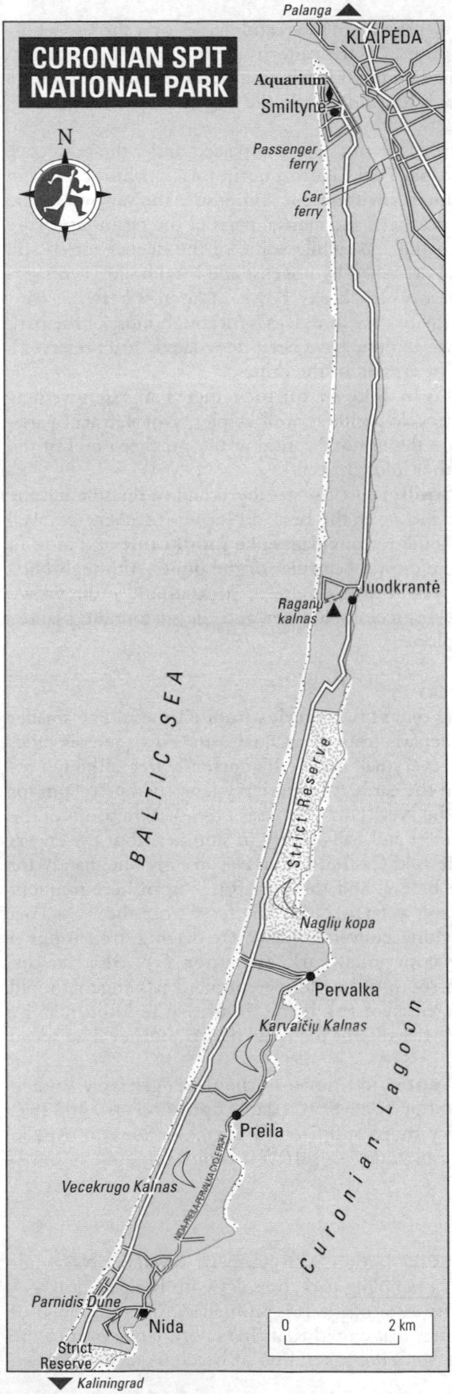

CURONIAN SPIT NATIONAL PARK

N

Palanga

KLAIPĖDA

Aquarium

Smiltynė

Passenger ferry

Car ferry

Juodkrantė

Raganų kalnas

BALTIC SEA

Strict Reserve

Naglių kopa

Pervalka

Karvaičių Kalnas

Curonian Lagoon

Preila

NIDA-SMILTYNĖ CYCLING ROUTE

Vecekrugo Kalnas

Parnidis Dune

Nida

Strict Reserve

Kaliningrad

0   2 km

---

office Tues–Sun 11am–2pm & 3–6pm; ⓦwww.muzikinis .teatras.lt), which hosts chamber concerts, musicals and occasional visits by Vilnius's symphony orchestras.

The Curonian Spit

A short hop by ferry from Klaipėda's port, the long, sandy promontory which makes up the **Curonian Spit** (Kuršių nerija; also known as "Neringa" after the sea goddess who allegedly built it) is one of the most exotic natural wonderlands in the Baltic. Formed over several millennia by deposits of wind- and wave-driven sand, the spit closed off the Nemunas delta from the open sea, forming the Curonian Lagoon in the process. Only the northernmost half of the 97-kilometre-long spit falls within the territory of Lithuania – the remainder belongs to Kaliningrad Province, part of German East Prussia until 1945, but now governed by the Russian Federation.

A sliver of land never more than 4km wide, the spit basically takes the form of an undulating line of huge, fifty-metre-high sand dunes, some looking starkly Saharan in their bareness, but most covered in a dense carpet of dark-green pines, stately silver birches and skinny, soil-starved limes. It's an impermanent landscape, with sea breezes driving sand up the western slopes of the dunes and over the other side, causing a gradual eastward drift of the spit's central ridge. Deforestation in the seventeenth century sped this process up so much that villages had to be moved from one generation to the next as homes were progressively swallowed up by the sands. Systematic re-planting of pines and grasses over the last century or so has served to stabilize the dunes. On the eastern side of the spit lies a scattering of villages that traditionally relied on the fish-teeming waters of the lagoon for a living (nowadays the main industry is tourism), while the western shore is one long, silky stretch of beach.

The whole of the Lithuanian part of the spit has been placed under the protective wing of the **Curonian Spit National Park** (Kuršių nerijos nacionalinis parkas) in order to preserve the pines-and-dunes environment and ensure the survival of the species for whom it is home. The northern and central parts of the promontory are nesting grounds for herons and cormorants, while some of the deeper forests still harbour a handful of elk, an animal described by novelist and local holiday-cottage-owner Thomas Mann – clearly an awe-struck city boy – as "a cross between cow, horse, deer, camel and buffalo, and with very long legs". Although most of the park is accessible to the public, some areas of dune have been designated "strict reserves", closed to visitors in order to prevent erosion of the dunes.

The best way to explore the spit is **by bike or on foot**: there's an extensive network of forest trails and surfaced cycle paths, as well as plenty of national park-maintained signboards with maps – the visitors' centre at the northern end of the spit (see below) can help with further information.

Ferries from Klaipėda arrive at **Smiltynė**, at the northern end of the spit and the site of a hugely popular aquarium. However, the best of Neringa's scenery lies well south of here, around neat, timber-built resort villages like **Juodkrantė** and most of all **Nida**, which allows access to the most spectacular of the dunes. Although Nida is do-able as a day-trip from Klaipėda it makes sense to stick around – the village has an invigorating, Vilnius-by-the-sea feel in summer, and the surrounding sands-and-pines landscape is a joy to explore.

Getting there and information

Getting to Neringa involves taking one of two **ferries** from Klaipėda. The smaller one, mainly for foot passengers, departs from the Old Castle Port (Senasis pilies uostas), just outside the Old Town, every half hour – it's currently free, although re-introduction of a nominal fee is on the cards. A larger ferry (and the one to aim for if you're taking a car) leaves from the New Port (Naujasis uostas), 2km south of the Old Town, operating hourly in winter and half-hourly in summer (foot passengers free; cars 20Lt). The ferry from the Old Castle Port arrives in Smyltinė, handy for both the Maritime Museum (see below) and the bus stop – from here more frequent **minibuses** run the length of the spit as far as Nida. The ferry from the New Port ends up a good 2km south of Smyltinė, convenient if you're driving straight down the spit. All visitors have to pay a national park **entrance fee** (3Lt/person, 15Lt/car) at the road barrier 5km south of Smyltinė – minibus passengers should disembark and make for the ticket kiosk, or risk being shouted at in Lithuanian by the driver. Car drivers should keep the receipt for their return journey. The speed limit on the spit is 40km/hr.

The **National Park Visitors' Centre**, just north of the passenger ferry landing at Smiltynės plentas 11 (May–Sept Tues–Sun 10am–6pm; ☎8-46/402257, ⓦwww.nerija.lt), offers rudimentary **maps** and friendly advice on how to explore the spit; otherwise the tourist office in Nida (see p.161) is your best source of information.

Smiltynė

Lying a ten-minute ferry hop across the lagoon from Klaipėda, **SMILTYNĖ** is not really a settlement as such, more of a rambling park, popular with Klaipėda folk as a recreation venue. Running along its eastern side is a promenade offering views of the merchant ships and loading cranes that crowd Klaipėda's port, while over to the west lies the start of the Curonian Spit's unbroken line of beach. Ranged between the two there's a respectable clutch of attractions, beginning with the **Fishermen's Farmstead** (Žvejų sodyba; free), just north of the ferry landing, a quaint ensemble of nineteenth-century, wooden buildings – a reed-roofed dwelling house (occasionally open) accompanied by a sauna, a fish-smoking shed and a potato cellar.

Another five minutes' walk north, a gun battery built to beef up Klaipėda's defences in the mid-nineteenth century provides the setting for the **Maritime Museum** (Jūrų muziejus; June–Aug Tues–Sun 11am–7pm; May & Sept Wed–Sun 11am–7pm; Oct–April Sat & Sun 11am–6pm; 6Lt; ❷www.juru.muziejus.lt), which is really an aquatic zoo with a few history-related displays tacked on for good measure. An enormous place, resembling a red-brick doughnut, surrounded by huge earthen ramparts, the building is now garrisoned by all manner of water-dwellers – personable seals loll around in the inner moat, while the circular central enclosure accommodates everything from piranha fish to penguins. Across the central courtyard, a display of nautical artefacts and model ships is less memorable than the atmospherically lit powder magazines in which it is housed. In a modern building

Mystical figures, Lithuania △

next door to the museum is the popular **Aquarium** (Akvariumas; May–Sept shows at noon, 2pm & 4pm; Oct–April shows at noon & 3pm; 15Lt), where Black Sea dolphins and Baltic sea lions are put through the hoops. To get to Smiltynė's delicious, fine-sand **beach**, simply follow paths through the forest just west of the ferry landing – you'll hit it in ten minutes.

Juodkrantė and beyond

Fourteen kilometres south of Smiltyne, **JUODKRANTĖ** was the favoured resort of well-to-do Germans from Klaipėda during the inter-war years and still has an air of gentility about it, with its trim, big-balconied, wooden villas, well-tended gardens and seafront park. At the southern end of the resort are a few rows of wooden fishermen's houses, watched over by a red-brick church, the strange, twisting spire of which looks as if it was designed to drill holes in the sky. Immediately opposite, a **gallery** (Tues–Sun 10am–6pm; free) belonging to the Lithuanian Art Museum hosts exhibitions of art and photography in a fragrant, pine-beamed interior.

From the centre of Juodkrantė a path winds up onto **Witches' Hill** (Raganų kalnas), a wooded ridge dotted with wooden sculptures made by contemporary folk artists from all over the country and depicting sprites and demons from Lithuanian folklore. There are lots of sculptures of the sea goddess Neringa and her fisher-lover, although the most attention-grabbing work on display has a muscular St George slaying an intricately chiselled, fish-scaled dragon. Trails lead on further into the forest, continuing over the ridge towards the spit's western coast, where – after a good twenty-minute walk – you'll find Juodkrantė's **beach**.

The coast around Juodkrantė is famous for being one of the prime Baltic nesting grounds for **cormorants**; they gorge themselves on the Curonian Lagoon's marine life – much to the chagrin of local fishermen.

Practicalities

Smiltynė–Nida **minibuses** pick up and drop off on Rėzos, Juodkrantė's single main street. The **tourist office** is at no. 54, inside the *Ažuolynas* **hotel** (☎8-469/53310, ☏53316; ❺), a big concrete place with comfy en-suites in four big accommodation blocks and a small swimming pool on site. More intimate is the *Kuršių Kiemas*, Miško 11 (☎8-469/53004, ✉kkiemas@takas.lt; ❸), a nicely renovated, old building near the northern entrance to the village, offering neat en-suites with TV and fridge. The smartest place to stay is the *Villa Flora*, at the northern end of the village at Kalno 7A (☎8-469/53026, ☏53421; ❻), a modern building in the style of a traditional, wooden villa, with smart rooms. There are also a number of private rooms (❶) available around town, bookable through the tourist office.

The *Villa Flora* boasts the most varied **restaurant** menu, although the locally caught fish on offer at *Žvejonė*, Rėzos 30, tastes all the better for being served up in a delightful flower-filled garden. You can tuck into cheap Lithuanian staples like *cepelinai* at *Pamario takas*, Rėzos 42.

South of Juodkrantė

Beyond Juodkrantė the southbound road heads inland and follows the spit's central wooded spine. Parking places have been strategically placed along the route so you can pull over and admire the tawny-coloured dunes off to the left; most of them fall within one of the national park's strict reserves, so you can't actually get up close to them on foot. After 15km, a turn-off heads east to the village of **PERVALKA**, a sleepy place consisting of a few (largely modern) holiday cottages and the odd café and also marking the northern end of the Nida–Preila–Pervalka cycle route (see p.160).

Nida

The ancient fishing village of **NIDA**, 35km or so south of Smiltynė, has been the main focus for tourism on the spit ever since the mid-nineteenth century, when the first German visitors were drawn here by the promise of unspoilt seaside rusticity. The Germans were quick to rediscover the place in the early 1990s, and it's now the country's most cosmopolitan resort, attracting a healthy cross-section of Lithuanians and outsiders. Despite some ugly Soviet architecture at its heart, it still possesses an impressive stock of traditional timber houses, many of their reed-thatched roofs sporting the wooden, horse-head crosspieces characteristic of Curonian homes.

Some of the prettiest of Nida's houses are to be found just south of the main square, along narrow streets like Lotmiškio and Naglių. Here you'll find neat lines of wooden fishermen's houses, attractively painted in a variety of maroons, yellows and blues, their tidy, picket-fenced gardens packed with flowers and fruit trees. One of the best examples, at Naglių 4, is now the **Fishermen's Ethnographic Homestead** (Žvejo etnografinė sodyba; May–Sept Tues–Sun 11am–7pm; 1Lt), a plain, wooden structure laid end-on to the road. The reconstructed interior provides a fascinating insight into the domestic life of Curonian fishermen in the nineteenth century. Oblong dwellings such as this were designed to accommodate two households, one at each end, each with their own kitchen, sitting room and bedroom. Curonian families were very much into colour-coordinated interiors if the furnishings on display here are anything to go by – wooden chests, wardrobes and bedsteads are painted the same bright blue as many of the house exteriors. Walls were left bare except for uplifting religious mottoes, neatly embroidered and framed.

The Curonian Spit Livelihood Exhibition

East of the main square lies Lithuania's most fashionable yacht marina, the starting point of a seaside path that heads north past well-tended lawns and flowerbeds. Cutting inland after five or ten minutes brings you to the junction of Pamario and Kuverto, where the **Curonian Spit Livelihood Exhibition** at Kuverto 2 (Kuršių nerijos gyventojų verslų ekspozicija; May–Sept Tues–Sun 11am–7pm; 3Lt) contains more on the lives of Nida's fisherfolk. Most likely to hold your attention are the skilfully rendered scale models of traditional craft, including one of the sail-powered sledges once used for crossing the lagoon in winter and the *kurėnas*, a fishing boat particular to the region and characterized by a tall, oblong main sail and big lee boards like the gills of a fish. There's a large collection of the metal weather vanes that have decorated local fishing vessels ever since 1844, when new laws specified that each boat had to display a sign showing which of the Curonian fishing villages it belonged to. Originally this consisted of a simple two-colour design rather like a flag, but with time, fishermen began to add pictorial details – shapes representing buildings, trees, lighthouses, churches and horses – hence the highly stylized weather vanes still made today. Looking more like something out of a horror film are the inter-war photographs of villagers laying nets to catch crows, swarms of which descended on the spit every autumn. Tasting a bit like wild pigeon, the crows were prized as a delicacy by the locals – and giving a crow as a present was considered a special way of saying thank you. Once caught, they were killed by administering a swift bite to the neck. You might be relieved to know that crow no longer forms part of the local diet.

Five minutes' north of here along Pamario, Nida's ruddy-coloured **parish church** looks like an organic extension of the forest that surrounds it, its bell tower sprouting ten mini-pinnacles resembling pine cones. The nearby graveyard contains a fair number of traditional wood-carved crosses, many fashioned into abstract, thistle-like forms, a symbol of re-birth that goes back to pre-Christian times.

Thomas Mann's House

Carrying on up Pamario and bearing right into Skruzdynės brings you to the most famous of Nida's wooden houses, **Thomas Mann's House** at no. 17 (Tomo Manno namelis; May–Sept Tues–Sun 11am–5pm; 3Lt), a thatched cottage of almost fairy-tale loveliness, where the writer spent his summers from 1930 to 1932. The rather disappointing museum within contains a few photos of Mann and family and various editions of his books, including *The Story of Jacob* (1933), and *Young Joseph* (1934), both of which were largely written here. Mann first visited Nida in 1929 on an excursion from the nearby summer resort of Rauschen (now Svetlogorsk in Kaliningrad Province), and was immediately enchanted by the landscape and its people – whom he described as "not exactly good-looking, but friendly". He engaged Klaipėda architect H. Reissmann to build a summer house straight away, ready for his return the following year. When he arrived to take up residence in July, 1930, the locals lined the streets to greet him, an event recorded by press cuttings on show in the museum.

The dunes

The highlight of any trip to Nida are the **dunes**, which begin just south of the village. From the southern end of Naglių a shore path runs to a flight of wooden steps that forges up past wild raspberry bushes onto the shoulder of the fifty-metre-high **Parnidis Dune** (Parnidžio kopa), one of the biggest that Neringa has to offer. The summit is marked by a modern **sundial** in the form of an imposing obelisk decorated with rune-like inscriptions. Blown off its pedestal by a gale in 1999, it has been only partially reconstructed, and now looks like the mysterious remnant of some ancient civilization.

From the summit extends a rippling sandscape of semolina-coloured dunes, their flanks mottled with patches of grey-green moss and purplish thistle flowers. The eastern, lagoon-facing sides of the dunes are roped off in order to prevent subsidence, although you can strike out southwards for about 1.5km before coming up against the boundary of a strict nature reserve – a glorious pale-sand wilderness into which you are not permitted to venture, stretching as far as the Russian border some 2km beyond.

You can walk west from the sundial – or indeed take any of the paths leading westwards from Nida – to reach the **beach** on the spit's far shore, where you'll find a handful of food and drink shacks. It's a glorious place for a stroll even on bad-weather days, when gunmetal seas roll in under glowering skies. Running parallel to the strand and handy for exploring the woods just behind the beach is a north–south foot- and cycle-path.

The Nida–Preila–Pervalka cycling route

One of the best ways to explore the Curonian Spit's tranquil woodland is to follow the **Nida–Preila–Pervalka cycle route** (dviračių takas Nida-Preila-Pervalka), a sixteen-kilometre-long, asphalted path that leads through the mixed birch and pine forest on the eastern side of the spit. As popular with walkers as it is with cyclists, it provides access to a wonderfully serene landscape, with numerous opportunities for climbing up and down trail-side dunes.

Leaving Nida via the *Skalva* hotel at the northern end of the village, the path forges inland for the first few kilometres, running beneath the forest-blanketed western slopes of the spit's central ridge. After about 5km you'll catch sight of Vecekrugo kalnas, at 67m high, the park's highest point. The pine-covered dune gets its name ("Old Pub Hill") from an inn that used to stand at its foot, catering to a local population whose villages have long-since vanished under the sands. After another 3km the trail rejoins the shores of the lagoon, running alongside the reedy Preila Bay before entering **PREILA** itself, a single street of lush-lawned, seaside suburbia, harbouring a couple of simple snack bars. From here it's another 6km to Pervalka, passing another lofty dune, Karvaičių kalnas, en route. Somewhere under the dune's western slopes lies the village of Karvaičiai, abandoned in 1797 owing to shifting sands, but still very much remembered as the birthplace of Liudvikas Rėza (1776–1840), the Königsberg-educated poet and publisher who kick-started the process of cultural revival in Lithuania Minor.

Practicalities

The **tourist office** is right in the middle of the village inside the cultural centre on the main square at Taikos 4 (Mon–Fri 9am–1pm & 2–6pm; ☎8-469/52345). Numerous ad-hoc establishments offering **bike rental** (*dviračių nuoma*) sprout up in the centre during the summer. The cheapest accommodation is a **room** in a private house (❶); ask the tourist office to book you into one. Also, Litinterp back in Klaipėda (see p.152) can book rooms in advance, but at a slightly higher fee.

The best of the numerous small **hotels** in town are the *Rasytė*, Lotmiskio 11 (☎8-469/52592; ❺), a wooden house in the heart of the old fishing settlement with modern, TV-equipped rooms; and *Miško Namas*, Pamario 11 (☎8-469/52290, ⑩www.miskonamas.com; ❺), offering similarly comfy quarters in a picturesque timber building north of the centre – both require advance booking. Primly modern in comparison is the thirty-room *Linėja*, Taikos 18 (☎8-469/52390, ⑩www.pajuris.lt; ❻), which has smart en-suites with TV and is conveniently central. *Nidos Smiltė*, Skruzdynės 2 (☎8-469/52221; ❶–❻), offers simple doubles with shared facilities, more sophisticated en-suites, or spartan cabins in the affiliated Nidos Pūsynas holiday settlement nearby. Handy for the beach on the western side of town are *Auksinės Kopos*, Kuverto 17 (☎8-469/52212; ❹), a large, modern building near the main road, offering rather basic en-suites with TV; and the nearby *Nidos Rūta*, Kuverto 15 (☎8-469/52367; ❹), slightly smarter and more comfortable.

For **eating** and **drinking**, try the wonderfully relaxing garden café of the *Rasytė* guesthouse (see above), which has a substantial menu of meaty main courses, or the nearby *Sena sodyba*, Naglių 6, which serves up omelettes, pancakes and potato dishes in a miniature orchard. A modern pavilion with a thatched-roof makeover, *Ešerinė*, Naglių 2, offers less in terms of atmosphere, but has a satisfying range of main courses and is an enjoyable place for a beer. *Seklyčia*, Lotmiško 1, is Nida's fanciest eatery, a big wooden villa with lots of seating both inside and out; the fish dishes are excellent and you can still get cheap staples like *cepelinai*. *Reidas*, Naglių 5, is the best place for grilled fish, and turns into a great drinking venue in the evenings, with live rock cover bands and dancing. The disco-bar above the hydrofoil terminal caters for techno-fixated teenagers and sundry late-night drinkers.

The cultural centre on the main square hosts films and concerts throughout the summer season, and serves as the main venue for the **Thomas Mann Cultural Festival in July** (⑩www.mann.lt), featuring solo recitals, chamber music and Mann-related literary symposia.

Palanga and around

A short drive up the coast from Klaipėda, **PALANGA** is Lithuania's favourite beach resort and summertime playground, a self-contained empire of ice cream and candy floss visited by everyone from bucket-and-spade-wielding families to drink-fuelled party animals and the Vilnius-based social and cultural elite. On summer evenings you can see all of them parading up and down the bar-lined central strip, Basanavičiaus.

This erstwhile fishing village was first developed as a resort by Polish-Lithuanian aristocrat Jozef Tyszkiewicz (1835–1891), who invited the doyen of wooden architecture, Stanislaw Witkiewicz, to Palanga to build a Kurhaus, and though the building no longer stands, Witkiewicz's trademark style, full of spindly balustrades, pointy gables and fanciful turrets, can still be seen in many of the town's older villas. Originally patronized by well-to-do Poles, Palanga became the resort of choice for Lithuanians after World War I – it was cheaper than Juodkrantė and Nida, which tended to be monopolized by the Klaipėda Germans.

Aside from the beach and the fast-paced nightlife, ample reason to visit is provided by the lush and leafy **Botanical Gardens**, laid out by Jozef Tyskiewicz's son Felix, and an absorbing **Amber Museum** in the Tyskiewicz Palace. Tyskiewicz's **Winter Garden** at nearby **Kretinga** is an easy half-day excursion from town.

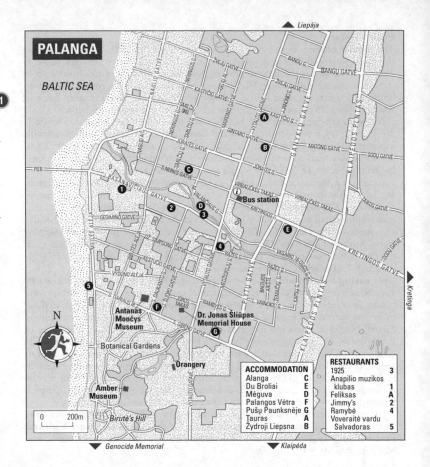

PALANGA

BALTIC SEA

BANGŲ G.

ZVEJŲ GATVE

KASTYČIO GATVE

NAGLIO GATVE

NERINGOS G.

VYTAUTO GATVE

GANYKLŲ GATVE

SMILČIŲ SKG.

SMILČIŲ G.

GINTARO GATVE

KASTYČIO G.

Ⓐ

MATONO GATVE

JŪRATES GATVE

Ⓑ

SODŲ GATVE

PIER

S. NERIES GATVE

JŪRATES G.

Ⓒ

VIRBALIČKES TAKAS

KLAIPEDOS PLINTAS

ZAIKOS GATVE

BASANAVIČIAUS GATVE

VALANČIAUS G.

ℹ Bus station

VIRBALIČKES TAKAS

❶

❷

Ⓓ❸

KRETINGOS G.

Ⓔ

KRETINGOS GATVE

MEILES ALEJA

GEDIMINO GATVE

S. SIMPSONO G.

❹

RAZES G.

VASARIO 16-OSIOS G.

KLAIPEDOS PLINTAS

▶ Kretinga

KESTUČIO GATVE

VYDUNO ALEJA

DAUKANTO G.

VYTAUTO GATVE

MEDZIOTOJŲ G.

PLYTŲ GATVE

BATLIŲ G.

RAZES G.

IZNADŲ G.

KAPSŲ G.

ZNADŲ G.

❺

S. DARIAUS IR

JŪROS TAKAS

RAMBYTES G.

L. VAINEIKIO G.

N

Antanas
Mončys
Museum

Ⓕ

GIBENO GATVE

Dr. Jonas Šliūpas
Memorial House

Ⓖ

Botanical Gardens

Orangery

Amber
Museum

VYTAUTO GATVE

ACCOMMODATION	
Alanga	C
Du Broliai	E
Meguva	D
Palangos Vetra	F
Pušų Paunksneje	G
Tauras	A
Žydroji Liepsna	B

RESTAURANTS	
1925	3
Anapilio muzikos klubas	1
Feliksas	A
Jimmy's	2
Ramybe	4
Voveraite vardu	
Salvadoras	5

0   200m

Birute's Hill

Palanga is served by regular municipal **buses** from Klaipeda bus station, though these tend to stop at every minor halt en route; it's best to take one of the faster minibuses also from Klaipeda bus station – these run from 7.30am to 10.30pm and depart when full. There's a handful of direct services from Vilnius and also four daily buses from and to Liepāja in Latvia (some of these are based in Kaliningrad, so destination boards will be in the cyrillic script).

Arrival, information and accommodation

Palanga's **bus station** is just off Vytauto gatve, the main street running north–south through town. Right in the bus station forecourt, at Kretingos 1, is the **tourist office** (Mon–Fri 9am–1pm & 2–6pm; June–Sept also Sat & Sun 9am–1pm & 2–4pm; ☏8-460/48822), which can book you into a **private room** (❶). The Litinterp office in Klaipeda (see p.152) offers the same service, but charges slightly more (❷). If you're prepared to search yourself, you'll turn up rooms at even cheaper rates – there are plenty of *kambarių nuoma* ("rooms for rent") signs in the suburban streets northwest of the bus station; beware though that this can be a time-consuming business and not all hosts speak English.

A few unrenovated, Soviet-era hulks aside, Palanga is well stocked with modern, snazzily designed **hotels**. Owing to the resort's popularity, however, prices are high in peak season (June–Sept). Outside this period, rates may be thirty to fifty percent cheaper than those quoted below.

Alanga Nėries 14 ☎8-460/49215, ⓦwww.alanga.lt. Stylish and central, this is an excellent mid-range choice. ❸

Du Broliai Kretingos 36 ☎8-460/48047, ⓦwww.travel.lt/dubroliai. A classy, ten-room establishment with the feel of an exclusive club that anyone can join, a ten-minute walk east of the centre. ❹–❻

Mėguva Valančiaus 1 ☎8-460/48839. A central, no-frills establishment whose plain rooms offer a bed, WC, shower – and not much else. ❷

Palangos Vėtra Daukanto 35 ☎8-460/53032, ⓦwww.vetra.lt. Modern, bright en-suites in a new building in the southern part of the centre, right beside the Botanical Gardens. ❺

Pušų Paunksnėje Dariaus ir Girėno 25 ☎8-460/49080, ⓦwww.pusupaunksneje.lt. An apartment-hotel, with self-catering units suitable for couples or families of 3 or 4, owned by basketball superstar Arvydas Sabonis. The furnishings look as if they've come straight out of an upmarket design magazine. The name means "in the shade of the pines", which is a reasonably accurate description. ❼

Tauras Vytauto 116 ☎8-460/49111, ⓦwww.feliksas.lt. Twenty minutes' walk south of the centre, but handy for the wilder reaches of the Botanical Gardens, this smallish, friendly place comes with unassuming, standard en-suites and a handful of plusher rooms with TV. ❸–❺

Žydroji Liepsna Gintaro 36 ☎8-460/52441, ⓔzydroji_liepsna@is.lt. A medium-sized hotel occupying a downtown apartment block just north of the bus station. Rooms at the "Sky-blue Flame" are on the chintzy side, but eminently comfortable. ❸

The Town

Palanga is made up of an easily navigable grid of broad avenues lined with lime trees and pines. The main reference point is the pedestrianized **Basanavičiaus**, the resort's premier promenading ground, lined with a garish succession of amusement arcades, cafés and bars. At its western end is the simple, wooden **pier** (jūros tiltas), which stretches out to sea for almost half a kilometre – a stroll to the end of it is considered an essential part of the Palanga experience, and does at least provide you with a wide-angle view of the dune-backed beach, which stretches as far as the eye can see in either direction.

Once you've cast an eye over the seascape, you really need to make a beeline for Count Felix Tyszkiewicz's **Botanical Gardens**, a huge expanse of parkland that drapes itself across the southern end of town. Comprising clipped lawns, a myriad different tree species and untamed forest, the park was laid out in 1897 by much-travelled Frenchman Edouard André, whose landscaped gardens can be seen in locations as diverse as Sefton Park in Liverpool and Evksinograd in Bulgaria. Over on the northeastern side, beyond a bow-shaped lake, the **Orangery** (Oranžerija; Tues–Sat 10am–6.30pm; 2Lt) houses a diverse collection of cacti, umpteen varieties of begonia and fig, and spectacular, exploding-firework bromelias. In the centre of the park, the neoclassical Tyszkiewicz Palace hosts orchestral concerts on its colon-naded portico, and the tastefully refurbished interior harbours an enjoyable **Amber Museum** (Gintaro muziejus; Tues–Sun 10am–6pm; 5Lt) – it's a real tour de force, presenting the natural history of the substance in easily digestible style, before bombarding the visitor with an array of examples, as well as prehistoric insects trapped in amber pieces and roomfuls of amber jewellery.

Just southwest of the palace, a Christmas pudding-shaped mound known as **Birutė's Hill** (Birutės kalnas) is associated with the story of pagan princess Birutė, who was keeper of the hill's pagan shrine until forcibly abducted by her suitor, Grand Duke Kęstutis. It's said that Birutė's heart softened during the journey to Kęstutis's capital, Trakai (where they were married and Birutė gave birth to the future Grand Duke Vytautas the Great), but she returned to her hilltop shrine in Palanga after Kęstutis's death to keep pagan traditions alive in a slowly Christianizing country. Despite Birutė's status as a standard bearer for the old gods, both she and Kęstutis are pictured in the stained glass that adorns the octagonal nineteenth-century chapel at the hill's summit. Following paths due south from here will bring you after ten minutes to a small and easily missed **Jewish**

Amber

According to Lithuanian folklore, amber came into being when king of the gods Perkūnas discovered that Jūrate, queen of the Baltic Sea, was having an affair with mortal fisherman Kastytis, despite being betrothed to water-god Patrimpas. Perkūnas showed his displeasure by zapping Jūrate's undersea palace with a thunderbolt, scattering a myriad of golden-coloured fragments across the Baltic.

The scientific version of events is rather different, maintaining that amber is essentially the fossilized resin of fifty million-year-old pine trees, deposited on the Scandinavian side of the Baltic, and washed up on the shores of Lithuania, Latvia and Estonia. Taking the form of translucent nuggets of orangey-brown, amber is usually clear, although it sometimes includes pine needles or insects caught in the resin before it solidified, allowing today's scientists the chance to study creepy-crawlies that may have died out millennia ago.

Valued as an ornament ever since Neolithic times, amber provided the ancient Baltic tribes with an important means of exchange, putting them at the supply end of trade routes that extended south to Rome, Byzantium and beyond. Although amber can still be found all along the Baltic coast, the richest deposits are in the Russian province of Kaliningrad – as much as ninety percent of the world's amber is thought to lie underneath the town of Yantarny, where it is mined on an industrial scale.

In all three Baltic states, charms, bracelets and necklaces made from amber remain the principal diet of souvenir stalls and gift shops. It can also be picked up in its raw form on Baltic beaches if you're lucky – fragments of the stuff are usually washed up after storms, when you'll see lots of people, gimlet-eyed, earnestly searching the sands.

Genocide Memorial (Žydų genocido vieta), marking the spot where the bulk of Palanga's Jews were murdered by German troops and Lithuanian auxiliaries in the summer of 1941. A simple granite block rears up out of the grass, bearing a Star of David and an inscription so worn that it's now illegible – the figure of 105 (the number of victims) is all that can be made out.

Returning from the park towards central Palanga along Vytauto gatvė will take you past the **Dr Jonas Šliūpas Memorial House** at no. 23 (Dr Jono Šliūpo memorialinis namas; Wed–Sun 11am–5pm; 2Lt), a charming nineteenth-century dwelling which honours one of Palanga's former mayors. The Šiauliai-born Dr Šliūpas began his political career in the 1890s with the clandestine distribution of Lithuanian-language magazine *Aušra*, an epoch-defining publication which brought together all the leading intellectuals of the day. Escaping Tsarist persecution, he emigrated to the USA, where he began to canvass international support for the Lithuanian national movement. Old photographs recall the man and his times. Other snaps record the motorcade bearing a bemused Lord Baden Powell through the streets of Palanga in 1933 – as one of the few internationally known personalities who bothered to set foot in inter-war Lithuania, he was accorded the status of a visiting head of state.

A block west of here, at Daukanto 16, the **Antanas Mončys Museum** (Antano Mončio muziejus; Tues–Sun noon–5pm; 4Lt) celebrates the work of emigre sculptor Mončys (1921–1993) with an impressive display of his anguished, skeletal creations. The gallery space downstairs is dedicated to seasonal exhibitions by contemporary Lithuanian artists.

Eating and drinking

Pretty much everything you need is on or near the two main streets, Vytauto and Basanavičiaus; there are innumerable snack stalls selling hot dogs and *čeburekai*, and probably more pizzerias than in the rest of Lithuania put together. Many eating and drinking venues feature live music in summer – if you're lucky you'll be treated to classy jazz or pop-rock covers, although more often than not be prepared for Lithuanian techno or medallion-man balladeering.

1925 Basanavičiaus 4. Currently one of the classier places on the main strip: a little yellow wooden house with an intimate, if slightly ersatz, rustic-style interior. The Lithuanian food (with the accent more on meat than fish) is well presented and includes plenty of tasty salads. The music is unobtrusive and it's a good place for a civilized meal or drink.

Anapilio muzikos klubas Birutės 34A. Café and cultural centre housed in an extravagantly turreted and gabled wooden mansion, at the bottom of a leafy park just off the west side of Birutės. Standard range of snacks and meaty main courses, and creaky verandah on which to enjoy a relaxing drink. Bohemian clientele drawn by live music, film shows and theatre at weekends.

Feliksas Vytauto 116. Smart café-bar with dark-wood interior. Hosts frequent live jazz, easy-listening crooners or piano-tinklers on summer evenings. There's another branch at Daukanto 35.

Jimmy's Basanavičiaus 19. American eatery in verandah-ed timber house offering ribs, chicken wings and juicy steaks, alongside a range of salads that make good vegetarian lunches. Sangria and tequila on the drinks list, as well as bottled American beers.

Ramybė Vytauto 54. Slightly more laid-back than some of the places along Basanavičiaus, with jazzy sounds on the stereo and jazzy clientele laying into the scrumptious pancakes.

Voveraitė vardu Salvadoras Meilės 24. Roomy café-bar-restaurant-club which looks like a cross between an interior design show room and the bridge of a spaceship. The name ("Salvador the Squirrel") doesn't make much sense either.

Kretinga

Occupying hilly ground 12km east of Palanga, **KRETINGA** is visited primarily for its Winter Garden and perhaps its monastic heritage. It has been one of the most important monastic centres in the country since 1602, when a community of Bernardines established themselves here under the patronage of the Grand Hetman (supreme military commander) of Lithuania, Jan Karol Chodkiewicz (Katkevičius in Lithuanian). Closed down by the communists in 1945, the monastery was re-founded by the Franciscans in 1993 and is flourishing once more. The lean-spired **monastery church of the Annunciation** still dominates the spacious town square, Rotušė aikštė.

Heading north past the church brings you after ten minutes to **Tyszkiewicz Palace** (Wed–Sun 10am–6pm; 4Lt), an outwardly undistinguished mansion built by Jozef Tyszkiewicz in the 1890s and now mostly occupied by an agricultural college. Nowadays, visitors flock here from their coastal hotels to see Jozef Tyszkiewicz's **Winter Garden**, a narrow, glass-enclosed chamber packed with palms, ferns, cacti and climbing plants, and overlooked by three elegant tiers of cast-iron balcony. The centrepiece at ground level is a fountain, surrounded by Graeco-Roman pillars that have been encrusted with pebbles to provide a grotto effect. A handful of the palace's ground-floor rooms have been opened up for visitors: in the Blue Room a frieze of haughty-looking gryphons makes more of an impression than the collection of anonymous-looking nineteenth-century paintings, while the Red Room (which originally served as the music room), is filled with photographs of the whiskery Czech musicians imported by Jozef to play in his private brass band.

Practicalities

In summer, minibuses shuttle between Palanga bus station and Kretinga's main square from about 7.30am until 10.30pm. Regular services from Klaipėda use Kretinga bus station, just west of the centre on the opposite side of the river.

There's a small **tourist office** at Rotušės aikštė 3 (Mon–Fri 9am–5pm; ☎8-458/51341, ✆itc@kretinga.omnitel.net). Most people visit Kretinga as a day-trip from Palanga, but if you want to stay try the *Gelmė*, Žemaičių 3 (☎8-258/76931; ❶), just off the southeastern corner of Rotušės. *Pas Grafą*, the **café–restaurant** inside the Winter Gardens (open until 10pm), is a wonderful place to indulge in coffee, cakes or main-course meat or chicken dishes among the palm branches.

The Žemaitija National Park and around

Lying in a gently rolling landscape of glacier-smoothed uplands, 50km east of Palanga, the **Žemaitija National Park** is one of the country's smallest, most compact conservation areas, comprising the placid waters of Lake Plateliai and the belt of pastureland, forest and bog that surrounds it. Barely 5km from north to south and 2km across, Lake Plateliai is one of the more attractive bodies of water in this

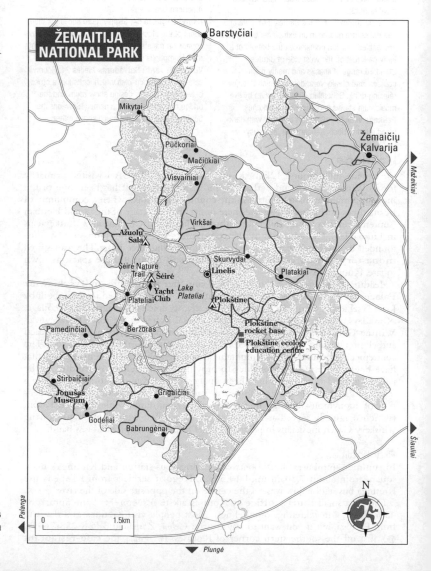

part of Lithuania – its eastern shore is smooth and sandy, while the western shore is broken up by a confusion of tree-smothered promontories. Around 30 percent of the park's territory is made up of agricultural land and 45 percent woodland – largely spruce and pine, although there's a sufficient number of deciduous trees (mostly birch, ash, alder and oak) to produce a much more varied range of greens than you might find elsewhere in Lithuania. Although there's only a handful of signed paths, the region's country lanes and dirt roads make it a wonderful environment for woodland walks and bike rides, while the waters of the lake are perfect for messing about in rowing boats or pedaloes. In addition, there's a strong tradition of **folk art** in the area, with many a garden or driveway sporting a wayside shrine, often painted, wooden figurines representing the Virgin, St George or other popular saints.

The village of **Plateliai** on the lake's western shore is the park's main service and information centre and most of the park's accommodation is in or near the village. You can access nearly all of Lake Plateliai's western side on foot or by bike from Plateliai, although to explore the park in any greater depth you'll probably need your own transport.

One of the places you'll want to aim for is **Žemaičių Kalvarija**, a blissfully bucolic village and one of Lithuania's most popular Catholic pilgrimage centres. Among the more offbeat attractions that Žemaitija has to offer are the disused, Soviet-era rocket base at **Plokštinė**, southeast of Lake Plateliai, and the eccentric collection of open-air sculpture and naive art that is **Orvydas's Garden**, well northwest of the park near the town of Salantai. Good times to visit the area are **Shrovetide** (Užgavėnės), when masked revellers take to the streets of Plateliai; **St John's Eve** (Rasos), when folk music, bonfires and beer tents take over the shores of the lake; or early July, when religious celebrants descend on Žemaičių Kalvarija for ten days of calvary processions.

The main access point to Žemaitija is the town of **Plungė**, just south of the park border. It's linked **by bus** to Žemaičių Kalvarija and is served by numerous intercity buses, as well as the twice-daily Vilnius–Klaipėda express train. If you're visiting the national park by car, note that the majority of roads in the park are unsurfaced once you get away from the Plungė–Mažeikiai highway on the eastern side of the park, and the Plungė–Plateliai route to the west.

Plungė

Lying astraddle the main Klaipėda–Šiauliai rail and road routes, the market town of **PLUNGĖ** is the main jumping-off point for Žemaitija National Park. The town itself isn't up to much, but it's worth making time for a visit to the **Žemaitija Art Museum** (Žemaičių dailės muziejus; Wed–Sun 10am–5pm; 2Lt), housed in **Oginski Palace** (Oginskių dvaras) on Dariaus ir Girėno, a short walk southwest from the train and bus stations. Oginski Palace was built for Polish-Lithuanian aristocrat Count Michał Oginski in the late nineteenth century. Set amid landscaped gardens, this creamy-coloured neo-Renaissance pile – complete with Graeco-Roman-style statues perched along the roofline – provides a suitably elegant setting for some superb examples of local folk art, with tree trunks carved, to totem pole-like effect, into likenesses of Christian saints and pagan deities. A roomful of musical instruments recalls the days when keen arts patron Oginski established a private music school in the palace, dedicated to nurturing local talent – pioneering Lithuanian composer Mikalojus Konstantinis Čiurlionis (see p.124) was a teenage boarder. Behind the palace, and beyond a lily-filled pond, the grandiose red-brick stable block (*žirgynas*) stands in eloquent testimony to the count's enthusiasm for all things equine. Once you've strolled through the overgrown, tree-shaded palace park, there's not a great deal else to get excited about in Plungė: the central town square, Senamesčio aikštė, is now totally modernized, and you wouldn't know that in the nineteenth century it was a vast, open space in which Žemaitija's biggest agricultural fair was held.

The sole **hotel** in town is the medium-sized *Beržas*, just off the square at Minios 2 (☎8-218/56840; ❶–❸), where you can choose between poky rooms with shared facilities, or slightly more salubrious en-suites. For **eating**, try the smart, comfortable *Katpėdėlė*, on the main square, popular with daytime shoppers for its mixture of cheap canteen stodge and patisserie-style nibbles; or *Galera*, opposite the train and bus stations, which doles out pork-and-potato standards, decent beer, and becomes a late-opening disco-bar at weekends.

Plateliai and around

Twenty kilometres north of Plungė, the lakeside village of **PLATELIAI** revolves around a sleepy main square. Just to the south is the wooden parish church dating from 1744, its free-standing bell tower resembling a fortress or a fire-station lookout. Behind the church, a small park surrounds a venerable tree known as **Witch's Ash** (Raganos uosis) – with a girth of 7m, it's thought to be Lithuania's stoutest example of the species. Across the road stands a beautifully restored **Granary** (Dvaro svirnas; ask the National Park Information Centre about access), now used for seasonal art exhibitions and a permanent display of local crafts, including a veritable crowd of wood-carved saints and examples of the devilish masks worn by Shrovetide revellers.

North of the main square, a surfaced road veers down towards the lakeside, where the Yacht Club (Jachtklubas) rents out **rowing boats** and pedaloes (10Lt/hr). It's well worth venturing out onto the water to savour the superb landward views of the wooded bays and peninsulas that characterize the lake's western shore. North of the Yacht Club lies an enchanting area of virgin forest traversed by the **Šeirė Nature Trail** (Šeirės gamtos takas), a five-kilometre-long, figure-of-eight circuit whose starting-point is marked by a national park information board on the Yacht Club access road, about 500m back from the lake. The trail passes through dark, dense forest before bridging a section of Gaudupis Bog (Gaudupio pelkė), a squelchy expanse of mosses punctuated by the odd stunted pine, and culminating at Piktežeris, a beautiful blue, spruce-encircled lake, marking the northernmost extent of the trail.

From the southern end of Plateliai, it's an easy two-kilometre walk to the next village, **BERŽORAS**, site of another eighteenth-century wooden **church**, resembling an enormous stable with wonky crosses perched on its roof. Just east of the village lies a small **beach**, picturesquely situated in a bay between the densely wooded Kreiviškių and Auksalės peninsulas. Southwest from Beržoras a dirt road leads across undulating pastures to the hamlet of **GODELIAI**, 5km distant, where local couple Regina and Justinas Jonušas have established a **Museum of Folklore and Ethnography** (Tautodailės ir etnografijos muziejus; enquire at National Park Information Centre about opening times; donation requested) in their farmstead. The main house holds examples of Justinas's own wood sculptures, as well as innumerable other pieces he's salvaged from decaying wayside shrines, while a barn across the way is packed with all manner of agricultural tools, wardrobes, hatboxes and handbags salvaged from local households.

Practicalities

The **National Park Information Centre**, on Plateliai's main square at Didžioji 8 (May–Aug Mon–Fri 8am–5pm, Sat 9am–5pm; Sept–April Mon–Fri 8am–noon & 1–5pm; ☎8-448/49231, ⍟www.zemaitijosnp.lt), sells maps, dishes out advice on what to see in the park and rents bikes (4Lt/hr). In addition, it can book **rooms** in local farmhouses (❶), most of which are in Plateliai or in the nearby village of Beržoras, and also runs the **hostel**-style *Dvaro svetainė* (35Lt), 200m south of the square at Didžioji 19, and the *Plokštinė Ecology Education Centre* (Plokštinės ekologinio ugdymo centras; 30Lt), a former barracks set amidst atmospheric wood- and swamp-land 7km east of Plateliai – both places deal in sparsely decorated, but satisfactory, rooms with shared WC/shower. Offering more comfort, 2km south of Plateliai in Beržoras, *Marija Straukienė* (☎8-448/49152, 698/03485 or 612/74973; ❸) has a lakeside ensemble of reed-thatched **holiday houses** with ultra-swish, hard-floored interiors – you can opt for a double room (❷) or an entire house (❹) – and guests can rent bikes. Further afield (and a good 10km from Plateliai by road), the *Hotel Linelis*, on the opposite shore of the lake (☎8-448/49422; ❷), offers a choice between modernized rooms with pristine bathrooms and dinky balconies, or Soviet-era en-suites with lino floors and weird wallpaper, and there's both a restaurant and a sandy beach on site – to get there, take the road to Žemaičių Kalvarija and turn right at the northeastern shoulder of the lake, when you see the sign for "Poilsavietė".

If you don't mind rough **camping**, there's a handful of designated sites around Lake Plateliai where you can pitch tents and light fires – a national park warden calls round every day or so to empty rubbish bins and collect fees (5Lt for tent and vehicle). The nearest site to Plateliai is the *Šeirė stovyklavietė*, just north of the Yacht Club; also within striking distance is the *Ąžuolų sala* site, 3km north, an idyllic lakeside spot well signed off the road. Over on the opposite side of the lake, the *Plokštinė* site occupies a part-sandy, part-forested spot, 2km south of *Hotel Linelis*.

For **eating** and **drinking**, try *Senas Ąžuolas* on Plateliai's main square, which has a full range of soups, potato pancakes and meaty main courses, and is also a reasonable place to drink, while *Šašlykinė*, a pavilion in the forest just off the Yacht Club access road, does a reasonable line in Caucasian-style, skewer-grilled kebabs.

Plokštinė rocket base

It's perhaps not surprising that the Soviet authorities should consider the sparsely populated wilderness of forests and bogs in the **Plokštinė** area, southeast of Lake Plateliai, to be the perfect place to hide a rocket base. Built in 1962, the facility at Plokštinė was one of the first such silo sites in the Soviet Union, housing four nuclear missiles capable of hitting targets throughout western and southern Europe. Closed down in 1978 and left to rot for over three decades, the base has now been re-opened to the public as the so-called **Militarism Exhibition** (Militarizmo ekspozicija; May–Aug tours daily at 9am, 11am, 1pm, 3pm & 5pm; 4Lt; Sept–April advance booking required; contact the National Park Information Centre). It's accessible via a dirt road which leaves the Plateliai–Plungė road just south of Beržoras – to register for a tour and pick up a guide, head first for the Plokštinė Ecology Education Centre (Plokštinės ekologinio ugdymo centras), which occupies a former barrack blocks just south of the base.

There's not much to see on the surface, save for an unwelcoming family of grey domes, and it's only on descending into the facility's subterranean areas that the size of the base becomes apparent: a seemingly endless sequence of concrete-floored, metal-doored rooms, passages and stairways. It's rather like exploring a cave system in which the showpiece cavern is one of the silos themselves – a vast, metal-lined cylindrical pit deep enough to accommodate 22m of slender, warhead-tipped rocket. Peering into the abyss from the maintenance gallery can be a numbing experience – especially when you consider that most similar silos around the world are still very much in working order.

Žemaičių Kalvarija

Marking the northeastern corner of the park, about 20km out from Plateliai, the attractive village of **ŽEMAIČIŲ KALVARIJA** consists of a twin-towered hilltop church surveying a greeny-yellow collage of wooden houses, haystacks and fields of horses. It's also one of the most important Catholic pilgrimage sites in the country, thanks to a three-and-a-half-centuries-old tradition of calvary processions, which draw thousands of celebrants every year between July 2 and July 12.

The village owes its prominence to Bishop of Žemaitija Jerzy Tyszkiewicz, who in 1644 invited the Dominicans to establish a monastery and a school here. They brought with them an image of the Madonna, whose supposed prayer-answering powers soon transformed the settlement into the most popular shrine in Žemaitija. They also started the construction of nineteen calvary chapels around the village, forming a five-kilometre-long processional route that has been the focus of religious ritual ever since. During the communist period local party bosses organized free folk festivals during the procession season in the hope that they would divert popular attention away from Žemaičių Kalvarija – a strategy that never met with more than limited success. Nowadays, people from all over the country throng to the village to take part in formal processions led by banner-wielding ecclesiastics, or to embark on a private circuit of the chapels, often approaching each chapel on their knees as a sign of devotion and sacrifice.

Scattered throughout the village, many of the chapels look like barns or outhouses and some are only recognizable from the wrought-iron crosses on their roofs. The chapel interiors, decorated with scenes from the Passion, are almost invariably closed outside the procession season, but the padlocked structures still provide an excellent excuse for a round-the-village stroll. Most of the chapels are concentrated on the hillocks around the church – there's an especially attractive cluster near the town graveyard due west, and an outer loop of chapels dotting the cornfields just off the road to Barstyčiai to the northwest. Žemaičių Kalvarija's gleaming-white, nineteenth-century church is always closed outside prayer times, although the local priest might open it up to show you a much-revered image of the Virgin on the high altar.

Žemaičių Kalvarija is 2km off the main Plungė–Mažeikiai road. There are only two **buses** a day from Plateliai, but about seven daily Plungė–Mažeikiai services trundle past the turn-off – some enter the village to pick up and drop off. A small **Žemaitija National Park Information Centre** stands just south of the church at Alsėdžių 3 (usually summer Mon–Fri 9am–5pm; ☎8-448/43200), although it's sporadically staffed and less well equipped than the main one in Plateliai. There's a rudimentary **café** in the cultural centre opposite the church, and a couple of food shops on the main street nearby.

The Orvydas Garden

Twenty-five kilometres northwest of Plungė on the Skuodas road and well outside the territory of the national park, the undistinguished country town of Salantai would be a mere dot on the map were it not for its proximity to the **Orvydas Garden** (Orvydų sodyba; daily dawn till dusk; donation requested), an open-air sculpture park that ranks among the most off-beat and eccentric art collections in the whole Baltic region. It's located 2km southwest of Salantai on the Plungė road and is served by the four daily Plungė–Salantai–Skuodas buses. The garden is on the farm of **Vilius Orvydas** (1952–1992), a self-taught sculptor who specialized in the larger-than-life, tree-trunk-sized statues of religious and mythical subjects typical of Lithuanian folk art. He also collected graveyard crosses, religious sculptures from wayside shrines and Catholic-related folk art in order to save them from an atheistic Soviet regime that either had them destroyed or left them to decay where they were. Orvydas arranged these objects in his own garden, adding landscape features such as ponds, pathways and rocks carved with strange, rune-style signs. During the last years of the Soviet Union, the garden became a cult site among Lithuanian intellectuals who saw Orvydas's magpie activities as a sign of defiance; since independence, Orvydas has been acclaimed as an outstanding practitioner of naive, non-academic sculpture and landscape art – and you'll see coffee-table books devoted to the man and his garden in Vilnius bookshops. As a privately owned site (Orvydas's son still lives on the property), the garden has none of the touches, such as labelling or logical ordering, that you might expect to find in a state-run collection; indeed, in large parts it looks almost derelict and uncared for. Strolling around the garden is certainly a strange experience: like the Hill of Crosses (see p.146), its power rests in its seemingly unplanned, cluttered nature, with the presence of a Soviet-era rocket and a World War II tank adding to the junkyard feel.

Travel details

Buses

Klaipėda to: Kaunas (12 daily; 3–3hr 30min); Palanga (minibuses; every 30min–1hr; 30min); Šiauliai (3 daily; 3hr); Šilutė (2 daily; 1hr 20min); Vilnius (12 daily; 4–5hr).
Nida to: Juodkrantė (hourly; 30min); Kaunas (1 daily; 4hr); Smiltynė (hourly; 45min); Vilnius (1 daily; 6hr).
Palanga to: Kaunas (9 daily; 3hr 45min); Klaipėda (minibuses; every 30min–1hr; 30min); Kretinga (minibuses; every 30min–1hr; 20min); Panevėžys (3 daily; 5hr); Šiauliai (3 daily; 3hr); Vilnius (7 daily; 5hr 45min).
Plateliai to: Plungė (Mon–Sat 6 daily, Sun 3 daily; 25min); Žemaičių Kalvarija (2 daily; 40min).
Plungė to: Klaipėda (5 daily; 1hr 40min); Kretinga (9 daily; 1hr); Palanga (4 daily; 1hr 25min); Plateliai (Mon–Sat 6 daily, Sun 3 daily; 25min); Salantai (4 daily; 40min); Šiauliai (3 daily; 1hr 40min).
Smiltynė to: Juodkrantė (hourly; 15min); Nida (hourly; 45min).

Trains

Klaipėda to: Kaunas (1 daily; 6hr 30min), Plungė (6 daily; 2hr); Šilutė (2 daily; 1hr 30min); Vilnius (2 daily; 5hr).

Plungė to: Klaipėda (6 daily; 2hr); Šiauliai (4 daily; 1hr); Vilnius (2 daily; 3hr).

Flights

Palanga to: Kaunas (4 daily; 40min).

International buses

Klaipėda to: Kaliningrad (3 daily; 4hr); Liepāja (3 daily; 4hr).
Palanga to: Kaliningrad (3 daily; 4hr 30min); Liepāja (3 daily; 3hr 30min).

International ferries

Klaipėda to: Arhus (1 weekly; 45hr); Karlshamn (6 weekly; 16hr); Kiel (6 weekly; 21hr); Sassnitz (3 weekly; 20hr).

International flights

Palanga to: Billund (5 weekly; 2hr 25min); Hamburg (1 daily; 2hr 20min); Malmö (5 weekly; 2hr); Oslo (5 weekly; 2hr 25min).

Latvia

Latvia Highlights

* **Rīga Old Town** A nest of narrow streets lined with an engaging ensemble of buildings reflecting eight centuries of history. **See p.196**

* **Art Nouveau Architecture, Rīga** Nymphs, caryatids and a host of other creatures peer down from the richly ornamented facades of Rīga's nineteenth-century Centre. **See p.209**

* **Cape Kolka** A hauntingly beautiful horn of land extending into the Baltic Sea and flanked by semi-deserted sandy beaches. **See p.239**

* **Kuldīga** An attractive huddle of half-timbered houses set beside the foaming River Venta, Kuldīga represents small-town Latvia at its most picturesque. **See p.247**

* **Rundāle** A veritable Versailles of the north, this stupendous eighteenth-century palace is filled to the rafters with sumptuous Baroque and rococo furnishings. **See p.232**

* **Gauja National Park** The River Gauja cuts its way through pine-carpeted sandstone hills to create this paradise for hikers, canoeists and nature lovers. **See p.261**

* **Latgale** A sparsely populated area of rustic villages and rolling hills, this is one of the most delightful rural landscapes in the region. **See p.277**

Introduction and basics

The history of Latvia, like that of its neighbour Estonia, is largely one of foreign occupation. The indigenous Balts were overwhelmed at the start of the thirteenth century by German crusading knights, who massacred and enslaved them in the name of Christianity. The Germans continued to dominate both land and trade even after political control passed to the Polish-Lithuanian Commonwealth, then Sweden and finally Russia. During the second half of the nineteenth century the Latvians began to reassert their identity, achieving independence following the 1918–20 war, in which they beat off both the Soviets and the Germans. This hard-won independence was extinguished by Soviet annexation in 1940. As conditions in the Soviet Union relaxed during the late 1980s, demands for increased autonomy turned into calls for independence, and on August 21, 1991, as the attempted coup against Gorbachev disintegrated in Moscow, Latvia declared its independence for the second time.

Where to go

The most obvious destination in Latvia is its capital, **Rīga**, a boisterous, mercantile city whose Gothic red-brick heart is girdled by one of the richest collections of Art Nouveau apartment blocks anywhere in Europe. The Latvian capital is also known for its varied and often wild nightlife, and offers easy access to the sands of **Jūrmala**, a seaside suburb northwest of the city.

One of the most scenic stretches of the Latvian countryside can be found just east of Rīga, where the **River Gauja** winds its way through wooded sandstone hills, passing medieval castles at **Sigulda** and **Cēsis** en route.

Further southeast, Latvia's gritty second city **Daugavpils** is very much an acquired taste, but it does possess an enchanting rustic hinterland in the shape of **Latgale**, a region of rippling hills and beguiling villages, of which **Aglona** – Latvia's most popular Catholic pilgrimage centre – is the most obvious target.

South of Rīga lies a flat-as-a-pancake region of rich farmland, dotted with the country palaces of the eighteenth-century Baltic aristocracy, with the rococo finery of **Rundāle Palace** making a rewarding daytrip from the capital. On the west coast, the port cities of **Ventspils** and **Liepāja** offer a good deal in the way of historical attractions and cultural diversions, although neither can compare with the country-town charm of **Kuldīga** just inland. For the best in deserted beaches, dunes and sea views, head for **Cape Kolka** in the far northwest.

Costs, money and banks

The Latvian capital, Rīga, has the highest cost of living of any city in the Baltics, and – although it's not yet as expensive as Western Europe, your daily spend here will be greater than in Vilnius or Tallinn. Things are different outside Rīga, where you can live exceedingly well on very little.

Costs

Wherever you stay in Latvia, **accommodation** will take a major chunk out of your daily budget. In Rīga, hostel beds start at £7/$10, while private rooms and the cheapest hotels cost around £27/$40 for a double. Comfortable, mid-range hotels start at around the £60/$90 mark for a double, and anything more stylish costs considerably more than this. Out in the provinces you won't find much in the way of hostels, but the price of a double room can fall to £10/$15 in a rustic B&B, £20/$30 in a hotel.

Public transport costs are comparatively low: short journeys by bus or train (Rīga–Jūrmala or Rīga–Sigulda for example)

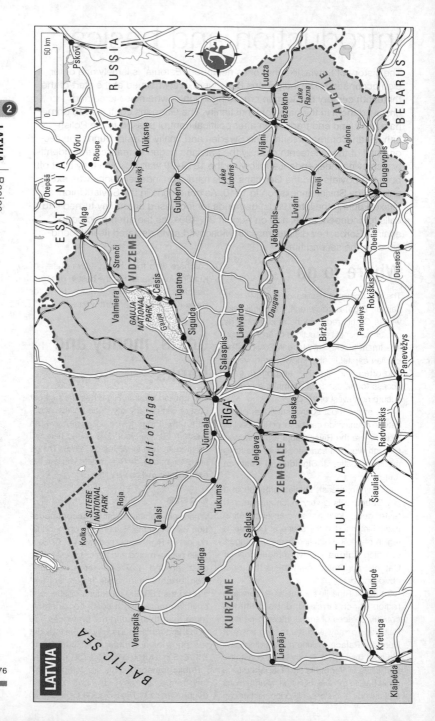

Ⓦ **www.lv** General directory of web resources.

Ⓦ **www.art.lv** Gallery listings and links to individual painters and sculptors.

Ⓦ **www.balticshop.com** Online Latvian store selling woolly mittens and folk CDs.

Ⓦ **www.culture.lv** Culture portal with a multitude of links.

Ⓦ **http://folklora.lv** The lowdown on the Latvian folk scene, with guides to performers and an introduction to traditional instruments.

Ⓦ **www.latinst.lv** Web page of the Latvian Institute, a state-funded organization that distributes all kinds of information about Latvian culture, much of which is available on this site.

Ⓦ **www.latvians.com** Web-zine aimed at Latvians and their descendants all over the world, with lots of readable features and comment.

Ⓦ **www.latviansonline.com** Stimulating source of news and views from Latvians all over the globe.

Ⓦ **www.lmuza.lv** Serious music site with concert listings and background features on classical and folk performers.

Ⓦ **www.tornis.lv** Alternative rock site with background features and up-to-date gig schedule.

Ⓦ **www.virtual.lv** Latvian maps and city plans online.

Ⓦ **www.virtualriga.lv** City guide with what's on info and topical news content.

are unlikely to break the £0.70/$1 barrier; while intercity journeys from Rīga to Ventspils, Liepāja or Daugavpils rarely exceed £3.50/$5.25.

If you're shopping in markets for picnic ingredients during the daytime and sticking to the cheaper cafés and bars in the evening, then £6/$9 per person per day will suffice for **food and drink**. For a sit-down lunch and a decent dinner followed by a couple of night-time drinks, you'll need at least £20/$30 per person per day in Rīga, £15/$22.50 outside the capital.

Currency

Latvia's unit of currency is the **lats** (plural lati), abbreviated to Ls and divided into 100 santimi. Coins come in denominations of 0.01, 0.02, 0.05, 0.10, 0.20, 0.50, 1 and 2Ls and notes in 5, 10, 20, 50, 100 and 500Ls. At the time of writing £1 was worth 0.9Ls and $1 was worth 0.6Ls.

Banks and exchange

Major **banks** (*banka*) like Hansabanka, Latvijas Krājbanka and Unibanka will change money, cash traveller's cheques (Thomas Cook and American Express preferred) and some give advances on major credit cards. **Opening times** are usually Mon–Fri 9/10am–5/6pm,

with some banks in big cities opening 10am–3pm on Saturday. Outside these hours you can change cash in **currency exchange offices** (*valūtas maiņa*), many of which are little more than kiosks found in unlikely locations like food shops or gambling arcades. These are often open until around 10pm at night, and one or two in Rīga are open 24 hours. You'll find **AIM cash machines** (*automāts*) liberally dotted around most town centres.

Credit cards can be used in a growing number of bars, restaurants and shops in Rīga and other cities, as well as in most petrol stations, but are not widely accepted in small towns and villages.

Communications

The **Latvian postal service** (*Latvijas pasts*) is reasonably reliable, even if post offices themselves tend to be gloomy and disorganized places, with a confusing array of different counters. **Opening times** are generally Monday to Friday 8am–7/8pm, Saturday 8am–4pm. City-centre post offices may also be open Saturdays 8am–6pm and Sundays 8am–4pm. Cards (0.20Ls) or letters (0.30Ls) to Europe take about seven days to arrive; cards (0.30Ls) and letters (0.40Ls) to North

America or Australasia take fourteen days. Most post offices have a fax (*fakss*) counter where you can send documents for a few santimi.

Phones

The Latvian telephone system is generally hitch-free and easy to use: all numbers in the country are seven-digit and there are no separate area codes. Direct international calls are possible from all phones – dial 00 followed by the country code, area code and number.

Town centres are well supplied with **public telephone boxes**, operated using magnetic cards (*telekarte* or *zvaņu karte*). These come in 2, 3 and 5Ls denominations and can be bought at the post office or from newspaper kiosks. A 2Ls card should just about stretch to a three-minute call to Europe, the US or Australasia.

Mobile phones

For general information on using mobile phones in the Baltic States, see p.29. If you have a **GSM mobile phone** it's possible to avoid heavy call costs by purchasing a pre-paid SIM card from one of the local operators such as Amigo, Okarte or Zelta Zivtiņa. This will provide you with a Latvian telephone number and allow you to make local calls at the local rate. In each case it costs 5–6Ls for the SIM card and your first few minutes of airtime, after which you can buy top-ups in increments of 2, 3, 5Ls and above. Starter packs and top-up cards can be bought from newspaper kiosks and supermarket checkouts just about everywhere in the country.

Internet access

Rīga and other cities are well served by **Internet cafés** (*interneta kafejnīca* or *interneta klubs*), although they're not very common in smaller towns. Internet access is also available in public libraries, although you may have to wait to use a terminal. Thirty minutes of surfing time rarely costs more than 1Ls.

Media

For a country containing little over 1.5 million native speakers, Latvia can boast an aston-

ishing array of **newspapers** and magazines. Best by far of the national dailies is *Diena* ("The Day"; ⊚ www.diena.lv), a well-designed and -written broadsheet whose Friday listings supplement *Izklaide* contains what's on details for the whole country. Latvia's Russian-speaking inhabitants have a handful of dailies of their own, of which *Telegraf* is the most influential.

As far as **magazines** are concerned, *Rīgas laiks* is a good-looking but intellectually obscure cultural monthly; it's more a fashion accessory than something you would ever dream of reading. More down-to-earth, but impeccably stylish with it, *Santa* and *Ieva* are the most broad-based of the women's interest titles. If you're interested in architecture and interior design, *Latvijas Architektūra* is worth getting just for the photos, while *Studija* is a highly recommended fine arts magazine with English-language summaries.

As for **television**, most people tune in to state-owned terrestrial channels LTV1 and LTV7 for serious news and culture, and to privately owned LNT and TV3 for game shows and imported dramas. English-language films are shown in the original language with Latvian subtitles on LTV7 only – all other Latvian channels show them dubbed. Many hotels and households are equipped with a multitude of cable channels, offering a broad range of English-, German- and Russian-language programming.

Getting around

Latvia's public transport network is, on the whole, efficient and comprehensive. Travelling by **bus** is generally slightly quicker, but also a little more expensive, than by **train**. For details of travelling between Latvia and the other Baltic States, see p.27.

Trains

Latvia's train network is exceedingly useful if you're making short trips in and around the Rīga region: there are regular services to Jūrmala, the Gauja National Park and the Daugava Valley towns, putting lots of destinations within comfortable day-trip range. Most carriages feature hard, wooden seating, so bring a cushion if you're accustomed to travelling in comfort. Long-distance journeys are in any case better attempted by bus: trains from Rīga to the west Latvian cities of Liepāja and Ventspils have been discontinued, and services to the southeastern urban centres of Daugavpils and Rezekne take three to four hours to arrive and don't have a buffet car – so you'll need to bring your own food and drink.

Train **tickets** (*biļete*) should be bought in advance if the ticket office is open – if not, pay the conductor. All but the smallest of train stations will have the **timetable** (*kustības saraksts*) written up on a board – departures are listed under *atiešana* or *atiet*, arrivals under *pienākšana* or *pienāk*. *Darbdienās* means on working days, *brīvdienās* or *svētdienās* means on Sundays and public holidays; the words *nepietur stacijās* mean "doesn't stop at". Trains with four-digit route numbers stop at virtually every halt; those with three-digit route numbers are "fast" trains that miss some of the smaller stations out – although even these are unlikely to travel at speeds exceeding 60km/hr.

Buses

Latvia is covered by a comprehensive bus network; frequent services run between the main cities and even the smallest villages are served by at least one bus a day. Buses on the intercity routes are reasonably comfortable; those working on rural routes may well be ancient contraptions with sagging seats. At the bigger bus stations **tickets** should be bought in advance wherever possible; if you're catching the bus from an intermediate stop-off rather than its point of origin, you'll have to pay the driver. Normally **luggage** is taken on board, though if you have a particularly large bag you may have to pay extra to have it stowed in the luggage compartment.

Departure boards at bus stations are fairly easy to understand, with most of the terminology the same as that used in railway stations (see above). **Express buses** are usually shown on timetables with the letter "E"; buses that only travel on a certain day of the week are marked with an initial denoting the day in question ("P" means *pirmdiena* or Monday, for example, see p.450 for the full list of days in Latvian).

Information provided in bus stations rarely covers the times of return buses from the particular place you're heading for, making it difficult to plan day-trips with any certainty – a problem made worse by the fact that station staff outside Rīga rarely speak any English. If in doubt, telephone the tourist office of the place you're aiming for and ask them for advice on how to get back – they're usually quite happy to help. Timetable information is available on ⓦwww.ikase.lv and ⓦwww.118.lv – although they're in Latvian only for the time being.

Driving

Road conditions in Latvia can vary dramatically. There are no two-lane highways, apart from a brief stretch between Rīga and Jūrmala. Roads linking major towns are usually in a reasonable state, but off the beaten track, conditions deteriorate rapidly. The biggest hazard is reckless drivers – Latvia's road casualty rate is shocking.

To bring a car into Latvia you need a valid Green Card or third-party insurance policy. **Speed limits** are 50kph in built-up areas, 90kph on the open road, and 100kph on highways. In towns it's forbidden to overtake stationary trams. The wearing of seatbelts is compulsory, and headlights should be switched on at all times. It's illegal to drive with more than 0.05 milligrams of alcohol in the blood (which is roughly equivalent to one and a half pints of beer).

Though most towns and major highways are well provided with round-the-clock **petrol stations** (*degvielas stacija*), there are few in rural areas – carry a spare can. Petrol costs around $0.70 for a gallon.

For **car rental**, Western rates apply, though you may get a better deal from small, local firms – bear in mind though that with the latter, contracts can be dubious, insurance coverage sketchy and the cars themselves not necessarily maintained properly. Details of major car rental firms are given on p.27.

Accommodation

The last decade has seen a hotel-building boom in Rīga, ensuring that the mid-range and business ends of the market are

Accommodation price codes

The hotels and guesthouses listed in the Latvian chapters of this guide have been graded according to the following price bands, based on the cost of the least expensive double room in summer.

- ❶ Under 18Ls
- ❷ 18–24 Ls
- ❸ 24–32 Ls
- ❹ 32–44 Ls
- ❺ 44–60 Ls
- ❻ 60–80 Ls
- ❼ 80–120 Ls
- ❽ Over 120 Ls

increasingly well catered for. Outside the capital things are less predictable, and there's a lack of decent budget hotels or youth hostels, whichever part of the country you're in. In rural areas, the number of affordable guesthouses and rural homestays is on the increase, and there are plenty of idyllic camping opportunities if you don't mind roughing it a bit.

Hotels

Latvian hotels (*viesnīcas*) are yet to be graded according to the international 5-star system, and room prices are not always an accurate indication of the quality of accommodation you're going to get – if you want things like Sat-TV and full-size bathtubs, it always pays to ask before making a reservation.

In general, the **cheapest hotels** tend to be Soviet-era establishments that haven't been refurbished for a couple of decades – usually these come with gloomy furnishings and en-suite shower and WC, although a few places have a handful of cheaper rooms with shared toilet facilities in the hallway. In Rīga you'd expect to pay 25–35Ls for a double in these places, 15–20Ls in the provinces.

In the capital at least, there's a broad range of **mid-price hotels** – either reconditioned Soviet-era places or new establishments built in the last ten years – offering plush carpets, TV and a neat-and-tidy bathroom. There's a growing number of such establishments in provincial cities and popular areas like Jūrmala and the Gauja Valley. A double will cost 50–60Ls in the capital, 30–40Ls elsewhere.

Latvia can also claim a good choice of **upmarket hotels** that would merit four or more stars in any other European country,

and charge room rates to match – for the time being, however, these are all limited to the capital. Some hotels in Rīga offer cut-price rates at weekends and in off-season periods, such as autumn and early spring – it always pays to ask.

Guesthouses and rural homestays

Outside the big cities there's an increasing number of family-run places calling themselves a **guesthouse**, or *viesu nams*. Standards vary widely from place to place – some guesthouses are small hotels in all but name, while others are simply suburban houses or rural farmsteads that rent out rooms and are similar to B&Bs (see below). They're usually a good deal cheaper than mid-range hotels and offer a friendlier, more intimate atmosphere to boot.

Most tourist offices outside Rīga will have a list of local households offering **B&B**, and in most cases will make reservations on your behalf – the hosts themselves rarely speak much English. Many of these B&Bs are in rural areas and may indeed be run by a farming family – as such they represent a great way to experience the countryside, but you'll probably need your own transport to make full use of them. One agency that deals exclusively with **rural homestays** and can fix up your whole holiday in advance is Lauku ceļotajs, Kuģu 11, Rīga (☎761 7600, ⓦwww.celotajs.lv).

Hostels and private rooms

Although there's no genuine network of youth hostels in Latvia, it's usually possible to find rooms in **student halls of residence** in Rīga and a handful of provincial towns.

Conditions can be on the spartan side, but at least prices are low, with doubles costing 10–15Ls and dorm beds considerably less.

One other budget option in Rīga are **private rooms** rented out by locals with flat-space to spare. Most of these are located in ageing apartment blocks and you'll probably be sharing your host's bathroom – but at 15–20Ls per person they're better value than many of the city's hotels. See the Rīga account for further information.

Campsites

The most basic form of campsite in Latvia is a **tent site** (*telšu vieta*), which, as its name suggests, is basically a meadow where you're allowed to pitch a tent – additional facilities such as earth toilets or a water tap may or may not be provided. A nominal fee of 0.50–0.60Ls is charged for using these places. Several national parks (notably the Gauja National Park; see p.261) provide tent sites free of charge, and even supply free wood for bonfires – the idea being that this prevents campers from illegally chopping timber themselves.

One step up from a *telšu vieta* is a **kempings** (campsite), where – alongside tent space – accommodation consists of two- or four-person cabins, with shared toilets and washing facilities. On average, a two-person cabin costs 15–20Ls. Campsites offering modern toilet blocks and showers are something of a rarity in Latvia, although the new site in Ventspils (see p.251) is about the best the Baltic region has to offer.

Eating and drinking

Traditionally, Latvian cuisine is rich in meat and dairy products, with pork, cheese and sour cream forming the mainstay of most main courses. In recent years, however, chicken, fish, and fresh salads have started appearing on menus, providing some respite for those who haven't just come to the Baltics to bulk up on body fats. As you'd expect, Rīga boasts the best range of restaurants, cafés, bars and pubs, and can boast a growing stable of ethnic-influenced eateries; the further away you travel from the capital, the narrower the choice, with most establishments concentrating on a tried-and-tested repertoire of traditional Latvian fare.

Where to eat

The word *restorāns* (restaurant) usually denotes a smartish, starched-tablecloth establishment – and although there are plenty of these in Rīga, many Latvians prefer to eat in the more informal (and cheaper) surroundings of a *krogs* or *krodziņš* (pub-like taverns often decked out in folksy wooden furnishings), or in a *kafejnīca* (a catch-all term covering anything from a greasy spoon to an elegant coffee-and-cakes café). Many kafejnīcas are in fact sizeable, self-service restaurants in which a handsome selection of traditional eats are displayed at the counter and you simply point to what you want – an excellent way to fill up at an affordable price.

Snacks and starters

Certain Latvian staples crop up on most menus and function rather well as either snacks, starters, quick lunches – or simply an accompaniment to a round of drinks. An ever-present staple in just about all kafejnīcas, restaurants and supermarket deli counters is *rasols*, a salad containing diced meat, bits of herring, potatoes, peas, carrots and gherkin – all drenched in a mixture of sour cream and mayonnaise. Other ubiquitous snacks include *pīrāgi* or *pīradziņi* (parcels of dough with various stuffings, usually cabbage and/or bacon bits), and *pelmeņi* (meat-filled pockets of pastry akin to ravioli). Also common are savoury pancakes (*pankūkas*), usually filled with cheese or ham – *kartupeļu pankūkas* are potato pancakes.

One typically Latvian dish that is frequently ordered alongside a round of beers but functions perfectly well as a snack in its own right is *pelēkie zirņi* (mushy grey peas cooked in smoky-bacon fat). *Zirņu pikas*, in which peas and bacon bits are mashed and moulded into balls, is a posher variation on the same theme. Other indigenous specialities include pork in aspic (*cūkas galerts*) and smoked sausage (*žāvēta desa*). Some Baltic Sea fish-dishes likely to find their way onto starter menus include sprats with onions (*šprotes ar sēpoliem*), herring (*siļķe*) and fried, smoked or salted eel (*zutis*). Popular soups (*zupas*) include *kāpostu zupa* or cabbage soup, and *soļanka*, a meat, vegetable and gherkin broth of Russian origin.

Whatever you order it will come with several slices of bread (*maize*), including some of the delicious, dark, rye bread (*rupjmaize*) for which the Baltic region is famed.

Main courses

A main course based on **meat** (*gaļa*) usually comes in the form either of a *fileja* (fillet) or *karbonāde* (chop, often a lightly battered schnitzel). *Cūkas fileja* is a pork fillet, *teļa* veal, *liellopu* beef, and *cālīšu* chicken. Cuts of pork and other meats usually come with a nice rind of fat round the edge – giving people only lean meat was traditionally considered rather rude.

Common varieties of **fish** (*zivs*) include *lasis* (salmon), *forele* (trout) and *zandarts* (pike-perch). Main courses are usually served with boiled potatoes or french fries, accompanied by a coleslaw-style salad or a pile of pickled vegetables. Popular garnishes include lashings of sour cream (*krējums*), or a ladleful of mushroom sauce (*sēņu merce*).

Desserts

One traditional Latvian dessert that crops up almost everywhere is *ķīselis*, an oat-porrige sweetened with seasonal fruit and forest berries. Otherwise, dessert menus tend to concentrate on more familiar items such as ice cream (*saldējums*), gateau (*torte*) and all manner of cakes (*kūkas*). Pancakes (*pankūkas*) come with a variety of fillings, notably *biezpiens* or curd cheese, which is slightly sweetened to form a cheesecake-ish taste. Little chocolate-coated cubes of *biezpiens* (Kārums is the best-known make) can be picked up from supermarket chiller cabinets – they're absolutely delicious.

Drinking

Traditionally Latvian drinking culture revolves around the **kafejnīca** or café, which serves non-alcoholic drinks and closes early in the evening, and the **krogs** or tavern, where serious evening boozing sessions take place. Nowadays, the range of internationally styled bars and pubs in Rīga and other big cities has massively broadened the range of venues available – and the global choice of drinks you can consume in them.

The main alcoholic drink in Latvia is **alus** (beer), which comes either as *gaišs alus* (the regular, lager-like brew) or as *tumšs alus* (a strong dark porter). The biggest and best of the breweries are Aldaris, from Rīga, and Cēsu from Cēsis.

One Latvian spirit you should definitely try at least once is **Rīgas melnais balzāms**, or Rīga black balsam, a bitter-tasting potion brewed according to a two-and-a-half-centuries-old recipe that combines various roots, grasses and herbs. It's a bit of an acquired taste when drunk neat, but combines rather well with cola and other mixers. Decent **vodka** is easy to get hold of in Latvia – world-renowned brands such as Stolichnaya and Moskovskaya are made under licence in the same distillery as melnais balzāms. The local **sparkling wine**, Rīgas šampanietis, is both potent and cheap.

One traditional non-alcoholic beverage that is making something of a come-back is **kvass**, a drink made from malt extract, resembling cola in colour and just as popular locally. **Coffee** (*kafija*) and **tea** (*tēja*) are usually served black – if you want milk (*piens*) you'll have to ask. *Ar cukuru* means with sugar, *bez cukura* means without.

Opening hours and public holidays

Shops are usually open Monday to Friday 10am–7/8pm, Saturday 10am–4/5pm, though some close for an hour around lunchtime. Supermarkets and food shops often stay open until 10pm and also open on Sunday.

Museums and galleries are usually open Tues–Sun or Wed–Sun 10am–5pm, with the addition of the odd hour or two in summer. Latvia's Lutheran **churches** can be very hard to get into outside Sunday service times, unless – like those in central Rīga for example – they're of particular cultural and historic importance, in which case they'll be open on a nine-to-five basis every day of the week.

Holidays and remembrance days

National holidays

All banks and offices, as well as most shops, are closed on the following public holidays. Big supermarkets and food stores in Rīga may well stay open, apart from on January 1, when there is a genuine national shut-down

Jan 1 New Year's Day

Good Friday

Easter Sunday

Easter Monday

May 1 Labour Day

Mothers' Day (second Sunday in May)

June 23–24 Midsummer celebrations

Nov 18 Independence Day

Dec 24–26 Christmas

Dec 31 New Year's Eve

Remembrance days

A number of dates in the Latvian calendar are set aside for remembering specific events or particular groups of people who made some contribution to the nation. Shops and businesses remain open on the following dates, although some individuals take all or part of the day off to attend commemorative events or to lay flowers or wreaths.

March 16 Latvian Legion

March 25 Deportations of 1949

May 4 Declaration of Independence

May 8 Victims of World War II

June 14 Victims of Communist Terror

July 4 Holocaust Day

November 11 Lāčplēšis Day (Independence 1918–19)

Orthodox churches, in contrast, are much more accessible, and there's usually an attendant selling candles and icon-bearing postcards during the daylight hours.

Festivals

In pagan times, Latvian festivals were closely related to the position of the sun, with solstices and equinoxes providing the main occasions for ritual celebration. Many of these practices still exist, although they dovetail so neatly with the Christian calendar that they're no longer recognizeable as the pagan holidays they originally were.

The run-up to **Easter** (*Lieldiena*) is marked by street hawkers selling bunches of catkins (*pūpoli*), which, as well as serving as a symbol of the coming spring, are also used to thrash your nearest and dearest on the morning of Palm Sunday (*Pūpolsvētdiena*). In days gone by, rural communities celebrated Easter itself by gathering beside the village swing – a huge wooden platform capable of bearing whole families – and taking it in turns to swoop up and down to the accompaniment of suitably rhythmic chants. A fertlity ritual of ancient, pre-Christian origins, the practice is kept alive by folkloric societies.

The one big ritual event which is still celebrated en masse is **Jāņi** or Midsummer's Eve, when urban Latvians head for the countryside to spend the whole night drinking beer around a bonfire and singing ancient sun-worshipping songs known as *līgotne* – named after the swaying "līgo, līgo" refrain that almost all of them feature. Traditionally, Jāņi represented the last chance for a booze-up before the hard work of the harvest season began, and it's the hedonistic aspect of the occasion that has made it enduringly popular – and also explains why there are so many drunk drivers careering around Latvia's roads on midsummer morning.

At some stage in summer or autumn each town and village has a **graveyard festival** (*kapu svētki*), when family plots are tidied up and picnics are eaten beside the graves – urban dwellers often go back to their home village to take part.

Latvian **Christmas** (*Ziemassvētki*) is nowadays the commercialized occasion that it is in the rest of Europe, and few families still celebrate Christmas Eve by tucking into the traditional fare of boiled pig's head and peas. A couple of practices connected to the winter solstice are still enacted by folklore societies, especially at the open-air museum in

Arts festivals

All-Latvian Song and Dance Festival
Rīga and locations countrywide. Held
every five years (the next is due in
2008) and featuring as many as
30,000 singers.

International Bach Festival Rīga,
March.

Baltic Ballet Festival Rīga, March;
ⓦwww.ballet-festival.lv.

Opera Festival Rīga, June;
ⓦwww.music.lv/opera.

Organ Music Festival Rīga, July.

Early Music Festival Rīga, Bauska &
Rundale, July.

Sigulda Opera Festival Sigulda, July;
ⓦwww.sigulda.lv.

Sacred Music Festival Rīga, August.

Liepājas dzintars rock festival
Liepāja, August.

**International Chamber Choir
Festival (Rīga dimd)** Rīga,
September; ⓦwww.culture.lv
/choirfestival.

**International Chamber Music
Festival** Rīga, September.

Arēna New Music Festival Rīga,
October; ⓦwww.arenafest.lv.

Rīga (see p.218), where you can see mummers masked as bears, horses, cranes, goats or the grim reaper going from house to house to drive away evil, and a yule log (*bļuks*), symbolizing the misfortunes of the previous year, is dragged around by celebrants before being ritually burned. **New Year** (*Jaungads*) is marked by the familar round of boozing, partying and firework displays.

Entertainment

Although most Latvian cities can muster a theatre, a cinema and the odd music venue, the bulk of the country's entertainment options are concentrated in Rīga, a culture-saturated metropolis with something to satisfy most tastes. Details of where to catch opera, ballet, orchestral music and theatre in the capital can be found on p.224.

Choral singing and classical music

Choral singing has played a central role in Latvian culture ever since 1868, when 150 singers attended the first-ever national song festival in Valga. The nurturing of an indigenous folk-song tradition was seen as an important way of opposing the domination of German-language culture and it helped to keep Latvian traditions alive during the Soviet period. Nowadays, there's hardly a village, factory or government department without a choir, most of them performing material which is deeply rooted in Latvia's rich folk tradition (for more on folk music, see p.422). The nation's choirs get together every five years to participate in the **All-Latvian Song and Dance Festival**, when the sound of thousands of massed voices issuing forth from the open-air song bowl in Rīga's Mežaparks can be a truly visceral experience. If you can't make it to the festival (the next is due in 2008), there are plenty of opportunities to hear top-quality choirs in Rīga. Prominent among these are the all-female **Dzintars**, and the mixed choir, **Ave Sol**, both of whom perform startlingly modern arrangements of archaic Latvian songs, as well as specially commissioned contemporary compositions.

One outstanding modern composer known for his choral as well as orchestral works, is **Pēteris Vasks** (b.1946), whose journeys into contemplative, deeply spiritual territory have earned comparisons with the likes of Gorecki, Tavener and Pärt. His works are regularly performed in Rīga, and the city's record shops are full of his CDs. One of the best-known interpreters of Vasks' work is the Rīga-born violin virtuoso **Gidon Kremer** (b.1947), whose multinational chamber ensemble Kremerata Baltica has garnered an international reputation for its performances of contemporary classical music. Tickets for Kremer performances sell out fast in Rīga – again, there are plenty of CDs in the shops if you miss out.

Club culture and popular music

Rīga's club scene offers a bit of everything, from cavernous mega-clubs pumping out frenetic techno to thousand-strong herds, to more intimate alternative spaces where you can hear anything from hip-hop and reggae to post-industrial noise. A lot of the latter places offer a regular programme of live music, with the result that the underground gig scene is slightly more vibrant here than in Tallinn or Vilnius. There's also a respectable range of mid-sized venues hosting performances by Latvia's sizeable stable of home-grown, pop-rock acts.

Ever since the 1960s, Latvia has developed a strain of melodic, lyrical pop that has gone against the grain of both Soviet show-biz culture and Western rock, and has been embraced as an important element in national identity as a consequence. Central to its evolution has been **Imants Kalniņš**, a classically trained composer (his symphony no. 4 is widely held to be on a par with most contemporary classical production), who has written songs for just about every Latvian pop performer of consequence from the late 1960s onwards. His 1967 song *Dziesma par četriem baltiem krekliem* ("Song About Four White Shirts") – recorded by the group Menuets for the cult film *Elpojiet Dziļi* ("Breathe Deeply") – was banned by the authorities because the shirts in question were taken as a metaphor for Latvian dignity in the face of Soviet oppression, and he's been a symbol of national integrity ever since. Kalniņš' wide-ranging oeuvre is difficult to pin down, but if you crossed Paul Macartney with Leonard Cohen something resembling Kalniņš would probably come out the other end. Your best bet is to get hold of best-of compilation *Dziesmu izlase* and make up your own mind.

Few subsequent songwriters have enjoyed similar stature, save perhaps for **Ainars Mielavs**, originally lead singer with rousing folk-pop practitioners **Jauns Mēness** – their early 1990s albums represent the high point of Latvian rock. Mielavs is now a solo performer of adult-oriented, mellow songs, and also heads leading folk label Upe records (see p.426). Latvian pop's current international standard bearers are **Brainstorm**, one of the few groups to appear in the Eurovision Song Contest (they came third in 2000) and survive with their career unscathed. They've recorded numerous albums of bright, infectious, indie-influenced melodies, some of which come in both Latvian and English versions, and they have a sizeable fan base in central Europe and Scandinavia.

Alternative rock culture runs deep in Rīga, although few groups stay together long enough to leave a lasting mark. Eager album buyers looking for non-mainstream souvenirs should check out CDs by gritty anarcho-punk trio **Inokentijs Marpls**, ambient electro-experimentalists **Latvias Gāze**, and jazzy post-rock soundsmiths **sattlelites.lv**.

No discussion of Latvian music would be complete without mention of composer, impresario and all-round national institution **Raimonds Pauls**. His recently re-released album *Tik Dzintars Vien* – recorded in 1970 but recalling European popular songs of the 1950s – is a landmark in Latvian easy-listening. He went on to become a big star in the Soviet Union, penning albums for astronomically popular, variety-show warblers like (Latvian) Laima Vaikule and (Russian) Alla Pugacheva. You might want to give his latter-day work a wide berth, though, ranging as it does from Eurovision-style pop-pap to cocktail-bar piano-tinkling of the queasiest kind.

Cinema

Latvian cinemas show feature films in the original language – with subtitles in both Latvian and Russian blotting out the bottom third of the screen. During the Soviet period, Rīga's film studio turned out an average of eight features a year, but with the collapse of state funding after 1990 the tally has shrunk to one or two low-budget affairs. The most successful domestic effort in recent years has been *Summer of Dread* (*Baiga Vasara*; 2000), a drama set in Latvia on the eve of the Soviet occupation of June 1940 – a version with English subtitles was recently doing the rounds of Rīga's video stores. Ask locals to name their favourite Latvian film of all time and they'd probably plump for 1973's *Blow, Wind!* (*Pūt Vējiņi!*), a lavishly costumed tale of love and death set in pre-

Christian Latvia, and featuring a rousing score by Imants Kalniņš – the soundtrack CD is worth having on its own.

Internationally, Latvia is more famous for its documentaries than its feature films. This is almost entirely due to the career of **Juris Podnieks**, whose 1986 work *Is it Easy to be Young* – an unflinching investigation into the lives of directionless, delinquent youth in Rīga – eloquently stripped bare the inner psychoses of a disintegrating society and attracted massive audiences throughout the USSR as a result. He subsequently devoted his efforts to documenting the death throes of Soviet communism – his five-part TV series *Hello, Can you Hear Us?* (1989) was a disturbing portrait of a multinational empire on the skids, while *Homeland* (1992) dealt movingly with the drive to independence in the Baltic States. Production of the latter was marred by the deaths of two of Podnieks' cameramen – shot while filming the Soviet attack on the Latvian Interior Ministry in January 1991 (see p.207). Podnieks himself died in a freak scuba-diving accident in summer 1992.

A major showcase for new Latvian films (whether dramas or documentaries) is the **Lielais Kristaps festival** (organized by the Latvian National Film Centre; ⓦwww.nfc.lv), a not-quite-annual affair that's held whenever enough films are produced to justify it.

Spectator sports

Most international team games enjoy moderate popularity in Latvia, although it's **ice hockey** that generates most in the way of mass enthusiasm. The sport's big breakthrough in the public consciousness came during the world championships of 2000, when an unfancied Latvian team defeated title favourites Russia in the group stages, sending thousands of Latvians out onto the streets of Rīga in celebration. The Latvians have remained in the world's top ten ever since, but are yet to break through to the medal-winning stages of a major competion. The Ice Hockey World Championships, due to take place in Rīga in 2006, may provide their best ever chance. League games in Latvia itself are lacklustre affairs (the best

Latvian players ply their trade in North America), and the best way to enjoy the sport is to catch a major international encounter on the big screen in a crowded pub. The distinctively maroon Latvian hockey jerseys make highly desirable souvenirs, and can be bought from some of the Rīga souvenir shops listed on p.226. Still on the subject of winter sports, Latvia has a couple of decent **bobsleigh** crews, and the national track at Sigulda is used annually for international world cup meetings.

After a decade of under-achievement, the Latvian **football** team astonished everybody (not least themselves) by qualifying for the 2004 European Championships, beating a highly rated Turkish team in the play-offs. International matches are played in Rīga in front of sizeable crowds (see p.225), but domestic league games are poorly attended. Top team **Skonto Rīga** have won the national league title ten times since the regaining of independence, and the lack of meaningful competition has kept the crowds away. Owing to Latvia's harsh winters, the football season runs from April to October.

Directory

Addresses In Latvian addresses, the name of the street precedes the number. The word for street itself (*iela*) is often omitted from the sentence.

Contraceptives The best place to look for condoms (*prezervatīvi*) is near the check-out of big supermarkets.

Emergencies Police ☎02; ambulance ☎03; fire ☎01.

Left luggage Most bus stations have a left-luggage counter (*Bagāžas novietne* or *Rokas bagažas glabātava*), with a daily charge of about 0.50–1Ls per item, depending on size.

Tipping Tipping is only expected in restaurants or in the smarter cafés with waited tables, in which case you add ten percent to the bill or round it up to the nearest convenient figure.

Toilets Public toilets can be found at most bus stations. Ladies are *dāmas*; gents are *kungi*.

2.1

Rīga and around

With just over 743,000 inhabitants, almost one third of the country's population, **RĪGA** is the biggest city in the Baltics, offering a degree of cosmopolitan bustle, sophistication and sheer urban chaos that neither Tallinn nor Vilnius can really compete with. It's also one of the best-looking Baltic cities, its rich history as a military, ecclesiastical and, above all, mercantile powerhouse having bequeathed the city a legacy of fine architecture: medieval red-brick churches and gabled merchants' houses rise above the alleyways of the Old Town, while the surrounding nineteenth-century streets hold some remarkable examples of Art Nouveau, as well as buildings in National Romantic style, a local offshoot of Art Nouveau, in which architects drew on Latvian folk symbols for ornamental inspiration. And you don't need to wander far from the centre to find neighbourhoods full of tumbledown wooden houses and cobbled back streets.

Almost totally absent from the capital are the national characteristics that many Latvians ascribe to themselves – an enduring attachment to wholesome peasant values and a love of nature, to name but two. Since its very inception, Rīga has dedicated itself to commerce and wheeler-dealing. Hard-headed mercantile instincts have always served to bond together Rīga's ethnically diverse population: currently, half of the city's inhabitants are Latvian, while the other half are either Russian or Russian-speaking, giving the city a strangely schizophrenic character – the two

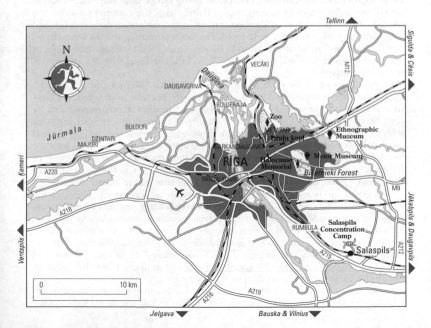

communities get on peaceably enough, but tend to lead separate lives, reading their own newspapers and watching their own TV stations, and often displaying a staggering indifference to each others' language and culture.

Boasting historic buildings on almost every corner and a strong hand of set-piece museums, such as the moving Occupation Museum and compelling Museum of Medical History, **downtown Rīga** can easily fill two or three days of your holiday time; longer if you're drawn towards the more offbeat attractions of the city's **suburbs**, such as the impressive Open-air Ethnographic Museum. Also within easy reach are the beguiling beach resort of **Jūrmala**, 20km to the northwest, and the Holocaust memorial sites at **Rumbula** and **Salaspils**, just outside the city to the southeast. You could even use the city as a base for exploring sizeable chunks of north and central Latvia, much of it no more than a couple of hours' journey away.

Some history

Rīga was founded by **Albert von Buxhoeveden**, a priest from Bremen who arrived in 1201 with twenty shiploads of crusaders to convert the Baltic tribes to Christianity. Taking over a site previously occupied by Livonian fishermen, Albert lost no time in building a fortified settlement strong enough to withstand the frequent raids made by Livonians and Latvians, and civilians from northern Europe flocked to the new town to take advantage of the new opportunities for business and trade. As the headquarters of the crusading effort in the Baltics, Rīga was home to three often quarrelsome groups – the church, the knights of the Livonian Order, and the increasingly assertive citizenry. With the last refusing to put up with the dictates of the other two, Rīga became a self-governing municipality owing symbolic fealty to the Order, whose Grand Master continued to base himself in Rīga's castle. Eager to exploit this new freedom of manoeuvre, the city joined the **Hanseatic league**, a loose alliance of north-German trading cities, in 1282 (see box on p.302 for more on this). Civic life was to remain in the hands of a German-speaking mercantile elite for the next six hundred years.

Rīga grew rich on the trade of timber, furs and flax, which were floated down the Daugava River on enormous rafts before being loaded onto ships and exported west. Perennially suspicious of the grasping Baltic clergy, the citizenry provided fertile ground for the spread of **Protestantism** in the early sixteenth century and Rīga became a bastion of the new creed. The city's remaining monks were chased out in 1524, and most of the churches were vandalized by Protestant mobs at around the same time – which explains why so little medieval religious art survives in the city today.

Squeezed between the expanding states of Russia, Sweden and Poland, the Livonian Order collapsed in 1562 and Rīga briefly became an independent city-state before being absorbed into the **Polish-Lithuanian Commonwealth** by King Stefan Bathory in 1582. Bathory seriously considered re-Catholicizing Rīga with the help of the Jesuits, so anxious locals were not sorry to see the Poles kicked out by the **Swedes** in 1621. For almost a century Rīga was the main base for Swedish military campaigns in the Baltics, stimulating trade and filling the coffers of the city's merchants. The Swedes met their nemesis, however, in the shape of **Peter the Great of Russia**, who captured Rīga in 1709 after a nine-month siege.

Even under the Russians Rīga remained culturally a German city, although the seventeenth century saw an influx of **Latvian-speaking** peasants from the surrounding countryside. The German and Latvian populations were largely segregated, and knowledge of German remained the only route to social advancement. Even those Latvians who made it into business were denied acceptance by the urban elite (the city authorities argued that as the descendants of serfs, Latvians had no right to be considered free burghers), and it wasn't until the 1780s that the right of Latvians to own property in the city was recognized.

During the nineteenth century, Rīga developed into a major industrial centre, the population growing from just under 30,000 in 1800 to half a million by the century's close. Significant numbers of Russians were brought to Rīga to work in the factories, and with a deliberate policy of **Russification** now being applied to the Tsarist Empire's western cities, Russian was made the main language of instruction in schools. Although denied any real political influence, the burgeoning Latvian population was determined to make its presence felt, with events like the first all-Latvian song festival (held in the city in June 1873) signalling their increasing cultural self-confidence. On the eve of World War I the Latvians were the biggest ethnic group in the city – the Germans had in the meantime been pushed into third place behind the Russians.

Having spent much of World War I as a front-line city and having been badly damaged, Rīga was abandoned by the Russians in September 1917 and German Kaiser Wilhelm II arrived in person to take possession of the city. The collapse of Germany just over a year later ushered in a period of extreme chaos. Latvian independence was proclaimed in the National Theatre on November 18, but with no army at their disposal, the new government had to hand the city over to the **Bolsheviks** on January 3, 1919. Home-grown Latvian revolutionary Pēteris Stučka presided over four months of communist terror – during which the bourgeoisie were made to perform demeaning tasks (or were simply taken away to be shot) – before being chased out by a combined force of Latvians, White Russians and Germans. This marriage of convenience didn't last long, however, and the White Russians and Germans were finally seen off by the Latvians in November, 1919, with the assistance of a British naval bombardment.

Now the capital of an independent Latvia, Rīga entered the new era a massively changed city. Industry was in ruins, and the population had fallen by half since 1914. The city recovered quickly, however, and for much of the 1920s and 1930s Rīga enjoyed something of a belle époque, earning the city the sobriquet of "Little Paris". The city's cosmopolitan mix was boosted by an influx of anti-Bolshevik refugees from Russia, whose taste for old-world etiquette and lavish entertaining led American diplomat George Kennan to remark that Rīga was "the only place where one could still live in Tsarist Russia".

World War II – during which Rīga was occupied by the Soviets, then by the Germans – once again left the city impoverished, a situation that didn't radically improve when the Soviets returned to stay in October 1944. The communists dedicated themselves to the development of heavy industry in Rīga and radically changed the ethnic profile of the city by importing a (largely Russian-speaking) workforce from all over the Soviet Union. By the late 1980s the influx of Russian immigrants had reduced the Latvians to a minority in their own capital.

Most of Rīga's non-Latvians were unenthusiastic about leaving the Soviet Union when the independence drive took off in the late 1980s, but few supported the use of OMON troops and tanks to seize control of key buildings in January 1991, an action which cost five innocent lives and destroyed any shred of credibility communist rule still had.

With the Soviet Union buried well over a decade ago and and the promise of EU membership attracting huge levels of foreign investment, Rīga has become something of a boom town, with gleaming office blocks sprouting up on vacant lots everywhere and real estate prices going through the roof. New wealth has been slow to trickle down to the majority, however, and while there's no shortage of flashy, fuel-guzzling, four-wheel-drives bouncing their way around Rīga's badly paved streets, many denizens of the capital continue to eke out a living on meagre wages.

Arrival, information and city transport

Rīga's smart, modern **airport** (Rīgas lidosta) is 8km southwest of the Old Town. Head straight out of the arrivals hall and cross the car park to find the bus stop, from where bus #22 (2–3 every hour; 0.20Ls; pay the conductor) runs to Abrenes iela on the southeastern fringes of the centre, passing the bus and train stations on

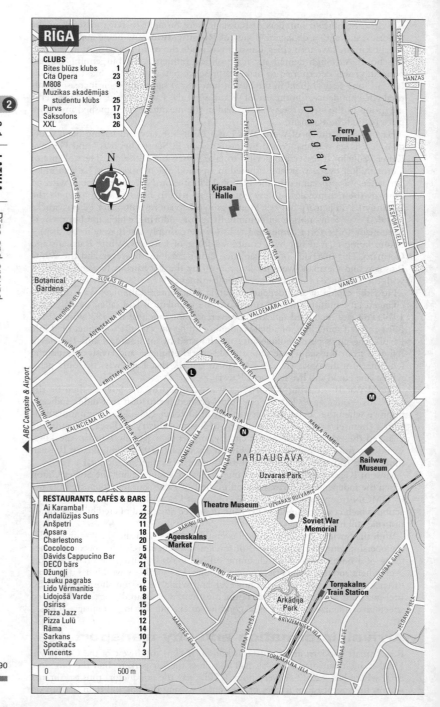

RĪGA

CLUBS
Bites blūzs klubs	1
Cita Opera	23
M808	9
Muzikas akadēmijas studentu klubs	25
Purvs	17
Saksofons	13
XXL	26

RESTAURANTS, CAFÉS & BARS
Ai Karamba!	2
Andalūzijas Suns	22
Anšpetri	11
Apsara	18
Charlestons	20
Cocoloco	5
Dāvids Cappucino Bar	24
DECO bārs	21
Džungļi	4
Lauku pagrabs	6
Lido Vērmanītis	16
Lidojošā Varde	8
Osiriss	15
Pizza Jazz	19
Pizza Lulū	12
Rāma	14
Sarkans	10
Spotikačs	7
Vincents	3

0   500 m

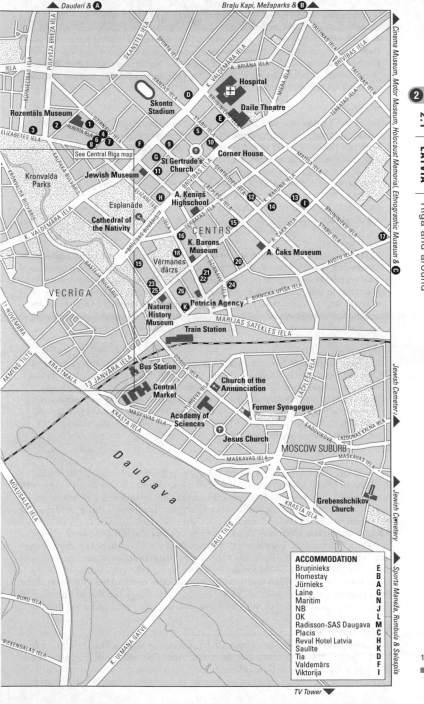

Dauderi & **A**

Braļu Kapi, Mežaparks & **B**

Cinema Museum, Motor Museum, Holocaust Memorial, Ethnographic Museum & **C**

Rozentāls Museum

Skonto Stadium

Hospital

Daile Theatre

Corner House

St Gertrude's Church

Jewish Museum

A. Keniņš Highschool

Cathedral of the Nativity

Esplanāde

Kronvalda Parks

CENTRS

K. Barons Museum

A. Čaks Museum

Vērmanes dārzs

VECRĪGA

Natural History Museum

Patricia Agency

Train Station

Bus Station

Central Market

Church of the Annunciation

Former Synagogue

Academy of Sciences

Jesus Church

MOSCOW SUBURB

Daugava

Grebenshchikov Church

Jewish Cemetery

Jewish Cemetery

Sporta Maneža, Rumbula & Salaspils

TV Tower

ACCOMMODATION

Bruņinieks	E
Homestay	B
Jūrnieks	A
Laine	G
Maritim	N
NB	J
OK	L
Radisson-SAS Daugava	M
Placis	C
Reval Hotel Latvia	H
Saulite	K
Tia	D
Valdemārs	F
Viktorija	I

Moving on from Rīga

Rīga is a major transport hub, with a multitude of **bus** routes fanning out across the Baltic region and beyond. There are several daily buses to Vilnius and Tallinn and plenty of direct services to Germany, France, the Netherlands and Great Britain. There are also overnight **trains** to Russia, the Ukraine and Belarus; and **car ferries** to Scandinavia and Germany.

By bus

Rīga's **bus station** (@www.autoosta.lv) is relatively user-friendly, with easy-to-read departure listings and an English-speaking information office in the main ticket hall. Domestic tickets are sold from the ticket counters immediately opposite the main entrance; international services are handled by a cluster of offices just around the corner on the right. The main **agents** for international tickets are Eurolines (☎721 4080, @www.eurolines.lv) and Ecolines (☎721 4512, @www.ecolines.lv); both have outlets at the station, and Ecolines also has an office at Čaka iela 45 (☎727 4444). Facilities in the station are limited to a coffee shop and a couple of newsagents in the ticket hall.

By train

Rīga's recently renovated **central station** feels more like a vast shopping mall than somewhere to get a train. With all the cafés and bakeries around, you'll certainly have no trouble stocking up on supplies for the trip. There are daily or thrice-weekly services to Vilnius, Moscow, St Petersburg, Minsk, Vitebsk, Lvov and beyond – all of which require at least one night on the train. **Tickets** for international services are bought from the "Starptautiskie vilcieni" counters; those for journeys within Latvia are purchased from windows marked "Iekšzemes vilcienu biļešu kases".

By ferry

The **ferry terminal** at Eksporta iela 3A (tram #7 from the bus station or National Opera to Ausekla iela) is a pretty joyless place, with ticket counters, an exchange office and a duty-free shop – but not much else. Last-minute food or souvenir shopping should be done before you get here. The thrice-weekly **ferry to Stockholm** is operated by Rīgas Jūras Līnija, which has a ticket office at the terminal (☎720 5460, @www.rigasealine.lv). Latlines, Zivju iela 1 (☎734 9527, @www.latlines.lv), sells tickets for the twice-weekly ferry **to Lübeck**.

the way; bus #22A (1–2 every hour; 0.25Ls; pay the driver) runs to "Katedrāle" – the Russian Orthodox cathedral just east of the Old Town. A taxi to the centre will cost around 5–7Ls. The taxi booking office inside the arrivals hall will reserve you a taxi for an additional 2Ls – a useful way of jumping the queue if things are busy, but not worth bothering with otherwise.

Rīga's main **train station** (Centrālā stacija) and **bus station** (Autoosta) are within 200m of each other, five minutes' walk south of the Old Town. Taxi drivers outside both stations aren't keen on ferrying passengers short distances, and will demand a minimum of 3–4Ls to take you anywhere in the city centre.

The **ferry terminal** (Jūras pasažieru stacija) is 1500m north of the Old Town at the end of Eksporta iela. Trams #5, #7 or #9 run from the stop 100m east of the terminal on Ausekļa iela to the edge of the Old Town (two stops; pay the conductor; 0.20Ls).

Information

The main **tourist office** is on the Old Town's main square, Rātslaukums (daily 10am–7pm; ☎703 7900, @www.rigatourism.com). The staff speak English and can give you accommodation lists, although they don't book hotels on your behalf. In addition, there are tourist information booths at the airport (just outside the arrivals hall; Mon–Sat 10am–6pm; ☎720 7800) and the bus station (Mon–Fri 9am–6pm, Sat & Sun 10am–5pm; ☎722 0555). All three offices sell the **Rīga Card** (8Ls for 24hr, 12Ls for 48hr, 16Ls for 72hr), which allows unlimited use of public transport, entry to the major museums, a guided tour of the city and discounts in some restaurants – worth buying if you intend to do a fair amount of sightseeing. A handy source of information is the English-language guide *Rīga in Your Pocket* (from news kiosks; 1.20Ls; ⓦwww.inyourpocket.com), which contains restaurant and bar listings and Yellow Pages-style information, updated every two to three months. Also useful is the magazine-format *City Paper* (from news kiosks; 2.30Ls; ⓦwww.balticsworldwide.com), published bi-monthly, and offering a good mix of listings and readable features – it covers Tallinn and Vilnius into the bargain.

City transport

The centre of Rīga is easily walkable and outlying attractions are served by **bus**, **tram** or **trolleybus**. All run from around 5am until 11pm. Key stops are Stacijas laukums (the square immediately in front of the train station) and Katedrāle, the part of Brīvības iela adjacent to the Orthodox cathedral. Flat-fare, single-journey **tickets** cost 0.20Ls and are purchased on board from the conductor. Some routes are operated by express buses, which only stop at selected points; tickets for these cost 0.25Ls and can be bought from the driver. Speedier still are the minibuses (*taksobuss* or *mikroautobuss*; 0.25–0.30Ls; pay the driver), which run along the main boulevards joining the centre to the suburbs, in many cases duplicating the routes operated by trams and buses. **Travelcards** (available from news kiosks) will prove useful if you're sticking around for some time, although there's a bewildering variety available. The most useful perhaps is the five-day pass (*biļete piecām dienām*; 2.80Ls), covering all tram and trolleybus routes, though not buses.

Taxis are generally cheap: the basic fare is around 0.40Ls plus an additional charge of 0.30Ls per kilometre during the day and 0.40Ls between 10pm and 6am. Although rip-off merchants are the exception rather than the rule, some drivers will take advantage of foreigners by switching the meter off and demanding a set price. You'll find taxi ranks at all the main entry points to the Old Town, although it's usually cheaper to phone for a taxi in advance rather than picking one up from a rank. See "Directory", p.227, for recommended taxi firms.

Accommodation

Rīga has undergone a hotel-building boom in the years since independence, and there's no shortage of middle- to upper-bracket establishments to choose from. The outlook for budget travellers is less promising, the majority of cheap city-centre **hotels** having been closed down and redeveloped over the last decade. The number of hostel beds is minimal for a city of this size, and the only other source of cheap, central accommodation is a **private room** with a local family. One of the most reliable room-rental agencies is Patricia Ltd, Elizabetes 22–6 (Mon–Fri 9.15am–6pm, Sat & Sun 10.15am–1pm; ☎728 4868, ⓔtourism@parks.lv); private rooms within walking distance of the Old Town start at 15Ls per person, 3Ls more if you pay by credit card. Breakfast is 3Ls.

The sole **campsite** is ABC, 6km southwest of the centre at Šampētera 139A (☎789 2728, ⓦwww.janisnaglis.lv), with space for tents and caravans, plus well-appointed cabins with TV (20–30Ls). Located immediately before the airport turn-off, it's clearly signed off the main Jūrmala highway if you're driving west. Buses #22 and #22A pass nearby.

Student hostels

There are no youth hostels as such in Rīga, only some hostel-style accommodation in student dorms. Staff at these places don't always speak much English and often behave as if they've never seen a backpacker in their lives before, but will sort you out with a bed if you're patient. Advance bookings are feasible if you're lucky enough to find a common language.

Latvijas Universitātes dienesta viesnīca Basteja 10 ☎721 6221. A university-owned establishment that functions as a hotel for visiting teachers during the academic year (when you will be lucky to find a space), and a hostel for all-comers in July & August – when it fills up quickly owing to its Old Town location. Rooms are sparsely furnished and plain, but clean. Beds from 8Ls per person, doubles with en-suite shower 20Ls.

Placis Laimdotas 2A ☎755 1824, ✉placis@delfi.lv. A student dorm a good 6km northeast of the Old Town, but easy enough to get to on public transport. A mixture of singles (16Ls), doubles (22Ls) and triples (15Ls), and a cafeteria on site. To get there, take bus #1, #14 or #32 from Katedrāle, or trolleybus #4 from Stacijas laukums, to the Teika stop – the hostel is five minutes' walk beyond the Teika cinema.

Hotels

There's no shortage of hotels in and around the Old Town, though the range is somewhat limited, with a glut of mid-price establishments offering neat but rather bland rooms, with little to distinguish them. Places of charm and character do exist, though – typically in the more expensive categories.

Generally speaking, you'll be hard pushed to find a double room in the Old Town for less than 50Ls. Cheaper deals do exist in the grid of streets that make up the Centre, although many of the hotels in this part of Rīga haven't renovated their rooms since the communist period and can be slightly gloomy. Providing you don't mind being a ten-minute tram ride away from the sights, there's a growing choice of accommodation in Pārdaugava, just across the river from the Old Town, and there are a couple of choice picks elsewhere in the city – notably in the northern suburbs of Mežaparks and Sarkandaugava.

Some hotels cut their prices in winter (typically October–March), while others offer weekend **discounts** – it always pays to ask. **Breakfast** is included in the price in the listings below unless otherwise stated.

The Old Town

Ainavas Peldu 23 ☎781 4316, ⊕www.ainavas.lv. A small, intimate and characterful hotel in a restored medieval house, offering attractive en-suite rooms, each decorated in different pastel colours – hence the place's name, which means "Landscapes". **❼**

Centra Audēju 1 ☎722 6441, ⊕www.centra.lv. Spacious, smart rooms, decorated in modern, minimalist style, with shower and TV, each offering good views of the Audēju iela street scene below. Good value for the location. **❻**

Forums Vaļņu iela 45 ☎781 4680, ⊕www.hotelforums.lv. A medium-sized hotel across the road from the bus station, offering plush though cramped en-suite rooms, with wine-red carpets, wooden furnishings and TV. **❺**

Grand Palace Hotel Pils 12 ☎704 4000, ⊕www.schlossle-hotels.com. A luxury hotel in a wonderful old building, stuffed full of antique-effect furniture, just off Doma laukums. Rooms from 130Ls. **❽**

Gutenbergs Doma laukums 1 ☎781 4090, ⊕www.gutenbergs.lv. Affordable and superbly situated, this comfy, medium-sized place fills up

fast. Faux-rustic rooms in one wing, more chintzy affairs in the other. The restaurant's summer terrace, with views of the Old Town's roofscape, is a major plus point. **❻**

Konventa Sēta Kalēju iela 9/11 ☎708 7501, ⊕www.derome.lv. A charming, 140-room hotel in the heart of the Old Town, with modern en-suite rooms surrounding the beautifully restored courtyard of a former convent. Some of the doubles are apartment-style, with kitchenettes. **❺**

Metropole Aspazijas 36/38 ☎722 5411, ⊕www.metropole.lv. Between the opera and the train station, this stately old hotel has been going since 1872 and was given a complete facelift in the 1990s. Rooms are fully equipped, but something seems to have gone wrong in the interior design department – Scandinavian minimalism meets overpowering chintz. **❻**

Park Hotel Rīdzene Reimersa 1 ☎732 4433, ⊕www.parkhotelridzene.com. A classy, fully equipped and well-run luxury hotel, nicely situated in the belt of parkland surrounding the Old Town. Doubles from 150s. **❽**

Radi un Draugi Mārstaļu iela 1/3 ☎722 0372, ⊕www.draugi.lv. Neat and cosy rooms in an

excellent downtown location, with en-suite bathrooms, TV and tea-making facilities. Decor is on the bland side, but it's superb value for the location. Reservations advisable in summer. ❹
Rolands Kaļķu 3A ☏ 722 0011, ⓦ www.hotelrolands.lv. Bang on the Old Town's main street, this unabashedly modern establishment offers bright, chintz-free rooms, all with tea and coffee makers and most featuring proper tubs in the bathrooms. Doubles from 130Ls. ❽
Saulīte Merķeļa 12 ☏ 722 4546. Cheapie directly opposite the train station, with cramped rooms, lino floors, battered furniture, and shared toilets in the hallway – but clean and safe nevertheless. There are a few more expensive "comfort" rooms with en-suite WC and showers. Breakfast 1.50Ls extra. ❶–❷
Vecrīga Gleznotāju iela 12/14 ☏ 721 6524, ⓦ www.vecriga.lv. A ten-room hotel on a quiet Old Town street. Standard en-suites with TV, most with bathtubs rather than showers. ❻

The Centre

Bruņinieks Bruņinieku 6 ☏ 731 5140, ⓦ www.bruninieks.lv. Smart, modern en-suites in a medium-sized establishment just off busy Brīvības iela, the Centre's main artery. It's a twenty-minute walk from the Old Town, but buses and trolleybuses are plentiful. Tram #11 from Radio iela to the Brīvības stop. ❺
Laine Skolas iela 11 ☏ 728 8816, ⓦ www.laine.lv. Occupies several floors of an apartment block ten minutes' walk northeast of the Old Town, in a relatively quiet street. Sparsely furnished, but acceptable, doubles use hallway WC and showers, while the more stylish renovated rooms are en-suite. ❸–❹
Reval Hotel Latvia Elizabetes 55 ☏ 777 2222, ⓦ www.revalhotels.com. A twenty-seven-floor block, once part of the Soviet state-run Intourist organization, now privatized and fully refurbished. Neat en-suites, great views from the upper floors. ❼
Tia Valdemāra iela 63 ☏ 733 3918, ⓦ www.tia.lv. A modern block some fifteen minutes' walk northeast of the Old Town with no-frills but neat rooms, all with TV and shower. ❹
Valdemārs Valdemāra iela 23 ☏ 733 4462, ⓦ www.valdemars.lv. A venerable Art Nouveau building with simple, clean en-suites decked out in gloomy brown colours. Some of the better rooms have elegant 1920s–30s furnishings, while the main stairwell boasts Art Nouveau stained glass. Breakfast 2Ls extra. ❸–❹
Viktorija Čaka iela 55 ☏ 701 4111, ⓦ www.hotel-viktorija.lv. Historic pre-World War I structure ten

minutes' west of the train station along the grimy but animated Čaka iela. Renovated rooms are simple, neat, carpeted affairs with modern bathrooms. Cheaper unrenovated rooms have creaky parquet floors and shared facilities. ❶–❹

Pārdaugava

Maritim Slokas 1 ☏ 706 9000, ⓦ www.maritim.lv. This 239-room cruise liner of a hotel, complete with all creature comforts, would be overpriced for this part of Rīga were it not for its position overlooking the savannah-like expanses of Uzvaras park. A nice place to stay in summer when the park is at its lushest – at other times of year this area can be miserable. Tram #2, #4 or #10 from the Central Market. ❻–❼
NB Slokas 49 ☏ 781 5333, ⓦ www.nb.lv. Mid-sized modern place offering trim en-suites with TV, 4km northwest of the city centre and just round the corner from the Botanical Gardens (see p.216). The ground floor doubles as a pool club. Tram #5 from 13. Janvāra iela to Konsula iela. ❹
O.K. Slokas 12 ☏ 786 0050, ⓦ www.okhotel.lv. On a drab Pārdaugava street but within walking distance of most of the area's green spaces. Nicely refurbished rooms with en-suite shower and TV, although some of the greens and reds take a bit of getting used to. Tram #4 from the Central Market or #5 from 13. Janvāra iela to the Kalnciema stop. ❺
Radisson-SAS Daugava Kuģu 24 ☏ 706 1111, ⓦ www.radissonsas.com. Comfort and quality in this 250-room monster. Great views of the Old Town skyline. ❼

Mežaparks and Sarkandaugava

Homestay Stockholmas iela 1 ☏ 755 3016, ⓦ www.homestay.lv. A welcoming B&B set in the leafy garden suburb of Mežaparks, offering four comfortable rooms and a home-from-home atmosphere. Tea- and coffee-making facilities in every room, free Internet access, and use of fridge and washing machine if you ask nicely. Reserve well in advance. Tram #11 from Radio iela to Visbijas prospekts. ❷
Jūrnieks Sofijas 8 ☏ 739 2350, ⓦ www.jurnieks.lv. Recently refurbished and civilized cheapie with small neat rooms, all with shower and TV. "Lux" rooms come with a lounge and only cost a few lats extra. A twenty-five-minute tram ride from the centre, this place can feel a bit isolated, but it's handy for Dauderi (see p.218) and Mežaparks (p.216). English-language skills are not the staff's strong point, and breakfast costs extra. Tram #5 or #9 from 13. Janvāra or the National Opera to Allažu iela. ❶

The City

The majority of Rīga's historical buildings are concentrated in the **Old Town** (Vecrīga), a compact web of narrow, cobbled streets, medieval merchant houses and brick-built churches squatting on the eastern bank of the broad **River Daugava**. To the east, the spacious belt of **parkland**, with its sedate nineteenth-century buildings sheltering beneath beech, elm and lime trees, couldn't be more different. Beyond here, streets radiate outwards through the so-called **Centre** (Centrs), the nineteenth- and early twentieth-century extension of the city and its commercial and administrative heart – a gritty, grey area redeemed by the innumerable gems of Art Nouveau architecture lining its streets. Further afield, Rīga's suburban sprawl harbours a number of quirky sights, such as the engaging Open-air Ethnographic Museum and the charming Dauderi museum dedicated to former president Ulmanis, while sizeable stretches of park in **Pārdaugava** and **Mežaparks**, and woodland around **Biķernieki**, present plenty of opportunities for strolling. Just to the southeast of the city lie the sombre Holocaust memorial sites at **Rumbula and Salaspils**.

The Old Town

World War II bombardment and insensitive post-war restoration notwithstanding, Rīga's **Old Town** still looks and feels like the warren it was in the Middle Ages. Nineteenth-century German guidebook writer, J.G. Kohl, could easily have been addressing today's tourists when he compared it to a "huge mass of rock, bored through, with holes for houses", adding that "the temperature of the town is that of a cavern, and there are parts of it which the sun has not seen for centuries".

The main thoroughfare is the dead-straight **Kaļķu iela**, which cuts through the Old Town from northeast to southwest. Many of the Old Town's attractions are located away from this strip in a maze of crooked alleyways – which explains the zigzagging itinerary described below.

Doma laukums

At the core of the Old Town, just off Kaļķu iela to the north, **Doma laukums** (Cathedral Square) is dominated by the red-brick bulk of Rīga's Romanesque **Cathedral** (Rīgas dome; Tues 11am–6pm, Wed–Fri 1–6pm, Sat 10am–2pm; 0.50Ls). The biggest cathedral in the Baltics, it was begun in 1211 by Albert von Buxhoeveden, the warrior-priest who founded Rīga and became its first bishop. Although much tinkered with by his successors, it remains an exuberant expression of medieval ecclesiastical power, bowling successive generations of visitors over with its combination of sheer size and decorative finesse – particularly fine are the intricate brickwork chevrons and zigzag patterns that cover the outer walls. Post-medieval add-ons have bestowed a degree of eccentric grandeur on the building – especially the enormous Renaissance gable at its eastern end and the bulbous Baroque belfry rising improbably from the roof – a feature which inter-war English resident Peggie Benton likened to "a Georgian silver teapot".

In true Lutheran style, the **interior** is relatively austere, its most eye-catching features being a florid pulpit from 1641, bristling with statues of saints and trumpet-wielding angels, and a magnificent nineteenth-century organ with 6768 pipes – said to be the fourth largest in the world (and *the* largest in the world when it was first installed in 1884); its stentorian tones can be heard at weekly organ recitals – pick up a schedule at the cathedral entrance or at the tourist office. The pillars of the nave are decorated with carved coats of arms, while its walls are lined with German memorial slabs, mostly dating from the period after the Reformation. A much older gravestone is that belonging to Meinhard, Bishop of Uexküll, occupying a pinnacle-capped niche on the left-hand side of the choir. Meinhard was the first German ecclesiastic to make his way to Latvia in an attempt to convert the local heathens, building the region's first church southeast of Rīga in 1188, and paving the way for Albert von Buxhoeveden's crusading hordes.

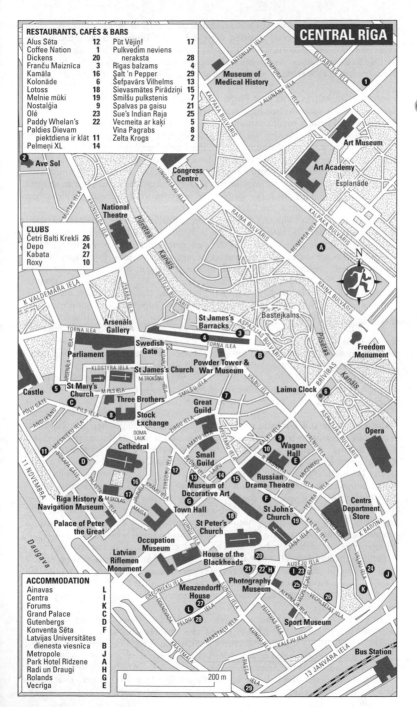

CENTRAL RĪGA

RESTAURANTS, CAFÉS & BARS

Alus Sēta	12	Pūt Vējiņ!	17
Coffee Nation	1	Pulkvedim neviens	
Dickens	20	neraksta	28
Franču Maiznīca	3	Rīgas balzams	4
Kamāla	16	Šalt 'n Pepper	29
Kolonāde	6	Šefpavārs Vilhelms	13
Lotoss	18	Sievasmātes Pīrādziņi	15
Melnie mūki	19	Smilšu pulkstenis	7
Nostaļģia	9	Spalvas pa gaisu	21
Olé	23	Sue's Indian Raja	25
Paddy Whelan's	22	Vecmeita ar kaķi	5
Paldies Dievam		Vina Pagrabs	8
piektdiena ir klāt	11	Zelta Krogs	2
Pelmeņi XL	14		

CLUBS

Četri Balti Krekli	26
Depo	24
Kabata	27
Roxy	10

ACCOMMODATION

Ainavas	L
Centra	I
Forums	K
Grand Palace	C
Gutenbergs	D
Konventa Sēta	F
Latvijas Universitātes	
dienesta viesnīca	B
Metropole	J
Park Hotel Rīdzene	A
Radi un Draugi	H
Rolands	G
Vecrīga	E

Museum of Medical History

Art Museum

Art Academy

Esplanāde

Ave Sol

Congress Centre

National Theatre

St James's Barracks

Arsenāls Gallery

Swedish Gate

Parliament

St James's Church

Powder Tower & War Museum

Freedom Monument

Laima Clock

Castle

St Mary's Church

Three Brothers

Stock Exchange

Great Guild

Opera

Cathedral

Small Guild

Wagner Hall

Russian Drama Theatre

Riga History & Navigation Museum

Museum of Decorative Art

St John's Church

Centrs Department Store

Palace of Peter the Great

Town Hall

St Peter's Church

Occupation Museum

Latvian Riflemen Monument

House of the Blackheads

Photography Museum

Menzendorff House

Sport Museum

Bus Station

0   200 m

13 JANVĀRA IELA

Daugava

The remaining three sides of Doma laukums are occupied by an odd collection of buildings from various eras, grandest of which is the **Latvian Stock Exchange** (Latvijas birža), on the corner with Pils iela, a stately mid-nineteenth-century structure decked out in hues of maroon and green and decorated with reliefs of Graeco-Roman demigods serving as allegories of various industries and trades.

Herdera laukums and the Rīga History and Navigation Museum

Doma laukums extends around the western side of the cathedral and runs into **Herdera laukums**, a small triangular space named after the German philosopher Johann Gottfried von Herder (see box opposite), who once taught in the cathedral school. Herder was a well-known critic of the harsh feudal system under which the Latvian peasantry lived, and notoriously likened the German presence in the Baltics to the Spanish conquest of Peru in terms of the damage done to indigenous culture. A bust placed here in his honour was removed after World War II in an attempt to de-Germanize Rīga's history – only to be returned to its pedestal in 1959 when a fraternal delegation from the GDR flew into town.

On the eastern side of Herdera laukums is the grilled entrance to the cloister known as the **Cross Gallery** (Krusteja; April–Oct daily 10am–5pm; 0.50Ls), a surviving part of the monastery that was attached to the cathedral before the Reformation. Its rib-vaulted arcades are stuffed with all manner of post-medieval junk, from coats of arms to seventeenth-century cannons. Much of this is overspill from the adjacent **Rīga History and Navigation Museum** (Rīgas vestures un kuģniecības muzejs; entrance round the corner on Palasta iela; Wed–Sun 11am–5pm; 1Ls), which charts the importance of seafaring in Rīga's development through an impressive collection of model ships. These range from the Viking longboats that regularly visited the Daugava estuary in the ninth century to the tugs, tankers and trawlers turned out by the local shipyards some thousand years later. A further section of the museum is devoted to twentieth-century urban life, vividly recalled through old photographs, theatre posters and inter-war fashions. The top floor gathers archeological finds, with a worthy display of local weapons and tools enlivened by a small collection of ancient Egyptian artefacts – including the 3400-year-old tombstone of Merire, keeper of the pharaoh's seal, seen here sporting a fetchingly Beatle-esque mop-top.

Continuing southeast along Palasta from the museum, you come to the former **Palace of Peter the Great** at no. 9, a plain-looking building where the Tsar lived for all of three months in 1711. Peter first visited Rīga in 1697 during the so-called Grand Embassy, when he traversed northern and western Europe accumulating the kind of technological and military knowledge that would help Russia become a great power. He was prevented from studying Rīga's fortifications by local officials, an incident (subsequently dubbed the "insult at Rīga") which so rankled, that Peter is said to have hurled the first grenade at the city himself when besieging it twelve years later. When Princess Sophie von Anhalt-Zerbst (the future Catherine the Great) stayed in the palace in 1744, her guard of honour was commanded by a certain Hieronymous Friedrich von Munchhausen (1720–1797), the bogus baron who went on to regale European society with improbable tales of his adventures while in imperial service.

Turning left into Jauniela takes you back towards Doma laukums, passing on the way the haughty female head that presides over the arched doorway of **Jauniela 25**. One of the most striking Art Nouveau buildings in the Old Town, it used to be the home of *Pie Kristapa*, Rīga's most famous restaurant during the Soviet period, now standing empty.

Just before you rejoin Doma laukums, a brief detour down the narrow Krāmu iela will bring you to the **Museum of the Barricades** at no. 2 (Wed–Sun 11am–5pm; 0.50Ls), displaying pictures and diagrams recalling the tension-filled days of January 1991, when it was feared that Soviet military action would crush the Latvian independence movement. Photographs of crowds brandishing Estonian and Lithuanian flags alongside the Latvians' own show the level of pan–Baltic solidarity at the time – a sentiment that has now all but evaporated.

Johann Gottfried von Herder (1744–1803)

Although ruled by a German-speaking aristocracy for seven hundred years, the Latvians retained a rich national culture, including a vast repertoire of folksongs that were passed down orally from one generation to the next. Ironically, the first person to systematically put these songs down in writing was a German, **Johann Gottfried von Herder**.

Born in the small East Prussian town of Mohrungen (now Morąg in Poland), Herder studied medicine and theology in Königsberg before arriving in Rīga to teach at the cathedral school in 1764. Herder's interest in folklore was initially focused on Germany, a country then divided into petty principalities, each ruled by an aristocratic elite that preferred French manners and culture to their own. Herder maintained that the rediscovery and propagation of authentic folkore would provide the German people with the cultural confidence that they lacked. The five years Herder spent in Rīga were enough to persuade him that the folk cultures of other nations – including the Latvians and Estonians – deserved to be taken just as seriously.

Believing that the very soul of a nation resided in its folk poetry, Herder spent the rest of his life collating traditional songs of peasant cultures from the Baltics to the Balkans. Many of these were collected together in his *Stimmen der Völker in Liedern* ("Voices of the Peoples in Song"). A large number of these songs were of an epic nature, recalling heroic struggles against powerful enemies or foreign occupiers, and they went down a storm with a Europe-wide public hungry for an exotic, romantic read.

When an ethnic Latvian intelligentsia began to emerge in the late nineteenth century, Herder's work provided the foundations upon which a modern national culture could be built. The poet and journalist Andrējs Pumpurs (see p.275) came up with just the kind of national epic that Herder had been so enthusiastic about and concocted the tale of superhuman warrior *Lāčplēsis* (published in 1888) by weaving several folk tales into a single narrative and adding his own material. His near-contemporary Krišjānis Barons (see p.212) carried out the more painstaking task of systematically collecting over one million folk songs, thereby bequeathing a vast library of indigenous literature to the nation. The songs collected by Barons still form the staple diet of Latvia's choral societies, and remain central to the country's self-image to this day.

Pils laukums

From Doma laukums, Pils iela runs west to leafy **Pils laukums** (Castle Square), the site of Riga's **Castle** (Rīgas pils). The castle began life as the headquarters of the Livonian Order, and now serves as the official residence of the Latvian president and also accommodates three museums. It's had a somewhat chequered history: the original thirteenth-century construction was demolished in 1484 by Rīga's municipal authorities, who were eager to celebrate the Livonian Order's declining influence over life in the city, and even sent individual bricks to other Hanseatic cities as a mark of their success. In 1491, the Order forced the townsfolk to rebuild it, and after numerous later additions, the castle ended up looking like the rather nondescript office block it is today. Beyond the discreet front door lies the first of the three museums, the **Foreign Art Museum** (Ārzemju mākslas muzejs; Tues–Sun 11am–5pm; 1.20Ls); its occasional visiting exhibitions are usually more interesting than its permanent collection – which comprises plaster copies of Greek and Roman sculptures plus a smattering of minor Flemish and Dutch paintings. A couple of floors above is the considerably more colourful **Latvian History Museum** (Latvijas vēstures muzejs; Wed–Sun 11am–5pm; 0.70Ls), containing a well-presented display of Neolithic pots, early Latvian weaponry and medieval jewellery – the necklaces and headbands made from coil-like strips of metal look surprisingly contemporary. A room full of ploughs, rakes and wicker baskets evokes the back-breaking toil endured by nineteenth-century villagers, although the traditional Latvian taste for the fine things in life is evident in the display of folk costumes from all over the country – exquisitely embroidered belts and bonnets for the ladies, sober grey or blue tunics for the blokes. Still on the same floor, the **Museum of Writing, Theatre and Music** (Rakstniecības, teātra un mūzikas muzejs; Wed–Sun 11am–5pm; 0.50Ls) isn't as exciting as it sounds, consisting as it does of a stuffily didactic display devoted to the big names of Latvian literature – useful if you're writing a thesis but not much fun otherwise.

From the Three Brothers to the Swedish Gate

Heading back east from Pils laukums along Mazā Pils iela takes you past the trio of venerable houses known as the **Three Brothers** (Trīs brāli). The first of the three at no. 17, which looks like a Cubist painter's nightmare and appears to be toppling into its neighbours, is also the oldest, dating from the early 1400s. While the slight, green brother at no. 21 is a little on the unassuming side, the middle sibling at no. 19 is a handsome, yellow-ochre structure with an elegant Renaissance portal and a wood-beamed interior that now harbours the **Latvian Architecture Museum** (Latvijas arhitektūras muzejs; Mon–Fri 10am–6pm), hosting small but worthwhile temporary exhibitions.

A left turn into Jēkaba iela at the end of Mazā Pils iela leads to the thirteenth-century red-brick **St James's Church** (Jēkaba baznīca), the seat of Rīga's Roman Catholic archbishop. As the centre of efforts to re-Catholicize Rīga in the late sixteenth century, St James's was trashed by the townsfolk on Christmas Day, 1584, and its rich inventory of Renaissance artworks destroyed. In a totally unconnected piece of urban lore, the church was famous for possessing bells which would supposedly peal of their own accord whenever a two-timing woman walked past. You can no longer test out the veracity of this belief – the bells were melted down to provide Russia with munitions in World War I and the church has been chime-free ever since.

Next door at Jēkaba 11 is Latvia's **Parliament** (Saeima), a rather workmanlike neo-Renaissance building that you wouldn't normally notice were it not for the discreet purr of ministerial motorcars on the cobbled street outside. Built in 1867 as an assembly hall for the Barons of Vidzeme (a region in eastern Latvia), and accordingly dubbed the Ritterhaus or "Knights' House", it became the headquarters of Peteris Stučka's Bolsheviks during their brief reign over Rīga in spring 1919, only to be taken over by the British Mission to the Baltic States when the Reds retreated. Stučka's headed notepaper was still on the desks when the mission moved in – its members immediately used it to write jokey letters home. Attendance at the mission's not infrequent parties was considered de rigueur by any party animal still left standing in the war-scarred city. When mission head Stephen Tallents held a reception for Latvian parliamentarians in May 1920, he commented drily that "the drinks were vodka, port and beer. Some of our guests drank them separately, others preferred them mixed."

At its northern end, Jēkaba iela opens out onto Torņa iela, where a left turn brings you to the **Arsenal Gallery** (Arsenāls; Tues–Sun 11am–5pm), the place to catch high-profile contemporary art shows. Heading in the opposite direction along Torņa iela takes you past **St James's Barracks** (Jēkaba kazarmas), a two-hundred-metre-long block built in the seventeenth century by the Swedes and now occupied by a string of upmarket shops and offices. Fired by cultural patriotism and revolutionary fervour, Latvian units of the Russian army invited Rīga's artists to establish a commune in the barracks in 1917. It was soon closed down by the city authorities, but its members went on to dominate the Latvian cultural scene during the inter-war years.

Over the road from the barracks is another legacy of Swedish rule, the **Swedish Gate** (Zviedru vārti), a simple archway beneath a three-storey town house. The only surviving city gate, it no longer leads anywhere in particular, although the alleyways on the other side – Aldaru iela and Trokšņu iela – are as picturesque as any in this part of town.

The Powder Tower and the Latvian War Museum

At the end of Torņa iela is the **Powder Tower** (Pulvertornis), a portly fourteenth-century bastion whose red-brick walls are still embedded with cannonballs from various sieges. In the years before World War I the tower served as the headquarters of the German-dominated Rubonia student fraternity, one of whose leaders was Alfred Rosenberg, future ideological mentor to Adolf Hitler and leading exponent of the idea of German superiority over the peasant races of Eastern Europe – Latvians included. Somewhat appropriately, the tower now forms part of the adjacent **Latvian War Museum** (Latvijas kara muzejs; Wed–Sun: May–Sept 10am–6pm; Oct–April till 5pm; 0.50Ls; English-language leaflet 0.50Ls), a well-presented array of guns, uniforms and sundry photographs that provides a thorough introduction to modern Latvian history. The narrative kicks off with World War I and the Latvian Riflemen – local units who fought with the Tsarist armies before defecting to the Bolsheviks (see p.204). A touching series of pictures shows Riflemen enjoying their days off in post-revolutionary Moscow, riding bikes, playing chess, or hanging out with their sweethearts in the park. Other Latvian units, left in limbo by the collapse of the Russian Empire, headed for home to fight for Latvian independence – notably the Troickas Battalion, whose epic 1920 voyage through Siberia to Vladivostok, and then by sea to Liepāja, is given extensive treatment. The establishment of the inter-war state (when both Germans and Bolsheviks had to be beaten off) gets equally thorough coverage: it comes as a bit of a surprise to see Latvian aeroplanes of the 1920s sporting swastikas until you learn that this common folk symbol was politically neutral at the time. Space is also devoted to the Latvian Legion – volunteers who served with the German Waffen SS during World War II. Most poignant of all is the room devoted to the anti-Soviet partisans of the 1944–56 period: cheery black-and-white portraits of optimistic young fighters are juxtaposed with Russian intelligence photographs of those who were later captured and summarily shot.

The Great and Small Guilds

From the Powder Tower, Meistaru iela runs down to the **Great Guild** (Lielā Ģilde) on the corner of Meistaru and Amatu, once the centre of commercial life in Hanseatic Rīga. The building owes its present neo-Gothic appearance to a nineteenth-century facelift, its main hall now pressed into service as the major venue for concerts by the Latvian National Symphony Orchestra. Immediately next door is the smaller but infinitely more arresting **Small Guild** (Mazā Ģilde), a playfully asymmetrical building featuring a castellated turret on one side and a jaunty spire on the other. A statue of the guild's patron, St John, occupies a niche beneath the spire. Rīga's business class had been divided into these two guilds since the fourteenth century, when the richer traders organized the Great Guild in order to differentiate themselves from shopkeepers and artisans, who quickly formed themselves into the Small Guild. Both guilds were exclusively German institutions – Latvian-speaking Rīgans had to make do with the significantly less prestigious Guild of Fishermen and Boatmen, which collected together all those who worked on and around the Daugava River. Between them the guilds regulated almost all commercial activity in the city until the mid-nineteenth century, after which they survived as social clubs until dying out completely in the 1930s, largely owing to lack of interest.

Opposite the Great and Small Guilds stands a yellow building known as the **Black Cat** (Melnais Kaķis), a wonderfully fluid piece of late Art Nouveau named after the lithe feline forms that ornament its two fanciful turrets. According to urban legend, the building's owner had been black-balled by the Great Guild, and so arranged for a cat statuette to be placed on his rooftop, profering its behind in the guild's general direction. After a successful legal action by the guild, the beast had to be repositioned with its cheeks pointing the opposite way.

Kaļķu iela and Skārņu iela

South of the guilds, Meistaru joins up with **Kaļķu iela**, the Old Town's main thoroughfare and its most popular evening promenading ground. Numerous narrow streets lead off the southern side of Kaļķu; the most graceful is **Skārņu iela**, which curves past a row of medieval buildings, their pastel-painted facades providing the photogenic backdrop to a clutch of souvenir stalls.

At Skārņu 10, the austere stone interior of the thirteenth-century chapel of St George provides a suitably atmospheric home to the **Museum of Decorative and Applied Arts** (Dekoratīvi lietišķās mākslas muzejs; Tues–Sun 11am–5pm; 0.70Ls), which showcases crafts as diverse as textile weaving, glassware and book binding. During the inter-war years, Rīga's crockery factories employed some of the country's best artists to design their tableware, and plates by the likes of Aleksandra Beļcova, Romans Suta and Sigismund Vindbergs – imaginatively mixing folksy Latvian motifs with more modern abstract forms – deservedly occupy centre stage here. Next door to the museum is the thirteenth-century **St John's Church** (Jāņa baznīca), the red and green brickwork of its stepped gable catching the late afternoon sun to spectacular effect. Legend has it that two monks chose to be immured in the southern facade during the church's construction, where they lived on food delivered through a hole in the wall – an extreme act of ascetic piety not unknown in the Middle Ages. The Gothic interior, whose rib-vaulted ceiling has recently been repainted in jolly primary colours, is a popular venue for chamber concerts.

St Peter's Church

Looming up on the western side of Skārņu iela is **St Peter's Church** (Pētera baznīca; Tues–Sun 10am–5pm), an imposing red-brick church whose graceful three-tiered spire is very much the city's trademark symbol. Although of thirteenth-century origins, the main body of the church acquired its present shape in the early 1400s and, notwithstanding the addition of some Baroque statues on either side of the main door, has remained pretty much the same ever since. The history of the spire is another story, however, beginning in 1491 with the construction of a 137-metre wooden spire – the highest in Europe at the time. It collapsed just under two hundred years later and was rebuilt twice in Baroque style before being destroyed by German shelling in 1941. Today's 123-metre spire is a steel replica of the eighteenth-century version, its three slender tiers seeming to sprout from a succession of onion domes. A lift (same times as the church; 1.50Ls) takes visitors to a gallery in its upper reaches, where you can enjoy a panoramic view of the city from the observation platform. After this, the impressively lofty church interior is a bit of a come-down, rioting Protestants having destroyed its original medieval furnishings in the 1520s.

Town Hall Square and the House of the Blackheads

From the main door of St Peter's you look directly across Kungu iela towards **Rātslaukums** (Town Hall Square), whose buildings were largely destroyed in World War II and subsequently replaced by ponderous, Soviet-style blocks. Since independence, however, the square has been the focus of an ambitious rebuilding effort centred on the late-Gothic **House of the Blackheads** (Melngalvju nams), shelled by the Germans in 1941 and totally demolished by the Soviets at the war's end. Work began in 1995 to rebuild the House from scratch and was completed on time for Rīga's eight-hundredth birthday celebrations in 2001. It's a wackily asymmetrical affair, comprising two joined buildings, one set back slightly from the other, both of which boast enormous stepped gables studded with ornate windows and statue-bearing niches. Although you wouldn't know from the present-day replicas, the building on the right was originally the older of the two, begun in the fourteenth century and progressively tinkered with over the next two hundred years; the one on the left was tacked on in 1891, in conscious imitation of the original.

The House was initially used as a meeting place by several of Rīga's guilds, but gradually became associated with just one of them – the group of unmarried merchants that took the name "Blackheads" in honour of their patron, the Roman warrior-saint of North African origin, Maurice. A rowdy bachelors' drinking club, and the scene of grandiose feasts such as the Fasnachtsdrunken ("Carnival Drinking Bout"), celebrated on the Saturday before Shrove Tuesday, the House was both a focus of civic life and a symbol of Rīga's cosmopolitan, mercantile identity. For centuries it was a magnet for tourists and foreign conquerors alike – both Peter the Great of Russia (1709) and Kaiser Wilhelm of Germany (1917) made it their first port of call in order to stamp their authority on the city. Since it was the smartest auditorium in Rīga, the House was also a major concert venue – as musical director of the City Theatre in the late 1830s, Richard Wagner frequently brandished his baton here, sometimes conducting his composition *Nikolai: Hymn of the People* (written in honour of Tsar Nicholas I) as a show-stopping finale. The Blackheads as an organization survived until 1940, when the last of its members were repatriated along with the rest of Latvia's Germans. Today, the House is resuming something of its former social role, with its main hall serving as the venue for chamber concerts, and the ground floor shared between the Rīga tourist office (see p.192) and an upmarket café, pretentiously decked out in reproduction nineteenth-century furnishings.

On the other side of the square, the similarly war-ravaged **Town Hall** was also rebuilt in 2001, although without the same commitment to accuracy – it's essentially a twenty-first-century office block with a neoclassical portal tacked on for good measure. Presiding over the flagstoned square between the Town Hall and the House of the Blackheads is a **statue of Roland**, the legendary eighth-century knight who died defending a Pyrenean mountain pass against invading Arabs – an act immortalized in the epic medieval romance *The Song of Roland*. The cult of Roland was immensely popular in northern Europe, and Rīga honoured him with a statue on this spot in the fourteenth century – although the current version is a modern replica of a nineteenth-century incarnation.

The Occupation Museum

The western end of Rātslaukums is dominated by a squat, forbidding structure built to house the now-defunct Museum of the Latvian Riflemen, local troops who fought with the Bolsheviks during the Russian Civil War (see box on p.204). After independence, donations from Latvians abroad paid for its transformation into the **Museum of Latvia's Occupation** (Latvijas okupācijas muzejs; ⊛www .occupationmuseum.lv; daily 11am–5pm; free), a moving and in parts disturbing display devoted to Latvia's occupation by the Nazis and the Soviets respectively. Portraits of Hitler and Stalin hover, demon-like, above the entrance to the exhibition – it was their decision to parcel up Eastern Europe into mutual spheres of influence in 1939 that condemned Latvia (along with Estonia and Lithuania) to the first period of Soviet occupation, which began in June 1940. Germany's declaration of war on the Soviet Union a year later ushered in four years of Nazi control (a photograph on display here shows Latvian girls in national costume welcoming the German troops with flowers), after which the Soviets returned in 1944 – and stayed for another 45 years. Contemporary photographs, propaganda posters and political proclamations recall these events in punchily effective style. The Soviets tried to rob Latvia of its ethnic identity by deporting a large proportion of its citizens to Siberia, implementing a first wave of mass arrests in June 1941, and a second in March 1949. The victims were often chosen arbitrarily – one of the Soviet warrants on display here gives the reason for arrest as simply "belonging to the Latvian national-ity". Most of the deportees lived in log-cabin work camps that they had to build themselves – the interior of a typical barrack block has been reconstructed here to give an idea of the harshness of camp life. Display cases contain examples of the artefacts made by deportees to make the experience of exile bearable – beautiful hand-drawn Christmas cards, carved wooden chess sets, and most poignantly of all, the bizarre, balaclava-like face masks fashioned from scraps of material in a desper-ate attempt to ward off the Siberian winter.

Latvian Riflemen's Square and 11 Novembra Krastmala

A further echo of Soviet culture can be found in the windswept car park immedi-ately west of the museum, which still bears the heroically Communist name of **Latvian Riflemen's Square** (Latviešu strēlnieku laukums), and where the rifle-men themselves are commemorated with a suitably red, granite monument. Depicting three stern figures buried in enormous greatcoats, it's one of the last examples of ideological sculpture left in the city. The natural gathering point for pro-communist, anti-independence protesters in 1991, the square is nowadays just a bus stop.

Northwest of the Riflemen's Square, along the right bank of the Daugava extends the traffic-choked strip of **11 Novembra Krastmala**, named in commemoration of the defeat of von der Goltz's Germans outside Rīga in November 1919, rather than the end of World War I in November 1918. The pleasant riverside walkway on the far side of the road is punctuated with steps leading down to the water's edge and provides a good vantage point from which to observe the traffic pulsing across Rīga's bridges – with the futuristic Vanšu tilts suspension bridge to the north and

The Latvian Riflemen

Considered heroes by Latvian patriots and Soviet loyalists alike, the **Latvian Riflemen** (Latviešu strēlnieki) continue to occupy a paradoxical place in the nation's heritage. Made up of local recruits, the unit was created by the Russians in 1915 and charged with the task of defending central Latvia against the advancing Germans. The Russian military authorities considered the creation of ethnic Latvian infantry units an effective way of harnessing local patriotism to the Tsarist cause and, initial-ly at least, were not disappointed. The riflemen often bore the brunt of the heaviest fighting and soon became a symbol of military pride to the folks back home. Increasingly aware that they were being used as cannon-fodder by their Tsarist com-manders, however, the riflemen came under the sway of revolutionary propaganda as the war dragged on. Radicalized by Bolshevik agitators, Latvian Riflemen played a key role in Lenin's siezure of power in November 1917.

Many of the riflemen simply drifted back to Latvia as World War I drew to an end, but those who remained loyal to the new Soviet state soon became a byword for Bolshevik discipline and were regarded by Lenin as the only revolutionary troops he could really trust. When anti-Bolshevik socialists attempted a coup in June 1918, the Latvians under General Vacetis were charged with defending the Kremlin – and saved the regime in the process. Latvian forces were also entrusted with the deli-cate task of shooting the Tsar and his family in Ekaterinburg on July 16, 1918 (their Russian counterparts were considered too sentimental to undertake the job in hand).

The importance of the Latvian Riflemen to the Soviet regime was not lost on the Western powers, and in summer 1918 the British representative in Moscow, Robert Bruce Lockhart, aided by Sidney "Ace of Spies" Riley, briefly entertained the idea of bribing the Latvians into deserting the Bolsheviks. Agents of the Soviet security services or Cheka (which counted numerous Latvians among its leaders) soon infil-trated the Lockhart plot and it was quickly abandoned.

the elegant five-arched span of the railway bridge to the south. Until the building of the latter in 1872, the only Daugava crossing was a pontoon affair, laid out every spring and packed up again in the autumn. In winter, people simply drove their carts across the ice.

Heading towards Vanšu tilts, you'll come across a glass-covered shrine holding a wooden statue of St Christopher bearing the Christ child on his broad shoulders. Known as **Lielais Kristaps** or "Big Christopher", it's very much a symbol of the city.

The Menzendorff House and Grēcinieku iela

Immediately east of Ratslaukums, on the corner of Grēcinieku and Kungu, is the so-called **Menzendorff House** (Mencendorfa nams; Wed–Sun 10am–5pm; 1.20Ls), an impeccably restored merchant's house decorated in grand style and adorned with period furniture and artefacts. Built by alderman Jürgen Helm in 1695, the house got its name from the Menzendorff delicatessen, which occupied the ground floor of the building in the years before World War I and kept Rīga society supplied with Swiss chocolates and other luxury nibbles. The four-storey interior was turned into flats after World War II and allowed to decay, but was completely renovated in the 1980s and pretty much restored to its eighteenth-century self – complete with creaky pine floors, mullioned windows and chunky Baroque wardrobes. It provides a charming insight into the world of Rīga's mercantile elite – and with house plants adding that homey touch, it will probably give you a few interior design ideas into the bargain.

East of the Menzendorff House, **Grēcinieku iela** threads its way past a clutch of shops and bars. With a name that translates as "Sinners' Street", Grēcinieku was for a long time Rīga's pleasure quarter, a tradition that still holds true today if excessive alcohol consumption counts among the major vices – several of the Old Town's most popular bars are located here. Grēcinieku gives way to Audēju iela, where swarms of shoppers are daily sucked up into the city's main multi-storey shopping mall, **Centrs**, a wedge of grey concrete that was considered a bold piece of modern architecture when it first opened in the 1920s.

From Grēcinieku iela to the Central Market

On the southern side of Grēcinieku and Audēju lies a warren of narrow streets lined with ancient, mostly unrestored, merchants' houses. Turning off Grēcinieku into Marstaļu and taking a sharp left into Alksnāja iela brings you to the **Photography Museum** (Fotogrāfijas muzejs; Wed–Sun 9am–5pm; 0.50Ls), which offers an entertaining jaunt through the history of photography in Latvia. Things get under way with Tsarist-era family portraits and an early photojournalist's record of President Ulmanis's arrival in Rīga in 1919, greeted by head of the British Mission (and temporarily governor of Rīga) Steven Tallents. Moving on to the 1920s and 1930s, glamour photos and publicity shots of Latvian actresses reveal what an exciting place inter-war Rīga must have been. There's surprisingly little in the display relating to Eižens Finks, the 1930s clairvoyant and celebrity photographer of Romany origin who became the subject of a Latvian musical (*Sfinks*) in 2002. However, there is a small section devoted to the desirably sleek and silvery Minox, a miniature camera developed by Rīga's VEF factory in the 1930s and displayed – with understandable pride – as a shining example of how technologically advanced the Latvian republic was before the Soviets took over.

A little further along Alksnāja, the **Sports Museum** (Sporta muzejs; Mon–Fri 10am–6pm, Sat 10am–5pm; 0.40Ls) at no. 6 is largely given over to changing exhibitions, although there's bound to be something on display recalling the phenomenal line of Latvian-trained javelin throwers who won Olympic medals for the Soviet Union – Inese Jaunzeme (gold in 1956), Jānis Lūsis (bronze in 1964, gold in 1968, silver in 1972), Lūsis's wife Elvīra Ozoliņa (gold in 1960) and Dainis Kūla (gold in 1980) – as well as the country's only post-independence gold medallist, gymnast Igors Vihrovs, granted his gong for floor exercises in Sydney in 2000.

Emerging at the southern end of Alksnāja and crossing the busy 13. Janvāra iela, you come to the **Central Market** (Centrāltirgus), an animated, seven-days-a-week affair housed in five hulking pavilions, each the size of a small football pitch. The pavilions are reconditioned World War I zeppelin hangars, built near Liepāja by the Germans and re-erected here in the 1920s, with ochre Art Deco facades tacked on at each end lending an air of architectural extravagance. Inside, stallholders sell top-quality farm produce from all over Latvia – as well as excellent honey and cheeses, you'll come across rows of animal carcasses waiting to be carved into cutlets in the meat hall (*gaļu pavilions*), and gurgling tanks full of eels and carp in the fish hall (*zivu pavilions*). Outside the hangars, Rīgans who can't afford supermarket prices throng around the fruit, veg and flower stalls, or peer into the jumbled window displays of kiosks selling everything from alarm clocks to zebra-print underwear.

East of the Old Town: the park belt

From the eastern edge of the Old Town, the broad asphalt stripe of **Brīvības bulvaris** ("Freedom boulevard") and its extension, Brīvības iela, forge a path out to the suburbs and beyond, cutting through a sequence of parks marking the boundary between medieval Rīga and the nineteenth-century parts of town to the east. The parks come in two parallel strips running roughly northwest to southeast: the first, comprising **City Park** and **Kronvalds Park**, is bordered to the east by **Raiņa bulvāris**, a busy street lined with imposing nineteenth-century mansions – mostly occupied by banks, foreign embassies and Rīga University. Beyond Raiņa lies the second strip of parkland, made up of **Esplanāde** and **Vērmane's Garden**. Landscaped when the city walls were demolished in the 1850s, the whole area is now a much-loved green belt, characterized by well-tended lawns, stately rows of trees and the odd formal flowerbed. It's packed with promenaders whatever the season – although it may no longer offer the kind of nocturnal thrills that Graham Greene encountered in the early 1930s, when he noted with excitement that "all the lights in Rīga were dimmed by ten: the public parks were quite dark and full of whispers. Giggles from hidden seats, excited rustles in the bushes. One had the sensation of a whole town on the tiles".

Marking the start of Brīvības on the corner of Aspazijas bulvaris is the **Laima Clock**, an unassuming four-metre-high pillar erected in the 1930s to advertise the Laima chocolate factory, and still sporting its original Art Deco logo. It's a much-loved monument to inter-war Rīga and is also the place at which half the city agrees to meet in the evening.

The Freedom Monument

Dominating the view as you head east along Brīvības iela is the defiantly modernist **Freedom Monument** (Brīvības piemineklis). Unveiled on November 18, 1935, it's a soaring allegory of Latvian independence and has occupied an important place in the national psyche ever since. A red granite pedestal bearing reliefs of Latvian heroes and inscribed with the words *Tēvzemei un brīvībai* ("for fatherland and freedom") provides the base for a slender fifty-metre-high column, crowned by a stylized female figure affectionately known as "Milda" – the most popular female first name in the country between the wars, Milda became emblematic of Latvia as a whole. She holds aloft three stars symbolizing the three regions of Latvia – Kurzeme, Vidzeme and Latgale – a constant source of puzzlement to Latvian schoolchildren who have always been taught that the country is made up of four regions, not three. (The reason for this confusion lies in the fact that the fourth region, Zemgale, fell within the administrative boundaries of Kurzeme for most of its history and is therefore overlooked in Milda's case.)

Oddly, the Soviets never attempted to demolish this rallying point for Latvian patriotism – unsurprisingly, it was the scene of the first pro-independence demonstrations in August 1987. During the 1990s it became the focus for gatherings of former SS Latvian volunteers on **March 16** – the official day of remembrance for World War II veterans. A government keen to ingratiate itself with both Nato and the EU banned the event after 2001, although the general public still gravitate towards the Freedom Monument for a bout of flower-laying on the same date.

A floral tribute of an altogether different kind took place beside the monument on November 8, 2001, when an ethnic Russian schoolgirl from Daugavpils, Alina Lebedeva, accosted the heir to the British throne, Prince Charles, swatting him in the face with a carnation. A protest against British participation in the war in Afghanistan, the gesture earned Lebedeva the charge of "endangering the health of a foreign dignatory", an offence carrying a maximum penalty of fifteen years in jail. In the event, however, a Rīga city court found her guilty merely of "hooliganism", and gave her a suspended sentence.

The City Park and Bastejkalns

On either side of Brīvības, paths dive into the **City Park** (Pilsētas parks), the first of the wedges of greenery that extend along the eastern boundaries of the Old Town. A ribbon of well-tended lawns patrolled by ducks, it's split by the serpentine form of a rather stagnant-looking **City Canal** (Pilsētas kanāls) – what's left of Rīga's moat. The main feature of the park on the southeastern side of Brīvības is the coolly imperious Rīga **Opera House**, built in 1887 and recently restored to something approaching its belle époque splendour.

Northwest of Brīvības, paths wind their way around **Bastejkalns** (Bastion Hill), a low knoll which began life as a pile of left-over rubble after the city defences were dismantled and was subsequently grassed over. It is also a reminder of Rīga's more recent history: on January 20, 1991, five people were killed here by sniper fire as Soviet OMON troops stormed the Latvian Ministry of the Interior on nearby Raiņa bulvaris during an attempted crackdown on Latvia's independence drive. Stones on the northern side of the hill mark the spots where they fell – the victims were Gvido Zvaigzne and Andris Slapiņš (cameramen attached to the film crew of acclaimed documentarist Jūris Podnieks), teenage schoolboy Edijs Riekstiņš and militiamen Sergejs Kononenko and Vladimirs Gomanovics.

Further over to the northwest, progress through the park is briefly broken by the busy thoroughfare of **Valdemāra iela**, the far side of which is overlooked by the **National Theatre** (Nacionālais teātris), a pair of muscular Titans bearing the weight of its newly renovated, neo-Baroque facade. It was here that Latvian independence was proclaimed on November 18, 1918, although the nation's new leaders had to hastily evacuate a city that was soon overrun by the Bolsheviks. The resolutely modern **Rīga Congess Centre** (Rīgas kongresu nams), which stands at the corner of Kronvalds Park (Kronvalda parks) 200m further north, played host to another generation of Latvian leaders in 1988, when it served as the venue for the first-ever congress of the Latvian Popular Front.

Museum of Medical History

Heading northeast across Kronvalds Park from the Congress Centre and crossing over Kalpaka bulvaris takes you to one of Rīga's most compelling museums, the **Stradiņš Museum of Medical History** (Stradiņa medicīnas muzejs; Tues–Sat 11am–5pm; closed on last Fri of month; 1Ls), on the corner of Kalpaka and Antonijas iela. Based on the collection of the Latvian physician Pauls Stradiņš (1896–1958), it's packed with eccentric oddities, beginning with a series of dioramas illustrating man's first forays into medicine – in one of them, a witch-doctor is trepanning a patient by hammering a pointed stick into his skull with a rock. A re-creation of a medieval street scene has plague victims grimacing from upstairs windows, and a man having his leg sawn off with the aid of a prayer book rather than an anasthetic. Upstairs, a re-created dental surgery of the 1930s will probably have you vowing never to visit the dentist's again, while a nearby section on the Soviet space programme includes a cabin built to accommodate space dog Veterok

("Breeze") – presumably never used, as these experimental animal flights were strictly one-way affairs. The canine theme concludes with the museum's most notorious exhibit, the (stuffed) **two-headed dog** of Dr Demihov, the eccentric Soviet scientist who pioneered a range of organ transplants in animals, few of which lived to tell the tale. Looking more like a creature from the novels of Mikhail Bulgakov than a monument to scientific progress, this particular specimen was produced by grafting the head and torso of a small dog onto the back of a larger one, ostensibly in order to see whether the vital functions of a weakened animal could be sustained by attaching it to a stronger host (apparently the dogs were so enraged they almost bit each other to death before being put down).

The State Art Museum

Heading back southeast along Kalpaka brings you face to face with the stern, red-brick bulk of the **Art Academy** (Mākslas akademija), a building so perfectly neo-Gothic that it was used to represent London locations in Soviet-made Sherlock Holmes adventures. Immediately northeast, the junction of Valdemāra and Elizabetes is dominated by the **State Art Museum** (Valsts mākslas muzejs; Wed–Mon 11am–5pm; 1.50Ls), a grandiose, neoclassical edifice with an imperious-looking Athena gazing down from above the entrance. A staircase ascends from an ostentatious, second-empire-style lobby to the galleries, where you'll find an exhaustive overview of Latvian painting and sculpture, although the collection stops short in the 1950s (artists have to be dead before they're allowed in here, as the local wags have it).

Prime among the past masters is the St Petersburg-educated **Jānis Rozentāls** (1866–1916), who employed a lively impressionistic style in documenting the Latvian landscape and its people – although the most famous of his works on show here (and one that most Latvians would instantly recognize) is the comparatively dour *Coming from Church after the Service* (1894), depicting sober village folk togged up in their Sunday best. Others who sought to capture the character of the Latvian countryside were **Jānis Valters** (1869–1932) and **Vilhelms Purvītis** (1872–1945), both represented here by a number of post-impressionistic canvases featuring, for the most part, forests. The diversity of Latvian inter-war art on display owes a lot to the activities of the Rīga Artists' Group, an organization that brought together most of the painters who had been involved in the St James's Barracks commune (see p.200) – look out for the brooding expressionist works of **Jēkabs Kazaks** (1895–1920), and the angular, cubist pictures of **Niklāvs Strunke** (1894–1966). The most revolutionary artist of the period was **Gustavs Klucis** (1895–1938), an enthusiastic Bolshevik who chose a career in the Soviet Union rather than life in inter-war Latvia – constructivist collages like *Lenin and Socialist Reconstruction* (1927) and *More Coal and Metal* (1932) are masterpieces of the agitprop genre. The leading Latvian woman artist of the twentieth century, **Aleksandra Belcova** (1892–1981), is represented by a striking series of female portraits, combining the glamour of glossy magazine covers with a palpable atmosphere of listlessness and boredom.

Esplanāde

Stretching southeast of the State Art Museum is the **Esplanāde**, a park planted with rows of lime trees at the close of the nineteenth century and popular with strollers and pram-wielding parents ever since. Rising above the trees at its south-eastern end are the neo-Byzantine domes of the **Cathedral of Christ's Nativity** (Kristus dzimsanas katedrāle), built for the city's expanding Russian community in 1884 and turned into a planetarium during the Soviet period, when most of its interior furnishings were destroyed. Its walls are currently being redecorated with swirly geometric designs – rich in browns, maroons and greens, they look a bit like Victorian wallpaper patterns.

A little way west of the cathedral is a pink granite statue of **Jānis Rainis** (1865–1929), the poet and playwright whose dour, socially engaged works form the staple diet of Latvian schoolchildren. An empty pedestal on the eastern side of the cathedral was once graced by a statue of **General Barclay de Tolly**, the Livonian baron of Scottish descent who was commander-in-chief of the Russian armies during the Napoleonic wars. The statue itself was evacuated – along with other Tsarist-era public sculptures – by the retreating Russian army in World War I, only to enjoy something of a second coming in 2001, when local businessman Yevgeny Gomberg commissioned a replica of the work and began to campaign for its reinstatement. Gomberg previously financed the restoration of an equestrian statue of **Peter the Great**, which once stood on the site now occupied by the Freedom Monument, and briefly displayed it in the Esplanāde in 2001 before returning it to storage. He then offered it as a gift to the city of St Petersburg, but the Rīga city authorities stymied the move – the Russians, however, commissioned a copy of the statue, which now stands outside St Petersburg's Constantine Palace, where it is affectionately known as "the Rīga Peter". In Rīga itself, ethnic Latvians weary of Russian imperial symbols regard the re-emergence of both statues as something of a provocation, and it remains to be seen whether either sculpture will ever be seen in public again.

Vērmanes dārzs and the Natural History Museum

Continuing southeast along Elizabetes iela, you soon come to the next park, **Vērmane's Garden** (Vērmanes dārzs), occupied by residential houses until 1812, when the Tsarist authorities burned them down to provide the army with a field of fire from which to defend the city against the advancing French. This may have been a huge miscalculation – it's said that one of the Russian scouts saw dust rising from a herd of cattle just south of the city and mistook it for Napoleon's cavalry; the cavalry however weren't actually anywhere near Rīga and decided to give it a miss. Five years later, the wasteland was redeveloped as a park by the wife of Rīga merchant, A. Wöhrmann (transliterated as "Vērmane" in Latvian, hence the park's name), although for decades it was reserved for Rīga's elite – the plebs had to content themselves with observing the Sunday promenade from behind the railings. Nowadays, the park is a favoured meeting point for elderly chess players, who hog all the benches of a little-used outdoor theatre in the park's northwestern corner.

Leaving Vērmane's Garden at the southernmost corner and crossing Barona iela brings you to the **Latvian Natural History Museum** at Barona 4 (Latvijas dabas muzejs; Wed–Sun 10am–5pm; 0.60Ls), which has three floors of exhibits covering everything from moths to mammoth tusks, all exhaustively labelled in Russian and Latvian. If you head southwest from here along Barona and cross the canal you end up back in the Old Town.

The Centre (Centrs)

East of the Vērmanes dārzs and Esplanāde parks is the district known as the **Centre** (Centrs) – a name that never fails to confuse first-time visitors, who, not unreasonably, assume that Rīga's centre is somewhere in the Old Town. Although it's a largely residential area, the reason it's called "the Centre" is because it contains the city's most important shopping and commercial district – concentrated in the region enclosed by **Valdemāra iela** to the northwest and **Čaka iela** to the southeast. The boulevards that characterize the Centre bear witness to a period of rapid urban expansion that began in the mid-1800s and lasted right up until World War I. With Rīga growing into a major industrial city, rows of four- and five-storey apartment buildings were erected to house the expanding middle class, and the single-storey wooden houses which then predominated were gradually cleared.

These long lines of apartment blocks look a little grey and unwelcoming on first sight, but as you get up close a wealth of **Art Nouveau** embellishments come to light: florid stucco swirls adorning doorways, stylized human faces incorporated into facades and towers fancifully placed on top of buildings. It always pays to look

Sergei Mikhailevich Eisenstein 1898–1948

Cinema pioneer Sergei Eisenstein was born in Rīga in 1898. He grew up at Valdemāra 6 (a plaque outside the Zvaigzne bookshop marks the spot), and was educated at the gymnasium just down the road at Valdemāra 1 (which still serves as a high school). His report cards gave little indication of his future calling – he only ever got average marks for art and, appropriately for someone who went on to become a master of propaganda, his best subject was theology. However, the development of Eisenstein's visual imagination is apparent in the letters he wrote to his mother, who had moved to St Petersburg in 1909 – in these Eisenstein recounts the events of the week in vivid film-storyboard style, with cartoon strips and caricatures.

During World War I, the Eisensteins were evacuated to Russia, Sergei going on to study art in Moscow after the war, before specializing in film. Many observers have interpreted his choice of the new and revolutionary form of cinema as a rebellion against the florid architectural style of his father. His cinematic trademark – the employment of a vigorous, jump-cut editing style he called "the montage of attractions" – must have seemed like a slap in the face to the Art Nouveau generation.

Cinema was regarded as the most politically effective art form of all by Soviet Russia's new rulers, and Eisenstein quickly established himself as its greatest practitioner. His first feature film, *Strike* (1924), was an attack on the evils of capitalism, while *October* (1928), offered up an over-dramatized reconstruction of the Bolshevik seizure of power – it's said that more people were injured during the making of the film than during the event itself.

During the inter-war years Eisenstein's films were rarely seen in the city of his birth. Playwright and socialist MP, Jānis Rainis (see p.227), campaigned succesfully to have Eisenstein's greatest masterpiece *Battleship Potemkin* (1925) shown in Rīga, despite the hostility of government censors towards such outright Soviet propaganda. Things changed when Latvia was sucked into the Soviet sphere of influence in 1939, and Eisenstein's epic of medieval Russia's struggle against the Germans, *Alexander Nevsky*, arrived in local cinemas at a time of growing anti-German feeling. "At each reverse suffered by the Teutonic Knights," wrote British diplomat's wife Peggie Benton, "the Latvian audience stamped their feet and clapped until the management had to silence them by turning on the lights."

up to catch details that might otherwise pass by unnoticed – and if the number of scantily clad nymphs gazing down from the Centre's facades is anything to go by, Sigmund Freud would have had a field day analyzing the architectural tastes of Rīga's bourgeoisie.

Along Elizabetes iela to Alberta iela

The biggest concentration of Art Nouveau buildings lies in the northwestern corner of the Centre, the majority of them designed by **Mikhail Eisenstein**, the architect father of cinema pioneer Sergei (see box above). One of Eisenstein-père's most famous creations lies just north of the Esplanāde park at **Elizabetes 10A and 10B**, an apartment building adorned with plaster flourishes and gargoyles and topped by two vast, impassive faces. Eisenstein was also responsible for just about everything on the even-numbered side of **Alberta iela**, one block north of here, a uniquely exotic terrace of town houses, each of which is stylistically different from the next. The most extrovert of the lot is the florid neo-Egyptian affair at no. 2A, although the fact that the facade is slightly higher than the building itself makes it look more like a film set than a real building. At ground level things are more reassuring, with a brace of contented-looking sphynxes standing guard either side of the entrance.

The most striking of the buildings on the opposite side of the street is the dark-grey apartment block at no. 11 designed by Eižens Laube, the prime exponent of

National Romanticism. Following hard on the heels of Art Nouveau in Rīga, this new style sought to establish a truly Latvian form of architecture through the inclusion of folksy touches like shingled roofs, irregular window frames and pointy gables – all of which are employed here to monumental effect.

The Rozentāls and Blaumanis Museum

Laube also helped to design the neo-Gothic building looming over the corner of Alberta iela and Strēlnieku iela. Prominent among the pre-World War I yuppies and arty types who were attracted to such real-estate developments was painter Jānis Rozentāls (1866–1916) – his top-floor apartment is now open to the public as the **Jānis Rozentāls and Rudolfs Blaumanis Museum** (Jāṇa Rozentāla un Rudolfa Blaumaṇa memoriālais muzejs; entrance round the corner on Strēlnielku iela; Thurs–Mon 11am–5pm; 0.70Ls). Reached via a wonderful twirling staircase, very much an attraction in itself, the museum is packed with period furnishings and evocative pictures of Rīga at the beginning of the twentieth century. In many ways the father of Latvian painting, Rozentāls (1866–1916) is primarily known for his large-format landscapes, although the smaller canvases gathered together here are full of intimacy and warmth – especially the portraits of his friends, children and Finnish mezzo-soprano wife. The family spent their summers in Finland, and pictures of the Rozentāls lolling around lakeshores fill the light-flooded attic studio where Rozentāls received students. The guest room next door was set aside by Rozentāls for his friend Rudolfs Blaumanis (1863–1908), the journalist, playwright and master of the Latvian realistic novel, who, despite enjoying a towering reputation among the local intelligentsia, never earned enough money to rent his own big-city pad. The room is largely bare save for a few facsimile manuscripts and a glass case containing a huge bearskin coat – donated by Rozentāls to help the tubercular Blaumanis ward off the winter chill.

The Museum of Latvia's Jews

A five-minute walk east of Alberta iela is the small but compelling **Museum of Latvia's Jews** (Muzejs Ebreji Latvijā; Mon–Fri noon–5pm; donation requested), located on the third floor of the Jewish community's cultural centre at Skolas 6. Built around documents amassed over many years by two Rīga-based Holocaust survivors, Zalman Elelson and Margers Vestermanis, the display commemorates a community that on the eve of World War II made up eleven percent of Rīga's population – the second-largest ethnic group in the city after the Latvians themselves – before being all but wiped out by the Nazis.

Until the twentieth century there was little evidence of anti-Semitism in Latvia, a point pressed home by the following quote from the 1881 article, *A Word on the Baltic Jews*, by nineteenth-century national ideologue Krišjanis Valdemārs: "Not one Latvian, neither wise nor fool, in the townlet or on the land, neither thought nor spoke about Jews being injurious to them. I myself perceived that Jews do somewhat to the benefit of Christians but nothing to the detriment." As photographs in the exhibition show, Jewish volunteer batallions fought on the Latvian side in the 1918–20 War of Independence and numerous Jewish politicians stood for mainstream Latvian parties in the years that followed. Although many Jews spoke German or Latvian (and frequently both), Rīga was also an important centre of Yiddish culture in the inter-war period, known above all as the home town of the quality colour magazine *Yidishe Bilde*, the Jewish *National Geographic* of its time. All of this was snuffed out when the Germans moved into Latvia in 1941: most of the city's Jews were herded into ghettos southeast of the Old Town (see p.214), then taken to forests outside the city and shot. Viewed against this background, the museum's photographs of Jewish life in the 1930s – banal pictures of football teams, trips to the beach and family picnics – assume a tragic and profoundly moving significance. There are also some deeply disturbing pictures of the Holocaust itself, including images of a massacre of Jews on Liepāja beach in July 1941, filmed dispassionately by an amateur German cameraman.

St Gertrude's Church to Čaka iela

Running parallel to Skolas is Baznīcas iela, sloping gently uphill towards the redbrick, neo-Gothic **St Gertrude's Church** (Sv Ģertrūdes baznīca), its green-capped spire encrusted with nobbly quatrefoil shapes. Immediately opposite, an Art Nouveau apartment block on the corner of Ģertrūdes iela and Baznīcas iela looks like something out of the Brothers Grimm, with sprites and gargoyles sprouting from its upper storeys.

A few steps southeast is the Centre's main artery, **Brīvības iela**, along which trolleybuses trundle laboriously towards distant suburbs. There's a sprinkling of National Romantic buildings along its length, although few have more historical significance for the Latvians than the so-called "**house on the corner**" at no. 61, a gaudily balustraded building used by the Soviet secret police during the 1940–41 occupation and still in use as the headquarters of the Latvian police.

Jollier by half is the **A. Ķeniņs Highschool** (A. Ķeniņa ģimnāzija), another block southeast at Tērbatas 15. Built in 1905 by Laube and Pēkšēns, it combines bold modernism (as seen in the irregular hexagonal window frames) with fanciful folkloric touches, including ground-floor archways so low that they look as if they've been made with a race of urban elves in mind.

Parallel to Tērbatas iela to the southeast is **Barona iela**, home to some of the Centre's smarter shops. Hogging most of the architectural limelight is the deliciously gaudy Art Nouveau office block at the junction of Barona and Blaumaņa, a veritable bestiary in vertical form, the facade of which features bat-like demons just above ground level, lions and hogs further up and dragons crowning the battlements at the top. Providing an escape from the daytime bustle is the **Krišjānis Barons Memorial Museum** (Krišjāņa Barona memoriālais muzejs; Wed–Sun 11am–6pm; 0.50Ls) at no. 3, the flat where the eponymous writer and ethnographer lived for four years following World War I. Barons' great service to Latvian culture was the cataloguing of over one million traditional Latvian *dainas* – four-line folk poems that country people knew by heart but had never been systematically recorded before. Barons wrote each *daina* on a tiny piece of paper, bundles of which were then placed in specially made chests of drawers – a pair of them are preserved here. Elsewhere there are pictures of people and places associated with Barons, although it's the chance to see the flat's well-preserved 1920s interiors that make a visit here worthwhile.

Moving a block to the southeast, you come to the last of the Centre's big lateral boulevards, **Čaka iela** and its extension, Marijas iela. Čaka takes its name from the poet Aleksandrs Čaks (1901–1950), who broke with Latvian literature's traditional obsession with the countryside to pen eulogies to the edgy urban landscape of inter-war Rīga. He was particularly enthralled by the low-life atmosphere of the street that now bears his name, calling it "forever the merchant... buying and selling anything from a piece of junk to human flesh". Although it's a fairly normal shopping street during the day, Čaka iela is still associated with the kind of raffish activities immortalized by Čaks, with its street prostitutes, all-night gambling arcades and seedy cafés drawing a shadowy clientele during the hours of darkness. From 1937 until his death, Čaks lived in a flat at the junction of Čaka iela and Lāčplēša iela, now the **Aleksandrs Čaks Memorial Museum** (A. Čaka memoriālais muzejs; entrance at Lāčplēša 48/50; Wed–Sun 11am–5pm; 0.40Ls). The poet's cosy sitting room, stuffed with prints, paintings and other objets d'art, is a charming period piece.

Southeast of the Old Town

Immediately southeast of the Old Town, the bustling area around the Central Market (see p.206) gives way to a quiet, run-down district seemingly untouched by

213

Daugava riverfront, Rīga △

the post-Soviet economic changes so evident in other parts of the centre. Many of the disparate sights in this part of town have a deep historical resonance – the prime reason for venturing here.

The principal landmark in this area of greying, nineteenth-century apartment blocks is the **Academy of Sciences** (Latvijas zinātņu akademija) at the junction of Turgeņeva and Gogoļa, built during the early 1960s and nicknamed "Stalin's Birthday Cake" because of its resemblance to the monumental, pseudo-Baroque structures that sprang up all over Moscow in the 1940s and 1950s. Constructed from enormous, gingerbread-coloured chunks of stone, this unloved communist heirloom radiates a melancholy beauty.

Standing in the academy's shadow on the opposite side of Gogoļa is the green-domed Orthodox **Church of the Annunciation** (Tserkva blagoveshtenya), one of the city's more atmospheric places of worship, largely because it's so dark inside – you can't see much apart from the gilded icon frames glittering in the candlelight. Round the other side of the academy on Elijas iela is the ochre-painted **Jesus Church** (Jēzus baznīca), surrounded by a horseshoe of grubby flats. Dating back to 1635, this is Rīga's oldest wooden church, though it's been rebuilt following fires a couple of times since then. The interior is unusual, with a circular central hall supported by wooden pillars.

The Great Synagogue and the Moscow Suburb

A block northeast of the Jesus Church, at the intersection of Gogoļa and Dzirnavu, stand the remains of Rīga's **Great Synagogue**, deliberately set alight on the night of July 4, 1941 (just three days after the Germans entered the city) with, it is thought, about a hundred worshippers still inside. The attack was thought to be the work of Viktors Arājs, leader of the Latvian security team that worked in tandem with the German SS and played a major role in murdering Rīga's Jews. Living in Germany under an assumed name after the war, Arājs was unmasked in 1979, extradited to Latvia and sentenced to life imprisonment (he died in 1988). The walls of the synagogue have been reconstructed to a height of a few metres to serve as a memorial and there's a lone boulder in the adjoining park inscribed with the simple legend "1941. 4/VII".

East of here stretches the so-called **Moscow Suburb** (Maskavas forštate), so named because the main road to Moscow ran through it. The area was inhabited by many of Rīga's Jews and is the site of the wartime ghetto to which they were confined by the Nazis. The erstwhile core of the ghetto is a good 400m east of the Great Synagogue, in the area now bounded by Lāčplēša, Maskavas, Lauvas and Kalna ielas. The Nazis started clearing the ghetto almost immediately after its establishment in September 1941 and by December of the same year almost all of its 25,000 inhabitants had met their deaths in the Rumbula and Biķernieki forests (see pp.217 & 219), just east of the city. The ghetto was then re-populated by Jews from Western Europe, brought here to work as slave labourers, until they, too, were considered surplus to Nazi requirements and murdered. It's now an area of gritty apartment blocks and warehouses, and there's a dearth of memorials to those who lived and suffered here, save for a lone inscription at the entrance to the former **Jewish cemetery** (Ebreju kapi; tram #3, #7 and #9 from the Central Market to the Balvu iela stop) at the corner of Maskavas iela and Ebreju iela. Shorn of its gravestones in World War II, it's now a grassy park.

The Grebenshchikov Church and Rabbit Island

On the southern edge of the former ghetto at Krasta 73 is the gold-domed **Grebenshchikov Church** (Grebenščikova baznīca), built in 1814 for the Old Believers, a dissenting sect which broke away from the Orthodox Church during the seventeenth century and many of whose members fled Russia to escape persecution. There are still enough Old Believers around in Rīga to maintain a small congregation, although the church is rarely open outside prayer times – 7/9am and 5pm seem to be your best bet.

Immediately south of the Moscow Suburb, the main road to Vilnius bridges the Daugava, crossing a long thin landmass known as **Rabbit Island** (Zaķu sala) on the way. You can't walk across the bridge, but there's a bus stop halfway along it (served by trolleybus #20 from Raiņa bulvaris, or buses #40 or #40A from Gogoļa iela) from which you can descend to the island and walk south to **Rīga's TV Tower**, a 368-metre concrete tripod with a viewing platform halfway up – come prepared for stunning views across the Daugava River towards the pitched roofs and belfries of the Old Town skyline.

Pārdaugava

Immediately west of the Old Town, trams #2, #4, #5 and #10 rattle across the Akmens tilts ("Stone Bridge") towards the downbeat suburb of **Pārdaugava** (literally "Across the Daugava"), characterized by rickety old wooden houses and 1950s-era apartment blocks. It's well worth making the trip, however – there's a handful of quirky museums and some beautiful **Botanical Gardens**; furthermore, the Pārdaugava riverbank affords majestic **views** back towards the city centre – revealing a spire-studded skyline that appeared to Laurens van der Post in the early 1960s "as tranquil and translucent as any of Vermeer's views of Delft".

The Railway Museum, Uzvaras parks and the Latvian Theatre Museum

Four hundred metres beyond the western end of Akmens tilts, an unassuming brick warehouse at Uzvaras 2/4 accommodates the **Latvian Railway Museum** (Latvijas dzelzceļa muzejs; Wed–Sat 10am–5pm; 0.50Ls), a small collection of old train tickets and timetables, enlivened by a model railway of which the curator is extremely proud – it features a faithful reconstruction of Līvberže station (on the Rīga–Ventspils line) that he made himself.

From here, Bāriņu iela forges west across the grassy expanse of **Uzvaras parks** ("Victory Park"), passing the most overstated of Rīga's Soviet-era monuments, erected in honour of the Red Army's victory in World War II. Its giant concrete needle spangled with shiny five-pointed stars might at first glance be taken for some outsize advertisement for a nightclub – though at ground level there's no mistaking the political message hinted at by the statue of Victory being saluted by machine-gun-toting Soviet soldiers. Just beyond the western corner of the park, at the junction of Bāriņu and Smilģa, the **Latvian Theatre Museum** (Latvijas teatra muzejs; Wed–Sun 11am–6pm; 0.50Ls) occupies the former home of actor and theatre director Eduards Smilģis (1886–1966), whose book-lined study is preserved in its original state – complete with a shrine to Italian poet Gabriele d'Annunzio, the high-priest of decadence and egoism who exerted such a big influence over early-twentieth-century arty folk. Elsewhere there's a well-presented history of Latvian stagecraft, including set designs, opera costumes and fanciful fairy-tale creatures from Rīga's puppet theatre. It's worth taking a peek at some of the nearby streets before moving on: **Smilģa iela** is rich with examples of pre-World War I wooden architecture, while Bāriņu iela leads to **Agenskalns covered market** (Agenskalņa tirgus), a deliciously doom-laden, red-brick pavilion that looks like something out of a horror movie.

Arkādijas parks and Torņakalnis

At its southern end, Uzvaras parks runs into **Arkādijas parks** ("Arcadia Park"), a smaller but prettier stretch of greenery arranged around a winding waterway popular with ducks. Just across the railway tracks to the east, **Torņakalns train station** was a key embarkation point in the deportations of 1941 and 1949, when thousands of Latvians were loaded into cattle trucks and shipped to Siberia. A cluster of knobbly granite shapes, erected behind the station by sculptor Pauls Jaunzems, serves as their memorial.

The Botanical Gardens

Some 2km northwest of Akmens tilts, and best reached by riding tram #5 to the Konsula iela stop, Rīga's **Botanical Gardens** (Botāniskais dārzs; daily: May–Sept 9am–8pm; Oct–April 9am–5pm; 0.50Ls) is a beautifully laid-out park which receives only a fraction of the visitors it deserves. The outdoor parts of the garden can be a bit dull until mid-May, when magnolias and rhododendrons presage the explosion of colour that lasts right through the summer. The central Palm House makes for a worthwhile excursion whatever the time of year, with halls filled with cacti and subtropicals and a central chamber housing a soaring pair of South American araucaria.

North and east of the city centre

North and east of the city centre sprawl industrial estates and concrete residential zones, softened here and there by sizeable patches of woodland. A great deal of interest is hidden away in these suburban areas. To the north lie the monumental inter-war sculptures of the **Braļu kapi cemetery** and the dense woodland of the **Mežaparks** recreation area; both are on the same tram route, making a combined outing feasible. To the east are a small, but rewarding **Cinema Museum**, a fascinating **Motor Museum** and a moving **Holocaust Memorial**, all grouped in or near the deep-green swathe of Biķernieku forest – and close enough together to be do-able as one trip if you're prepared to wait around for buses and do a bit of walking. Further out are the former presidential summer house, now a quirky museum of inter-war life, at Dauderi; and the enthralling collection of village architecture at the **Open-air Ethnographic Museum** near Lake Jugla.

Braļu Ķapi and around

Some 4km northeast of the centre, **Braļu kapi** ("Brothers' cemetery"; tram #11 from Radio iela) was planned in 1915 as a shrine to the Latvian soldiers then serving in the Tsarist army – by the time it was finished a decade later, it had become a powerful symbol of the newly independent Latvian state and the price in blood that had been required to build it. It remains a strongly evocative spot, its rows of graves guarded by the hulking, muscular creations of sculptor Kārlis Zāle, who blended folkloric traditions with modernism to produce a heroic national style. His monumental *Mother Latvia* (Māte Latvijā) towers over one end of the cemetery, with accompanying pieces *Two Brothers* (Divi Braļi) and *Wounded Horseman* (Ievainotais Jatnieks) driving home the message of comradeship and sacrifice.

On either side of Braļu kapi lie larger, rambling civilian cemeteries set in pleasant, park-like woodland. On the northern side, **Meža kapi** (Woodland cemetery) is full of wooden benches, provided so that Latvians can sit and commune with their ancestors – indeed certain days of the year are set aside as cemetery holidays (each town or region will pick a different date), when entire graveyards can be full of families cleaning up the tombs, tending shrubs or munching picnic fare. Immediately south of Braļu kapi, many of Latvia's leading writers, artists and stage performers are buried in **Raiņa kapi**, so named because it centres on the granite tomb of Latvia's most respected man of letters, Jānis Rainis (see p.227). When Colin Thubron came to pay his respects here in the early 1980s, his Latvian companion complained that Rainis "would be a Goethe or a Shakespeare if he'd been born anywhere else. But he wrote in Latvian... and who reads that?".

Mežaparks and the zoo

From Braļu kapi, tram #11 meanders through northeastern Rīga for another 3km before terminating at **Mežaparks**, a prosperous garden suburb that has been popular with the city's upper crust for well over a century. Mežaparks means "Forest Park", although it was originally known as Kaiserwald in honour of Swedish King Gustavus Adolphus, who landed his invasion force here in 1621. Occupying a wooded, hilly site right beside the tram stop is Rīga's **zoo** (Rīgas zooloģiskais dārzs; daily: mid-April to mid-Oct 10am–6pm; rest of year 10am–4pm; 2Ls), with a pleasant if predictable collection of elephants, camels and zebras enlivened by a pair of Amur tigers, their cage sponsored by a well-known brand of cat food. Beyond the zoo, you can follow paths into a sizeable expanse of woodland and park, somewhere in the middle of which sit both a funfair and the **Song Stadium**, built to accommodate the mind-bogglingly enormous choirs that perform at the National Song Festivals held every five years (the next one is due in 2008) – when over 10,000 people might be singing their hearts out on stage at any one time.

The Cinema Museum

Back in the Soviet era, Latvia churned out several feature films a year, all of which were made at the Rīga Film Studios (Rīgas kinostudija), located 6km east of town in woods just off the upper reaches of Brīvības iela. Hardly anything of a celluloid nature is produced here any more, and the main studio has been converted into a roller-skating rink, but the memory of the local movie industry is lovingly kept alive in the **Latvian Cinema Museum** (Latvijas kinomuzejs; Tues–Sat 11am–5pm; 0.50Ls), which occupies a suite of back rooms down the corridor from the rink. As well as photographs of Latvian film stars through the ages, there are posters and stills recording the landmarks of Latvian cinema, notably the silent adaptation of folk epic *Lāčplēsis* (1930) and the first-ever sound film in Latvia, *Zvejnieka dēls* ("The Fisherman's Son"; 1940). The history of cinema in general is celebrated by a collection of antique cameras, and the curator will play videos of early films by the Lumiere Brothers and Georges Méliès. To get to the museum, catch **bus** #21 from Stacijas laukums or from opposite Katedrāle to the Rīgas Kinostudija stop, and follow the signs to the "*skrituļslidotava*" ("skating rink").

The Motor Museum

A fifteen-minute walk southeast of the Cinema Museum (alternatively ride bus #21 for two more stops to Pansionāts, then bear right down the broad sweep of Eizenšteina iela) lies a smart, brick-and-glass pavilion holding the **Motor Museum** (Rīgas motormuzejs; Tues–Sun 10am–6pm; 0.50Ls) at Eizensteina 6, an eye-opening round-up of Latvian – and Soviet – transport history. The wide-ranging collection's most venerable exhibit is the fire engine made by Rīga's Russko-Baltiiski engineering factory in 1912, although it can't compete in the beauty stakes with the Hansa Renntorpedo, a wonderfully streamlined sports car built for a high-speed Berlin-to-Moscow ride in 1914, and impounded by the Russians when the outbreak of World War I caught the drivers in mid-trip. The Ford family cars made under licence by the Latvian Vairogs ("Shield") firm in the 1930s look frumpily utilitarian in comparison with the luxury motors favoured by fat cats in Bolshevik Russia during the same period: note the sleek 1934 Lincoln used by writer Maxim Gorky and the 1939 Rolls Royce Wraith used by Stalin's Foreign Minister, Molotov. Eloquently summing up the Kremlin's love affair with big cars is the somewhat crumpled 1966 Rolls Royce Silver Shadow owned by notorious speed freak Leonid Brezhnev, who pranged it himself during one of his customary nocturnal drives around Moscow.

Biķernieku forest and the Holocaust Memorial

Behind the Motor Museum, paths lead into the deep evergreen cover of the **Biķernieku forest** (Biķernieku mežs), site of the winding, overgrown racetrack where Soviet motorcycling championships were once held. It's since become a popular venue for woodland strolls – prams and pushbikes are the only vehicles likely to be put through their paces here nowadays.

The southwestern end of Biķernieku forest, traversed by the dead-straight Biķernieku iela, was used by the Nazis as a mass murder and burial ground in

World War II – thousands of Jews from all over Europe were shot here between 1941 and 1944. The sixtieth anniversary of the first wave of exterminations (which actually began not here but in Rumbula forest; see opposite) was marked on November 30, 2001, by the unveiling of an impressive new **Holocaust Memorial**, just off the southwestern side of Biķernieku iela. A profoundly beautiful piece of plein-air sculpture, it's well worth a trip from central Rīga to see. The memorial's central feature is an angular concrete canopy covering a black slab, on which an inscription in Latvian, German, Hebrew and Russian quotes Job 16.18: "Oh earth, cover not my blood, and let my cry have no peace". Radiating out from the slab is a garden of jagged stones marked out into plots – each inscribed with the name of the European city the victims came from. Some visitors place small pebbles on or around individual stones in a personal act of remembrance. In the forest around the memorial, mass graves are marked by raised beds of grass, each with a rough-hewn rock planted in the middle.

Trolleybus #14 (from opposite Katedrāle) goes past the memorial, but there's no stop beside the site itself – you need to get off at the Keguma iela stop and continue east along Biķernieku iela on foot (1km), or stay on the bus until the Eisenšteina iela stop and walk back along the same road (1.5km). If you've just been to the Motor Museum, you can walk to the memorial by following forest paths from the former racetrack (see p.217), although you'll probably need a decent Rīga city map to navigate your way through the woods – there aren't any signs.

The Ethnographic Museum

Twelve kilometres east of the centre on the Tallinn road, but easily reached by public transport, the **Latvian Open-air Ethnographic Museum** (Latvijas etnogrāfiskais brīvdabas muzejs; daily 10am–5pm; 1Ls) brings together over a hundred traditional buildings from all over Latvia, reassembled in a partly forested setting by the shores of Lake Jugla. It's a big site, and you'll need a couple of hours and an appetite for woodland strolling to get the best out of it. Consider buying the English-language plan (0.70Ls) at the entrance – you could quite easily get lost in the eastern reaches of the museum without it. The display captures perfectly the atmosphere of nineteenth-century rural life, when the majority of Latvians lived in isolated farmsteads rather than villages or towns. Although most of the timber-built houses look comfortably large, much of the space was devoted to storing grain or keeping animals, and families lived in cramped, spartan quarters at one end of the building, their tiny beds crammed into corners. Open hearths were used for smoking meats and drying hay, which was then stored in the loft. Farmsteads had to be self-sufficient in everything – and the re-created kitchen gardens here are full of every manner of vegetable, fruit tree and medicinal herb. The oldest of the buildings in the museum is a sixteenth-century church from Vecborne near Daugavpils, its interior featuring a painted, wooden ceiling filled with jovial-looking angels.

On **summer** weekends, blacksmiths and other craftsmen demonstrate their work, while around **Christmas** time, folk groups from all over Latvia converge on the museum to perform yuletide songs and dances. There's a traditional-style **inn** just up from the entrance serving grey peas (*ziņi*) alongside regular coffee-and-cake fare. To get to the museum, take **bus** #1 from Brīvības iela, and get off at the first stop after passing the shores of Lake Jugla on your right.

Dauderi

Hidden away behind the Aldaris brewery, 6km north of the city centre in the suburb of Sarkandaugava, the fanciful neo-Gothic mansion of **Dauderi** (Tues–Sun 11am–5pm; 0.50Ls; tram #5 or #9 from the National Opera to the Aldaris stop) served as the summer residence of Latvian president Karlis Ulmanis from 1937 to 1940 and now houses a modest tribute-museum to Ulmanis and the independent Latvia over which he presided. The display is a charmingly un-themed mish-mash which ranges from Latvian military medals to postcards of inter-war Rīga. One room is filled with paintings by Niklavs Strunke, one of the foremost modernist artists of the 1920s and 1930s, alongside the beautifully calligraphed, hand-illustrated letters he sent to his friends. Most rewarding of all are the rooms themselves, stuffed with period furniture and objets d'art – one of the upstairs salons boasts cherub-encrusted ceilings and a rather unusual nineteenth-century oven, the ceramic-tiled exterior of which is decorated with scenes of dwarves chopping firewood.

Rumbula and Salaspils

Thick woodland southeast of Rīga provided Latvia's Nazi occupiers with the cover they needed to murder tens of thousands of Jews; they were either shot at **Rumbula forest**, 11km southeast from the city centre, or crowded into **Salaspils** concentration camp, 3km further on. Both sites are now home to dignified memorials, with the serenity of the surrounding pines helping to concentrate the mind on themes of remembrance.

Located on or near the highway to Daugavpils, Rumbula and Salaspils are easy to reach **by car** from central Rīga. They're also just one stop apart on the Rīga–Ogre–Lielvārde **train** route, so it's not hard to combine them in a single trip, providing you swot up on timetable information before setting out – not all trains stop at Rumbula and Dārziņi and there's no information on arrivals or departures at the halts themselves. You can also get to Rumbula by a combination of **tram and bus** from central Rīga (see below).

Rumbula forest

Some 11km from the city centre, **Rumbula forest**, a once dense area of woodland, is now broken up by a patchwork of post-war factories, housing projects and vegetable plots. As many as 28,000 Latvian and Lithuanian Jews were brought to be shot in Rumbula on November 30, 1941, and mass killings continued here throughout the war. A **memorial site** now occupies a wooded knoll beside the road, and a newish-looking stone engraved with the words "To the Jewish Victims of Fascism" marks the entrance. A communist-era tablet among the trees further on refers to those who were murdered here simply as "Soviet citizens", a typical example of the USSR's refusal to grapple with the racial issues which underlay the Holocaust. A restful place surrounded by birches, but lacking in a single big memorial, the site consists of a central plaza, the main focus for the laying of wreaths, and a surrounding area of park where several raised beds planted with grass (each with rough-hewn rocks sprouting out of them) mark individual massacre sites.

To get here **by car**, head southeast from central Rīga along Maskavas iela (the main highway to Daugavpils) for 11km and you'll find the site right at the city limits, just past a used car lot and opposite a petrol station. The easiest way to get here **by public transport** is to take trams #7 and #9 from the Central Market to the Kvadrāts terminus, followed by bus #15 to the Rumbula terminus (from where you walk back the way you came for 100m and cross the road). Alternatively, catch a train to the Rumbula halt, which is just east of the memorial site – although be warned that this is no more than an unmarked platform in the middle of a meadow and you may well miss it altogether.

Salaspils

Between October 1941 and October 1944 an estimated 100,000 people met their deaths in **Salaspils concentration camp**, hidden in dense woodland 14km southeast of Rīga and 3km short of the town of Salaspils itself. The camp was originally intended as a transitional camp in which Jews from Germany, Austria and Czechoslovakia could be held before their deportation to work camps and extermination sites elsewhere, but was increasingly used as a killing zone as the war went on. At the centre of the site is a long, concrete hall, mounted on pillars and slightly tilted to form a gently ascending processional way, intended to concentrate the visitor's mind on the journey from life to death. At the end of the hall a staircase drops down into a small museum space, containing a series of gripping illustrations evoking the harshness of camp life by K. Būss, a Latvian political prisoner interned here. Outside, a long, black concrete slab containing a slowly ticking metronome is the main focus for wreath laying, remembrance and prayer. The surrounding terrain is peppered with concrete tablets marking the locations of the barrack buildings where the prisoners were held. An ensemble of heroic statues intended to depict the uncrushable human spirit comes across as tastelessly Soviet – one angular-jawed example is entitled "Red Front", as if to suggest that resistance to Nazi barbarity was entirely the preserve of the communists.

You can get to the memorial by taking a suburban **train** to the Dārziņi halt – there's currently no station signboard in evidence, but you'll recognize it from the fact that it's the first station out of Rīga that is completely surrounded by pine forest. From here a signed path leads to the memorial site – a fifteen-minute walk through peaceful woodland. Approaching the site **by car** along the Daugavpils-bound highway, you'll see a long concrete slab 15km out on the northern side of the road pointing the way to the site – assuming you're in the eastbound lane, however, you'll have to carry on for another couple of kilometres and do a U-turn.

The Botanical Gardens at Salaspils

Two more stops down the train line from Dārziņi is **SALASPILS** itself, a drab dormitory town rescued from obscurity by the presence of Latvia's **National Botanical Gardens** – (Latvijas botāniskais dārzs; daily: April–Sept 8am–8pm; Oct–March 9am–4.30pm; 0.60Ls), a large expanse of undulating grassland, flowerbeds and shrubs, the main entrance to which lies immediately opposite Salaspils train station. The site places an understandable emphasis on the indigenous flora of Latvia, and that quintessentially Baltic conifer, the juniper, is represented here in almost all its possible varieties. Near the centre of the gardens is an orangery, from which cacti, aloes, yucca and figs look as if they're about to mount a mass break-out. The eastern part of the garden contains examples of what a typical Latvian family might cultivate in their village plot – common herbs like thyme, garlic and hyssop rub shoulders with plants associated with traditional folk medicine, such as euphorbia (for stimulating the nerve system) and poppies (for putting it to sleep).

Eating

The majority of Rīga's **restaurants** serve international cuisine. Establishments offering indigenous meat-and-potatoes fare do exist, but most of these are self-service cafeterias rather than restaurants in the traditional sense – they're good sources of filling and cheap food nevertheless. Restaurant **prices** are on the whole higher than in Vilnius or Tallinn, but still significantly lower than in Western European capitals, unless you're eating in a particularly upmarket establishment. On average, main courses cost around 2–3Ls in the self-service places, 3–6Ls in full-blown restaurants; a three-course meal with drinks will be somewhere in the 10–18Ls range – more if you're ordering bottles of wine. We've included telephone numbers for those restaurants where reservations are recommended at weekends.

For livelier eating options check out the **bars** listed under "Drinking" below – many offer substantial eats at reasonable prices. Most of Rīga's **cafés** also offer a range of hot meals, which can often be just as good as anything on offer in a restaurant, and cheaper to boot. All eating establishments listed below are **open** daily till 11pm, unless otherwise stated.

If you're **self-catering**, you can pick up fruit, veg and other basics at the Central Market just beyond the bus station (see p.206), or at supermarkets like Rimi, at

Audēju 16 and Matīsa 27. There are 24-hour food and drink shops in the Old Town at Kramu 2 and Grēcinieku 10; and in the Centre at Barona 6 and Brīvības 68.

Cafés and snacks

Old Town

Franču Maiznīca Basteja. A French patisserie right opposite Bastejkalns hill. The perfect place to pig out on melt-in-the-mouth croissants and brie-filled baguettes. Mon–Sat till 10pm, Sun till 9pm.

Kolonāde Brīvības 26. A charming parkside pavilion conveniently sited on the eastern fringes of the Old Town, offering self-service coffees, breakfast pastries and cakes. Outside seating to the rear. Open till 10pm.

Nostalģia Kaļķu 22. Arch, Soviet-styled café occupying extravagantly stuccoed rooms, complete with monumental socialist-realist frescoes. Full range of drinks, and substantial meals. Till 2am.

Olé Audēju 1. Bright cellar café underneath the *Centra* hotel (see p.194), serving up excellent-value buffet lunches. Till 5pm.

Pelmeņi XL Kaļķu 7. A popular fast-food joint on the Old Town's main street offering *pelmeņi* filled with meat or cheese. Till 4am.

Sievasmātes Pirādziņi Kaļķu 12. A no-nonsense cafeteria doling out cheap and tasty *pīrodziņi*. Till 9pm.

Smilšu pulkstenis Cnr of Meistaru iela and Mazā smilsu iela. A cosy café conveniently located just off Livu laukums, serving decent tea and coffee, delightful pastries, and an impressive array of cakes. Till 9pm.

The Centre

Ai Karamba! Pulkveža Brieža 2. A cross between a funky London café and an American diner, with tables tightly packed into a cosy interior. Toasted sandwiches, pasta and salads. Popular with a younger crowd, it's also a good place for a drink. Till midnight.

Apsara Elizabetes iela. Quaint wooden pavilion on the eastern side of Vērmanes dārzs park, with a big range of speciality teas, and comfy cushions to sit on. Till 10pm.

Charlestons Cappuccino Bar Blaumaņa 38/40. Great coffee, some excellent salads, and dangerously delicious cakes.

Coffee Nation Valdemāra 24. Not the greatest range of nibbles, but good for quality coffee in a funky environment. One of the few places in town where you can get a decent drop of the brown stuff to take away. Also at Barona 24 and the train station. Till 10pm.

Dāvids Cappucino Bar Upīša Pasāža. Civilized environment in which to drink decent coffee and

tuck into tasty cakes, in an arcade just off Čaka iela. Till 9pm.

Osiriss Barona 31. A stylish, intimate café in the Centre, with coffee, cakes and a full menu of mouth-watering international eats. Till midnight.

Rāma Barona 56. A vegetarian bistro run by Hare Krishna devotees. The food is a bit unexciting sometimes, but it's wholesome, filling and dead cheap. Can get crowded at lunchtimes. Till 7pm.

Self-service cafeterias

Anšpetri Dzirnavu 57. An order-at-the-counter canteen behind the *Hotel Latvia*, featuring lots of stodge and a few salads. Open 24hr.

Džungļi Antonijas 13. A small but solid choice of hot food, alongside substantial salads. A handy bolt-hole for the Art Nouveau part of town.Till 9pm.

Lido Vērmanītis Elizabetes 65. A classy cafeteria serving all manner of tasty Latvian meat-and-potato dishes, pancakes and salads, with an interior decked out in country-cottage style. There are similar *Lido*-owned establishments all over the city, among them *Staburags*, Čaka 55; *Dzirnavas*, Dzirnavu 76; and *Līdo Atpūtas Centrs*, Krasta 76, a vast eating and entertainment complex – complete with real-size reproduction windmill – 3km southeast of the centre on the Daugavpils road.

Šefpavārs Vilhelms Šķūņu 6. A few steps from Doma laukums, a self-service place where you create your own savoury or sweet pancake. Till 10pm.

Restaurants

Old Town and around

Kamāla Jauniela 14. Smart, but not overpriced, vegetarian restaurant just round the corner from Doma laukums, serving Indian and Middle Eastern dishes in a room stuffed with cushions and exotic textiles.

Lotoss Skārņu 7. A funky little place with a great view of Skārņu iela's row of medieval buildings. Modern European menu, excellent salads.

Melnie mūki Jāņa sēta 1 ☏721 5006. An elegantly converted medieval building offering an imaginative range of top-notch international fare. Till 2am.

Pūt Vējiņ! Jauniela 18. Excellent pork, chicken and steak dishes in the homely grill-pub on the ground floor and moderately priced Latvian specialities in the low-key restaurant upstairs. Till midnight.

Salt 'n Pepper 13. Janvāra 33. Laid-back bar-restaurant with a bit of everything, from hearty breakfasts through lunchtime soups to an international array of main meals. Situated in a corner by the river, it's the perfect vantage point from which to observe trams and trains rattling their way across the Daugava bridges.

Sue's Indian Raja Vecpilsētas 3. Authentic Indian food, good service and an atmospheric warren of rooms.

Vecmeita ar kaķi Mazā pils 1. Informal but chic cellar restaurant just off Doma laukums, offering up pork-based Latvian favourites alongside healthy salads and pasta dishes. Nicely priced for the area.

Zelta Krogs Citadeles 12. Mixed European-Latvian cuisine in a relaxing spot just behind the Ave Sol concert hall. Plenty of salads, pasta and vegetarian pancakes, all at reasonable prices. Till 10pm.

Centre

Charlestons Blaumaņa 38. A stylish but not-too-formal restaurant with a wide-ranging menu that runs the gamut of global eats from steak through ribs to Italian pasta. Till midnight.

Lauku pagrabs Antonijas 9. Located in a basement just round the corner from the Art Nouveau buildings on Alberta iela, this is one of the few restaurants in Riga dedicated to Latvian cuisine pure and simple – the pork and sauerkraut

are especially recommended – and prices are quite cheap, too.

Lidojošā Varde Elizabetes 31A ☎732 1184. A bright basement restaurant with a couple of dark, atmospheric corners and a terrace on the street outside. The eclectic international menu features plenty of tasty salads and vegetarian choices, but the place's popularity with the expat community means that prices are creeping up (though you can still get main courses from around 3Ls) and you often need to book in the evening. Till 1am.

Pizza Jazz Raiņa 15. Big pizzeria just across the park from the Old Town. Breezy service and cheap, filling fare make up for antiseptic surroundings and piped rock-pop sounds. There's another branch at Brīvības 86. Till midnight.

Pizza Lulū Ģertrūdes 27. A fashionable little American-style pizzeria where you can eat well at a reasonable price. Can get crowded. Open 24hr.

Spotikačs Antonijas 12. A Ukranian restaurant with folksy cottage decor, serving cheap and tasty fare such as *vareniki* (meat-filled dumplings) and *golubtsi* (cabbage leaves stuffed with mincemeat) augmented by more solid pork and veal dishes, garnished with buckwheat and bacon bits.

Vincents Elizabetes 19 ☎733 2634. The nouvelle-ish cuisine is excellent, but you're unlikely to escape with a bill of less than 20Ls per person. Till midnight.

Drinking

Rīga offers innumerable opportunities for bar-hopping, with the Old Town in particular offering a multiplicity of supping venues that fill up with fun-seeking locals seven nights a week. There's a healthy scattering of characterful bars in the Centre, although they're somewhat more spread out – so it makes sense to aim for one in particular rather than expect to crawl your way through several. Most places are open until midnight or later on weekdays, with closing times of 2am or later being the norm on Fridays and Saturdays. Drinks are affordable even in the most stylish of places and there's usually a food menu of some sort. Bars regularly featuring live music or DJs have been included under "Clubs and live music" (see opposite).

Old Town

Alus Sēta Tirgotu iela 6. A justifiably popular pub with huge meals served from the grill. A good place to sample good, cheap Latvian ales accompanied by the national beer-snack – *zirņi* (peas garnished with bacon). Outdoor seating in warm weather. Till 1am.

Dickens Grēcinieku 11. Brit-pub with wide range of international beers. It heaves with expats and locals at weekends, but can seem like a characterless city-centre boozer at other times – the nostalgic adverts for train sets hanging on the walls might cheer you up. Pricey pub grub in the businessmen-oriented restaurant

at the back. Sun–Thurs till midnight, Fri & Sat till 2pm.

Paddy Whelan's Grēcinieku 4. A big, lively Irish pub occupying lovely stucco-ceilinged rooms, popular with young locals and expats alike. Head upstairs to the laid-back *Paddy Go Easy* bar for a quiet pint. Sun–Thurs till midnight, Fri till 2am, Sat till 1am.

Paldies Dievam piektdiena ir klāt ("Thank God it's Friday") 11. Novembra krastmala 9. Brash cocktail bar with kaleidoscope-coloured interior and Caribbean-themed food. Sun–Thurs till 2am, Fri & Sat till 4am.

Pulkvedim neviens neraksta Peldu 26/28. Taking its name from the Gabriel Garcia Marquez novel *Nobody Writes to the Colonel*, this hip bar with industrial-chic decor functions as a café-restaurant during the day and becomes a club at night (see "Clubs and live music" below). Sun–Thurs till 3am, Fri & Sat till 5am.

Rīgas balzams Torņa 4. A roomy, chic cellar bar serving up Rīga's favourite firewater – the black, syrupy *balzams* – either on its own or in a mind-boggling number of mixer combinations. Till midnight.

Spalvas pa gaisu Grēcinieku 2. A snazzy and spacious café-bar with loungey corners, loud music and good cocktails. Full menu of food, including some delicious sweets.

Vīna Pagrabs Pils 22. Cheap drinks, bench seating and alternative background music in friendly brick-lined cellar. Till 11pm.

Centre

Andalūzijas Suns Elizabetes 83–85. Named after *Un Chien Andalou*, the Surrealist film made by

Salvador Dalí and Luis Buñuel, this roomy café-bar is equally suited to an evening meal or a beery night out. The menu lists some eclectic dishes, with main courses from around 3Ls and some good vegetarian options. Sun–Wed till 1am, Thurs–Sat till 3am.

Cocoloco Stabu iela 6. A relaxing bar-restaurant with simple decor, Jamaican-influenced food and reggae rythms booming out on weekend evenings. Till midnight.

DECO bārs Dzirnavu 84. Great cocktails, music, dancing and excellent service, attracting a seemingly endless string of stylish patrons. Sun–Thurs till 2am, Fri & Sat till 6am.

Sarkans Stabu iela. A designer café-restaurant on three floors attracting a trend-conscious but laid-back crowd. The international food menu has plenty of vegetarian choices, and some decent breakfasts. Sun–Thurs till midnight, Fri & Sat till 4am.

Nightlife and entertainment

With an ever-increasing number of **nightclubs** and **music bars** in the city, you can go out partying in Rīga every night of the week. More refined cultural tastes are catered for, too, with a wealth of top-notch classical music, a spread of good cinemas and some enjoyable theatre. If watching clowns, acrobats and chimps in drag is your idea of a day out, then Rīga's circus at Merķeļa 4 (☎721 3479) is one of the oldest purpose-built circuses still operating in Europe and remains delightfully old-fashioned, if a bit grotty – performances usually kick off at lunchtime or mid-afternoon.

Rīga in Your Pocket (see p.193) carries advance **information** on classical music and theatre events, although the *Baltic Times* is better for week-by-week listings. If you can read Latvian, you'll find the most comprehensive run-down in the *Izklaide* supplement, given away with the *Diena* newspaper every Friday.

Clubs and live music

Most **dance venues** concentrate on a commercial diet of techno, Euro-hits and golden oldies, although more specialized styles of music might receive an airing in the smaller clubs, especially on weeknights. **Live music** is largely limited to the middle-of-the-road pop-rock groups that Latvia seems to churn out in ever greater numbers, with gigs taking place in a wide range of music bars and clubs. Bigger touring acts perform at the Skonto Halle sportshall on Melngaiļa iela, the Ķipsala Halle exhibition hall on Ķipslas iela, or the Kongresu nams (Congress Centre) in Kronvalda park – check posters and press for details. Clubs and music venues charge an entry fee of anything from 1–5Ls depending on what's on – once inside, drinks shouldn't be too much more expensive than in regular bars.

Bites blūzs klubs Dzirnavu 34A. Relaxed music pub with live acts most nights – performed by visiting bluesmen or by the house band. Fri & Sat till 2am. Sun–Thurs till 1am.

Četri Balti Krekli Vecpilsētas 12. Large, upmarket cellar bar, restaurant and disco known for its Latvian-only music policy and correspondingly popular with an older crowd keen to escape the

techno on offer elsewhere. The better-known domestic bands perform here. No trainers. Daily till 3am.

Cita Opera Raiņa 21. Classy, upmarket disco popular with Latvian yuppies and smarter students. Frequent live performances by Latvian pop-rock acts. Daily till 4am.

Depo Valnu 32 ☉www.klubsdepo.lv. Post-industrial cellar space with alternative DJ nights and live bands. Functions as a laid-back café during the day. Daily till 3am.

Kabata Peldu 19. A basement club in Old Rīga, with a small dance floor and live bands, popular with late teens and early twentysomethings. Daily till 3am.

M808 Lāčplēša 5 @http://m.808.lv. Small and friendly cellar club fifteen minutes' walk northeast of the Old Town, offering a more cutting-edge brand of techno than the bigger downtown clubs. Fri, Sat and some other nights (look out for posters) till 5am.

Muzikas akadēmijas studentu klubs Raiņa 23. Riotous student discos once a week (usually Fri) and occasional gigs in the basement of Rīga's Music Academy. Friendly crowd, with cheap drinks at the bar. Days and times vary.

Pulkvedim Neviens Neraksta Peldu 26/28. Different breeds of DJ on different nights of the week, laid-back artsy crowd and frequent live bands. Fri & Sat till 5am, Sun–Thurs till 2am.

Purvs Matīsa 60. Stylish gay club whose name means "Swamp". Erotic performances, sometimes with audience participation. Wed–Sun till 6am.

Roxy Kaļķu 24. Vast city-centre place blasting out Euro-pop and Russian techno to an undiscerning, fun-seeking crowd of expats and beautiful young things. Bar, billiards and "erotic" dancers. Daily till 6am.

Saksofons Stabu 43. The only real alternative rock bar in town, with local bands – ranging from the inspirational to the atrocious – playing almost every night. The cocktails are cheap and potent. Daily till 2am.

XXL Kalniņa 4. Gay club and restaurant attracting a mixed, dance-oriented crowd. Good food and wild decor. Open daily 4pm–6am, cover charge Tues–Sat 1–5Ls. Daily till 6am.

Classical music and theatre

Classical music in Rīga is of an exceptionally high standard. Performances are reasonably accessible – tickets are unlikely to cost more than 5–6Ls (unless you're visiting the opera; see below) and you rarely need to book weeks in advance. The Latvian National Symphony Orchestra and the Latvian National Opera are the biggest shows in town, but be sure to look out for performances by Kremerata Baltica, a chamber ensemble put together by the Rīga-born violinist Gidon Kremer; and the world-famous choral group, Ave Sol. The box office in the Great Guild (see below) handles information and tickets for most – but not all – classical music events in town; otherwise you'll have to contact the venues themselves. One major festival worth noting is the **Riga Opera Festival** (middle two weeks of July), when the best of the previous season's productions are reprised. Rīga can offer a rich and varied diet of **theatre**, although you'll probably need a working knowledge of Latvian or Russian to appreciate it to the full.

Concert and opera venues

Ave Sol Concert Hall (Koncertzāle Ave Sol) Citadeles 7 ☏702 7570. Home of Ave Sol, one of the best choral ensembles in the Baltic States. Also hosts concerts by other choirs and chamber musicians.

Great Guild (Lielā Ģilde) Amatu 6 ☏722 4850, @www.music.lv/orchestra. Main venue for the Latvian National Symphony Orchestra, who usually play here on Saturday evenings unless they're away on tour. Frequent Saturday- or Sunday-lunchtime concerts aimed at children and families, featuring popular classics. Box office Tues–Sat noon–6pm, Sun 2hr before performance.

House of the Blackheads (Melngalvju nams) Rātslaukumā 7 ☏704 4300. Solo recitals and chamber music.

Latvian National Opera (Latvijas Nacionālā Opera) Aspazijas bulvaris 3 ☏707 3777, @www.opera.lv. The main auditorium – lavishly refurbished in late-nineteenth-century style – stages classic operatic productions and is also home to the Rīga Ballet (Rīgas Balets). The New Hall (Jaunajā zāle) hosts anything from chamber music to civilized, sit-down pop-rock. Opera tickets range from 8Ls in the stalls to 30Ls for the best boxes. Box office daily 10am–7pm.

Rīga Cathedral (Rīgas Doms) Doma laukums ☏721 3498. Recitals given on the sonorous cathedral organ every Friday, sometimes midweek as well. Tickets can be obtained from the office opposite the west door.

Small Guild (Mazā Ģilde) Amatu 3/5 ☏722 3772. Chamber music.

St John's Church (Jāņa baznīca) Skārņu 24 ☏722 4028. Chamber music and choral concerts.

St Peter's Church (Pētera baznīca) Skārņu 19.
More chamber music.
Wagner Hall (Vagnera zāle) Vāgnera 4 ☏721
0814. Orchestral music and chamber concerts.

Theatres

Daile Theatre (Dailes Teātris) Brīvības 75 ☏729
4444, ⊚www.dailesteatris.lv. Big, modern
auditorium hosting a mixture of classical drama,
musicals and comedy. Small-scale productions in
the adjoining Mazā zāle or "small hall". Box office
Mon–Fri 10am–6.30pm, Sat & Sun 11am–6pm.
Kabata Peldu 19 ☏722 3334. Contemporary
fringe productions in small, intimate venue.
National Theatre (Nacionālais Teātris)
Kronvalda bulvaris 2 ☏732 2759. Elegant pre-
World War I building with mainstream classical
drama on the main stage, and more experiemental
stuff in the *Aktieru zāle* studio theatre.
New Theatre (Jaunais Teātris) Lāčplēša 25
☏728 0765. Usually considered the best place to
see contemporary plays by international
playwrights.
Puppet Theate (Leļļu teātris) Barona 16/18
☏728 5355. Great puppets, great stage designs,
great fun for children of all ages. Productions
usually kick off at 11am or 3pm.
Russian Drama Theatre (Krievu drāmas
teātris) Kaļķu 16 ☏722 5395, ⊚www.trd.lv.
Varied Russian-language programme featuring
everything from Chekhov to musical cabaret. Box
office Mon–Fri 9.30am–6pm, Sat 10am–3pm.

Cinema

Big-name movies arrive in Rīga almost immediately after their release in Western
Europe. **Films** are usually shown in the original language with Latvian and Russian
subtitles, unless they're art-house movies that are in Rīga for a short run only – in
which case they'll have Latvian-language voice-over.

Tickets cost somewhere in the 2Ls–2.50Ls range, although most cinemas reduce
their rates by thirty to fifty percent on at least one day a week – usually Mondays or
Tuesdays.

Daile Barona 31 ☏728 3854. Reasonably modern
cinema with first-run Hollywood movies on two
screens.
K. Suns Elizabetes 83/85 ☏728 5411.
Mainstream commercial films.
Kino 52 Lāčplēša 52 ☏728 8778. Classy,
comfortable place with a moderately arty
programming policy and discounts for ISIC card
holders.
Kinogalerija Jaunielā 24 ☏722 9030. Regular
programme of non-mainstream films, in the only
cinema still to be found in the Old Town.
Oskars Skolas 2 ☏733 3643. Mainstream
commercial films, late showings at weekends.
Rīga Elizabetes 61 ☏728 9755. The oldest of Rīga's
surviving cinemas (formerly the Splendid Palace),
and still a plush, atmospheric place. Commercial
films and the occasional art-house choice.

Spectator sports

International **football** matches, as well as those featuring leading club side Skonto
Rīga, are held at the Skonto stadium, fifteen minutes' walk north of the Old Town
at Melngaiļa iela. Despite winning the domestic title ten years running, Skonto
Rīga have a poor record in European competition. However, they often play pre-
season friendlies against moderately good European sides over the summer – look
out for street posters advertising these.

Big **ice hockey** and **basketball** matches take place in the Sporta maneža indoor
arena, 3km southeast of the Old Town beside the Maskavas dārzs park (trams #7,
#9 from the Central Market to the Balvu iela stop). A new ice-hockey stadium is
being built on Skanstes iela 2km northeast of the centre and will be the main venue
for the 2006 world championships.

Shopping

Rīga's Old Town possesses a reasonable selection of fashion boutiques, souvenir
shops and bookstores. The more mainstream high-street clothes, shoe, and toiletries
shops are concentrated in the streets east of here – Čaka, Barona, Tērbatas and
Brīvības ielas. Great for browsing for cheap clothes, fake designer watches and

Russian fur hats is the vast **Central Market** (Centraltirgus; see p.206), though you're unlikely to turn up anything of quality.

Rīga is an excellent place in which to stock up on **traditional hand-knitted woollens** (mostly hats, gloves, socks and scarves, plus sweaters). Many are decorated with traditional Latvian geometric patterns – often sun, star and fir-tree shapes, symbolizing nature's bounty. The same designs crop up on tablecloths, linen garments and other textiles, many of which are hand-embroidered. You'll find all of the above in souvenir shops and on the occasional street stall, alongside pendants, necklaces and bracelets made from the ubiquitous Baltic amber, and handmade ceramics – including candle-lit lanterns in the form of tiny clay houses.

Souvenirs

Laipa Laipu 2/4. Reasonable across-the-board selection of linenwear, woollens, amber jewellery and wooden toys.

Senā Klēts Merķeļa 13. A treasure trove of Latvian ethnography, with traditional folk costumes, tablecloths, bedspreads and more. Quality handiwork, high prices. Located inside the Latviešu biedrības nams (Latvian Society House), so not immediately visible from the street.

Tīne Vaļņu 2. Big store on two levels, selling ceramics, amber trinkets, linen goods and plenty of woolly mittens and socks.

Books

Jāņa Rozes Bastēja 12 & Barona 5. Good choice of tourist-oriented guidebooks and photo albums, and a decent range of English-language paperbacks.

Jāņa Sēta Elizabetes 83/85. The best place in the Baltics for maps and travel guidebooks.

Valters un Rapa Aspazijas 24. Big bookstore selling stationery, calendars, and coffee-table books about Rīga.

Zvaigzne ABC Valdemāra 6. Educational literature specialist: a good place to find dictionaries and Latvian language textbooks.

Music

Randoms Kaļķu 4. Big mainstream music store, where you'll find most Latvian classical, folk and pop titles, as well as familiar international stuff.

Upe Vāgnera 5. Folk and world music store run by the Upe record label, and the best place to seek out many of the CDs recommended in our "Baltic Folk Music" section (see Contexts p.422). The Upe store at Valnu 26 is good for rock, classical and jazz.

Listings

Airlines Aeroflot, Ģertrūdes 6 ☎278 774, ⊛www.aeroflot.ru; AirBaltic, Kaļķu 15 ☎720 7777, ⊛www.airbaltic.com; British Airways, Torņa 4/IIIA ☎732 6737, ⊛www.ba.com; Estonian Air, Kaļķu 15 ☎721 4860; Finnair, Barona 36 ☎724 3008, ⊛www.finnair.com; LOT, Mazā Pils 5 ☎722 7234, ⊛www.lot.com; Lufthansa, at the airport ☎720 7183, ⊛www.lufthansa.com; SAS, see under AirBaltic.

Airport 8km southwest of the centre at the end of bus routes #22 and #22A. Airport information on ☎720 7136, ⊛www.riga-airport.com.

Car rental Avis, at the airport ☎720 7353, ⊛www.avis.com; Europcar, Basteja 10 ☎722 2637, ⊛www.europcar.lv and at the airport ☎922 2637; Hertz, at the airport ☎720 7980, ⊛www.hertz.com.

Embassies and consulates Belarus, Jēzusbaznīcas 12 ☎732 5321, ⊛www.belembassy.org; Canada, Doma laukums 4 ☎722 6315, ©canembr@bkc.lv; Estonia, Skolas 13 ☎781 2020, ©embassy.riga@mfa.ee; Ireland, Brīvības 54 ☎702 5259; Lithuania, Rūpniecības 24

☎732 1519, ©lithemb@ltemb.vip.lv; Russia, Antonijas 2 ☎733 2151, ⊛www.latvia.mid.ru; UK, Alunāna 5 ☎777 4700, ⊛www.britain.lv; USA, Raiņa 7 ☎703 6200, ⊛www.usembassy.lv.

Exchange Round-the-clock service at Marika, Basteja 14, Brīvības 30, Merķeļa 10.

Hospital The main emergency department is at Hospital No. 1 (Rīgas pirmaja slimnīca) on Bruņinieku iela, although for all but the most urgent complaints you'd do far better to book an appointment with one of the English-speaking doctors at Diplomatic Service Medical Centre Elizabetes 57 (722 9942); or Ars, Skolas 5 ☎720 1001.

Internet access Dualnet Café, Peldu 17 (24hr); Interneta Kafejnīca, Elizabetes 75 (Mon–Fri 10am–10pm, Sat & Sun 10am–9pm).

Laundry Vienmēr Tirs, Tallinna 59 and Barona 52.

Left luggage in the basement of the train station (daily 4.30am–midnight) and at the bus station (daily 6.30am–9pm).

Libraries British Council, Blaumaņa 5A (Tues, Thurs & Fri 11am–5pm, Wed 11am–6pm, Sat 10am–3pm, ⊛www.britishcouncil.lv).

Parking 24hr guarded car parks at Prāgas 2, Basteja bul. 8, Republikas laukums 2.

Pharmacies 24hr service at Rīgas Vecpilsētas Aptieka, Audēju 20; and at Rudens, Ģertrūdes 105.

Photographic developing and supplies Kodak Laboratorija, Audēju 1.

Police Emergency number ☎02.

Post office Main office at Brīvības 19 (Mon–Fri 7am–11pm, Sat & Sun 8am–10pm).

Taxis Ranks can be found at the junction of Kaļķu and Aspazias, and at the junction of Audēju and Aspazijas. Otherwise call Rīga Taxi ☎800 1010; or Rīgas taksometru parks ☎800 1313.

Travel agents Latvia Tours, Kaļķu 8 (☎708 5001, ⊛www.latviatours.lv), and Via Rīga, Barona 7/9 (☎728 5901, ⊛www.viariga.lv), for international airline and ferry tickets, car rental and excursions within Latvia. SJCB, Lāčplēša 29 (☎728 4818, ⊛www.sjcb.lv), specializes in student and youth travel. Country Holidays/Lauku ceļotājs, Kuģu 11 (☎761 7600, ⊛www.country.holidays.lv), arranges accommodation in country cottages and rural hotels throughout Latvia.

Northwest of Riga: Jurmala

JŪRMALA or "Seashore" is the collective name for a string of small seaside resorts that begins just beyond the estuary of the River Lielupe, 15km northwest of Rīga, and straggles along the Baltic coast for a further 20km. Originally favoured by the Tsarist nobility, Jūrmala had become a virtual suburb of Rīga by the 1920s and 1930s, when anyone who could afford it would rent a holiday house here for the duration of the summer. Jūrmala's seasonal citizens would commute to Rīga by train every morning, returning late in the afternoon to change into sanatorium-style pyjama suits in which they would then promenade down to the beach. The resorts' simple, timber-built holiday villas appealed to the "back-to-nature" instincts of the local elite – indeed the lack of modern plumbing ensured that most of them had to perform their morning ablutions in the sea. After World War II, Jūrmala became popular with Soviet citizens from all over the USSR, not least because it was considered more Westernized and sophisticated than resorts elsewhere in the Union. Today, its sandy beaches backed by dunes and pine woods seethe with people at weekends and on public holidays. Despite the presence of a few decaying Soviet-era hotels, it's a delightfully low-rise area on the whole, with brightly painted wooden houses and tasteful modern holiday homes nestling beneath the trees. The main centre is the small town of **Majori**, where a handful of outdoor cafés cater for a constant stream of summertime visitors; elsewhere, Jūrmala is wonderfully underdeveloped and laid-back.

Majori, the beach and beyond

About 20km out from Rīga and connected by train, **MAJORI** is Jūrmala's most urbanized resort and main service centre. Cafés and boutiques line Jomas iela, the pedestrianized main street that conveys new arrivals from the station square northeast towards the beach. About 800m down Jomas, a left turn into Pliekšāna iela brings you to the **Rainis and Aspazija Memorial Summerhouse** (Raiņa un Aspazijas memoriālā vasarnica; Wed–Sun 11am–6pm; 0.50Ls), in which Latvia's leading literary couple, Jānis Rainis (1865–1929) and Elza "Aspazija" Rozenberga (1865–1943), spent three summers in the late 1920s. Rainis was an anti-Tsarist newspaper editor before World War I, who suffered exile in Siberia as a result of his support for the 1905 Revolution, before going on to write poetry, novels and plays, becoming Latvia's "national" writer in the process. His wife Elza was his equal as a playwright, her allegorical drama *Sidabra Šķidrauts* ("The Silver Veil") causing riots in 1905 because of its perceived anti-Tsarist message. She earned the nickname Aspazija (after the brainy and beautiful wife of Pericles) because her hidebound male contemporaries considered it unusual for Latvian women to be both good-looking and intelligent at the same time. There's an absorbing collection of heirlooms, photographs and manuscripts relating to the pair, and a chance to peruse the relaxing sun-lit verandah where Rainis scribbled his verse.

Another five minutes' walk down Jomas brings you to **DZINTARI** – allegedly a separate town from Majori, although there's no appreciable boundary between the two – a locality rich in pre-World War I holiday villas, many adorned with mock-medieval spires and towers. Running parallel to Jomas to the north is Jūras iela, from where paths lead over the dunes to the **beach**, a pale grey ribbon of sand stretching as far as the eye can see in either direction. Despite being prone to strong winds, it's packed with people sunbathing, playing beach volleyball or drinking in al-fresco cafés in July and August, and is a popular – if bracing – place for a stroll throughout the year. During the inter-war years the beach was given over to naturist bathing every morning, with different time slots reserved for each sex. Patrolling policemen (considered neuter for the occasion) ensured that segregation was maintained, although American travel writer E. Alexander Powell observed that during women's hour on Sundays the dunes behind the beach were full of "gentlemen equipped with telescopes, binoculars and opera glasses".

Some of the most beautiful, least crowded parts of the beach are at the eastern end of Jūrmala, near the point at which the Lielūpe River curves round to meet the sea. You can get there by alighting from the train at **BULDURI**, 4km east of Majori, and walking northeast through the pines. Bulduri itself was once named "Edinburg" after Prince Alfred, Duke of Edinburgh and second son of Queen Victoria (he married Marie, daughter of Tsar Alexander II of Russia, in 1874) – always considered to be Jūrmala's upmarket end, it's currently home to some of the most expensive real estate in Latvia.

Practicalities

Trains to Jūrmala leave from platforms 3 and 4 of Rīga's central station (every 30min 5am–11pm). The **tourist office**, in Majori at Jomas 42 (June–Sept daily 9am–9pm; Oct–May Mon–Fri 10am–5pm; ☎776 4276, ⊛www.jurmala.lv), can arrange **private rooms** (❶) and give advice on **hotels** – which are spread thinly throughout the Jūrmala area rather than concentrated in one particular locality. Two worth considering are the *Baltija*, in Dzintari at Dzintaru prospekts 11 (☎776 2338, ⊛www.eunet.lv/baltia; ❸), a Soviet-era beachside hotel with prim en-suites, many with sea views; and the *Majori*, Jomas 29 (☎776 1380; ❻), a tastefully done-up Art Nouveau villa opposite Majori train station, offering swanky en-suites with TV.

There's no end of **eating and drinking** spots in Majori, most serving up *šašliki* (Caucasian kebabs) and beer to the accompaniment of Russian pop music. *De La Presse*, Jomas 57, is one of the classier places on the main strip, perfect for a daytime coffee or a full evening meal, while *Al Thome*, just north of Jomas at Pilsoņu iela 2, does excellent Lebanese cuisine on a terrace overlooking the beach. *Haizivs un bullis*, a good 3km east of Majori at Bulduri prospektas 31, is the best place to sample succulent fish and steaks. The open-air stage next to the concert hall at Dzintari hosts perfomances over the summer ranging from Russian-language crooners to the Latvian Symphony Orchestra – consult the tourist offices or street posters to find out what's on.

Travel details

Trains

Rīga to: Daugavpils (4 daily; 4hr); Majori (every 20–30min; 45min); Rēzekne (1 daily; 4hr); Salaspils (every 30min–1hr; 30min).

Buses

Rīga to: Aglona (3 weekly; 4hr 30min); Ainaži (9 daily; 2hr 30min–4hr); Bauska (every 30–40min; 1hr 10min); Bebrene (3 weekly; 4hr); Cēsis (hourly; 1hr 50min–2hr 5min); Daugavpils (12 daily; 3hr 30min–4hr); Kolka (3 daily; 3hr 30min–4hr 30min); Kuldīga (Mon–Sat 9 daily, Sun 6 daily; 2hr 30min–3hr 45min); Liepāja (hourly; 4hr); Limbaži (12 daily; 1hr 40min–2hr); Mazsalaca (3 daily; 3hr 30min); Rēzekne (4 daily; 4hr); Sigulda (hourly; 1hr 10min); Valmiera (12 daily; 2–3hr); Ventspils (hourly; 4hr).

International trains

Rīga to: Lvov (3–4 weekly; 24hr); Moscow (2 daily; 16–17hr); St Petersburg (1 daily; 13hr); Vilnius (3 weekly; 7hr).

International buses

Rīga to: Berlin (1 daily; 20hr); Hamburg (4 weekly; 24hr); Kaliningrad (2 daily; 10hr); Kaunas (3 daily; 4hr 30min–5hr 20min); Klaipėda (2 daily; 5hr 30min–6hr); Köln (1 daily; 32hr); Minsk (2 daily; 12–14hr); Paris (3 weekly; 40hr); Pärnu (4 daily; 3hr 30min); St Petersburg (2 daily; 12hr); Šiauliai (4 daily; 3hr 15min); Stuttgart (4 weekly; 32hr); Tallinn (6 daily; 5–6hr); Tartu (1 daily; 5hr); Vilnius (4 daily; 5hr–5hr 30min).

International flights

Rīga to: Copenhagen (5 daily; 1hr 30min); Frankfurt (1 daily; 2hr 20min); Helsinki (4 daily; 1hr 10min); Kiev (1 daily; 4hr); London (5 weekly; 3hr 20min); Moscow (1 daily; 3hr); Prague (1 daily; 2hr); Stockholm (4 daily; 1hr 30min); Tallinn (1 daily; 50min); Vienna (1 daily; 2hr); Vilnius (3 weekly; 1hr); Warsaw (1 daily; 1hr 20min).

International ferries

Rīga to: Lübeck (3 weekly; 36hr); Stockholm (3 weekly; 16hr).

2.2

Western Latvia

Western Latvia has a rich variety of attractions, ranging from vibrant port cities to historic palaces and plenty of quirky market towns, not to mention long, sandy beaches – the region's 320-kilometre-long coastline amounts to virtually one long, continuous strand. Inland there are innumerable areas of genuine wilderness, especially in the slightly hillier north, where squelchy bogs and deep forest break up fields of crops and stretches of grazing land. The southwest is made up of Latvia's most fertile arable land, its farms producing bountiful harvests of grain, potatoes and sugar beet.

The region consists of two ethnographically distinct areas. **Zemgale**, extending south from Rīga to the Lithuanian border, is named after the Zemgaļi (Semgallians), one of the original Baltic tribes that subsequently coalesced to form the Latvian nation. Over to the west, **Kurzeme** – usually rendered into English as **Courland** – gets its name from the Kurši (Cours), a tribe that once held sway over the western seaboard of both Lithuania and Latvia and established the area's enduring reputation for fishing, seamanship and trade. From the 1560s onwards, both Zemgale and Kurzeme were united to form the **Duchy of Courland**, which exploited Polish, Swedish and Russian rivalries to ensure over two centuries of semi-independence.

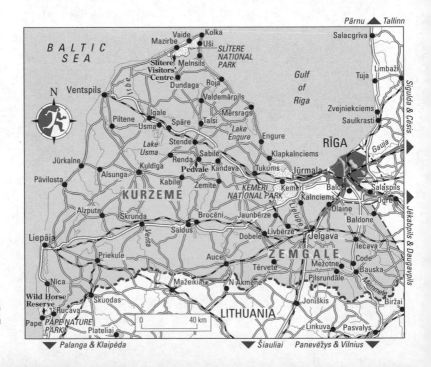

Much of western Latvia is within day-trip distance of Rīga. Easily reached are the Baroque palaces at **Rundāle** and **Jelgava** south of Rīga, providing some insight into the lavish tastes of Courland's eighteenth-century dukes. Nearby, the aristocratic seat of **Mežotne** provides a cool neoclassical riposte. West of the capital, the green, rolling countryside of Kurzeme enfolds attractive rural centres like **Tukums**, **Talsi** and, best of all, **Kuldīga**, a taste of small-town Latvia. All this contrasts with the hurly-burly of western Kurzeme's great port cities, **Ventspils** and **Liepāja**. The best of the region's wild, unspoiled nature is to be found in the beaches and forests of the **Slītere National Park** around Kurzeme's northernmost point; the desolate beauty of **Cape Kolka**; the bogs of the **Ķemeri National Park** just west of Rīga; and the reedy environs of the **Lake Pape Nature Reserve** south of Liepāja.

Zemgale

The region of **Zemgale** occupies central Latvia, cut through by the busy Rīga–Vilnius road. The landscape is largely flat and unremarkable, made up of arable farmland, but whatever Zemgale lacks in terms of natural beauty is more than made up for by the presence of two sumptuous palaces: park-girdled, neoclassical **Mežotne** and the splendid Baroque–Rococo confection that is **Rundāle**. Both lie just outside the small town of **Bauska**, the major transport hub for the area. All three places can be visited as a day-trip from Rīga, providing you make an early start.

Zemgale's only real city – and a more exciting urban prospect than Bauska – is **Jelgava**, 55km southwest of Rīga. One-time capital of the Duchy of Courland, it's home to a fine ducal palace, though sadly many of its other venerable buildings were destroyed in World War II. A short hop from here is **Tērvete Nature Park**, offering some particularly rewarding woodland walks.

Bauska

The main road to Vilnius ploughs right through the middle of **BAUSKA**, 75km south of Rīga. A historic fortress town commanding the confluence of the Mēmele and Mūsa rivers, Bauska is nowadays a rather bland market centre serving the local agricultural communities. The town gets its fair share of visitors though, firstly because it's the last sizeable settlement before the Lithuanian border 25km beyond, and secondly because its bus station is the place from which to catch services to Rundāle and Mežotne. Before pushing on, it's well worth seeing the semi-ruined **Bauska Castle** (Bauskas pils), its stark, grey presence looming over parkland fifteen minutes' walk west of the town's main T-junction. Built by the Livonian Order in 1443, the castle served a succession of rulers until Peter the Great ordered its destruction in 1706. The interior is currently undergoing reconstruction, although you can climb up to a viewing platform on one of the towers (May–Oct daily 9am–6pm; 0.50Ls) for a good view of the Mēmele and Mūsa; they converge just upstream to become the Lielupe ("Great River"), which flows into the Baltic Sea just west of Rīga.

If you've got a bit of time to kill, check out the **Museum of Regional Studies and Art** (Bauskas novadpētniecības un mākslas muzejs; Tues–Fri 10am–5pm, Sat & Sun 10am–4pm; 0.50Ls), just off the flagstoned main square at Kalna 6. Its old sepia photographs of firemen, brass bands and schoolchildren eloquently sums up Bauska's small-town sense of community.

Practicalities

Bauska's **bus station** is at the southeastern end of town, ten minutes' walk away from the **tourist office** on the main square, Rātslaukums 1 (Mon–Fri 9am–6pm, Sat & Sun 9am–2pm; ☎392 3797, ⊛www.bauska.lv), stocked with information on sights and accommodation throughout Zemgale. The only **place to stay** in town is the *Hotel Bauska*, beside the bus station at Slimnīcas 7 (☎392 4705; ❶), where you

The Duchy of Courland: a brief history

The original inhabitants of Courland were the **Livs** (see p.240), a Finno-Ugric tribe related to the Estonians who arrived in the wake of the last ice age and are still around – albeit on the verge of extinction – in the isolated fishing villages of the extreme north. Very much in the majority until the early Middle Ages, the Livs were gradually forced out of western and central Courland by the **Kurši**, one of the bedrock Baltic tribes that make up the modern Latvian and Lithuanian nations. The Kuršl succumbed to the Livonian Order in 1267 and Courland disappeared as a distinct entity until 1562, when the last Grand Master of the Livonian Order, **Gottfried Kettler** – faced with the prospect of Livonia's collapse under pressure from the Swedes and the Russians – dissolved the Order and created the **Duchy of Courland** to serve as a new power base. In need of a strong ally, Kettler made Courland a vassal of the Polish-Lithuanian Commonwealth, while retaining internal autonomy for himself and his successors.

Extending from the Baltic coast in the west to the River Daugava in the east, Courland under the Kettlers was a generally peaceful and prosperous place, with towns like Jelgava, Ventspils and Kuldīga growing fat on the profits of expanding trade. The duchy even enjoyed a brief spell as a transatlantic trading power when ambitious **Duke Jakob** (ruled 1642–1682) received an unusual gift from his god-father, King Charles I of England in the shape of the Caribbean island of **Tobago**. Merchantmen bearing Courland's standard – a black crayfish on a red background – were seen in ports all over northern Europe. Jakob's dreams of empire soon faded, however: the Swedes, unwilling to tolerate the existence of a rival maritime power in the Baltic, forced Jakob to disband his fleet in 1658. The overseas colonies were abandoned – although the waters around the Tobagan town of Plymouth are still known as Great Courland Bay.

Eventually, the rise of Russia and the decline of Poland seriously compromised Courland's independence. Peter the Great married his niece, **Anna Ioannovna**, to Duke Frederick Wilhelm in 1710 and sent his troops to take control of the region when the duke died childless two months later. Anna herself became Empress of Russia in 1730 and presented the dukedom to court favourite **Ernst Johann von Bühren** (1690–1772) – better known by his Russified name of **Biron** – marrying him off to one of her ladies-in-waiting, Benigna Gottlieb von Trotta-Treyden. Flush with

can choose between bare-bones en-suites or rooms with TV – breakfast isn't included, but there's a café next door. *Kafejnīca pie Rātslaukuma*, on the main square at Plūdoņa 38, is a good place for a cheap, filling **meal**.

Rundāle Palace

Rising above rich farmland 13km west of Bauska, **Rundāle Palace** (Rundāles pils; daily: May–Oct 10am–6pm; Nov–April 10am–5pm; ⊚www.rpm.apollo.lv; 1.50Ls) is one of the architectural wonders of Latvia, a haughty slab of Baroque masonry filled to the gills with rococo furnishings. This monument to eighteenth-century aristocratic excess is all the more impressive for its situation – plonked incongruously among the more modestly proportioned farmhouses and cottages of the Latvian countryside. The site was bought in 1735 by Empress Anna's fancy-man, Duke of Courland **Ernst Johann von Biron**, who named it *Ruhetal* (German for "Vale of Peace") and engaged Francesco Bartolomeo Rastrelli, architect of the Winter Palace in St Petersburg, to build the 138-room summer hideaway that you see today. Most of the construction work was completed by 1740, but Biron was exiled to Siberia in the same year, and it wasn't until his return in the 1760s that the interiors were finally decorated in the opulent, rococo style that was all the rage at the time. On the abolition of the duchy in 1795, Biron's son Peter was thrown out wealth and success, Biron commissioned Italian architect Rastrelli to design sumptuous palaces at **Rundāle** and **Jelgava**. With the death of Anna Ioannovna in 1740, Biron fell from grace and was exiled to Siberia by new Empress Elizabeth. Finding favour again under Catherine the Great and resuming his ducal office in 1764, he went on to supervise the completion of Rundāle Palace and presided over a glittering court at Jelgava. Before long, Jelgava's palace had become a popular stop-off for society folk travelling from Western Europe to St Petersburg. One house guest was Casanova, whose ability to sound off on subjects he knew nothing about tricked Biron into believing he was an internationally recognized authority on mining techniques – somewhat improbably, Biron paid the Venetian charmer 200 ducats to write a report on the minerals of Courland. Biron's son and successor Peter was no less gullible a host, giving board, lodging and lavish gifts to bogus faith-healer Cagliostro.

With Courland's formal incorporation into the Russian Empire in 1795, the duchy was finally extinguished. Shifts in sovereignty made little difference to local society, with the Latvian-speaking majority remaining subject to a Germanized landowning elite. Life continued to be centred on the great manor houses, and the nobles themselves overcame isolation by devising a busy round of social events, attending society gatherings in provincial towns like Jelgava and Aizpute (where balls usually lasted three days in order to justify the travelling involved) and decamping to the seaside in July. Their easy-going hospitable nature was much appreciated by German guidebook writer J. G. Kohl, who summed up a visit to Courland in the 1840s by asking, "What gentleman or lady values time? The whole day is made up of leisure. No one looks at the clock, except to know when it will be dinner time, or whether tea may soon be ordered."

The duchy was briefly resurrected in March 1918, by Kaiser Wilhelm, who believed that a chain of German-dominated states could be established along the Baltic seaboard prior to their outright incorporation into the Reich. Even after the defeat of Germany in November 1918, this dream was kept alive by a Baltic German army of General von der Goltz, who based themselves at Liepāja, then Jelgava, before finally being beaten off by the Latvians in November 1919.

of Rundāle (he took most of the moveable furnishings to Żagań in Silesia, where they were destroyed in World War II), and the palace was given to Catherine the Great's favourite, Platon Zubov. It remained in private hands until 1920 and thereafter fell into disrepair, but meticulous restoration, begun in 1972, has returned large chunks of the palace to their former glory. With only about a third of the palace open to the public, Rundāle is very much a work in progress. Judging by the fanatical dedication to detail deployed thus far, completion of the rest of the palace will probably take decades.

The grandeur of Rundāle unfolds gradually: after you've passed through a belt of orchards and crossed a small moat, a wine-red gatehouse heralds the entrance to an oval-shaped outer courtyard. At the far end of this a brace of regal-looking lions guard the entrance to the inner courtyard, closed off on three sides by the ochre wings of the palace itself. Inside, you ascend a cherub-encrusted staircase to the **state rooms**, where the original decorations – wall and ceiling paintings by St Petersburg-based Italians Francesco Martini and Carlo Zucchi, stuccowork by Johann Michael Graff – have been faithfully re-created by modern-day restorers.

First up is the **Gilded Hall**, a long, showpiece chamber intended for ceremonial receptions, with exuberant ceiling frescoes swirling above a row of mirrors, each topped by a relief of birds fighting over berries. This leads on to the **White Hall**, a ballroom the size of a basketball court, with a stucco frieze depicting cherubs in a range of rather unlikely pastoral situations – tootling away on flutes, riding goats or warding off big-tusked boars. Side chambers are devoted to displays of fancy porcelain, the asymmetrical rococo shelving so ornate that it upstages the vases themselves. Other highlights include the **Rose Room**, with its fanciful ceiling paintings of sundry Apollos chasing buxom nymphs, and the **State Bedchamber**, whose gargantuan pair of tiled stoves give some idea of how difficult it must have been to keep the palace warm during the dark Baltic nights. In contrast to all this magnificence, a suite of **unrenovated rooms**, full of chipped plaster and peeling wallpaper, point up the enormity of the task faced by restorers. Finally, stairs descend towards the **kitchen**, where spits big enough to skewer an entire family of buffalo are lined up in front of gaping fire grates.

Practicalities

Getting to the palace is easy enough: it's a well-signed thirteen-kilometre drive west of Bauska on the Eleja road. There are ten to twelve daily buses (fewer on Sundays) from Bauska – make sure you catch a service that's going to Pilsrundāle or Rundāles pils ("Rundāle Palace") rather than simply the village of Rundāle, which is 3km further west. Get off the bus when you see a big hedge: the palace gates are hidden just behind it. You can eat well at the rather formal **restaurant** in the palace itself, serving up superb cuts of veal and steak, as well as freshwater fish; there's also a basic food store by the bus stop.

Mežotne Palace

Ten kilometres northwest of Bauska and another easy jaunt by local bus, the cool, lemon-yellow slab of **Mežotne Palace** (Mežotnes pils; daily 9am–5pm; 0.70Ls) could almost be seen as a restrained neoclassical response to the lavish ostentation of Rundāle. It began life as the country estate of Princess Charlotte von Lieven, who was given the land by Catherine the Great in 1795 in recognition of her services as governess to the imperial children. The princess visited Mežotne only once, but the palace stayed with the Lieven family until the Land Reform of 1920 (when most Baltic German aristocrats were kicked off their lands), after which it became an agricultural college. It was badly damaged in World War II and subsequently various parts of the building served as a library, post office and residential flats. Now lavishly restored, it functions primarily as a hotel and conference centre, although several state rooms are open to the public. Decked out in pastel shades of ochre, pink and eau-de-nil, the interiors exude an easy-going elegance, with decoration limited to stucco friezes of personable gryphons, their paws raised as if in friendly greeting. There's a small display of engravings showing how the estate looked at the time of the Lievens and a forest-green ballroom framed at each end by ionic columns. One space you'll want to return to again and again is the so-called **Cupola Room**, a light-filled chamber said to be modelled on the Pantheon in Rome and featuring a dome held up by Titans – it also offers panoramic views of the palace park from its windows. The park itself is a terrific place for a stroll, stretching away along the bank of the River Lielupe and densely wooded at its far end.

The palace **hotel** (☎392 8984 or 392 8796, ✉mezotnpils@apollo.lv; ❺), is one of the most charming in Latvia, offering eight double rooms and five three- to four-person apartments (70–80Ls), each decorated in olde-worlde style – expect things like cast-iron bedsteads, Thonet furniture and your great-grandmother's wallpaper.

Jelgava and around

Straddling the road between Rīga and Kaliningrad, **JELGAVA** is a predominantly post-war, concrete city, although a reconstructed ducal palace and a smattering of other old buildings make a short stop-off here worthwhile. Jelgava was founded by the Livonian Order in 1265. The Livonians named it Mitau and used it as a base

Mežotne Palace △

from which to mount successive campaigns against the pagans of Zemgale just to the south. In the seventeenth and eighteenth centuries, it was the capital of the Duchy of Courland and became an important social centre: Duke Jakob resided here for at least part of the year, and his successor Friedrich Casimir founded an (albeit short-lived) opera house. By the nineteenth century most of Courland's German barons owned town houses in Jelgava and spent the coldest months here rather than on their country estates, turning winter into one long round of parties and balls – young Tsarist officers considered Jelgava a dream posting owing to its seemingly endless supply of charming debutantes. Sadly, little architectural evidence of Jelgava's golden age survives today: Baltic German forces under General von der Goltz put much of the town to the torch in November 1919 and World War II bombing raids largely put paid to what was left.

The City

The city centre lies on the west bank of the River Lielupe. Its principal land-mark is a grizzled, seventeenth-century tower, the last surviving remnant of the war-ravaged **Church of the Holy Trinity** (Sv Trīsvienības baznīca). Just round the corner, at Akadēmijas 10, is the **Museum of History and Art** (Vēstures un Mākslas Muzejs; Wed–Sun 10am–5pm; 0.50Ls), a neoclassical building, pin-striped with cream pilasters and topped by a thrusting clock tower. It was built in 1775 to house Duke Peter von Biron's Academia Petrina, an ambitious attempt at turning Jelgava into an internationally renowned university town that never quite caught on. The museum recalls the glory days of the Duchy of Courland through a display of old furniture mutely presided over by Duke Jakob in dummy form.

A few steps to the south, the corner of Akadēmijas and Raiņa is dominated by the bright-blue domes of the **Orthodox Cathedral of SS Simeon and Anna** (Sv Simeona un Sv Annas pareizticīgo katedrāle), built on the site of a wooden chapel originally used by Anna Ioannovna and her Russian entourage. Dating from the 1890s, the current structure was used as a warehouse during the Soviet period and after extensive restoration in the 1990s the interior is now decked out once more in vibrant greens and blues.

Twice rebuilt almost from scratch following devastation in both world wars, the Baroque **Jelgava Palace**, with its dignified, maroon-and-cream facade, graces the riverbank east of the city centre, next to the main Rīga road. The palace was built by Rastrelli for Count Ernst Johann von Biron in 1738 and was intended as an urban equivalent to the edifice then taking shape at Rundāle. Now part of the Latvian University of Agriculture, its student-trampled corridors and lecture rooms retain little in the way of original features. For some idea of what the palace looked like before World War I, visit the small **palace museum** (9am–4pm: May–Oct daily; Nov–April Mon–Sat; 0.50Ls), displaying photographs and prints recalling the days when Jelgava was a popular stop-off for society folk travelling from Western Europe to St Petersburg. To access the museum, go into the main courtyard and through the doors on the right.

If asked, the museum curator will open up the **Burial Vault of the Dukes of Courland**, beneath the east wing of the palace, where all the duchy's rulers, from Gottfried Kettler to Peter Biron, are lined up in a series of richly decorated cas-kets. Hogging the limelight is the burnished copper affair belonging to Ernst Johann von Biron, adorned with a dull-grey death's head and mounted on feet in the form of snarling lions. According to the memoirs of Ernst von Salomon, a vol-unteer with von der Goltz's army, the vault was broken open by Bolsheviks in 1919 and "the bodies propped up against the walls with German steel helmets on their heads and riddled with shots". This seems to be borne out by a grisly photo on display in the adjoining anteroom, where you can also view the richly embroi-dered burial shrouds in which seventeenth-century dukes were originally laid to rest.

Practicalities

Jelgava is easily reached from Rīga; trains leave every hour from the central station and minibuses every fifteen to thirty minutes from the bus stand just opposite. Jelgava's **bus station** is right in the city centre, about 400m west of the tower of the Church of the Holy Trinity. The **train station** is about 1km to the south: bear left down Zemgales prospekts to reach the centre. There's a **tourist office** near the bridge over the Lielupe at J. Čakstes bul. 7 (Mon–Fri 9am–5pm; ☏302 3874, ⊠ticjelgav@tvnet.lv).

The city's best **hotel** is the *Jelgava*, also near the bridge at Lielā 6 (☏302 6193, ⓦwww.zl.lv/hoteljelgava; ❶–❷); staff tend to direct you towards the more expensive, renovated doubles with en-suite bathroom and TV, although the cheaper rooms with older furnishings and shared facilities are perfectly habitable. Less comfortable are the eight-room *Brīze*, 2km west of the centre at Atmodas 9 (☏308 2979; ❶), and the *Akva Motel*, a similar distance southeast on the far side of the railway tracks at Birzes 49 (☏302 3444; ❶).

Good for a relaxing, sit-down **meal**, *Tobago*, just beyond the tourist office at Čakstes bul. 7, has all manner of steak and fish and an attractive riverside position. More informal is *Silva*, on pedestrianized Driksas iela at no. 7, a stylish order-at-the-counter canteen with the added advantage of a drinks bar and an outdoor terrace. For cheap meat-and-potatoes fare try run-of-the-mill café *Lido*, Lielā 17.

Tērvete

Some 30km southwest of Jelgava, **Tērvete Nature Park** (Tērvetes dabas parks; daily: April–Aug 9am–6pm; Sept–Nov 9am–5pm), just outside the town of **TĒRVETE**, is one of Latvia's most popular rural attractions. Measuring little more than 3km across in any direction, the park is made up of riverside meadow and woodland, criss-crossed by well-marked trails. Tērvete holds a cherished place in the hearts of many Latvians, many of whom were brought up on the well-loved children's stories written by author **Anna Brigadere** (1861–1933); Brigadere lived in the nearby hamlet of Plavnieki and evoked the beauty of the region in her writings. The park is dotted with wooden statues of dwarves, goblins and other characters from Brigadere's stories, making it a popular outing with young families.

Buses from Jelgava drop you at the northeastern end of the village; bear right down the gently sloping lane, then right again at the T-junction to reach the **tourist office** (Mon–Fri 8am–5pm; ☏376 3472) and, a little way beyond, a kiosk marking the **park entrance** – either place will sell you a ticket (1Ls) and a map detailing the main trails (0.30Ls).

Opposite the park entrance, a traditional-style log cabin with shingle roof accommodates the **Tērvete History Museum** (Tērvetes Vēstures muzejs; May–Sept Wed–Sun 10am–5pm; 0.50Ls), containing an absorbing collection of handmade, wooden farm utensils and traditional textiles. The same ticket allows you to climb the adjacent **viewing tower** for a 25-metre high panorama of the surrounding tree-tops. On the other side of the park entrance a path leads down to the **Anna Brigadere House Museum** (Anna Brigaderes māja muzejs Sprīdīši; May–Sept Tues–Sun 10am–5pm; 0.50Ls), a cottage presented to the writer in 1922 to mark 25 years of literary work and subsequently used by Brigadere as a summer house. Decorated in flowery period wallpaper, embroidered cushions and furnishings that exude rustic chic, it looks like the ideal place to spend the holidays. Displays of first editions and their accompanying artwork recall the best-known of Brigadere's creations, a Tom Thumb-sized character named Sprīdītis (*sprīdis* means the span of one hand in Latvian) who wins the hand of a beautiful maiden by overcoming a series of seemingly impossible tasks set by the girl's father. The tale began life as a pantomime script, hastily penned in November 1903 for the director of the Latvian Theatre in Rīga, desperate for a crowd-pleasing childrens' production to run over the Christmas season. As well as making great bedtime story material, Sprīdītis's exploits (including plenty of David-meets-Goliath encounters with giants and bears) have since become an enduring metaphor for Latvia's struggles against more powerful neighbours. Older kids move on to Brigadere's autobiographical *Dievs, Daba, Darbs* ("God, Nature, Work"), which is a much more lyrical read than its dour title suggests and remains a staple of the Latvian school curriculum.

Once you've digested the museums you can start exploring the **trails**, which fan out from the entrance kiosk in all directions, crossing horse-grazed pastures and bridging gurgling streams. Immediately north of the entrance, chunks of ruddy masonry crowning the **Tērvete Castle Mound** (Tērvetes pilskalns) bear witness to the presence of the Livonian Order, which fortified the spot after their thirteenth-century defeat of the indigenous Zemgaļi – there's a replica of the kind of stockade fort favoured by the latter in the woods ten minutes' further north. Twenty minutes' walk west of the entrance, **Rūkīšu mežs** ("Dwarf Forest") features paths lined with wooden sculptures of mushrooms and dwarves, as well as a dwarf village with little timber houses and a windmill – a popular children's play area. Marking the extreme northeastern extent of the park, a good fifty minutes away from the entrance, **Gulbju ezers** ("Swan Lake") is a favourite springtime stop-off for migrating bitterns, whose distinctive call is similar to the sound produced by blowing across the top of a bottle.

A couple of **cafés** just outside the park open on summer weekends; otherwise the shop next to the tourist office will pour you a coffee and sell you basic foodstuffs. The nearest **place to stay** is the welcoming, six-room *Klingeri* guesthouse (☎376 8567; ❶), 6km northwest of Tērvete – head along the Dobele road and look for a right turn after about 3km. If you have a tent, you can **camp** beside Gulbju ezers for less than 1Ls.

Northern Kurzeme: Cape Kolka, Talsi and around

Separating the Gulf of Rīga from the open Baltic Sea, the horn-shaped land mass of **northern Kurzeme** is endowed with one of the most captivating stretches of coast in the country: an almost uninterrupted ribbon of white sand backed by pines and spruce trees. The main focus for visitors is **Cape Kolka**, at the northernmost tip, a short, sandy spit jutting out into the Baltic Sea, backed by an enchanting hinterland of dunes, bogs and forests. A ten-kilometre belt of territory around the cape is protected by the **Slītere National Park**, the well-maintained walking trails of which provide access to the best of the local landscape. Although a good 70km south of Kolka, the attractive lakeside town of **Talsi** is the main service centre and transport hub for this part of Kurzeme.

Despite the presence of a few thriving fishing ports, such as Mērsrags and Roja, most of the settlements in Latvia's far northwest have an eerie, semi-abandoned air – the result of decades of rural depopulation. During the Soviet period, the whole of this shore was a sensitive border area and resources like schools and hospitals were deliberately concentrated inland in order to dissuade people from moving to the coast.

The best way to get to northern Kurzeme from Rīga **by car** is to head for Jūrmala (see p.227) and simply keep going – the scenic coastal road goes all the way to Cape Kolka. You could easily see Cape Kolka and be back in Rīga by nightfall, though it's well worth sticking around for a day or so to fully appreciate the beauty of the area. If you're reliant on public transport you'll have no choice but to stay overnight – the three daily **buses** from Rīga all set off in the afternoon (and a couple of them seem to travel all over Kurzeme before arriving). It's advisable to book accommodation in advance, especially at weekends, as places to stay are thin on the ground – Talsi tourist office can help make bookings. Jāņa Sēta's 1:100 000 **map** of the Talsi region (Talsu rajons) covers the whole of northern Kurzeme and is essential if you're exploring the area in any depth.

The Gulf of Rīga

The road from Rīga to Cape Kolka sticks to the coast for most of its 150-kilometre length, providing plenty of opportunities for scenic stop-offs. After leaving the urbanized sprawl of Jūrmala, the Kolka road passes through a series of small settlements whose beaches are popular with day-trippers keen to escape the more crowded stretches of sand further east. The first of these, some 10km out of Jūrmala, is **Lapmežciems**, a fishing village renowned for its smoked fish – which can be sampled at a string of roadside cafés. The village also abuts the eastern corner of Lake Kanieris, a brackish stretch of water separated from the Gulf of Rīga by a one-kilometre-long, thick bar of sand. The marshy shores of the lake attract white-tailed eagles, ospreys and bitterns, and are particularly popular with migrating cranes in the autumn. Further on, the stretch of coast between **Ragaciems** and **Klapkalnciems** is particularly beautiful, with a wonderful beach backed by pines – there are a couple of secure car parks along the road if you want to rest up for a while. The next settlement up the coast, **Apšuciems**, is likewise bordered by huge, pine-covered dunes.

Forty-five kilometres beyond Apšuciems, the working port of **MĒRSRAGS** marks the turn-off for **Lake Engure** (Engures ezers) just inland. The lake, 20km long and 4km wide, is one of the most important nesting sites for migratory birds in this part of Latvia: the reedy northern and eastern shores are particularly popular with grebes, bitterns, mute swans and 23 different species of goose. There are no paths, however – your best bet is to head for the birdwatching tower on the northern shoulder of the lake, 5km west of Mērsrags.

Forty kilometres further north, **ROJA** has the gruff feel of a working fishing port, but is surrounded by sand-and-forest scenery as inviting as any along this coast – it's also near enough to Kolka to serve as a base from which to explore the region. The best choice of the **hotels** is the *Roja* at Jūras iela 6 (☎323 2226, ✆rojahotel@inbox.lv; ❶–❷), offering simply furnished but bright en-suites with TV, plus a handful of cheaper rooms with shared facilities in an adjoining cottage. Less comfortable is the *Hotel Zītari*, at the southern end of Roja's main street at Selgas iela 57 (☎326 9256; ❷), with rooms above a shop. The **bus station**, in the town centre, has good connections with Talsi (see p.241).

Cape Kolka and around

Buses from Rīga stop 2km short of **Cape Kolka** in **KOLKA** village, which, like most settlements in these parts, consists of a single street running parallel to the coast. To reach the cape, head to the northern end of the street and turn right. Apart from a pile of rubble left over from an old lighthouse, there's nothing much here, but it's a uniquely beautiful spot nevertheless, with a desolate, end-of-the-world feel about it. Looking out to sea, you'll catch sight of the Kolka lighthouse rising up from a small island 6km to the northeast. In certain conditions, currents from the Gulf of Rīga meet counter-currents from the Baltic Sea to produce a chevron pattern of wavelets. In spring, the cape is an important collection point for migrating birds, with thousands of geese and ducks joined by herons, buzzards and eagles.

There's also a lot more in the vicinity to enjoy, whether it's the fishing villages west of the cape, **Vaide**, **Košrags** and **Mazirbe** (see p.241), where time seems to have stopped still, or the distinctive landscape inland, shaped over millions of years: at the end of the last ice age, the sea extended all the way to the Zilie Kalni (Blue Hills), a seventy-metre-high escarpment that lies about 10km inland from the present-day coast. Since then the sea has been in slow retreat, leaving behind the rippling succession of duney ridges that characterize the landscape today. Many of these ridges are covered in forest, but there are also large tracts of heath and bog – notably Bažu bog (Bažu purvs), just off the main Rīga–Kolka road, though it's a protected reserve and is closed to the public. The whole area falls under the protection of the **Slītere National Park** (Slīteres nacionlais parks; ✆www.slitere.gov.lv),

The Livs

The **Livs** (Lībi in Latvian; Livod in their own language), despite being the longest-established of Latvia's indigenous peoples, are the closest to extinction. A Finno-Ugric people closely related to the Estonians, the Livs settled in Latvia just after the last ice age, several millennia before the Latvians, who have only been here a mere 4000 years. The Livs remained in possession of northern Latvia and its coastline right up until the Middle Ages – the fact that the thirteenth-century German crusaders named one of their Baltic provinces "Livonia" suggests that the Livs were still in the majority at the time. Gradually, however, the Livs were assimilated by the Kurši and other Latvian tribes, and by the eighteenth century the fishing villages of northern Kurzeme were the only parts of Latvia where their culture survived. With the advent of mass schooling in the nineteenth and twentieth centuries, the Liv language suffered a severe blow. German and then Latvian were the only languages of educational and career advancement, and the Livs increasingly regarded their own tongue as a social hindrance and resigned themselves to assimilation by the Latvian-speaking majority. During the Soviet period, when the coast was militarized and fishing discouraged, most young Livs left the Kolka region for the big cities, intermarried with Latvians and left their culture behind.

Estimates differ as to how many Livs still exist. The number of native speakers can be counted on the fingers of one hand, although a couple of hundred urbanized Latvians of Liv descent declare themselves as Livs in official documents and actively study the language in an attempt to revive it. The main Liv cultural organization, Livod it (Union of Livs), has a membership of around 250. The Liv House in Mazirbe teaches Liv language and songs to anyone of Liv descent who's interested, and also organizes the annual Liv Festival in Mazirbe at the beginning of August. However, the long-term outlook for the language's survival is bleak in the extreme and it looks set to become the object of academic curiosity rather than a living tongue.

which maintains a modest visitor centre at Slītere lighthouse (see opposite). The park is also a haven for roe deer, elk, wild boar and lynx.

One of the best sea views to be had in the area is from **Ēvaži cliff** (Ēvažu stāvkrasts), a bank of moss- and tree-covered dunes that rises above the seashore 5km south of Kolka, just off the Rīga road, and is reached by a short trail just opposite the Novakari bus stop. From the top, you get a great view of the coast all the way down to Roja. Walking back to Kolka along the beach is a great way of taking in the pines-and-sands landscape.

Accommodation in Kolka is limited to the *Zītari*, next to a supermarket of the same name at the southern entrance to town (☎327 7145; ❷), with acceptable ensuites but indifferent service; and the more basic but much friendlier *Ūši*, well signed at the northern end of the main street (☎327 7350, ⓦwww.kolka.info.lv; ❶), offering two sparsely furnished rooms, a communal kitchen and tent space in the garden. There's a **café** serving meat-and-two-veg main courses at the *Zītari*.

West of Kolka

West of Kolka the main Ventspils-bound road runs a couple of kilometres inland to a string of sleepy fishing villages, connected to the outside world by a dirt road. The first you come to is **VAIDE**, a dune-encircled collection of fishermen's cottages and holiday houses about 7.5km west of Kolka. Aside from another glorious stretch of white sand, Vaide's main attraction is the **Horn Museum** (Ragu kolekcija; daily 9am–8pm; 0.40Ls), a forest ranger's large collection of elk and stag antlers, gleaned from the forest and artfully arranged in an attic. You can pitch a tent in the meadow behind the museum for 0.50Ls.

From Vaide you can continue westwards via a dirt road – a great ride through coastal heath and forest (if your suspension's up to it) – or return to the main road, turning off again after 6km for the village of **KOŠRAGS**, where wooden fishermen's houses huddle around sand-paved streets. There's a highly attractive **B&B** here, *Jauntilmači viesu nams* (☎941 2974 or 362 1427, ✆www.kolka.lv; ❸), offering smart, fully equipped rooms and an on-site sauna. A further 3km beyond Košrags lies the village of **MAZIRBE**, set back from a beautiful stretch of dune-backed beach. Like all the villages along this part of the coast, Mazirbe is inhabited by descendents of the Livs (see box opposite), although you're unlikely to find anyone here who still speaks the language. The study of Liv culture is kept alive by the **Liv House** (Lībiešu Tautas Nams/Līvlist Roukuoda), a modernist white cube built in 1939 with financial support from other Finno-Ugric nations – as a polyglot inscription in Estonian, Finnish and Hungarian attests. Towards the southern end of the village, the **Rāndali Ethnographic Collection** (Etnogrāfiska kolekcija Rāndali) has a small display of Liv costumes, while a little further on, on the far side of the Kolka–Ventspils road, Mazirbe **parish church** sports a highly personable pebble-dashed exterior and a lovely wooded cemetery. Back in the village, there's a cosy **B&B**, *Kalēji* (☎324 8374; ❶), with tent space in the grounds, and a **food shop** opposite the Liv House.

After Mazirbe the main road continues southwest towards Ventspils, while another route forks south towards Talsi, climbing up the Zilie Kalni escarpment. Taking the latter route, you'll pass a sign to the **Pēterezers Nature Trail** (Peterezera dabas taka) on your right after about 4km. This enjoyable boardwalk trail takes you up and down some of the region's trademark dune ridges and across heath before arriving at Pēterezers, a shallow lake edged by dark pines. Returning to the road and continuing up the hill for another 5km brings you to **Slītere lighthouse** (Slītcres bāka; Wed–Sun 10am–6pm, 0.30Ls), a stocky cylinder dating from 1849 and now containing a display of photographs of lighthouses throughout the world. You aren't allowed all the way to the top of the lighthouse, but you get a good view of the surrounding countryside from the penultimate floor, with a lush plateau of farmland to the south and wooded wilderness stretching seawards to the north. On the ground floor is the **Slītere National Park Visitors' Centre** (same times), where you can buy brochures and rudimentary maps. Immediately behind the lighthouse, a wooden stairway leads down the escarpment towards the start of the **Slītere Nature Trail** (Slīteres dabas taka), which winds through a lush expanse of mixed forest with occasional stretches of semi-bog, the undergrowth thick with bird's-eye primrose and all manner of ferns. The trail's only drawback is its short length, taking barely thirty minutes to complete.

Talsi

Seventy kilometres south of Kolka and 5km north of the Rīga–Ventspils highway, **TALSI** is the administrative capital and transport hub of northern Kurzeme – you'll probably change buses here if you're travelling between the Kolka area and the west coast. It's in any case a rewardingly pretty market town, ranged across a series of low hills. The town's cobbled streets slope down towards a neck of land separating two small lakes, Lake Talsi (Talsu ezers) to the south and Lake Vilkmuiža (Vilkmuižas ezers) to the north.

Squatting on a ridge to the northeast, the stocky white **Lutheran Church** (Luteranu baznīca) is famous for being the workplace of pastor Karl Amenda (1774–1836); a friend of both Beethoven and Mozart, he assisted in the care of the latter's children after the composer's early demise. Rising above the east bank of Lake Talsi, **Talsi Castle Mound** (Talsu pilskalns) was the site of a Liv fortress before falling in the tenth century to the Kurši, for whom Talsi was a key strategic stronghold until the arrival of the Livonian Order in 1263. Occupying a restored nineteenth-century manor house just east of the Castle Mound, the **Talsi District Museum**, K. Mīlenbaha 19 (Tues–Sun: April–Oct 11am–5pm; Nov–March 11am–4pm; 0.50Ls), harbours an enjoyable collection of local crafts, and the surrounding manor park is the perfect place for a relaxing stroll.

Practicalities

Talsi's **bus station** is ten minutes' walk northwest of the centre on Dundagas iela: walk downhill and bear left to reach the main street, Lielā iela, where you'll find the **tourist office** at no. 19/21 (Mon–Fri 9am–12.30pm & 1.30–5pm; May–Sept also Sat 10am–2pm; ☎322 4165, ⊛www.talsi.lv), a good source of information on **accommodation** throughout northern Kurzeme, especially in the Kolka region. There's not much to choose from in town itself: *Hotel Talsi*, just east of the bus station at Kareivju 16 (☎322 2689 or 322 4596; ❸), offers basic en-suites in a frumpy building, while *Motel Mikus*, 5km south of town (☎329 2226; ❷), is marginally more comfortable, but not in that good a location – it's right beside the Talsi exit of the Rīga–Ventspils highway.

Campers should push on to the popular **camping** spot at sandy-shored, forest-shrouded **Lake Usma**, 30km west of Talsi on the Rīga–Ventspils highway and served by plenty of Talsi–Ventspils buses. Several well-equipped sites are dotted around the lake's serene, heavily indented shoreline: there's tent space and cabins for rent at *Mežmalas* (☎934 1582; cabins ❶), *Usmas kempings* (☎633 4500 or 916 3264, ⊛www.usma.lv; cabins ❷) and *Dzītari* (☎367 3759; cabins ❸).You can rent boats at all three, and *Usmas kempings* also has a small stock of bikes.

The best place for **eating and drinking** in Talsi is *Mara*, at Lielā 16, with a coffee shop and cafeteria-style eatery at ground level, and just below, a beer cellar, complete with full menu of grilled meats and salads. *Kafejnīca Depo*, tucked away below the church at Ezera iela 1, offers hearty meat-and-potato stodge in a cosy wooden-bench interior, while nearby *Kai*, Lielā 30, has a full menu of hot food, as well as a billiard room and late-night disco.

West of Rīga: Ķemeri and Tukums

The commuter rail line which loops northwest out of Rīga via Jūrmala (see p.227) puts a couple of worthwhile destinations within day-trip range of the capital. Fifty kilometres out of Rīga, **Ķemeri** was one of the show-pieces of the inter-war Latvian state – a high-society spa resort, which, despite several decades of decay – still retains something of its former elegance. More importantly, the town is the centre of the **Ķemeri National Park** and provides access to one of the most captivating wetland landscapes in the country in the shape of the **Great Ķemeri Bog**. The line's terminus is at **Tukums**, a quiet country town with a modest clutch of museums.

Ķemeri

An upmarket resort in the inter-war years and a popular health spa during the Soviet era, **ĶEMERI** has fallen off the tourist map since Latvia regained independence and nowadays has a rather abandoned air. However, a tangible sense of grandeur still lingers in the **spa park** (a fifteen-minute walk northeast across town from the train station), where manicured lawns and flowerbeds and elegant, tree-lined avenues seem tailor-made for hours of recuperative walks. At its centre stands the **Ķemeri Hotel**, a stately ocean liner of a building whose combination of smooth curves and castellated towers brings to mind some sort of Art Deco Camelot. Designed in the early 1930s by leading National Romantic architect Eižens Laube, it seems a world away from the Gotham City-style apartment blocks he built in central Rīga. The hotel is currently being restored and looks set to resume its role as playground of the Rīga elite when it reopens.

Northeast of the hotel a path leads off through densely forested parkland, arriving 1km later at the Meža Māja or Forest House, where the **Ķemeri National Park Visitors' Centre** (Mon–Fri 9am–5pm; ☎776 5386, ⊛www.kemeri.gov.lv) sells maps and advises on walks. Immediately north of here lies the start of the **Black Alder Wetland Path** (Melnalkšņu dumbrāja taka), an 800-metre-long boardwalk trail through dense and leafy woodland and over soggy (and sometimes rather smelly) soil, fed by the same sulphurous springs that provide the Ķemeri spa with its restorative waters.

Note that although very much a town in its own right, Ķemeri is in administrative terms part of Jūrmala – this accounts for the rather confusing signs reading "Jūrmala" which you'll see if you enter Ķemeri by road.

Great Ķemeri Bog

Lovers of bleak wilderness landscapes will want to make the trip to **Great Ķemeri Bog** (Lielais Ķemeru tīrelis), a 6000-hectare expanse of bog covered in springy sphagnum moss and punctuated by stunted birch trees and conifers. Leading out into the bog is a three-kilometre-long boardwalk trail, which starts a good 4km south of Ķemeri itself. To get there, head south from Ķemeri train station to the main Rīga–Ventspils road, turn right and follow it for 800m before turning left down a dirt road that leads past Ķemeri cemetery. Curving through the forest, the road eventually arrives at a national park signboard, where you veer right and follow the "laipa" sign to find the start of the trail.

The boardwalk leads out onto a patchwork of greens and tawny browns, and, further along, a glinting archipelago of ponds. Local flora worth looking out for include cranberries (picking them is strictly forbidden) and sundews, which use the sticky red hairs on their lower leaves to trap insects – that's if the creepy crawlies haven't already been gobbled up by the bog's community of wood sandpipers.

Tukums

Occupying a low hill above the River Slocene, **TUKUMS** is a tranquil country town whose transport links with the capital have made it something of a dormitory settlement for Rīga-based commuters. It's not a hugely exciting place by any means, but it's a useful stop-off if you're heading west from Ķemeri towards central Kurzeme, and a handful of moderately appealing museums make it worth a couple of hours of your time. Just off the southern end of Brīvības laukums, Tukums' sleepy central square, a rather undistinguished **Castle Tower** (Livonijas ordeņa pils tornis; Tues–Sat 10am–5pm, Sun 11am–4pm; ®www.tukumamuzejs.lv; 0.50Ls) is the last surviving remnant of a Livonian Order fortress, once a favoured residence of sixteenth-century Grand Master Walter von Plettenburg. Inside is a modest museum display, the highlight of which is a room full of exquisitely modelled dioramas illustrating different periods in the town's history.

North of here, behind a whitewashed **parish church**, quiet cobbled streets like Harmonijas, Darza and Zirgu, lined with wooden houses, look as if they haven't changed much since the inter-war years. The **Art Museum**, Harmonijas 7 (Mākslas muzejs; same times; 0.40Ls), is worth visiting for its themed seasonal exhibitions, although the permanent collection of canvases by local painters is somewhat lacklustre.

Three kilometres southeast of the town centre and reached by heading along Rīgas iela and turning right into Durbes iela, **Durbe Palace** (Durbes pils; Tues–Sat 10am–5pm, Sun 11am–4pm; 0.60Ls), set in landscaped parkland, is a sturdy-looking, seventeenth-century manor house graced with a wedding-cake portico and Ionic columns (grafted on in the 1820s). It's now a museum devoted to life in nineteenth-century Latvia and offers an absorbing display of agricultural implements and traditional textiles.

Perched on a hillock overlooking the Rīga–Ventspils highway 8km west of town, the soaring red-brick towers and pinnacles of **Jaunmoku Palace** (Jaunmoku pils; mid-April to mid-Oct daily 10am–6pm; rest of year Tues–Sun 10am–5pm; 0.70Ls) look like something out of a gothic horror story. Built as a country retreat for third-generation Baltic Scot, bone-meal magnate and mayor of Rīga, George Armistead (1847–1912), it now belongs to the Latvian Forestry Authority and has been converted into a hotel and conference centre. The interior still preserves some of its

Russian Orthodox church, Liepāja △

late-nineteenth-century decorations – look out for an august pair of ceramic stoves adorned with landscape scenes of Jūrmala and Rīga. Also on site is a museum of hunting and forestry, but it's of rather minor interest, featuring antlers of long-departed stags and cabinets filled with stuffed woodland creatures.

Practicalities

Situated at the end of the rail line that runs through Jūrmala and Ķemeri, Tukums is served by regular commuter trains from Rīga. The town has two **train stations**, Tukums I just east of town, and Tukums II just to the west: the former is marginally nearer the centre and next door to the **bus station**, which has regular connections to Rīga, Talsi and Ventspils. The **tourist office**, Pils iela 3 (May–Oct Mon–Fri 9am–7pm, Sat 9am–4pm, Sun 10.30am–3pm; Nov–April Mon–Fri 9am–5pm; ☎312 4451, ⓦwww.tukums.lv), has brochures on the whole region and can fix you up in B&B accommodation, either in Tukums or nearby villages (❶–❷).

The most obvious **hotel** choice is *Jaunmoku Palace* (see above; ☎310 7126, ⓦwww.lvm.lv; ❸), offering comfortable quarters and stately surroundings. Second-best is *Arka*, Pils iela 9 (☎312 5747, ⓦwww.infoline.lv/arka; ❸), which has a handful of pastel-coloured en-suites and hosts weekend discos in its beer-cellar-style restaurant. At the budget end, *Harmonija*, a fitness centre just north of the main square at Jāṇa iela 3A (☎310 7007; ❶), offers some neat en-suites and there's a sauna and small indoor pool on site. When it comes to **eating**, *Kafejnīca Margo*, Lielā 1, will sort you out with a cheap and tasty *karbonāde* (pork chop) or a salad.

The Abava Valley

Northwest of Tukums, the glacier-carved, U-shaped **Abava Valley** is one of the most picturesque spots in western Latvia – not least because it offers a welcome change from the flat arable landscape that dominates elsewhere. In the middle of the valley is the one-horse town of **Sabile**, conveniently placed for the most attractive stretches of the Abava River and also a short hike away from an extraordinary open-air art museum at **Pedvāle**. Further west lies **Kuldīga**, arguably Latvia's most appealing provincial town.

Five daily Rīga–Kuldīga **buses** run through the Abava Valley, and a handful of additional Rīga–Sabile and Sabile–Kuldīga services increase the range of options. If you're coming from the north, there are buses from Talsi to Sabile.

Sabile

Sheltering beneath a south-facing escarpment on the banks of the Abava River, **SABILE** is famous for being the northernmost location at which vines are cultivated. On the hill just north of town, **Sabile vineyard** (Sabiles vīnakalns) was founded in the seventeenth century by Duke Jakob of Courland, one of many pet schemes designed to lessen the duchy's dependence on foreign imports. It never produced much in the way of wine and soon fell into disuse, but was re-established in 1936 in order to carry out research into hardy strains of vine – the hundred or so bottles of plonk produced here annually are unlikely to make it as far as the supermarket shelves. If you want to inspect the wine terraces at close hand, you need to buy a ticket from the tourist office (0.15Ls) – worth doing if you want to stretch your legs and enjoy the view across Sabile's rooftops. Back on the main street, it's hard to miss the stately apricot-coloured form of Sabile's nineteenth-century **synagogue**, recently restored and pressed into service as a contemporary-art exhibition space managed by the open-air museum at nearby Pedvāle (opening hours vary according to what's on). At the western end of town, the seventeenth-century **Lutheran Church** (Luteranu baznīca), so white that it looks as if it's been carved out of a big lump of chalk, harbours a striking Baroque pulpit held up by a quartet of gryphon-headed snakes. Behind the church, a brisk five-minute ascent brings you to the summit of the pudding-shaped **Castle Hill** (Sabiles pilskalns), site of an ancient Latvian fortress and affording excellent views across the valley.

There's a **tourist office** in the town council building at Pilskalņa 6 (April–Sept Mon–Fri 10am–1pm & 1.30–6.30pm; ☏622 5644), though the advertised opening hours aren't always adhered to. For something to **eat**, try one of the couple of decent cafés along the main street: *Erika*, at Rīgas 11, does a good line in pork and chicken standards, while *Kafejnīca Zane*, Rīgas 8, has more in the way of salads and soups.

Pedvāle

Climb Sabile's Castle Hill (see above) and you can't fail to notice the big, Hollywood-style letters spelling out the name "**PEDVĀLE**" on the opposite side of the valley. The sign refers to Pedvāle Manor, an abandoned estate entrusted to sculptor Ojārs Feldbergs in the early 1990s on condition that he restore the buildings and open them up as a cultural centre. The result of his labours is the **Pedvāle Open-air Art Museum** (Pedvāles brīvdabas mākslas muzejs; May–Oct daily 9am–6pm; 1Ls; ⊛www.pedvale.lv), a sculpture park set in part-agricultural, part-virgin countryside. The park functions wonderfully well as a nature trail, too, whether you're interested in sculptures or not, with paths taking you down beside densely wooded streams and up over wildflower-carpeted hills, with several storks' nests scattered around for good measure.

To get to Pedvāle, cross the river from Sabile and head uphill – a left turn takes you to the **main entrance** at Firkspedvāle manor house, where there's a window selling tickets and Latvian-language site plans (0.50Ls). Spread over 2km are well over a hundred works, ranging from the profound to the pretentious, donated by abstract and conceptual sculptors from all over the world – including some throwaway pieces that you wouldn't allow within a ten-mile radius of your own garden. Many of the more memorable works are by **Ojārs Feldbergs** himself – an ever-expanding collection of brooding, deeply mysterious granite lumps. The collection of rocks dangling from poles that make up his *51 Heartstones* (51 sirdsakmens) is the most impressive work in the whole park, although the quietly enigmatic stone hut that is Ryan Hoover's and Kerin Rozycki's *Fire Inside* (Iekšējā uguns) runs it a close second. There's room for the odd joke too: Rasa Jansone's *Will o' the Wisp* (Malduguns), an archery target with the face of Lenin in the middle, may well raise a chortle, and it's no great surprise to discover that the installation advertised on the plan as *XXX by Mr Beaver* turns out to be a dam built by real-life furry critters.

If you want **to stay**, the restored manor house at Firkspedvāle (☏325 2249) has a handful of doubles, triples and quads all at 5Ls per person – all rooms are atmospheric affairs with wooden floors and beams, although showers/WCs are in the hallway. Housed in one of Firkspedvāle's outbuildings, the *Krodziņš Dāre* **pub-restaurant**, serves up everything from simple salads to substantial steak and trout dishes.

Carrying on southeast from Firkspedvāle and turning left after 3km will bring you to **Zviedru cepure** (⊛www.zviedrucepure.lv), a hill overlooking the Abava which boasts a dry toboggan run in summer and a 250-metre-long ski piste served by drag lift in winter. You can rent ski and snowboard gear on site.

Along the Abava to Renda

There are a couple of much-frequented local beauty spots just west of Sabile, beginning with the **Abava Falls** (Abavas rumba), 4km west of town and 500m from the road, a series of frothing rapids where the river descends what looks like a stairway of stratified rock. Back on the main road, another 15km brings you to the turn-off (near the Kaleši bus stop) for **Māra's Chambers** (Māras kambari), a series of sandstone hollows 2km away on the banks of the Abava, where it's thought that ancient Latvians made sacrifices to Māra the Earth Mother. Five kilometres beyond, the main road crosses the river at the village of **Renda** and leaves the Abava Valley, crossing low hills before dropping down towards Kuldīga.

Kuldīga

If you only have time to visit one provincial town in Latvia then it really ought to be **KULDĪGA**, 155km west of Rīga, a pretty little town of cobbled streets and half-timbered houses on the banks of the Venta. Kuldīga can also boast one of the natural wonders of Latvia right on its doorstep – a set of rapids known as the Venta Falls. Thanks to the navigability of the Venta River, Kuldīga was once one of most important trading towns in Kurzeme and a member of the Hanseatic League. The birthplace of Duke Jakob, Kuldīga's castle was a favourite residence of the dukes of Courland until its destruction by the Russians in the Great Northern War, after which Kuldīga settled back into the state of small-town tranquillity that still characterizes the place today.

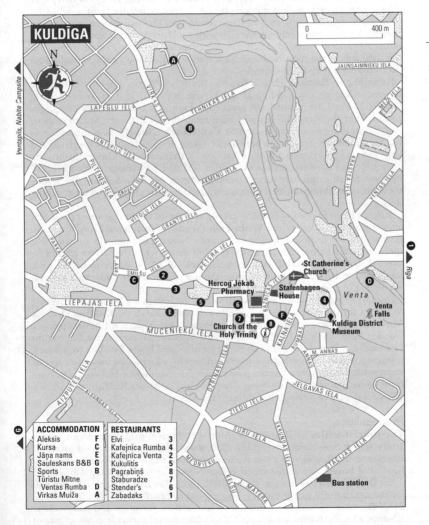

ACCOMMODATION		RESTAURANTS	
Aleksis	F	Elvi	3
Kursa	C	Kafejnīca Rumba	4
Jāņa nams	E	Kafejnīca Venta	2
Sauleskans B&B	G	Kukulītis	5
Sports	B	Pagrabiņš	8
Tūristu Mītne		Staburadze	7
Ventas Rumba	D	Stender's	6
Virkas Muiža	A	Zabadaks	1

The Town

Central Kuldīga is such a compact place that you can probably see all its sights in half an hour and still have time for a coffee, although the relaxing effect of its quiet streets and gingerbread-house buildings will make you want to stay longer. The most attractive of its jumble of well-preserved houses are concentrated on or around the junction of Baznīcas iela, Liepājas iela and Pasta iela. The creamy-yellow house on the corner of Baznīcas and Pasta is supposedly the oldest surviving wooden building in Kurzeme, dating from 1632, although it has been much rebuilt since. Of similar vintage is the single-storey timber building just opposite, at Baznīcas 5, formerly the town hall and now the tourist office. Heading east along Liepājas and taking the first left down Raiņa iela brings you to the seventeenth-century Catholic **Church of the Holy Trinity** (Sv Trīsvienības baznīca; Mon–Sat noon–1pm & 5–8pm, Sun 9am–1pm), a delightful stone building, sheltering in a neat garden square. The main focus of attention inside is a nineteenth-century altar rich with neoclassical detail, with urn-topped pillars and smooth-skinned angels framing a much older statue of the Virgin. On the right side of the nave, look out for a seventeenth-century confessional booth decorated with jolly floral squiggles.

Returning to Baznīcas iela and heading north, you'll pass a string of old stone houses, including the building at no. 17 which played host to Swedish King Charles XII in 1701 – when not preoccupied with planning military campaigns against Peter the Great, he enjoyed hunting in the local forests. At its northern end, Baznīcas curves its way around **St Catherine's Church** (Sv Katrīnas baznīca), an oft-rebuilt structure where Duke Jakob of Courland was baptized, and later married to Princess Louisa Charlotte of Brandenburg. Unfortunately, the church doesn't have regular opening times – if you do manage to find it open, look out for an exquisitely carved wooden altar by Nicholas Soffrens, the seventeenth-century Ventspils-based sculptor who worked for churches throughout the duchy.

A right turn at the end of Baznīcas takes you down to the bridge across the Venta, affording a superb view of the **Venta Falls** (Ventas rumba) immediately upstream. At less than 2m in height, they're not exactly Niagara, but provide a memorable spectacle nevertheless, curving across the 250-metre-wide river in an elegant S-bend. If the mid-nineteenth-century guidebooks of J.G. Kohl are to be believed, locals used to hang nets and traps from the top of the falls in order to catch fish attempting to jump their way upriver.

Occupying high ground on the south side of the bridge is a grassy park covering the site of the (now demolished) castle. In the middle stands the **Kuldīga District Museum** (Kuldīgas novada muzejs; Tues–Sun 11am–5pm; 0.40Ls), occupying a wooden house built in 1900 to serve as the Russian pavilion at the Exposition Universelle in Paris. Intended to show off prefabricated house-building techniques, it was successfully dismantled and re-erected here by a Liepāja businessman eager to impress his Kuldīga-born fiancée. The creaky-floored interior harbours a treasure trove of old photographs showing street life in Tsarist-era Kuldīga, as well as a colourful display of playing cards through the ages.

Practicalities

The **tourist office** at Baznīcas 5 (Mon–Fri 9am–5pm; July & Aug also Sat 10am–4pm & Sun 10am–2pm; ☎332 2259, ⊛www.kuldiga.lv) is a good source of information on Kurzeme as a whole. Accommodation options in Kuldīga include a handful of **hotels**: one of the nicest is *Jāņa Nams*, Liepājas 36 (☎332 3456, ☎332 3785; ❷), with neat en-suites, its sleek furnishings and fittings more than making up for the occasionally garish carpets. Also a good bet is *Aleksis*, Pasta iela 5 (☎332 2153; ❷), offering sweet little doubles with modern furniture and jazzy colour schemes, all with shower, some with TV too. Alternatively, snuggle down in one of the en-suites at the *Sauleskalni B&B* (☎332 2850, ⊛www.sauleskalni.com; ❷), with wooden floors and furnishings and set in idyllic countryside south of Kuldīga – it's signed off the bypass that carries through traffic on the Rīga–Ventspils route. A cheaper, but less attractive, option is the central *Kurša*, Pilsētas laukums 6 (☎332 2381 or 332 4342, ☎332 3671; ❶), a Soviet-era block on the main square featuring frumpy furnishings and unrenovated bathrooms – the more expensive rooms come with TV.

Hostel beds are available at *Virkas Muiža*, twenty minutes' walk northwest of the centre at Virkas iela 27 (☎332 3480; 4–10Ls per person depending on room size), and *Sports*, Virkas iela 13 (☎332 2671; 3Ls per person), but you may have difficulty finding an English-speaking member of staff and breakfast isn't included at either place. Dorm beds with breakfast are on offer at *Tūristu Mītne Ventas Rumba*, across the river from town right beside the Venta Falls (☎332 4168; 5–7.50Ls per person) – and you can pitch tents on the lawn outside. Otherwise, the nearest **campsite** is the *Nabīte*, about 12km northwest of town (signed off the Ventspils road; ☎949 6189), offering four-person cabins for 10Ls.

There are plenty of **places to eat** in town. *Kafejnīca Venta*, Pilsētas laukums 1, is the place to go for cheap pork chops and fries. *Elvi*, above the supermarket of the same name at Smilšu iela 20, has a healthier range of salads, while *Staburadze*, Liepājas 6, fills up with coffee-and-cake-seeking shoppers. For a relaxing drink and a great view, try *Kafejnīca Rumba*, a kiosk near the museum with an outdoor terrace overlooking the Venta Falls. *Kukulitis*, Liepājas 35, is the best place for take-away pastries. *Stender's*, a two-tier wooden pavilion at Liepājas 3, has the full range of meat-and-potato fare and is an enjoyable place for an evening **drink**, as is *Pagrabiņš*, occupying a cellar behind the tourist office at Baznīcas 5 and featuring steaks, salmon and trout on its menu.

Check posters to see if anything is happening at alternative **club** *Zabadaks*, on the western side of the Venta at Vijolīšu 24, one of the few places outside Rīga to host live bands.

Ventspils and around

Once the most hard-edged of port cities, **VENTSPILS** has undergone a dramatic makeover in recent years, its cutely cobbled pavements, neat flowerbeds and sculpture-scattered parks a happy foretaste of what perhaps other Latvian cities might look like in years to come. Huge sums have been chanelled into the city's transformation, with ambitious mayor Aivars Lembergs making full use of the revenues accrued by Ventspils from the oil transit business. Ventspils has been the main outlet for Russian oil exports since the early Sixties, although recent evidence suggests that this status can't be relied upon forever – the Russians boycotted Ventspils for several months in 2003 owing to disagreements about shipping costs. Keen to lessen their long-term dependence on the oil business, the city authorities have instead exploited Ventspils' tourist potential, restoring the medieval castle, cleaning up the beach area and constructing a children's adventure park. The resulting makeover has transformed the city into the number-one day-trip destination in Latvia – which is why you'll see more crocodiles of schoolchildren winding their way through the streets here than anywhere else in the country.

Arrival, information and accommodation

Ventspils **bus station** is conveniently located on the southeastern fringes of the centre on Kuldīgas iela. **Ferries** from Västervik dock some 400m from the centre, at the eastern end of Ostas iela. The **tourist office** at Tirgus 7 (May–Sept Mon–Fri 8am–7pm, Sat 9am–5pm, Sun 10am–3pm; Oct–April Mon–Fri 8am–5pm, Sat 10am–3pm; ☎362 2263, ☺www.tourism.ventspils.lv, ☺www.ventspils.lv) sells town maps. Although good-value, quality **accommodation** in Ventspils is on the rise, there's still not enough of it to go round in a city of this size – always book ahead if you can.

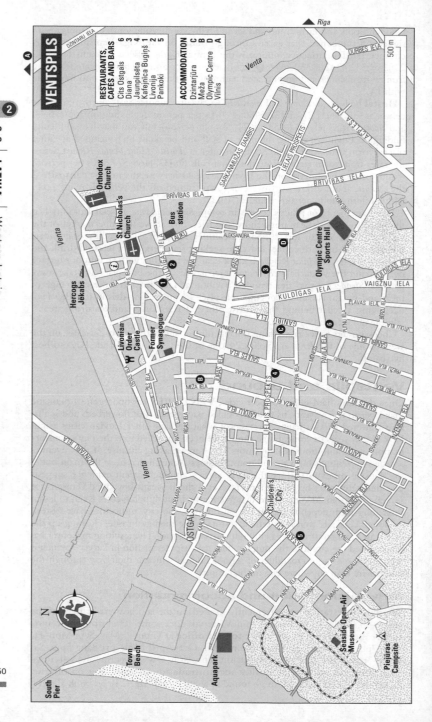

VENTSPILS

RESTAURANTS, CAFES AND BARS

Cits Ostgals	6
Diana	3
Jaunpilsēta	4
Kafejnīca Buģiņš	1
Livonija	2
Pankoki	5

ACCOMMODATION

Dzintarjūra	C
Meža	B
Olympic Centre	D
Vilnis	A

Hotels

Dzintarjūra Ganību 25 ☏362 2719. A seventy-room Soviet-era hotel offering perfectly habitable rooms with shower and TV, although the colour-clash decor is pretty dated. **3**

Meža Meža 13 ☏368 0745. A family-run guesthouse in a quiet street, with a home-from-home feel and a relaxing garden. Only one double, one triple and one quad. **1**

Olympic Centre (Olimpiskā centra viesnīca) Lielais prospekts 33 ☏362 2587. A former housing block converted into a bright, modern hotel in 2003, offering prim, affordable en-suites. **2**

Vilnis Talsu 5 ☏366 8880, ⓦwww.vilnis.lv. A smart, modern, business-oriented hotel offering serviceable en-suites with TV. It's a good 3km from the centre on the far side of the River Venta – take minibus #2 (destination Celtnieku iela) from opposite the bus station.

Campsite

Piejūras kempings Vasarnīcu 56 ☏362 7925, ⓦwww.camping.ventspils.lv. A large, well-tended campsite with tent and trailer pitches (1.50–3Ls respectively) and smart timber cottages sleeping four people – 20Ls per cottage with en-suite facilities, 10Ls per cottage without.

The City

Most of Ventspils' sights are spread out over 2km along the south side of the Venta estuary. Starting at the eastern end of this strip, there's a handsome collection of nineteenth-century buildings around **Rātslaukums**, the historic centre of the city. From here your best bet is to proceed westwards along the waterfront, taking in views of the bustling container port before arriving at the superbly restored **Livonian Order Castle**, now home to an absorbing history museum. Strolling west then south through the picturesque nineteenth-century suburb of **Ostgals** brings you eventually to the vast, green, open spaces of the **Children's City** play area, **Open-air Museum** and **Seashore Park**, which together provide much of the focus of Ventspils' blossoming tourist industry.

Rātslaukums and the waterfront

At the centre of Ventspils lies a tangle of narrow streets zeroing in on an unassuming **Town Hall Square** (Rātslaukums). On the square's eastern edge is the nineteenth-century **St Nicholas's Church** (Sv Nikolaja baznīca), the principal Lutheran place of worship in the city. It looks rather like a Greek temple with an observatory growing out of its roof and has a beautifully proportioned balustraded interior. From here Tirgus iela leads north to a market square thronging with shoppers on weekday mornings.

Beyond the market square lies **Ostas iela**, a waterfront promenade running along the southern bank of the River Venta and dotted with an impressive array of public sculpture. The eastern end starts with the *Sea Stone* (Jūras akmens), a rough-hewn lump of grey rock mounted on granite supports, and continues with several similarly inscrutable abstract pieces by local artists. You'll also come across two ends of a cow joined by a section of oil pipeline – one of a whole herd of bovine-related artworks placed throughout the city during 2002's "Cow Parade", a project designed to highlight the links between industrial Ventspils and its dairy-farming hinterland. Looking equally sculptural are the immense loading chutes and cranes of the cargo port on the opposite bank of the river. For a closer look at the port facilities, including the oil terminal just north of town, take a trip with the **Hercogs Jēkabs excursion boat** (May–Sept sailings roughly hourly between 10am & 7pm; Oct 5 times daily; 0.50Ls), which departs from a mooring just to the east of the cow.

The Livonian Order Castle

At the western end of Ostas iela, lanes lead back inland towards the egg-yolk-coloured bulk of the **Livonian Order Castle** (Livonijas ordeņa pils; daily: May–Sept 9am–6pm; Oct–April 10am–5pm; 1Ls), a medieval fortress and, later, Tsarist prison, that has become something of a Ventspils landmark in the wake of its much-publicized restoration in 2001. Inside is an exceedingly well-designed **museum of city history**, which makes up for a lack of genuinely dramatic artefacts through imaginative use of diagrams and touch-screen computers. The castle's renovated halls and galleries are a major attraction in themselves, especially the beautifully lit central courtyard overlooked by arched, red-brick galleries. Seasonal arts and crafts exhibitions are held in the main tower, where you'll also chance upon a clumsily painted fresco featuring weightlifters – a reminder that this part of the castle was used as a Soviet army gym in the 1960s.

West of the castle

Ten minutes' walk west of the castle lies a grid of cobbled streets and wooden one-storey houses known as **Ostgals** ("Port's End"), an attractively sleepy suburb dating from the mid-nineteenth century, when the Tsarist authorities encouraged local fishermen and farmers to build homes in the area, in order to prevent the Sahara-like encroachment of nearby dunes. Head south from here and you'll find it hard to avoid the hordes of little ones making a bee-line for **Children's City** (Bērnu pilsētiņa; free), a kiddies' playpark featuring all manner of slides, climbing frames and sandpits. The parkside café, *Pepija*, is appropriately furnished with toddler-sized chairs and tables.

From here it's a five-minute walk southwest along Vasarnīcu iela, lined with Tsarist-era summer houses, to the **Seaside Open-air Museum** (Piejūras brīvdabas muzejs; May–Sept daily 11am–6pm; Oct–April Wed–Sun 11am–5pm; 0.50Ls). Alongside a display of beached fishing boats of all eras and sizes there's a street of fishermen's cottages (each with a pair of crotch-high wading boots hung up in the hallway) and a nineteenth-century windmill whose mechanism is driven by wood-carved cogs. One of the museum's most popular attractions is the **narrow-gauge railway** (Mazbānītis), on which a steam-hauled train (0.50Ls extra) takes passengers on a brief circuit of the lawns and trees of the adjacent Seashore Park (Jūrmalas parks), its shrill whistle audible all over the western side of the city.

Immediately north of the museum lie the swimming pools and water slides of the **Aquapark** (Akvaparks; May–Sept daily 10am–10pm; 1.50Ls), while over to the west lies a glorious stretch of white-sand **beach**, with yet more swings and climbing frames for the kids. If it's not the right weather for sunbathing, consider strolling as far as the lighthouse at the end of the 800-metre-long **South Pier** (Dienvidu mols), which, together with the North Pier (Ziemeļu mols), just across the water, forms the so-called "Sea Gates" through which tankers and cargo ships lumber their way towards Ventspils' port.

Eating and drinking

Although culinary culture in Ventspils has yet to catch up with the visible signs of modernization elsewhere in the city, the generous sprinkling of cafés and restaurants in the centre are perfectly adequate if you're after a functional meal accompanied by a relaxing drink rather than fine dining.

Cits Ostgals Ganību 19. This relaxed pub attracts a cross-section of locals and offers a respectable range of soups, salads and main-course meals.

Diana Lielais prospekts 44. Pancakes stuffed with meat, cheese or fruit in a comfortable cafeteria.

Jaunpilsēta Saules 48. A self-service cafeteria, nicely poised between the city centre and the seaside areas. Big vats of soup and a decent salad bar.

Kafejnīca Bugiņš Lielā iela 1/3. A cosy café-bar

decked out in the style of a log cabin. A good place to tuck into pork-based favourites or snuggle down for an evening drinking session.

Livonija Kuldīgas iela 13. An odd mixture of old-fashioned restaurant and disco bar that at least offers a bigger choice of meat and fish dishes than the other places in the centre.

Pankoki Vasarnīcu 17. An old-fashioned serve-yourself café in a timber-built villa, specializing in sweet and savoury pancakes. Handy for the Open-air Museum.

Liepāja

Squeezed between a sandy seashore and the marshy Lake Liepāja (Liepājas ezers), the port city of **LIEPĀJA** has undergone several shifts in identity over the last century or so: bustling mercantile centre, then genteel bathing resort, Soviet garrison town and now cultural and commercial capital of Latvia's southwest. Its history is reflected in the city's engaging hodge-podge of architectural styles: wooden seaside villas rub shoulders with red-brick industrial buildings, crumbling barrack blocks and dockside cranes. Although tourism hasn't received as much investment here as in its west-coast rival Ventspils, there's still much to enjoy, including an attractive stretch of seaside gardens and long sandy beaches, a handful of worthwhile museums and churches and the grimly fascinating northern suburb of **Karosta**, once a Tsarist naval fortress and then a Soviet submarine base – virtually a walk-through history lesson.

Locals will tell you that Liepāja was the birthplace of Latvian rock music in the 1970s and 80s – although the rather staid **Liepājas Dzintars Festival** ("Liepāja's Amber"), held annually in mid-August, is about the only sign of this heritage you're likely to come across. The city is also famous for its **lingerie**, being the home city of Latvian textile giants Lauma – you'll see posters of young ladies clad (somewhat scantily) in the company's products all over the country.

Although served by regular **buses** from Rīga, Liepāja is too far away from the capital (220km) to make a comfortable day-trip. Luckily, there's enough to see and do here to make a stay of a couple of days an enjoyable option. Above all, the city is a good base from which to explore Latvia's south coast, notably the nature reserve at **Lake Pape**, 45km to the south.

Some history

Liepāja grew out of the village of Līva, a medieval fishing settlement subsequently taken over by the Livonian Order in the thirteenth century; they re-named it Libau and used it as a base from which to extend their rule over the Curonian coast. As one of the region's few ice-free ports, the city was developed by Tsarist Russia as a naval base in the late nineteenth century and was also one of the main departure points for passenger liners heading for the USA, taking thousands of Latvian, Estonian and Lithuanian migrants with them.

In 1919, with Rīga in the hands of the Bolsheviks, Liepāja became the seat of the Latvian Provisional Government. Unfortunately, it had to share the town with an army of Baltic Germans under General von der Goltz, who still entertained the dream of turning Latvia (or a large part of it at least) into a German-dominated statelet dependent on the Reich. The British, who needed both the Latvians and the Germans to stave off the westward advance of Bolshevism, sent the Royal Navy to Liepāja to keep the peace. When von der Goltz tried to have the Latvian government arrested, however, Ulmanis and his ministers were offered protection by the British, who installed them on a former Tsarist battle cruiser, the *Saratov*, anchored in Liepāja's port. A period of uneasy cohabitation unfolded, with British and German troops patrolling different parts of the city. Eager to offer Ulmanis a modicum of moral support, the British, French and Americans established diplomatic missions in Liepāja and were soon joined by representatives of international aid agencies. The city was even home to an English-language newspaper, *The Weekly Advertiser*, whose inaugural title page announced that "the sight of many a British sailor being led by street-arabs through our city and the idea that they might not be fairly dealt with, induced us to publish our small weekly". The situation changed when von der Goltz marched off to kick the Bolsheviks out of Rīga in May 1919. After a couple of months of confused diplomacy, the British persuaded the Germans to hand Rīga over to the Latvian government – who promptly sailed away in the *Saratov* to take up office in their newly liberated capital. Liepāja's brief period in the political limelight was over.

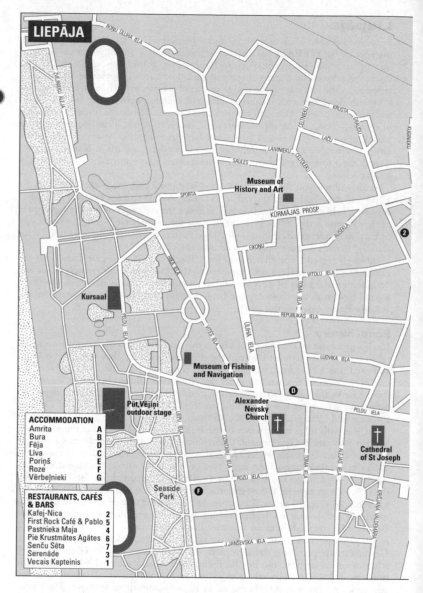

The Soviet navy established itself here after World War II and Liepāja was virtually closed to foreigners until 1990 – which goes some way to explaining why the tourist potential of its long, sandy beaches was never exploited.

Arrival, information and accommodation

Liepāja's **bus and train stations** occupy the same building at the northern end of Rīgas iela, some 1500m from the town centre. Catch any tram heading down Rīgas

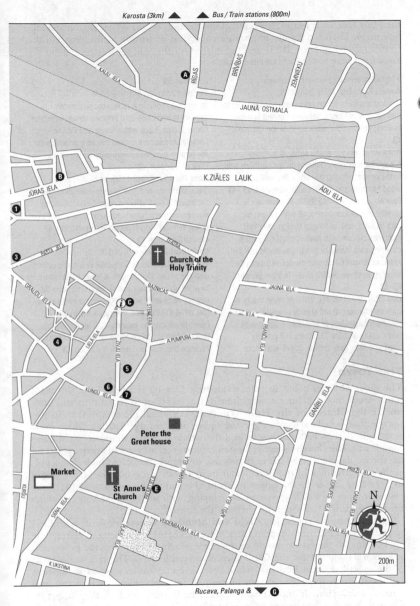

Karosta (3km) ▲   ▲ Bus / Train stations (800m)

Rucava, Palanga & ▼ **G**

iela to reach the centre (tickets 0.10Ls from kiosks or 0.12Ls from the driver) – get off when you see the grey spire of the Holy Trinity Church on your left. **Ferries** from Rostock and Karlshamn arrive at the Brīvosta terminal on Siļķu iela, 2km north of the centre – buses #3, #6, #10 and #15 run into town from Kalpaka iela, just inland.

The South Kurzeme **tourist information centre** (Lejaskurzemes tūrisma infor-mācijas birojs; Mon–Fri 9am–5pm; ☎348 0808, ✆ltib@apollo.lv), in the lobby of the *Hotel Liva*, Lielā iela 11, is a mine of information on the whole region and sells city maps. There's a rapidly improving collection of **hotels** in the city, and the tourist office can book **B&B** accommodation in the villages scattered along the coast from here to the Lithuanian border.

Hotels and guesthouses

Amrita Rīgas iela 7/9 ☏ 348 0888, ✉ info@amrita.lv. Smart en-suites measuring up to international business standard, housed in a new building ten minutes' walk north of the Old Town. ❻

Bura Jūras iela 22 ☏ 340 4858, ✉ bura@arcus.lv. A bold, contemporary building on the northern side of the centre, offering tidy en-suites with pale-wood furniture and pastel colour schemes. ❹–❺

Feja Kurzemes 9 ☏ 342 2688, ⓦ www.feja.lv. A handful of spacious rooms, all with TV and most with bathtub, and an interior design style that combines cubism with flowery chintz. If you're travelling as a family or group, you might ask for room no. 8, which has enough fold-out sofas to sleep up to seven people at 8–10Ls per person. ❸–❹

Līva Lielā iela 11 ☏ 342 0102, ⓦ www.liva.lv. A conveniently central but slightly charmless block offering a mixed bag of en-suites – some with new carpets and Sat-TV, others still proudly displaying their grey-brown, Soviet-era colour

schemes. ❹

Poriņš Palmu iela 5 ☏ 915 0596, ✉ porins@apollo.lv. A renovated nineteenth-century town house on a cobbled street, with nine comfy rooms, each with shower and TV. The homely atmosphere makes this very popular with the foreign business community, so it's best to book in advance. ❷

Roze Rožu 37 ☏ 342 1155, ⓦ www .parkhotel-roze.lv. A pair of renovated villas beside the seafront park offering repro furniture, roomy doubles with spacious bathrooms, and a handful of swish self-catering apartments. Apartments ❼, standard doubles ❹

Vērbeļnieki Pērkone ☏ 346 0217, ⓦ www.verbelnieki.lv. Cosy B&B in a rustic setting near the shore 15km south of town. Most rooms have en-suite shower and fireplace; all have TV. Liepāja–Nica and Liepāja–Klaipēda buses pass by (get off at the Pērkone stop, walk down into Pērkone village and bear right). If you're driving, turn right off the main highway when you see the Pērkone bus stop and follow the signs. ❷

The Town

The most obvious place to start exploring Liepāja is **Lielā iela**, the main north–south thoroughfare running through the centre of town. Its principal landmark is the **Church of the Holy Trinity** (Sv Trīsvienības baznīca), with its distinctive four-tiered belltower, a greying eighteenth-century structure which looks as though it's seen better days – indeed the whole structure shudders when trams rumble past. The church's weather-beaten exterior certainly doesn't prepare you for the rococo delights inside, where there's an exuberantly decorated high altar, a pulpit held up Atlas-like by the figure of an angel and an organ built by H.A. Contius in 1779 (and said to be the largest mechanical organ in the world until 1912), the clustered pipes of which appear to be dripping with molten gold. You can climb the **tower** (daily 11am–5pm) for views of the town.

South of here, the pedestrian **Zivju and Stendera streets** break off from Lielā to pass through the main shopping area of town. There's a scattering of picturesque old buildings in the side streets off to the east, including a half-timbered former inn at Kungu 24 where Peter the Great allegedly stayed in 1697. The visit formed part of the so-called Great Embassy, when Peter led a 250-man mission to Western Europe in order to study modern techniques in shipbuilding, architecture and fortress construction. It's not known whether he learned much in Liepāja, but he was back here as a conqueror ten years later.

Another 200m south, the neo-Gothic **St Anne's Church** (Sv Annas baznīca) contains a wonderfully delicate Baroque altar carved by Nicholas Soffrens in 1697. A three-tiered affair with a scene of the *Crucifixion* at the bottom, the *Deposition* in the middle and the *Ascension* at the top, the whole ensemble radiates a honey-coloured glow that is in marked contrast to the plain-grey tones of the rest of the – largely unadorned – interior. Head west from here, past Liepāja's animated covered **market**, to find the Roman Catholic **Cathedral of St Joseph** (Sv Jāzepa katedrāle), whose pinnacle-encrusted towers are a fanciful nineteenth-century addition to a structure of much older vintage. It's as ornate inside as it is out, its walls covered with floral designs, saints and harp-strumming angels, all rendered in bright reds and greens. To the right of the high altar there's a stunning side chapel, decorated with Art Nouveau stuccowork and hung with an intricate model ship.

From here Peldu iela heads west towards the beach, passing through a residential zone of timber villas where nineteenth-century industrialists spent their summers – some have been lovingly restored, others are slowly crumbling into the ground. At the junction with Ūliha iela you'll catch sight of the brittle spire of the Russian **Orthodox Church of St Alexander Nevsky** on your right – it's rarely open, but the turquoise exterior is pure eye-candy. Further west along Peldu and over to the left, the **Museum of Fishing and Navigation** at Hikes 9 (Zvejniecības un kuģniecības muzejs; Wed–Sun: summer 11am–6pm; winter 10am–5pm; 0.50Ls) is crammed with scale models of virtually every sea-worthy craft to have plied Baltic waters from Viking times onwards, culminating in a collection of sturdy ice-breakers produced by the Liepāja shipyards. The largest of the models is that of the British-built, Russian-operated ocean liner *Kursk*, which spent the years immediately before World War 1 conveying Latvian emigrants to North America on the Liepāja–New York–Halifax route. Further along Hikes lie some of the best pre served of Liepāja's belle époque villas, their filigree wooden window frames giving them the appearance of festive doily-trimmed cakes. Down an alley from a swan-stocked pond lies Liepāja's derelict **Kursaal** (Kūrmāja), a colonnaded, neoclassical facade hinting at its former grandeur. Extending south of the Kursaal is the **Seaside Park** (Jūrmalas parks), a well-tended area of lawns and leafy promenades separated by a line of dunes from the beach itself – as pristine a stretch of sand as you're likely to find on Latvia's west coast and a good spot for amber-hunting after storms.

Returning towards the town centre via the lime-tree-shaded Kūrmājas prospekts will take you past the **Museum of History and Art** at no. 9 (Vestures un mākslas muzejs; Wed–Sun: summer 11am–7pm; winter 10am–5pm; 0.50Ls), a didactically arranged assemblage of local artefacts occupying a villa built in 1901 for the Katzenelson family. The inlaid wooden floors and stuccoed ceilings of the interior provide an attractive setting for models of the Neolithic villages and fortresses that were once scattered along this stretch of coast, and a rather magnificent display of the eighteenth-century pewter tankards that were made for the town's guilds – encrusted with heraldic emblems and topped with statuettes of mermaids, they look like trophies awarded for some long-forgotten exotic sport. A words-and-pictures romp through Liepāja's history includes family snapshots of generations of Liepājans at work and play and chilling photographs of Latvians shot dead by Stalin's NKVD in 1941. There's also a colourful display of traditional Kurzeme costumes and a gallery that hosts seasonal exhibitions by some of Latvia's best contemporary artists. Further up Kūrmājas, a right turn into Graudu will take you past some recently spruced-up Art Nouveau apartment blocks – note the easily missed doorway at no. 44, guarded by fearsomely beaked birds sporting what look like Elizabethan ruffs.

Karosta

Four kilometres north of the Old Town lies **Karosta** (a contraction of "Kara osta", which means simply "Naval port"), a military suburb developed by Tsarist Russia in the late nineteenth century in order to guard against the growing threat of German sea power. Paradoxically, Karosta's expensively fortified port facilities and gun batteries were never put to the test – on the outbreak of war in 1914 the Russians withdrew their Baltic fleet to Tallinn and Helsinki and sank blockships in Karosta harbour in order to dissuade the Germans from bothering to capture it. Subsequently adopted by the Soviets as a submarine base, Karosta grew into a self-contained, Russian-speaking city inhabited by naval ratings, ancillary workers and their families. Many of the civilians are still here, left stranded by the pull-out of the military machine they served.

Today Karosta is a curious place, with stately, semi-abandoned boulevards bisecting a landscape of imposing Tsarist-era buildings (the best of which have been bagged by the Latvian armed forces), skeletal remains of ruined barracks and depressing lines of run-down housing blocks. Riven by unemployment and drug addiction, it's not the kind of place in which you want to linger at night.

The best way to get to there is to take **minibus #3** from Lielā iela to the terminus on Atmodas bulvāris, right in the heart of Karosta. Retracing the minibus route, turn left to find one of the Russian Empire's finest architectural heirlooms, the yellow-domed **Orthodox Cathedral of St Nicholas** (Sv Nikolaja pareizticīgo katedrāle). With a facade of ochre-coloured bricks speckled with turquoise, blue and green tiles, it looks as though it might be a shiny toy made for giants. The main object of veneration in the sparsely furnished interior is an icon depicting a placid *Madonna and Child* flanked by angelic beings bearing gifts.

Northwest of here, lanes lead down to the shore, where the **Northern Pier** (Ziemeļu mols) extends into the Baltic, providing amateur fishermen with a kilometre-long perch. Beyond the pier, paths lead north along a sandy shore overlooked by gun emplacements built by the Russians between 1894 and 1908. Long abandoned, they're now collapsing slowly into the Baltic Sea.

One Karosta-related experience you'll have to plan in advance is **"Behind Bars"** (Aiz restem), an increasingly popular interactive show held in the former jail on Cietoksna iela. Normally held a couple of times every weekend (the tourist office in Liepāja has schedules and sells tickets; 2Ls), the performance involves actors dressed up as Soviet prison guards herding groups of visitors into the cells at gunpoint, bellowing orders and initiating rounds of repeat-after-me Leninist sloganeering. The show is normally conducted in Latvian or Russian, but if you book well in advance the tourist office might arrange someone to translate for you.

Eating and drinking

Liepāja can boast a decent variety of places to eat and drink, mostly concentrated on or around Lielā iela and Graudu iela. Additionally, in summer, a handful of relaxing outdoor cafés open up in the seaside park, near the western end of Peldu iela.

First Rock Café Stendera 18/20. The social hub around which much of Liepāja's day and nightlife revolves, with an enjoyable pub-restaurant at ground level, café with roof terrace upstairs and a basement nightclub by the name of *Pablo* (ⓦwww.pablo.lv), regularly featuring live bands.

Kafej-Nīca Graudu 31/33. A laid-back venue for cheap, filling food or a quiet beer.

Pastnieka maja Brīvzemnieka 53. A reconditioned red-brick and timber building harbouring a snazzy pub-restaurant. Big outdoor terrace.

Pie Krustmātes Agātes Zivju 4/6. A tidy little café with self-service salads, soups and meaty main courses at very reasonable prices. Till 8pm.

Senču Sēta Stendera 13A. A cosy, characterful and traditional tavern with a full menu of pork chops, steaks and grilled fish, and a tiny tree-shaded terrace.

Serenāde Graudu 41. Decent coffee, fresh pastries and scrumptious cakes in the best of the downtown patisseries. Mon–Sat till 8pm, Sun till 4pm.

Vecais Kapteinis Dubelšteina iela 14. The top place to eat in town, offering a mouth-watering menu of trout and salmon dishes, as well as the usual pork-based staples. It's atmospheric too, with wooden beams, an open fireplace and brick-lined cellar.

Entertainment

Liepāja is the only Latvian city outside Rīga to have a **symphony orchestra** – it performs regularly at the Filharmonija, Graudu iela 50 (☎342 5538, ⓦhttp://lso.apollo.lv). You can also hear music – mostly musicals and rock opera – at Liepāja's **theatre**, Teātra 4 (☎342 0145, ⓦhttp://teatris.liepajanet.lv). Balle, Rozu laukums 5/6 (☎348 0638), is a comfortable, modern and central **cinema** showing mainstream films. In summer, all kinds of concerts take place at the Pūt vējiņi outdoor stage in the seaside park – most importantly it's the venue for Liepājas Dzintars (early to mid-August), which, although unlikely to set the pulse racing, is traditionally Latvia's biggest **rock festival**.

Lake Pape

Beyond Liepāja, a sandy sliver of beach backed by forest and coastal heath continues all the way to the Lithuanian border, some 60km to the south. There are any number of picturesque spots where you could stop off along the way, although it's the World Wildlife Fund-sponsored nature reserve at **Lake Pape** (@www.wwf.lv), just short of the border, that shows this part of the coast at its unspoiled, desolate best. Cut off from the sea by a bar of sand, the lake is surrounded by reeds, wetland forest and grassy meadow, grazed by a herd of wild horses, the only such herd in the country and one of the reserve's main attractions. The area also offers some rewarding walks – the best start from the lake's main settlement, **Pape village**, and wend along the seashore.

Lake Pape is best explored with your own transport, though getting to the lake by bus is just about possible. The main entry point to the region is the village of **Rucava**, on the main Liepāja–Klaipėda highway, 7km east of Lake Pape. International **buses** operating the Rīga–Liepāja–Klaipėda–Kaliningrad route all stop in Rucava, but beware that the timetable information displayed at Rucava's tiny bus station is only approximate – allow thirty minutes either side when moving on. From Rucava you could just about walk to the lake's main sights in the space of a day, though it's a hard slog.

The lake's eastern shore

Since 1999, the eastern shore of Lake Pape has been the centre of a project to reintroduce **wild horses** to Latvia. Wild horses died out in the area in the eighteenth century and the aim of the project is to re-create the kind of naturally grazed landscape that would have existed all over the Baltic States before the Middle Ages. Eighteen stocky, grey *konnik polski* (a type of horse with wild traits selectively bred in Poland in the 1930s) were imported initially and there are now over fifty horses living in five or six so-called "harems" or social units – with new groups being formed every time older males drive younger ones away to form harems of their own.

The best way to reach them if you're coming by car is from **Kalnišķi** on the main southbound highway. Take the signed dirt road that branches off from Kalnišķi, and after ploughing through forest for about 5km the road arrives at a ticket barrier (May–Sept daily 9am–5pm; 0.50Ls), where a warden will either guide you through the lakeside meadows, or simply give you advice on where you can walk and leave you to get on with it. Although they're far from tame, the horses are relatively unfazed by humans and are unlikely to scamper off on your arrival – they're certainly a delight to watch. The rush-shrouded shores of the lake itself lie about 1km west of the ticket barrier and are favoured by all kinds of **migrating birds** in spring. The arrival of the horses has helped to increase the numbers of visiting greylag geese, who favour the short-grass habitat created by grazing animals.

Pape village

Located on the low sandy ridge that separates the lake from the sea, the wind-battered village of **PAPE** was a thriving fishing port until the communist period (when the Soviet military sank ships in the narrow coastal waters and used the wrecks for target practice), and is now a sleepy, dune-enclosed settlement, with a largely Lithuanian-speaking population. You can walk from the horse reserve to Pape in about two hours by following paths running southwestwards beside the irrigation dykes. If you're driving, you'll have to return to the main road and head south to Rucava and the Pape turn-off. Just before arriving at the village from the Rucava direction, you'll pass a wooden observation tower offering panoramic views of the lake's reedy south shore – although don't be surprised if the bulk of Pape's birdlife is away at the quieter, northern end of the lake.

Pape itself is the starting point for wonderful seashore walks in either direction, particularly to the south, where the signed **Path of Natural Processes** (Dabas procesu taka) takes you through landscape of meadow, forest and dunes before returning to Pape along the beach – a circuit of 9km in all. About 1.5km into the trail (and just about accessible by car), a delightful **Vītolnieki Fishermen's Homestead Museum** ("Vītolnieki" zvejnieku sēta; May–Oct daily except Mon & Thurs; 0.30Ls) occupies the private house of a woman who has kept everything pretty much as it was in her grandfather's time. It somehow makes a difference to know that the simple wooden furnishings, cast-iron kitchenware and trunk-sized bedstead are still in use. There's more of a museum-style display in the outbuildings, with a collection of traps and baskets in the net-mending shed and a thousand-year-old, carved tree-trunk canoe in the granary.

Practicalities

The **tourist offices** in either Liepāja (see p.256) or in Rucava public library (Mon–Fri 9am–5pm; ☎349 4766) can book you into local **B&Bs** (❶). You can also stay in the WWF Nature House in Pape (Dabas māja; ☎947 5734; ❶), at the entrance to the village; it offers a handful of plain rooms and a kitchen and you can pich a tent in the grounds.

There are a couple of **food and drink** shops on Rucava's main square and a rudimentary day-time café in the nearby town hall. If you're planning on doing a lot of walking in the area then consider buying **map** no. 3113 in the 1:50,000 Latvias satelitkarte series, available from the Jāņa Sēta shop in Rīga (see p.226).

Travel details

Trains

Jelgava to: Rīga (hourly; 50min).
Rīga to: Jelgava (hourly; 50min); Ķemeri (every 40–50min; 1hr 5min); Tukums (every 40–50min; 1hr 25min).

Buses

Bauska to: Jelgava (6 daily; 1hr 20min); Mežotne (Mon–Fri 6 daily; Sat & Sun 4 daily; 25min); Rundāles pils (Mon–Fri 12 daily, Sat 10 daily, Sun 5 daily; 25min).
Jelgava to: Bauska (6 daily; 1hr 20min); Rīga (every 20min; 50min); Tērvete (6 daily; 30min).
Kuldīga to: Liepāja (Mon–Sat 5 daily, Sun 3 daily; 1hr 20min); Rīga (5 daily; 2hr 30min–3hr 30min); Sabile (Mon–Sat 11 daily, Sun 7 daily; 1hr); Ventspils (Mon–Sat 5 daily, Sun 3 daily; 1hr 20min).
Liepāja to: Pavilosta (1 daily; 1hr); Rīga (14 daily; 3hr 30min–4hr); Rucava (5 daily; 40–50min); Sabile (4 daily; 3hr); Ventspils (Mon–Sat 6 daily, Sun 4 daily; 2hr 50min).
Rīga to: Bauska (every 30min; 1hr 10min–1hr 30min); Jelgava (every 30min; 50min); Kolka (3 daily; 3hr 15min–4hr 30min); Kuldīga (5 daily; 2hr 30min–3hr 30min); Liepāja (14 daily; 3hr 30min–4hr); Mazirbe (2 daily; 4hr); Rucava (4 daily; 4hr 30min); Sabile (Mon–Sat 13 daily, Sun 6 daily; 2hr); Talsi (12 daily; 2hr 30min); Tukums (12 daily; 1hr 40min); Ventspils (14 daily; 3–4hr).
Sabile to: Kuldīga (Mon–Sat 11 daily; Sun 7 daily; 1hr); Liepāja (4 daily; 3hr); Talsi (Mon–Sat 9 daily; Sun 5 daily; 40min); Rīga (Mon–Sat 13 daily; Sun 6 daily; 2hr).
Talsi to: Kolka (3 daily; 1hr 15min); Rīga (12 daily; 2hr 30min); Roja (Mon–Sat 7 daily; Sun 5 daily; 1hr); Sabile (Mon–Sat 9 daily, Sun 5 daily; 40min); Ventspils (Mon–Sat 6 daily, Sun 4 daily; 1hr 40min).
Ventspils to: Kuldīga (Mon–Sat 4 daily, Sun 2 daily; 1hr 20min); Liepāja (2hr 50min); Rīga (14 daily; 3–4hr); Talsi (Mon–Sat 6 daily, Sun 4 daily; 1hr 40min).

International buses

Bauska to: Panevēžys (2 daily; 2hr 30min).
Jelgava to: Šiauliai (4 daily; 2hr 30min).
Liepāja to: Kaliningrad (1 daily; 8hr); Klaipéda (4 daily; 3hr 30min); Moscow (2 daily; 18hr); Palanga (4 daily; 3hr).

2.3

Eastern Latvia

astern Latvia is made up of two distinct regions with very different histories: **Vidzeme** (literally "the land in the middle"), conquered by the Knights of the Sword – and then taken over by their successor organization, the Livonian Order – in the thirteenth century, and dotted with the crumbling relics of their hilltop castles. The Livonian Order had much more difficulty imposing their authority on **Latgale**, the region to the southeast, a disputed borderland prone to frequent incursions from the Russians to the east and Poles and Lithuanians to the west. When the Livonian Order collapsed in the mid-sixteenth century, Vidzeme went to the Protestant Swedes, while Latgale was taken over by the solidly Catholic Polish–Lithuanian Commonwealth – and although the foreign overlords have long since departed, the spiritual divide remains to this day. Political and religious borders also aided the survival of Latgale's archaic dialect, which – unlike the speech of Vidzeme, more or less indistinguishable from mainstream Latvian – is even now almost unintelligible to their fellow countrymen.

The dominant geographical features of eastern Latvia are its two main river valleys: the gloriously unspoilt **Gauja**, northeast of Rīga, and the broad **Daugava**, to the southeast, the main transport corridor to Latgale and beyond. The combination of cliff-lined riverscapes and forest-clad hills make the **Gauja National Park** the one must-see natural attraction in the country, with the relaxing resort of **Sigulda** and the historic market town of **Cēsis** providing the ideal entry points. The settlements along the Daugava are as a rule much more industrialized, although there's a wealth of historical attractions along its banks – the ancient Latvian stockade fort of **Lielvārde** and the handsome provincial town of **Jēkabpils** being stand-out sights. The last big settlement on the Latvian stretch of the Daugava before the Belarussian border, the brooding industrial city of **Daugavpils** is very much an acquired taste, and a totally misleading introduction to the surrounding province of **Latgale** – a rustic paradise of forests and lakes which counts the Catholic pilgrimage centre of **Aglona** and the tranquil country town of **Ludza** among its highlights.

The Gauja Valley

Rising in an area of rolling uplands 90km due east of Rīga, the River Gauja winds its way through most of northeastern Latvia before emptying into the Baltic Sea a short distance north of the capital. The most exciting stretch of the valley is between the towns of Sigulda and Valmiera, where the river carves its way through hills of Devonian sandstone, leaving ruddy cliffs and steep, forest-covered banks in its wake. Even though the highest peaks in the region barely scrape altitudes of 100m above sea level, it's a spectacularly lumpy region by local standards, so much so that the Baltic Germans were moved to call it the "Livonian Switzerland".

Much of the Sigulda–Valmiera stretch falls within the boundaries of the **Gauja National Park** (Gaujas nacionālais parks; ⊛www.gnp.gov.lv), founded in 1973 to protect the region's diverse flora and fauna and establish a well-maintained network of walking routes. Given the park's proximity to Rīga, it's relatively easy to access, with regular trains and buses heading for **Sigulda** and the next major town upriver, **Cēsis**, either of which serves as a handy and attractive base for further exploration. Midway between the two, the **Ligatne Nature Trail** offers the opportunity to

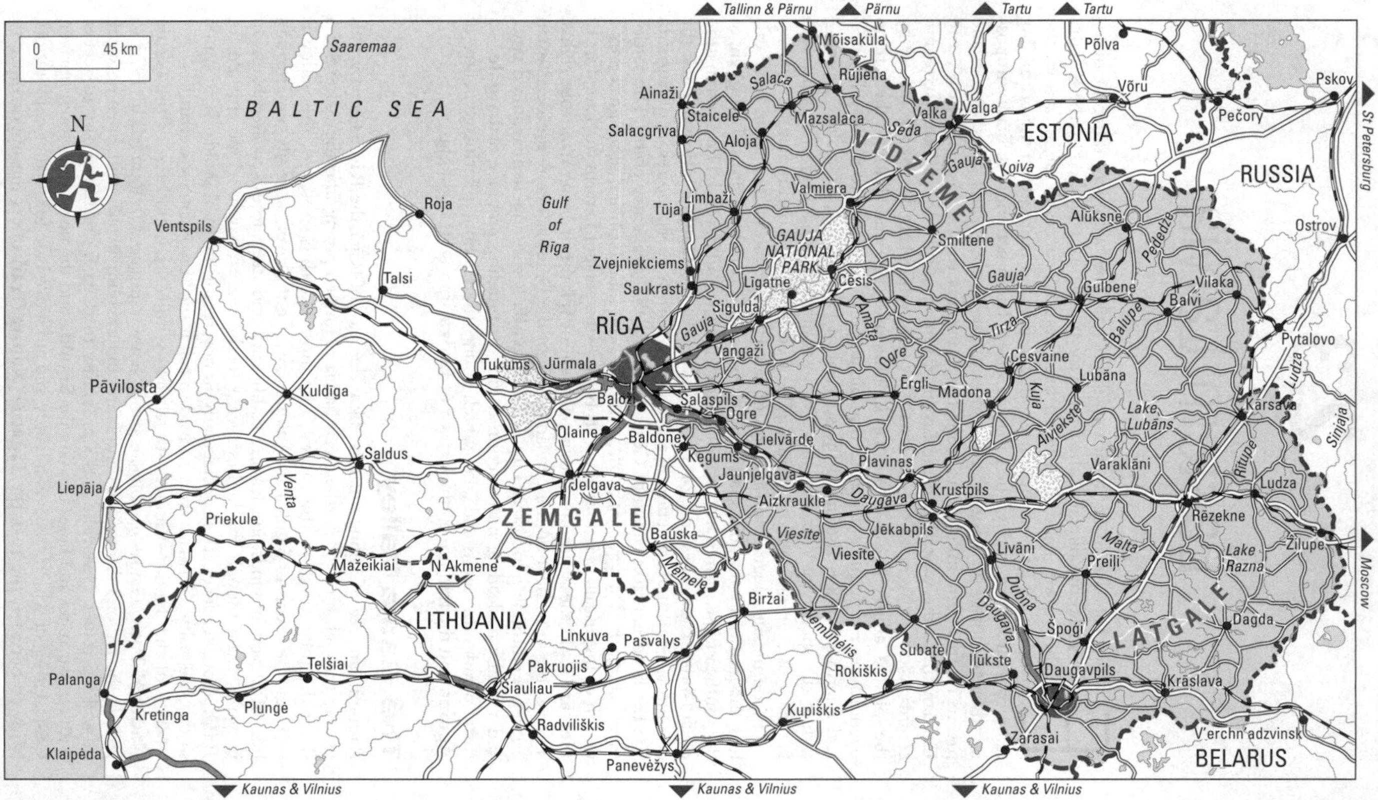
Tallinn & Pärnu
Pärnu
Tartu
Tartu
St Petersburg
Moscow
Kaunas & Vilnius
Kaunas & Vilnius
Kaunas & Vilnius
0
45 km
N
Saaremaa
BALTIC SEA
Gulf of Rīga
RĪGA
ESTONIA
RUSSIA
BELARUS
LITHUANIA
VIDZEME
ZEMGALE
LATGALE
GAUJA NATIONAL PARK
Mõisaküla
Põlva
Rūjiena
Võru
Pskov
Pečory
Ainaži
Staicele
Mazsalaca
Valka
Valga
Salacgrīva
Aloja
Salaca
Seda
Gauja
Koiva
Limbaži
Tūja
Valmiera
Alūksne
Ostrov
Smiltene
Pededze
Zvejniekciems
Saukrasti
Līgatne
Cēsis
Gulbene
Vilaka
Balvi
Sigulda
Amata
Tirza
Balupe
Pytalovo
Vangaži
Ogre
Cesvaine
Lubāna
Ludza
Roja
Ventspils
Talsi
Tukums
Jūrmala
Pāvilosta
Kuldīga
Baloži
Salaspils
Ērgli
Madona
Kuja
Kārsava
Lake Lubāns
Sinjaja
Olaine
Baldone
Lielvārde
Aiviekste
Ķegums
Plavinas
Varakļāni
Ritupe
Saldus
Jaunjelgava
Venta
Liepāja
Jelgava
Aizkraukle
Daugava
Krustpils
Rēzekne
Priekule
Bauska
Viesīte
Jēkabpils
Līvāni
Malta
Lake Razna
Zilupe
Mažeikiai
N Akmene
Mēmele
Preiļi
Biržai
Dubna
Nemunēlis
Dagda
Linkuva
Pasvalys
Špoģi
Subate
Ilūkste
Daugavpils
Telšiai
Pakruojis
Rokiškis
Palanga
Siauliau
Krāslava
Kretinga
Plungė
Radviliškis
Kupiškis
V'erchn'adzvinsk
Zarasai
Klaipėda
Panevėžys

Canoeing down the Gauja Valley

To experience the Gauja landscape at its best, you really have to see it from the river itself. The favoured craft is a canoe and in fact, **canoeing down the Gauja** has become one of Latvia's most popular outdoor holiday activities. True aficionados start at Strenči, northeast of Valmiera, and spend four to five days paddling their way downstream to Sigulda – a total distance of 95km. However, it's the 35-kilometre stretch between Cēsis and Sigulda that is the most scenic and correspondingly busiest, especially on summer weekends. Most people do the Cēsis–Sigulda trip in two to three days, overnighting at designated national park campsites spaced at convenient intervals along the way. The easiest way to start is simply to rent a canoe (and a tent if you don't have one) and set off, or if you prefer, you can opt for a guided canoe trip organized by one of the adventure tourism agencies listed below. The season lasts from early June to the end of August.

A number of agencies that rent out gear and organize trips are listed below; the tourist offices in Sigulda and Cēsis can advise on others. It's best to organize canoe rental and trips a few days in advance if possible – things get booked up quickly at summer weekends. Expect to pay 10Ls a day for canoe rental, 20Ls per person a day for a guided canoe tour.

Canoe rental contacts

Campo Blaumaņa iela 22/24, Rīga ☏922 2339, ⊛www.laivas.lv. Canoe rental, advice and guided canoe trips on the Gauja. They can also organize the transport of your canoe to and from the Gauja – at a cost of 0.25Ls per kilometre.

Cēsu Tūrisma Inventāra Noma Uzvaras 30, Cēsis ☏412 0458, ✉Ielde.pole @navigators.lv. Canoe (3–10Ls/day) and tent rental (1–2.50Ls/day).

Eži Valdemāra iela 1, Valmiera ☏428 1764, ⊛www.ezi.lv. Canoe rental and guided one- to three-day tours.

Makars Peldu 1, Sigulda ☏297 3724, ⊛www.makars.lv. Canoes (10–20Ls/day), rowing boats (1Ls/hr) and tents (1.50Ls/day) for rent. Guided one- to three-day tours.

---

examine the park's flora and fauna at close quarters, while the reconstructed lake-village at **Āraiši**, just south of Cēsis, provides a fascinating insight into the lives of the Latvians' ancient forebears.

Throughout the park you'll find a multitude of **forest and riverbank trails** suitable for exploration on foot or by bike, while **canoeing** down the Gauja itself is a particularly invigorating way of enjoying the scenery. Although the pistes at Sigulda and Cēsis are puny by alpine standards, the potential of the area as a low-level, laid-back **skiing** centre shouldn't be overlooked – given the rigours of the Baltic winter, at least snow cover is guaranteed.

Jāņa sēta's 1:100 000 *Gaujas nacionālais parks* **map**, on sale in local tourist offices, covers the whole region, and comes with smaller-scale inset maps of Līgatne, Āraiši and other key localities.

Sigulda and around

Sprawled across a plateau on the south bank of the River Gauja, **SIGULDA** is not so much a town as a vast leafy park with a few houses and apartment blocks tastefully scattered across it. Close to some of the most beautiful stretches of the Gauja Valley, it has been Latvia's most popular inland resort ever since the mid-nineteenth century, when the construction of the Rīga–Valka railway line put it within reach of vacationing St Petersburg folk. It's a great base for short- and mid-range walking, with a variety of woodland and riverbank trails within easy striking distance of the town centre. It's also the obvious starting point for visits to the reconstructed castle

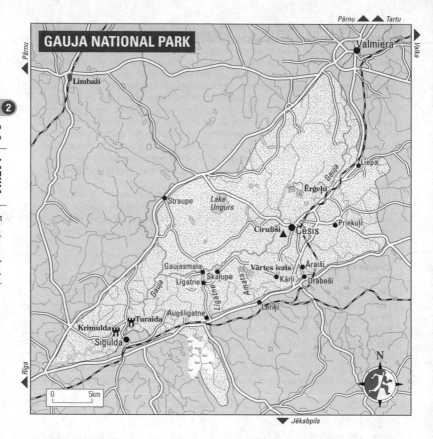

at **Turaida** and the nineteenth-century aristocratic seat of **Krimulda**, both of which adorn hilltops on the opposite side of the valley. In the colder months, **winter sports** enthusiasts flock here to experience the thrills of the country's only Olympic-standard bobsleigh track and its downhill ski runs. Key summer events include the **balloon festival**, which draws international competitors every May, and an **Opera Festival** in late July/early August, usually featuring top-rank performers from all over the Baltic States and Russia.

Arrival and information

Sigulda is an easy day-trip from Rīga, with **buses** and **trains** running almost hourly. If you're approaching from the east, catch a Cēsis–Rīga or Valmiera–Rīga bus – these don't actually pass through Sigulda's town centre, but pick up and drop off on the main highway 1km south.

Sigulda's centrally located **tourist office**, in the same building as the *Sigulda Hotel* at Pils 4A (☎ & ☎297 1335), can advise on local sights and activities, although the **Gauja National Park Visitors' Centre**, Baznīcas 3 (Mon 9.30am–4.30pm, Tues–Sun 9.30am–6pm; ☎797 1345, ⊛www.gnp.gov.lv), is better informed about hiking trails and sells a wider range of maps.

You can rent **bikes** from Buru sports, 1km south of the centre at the junction of Gāles iela and the main Rīga–Cēsis highway; and Eži, which has a summer-only kiosk at Pils iela 4. For **canoe** and rowing boat rentals see the box on p.263.

Accommodation

Despite Sigulda's popularity, it's primarily a day-trip or weekend destination and doesn't have as many **hotels** as you might think – those that do exist are generally neat, clean and invariably come with saunas. Less expensive accommodation is available in a handful of suburban **B&Bs** (❶–❷) – ask at the tourist office about these and they'll book you into one. **Hostel** accommodation is available at the Krimulda sanatorium (see p.268), a bus ride or forty-minute walk away on the north side of the valley, where beds are as little as 5Ls per person, but they're used to dealing with groups rather than individuals, so it's best to get the tourist office to ring them up and ask about vacancies before you head out. Campers are well catered for by the attractive riverside **campsite**, *Siguldas pludmale*, equipped with toilet blocks and electricity points, on the west side of town at Peldu 1 (☎797 3724, ⓦ www.makars.lv).

Aparjods Ventas 1B ☎770 5225, ⓦ www.aparjods.lv. Medium-sized place at the southwestern end of town just off the Rīga–Cēsis highway. Built in folksy style (complete with shingle roof), but the rooms inside are modern, with shower and TV. ❸

Ezeri ☎797 3009, ⓦ www.hotelezeri.lv. Cosy, small-scale place set in meadows south of town, offering tasteful en-suites. ❸

Līvkalns Pēteralas ☎797 0916, ⓦ www.livkalns.lv. Five pine-furnished rooms in a large, reed-thatched house on the eastern edge of town, within easy striking distance of the Satezele

Castle Mound. ❸

Senleja Turaidas iela 4 ☎797 2162. Drab Soviet-era block offering uninspiring but acceptable rooms with shower in a wonderful wooded riverbank location. Three kilometres out of town on the north side of the Gauja, just off the road to Turaida and Krimulda; Krimulda-bound buses stop off at the access road. ❶

Sigulda Pils iela 6 ☎797 2263, ⓦ www.hotelsigulda.lv. Nineteenth-century hotel bang in the centre, with smart, renovated en suites with TV, and a tiny indoor pool. ❸

The Town

From the train station **Raiņa iela** runs north through the centre of town, passing the bus station before forging through a swathe of parkland shaded by limes, oaks and maples. After about 800m, a right turn into **Baznīcas iela** takes you past the brilliant-white spire of the thirteenth-century **Lutheran church** (Luterānu baznī-ca) and on to **Sigulda New Castle** (Siguldas Jaunā Pils), a nineteenth-century manor house with medieval pretensions, sporting an ostentatiously crenellated tur-ret and now used as offices by the town council. Out in front, regimented flowerbeds lie in the shade of a monument to Atis Kronvalds (1837–1875), a promi-nent nineteenth-century publicist who energetically promoted Latvian-language education at a time when knowledge of German was seen as the only passport to a successful career.

Immediately north of the New Castle, a path leads across a long-dried-up moat to the ruins of **Sigulda Castle** (Siguldas Pilsdrupas), a thirteenth-century Livonian Order stronghold built from rough-hewn blocks of honey-coloured stone. Behind it lies an outdoor stage which is put to good use during the summer opera festival, and beyond that is a knobbly hillock which affords sweeping views of the Gauja Valley, with the fat red tower of Turaida castle (see p.267) spearing up out of the forest to the north.

More fine views across the valley can be savoured by following footpaths east from the castle ruins to Miera iela, then heading northwards to the ridge known as **Artist's Hill** (Gleznotāju kalns), which offers an expansive panorama of Turaida, Krimulda and the surrounding woodland – unsurprisingly it was a favourite spot with early-twentieth-century landscape painters Jānis Rozentāls and Vilhelms Purvītis. Southeast of here, paths descend steeply to meet the Vējupite stream, which flows into the Gauja a few hundred metres to the north. Heading south along the Vējupite will take you past the **Satezele Castle Mound** (Satezeles pil-skalns), a Liv stronghold associated with semi-legendary chieftain Dabrelis, who

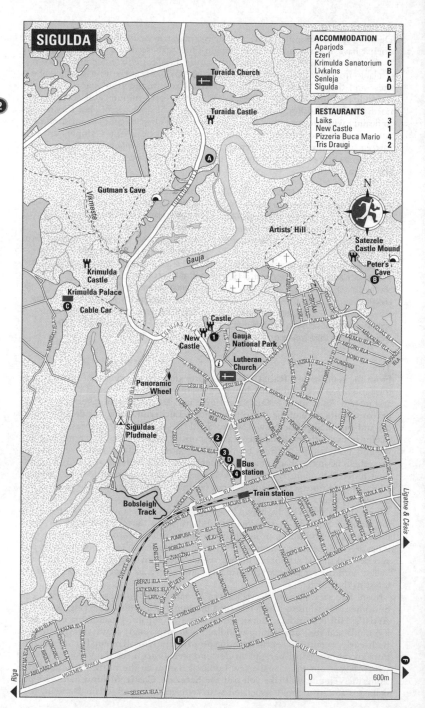

SIGULDA

ACCOMMODATION
Aparjods	E
Ezeri	F
Krimulda Sanatorium	C
Livkalns	B
Senleja	A
Sigulda	D

RESTAURANTS
Laiks	3
New Castle	1
Pizzeria Buca Mario	4
Tris Draugi	2

Turaida Church

Turaida Castle

Gutman's Cave

Vikmeste

Krimulda Castle

Krimulda Palace

Cable Car

Artists' Hill

Satezele Castle Mound

Peter's Cave

Gauja

Castle

New Castle

Gauja National Park

Lutheran Church

Panoramic Wheel

Siguldas Pludmale

Bobsleigh Track

Bus station

Train station

Līgatne & Cēsis

N

0   600m

fought unsuccessfully to stem the Teutonic advance in the early thirteenth century – a stepped pathway leads to the summit for more valley views.

Over on the western side of Sigulda, a five-minute walk from Raiņa iela along Cēsu iela, the ferris-style **Panoramic Wheel** (Panorāmas rats; May–Sept daily 9am–5pm; 1Ls) provides another way of getting to grips with the Gauja landscape, affording views across the valley to Krimulda and Turaida. South of the wheel, a steep, west-facing escarpment becomes a ski piste in winter and is the site of the town's state-of-the-art **toboggan and bobsleigh track** (Kamaniņu un bobsleja trase). As well as hosting World Cup luge and bobsleigh events in winter, the track is put to good use from May to October when you can descend the course in a "summer bob" – a thick-tyred, futuristic-looking silver kart – for 3Ls per person.

From Sigulda to Turaida

From central Sigulda, Gaujas iela descends towards the bridge over the Gauja, and then heads north along the northern bank of the river before climbing up to **Turaida castle**, some 3km distant. Sigulda–Krimulda buses pass along this route roughly every hour, but you're unlikely to take in much of the scenery through the window – walking at least part of the way seems a good idea.

Starting on the far side of the bridge from Sigulda, paths lead away from the main road and into the shadow of the densely forested escarpment that overlooks the valley from the northwest. Here, all kinds of alternative trails and interesting detours present themselves: you can head due west up to Krimulda (see p.268), or follow the path (built by American-Latvian youth in 1990, as the signboard proudly proclaims) that winds its way up the enchanting, wooded gully of the Vikmeste stream before emerging at the top of the ridge midway between Turaida and Krimulda. Alternatively, you can stick to the valley floor, following a level trail that runs past a sequence of small lakes and several sandstone caves. Despite its small, unexciting proportions, **Gūtman's cave** (Gūtmaņa ala) is the most famous of these fissures, not least because of the key role it plays in the story of *Turaida Rose* – a heady tale of love, death and Latvian virtue. National poet Jānis Rainis based his play *Love is Stronger than Death* (Mīla stiprāka pār nāvi) on the story and most Latvian schoolchildren know the plot by heart. The rose in question was a seventeenth-century local maiden named Maija, who fell in love with the Turaida castle gardener Viktor, while at the same time being subject to the unwanted advances of Polish army deserter, Adam Jakubovsky (the suitor is a Swedish officer in some versions of the tale). When Jakubovsky trapped her in Gutman's cave, she wound a scarf given to her by Viktor around her neck in the hope that it would shield her from evil. When the Pole struck out with his sword, however, the scarf unsurprisingly failed to provide the degree of protection expected. Maija's murder was initially pinned on Viktor, but he was released when a guilt-tormented Jakubovsky committed suicide.

Beyond the cave the path rejoins the main road for the final 800-metre climb to the **Turaida Museum Reserve** (daily: May–Oct 9.30am–6pm; Nov–April 10am–5pm; 1Ls), which comprises a partially reconstructed castle and extensive grounds scattered with outbuildings. Built on the site of a Liv stockade fort, Turaida was one of the bishop of Rīga's key strongholds from 1214 onwards, surviving numerous wars until finally reduced to rubble when lightning hit its gunpowder magazine in the early eighteenth century. Rebuilding began in the 1960s and the sight of Turaida's trio of red-brick towers, rising rocket-like from the jagged sea of pines, is one you'll see on many a Latvian tourist poster. The local history museum inside the castle (Tues–Sun 10am–5/6pm; 0.80Ls) is a bit of an anti-climax, with sundry cannonballs and suits of armour struggling to breathe life into a familiar narrative of indigenous Latvians and Livs being ousted by a cavalcade of foreign conquerors. Outside the castle, the eighteenth-century **Turaida Church** (Turaidas baznīca), an appealing little wooden building with a Baroque tower, is one of the best-preserved examples of Latvian native architecture in the country. Just outside the church, a plaque honouring the Turaida Rose is one of the most popular venues in the country for the post-wedding photo shoot.

Krimulda

Commanding superb views of the Gauja Valley 2.5km southwest of Turaida is the custard-coloured, neoclassical **Krimulda palace** (Krimuldas pils), seat of the Baltic German Lieven family in the nineteenth century and now a sanatorium. Though the palace is closed to visitors, the wooded ridge-top setting provides reason enough to visit. There's a neat park with flowerbeds on the western side of the building, while over to the east lie the fragmentary remains of **Krimulda castle** (Krimuldas pilsdrupas), a thirteenth-century stronghold perched dramatically on a rocky bluff overlooking over the valley.

As well as being served by Sigulda–Krimulda buses, the sanatorium can also be reached by paths from the Gauja Valley (notably from the Vikmestes taka; see p.267). The most stylish way to arrive, though, is by **cablecar** (Gaisa trosu ceļš; May–Sept weekends only 9am–5pm; 0.50Ls; ⓦwww.lgk.lv), which sets off from the terminal on Poruka iela in Sigulda every hour.

Eating and drinking

The best **restaurant** in Sigulda is in the New Castle (see p.265), offering an international menu, decent wine list and scenic outdoor terrace. More functional is the *Pizzeria Buca Mario*, behind the bus station; it's fast, cheap, but still civilized enough for a sit-down evening meal. Otherwise, try *Tris draugi*, Pils 9, a glass-fronted pavilion with a canteen-style food counter at one end and a bar open till 2am at the other, or *Laiks*, near the tourist office on Pils iela, a homely **pub** with daily food specials chalked up outside.

Līgatne Nature Trail and around

Twelve kilometres northeast of Sigulda, the **Līgatne Nature Trail** (Līgatnes dabas takas) provides one of the best ways to sample the sheer variety of the Gauja Valley landscape. Located on the south bank of the river, the trail meanders through a changing landscape of dense pine woods, evergreen forest and meadow clearings, and also gives access to some cliff-lined stretches of the riverbank itself. Entrance to the trail is 2km west of the village of **Gaujasmala** and 3km northwest of the village of **Līgatne**, which in turn is 5.5km north of its sister settlement on the main Rīga–Cēsis highway – variously called Augšlīgatne ("Upper Līgatne"), Līgatnes stacija ("Līgatne Station") or simply "Līgatne", depending on which map you look at. It's this place that Rīga–Cēsis **trains and buses** serve: once here, you can either walk to Līgatne proper (1hr), or wait for one of the six daily buses (three at weekends) which start at the train station, then call at Augšlīgatne's main bus stop before continuing to Līgatne proper, terminating at Gaujasmala. If you're approaching from the Cēsis direction, you can take one of the three daily Cēsis–Līgatne–Gaujasmala buses (weekdays only).

Līgatne and Gaujasmala

LĪGATNE village is a pretty little place hugging the banks of the Līgatne stream, a tributary of the Gauja, here overlooked by a handsome set of the region's trademark red sandstone cliffs. The village possesses a modest café and a couple of food shops for stocking up on picnic fare. From the main crossroads, Dārza iela winds west then north before coming to a T-junction after 2km: a left turn takes you to the Līgatne Nature Trail (see opposite), while a right turn leads directly into grubby **GAUJASMALA**, a village of Soviet-era apartment blocks, worth visiting on account of its **ferry** (pārceltuve; May–Sept: shuttle service 6am–11pm; 0.20Ls per person; 1Ls per vehicle). Basically a small open-topped raft, guided across the river by a fixed chain, it's one of the last such contraptions still in use in the Baltics.

There's a free **campsite** next to the riverbank, supplied with a couple of rudimentary earth toilets.

Līgatne Nature Trail

Established in 1975, **Līgatne Nature Trail** (May–Sept Mon 9.30am–5pm, Tues–Sun 9.30am–6.30pm; 1Ls) is basically an open-plan zoo of indigenous fauna, including brown bears and bobcats, with several large enclosures scattered, safari-park style, over a wide area. The animals spend the summer roaming their spacious quarters at Līgatne, returning to Rīga zoo (see p.217) for the winter. Getting from one enclosure to another involves passing through undulating terrain carpeted in sweet-smelling forest, and it's this that constitutes the trail's main appeal. There are two circular routes about 6km long – one for cars, one for pedestrians – both of which pass the principal enclosures; the information desk at the entrance will provide you with a map. Things are in any case well signposted along the trail and it's easy to find the most popular way-stations: a field full of aurochs (European bison) on the eastern side of the circuit, and a wooded hillside over to the west populated by brown bears – although extinct in Latvia by the late nineteenth century, the creatures began migrating back from Estonia in the 1970s. Elsewhere you'll see wild boar, roe deer, red deer and (if you're very lucky) lynx. A couple of subsidiary footpaths lead off the main trail and are well worth exploring: one track (the Gaujmalas taka or "Gauja bank trail") heads west from the information kiosk towards the riverbank, where you can admire the **Gūdu iezis** sandstone outcrop on the opposite bank, while another (the Neskartās dabas taka or "wild nature trail") branches off just south of the brown-bear enclosure and heads down **Paparžu grava**, a leafy gully whose name – "fern glen" – gives you some idea of what kind of undergrowth to expect.

The information kiosk at the entrance to the trail sells snacks, and there's a free riverside **campsite** at Katrīnas iezis 500m north of the kiosk. Back in Augšlīgatne, the *Mana Muiža* **hotel** beside the main Rīga–Cēsis highway (☎415 5505; ❸) has a handful of smart en-suite rooms and a decent **café–restaurant**.

The Amata Valley

Providing you have your own transport, it's easy to combine a trip to the Līgatne nature trail with a visit to the winding, steep-sided valley of the Amata River, a fast-flowing tributary which joins the Gauja 7km northeast of Gaujasmala. The most picturesque part of the valley is the rocky outcrop known as **Vārtes iezis**, reached by following the Skaļupes–Kārļi road out of Līgatne village, heading straight on for 10km, then taking a (signed) turn-off to the right, that leads after another 2km to a car park and a national park information board. Overlooking the car park from the west bank of the river, Vārtes iezis is on the edge of the Roču meža woodland reserve, an area of dense coniferous cover, most of which is closed to the public. However, you can gain a flavour of the landscape by following a footpath from the car park that crosses the Amata and works its way up onto the cliff-top before looping back down again. An equally attractive trail heads north from the car park and hugs the east bank of the river, which zigzags its way between a further stretch of forest-shrouded cliffs. Each of the trails takes under an hour to complete.

Cēsis and around

The well-preserved, laid-back market town of **CĒSIS** (pronounced "*Tsaah*-sis"), on a hillside, 35km northeast of Sigulda, is reckoned by many Latvians to come as close as you'll get to pre-war, small-town Latvia. The knot of narrow streets at its heart, characterized by sturdy stone houses and one-storey timber dwellings, was largely undamaged in World War II and spared any significant modernization in the years that followed. The town's other main draws are its moody **castle ruins**, fine

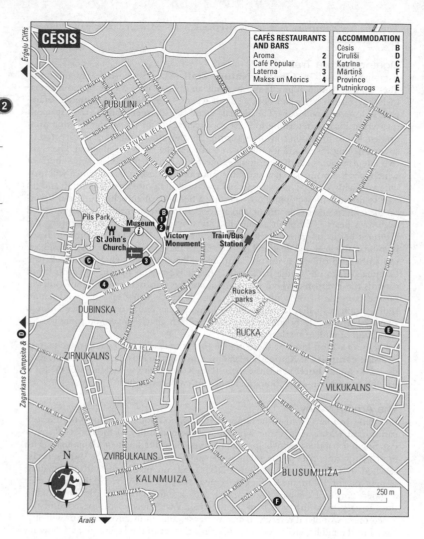

museum and convenience as a touring base for the rest of the Gauja Valley; particularly close at hand are Līgatne, the Iron Age settlement at **Āraiši** and **Ērģeļu cliff** being particularly close at hand. The Gauja riverbank 3km west of town is one of the main starting points for canoe trips heading downstream (see p.263), while the steep escarpment above it is the raison d'être of the popular downhill skiing resort of **Cīrulīši**.

Cēsis was one of the Livonian Order's key power centres, serving as the official seat of their grand master, as well as being an important trading post on the route to Russian towns Pskov and Novgorod. By World War I it had also garnered a reputation as a minor spa resort, encouraging the locals – no doubt carried away by the Gauja Valley's "Livonian Switzerland" tag – to dub it the "Davos of the Baltic", though rest-cures are now largely a thing of the past.

Arrival and information

Both **buses** and trains use the **train station** building 500m east of the main square, Vienības laukums: bus timetables and ticket windows are on the left-hand side as you enter from the street; train timetables and tickets are on the other. The helpful **tourist office** lies five minutes' west of the square at Pils laukums 1 (June–Sept Mon–Fri 9am–6pm, Sat & Sun 10am–5pm; Oct–May Mon–Fri 9am–5pm; ☎ & ℱ 412 1815, ⦿ www.cesis.lv).

Cēsu Tūrisma Inventāra Noma, at Uzvaras 30, rents out **canoes** and boats; see box on p.263 for more details. If you prefer to stick to dry land, **renting a bike** is also a good way of exploring the area (suggested trails are available from the tourist office). You can rent bikes from the above agency (6Ls/day) and also from the summer-only Eži kiosk at Lenču 7A.

Accommodation

Cēsis has a decent range of hotels, with a handful of stylishly modern establishments in the centre of town and a scattering of cheap-and-simple options in the suburbs. The nearest **campsite** is *Zagarkalns* (☎ 412 5225, ⦿ www.zagarkalns.lv), pleasantly sited on the shores of Lake Ungurs (Ungura ezers), 15km northeast on the Limbaži road; as well as space for tents, there are four-person cabins for 20Ls.

Cēsis Vienības laukums 1 ☎ 412 2392, ⦿ www.danlat-group.lv. A recently modernized inter-war hotel right on the main square, offering thick-carpeted en-suites with bathtubs, and high standards of service. ❹

Cīrulīši Kovārņu 22 ☎ 412 5476, ⦿ www.atputa-cirulisi.lv. A Soviet-era hotel and sanatorium near the ski slopes southwest of town. It looks pretty grim from the outside, but the rooms are all en-suite, clean and have new furniture. ❶

Katrīna Maza Katrīnas iela 8 ☎ 410 7700, ℮ hotelkatrina@apollo.lv. A modern but cosy eight-room place. Rooms are smallish with shower and TV, each decorated in a different colour. ❹

Mārtiņš Rīta 9 ☎ 412 3678, ℮ martins@martins.apollo.lv. B&B-style accommodation, twenty minutes' walk north of the centre, featuring neat en-suites with Sat-TV, friendly hosts, and a decent buffet breakfast. ❷

Province Niniera iela 6 ☎ 412 0849. A five-room hotel in conveniently central location. Soothing decor and smart en-suite rooms with TV. ❸

Putniņkrogs Saules 23 ☎ 412 0290. Located in a housing estate fifteen minutes' walk east of the centre, this hotel offers simple rooms with battered furniture and weird scraps of carpet, with WC/shower in the hallway – but it's basically clean and secure. Breakfast isn't included, though there's a café next door. ❶

The Town

Marking the eastern entrance to Cēsis's town centre is the broad square, **Vienības laukums**, dominated by the quirky, impressive **Victory Monument**, an obelisk licked by concrete flames and topped by what looks like a golden ping-pong ball. Erected in the 1920s, demolished by the Soviets in the 1950s (presumably for political rather than aesthetic reasons) and reconstructed in the 1990s, it commemorates June 1919's **Battle of Cēsis**, an impressive display of pan-Baltic cooperation in which an Estonian army, backed up by Latvian volunteers, defeated the Iron Division of German General von der Goltz. The Estonians chased von der Goltz's men all the way back to Rīga, only to be dissuaded from finishing them off entirely by the British, who argued that German troops might still come in useful in helping to fight off the Bolsheviks, proving difficult to dislodge from Latvia's southeastern corner.

Southwest of the square, Skolas iela descends towards the thirteenth-century **St John's Church** (Sv Jāņa Baznīca), a heavily buttressed structure containing the tombs of several masters of the Livonian Order, most notably Walter von Plettenberg (1494–1535). Something of a national hero among Baltic Germans, Plettenberg pushed back seemingly unstoppable Russian offensives at the beginning of the sixteenth century, winning a brief but significant respite for the Livonian Order – which struggled on for another fifty years before bequeathing its territories to the Poles and the Swedes. The narrow streets just west of the church are among Cēsis's most atmospheric, with one-storey wooden dwellings huddled over the cobbles.

Heading north from the church along Torņa iela, you soon come to **Cēsis castle** (Cēsu pils), a complex comprising the Livonian Order's original fortress, begun in the thirteenth century and now a picturesque ruin; and an eighteenth-century annexe which today holds the **Museum of History and Art** (Cēsu vēstures un mākslas muzejs; mid–May to mid–Sept Tues–Sun 10am–5pm; 0.50Ls), the admission fee to which also gives access to the castle ruins. The museum is one of the country's more entertaining historical collections, getting under way with intricately fashioned jewellery unearthed from twelfth-century Latvian graves – including necklaces festooned with bronze toggles and miniature horse shapes. Costumes in the ethnographic section, in rich red-grey check patterns and green-grey stripes, have an understated beauty about them, typical of Latvian folk art. After rooms devoted to local landscape painters and grainy photographs of 1919's Battle of Cēsis, steps climb to the summit of the Ladermacher tower, a fifteenth-century bastion affording sweeping views of the surrounding hills.

From the base of the Ladermacher tower a doorway leads out towards the medieval **castle**, built by the crusading Knights of the Sword in 1207 and subsequently inherited by their successor organization, the Livonian Order – whose first grand master, Hermann Balk, moved here in 1239. It continued to serve intermittently as the master's residence until the mid-sixteenth century, after which the conquering Swedes turned it into an administrative nerve centre for the whole of northeastern Latvia. The Russians took the castle in 1703, severely damaging it in the process and leaving it to fall into ruin. All that remains are a couple of stout, barrel-like towers, together with a scrap of the central keep.

On a forest-fringed bluff overlooking the Gauja Valley, 2.5km southwest of the town centre, **Cīrulīši** (reached on minibus #5 or #9) is the most popular downhill skiing resort in Latvia after Sigulda (see p.267), although its three short pistes and small snowboard park (all served by drag lift; passes 2Ls/hr) are unlikely to set the pulse racing.

Eating and drinking

The best **restaurant** in town is the formal, starched-napkin restaurant of the *Cēsis* hotel, with an eclectic menu of main courses at 6–8Ls and some superb sweets. *Café Popular*, in the basement of the same building, offers filling Latvian meat-and-two-veg meals at a third of the price; and *Laterna*, at Rīgas 25, has a big beer garden down a side alley and a decent menu of omelettes, pancakes and pork chops. *Aroma*, Lenču iela 4, is the prime venue for freshly made pastries and cakes, while the best place for a **drink** is *Makss un Morics*, a snug but stylish little bar at Rīgas 43. There's a **market** five minutes' northwest of the train/bus stations on Uzvaras iela.

Ērģeļu cliff

Of all the rocky outcrops overhanging the waters of the Gauja, **Ērģeļu cliff** (Ērģeļu klintis; Ērģļu klintis on some maps), 7km north of Cēsis, is probably the most dramatic, a wavy line of sandstone some 500m long and topped with dark-green conifers. To get there take Lenču iela from Cēsis's main square and keep going as far as Pieškalni – a car park on the far side of the village marks the end of the road. A further five minutes on foot brings you to the top of the cliff, from where you can follow trails either east or west along the summit – either way, expect some stunning views of the surrounding riverscape.

Āraiši

Seven kilometres south of Cēsis, the rustic lakeside village of **ĀRAIŠI** would be a charming enough spot for a stroll even without the added attraction of **Āraiši**

Lake Fortress (Āraišu ezerpils; May to mid-Oct daily 10am–6pm; 0.60Ls), a modern-day reconstruction of an Iron Age settlement. Built on a man-made island and joined to the lakeshore by a causeway, it's an exact replica of the ninth-century original that once stood on this very site. It's not really a "fortress", rather a compact village with fifteen dwellings, rendered defensible by its watery location. Shrouded by reeds and with the ruddy roof of Āraiši village church in the background, it couldn't be more picturesque. Locally available trees provided the raw material for almost everything in the lake dwelling, with the tiny log-built houses with bark roofs huddled together on wooden decking. The houses are currently bare inside, although the addition of sleeping benches, domestic artefacts and authentically attired mannequins is planned for the future.

Once you've had a look at the lake dwelling, there's plenty in the way of minor attractions to justify lingering a little while, beginning with the ruins of **Āraiši castle** (Āraišu pilsdrupas), sitting on a hillock immediately to the southeast. Built by the Livonian Order in the thirteenth century, it was abandoned after Ivan the Terrible's Russians sacked it in 1577.

Heading northwards around the lake brings you to **Āraiši village** and its slender-spired parish church, erected in the thirteenth century and rebuilt in the eighteenth – when a human skeleton was found bricked up in the wall. The discovery soon entered local folklore, with villagers claiming that the church's original architect had pledged to ensure the structure's longevity by immuring the next human being he saw, unaware that his own daughter was at that moment advancing up the street with his lunch. Finally, for a great view back towards lake, fortress and village, it's worth walking as far as the **windmill** on the low hill to the west, its overhanging wooden canopy looking like an upturned boat.

At least one daily Rīga–Cēsis **bus** passes through Āraiši itself; most other Rīga–Cēsis services use the main road 1km west of the site – get off at the Betes stop and walk via the windmill, clearly visible on the brow of the hill above the road. In addition, four daily Rīga–Cēsis **trains** call at the Āraiši halt, although it's 2.5km southeast of the village.

The Daugava Valley

Rising in the same part of western Russia as the Volga and the Dniepr, the 1020-kilometre-long **Daugava** is the longest and most majestic waterway in the country, flowing through Belarus and Latvia before emptying into the Gulf of Rīga. The Daugava Valley has been Latvia's main northwest–southeast **transport corridor** since time immemorial and until the twentieth century was busy with rafts and barges carrying timber, hemp, flax and hides downriver to the export markets of Rīga. Nowadays, goods travel via the main road and rail routes on the right bank of the Daugava, the river itself having been rendered unnavigable by the construction of a series of **hydroeletric projects**, that together provide for the bulk of the country's energy needs. The first of these, damming the river at Ķegums, was built by the Ulmanis regime in 1937 and was a symbol of Latvian technological progress at the time, although subsequent, Soviet-era projects have proved much more controversial. Upriver at Aizkraukle, the Pļaviņas Reservoir (Pļaviņu ūdenskrātuve) project involved flooding the most picturesque part of the Daugava Valley and only went ahead after patriotic-minded politicians had been purged from the Latvian Communist Party in the late 1950s. A project planned (but never completed) further upstream near Daugavpils provoked one of the first environmentalist protests in the Soviet Union in 1986, when Latvian intellectuals, grouped around cultural weekly *Literatūra un māksla*, successfully called for its cancellation.

Such ecological concerns are understandable given the importance of the Daugava landscape in Latvian culture. As the country's longest river it has inspired more mythic tales and folk songs than any other inland geographical feature. Nineteenth-century writer **Andrējs Pumpurs** (see box on p.275) set much of the action of his epic poem *Lāčplēsis* on the Daugava riverbank. Upriver from Rīga, the writer's home town, **Lielvārde**, with its Pumpurs museum and reconstructed Iron Age stockade fort, is the first of the riverside settlements worth a stop. Further upstream, the ruined castle at **Koknese** is an evocative place to ponder the river's history, although it's the prosperous market town of **Jēkabpils** that offers most in terms of sightseeing potential.

Getting up and down the valley is easy enough, with Rīga–Daugavpils **buses** passing through the main settlements on the right bank. Using the Daugava Valley rail route (served by Rīga–Daugavpils, Rīga–Rēzekne and some commuter trains), you can quite feasibly train-hop your way up the valley, visit a few sights, and still get back to Rīga before nightfall – although bear in mind that most of the train stations are some way away from the town centres they serve, so you'll need to employ a certain amount of leg power to get around.

Upstream to Lielvārde

Though not really worth a stop-off, the small town of **IKŠĶILE**, 40km out of Rīga, is worth a mention for its historical significance, for it was here that the first ever Christian church in the Baltics was built by German missionaries in 1188. It was sacked, however, by pagan Latvian tribesmen soon after the death of its founder, Meinhard von Uexküll (buried in Rīga cathedral; see p.196), giving warrior-priest Albert von Buxhoeveden the excuse he needed to launch his bloody crusade in 1201, subjecting the Latvians to centuries of Teutonic tutelage as a result. Ten kilometres beyond lies **OGRE**, a bland, modern town serving the hydroelectric plant at Ķegums 10km upstream, although – thanks to its dry microclimate – it was once a top spa destination for Rīga folk and the place where most of Latvia's TB sufferers ended up during the inter-war years.

The first town upstream from Rīga worth spending some time in is **LIELVĀRDE**, situated midway along a broad stretch of the Daugava – the Ķegums dam upstream causes the river to widen here. It's an uneventful little place with a rather nondescript town centre, but has a brace of intriguing sights on its riverside outskirts. The first of these, the reconstructed **Ancient Latvian castle** (Senlatviešu pils; April–Nov daily 10am–6pm; 0.50Ls), is right beside the Rīga–Daugavpils highway at the western entrance to town. Its outer perimeter bristling with sharpened stakes, this timber-built stockade fort is a reasonably authentic approximation of what twelfth-century strongholds would have looked like in general rather than the exact replica of one in particular. Quite small in scale, such forts supported only a small population of warriors in peacetime, filling up with civilians from the surrounding farmsteads in times of war. The simple log dwellings crowding the courtyard are all chimneyless – it's thought that the inhabitants only lit fires for the length of time it took to warm their heat-radiating hearthstones. With its dinky wooden ramparts, the whole scene looks more like an adventure playground for adults than a military installation – it's not difficult to see why the log-based civilization of the Latvian chieftains was so quickly brushed aside by the crusading Knights of the Sword.

About 2.5km southeast of the fortress, on the far side of the town centre, a tree-lined lane leads from the main road to the **Andrējs Pumpurs Museum** (Tues–Sat 10am–5pm; 0.50Ls), honouring the locally born author (see box opposite) of the epic tale of *Lāčplēsis*, bear-slaying hero and symbol of Latvia's resistance to outside rule. The display of photographs, facsimile manuscripts and first editions is less exciting than the museum's park-like setting, with a riverside path leading past wooden sculptures inspired by Pumpurs' poem to the cliff-top ruins of **Lielvārde castle**, a crusader stronghold built on the site of an earlier Latvian stockade fort.

Practicalities
Served by frequent commuter services from Rīga, Lielvārde **train station** is at the northwestern end of town, a five-minute walk from the ancient Latvian castle.

Andrējs Pumpurs (1841–1902)

A versatile journalist and poet, **Andrējs Pumpurs** is primarily remembered for *Lāčplēsis*, a composition in verse that weaves numerous Latvian folk tales into a harmonious, epic whole. Born at Birzgale, near Lielvārde, and receiving only an elementary education, Pumpurs worked as an agricultural worker and assistant land surveyor before heading for Moscow in 1876 to join the Slav Volunteer Regiment, a unit formed by idealistic young Russians to aid Serbia in its struggles against the Ottoman Empire. With combat experience in the Balkans under his belt, Pumpurs made easy work of an officer training course in Odessa and spent the rest of his years occupying a succession of administrative posts in the Russian army.

Despite unswerving loyalty to the Russian Empire, Pumpurs was a keen champion of Latvian culture and had been writing for the burgeoning Latvian-language press since his twenties. Pumpurs saw Latvian folklore in particular as a profound source of cultural and spiritual wealth, the study of which he believed would help the Latvians – a politically powerless people ruled over by Russian bureaucrats and German-speaking landowners – to regain a sense of self-respect. Enthused by the work of Elias Lönnrot in Finland and Friedrich Reinhold Kreuzwald (see p.393) in Estonia – both of whom had used traditional folk material to compose chest-beating epic poems – Pumpurs set out to produce a Latvian equivalent.

Like Kreuzwald, Pumpurs was prepared to invent the narrative himself if the folk fragments available to him didn't add up to the kind of epic story he was looking for. He chose an archetypal character from Latvian myth, born of man and female bear (and, in original folk versions, blessed with a pair of bear's ears), and transformed him into Lāčplēsis, the "Bear Slayer", a virtuous youth bestowed with almost superhuman strengths – including the ability to tear wild beasts apart with his bare hands.

Pumpurs then put Lāčplēsis through all manner of adventures – battling sorceresses, helping out good chieftains in their struggles against the bad – in order to showcase the richness and diversity of Latvian lore. Many of Pumpurs' protagonists were either his own inventions or composite figures drawn from numerous traditional sources, but they soon entered the national consciousness and are nowadays treated as authentic characters from national mythology – two of the most popular being Staburadze, the water nymph who lives in a crystal palace beneath the waters of the Daugava, and Laimdota, the sugar-and-spice Latvian girl who tends Lāčplēsis's wounds. However Pumpurs' overriding aim was to provide the Latvians with an action hero with whom they could identify in what he saw as their coming struggle with the Baltic German aristocracy. The world of fairies, witches and forest sprites that Lāčplēsis inhabits is a clear metaphor for an idealized, pre-conquest Latvia that existed before German-speaking crusaders arrived on their shores, and it's no accident that the bear-bashing protagonist fights his last battle against the unmistakably Teuton Black Knight. The story ends with Lāčplēsis making the ultimate sacrifice, dragging his adversary with him over a cliff and into the murky waters of the Daugava.

Buses working the Rīga–Jēkabpils–Daugavpils route pick up and drop off at stops at the northeastern end of town near the castle and at the southeastern end, near the lane to the Pumpurs Museum. Handily placed – just opposite the train station – is a comfortable **B&B** in the shape of *Oši*, (☎507 1855; ❷). The best place to pick up supplies is the Olvi supermarket, midway between castle and museum at Lielvārde's central crossroads, and it also has a **café** attached.

From Lielvārde to Jēkabpils

Beyond Lielvārde there's little to slow your progress until you get to **SKRĪVERI**, a further 30km upriver, where the roadside **Dendrological park** (Dendroloģiskais parks) gathers together more than 380 tree species from all over the world. First planted by lord of the local manor, Max von Sivers, in 1891, it remains surprisingly little visited and the expanse of parkland criss-crossed by trails has an appealing wild and untamed feel.

Ten kilometres beyond Skrīveri, **AIZKRAUKLE** was built from scratch in the 1960s to house workers at the nearby Pļaviņas hydroelectric project and has been burdened ever since with the unofficial title of ugliest town in Latvia. It's a good 4km west of the main road and rail lines – savouring the blur of housing blocks that appears on your right as you speed past is probably the best way to experience it.

Rather more interesting is the smaller town of **KOKNESE**, 20km further on, where a single street leads down from the train station and main road to the remains of a **riverside fortress** built by the German crusaders in 1209. The castle was robbed of its romantic cliff-top position by the rising water level resulting from the construction of the Pļaviņas dam, but the Daugava-lapped ruin still possesses undeniable charm. The dam also dwarfed the erstwhile majesty of **Staburags cliff**, which used to tower above the river just upstream from Koknese on the opposite bank. As the rock from which the eponymous hero of Andrējs Pumpurs's *Lāčplēsis* (see p.275) hurls both himself and the Black Knight, Staburags occupies an important place in the Latvian psyche – and its near-disappearance under the Pļaviņas reservoir was enough to persuade many Latvian patriots that the Soviet-era project was a deliberate attack on their national culture.

If you want to break your journey near Koknese, the **tourist office**, Blaumaņa 3 (Mon–Fri 9am–5pm; ☎516 1296, ✆tic@koknese.apollo.lv), can direct you to one of a handful of **B&Bs** in the surrounding villages, or you could head for *Kalnavoti*, on the main road just southeast of Koknese (☎911 7795; ❷), an eight-room guesthouse set in riverside meadows and serving up traditional fare in its pub-restaurant.

Jēkabpils

The main settlement on the middle stretch of the Daugava, **JĒKABPILS** managed to escape the kind of wartime destruction and post-war industrialization visited on most other places in the region and preserves the laid-back charm of a Latvian country town. With its one-storey wooden houses complete with neat cottage gardens, it exudes a palpable nice-place-to-bring-up-the-kids vibe.

Jēkabpils is made up of what were originally two separate towns – **Krustpils** on the northern bank of the river, and **Jēkabpils** immediately opposite on the south. While Krustpils dates back to the establishment of a castle here by the Archbishop of Rīga in the thirteenth century, Jēkabpils originated as a seventeenth-century sanctuary for Old Believers – schismatic Orthodox Christians fleeing persecution in Tsarist Russia (see p.395). Eager to take trade away from Krustpils, the ambitious Duke Jakob of Courland (whose territory then extended as far as the Daugava) bestowed free-town status on the new settlement in 1670 and also gave it its name – Jēkabpils being the Latvianized form of the original Jakobstadt, or "Jacob's town". Before long, the place had become the main stop-off point for rafters taking logs and furs downstream to Rīga and a cosmopolitan community of Latvians, Jews, Poles and Russians (both orthodox and schismatic) grew up to rake in the proceeds. These groups bequeathed the town a fine set of religious buildings in a variety of architectural styles, which – along with a pair of worthwhile museums – constitute the town's main sights.

Buses pick up and drop off on the main square in Jēkabpils, and the **train station** is on the Krustpils side of the river, 3.5km from the centre – consequently Krustpils (and not Jēkabpils) is the name used on train timetables and destination boards.

The Town

The town's prim main square is **Vecpilsētas laukums**; heading west of here, Brīvības iela passes a semi-derelict **Uniate church** (Uniātu baznīca) before arriving at the nineteenth-century **Orthodox Church of St Nicholas** (Sv Nikolaja baznīca), which presides over a walled enclosure at Brīvības 202. The church is rarely open, but its exterior is worth a brief once-over, especially its delicately carved wooden porch and cluster of domes resembling a huddle of bulbous-hatted priests. Five minutes' walk southeast of Vecpilsētas laukums is the equally personable **Old Believers' church** (Vecticībnieku baznīca) at Viestura 15, a bright-blue timber building, topped off by a trio of tiny cupolas. East of the main square, the comparatively sober **Lutheran church** (Luterāņu baznīca) marks the turn-off to the **Sēlian Farmstead Museum** (Sēļu sēta; May–Oct Mon–Fri 9am–5pm, Sat & Sun 10am–3pm; 0.30Ls) on the corner of Dambja and Filozofu, displaying buildings rescued from the villages of Sēlia – the rural region extending south from Jēkabpils as far as the Lithuanian border. The nineteenth-century reed-thatched farmhouses are almost upstaged by a functional grey slab of a windmill, that looks as if it could have been designed by Mies van der Rohe's country cousin and has a long pole attached to it so it can be pulled round on its axis to face the wind.

The chief attraction on the opposite side of the river is **Krustpils castle** (Krustpils pils), reached by crossing the bridge from Jēkabpils and turning left up Rīgas iela (a ride on buses #1, #4, #5 or #9 will save you a twenty-minute walk). Built shortly after the Teutonic conquest in 1237, it was extensively re-modelled in the sixteenth century, and received repeated batterings in wars between Swedes and Poles. However, its interior has been elegantly restored and now houses the **Jēkabpils History Museum** (Jēkabpils vēstures muzejs; Mon–Fri 9am–5pm, Sat 10am–3pm; 0.30Ls), harbouring the usual hodge-podge of archeological and ethnographic trinkets and a wealth of old furniture culled from the region's manor houses.

Practicalities

The **tourist office** in the town library, at Vecpilsētas laukuma 3 (Mon–Fri 10am–6pm; ☎523 3822, ⓦwww.jekabpils.lv), is short-staffed and doesn't always abide by its advertised opening times. The best **hotel** is the six-room *Hercogs Jēkabs*, Brīvības 182 (despite the three-figure street number, it's only five minutes' walk west of the main square; ☎523 3433, ⓔsaule@niko.lv; ❸), offering parquet-floored, pastel coloured en-suites with TV, some with river views. Next best is the riverside *Daugavkrasti*, 1.5km east of the centre at Mežrūpnieku 2 (☎523 1232; ❷); the rooms come with shower and TV, but the furnishings are beginning to show wear and tear. For **eating** and **drinking**, *Kafejnīca Ugurtiņa*, at the top of the main square, is a good daytime source of no-nonsense pork-and-potatoes staples, while *Kafejnīca Atpūta*, Viestura 5, has a wider-ranging menu and is snazzier all round, attracting a coffee-and-cake crowd in the daytime and cool young drinkers in the evening.

Latgale

Extending east from Jēkabpils to the Russian border, the region of **Latgale** (ⓦwww.latgale.lv) offers some of the most enchanting landscapes in the country: pleasantly rolling upland studded with lakes, girdled with a mixture of reed beds, pine trees and birch. Along with Vidzeme, Kurzeme and Zemgale it's one of the four main historical regions of Latvia and, although it no longer exists as an administrative unit, preserves a stronger sense of local identity than any other part of the country. The region's name comes from the Latgalians, one of the original Baltic tribes who settled in Latvia four millennia ago. Latgale still preserves an archaic dialect that differs sufficiently from standard Latvian for some to consider it a separate language (it's not officially recognized as such, but publication of Latgalian poetry and prose is an increasing preoccupation of the local literati).

Latgale's uniqueness is largely due to the fact that it was cut off from the rest of Latvia for large chunks of its history, thereby missing out on the process of cultural and linguistic unification that bound the other three regions together as a nation.

Most significantly, it was part of the Polish-Lithuanian state from 1561 until the first partition of Poland in 1772. During this period the tribes living in northern and western Latvia gradually standardized their languages into a mutually intelligible national tongue, while the isolated Latgalians stuck to their own archaic dialect. Latgale was also cut off from the Protestant culture then developing in the rest of Latvia, remaining under the sway of the **Catholic Church** – a faith to which the Latgalians are still passionately devoted to this day. Under Russian rule from 1772, Latgale was attached to the Vitebsk Gubernia (covering what is now most of eastern Belarus), distancing it even further from the main currents of Latvian culture. The Latgalian intelligentsia always regarded themselves as a legitimate branch of the Latvian national family, however, and in April 1917 the **Latvian-Latgalian Congress** convened in Rēzekne to declare Latgale's "independence" from Vitebsk and its unification with Latvian territories governed by Rīga. For the next three years Latgale was the scene of fierce battles between pro-Latvian forces and Bolsheviks invading from the east and it wasn't until 1920 that real political unity was achieved.

Latgale was always an ethnically mixed area, with Latgalian Latvians dominating the countryside and Russians and Poles congregating in the towns. Jews made up forty to fifty percent of the population in urban areas like Daugavpils, Ludza and Krāslava, though Nazi terror in World War II destroyed this centuries-old presence at a stroke. After the war, Latgale's cities were earmarked for industrialization, encouraging mass immigration from other parts of the Soviet Union – with the result that Russians are now the largest ethnic group in the region, making up some 43.5 percent of the population. The collapse of heavy industry following the fall of the USSR, coupled with rural backwardness, have conspired to make Latgale one of the poorest regions in the country, and tourist facilities are fairly basic.

The cities of **Daugavpils** and **Rēzekne** are the region's main transport hubs and service centres, although neither is likely to hold your attention for long. Rural Latgale is another matter, however, with the Catholic pilgrimage site of **Aglona** and the drowsy market town of **Ludza** providing access to the best of the lakeland scenery.

Daugavpils

Despite being Latvia's second city, **DAUGAVPILS** is usually dismissed by the rest of the country as an economically depressed backwater with few redeeming features. It's true that this erstwhile industrial powerhouse has fallen on hard times, but it remains – in parts at least – a ruggedly handsome city whose historical resonances run deep. If there is so much prejudice against Daugavpils it's probably because so few Latvian-speakers actually live there: over ninety percent of the population is Russian-speaking and although the street signs are in Latvian, you'll hardly ever hear the language used in everyday conversation. Starved of investment by a state that appears embarrassed by the city's failure to fit into the patriotic post-independence picture, Daugavpils has been left largely to its own devices.

Perhaps appropriately for a town with such a large Russian population, Daugavpils appears to have been founded by marauding Muscovite Ivan the Terrible, who sacked the Livonian Order fortress of Dünaburg, 19km upstream, and ordered its reconstruction on the site of the present-day city. An important garrison town under successive rulers, Daugavpils experienced its most rapid period of growth in the years before World War I, when a developing manufacturing industry sucked in migrant workers from all over the Russian Empire. The process repeated itself after 1945, when the Soviet authorities deliberately imported a non-Latvian workforce to feed the city's expanding factories, which produced everything from landmines to lawn mowers. Daugavpils took an economic battering in the immediate post-independence years, with hitherto unimagined social problems like mass unemployment, poverty and drug addiction engendering an atmosphere of despon-

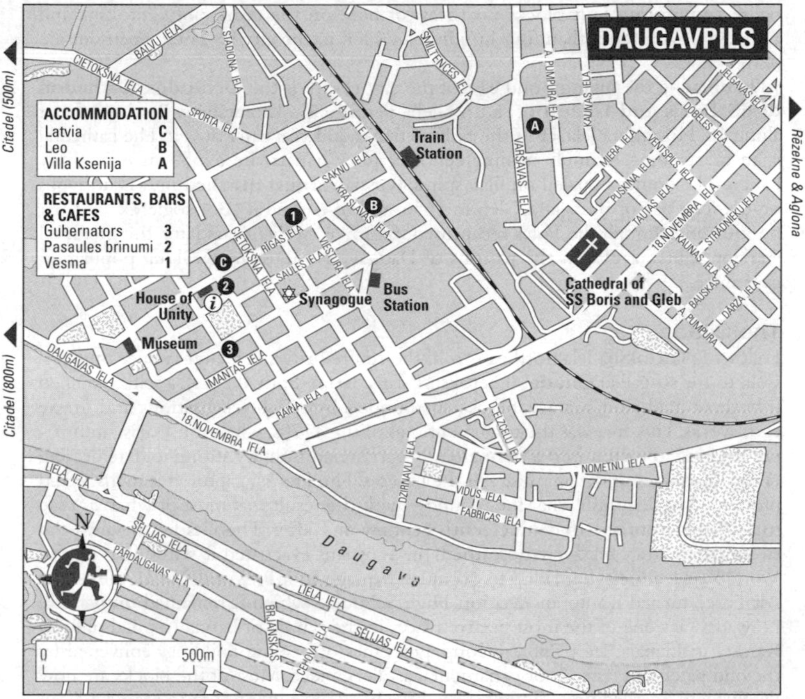

DAUGAVPILS

ACCOMMODATION
Latvia   **C**
Leo   **B**
Villa Ksenija   **A**

RESTAURANTS, BARS & CAFES
Gubernators   **3**
Pasaules brinumi   **2**
Vēsma   **1**

dency only now beginning to lift. However, it's by no means the unremittingly ugly city that many Latvians claim it to be, and with a downtown area full of robust nineteenth-century buildings, it has enough in the way of gruff charm to reward even the briefest of visits.

The Town

Slicing straight through the middle of Daugavpils' grid-iron city centre is **Rīgas iela**, a stately, pedestrianized strip lined with tastefully restored nineteenth-century apartment blocks. Midway along the street's 1.5-kilometre length, the grassy open spaces of **Vienības laukums** provide downtown Daugavpils with some kind of focus. It's overlooked by the nine-storey bulk of the **Hotel Latvia**, long considered one of the most graceless buildings in the country and – 2003 facelift notwithstanding – still something of an eyesore. Not much better is the grey-brown **House of Unity** (Vienības nams) immediately opposite, a combined theatre and administrative building, holding the dubious distinction of being the largest construction project undertaken by the inter-war Latvian state. From here it's a short hop southwest to the **Daugavpils Regional History and Art Museum** at Rīgas 8 (Daugavpils novadpētniecības un makslas muzejs; Tues–Sat 11am–6pm; 0.50Ls), with an absorbing ethnographic collection and a small display devoted to abstract painter **Mark Rothko**, who was born Markus Rothkowitz in Daugavpils in 1903. He was only 10 years old when his family left for Portland, Oregon, and there's consequently little of Daugavpils in the man's work, or indeed the man's work here in Daugavpils – you're best off going to London or New York to see that. A further reminder of the town's once-thriving Jewish community is provided by the smart, ochre **synagogue** four blocks northeast of here on the corner of Cietokšņa and Lāčplēša – with fewer than four hundred Jews left in the city, it's rarely open outside prayer times.

Dominating the high ground east of the city centre is the **Orthodox Cathedral of SS Boris and Gleb** (Borisa un Gļeba pareizticīgo katedrāle) – head northeast along 18. Novembra iela, cross the railway tracks and you can't miss it. The cathedral is an outstanding example of nineteenth-century Muscovite exuberance, its shiny bauble-like domes impaled on lilac spires. Russian armies marched into Daugavpils on the feast day of Boris and Gleb in 1656, and re-named it "Borisoglebsk" in their honour, and though the Poles recaptured the town twelve years later, the medieval warrior saints have been the patrons of Daugavpils's Russian-speaking population ever since.

The Citadel

Following Cietokšņa iela northeast from the centre brings you after twenty minutes' walk to the so-called **Citadel** (Cietoksnis; daily 10am–8pm; 0.20Ls), a self-contained suburb of grid-iron barrack blocks surrounded by red-brick bastions and grassy earthworks. This area was the town centre until the 1770s, when the Tsarist authorities decided to turn it into a permanently garrisoned military stronghold, relocating civilian activities to the southeast in the process. The French captured it in 1812 and proceeded to demolish what they found – with the result that most of what you see today dates from the mid-nineteenth century and after. The citadel survived the twentieth century relatively unscathed: the Russians evacuated it without a fight in World War I, and having failed to do much damage to it in World War II, the Soviet Air Force turned it into an Aviation High School – which it remained until 1990. Nowadays it's one of the most bizarre places in the whole of Latvia (topped only by Karosta in Liepāja; see p.258), its long, grey lines of peeling buildings enlivened by the odd patch of greenery or ornamental artillery piece. Most of the blocks are now derelict and boarded up, although some have been pressed into use to provide cheap housing for locals – as if to complete the experience of alienation, these sections are surrounded by security fences in order to ward off intruders.

Practicalities

Daugavpils' **train station** lies at the northeastern end of the main street, Rīgas iela, while the **bus station** is two blocks southeast of this thoroughfare; both are within easy reach of the helpful **tourist office** at Rīgas 22A – the entrance is round the back of this enormous building and you have to walk a block southeast in order to find it (Mon–Fri 9am–6pm, Sat 10am–4pm; ☎542 2818, ✆tourinfo @daugavpils.apollo.lv). The recently refurbished *Latvia* **hotel**, bang in the centre at Gimnazijas 46 (❻), offers comfortable TV-equipped en-suites in antiseptic tower-block surroundings; you'll get the same levels of comfort at the more intimate *Leo*, midway between bus and train stations at Krāslavas 58 (☎542 6565, ☎542 5325; ❹), although there are only five rooms, so ring in advance. *Villa Ksenija*, Varšavas 17 (☎543 4317, ✇www.villaks.lv; ❹) offers slightly cramped, but otherwise superbly comfortable, en-suites in a pre-World War I mansion twenty minutes' walk east of the centre.

For **eating**, there are plenty of cafés along the length of Rīgas iela, especially at the train-station end. *Vēsma* at no. 49 has an order-at-the-counter canteen with a good salad bar in one half of the building, and a smart café-bar in the other. *Pasaules brinumi*, Gimnāzijas 17, does a good line in salads, pork chops and pancakes. The spacious, cellar-bound *Gubernators*, Lāčplēša 10, is the liveliest place **to drink** in the centre, and has a full menu of hot meals to boot.

Aglona

Nestling picturesquely between a pair of lakes 45km northeast of Daugavpils and 10km east of the Daugavpils-Rēzekne highway, the one-horse village of

AGLONA is dwarfed by the twin-towered, late-Baroque basilica that stands on its outskirts. The most important Catholic shrine in Latvia, it can draw anything from 100,000 to 150,000 celebrants for the Feast of the Assumption on August 15, and remains popular with pilgrims throughout the year – Easter, Pentecost and September 8 (Birth of the Virgin) being the other key dates. Aglona's importance as a religious centre dates back to 1699, when Dominicans chose to settle in this tranquil spot, bringing with them a seventeenth-century image of the Virgin that soon developed a reputation for miraculous healing powers. The first (wooden) monastery burned down in 1766 and Aglona's burgeoning popularity with the Baltic Catholic faithful was considered sufficient reason to justify construction of the impressive basilica which dominates the landscape today. Aglona's holy aura was boosted further when a local woman claimed to have seen a vision of the Virgin on the hillock beside the basilica in 1798. During the Soviet period the monastery was closed down and pilgrimages discouraged, although the basilica was allowed to publicly celebrate its 200th anniversary in 1980. Thoroughgoing restoration was carried out in time for Pope John Paul II's visit in September 1993, when a massive paved area was laid down for outdoor masses.

The **basilica** has the severe appearance of a freshly iced, but otherwise undecorated, cake. Its distinguishing feature is the pair of chunky sixty-metre-high towers rising on either side of the main door – the basilica was by far the highest man-made object for miles around until the erection of the next-door TV transmission mast, a clear indication of where spiritual power in contemporary Latvia really lies. With the population of Latgale presumably far too busy watching soap operas and game shows to actually visit the basilica, it's no surprise to discover that it doesn't keep regular opening hours, and unless you arrive on Sundays, gaining admittance is rather a matter of luck. Inside, the icon-like image of the Virgin which graces the high altar is hidden behind a curtain – and only unveiled on holy days. If all this is a bit of a let-down you can always enjoy the scenery by following the paths around Lake Aglona immediately east of the basilica, or the larger, reed-fringed expanse of Cirīss to the west.

Getting to Aglona

Buses stop on what passes for a main square, 500m uphill from the basilica. If you're travelling **from Rīga**, it's best to aim first for the market town of **Preiļi**, 25km northwest of Aglona, and pick up a local bus from there – you should be able to see Aglona as a day-trip from the capital providing you set off early in the day and double-check return times at each stage of the journey. Preiļi's bus station is right on the central square, just across from a **tourist office** at Tirgus laukums 1 (Mon–Fri 9am–5pm; ☎532 2041, ✆www.preili.lv).

Approaching Aglona **from Daugavpils or Rēzekne**, note that Daugavpils–Rēzekne buses don't pass through Aglona itself, however much staff in local bus stations may persuade you otherwise; they stop off instead in the similarly named Aglonas stacija ("Aglona Station") on the main highway, a hamlet huddled around a barely used railway halt and not the kind of place you want to get stranded in. A handful of Daugavpils–Aglona and Rēzekne–Aglona services do exist, although they may set off too late in the day to allow sufficient time to look around and get back to town.

Driving to Aglona is much less complicated all round: the main turn-off from the Daugavpils–Rēzekne highway at Aglonas stacija is marked by a huge, unmissable white cross. For a more picturesque approach, turn off the highway at **Spoģi**, 30km out of Daugavpils, and head east via the tiny lake resort of **Višķi** – not all of this road is tarmacked, but it's a lovely up-hill-and-down-dale ride through rolling, partly forested countryside.

Accommodation, eating and drinking

There's a rudimentary **café** immediately opposite the bus stop, although *Zodiaks*, 400m north, has a nicer range of hot meals. If you want **to stay**, try *Tūjas*, Kalna 13

(☎537 5469; ❷), a smartish six-room B&B, offering unfussily furnished rooms, some with views of the basilica's twin towers; or *Jura Cakula viesu maja*, Ezera 4 (signed from the northern entrance to the village; ☎537 5465; ❶–❸), a big lakeside house offering B&B and boat rental. There's tent space at *Arkāda*, a lakeside **campsite** 2km northwest of the village off the Preiļi road (☎537 5498). Back in Preiļi itself, the *Preiļi* **hotel**, Raiņa 24 (☎530 7118; ❸), has some bland, but comfortable, en-suites, as well as some hostel-style beds at 3Ls per person. Offering smart, modern rooms with TV is the *Stalkers* **motel**, on the main Daugavpils–Rēzekne highway just south of Spoģi (☎547 9221; ❻).

Rēzekne

Despite being fortified by both Latgalian chieftains and the Livonian Order, **RĒZEKNE**, 90km northeast of Daugavpils, didn't really take shape until the nineteenth century, when it was laid out in the grid pattern beloved of the Tsarist Empire's town planners. Unfortunately, few historic buildings survive from any era: Rēzekne found itself among the most artillery-pummelled towns in Latvia in World War II, which helps to explain why it's unremittingly grey and modern today. That said, it's a relatively relaxing, leafy city, and with a decent museum and a couple of other cultural oddities to its name, it's worth a brief stop before moving on.

The City

Rēzekne's main point of reference is **Atbrīvošanas aleja** ("Liberation Alley"), the long, straight street which runs north–south through the centre of the city. Marking its mid-point is a roundabout, the central reservation of which is occupied by the region's most famous resident, **Māra of Latgale** (Latgales Māra), a statue of a woman brandishing a cross in celebration of victory over the godless Bolsheviks in 1920 and Latgale's subsequent absorption into the infant state of Latvia. The inscription on the statue's pedestal reads *Vienoti Latvijai* ("For Latvian Unity!"), just to drive the point home.

Photographs of the local woman who modelled for the original sculpture are on display at the **Latgale Museum of History and Culture** (Latgales kultūrvēstures muzejs; Tues–Fri 10am–5pm, Sat 10am–4pm; 0.50Ls), just north of the roundabout at Atbrīvošanas 102. The museum's collection is something of a nostalgic evocation of the Rēzekne of old: you can see sepia photographs of the handsome brick buildings that used to line Rēzekne's main street in pre-World War I days and re-creations of shop interiors – including the dressing table of a 1930s beauty parlour. Upstairs, a thorough chronology of arts and crafts in Latgale kicks off with Bronze and Iron Age necklaces and continues with several rooms devoted to contemporary ceramics – a traditional Latgale craft still alive and well. Among the glossily glazed pots and plates look out for the many-branched candlesticks, very much a local trademark.

Heading south from the roundabout and turning left into Pils iela brings you face to face with the stark ruins of Rēzekne's **medieval fortress**, crowning a hillock. It's a good spot from which to admire the red-brick **Catholic cathedral** on the far side of the river; not that interesting a building to merit a close-up encounter, it has a certain nobility when viewed from here.

Practicalities

Rēzekne has two **train stations**: Rēzekne II, just off the northern end of Atbrīvošanas aleja and about twenty minutes' walk north of the central roundabout, handles trains to and from Rīga and Ludza, while Rēzekne I, fifteen minutes' southwest of the roundabout, is currently served by the Vilnius–St Petersburg express only, which passes through three times a week in each direction. The **bus station** is ten minutes' walk south of the roundabout. Overlooking the roundabout, and offering some good views of the city from its upper floors, the tower-block *Latgale* **hotel** (☎462 2180; ❶), Atbrīvošanas aleja 98, doesn't offer much in the way of modern furnishings, but the en-suite rooms with TV are habitable enough – cheaper rooms come with shower/WC in the hallway. The best place for a quick bite is *Rūķītis*, on the corner of Atbrīvošanas aleja and 18. Novembra, an unpretentious little **café** offering the usual repertoire of salads, soups and pork chops, and some excellent ice cream. For a more relaxing evening meal, *Little Italy*, beside the roundabout at Atbrīvošanas aleja 100, serves up pizza, pasta and mainstream pork and chicken dishes in an elegant but not-too-formal environment.

Ludza

A short 25-kilometre ride from Rēzekne across a pleasing landscape of low hills and lakes, **LUDZA** is reckoned to be one of the most attractive small towns in Latvia, with neat rows of wooden houses draped across a neck of land separating three lakes. Overlooking the scene from a small hill are a pert, twin-towered Catholic church that – from a distance at least – looks like a souvenir-sized copy of the basilica at Aglona, and a ruined red-brick fortress, built by the Livonian Order to keep Russian invaders at bay. Head to the rugged shell of the three-storey keep to enjoy a sweeping panorama of the lakes, with Mazais Ludzas ezers ("Little Ludza Lake") over to the west, Lielais Ludzas ezers ("Great Ludza Lake") to the northeast and Dunakļu ezers further away to the north.

North of the fortress, on the far side of a bridge, the **Ludza District Museum** (Ludzas novadpētniecības muzejs; Mon–Sat 10am–5pm; 0.50Ls), at Kuļņeva 2, occupies the former villa of Yakov Petrovich Kulnev (1763–1812), a dashing cavalry officer who was the first Russian general to be killed in defence of the homeland during Napoleon's invasion of Russia of 1812 and became something of a national hero as a result. Alongside more Latagale ceramics, the display includes a fine collection of spiral headbands, necklaces and bracelets found in locally excavated tenth-century graves.

Behind the museum, Soikāna iela leads uphill onto a ridge running along the north side of the lake, arriving after ten minutes at an atmospheric, tree-canopied **Jewish cemetery**, with hundreds of Hebrew-engraved tombstones amid the long grass. Back in the eighteenth century, an estimated 59 percent of the town's population was Jewish, earning Ludza the title of "Latvian Jerusalem" – although the community thinned out in the 1930s owing to emigration to Rīga or America, and was annihilated completely by the Nazis in summer 1941. Back in town, there's a (currently unused) synagogue on the lakeside Ezerkrasta iela, just behind the tourist office, although there's nothing to indicate its former function.

Practicalities

Ludza can be reached by two daily trains and two daily buses from Rīga; otherwise public transport comes from Rēzekne. The **bus station** is right in the town centre, while the **train station** is a good twenty-minute walk south, at the top of Stacijas iela. The enthusiastic **tourist office**, Baznīcas 42/11 (Mon–Fri 8am–5pm; ☎570 7202), supplies brochures and town plans and can book you into B&B accommodation in villages throughout the district. **Accommodation** in Ludza itself is limited to the *Ezerzeme* hotel (☎572 2490; ❶), Stacijas 44, a Seventies-era grey block offering frumpy doubles with shared bathrooms and no breakfast; and *Motelis Pie kamīna* (☎572 5498; ❶), 2km south on the Zilupe road at Latgales 238, which, despite the motel tag, is a friendly five-room guesthouse. Ludza is bereft of decent cafés – there's a **food shop** near the tourist office on Baznīcas iela.

Travel details

Trains

Rīga to: Cēsis (4 daily; 2hr); Daugavpils (4 daily; 3hr 20min–4hr); Jēkabpils (8 daily; 2hr 30min); Lielvārde (16 daily; 1hr); Līgatne (4 daily; 1hr 15min); Rēzekne (2 daily; 4hr); Sigulda (14 daily; 1hr 5min–1hr 20min); Valmiera (4 daily; 2hr 20min).

Buses

Cēsis to: Līgatne (Mon–Fri 3 daily; 40min).
Daugavpils to: Aglona (3 daily; 1hr 20min); Ludza (Mon–Sat 2 daily; 2hr 30min); Rēzekne (7 daily; 2hr 10min).
Līgatne train station to: Līgatne village (Mon–Fri 6 daily, Sat 3 daily, Sun 5 daily; 15min).

Preiļi to: Aglona (6 daily; 55min).
Rēzekne to: Aglona (2 daily; 1hr 30min); Alūksne (4 daily; 3hr 10min–4hr 15min); Daugavpils (7 daily; 2hr 10min); Ludza (5 daily; 30–50min); Rīga (8 daily; 5hr).
Rīga to: Cēsis (hourly; 2hr); Preiļi (6 daily; 3hr 30min); Sigulda (Mon–Sat 15 daily, Sun 7 daily; 1hr 10min).
Sigulda to: Krīmulda (9 daily; 20min); Rīga (Mon–Sat 15 daily, Sun 7 daily; 1hr 10min); Saulkrasti (4 daily; 1hr); Turaida (10 daily; 15min).

International trains

Daugavpils to: Vilnius (Fri, Sat & Sun 1 daily; 3hr 30min).

Estonia

Estonia Highlights

✱ **Tallinn Old Town** A tightly-packed maze of narrow streets overlooked by proud merchants' houses and medieval church spires. **See p.308**

✱ **Kadriorg, Tallinn** A leafy park laid out by Peter the Great for his mistress, now home to the finest art museum in the Baltics. **See p.321**

✱ **Saaremaa** This popular holiday island offers the best of Estonia's maritime landscape, its starkly beautiful heathland dotted with windmills, lighthouses and even the odd meteorite crater. **See p.341**

✱ **Pärnu** Pärnu boasts a glorious white-sand beach and vibrant, summertime nightlife. **See p.351**

✱ **Lahemaa National Park** An unparalleled variety of unspoiled natural environments, from dense pine forests to bogs and desolate, boulder-strewn shores. **See p.364**

✱ **Tartu** An easy-going university town with plenty in the way of handsome historic architecture, quirky museums and a vibrant after-dark drinking scene. **See p.375**

✱ **Setumaa** Home to the Setu, a dwindling branch of the Estonian people attached to the Orthodox Church, Setumaa is one of the most rewarding and mysterious corners of the country, with bucolic villages and wooden churches set amid rippling hills. **See p.396**

Introduction and basics

It's a tribute to the resilience of the Estonians that during the short years since the Declaration of Independence in August 1991 they've transformed their country from a dour outpost of the former Soviet Union into a forward-looking, economically stable nation that boasts the highest rates of computer and mobile-phone ownership in the Baltic region. The creation of a viable modern nation state is even more impressive in the light of the fact that Estonians have ruled their own country for barely thirty years out of the past eight hundred. A Finno-Ugric people related to the Finns, the Estonians have had the misfortune to be surrounded by powerful, warlike neighbours. The first to conquer Estonia were the Danes, who arrived at the start of the thirteenth century; they were succeeded in turn by German crusading knights, Swedes and then Russians. Following a mid-nineteenth-century cultural and linguistic revival known as the National Awakening, the collapse of Germany and Tsarist Russia allowed the Estonians to snatch their independence in 1918. Their brief freedom between the two world wars was extinguished by the Soviets in 1940 and Estonia disappeared from view again. When the country re-emerged from the Soviet shadow in 1991, some forty percent of its population were Russians who had been encouraged to settle there during the Soviet era.

Where to go

Estonia's capital, **Tallinn**, is a fascinating combination of quaint medieval town and glitzy, go-ahead metropolis, with a choice of restaurants, bars and clubs big enough to bring out the hedonist in anyone. By way of complete contrast, the **Lahemaa National Park**, east of Tallinn, possesses one of the most enticing mixtures of forests, fishing villages and manorial estates in the Baltics, its deeply indented coastline pebble-dashed with an enigmatic collection of boulders.

Of the east Estonian cities, the gruff border city of **Narva** is worth visiting for its superb fortress, although it's the historic university town of **Tartu**, full of inviting museums, pubs and parks, that exerts most appeal. Tartu is also a great base from which to visit the unspoilt countryside of the south, with ski-resort **Otepää** and small-town **Võru** providing access to a rolling landscape of pudding-shaped hills – one of which, **Suur Munamägi**, is the highest point in the Baltics at a cloud-scraping 300m above sea level. In the far southeast, bucolic villages inhabited by the Russian sect of Old Believers and the Orthodox Estonian **Setu**

provide an insight into the country's racial and cultural diversity.

Most beach tourism is located on the west coast, where laid-back, genteel **Haapsalu** and boisterous, party-hard **Pärnu** are the main places to aim for. For a taste of the Estonian coast's desolate beauty, head for islands like **Hiiumaa** and **Saaremaa**, their landscape of lighthouse-scattered shores and inland juniper heaths perfect for hiking and cycling. As well as being a popular spa resort, Saaremaa's capital **Kuressaare** is home to one of the finest castles in the Baltics.

Costs, money and banks

Although costs are on the rise in Estonia's capital, Tallinn, it's still a reasonably inexpensive destination compared to cities in Western Europe – a day's sightseeing followed by a fun evening out is unlikely to break the bank. Things are cheaper still outside the capital, where a little money can go a long way.

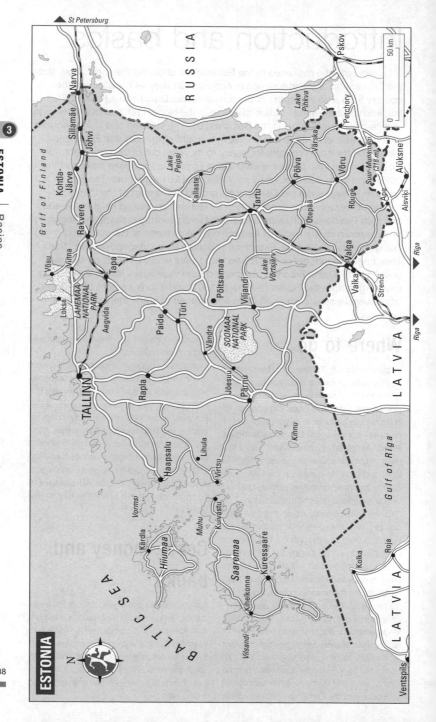

Estonia on the web

⚛**www.ee** General portal offering all manner of useful links.

⚛**www.einst.ee** A mine of cultural information, courtesy of the Estonian Institute.

⚛**www.estonica.org** Useful features on all aspects of Estonian life.

⚛**www.estoniatimes.com** A digest of the latest news and stories on Estonia from the world's press.

⚛**www.kultuuriinfo.ee** A good, general resource on the arts, including concert and exhibition schedules.

⚛**www.visitestonia.com** National Tourist Board site offering plenty of useful info and links to regional sites.

⚛**www.weekend.ee** Entertainment listings, including everything from high culture to clubbing.

⚛**www.1182.ee** Yellow Pages-style info for the whole country, including public transport timetables.

Costs

Accommodation is likely to prove your biggest expense in Estonia. In Tallinn, Tartu and resort areas, hostel beds cost between £7/$10 and £12/$18, private rooms around £20/$30 for a double. The cheaper hotels start at about the £30/$45 mark for a double, with comfortable, mid-range choices costing around £45/$68 – anything more stylish will be considerably more than this. In rural areas you won't find much in the way of hostels, but the price of a double room can fall to £15/$22 in a rustic B&B, £20/$30 in a hotel.

Public transport costs are comparatively low: an inter-city bus journey from Tallinn to Pärnu or Tartu will be somewhere in the region of £3.60/$5.50, while a one-way ticket from Tallinn to Kuressaare on the island of Saaremaa costs £7/$10.

If you're shopping in markets for picnic ingredients during the daytime and sticking to the cheaper cafés and bars in the evening, then £6/$9 per person per day will suffice for **food and drink**. In order to cover a sit-down lunch and a decent dinner followed by a couple of night-time drinks, you'll need at least £20/$30 per person per day in Tallinn, £15/$22.50 outside the capital.

Estonia is one Baltic country in which it's well worth having a student discount card: **ISIC-card** holders get discounts of ten percent in many hotels, reduced entry in museums and often up to thirty percent off theatre and concert tickets.

Currency

Estonia's unit of currency is the **kroon**, normally abbreviated to EEK (Eesti kroon – "Estonian Crown"), and is divided into 100 sents. Notes come in 1, 2, 5, 10, 25, 50, 100 and 500EEK denominations and coins in 0.05, 0.10, 0.20, 0.50, 1 and 5EEK denominations.

The kroon is currently pegged to the euro at a rate of 15.65EEK to 1€ and exchange rates are likely to remain reasonably stable. At the time of writing there are around 22EEK to £1, 13.5EEK to $1.

Banks, exchange and credit cards

With plenty of **ATMs** scattered around Estonia's town centres, you should have no problem drawing instant cash with a valid debit or credit card. Major **banks** (*pank*) such as Ühispank, Hansapank and Sampo Pank can change cash for a commission, cash traveller's cheques (Thomas Cook and American Express preferred) and give cash advances on most major credit cards for a commission of around three percent. Banks are usually **open** Monday to Friday 9am to 4/6pm – major banks in the cities often open on Saturday from 9am to 2 or 3pm.

Exchange offices (*Valuuta vahetus*) usually work longer hours and open on Sundays, too, and in many cases offer lower commission rates than the banks for cash transactions. **Credit cards** can be used in some of the more expensive hotels, restaurants and stores and in some petrol stations in Tallinn, and although you will find places that accept cards outside Tallinn, it's best not to count on it.

Communications

Estonian **post offices** (*postkontor*) are in the main efficient, easy to use, and often staffed by English-speakers. They are usually open Monday to Friday 9am–6/7pm and Saturday 9am–3pm. You can buy stamps (*postmark*) at post offices and at most newspaper kiosks. Sending a letter or postcard will cost 4.40EEK within Estonia, 6.50EEK to the rest of Europe, 8EEK to North America, Canada or Australasia.

Phones

You shouldn't have any problems using Estonia's smooth, problem-free telephone system. Direct international calls are possible from all phones – simply dial ☏00 followed by the country code. Public telephones (*telefoniputka*) all use magnetic cards (available in denominations of 30, 50 and 100EEK from post offices and newspaper kiosks) for both local and long-distance calls; a 50EEK-card should be sufficient to call Western Europe, a 100EEK-card to call the States. For English-language directory enquiries dial ☏1182 or ☏1188.

For general information on using mobile phones in the Baltic States, see p.29. If you have a **GSM mobile phone** you can cut the cost of local calls by buying a pre-paid SIM card from Estonian operators like EMT Simpel or Tele2 Smart. For 150EEK you'll get an Estonian phone number and a few minutes of call time – which you can top up by buying cards (available from newspaper kiosks) in increments of 100, 200 and 500EEK.

Internet

You'll find plenty of **Internet cafés** (*interneti kohvik*) in Tallinn and Tartu, but they're somewhat thin on the ground elsewhere in the country. Expect to pay 40–60EEK for an hour's surfing. Public libraries all have at least one Internet terminal available for public use free of charge, although they're often booked up in advance by the locals.

Media

Given a national population of 1,370,000 (of which only 67 percent are native Estonian speakers), the range of **newspapers and magazines** cluttering up Estonia's street kiosks is absolutely staggering, with titles covering every conceivable interest group from computer nerds to dog breeders and gardeners.

The most prestigious of the national dailies is *Eesti Postimees* (◉www.postimees.ee), founded in Tartu in 1867 and still required reading for the political and business elite – the Friday edition carries good cultural listings, too. Mass-market tabloids *Eesti Päevaleht* and *Sõnumileht* make up for lightweight news coverage with racy showbiz gossip. Best of the weeklies is *Eesti Ekspress*, which mixes political reporting with extensive cultural coverage and carries by far the best "what's on" information (found at the end of the TV section under the heading *Vaba aeg* – "Free Time").

The locally produced Russian daily *Molodezh Estonii* (◉www.moles.ee) is a reliable and readable guide to what's happening in politics and society. There's also a huge array of Moscow-published newspapers and magazines in the kiosks, including the seductively stylish Russian-language editions of major international fashion and design monthlies.

Locally produced **English-language publications** are thin on the ground. *Life in Estonia* is a glossy advert for everything Estonian and occasionally includes interesting interviews with leading national personalities, but is otherwise rather stodgy – it appears sporadically and is difficult to get hold of outside Tallinn hotels and bookshops. In another league entirely is *kunst.ee*, a superbly designed art monthly with a mixture of intelligent articles in Estonian and English.

As far as **television** is concerned, the state-run Eesti TV and the privately owned TV1, Kanal 2 and TV3 offer a pretty varied diet of home-grown and imported programming, although many Estonians (and most Estonian hotels) have cable packages offering a range of English, German, Finnish and Russian channels. All the Estonian stations show imported films and dramas in the original language with Estonian subtitles. For details of pan-Baltic media in the English language, see p.30.

Getting around

Given the relative lack of fast, two-lane high-ways, Estonia can be a slow country to get around. For all that, if you're relying on public transport you're more likely to use the well-organized and extensive bus network than Estonia's trains, which have been cut back so drastically in recent years that there are few useful passenger routes left.

Buses

Although car ownership in Estonia is on the increase, bus transport is still crucial to the lives of many citizens, and there's hardly a town in the country that isn't served by at least one daily bus from Tallinn. Buses link-ing the main cities are frequent, fast and comfortable, while those operating rural routes often look like museum pieces and rarely exceed speeds of 30km/hr. **Express buses** (marked with a red "E" on timetables) stop at fewer places en route and cost slightly more than regular services.

Tickets (*pilet*) can be bought from the driv-er or from the bus station ticket office in advance – buying tickets in advance is wise if you're travelling on a popular inter-city route at a weekend, when buses fill up quickly. Normally, **luggage** is taken on board – if you have a large bag you may have to pay 10–15EEK extra to have it stowed in the luggage compartment.

Prices differ according to the operating company, but are unlikely to put a major dent in your budget. Expect to pay 80–90EEK for major inter-city journeys such as Tallinn–Tartu and Tallinn–Pärnu, much less for shorter trips in the provinces. Buses from the mainland to the islands are more expen-sive, but the price of the ferry crossing is included in your ticket – expect to pay around 150EEK for the Tallinn–Kuressaare journey, 200EEK for Tartu–Kuressaare.

Timetables and information

Estonian **bus timetables** (*sõiduplaan*) are quite complicated at first glance, incorporat-ing lots of specific annotations that are important to get the hang of if you want to be sure that a particular service is travelling on a particular day. Days of the week on which a service runs are usually denoted by a letter (eg, "E" for *esmaspäev* or Monday; see p.453 for the days of the week in Estonian). The abbreviation "v.a." before a particular letter means "runs every day except...". *Iga päev* means "every day"; *tööpäev* means "working day" (ie Mon–Sat).

The Estonian for "departure" is *väljub*, and "arrival" is *saabub*. Some timetables simply list a departure time and nothing else; others may have four columns of timings, denoting time of departure, time of arrival at destina-tion, time of departure back to original start-ing point, time of arrival back at original starting point – very useful if you're planning a day out.

Although a few bus station employees speak English (especially in Tallinn), it's best to have a pen and paper handy to ease com-munication. The English-speaking telephone **information service** on ☏1182 handles inter-city bus information, while timetables for most of the national network are available on the Internet at ⊛www.bussireisid.ee – simply enter your point of departure under *lähteko-ht*, intended destination under *sihtkoht*, then click on *otsi!* ("search!").

Trains

Estonia's train network has been cut back to such an extent that Tallinn is now the only place in the country that has a permanently manned station – all the rest either have sporadically open ticket windows or are sim-ply unstaffed. The destinations you can reach by train are somewhat limited: regular commuter trains run westwards from Tallinn to the port of Paldiski, and there are less fre-quent long-distance services to Tartu, Pärnu, Valga and Viljandi. Moscow (daily) and St Petersburg (three times weekly) are the only international destinations covered. Trains are on the whole slower, less frequent and only slightly cheaper than buses, so unless you have a particular preference for rail travel, there's no compelling reason to use them.

For international services, **tickets** (*pilet*) should be bought in advance. For domestic services, you should buy them in advance if you're beginning your journey from a station with a working ticket office – otherwise, pay the conductor. Trains to Tartu and Valga contain first-class as well as second-class carriages; all others just have second class. Train **timetables** use pretty much the same terminology as those displayed in bus stations (see p.290).

Driving

Driving in Estonia is not too nerve-racking, with main roads in reasonable condition and traffic fairly light outside the towns. Reckless driving is the exception rather than the rule, but watch out for people showing off in BMWs and four-wheel drives. There's no motorway to speak of – just a few stretches of two-lane highway either side of Tallinn and another near Pärnu.

To bring a car into Estonia you need a valid Green Card. **Speed limits** are 50kph in built-up areas and 90 on the open road – some sections of highway allow speeds of 100kph or 110kph. The wearing of **seatbelts** is compulsory for the driver and all passengers and headlights should be switched on at all times. In towns it's forbidden to overtake stationary trams so that passengers can alight in safety, and it's against the law to drive after drinking any alcohol whatsoever. **Petrol stations** can be a little thin on the ground in rural areas, so it's advisable to carry a spare can.

Car rental costs around $60 per day from one of the big companies, as little as half that from some local firms – though their contracts can be dubious, insurance coverage sketchy and cars not necessarily maintained properly. If you are not the car owner a valid photo ID licence is required along with proof of insurance, the car's registration and a letter of authorization. Details of major car rental firms are given on p.27.

Ferries

Roll-on roll-off ferries operated by the state shipping line (✆www.laevakompanii.ee) connect the Estonian mainland with the main islands, with services from Rohuküla near Haapsalu to Hiiumaa (5–7 daily) and Vormsi (2–4 daily); and sailings from Virtsu serving Saaremaa (hourly). Prices are very reasonable: if you're travelling by bus, the cost of the crossing will be included in your ticket (see above); otherwise, expect to pay 20–25EEK per person one-way for these services; an additional 80–120EEK for a car,

30–50EEK per motorbike and 15–30EEK per bike. Although journey times are short (about 90 minutes to Hiiumaa, less than an hour to Saaremaa and Vormsi), ferries have a well-stocked cafeteria on board.

The small island of Kihnu, off Estonia's southern coast, is served by a couple of daily, privately operated ferries from the port of Munalaiu, northwest of Pärnu. Prices for these services are around 40EEK per person, 130EEK per car.

Cycling

Estonia, being predominantly flat, makes perfect cycling terrain, although there aren't any cycle lanes and – on the mainland at least – you can't expect much consideration from other road users. Things are slightly better on the islands, where cyclists are a common sight in summer and there's more in the way of prepared routes and signage. While motor traffic can still be a problem on the roads of the two biggest islands, Saaremaa and Hiiumaa, cyclists will have the country lanes to themselves on Vormsi and Kihnu, where there are far fewer cars.

Flights

Although there are no domestic services linking Estonia's inland cities, flying can be a quick way of getting to the islands, with Air Livonia (✆www.airlivonia.ee) operating daily turbo-prop flights from Tallinn to Hiiumaa and from Pärnu to Kihnu, as well as twice-weekly services from Pärnu to Ruhnu and Pärnu to Kuressaare on Saaremaa.

Accommodation

Tallinn can muster a growing stock of modern, comfortable hotels on a par with those in any Western European city, and similar establishments are also sprouting up in provincial cities. In addition, most towns have one or two reasonable budget hotels, and an increasing number of inexpensive guesthouses and B&Bs exist in rural areas and on the islands. Other cheap options include a handful of hostels, a few private rooms (mostly in Tallinn) and a healthy scattering of campsites – though the majority of these are basic in the extreme.

Hotels

Estonian hotels (*hotell*) come in all shapes and sizes, from the international-style blocks mushrooming all over Tallinn to the more characterful, mid-size places you're more likely to find in small towns and on the islands. Most of Estonia's hotel stock has been either refurbished or built from scratch in the last ten to fifteen years, and swish interior design and gleaming bathrooms tend to be the rule rather than the exception. A few unrenovated, Soviet-era establishments still exist here and there, and worn carpets and chipped furniture aside, they're still perfectly habitable.

Although the international five-star grading system has yet to be fully applied in Estonia (some of the upmarket establishments have awarded themselves stars, but most don't bother), prices are usually a reasonably accurate guide to room quality. A buffet breakfast is included in the price in almost all but the cheapest hotels, where you'll probably have to buy your own in a nearby café. You should be able to find plain, but clean, double rooms, often in old Soviet-era places or converted student hostels, for between 500 and 800EEK. For this price you'll probably get a basic en-suite shower unit and WC, although some of the cheaper places have one shower/WC shared between every two or three rooms. If you want newer furnishings and a TV in the room you'll be paying more like 700–1000EEK. Anything more than this will buy you comforts equivalent to international three- or four-star standard.

Hotel **prices** in the main cities and towns are the same all year round – although many offer weekend discounts and it never hurts to ask. In coastal areas, hotels are often twenty- to thirty-percent cheaper in the off-season (Oct–April) – even hotels that don't publicly advertise an off-peak rate will usually be open to bargaining during this period. Note that many hotels quote their prices in euros, though you can still pay in kroon.

Small hotels in rural areas may close altogether from October to April. Even those that claim to stay open during the winter may refuse to take bookings from individuals or groups of less than four or five – it's not worth their while turning the heating on if only one or two rooms are occupied.

Families are better catered for in Estonia than its Baltic neighbours: children under the age of 3 usually stay for free, while those under 14 (sometimes 16) get a thirty- to fifty-percent discount if sleeping in the same room as their parents. Many hotels offer two-room suites featuring a bedroom and a living room with fold-down beds – perfect for three- or four-member families.

One feature that all travellers will enjoy is the **sauna** – all hotels of any size will have one or more of these on site. They cost from 180 to 300EEK an hour to use, although guests might be allowed to use them for free during off-peak hours (ie early in the morning).

Provision of **no-smoking** rooms is becoming standard throughout the hotel industry and many smaller hotels are non-smoking throughout.

Guesthouses, B&Bs and private rooms

In Tallinn's suburbs, provincial towns and rural areas there's a growing number of small, family-run establishments offering homely bed-and-breakfast accommodation for lower prices than those offered by the hotels. If one of these places has five rooms or more, it's classified as a **guesthouse** (*külalistemaja*); otherwise it's a **B&B**

Accommodation price codes

The hotels and guesthouses listed in the Estonian chapters of this guide have been graded according to the following price bands, based on the cost of the least expensive double room in summer.

❶ Under 450EEK
❷ 450–600EEK
❸ 600–800EEK
❹ 800–1100EEK

❺ 1100–1500EEK
❻ 1500–2000EEK
❼ 2000–3000EEK
❽ Over 3000EEK

(*kodumajutus*). Standards in these places are hard to predict: the snazzier ones will have en-suite rooms with TV; others will offer simply furnished, but cosy, rooms with communal WC/shower in the hallway. Guesthouses and B&Bs based on working farms often go under the name of *turismitalu* or "tourist farmstead" – such places offer an excellent opportunity to observe rural life at first hand and may also offer horse riding and other activities as part of the package. Prices for guesthouses and B&Bs range from 300 to 600EEK a double depending on location and facilities.

Local tourist offices throughout Estonia provide information on local guesthouses and B&Bs and will in most cases make **reservations** on your behalf. You can also book rural B&Bs in Estonia through Latvian agency Lauku ceļotājs, Kuģu 11, Rīga (☏+371 783 0041, ⊛www.celotajs.lv). The Estonian Rural Travel Association, Vilmsi 53B, 10147 Tallinn (☏600 9999, ⊛www.maaturism.ee) is another source of information on rural B&Bs, but doesn't as yet offer a booking service.

In Tallinn, Tartu and Pärnu, another cheap alternative to hotels are **private rooms**. These usually involve staying in the spare room of an apartment-block dweller and sharing their WC/bathroom. Although you'll usually be greeted by a spick-and-span room and a friendly host, be aware that these standards can't be guaranteed. Prices are around 250EEK for a single, 450EEK for a double. The Rasastra agency in Tallinn (see p.306) can fix you up with rooms in all three cities; otherwise contact the Majutusbüroo in Pärnu (p.353) or the tourist office in Tartu (p.379).

Hostels and campsites

Estonia has a modest network of **hostels**, ranging from large, concrete buildings, with a multitude of three- to four-bed rooms, to small (often privately owned establishments) offering an unpredictable range of sleeping quarters – from sparsely furnished, bunk-packed dormitories to cosy doubles. Prices range from 150 to 250EEK per person.

The geographical distribution of hostels is somewhat haphazard: there's a good choice in Tallinn, a couple in the Lahemaa National Park, a couple in Pärnu – and a handful elsewhere. Most (but not all) hostels are members of the Estonian Youth Hostel Association (Narva mnt 16-25, 10120 Tallinn, ☏646 1455, ⊛www.baltichostels .net), which can provide information and make bookings.

The most basic form of **campsite** (*kämping*) in Estonia is a simple patch of ground where you're allowed to pitch a tent for 50–60EEK. Earth toilets may be provided, but running water usually isn't. These sites are particularly common in the Lahemaa National Park (where camping is actually free, provided you stick to the official park-run sites) – wardens call round every day to collect rubbish and drop off free supplies of firewood. Many small hotels and guesthouses in rural Estonia allow camping in the garden for about 60EEK – in these places you'll be allowed access to a toilet and running water.

Some larger campsites are equipped with toilets and washing facilities and also provide accommodation in three- to four-bed cabins for around 180 to 260EEK per person. Caravans are something of a novelty in Estonia, although there are at least a couple of sites (at Pärnu and near Võsu in the Lahemaa National Park) that have electricity points for trailers.

Eating and drinking

For centuries, rye bread, salted herring and beer formed the Estonians' staple diet, with roast pork making an appearance on festive occasions. Such staples are still the backbone of the eating and drinking scene, although nowadays there's a great deal else besides. As in much of northern Europe, calorific meat dishes and dairy products set the tone of Estonia's national cuisine, although you can find plenty in the way of salads and ethnic foods – especially in Tallinn and other cities.

Eating

Eating in towns and cities usually takes place in **restaurants** (*restoran*) with menus and table service, or in **cafés** (*kohvik*) where you order and pay at the counter. Cafés often provide a simpler repertoire of main courses than restaurants and are usually much cheaper – they're also good places to tuck into snacks and sweets. In rural or well-touristed areas you'll come across traditional **inns** (*kõrts*), which cater for both eaters and drinkers and concentrate on standard Estonian meat-and-potato dishes. In addition, a lot of **pubs and bars** (see "Drinking" overleaf) offer a full menu of cooked food. Restaurants and inns are usually open till 10pm in small towns and rural areas, 11pm or midnight in cities and resorts. Cafés usually close at around 7/8pm, earlier on Sundays. By and large, you should be able to have a decent meal (two courses and a drink) for around 150EEK in restaurants, 100EEK in cafés, although prices in the more upmarket establishments in Tallinn are creeping ever upwards. Watch out for restaurants and cafés offering excellent deals on a **dish of the day** (*päevapraad*) – details of which are usually chalked up on a board outside.

For **self-catering** and picnicking, basics like bread, cheese, smoked meat and tinned fish can be picked up in supermarkets, while the full range of fruit and vegetables is available at outdoor markets in most towns of any size. Most high streets have a bakery (*pagariäri*) where you can pick up bread and pastries.

Snacks, starters and salads

The most characteristic Estonian starter is *sült*, a mixture of pork bits set in jelly that is definitely an acquired taste – a family meal or festive occasion would be unthinkable without a big bowl of the stuff on the table. Salted herring (*heeringas* or *räim*), smoked eel (*angerjas*) and sliced sausage (*voorst*) frequently feature as restaurant starters or bar snacks and invariably come with a few slices of delicious dark rye bread (*leib*).

Soup (*supp*) is either eaten as a starter or a lunchtime snack in its own right; available pretty much everywhere is *seljanka*, a broth of Russian origin featuring meat, pickled vegetables and sometimes (in its Estonian version at least) fish. Other light meals that you'll come across – in cafés more often than in restaurants – include *pelmenid* (ravioli-like parcels of minced meat), *pirukas* (dough stuffed with bacon, cabbage or other fillings) and *pankoogid* (pancakes) which can come with cheese, meat or mushrooms.

Many cafés offer **salads** (*salat*), which can range from a sorry-looking bowl of peas and gerkhins drenched in sour cream to a healthy platter of greens and other ingredients, substantial enough to serve as a light meal in its own right – tuna salad (*tuunikasalat*) is one of the most common.

Main courses

The quintessential Estonian main course comprises **pork** (*sia*), potatoes (*kartulid*) and sauerkraut (*mulgikapsad*) – and during the Soviet era this was all that most restaurants ever bothered serving. Pork is most commonly served roasted or pan-fried in the form of a *karbonaad* – a chop coated in tasty batter. Cuts of pork usually come with a healthy rind of fat which, when properly cooked, can be quite delicious. Other meats that crop up regularly on menus are chicken (*kana*), steak (*biifsteik*) and a locally produced form of blood sausage known as *verevoorst*. Lamb (*lamba*) is much less common unless you're eating in a grill restaurant devoted to Caucasian cooking, in which case it will probably feature in a *šašlõkk* (shish kebab). Freshwater **fish** (*kala*) figures strongly on restaurant menus, with pan-fried trout (*forell*), perch (*ahven*) or pike (*haug*) being the most popular. Main courses are usually served with potatoes and seasonal vegetables and frequently come with lashings of sour cream (*hapukoor*).

Vegetarians are not well catered for, though a few places make a token effort – especially the growing number of (generally rather good) ethnic restaurants in Tallinn.

Desserts

Estonian cafés serve up a mouth-watering array of sweets, most of which crop up on restaurant menus, too. The satisfyingly smooth *mannapuder* (semolina pudding) rules the roost as far as indigenous desserts are concerned – it often comes garnished with local fruits and berries. Pancakes, usually filled with jam, are also ubiquitous. If you want a daytime nibble to go with your coffee then you can choose between a sticky bun (*sai*) or a slice of cake (*kook*) – the latter is a blanket term covering everything from chocolate cake and cheesecake to fruit flan.

One local delicacy you'll see in the best bakeries and delicatessens is *kringel*, a sweet loaf filled with dried fruit.

Drinking

An ever-increasing range of pubs and bars – most of which imitate Irish or American models – are beginning to take over the Estonian drinking scene, especially in Tallinn and other major centres. Many cafés (*kohvik*) only serve soft drinks and are closed by mid-evening, although some stay open later and offer alcohol too.

Estonians are enthusiastic drinkers, with **beer** (*õlu*) being the most popular tipple. The principal local brands are Saku and A. Le Coq, both of which are rather tame, lager-style brews, although both companies also produce stronger porters (*tume*). The strongest beers are found on the islands – best known is the deceptively sweet Saaremaa õlu (widely available in supermarkets, less so in bars), which has twice the alcohol content of regular brands. Inland, a number of smaller breweries continue to supply the pubs in their local areas, notably Wiru in the northeast – their Palmse porter is well worth trying. Beer is sold in measures of 0.3 or 0.5 of a litre, although many establishments outside Tallinn only stock 0.5 litre glasses, believing the consumption of lesser quantities to be an affectation.

Most common of the spirits is **vodka** (*viin*) – either the locally made Viru Valge or Russian brands – which is usually drunk with juice or a fizzy-drink mixer. Local alcoholic specialities include *hõõgvein* (mulled wine) and Vana Tallinn, a syrupy, medicinal-looking liqueur, best mixed with blackcurrant juice or black coffee.

Coffee (*kohv*) sometimes comes as espresso or cappuccino in the better cafés, although filter coffee is more common and it's usually served black, unless you specify *koorega* (with cream).

Opening hours and public holidays

Most **shops** are open Monday to Friday 9/10am–6/7pm and Saturday 10am–2/3pm.

Some food shops stay open until 10pm or later and are also open on Sundays. Museum and gallery opening times vary greatly from one place to the next, although they're usually closed on Mondays and frequently on Tuesdays as well. Estonia's Protestant churches generally close outside mass times unless they're of historical or artistic importance, in which case their opening hours will be similar to those of museums. Orthodox churches frequented by Estonia's Russian minority are much more likely to be open all day for the benefit of devout locals.

Public holidays

Most shops, banks and museums close on the following public holidays:

Jan 1 New Year's Day
Feb 24 Independence Day
Good Friday
May 1 May Day
Whitsun
June 23 Victory Day
June 24 St John's Day
August 20 Day of Restoration of Independence
Dec 25 & 26 Christmas

Festivals and events

Although traditional festivities and folk practices don't fill the Estonian calendar in the same way as they do in Latvia and Lithuania, there are several major seasonal events, many of which are closely related to the traditional work-cycle of the agricultural year.

As elsewhere in Europe, **Easter** is both a Christian feast and a much more general celebration of the coming spring, with painted eggs and general over-consumption of festive food setting the tone. Easter is celebrated with more gusto by Estonia's Orthodox minority, who mark the event by processing around churches with lighted candles at midnight on Easter Saturday – Orthodox Easter takes place two to three weeks after the Catholic/Protestant event.

Until recently, the other great springtime festival was **St George's Day** (Jüripäev) on April 23, traditionally the last chance to indulge in feasting and drinking before the sowing season – sadly it's not much observed nowadays. Celebrations of **St John's Day** (Jaanipäev) on June 24 have proved more enduring. Originally, the last chance for a knees-up before the hard work of the harvesting season began, St John's Day is still associated with hedonistic abandon – and for working Estonians it's the most important day off of the summer. On **June 23** most people head for the countryside with family and friends and spend the night drinking and carousing, staying up long enough to greet the sunrise on the longest day of the year.

Before World War II, late October was marked by the four-day holiday known as *kliistripühad* ("shutting the windows"), when people mended cracked window frames and sealed up draughty cavities in preparation for the coming winter. Early November is traditionally a period of remembrance roughly analogous to **All Souls' Day** in Catholic Europe, when families visit cemeteries to tidy graves and lay flowers. This period traditionally comes to an end on **St Martin's Day** (Mardipäev) on November 10, when – in some areas – children dressed as beggars do the rounds of neighbourhood houses asking for treats. **Christmas** (Jõulud) is pretty much the same as in the rest of Europe, with children hassling a fat, bearded bloke (Jõuluvana) for gifts while their parents pig out on roast pork (*seapraad*), gingerbread (*piparkoogid*) and mulled wine (*hõõgvein*).

Calendar of events and festivals

Jazzkaar Tallinn (@www.jazzkaar.ee). Top-name jazz concerts in Tallinn, with some events in Tartu as well. April.

Soup City Days (Supilinna päevad) Tartu. Three days of art and music in Tartu's run-down bohemian suburb. Last weekend in April.

University Spring Days (Ülikooli kevadpäevad) Tartu. Five days of partying and feasting, straddling May 1. Late April/early May.

International Dance Festival (Rahvusvahelisel tantsufestival) Tartu. Contemporary dance from all over Europe. Late May/early June.

Old Town Days Tallinn. Medieval parades and jousting tournaments. Early June.

Pühajärve Beach Party (@www.beachparty.ee). Pop festival with live bands and DJs on the shores of Lake Pühajärve, Otepää. June.

Early Music Festival Haapsalu (@www.concertogrosso.ee). Local and international ensembles perform in Haapsalu's cathedral. Early July.

Summer Music Festival Tartu. Classical, contemporary and jazz concerts at venues all over town. Early June to late August.

Hansa Days Tartu (@www.tartu.ee/hansa). Medieval-style fair with street musicians and tournaments. Late June.

Folklore Festival Viljandi (Viljandi pärimuusika festival; @www.folk.ee). Estonia's biggest ethno bash. July.

Folklore Festival Võru (@www.werro.ee/folkloor). Estonian and international ensembles. Mid-July.

Days of the Setu Kingdom (Setokuningriik) Obinitsa (@www.hot.ee/setokuningriik). Folk festival celebrating the culture of the Setu people in Estonia's far southeast. August.

Days of the White Lady Haapsalu (@www.daam.haapsalu.ee). Drinking and dancing in the castle courtyard. Mid-August.

Dark Nights Film Festival (Pimedate Ööde) Tallinn (@www.poff.ee). Contemporary art-house film festival. December.

Entertainment

Estonians takes their leisure time seriously, and there's a correspondingly wide range of classical music and serious theatre on offer, especially in the capital. Tallinn can also muster a huge choice of clubs, cinemas, and venues offering live jazz, rock and pop.

Classical music

Estonia's principal musical institutions – national symphony orchestra, chamber orchestra, opera and ballet – are all based in Tallinn, although they frequently perform in the provinces, most notably Tartu and Pärnu. The @www.concert.ee site carries schedule details.

Contemporary classical music occupies an important place in the regular Estonian repertoire, thanks in large part to local-born composer **Arvo Pärt** (b.1935), whose sparsely orchestrated, meditative pieces have earned him a towering international reputation. Having spent the 1960s experimenting with serialism and other modernist techniques, the devoutly religious Pärt began to develop a much more personal style in the 1970s, with works like *Summa* (1977), the *St John Passion* (1982) and *Stabat Mater* (1986) being acclaimed as classics of spiritually inspired minimalism. Clearly no stranger to the Estonian choral tradition, Pärt has also used German-language evensong and medieval Latin in his works.

Considerably more rooted in indigenous folk tradition is Pärt's near-contemporary **Veljo Tormis** (b.1930), whose choral works take their inspiration from the mesmeric, chant-like runic songs that form such an important part in Estonian musical heritage. The best-known of Tormis's works are *Curse Upon Iron* (1972), which combines sweeping orchestral passages with archaic, shamanistic drum beats; and *Karelian Destiny* (1989), a cycle of fairytale-esque narrative songs drawing on the heritage of Estonians, Finns and other related Finno-Ugric peoples.

Archaic sounds of another sort feature in the repertoire of **Hortus Musicus**, a world-renowned early music ensemble that is based in Tallinn and performs regularly in the city. Specializing in the music of the Renaissance and Baroque periods, they often dress up in the clothes of the period as well as playing as-authentic-as-possible instruments.

Clubbing and popular music

There's a growing and increasingly sophisticated choice of **club culture** to be sampled in Tallinn, where you'll find everything from heaving discos playing mainstream chart music to ironic retro clubs and all manner of niche DJ styles. There's a lot of activity outside the capital too, with the student-filled town of Tartu offering a particularly enjoyable range of clubs and the beach resort of Pärnu coming to life in the summer.

Some clubs in Tallinn and Tartu host live gigs by local pop-rock acts and there are a couple of music bars in the capital where you can hear competent cover bands churning out blues and R&B standards. The jazz scene is hampered by a lack of regular venues, although the **Jazzkaar festival** (held in Tallinn every spring; see p.297) is arguably the best such event in the Baltics, attracting major international names.

Estonia is full of competent middle-of-the-road **rock bands**, few of which display much in the way of character or quality. One exception is Jäärboiler (also known as Jäääär), whose intelligent blend of jazz, folk and rock is sufficiently involving to overcome any language barrier. However, the best in Estonian music is to be found out on the fringes – you'll find the easy-listening indie-pop of Dallas or the frenetic rhythmic assault of DJ collective Unabomba far more rewarding than anything in the mainstream.

Few Estonian pop-rock acts have made much of an impression internationally, save perhaps for the manufactured duo of Tanel Pader and Dave Benton, who had the dubious honour of winning the Eurovision Song Contest in 2001. Not a single Western record company showed interest in releasing their winning song, but they're still very much around in Estonia (separately rather than as a duo), producing albums every bit as bland as you would expect.

Cinema

Cinemas in Estonia show mainstream movies pretty much immediately after their release in Western Europe. They're shown in the original language, with Estonian subtitles.

During the Soviet period, the Tallinn Film Studio churned out several workmanlike films a year, many of which were made in Russian to appeal to a wider Soviet market. As far as the locals are concerned, the outstanding product of this era was the Estonian-language *The Last Relic* (*Viimne Reliikvia*; 1969), a cross between swashbuckler, sex comedy and musical, set among the religious struggles of the sixteenth century and intended to demonstrate that Estonian cinema was as capable of producing lavish historical epics as anyone. It's still great to look at and some of the countryside scenes could almost pass for an advertisement for the Estonian Tourist Board. There's certainly been nothing like it since, although Kristjan Taska's intelligent historical drama *Names in Marble* (*Nimed Marmortahvlil*; 2002), set in the post-World War I struggles between Estonians and Bolsheviks, points towards a rosier future for the industry.

Internationally, Estonia is known less for its full-length features than for its animated films, thanks largely to the efforts of the Tallinn-based studio Nukufilm (@www .nukufilm.ee). Established in 1957 by Elbert Tuganov, the studio has garnered a global reputation for its use of superbly fashioned dolls and puppets. Most of its output is intended for children, although some of the studio's more surreal products – especially recent work by Riho Unt and Mait Laas – goes down equally well with the European art-house crowd.

Spectator sports

Few Estonian teams have tasted success in the international arena, which probably explains the lack of excitement generated by even the most popular sports, **basketball and football**. The Estonian football team play their home matches in Tallinn and these are your best bet if you're looking for a modicum of atmosphere and a decent-sized crowd; domestic league games rarely attract more than a few hundred paying fans.

Estonia is not entirely without its sporting heroes, however: decathlete Erki Nool put the country on the map when he won Olympic gold in 2000, while cross-country skier Andrus Veerpalu brought back one gold and one silver medal from the 2002 Winter Olympics in Salt Lake City.

Directory

Addresses In Estonian addresses, the name of the street or square comes first, the number second. The following terms or their abbreviations are commonly encountered: *väljak* (square); *mantee* (mnt) – road; *puistee* (pst) – avenue; and *tänav* (tn) – street.

Contraceptives The best place to find condoms is at a pharmacy (*apteek*).

Emergencies Police ☎110, ambulance and fire ☎112.

Left luggage There's usually a left-luggage office (*pakihõid*) in big-town bus stations, charging 10–15EEK per item.

Tipping Tipping is only expected in Estonia if you're in a restaurant or smart café with table service, or if you've had a meal and/or big round of drinks in a bar. In these cases, round up your bill by ten to fifteen percent.

Toilets Public toilets (*tualettid*) can usually be found in bus stations. Gents are marked with a letter "M" or a ▼ symbol; ladies with an "N" or a ▲ symbol.

3.1

Tallinn

One of the best-preserved medieval towns in northern Europe, Estonia's human-scale capital of **TALLINN** rarely fails to make a favourable first impression. The Old Town's rough-paved alleys, slender steeples and barrel-shaped towers could have jumped straight out of the pages of a medieval illustrated manuscript. Tallinn is no historical theme park, however, but rather the commercial and political heart of an extraordinarily fast-changing nation, and the gleaming-new, glass-fronted banks, business parks and café-bars provide the back-drop to a work-hard-play-hard culture that imbues the city with a palpable, restless energy.

Despite being the capital of an independent Estonia from 1918 until 1940 and again from 1991, modern-day Tallinn is a more hybrid creation than many Estonians would care to admit. The city's name, derived from the Estonian *taani lin-nus*, meaning "Danish Fort", is a reminder of the fact that the city was founded by the Danes at the beginning of the thirteenth century, and since that time political control has been in the hands of foreigners for lengthy periods. The Germans have undoubtedly had the most lasting influence on the city; Tallinn was one of the lead-ing cities of the Hanseatic League, the German-dominated association of Baltic trading cities, and for centuries it was known to the outside world by its Teutonic name, Reval. Even when Estonia was ruled by the kings of Sweden or the tsars of Russia, the city's public life was controlled by the German nobility and its com-merce run by German merchants. During half a century of Soviet rule Russian speakers flooded into the city – even now they make up some 45 percent of the population and the Russian language persists as an ever-present shadow culture, heard constantly on the streets and in neighbourhood bars.

June, July and August are the most popular times to visit Tallinn, although the city's year-round cultural attractions and club culture ensure that it's a rewarding weekend destination whatever time of year you choose to visit. Specific seasonal attractions include the Advent period, when there's a **Christmas Market** selling handicrafts, gingerbread and other treats on Raekoja plats; and the **Old Town Days**, straddling the first weekend of June, when locals parade around in medieval garb, a knights' tournament is held to choose the May Count and there's a "rat race" in which contestants run round the streets carrying briefcases and mobile phones.

Some history

Tallinn began life as a trading post where Vikings came to buy furs and wax from Estonian tribes. It only became a defensible settlement with a permanent popula-tion in 1219, when it was conquered by empire-building Danish **King Valdemar II**, "the Victorious", who had just been given free licence by the Pope to subjugate the Estonian heathens. Valdemar built a castle and a cathedral on the rock known as Toompea, and a town of merchants and craftsmen soon grew up at its foot. Most of those who chose to settle in Danish-ruled Tallinn were of German or Flemish stock and they called the town Reval – a name that stuck until 1918. Estonians, drawn to the city to work as servants and labourers, were allowed to reside in the city, but not given full citizens' rights.

With the **Teutonic Knights** gobbling up more and more of Estonia from the 1220s onwards, the Danes hung on to Tallinn (save for one short period of Teutonic overlordship in 1227–38) until 1347, when cash-strapped King Valdemar III sold it – along with the rest of his remaining possessions in Estonia – to the Livonian Order for 19,000 silver marks. By this time the town had already become a member of the **Hanseatic League** (see box on p.302), which united German-speaking cities throughout northern Europe in a trading alliance – stimulating the emergence of a boisterous, self-confident mercantile culture. The townsfolk of Tallinn, resentful of the power wielded by the knights and bishops on Toompea, enthusiastically adopted Protestantism in the early sixteenth century; riots in September 1524 destroyed most of the town's medieval altarpieces and put monks and clergy to flight.

Weakened by the Reformation and squeezed by neighbouring powers, the Livonian Order dissolved itself in 1561, leaving Tallinn to be fought over by Russians and Swedes. The resulting **Livonian Wars** led to a decline in trade and despite serving the victorious Swedes as an important military and administrative centre, Tallinn's days as a mercantile powerhouse were over. Swedish control came to an end in 1710, when Peter the Great's armies took the city. For the next two centuries Tallinn was part of the **Russian Empire**. By the early nineteenth century it had established itself as the most fashionable bathing resort in the region, with the cream of St Petersburg society taking up residence in town for the whole month of July. The arrival of the railway in 1870, however, transformed Tallinn into an important port and industrial centre, effectively putting paid to its days as a seaside resort and Baltic folk trooped off to the beaches of Pärnu and Haapsalu instead.

Industrialization also changed Tallinn's **ethnic profile**, with more and more workers being drawn from the surrounding countryside. At the start of the nineteenth century barely one third of Tallinn's population had been Estonian, yet a hundred years later this proportion had more than doubled. Estonian-language

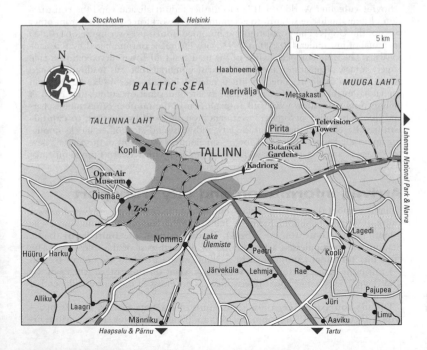

The Hanseatic League

In the thirteenth century, maritime traffic in the Baltic was controlled by the Danes, prompting cities across northern Europe to band together in an attempt to protect their trading and fishing rights. Gradually, a group of cities, centred on the German port of Lübeck, developed a common set of trading standards and ostracized those who didn't sign up to them. Delegates from these cities occasionally met at Lübeck to debate issues of common concern and their association became known as "Hansa", meaning "union" or "guild".

Despite being subject to the Danish crown throughout much of the thirteenth century, Tallinn eagerly signed up to the Hanseatic League in 1285. Other Baltic members included Tartu, Pärnu, Rīga, Ventspils and Cēsis.

The league was initially a loose alliance whose members could join and leave as they pleased, but in the fourteenth century the need to defend trade routes bound the Hansa members into a tighter union. The Hanseatic cities held annual assemblies and organized common defence, successfully prosecuting a war against the Danes in the 1360s. However, it remained a politically loose organization, with most of its member-cities owing allegiance to a variety of different north European rulers, whose interests often overrode those of the league.

The league's influence faded in the fifteenth century, when the exhaustion of the Baltic's herring stocks led to a slump in fishing and Hanseatic cities began competing amongst themselves for access to the same markets. With its members no longer tied to a common agenda, the league slowly folded through lack of interest.

parties won a majority of seats on the town council for the first time in 1904, turning Tallinn into the obvious focus of the Estonian national movement. The Germans, who had for so long formed the city's elite, now numbered less than ten percent of the total and were outnumbered by Russians.

Soviet rule after World War II led to further industrialization and the construction of dour, high-rise suburbs to accommodate a workforce imported from other parts of the USSR. The population mushroomed from a pre-war figure of 170,000 to a total of just under 420,000 in 1991, with Estonians outnumbered by Russian-speakers. The spire-studded skyline of the medieval Old Town survived Soviet rule largely intact, bequeathing the city a tourist potential that was readily exploited when Estonia finally regained its independence. Indeed, since 1991, the Estonian capital has established itself as a popular city-break destination, stimulating a rash of architectural renovation work and an explosion in the number of restaurants, bars and clubs. The influx of foreign investment brought about by a **return to capitalism** has also changed the face of the city, with glass-and-steel office blocks sprouting up on the fringes of the Old Town – an eloquent statement of the capital's new self-image as a young, dynamic society ready to deal with Western Europe on equal terms.

Arrival, information and city transport

Tallinn's **airport** (Lennujaam) is 3km southeast of the city centre and linked to Viru väljak, just east of the Old Town, by bus #2 (Mon–Sat every 20min; Sun every 30min; journey time 10min; 15EEK). **Trains** arrive at the **Balti jaam** (Baltic Station) on Toompuiestee, a five-minute walk northwest of the Old Town. The city's **bus terminal** (Autobussijaam) is 2km east at Lastekodu 46 – trams #2 and #4 run from nearby Tartu mnt to Viru väljak, right on the eastern fringes of the Old Town. The passenger **port** (Reisisadam) is northeast of the centre at the end of Sadama.

Tallinn's **tourist office**, a few steps south of Raekoja plats at Kullasseppa 4 (April–Oct Mon–Fri 9am–6pm, Sat & Sun 10am–4pm; Nov–March Mon–Fri

9am–5pm, Sat 10am–4pm; ☎645 7777, ⓦwww.tourism.tallinn.ee), provides well-informed advice about the city and a free city-centre sightseeing map and also sells a selection of more detailed maps and guides. You can also buy the **Tallinn Card** (ⓦwww.tallinn.ee/tallinncard) here, which entitles you to free use of public transport, entrance to all museums and main sights, a tour of the city, discounts on car rental and savings in some shops and cafés. A 24-hour card costs 205EEK, a 48-hour one 275EEK, and a 72-hour one 325EEK – well worth it if you're seriously planning to blitz your way round the museums. The excellent *Tallinn In Your Pocket* city guide (35EEK; ⓦwww.inyourpocket.com) carries informed restaurant and bar **listings**, as well as plenty of info on local services and shopping, and is available from shops and hotels.

Most of Tallinn's sights can be covered on foot and those slightly further out are served by an extensive **tram, bus and trolleybus** network. Services are frequent and cheap, though usually crowded, with tickets common to all three systems available from kiosks near stops for 10EEK or from the driver for 15EEK. Tickets

---

Moving on from Tallinn

Tallinn is the Baltics' main gateway to Scandinavia, with a host of ferries, hydrofoils and catamarans conveying passengers across the Gulf of Finland **to Helsinki**. Ferries take about 3hr 15min to make the crossing; hydrofoils and catamarans are faster, taking on average 1hr 30–40min, but only run when the gulf isn't frozen over – which roughly means from early March to late December, although beware that some winters last longer than others. There's also at least one ferry daily **to Stockholm** (16hr; overnight) and three weekly **to Rostock** between June and September. An easy ten-minute walk northeast of the Old Town, the **Passenger Port** (Reisisadam) is divided into four terminals: A, B, C and D. A, B and C are grouped together on the northern side of the port, at the end of Sadama; D is on the south side, which entails an extra ten-minute walk round the dock; bus #2 goes there every twenty to thirty minutes. Terminals A and D are equipped with cafés, exchange offices offering reasonable rates, and luggage lockers (Estonian coins required).

Most travel agents (see p.331) in the Old Town sell **tickets** to Helsinki and Stockholm, and the main operators have offices in the harbour-front terminals. The leading operators for Helsinki are Eckerö Lines at terminal B (car ferries; ☎631 8606, ⓦwww.eckeroline.ee); Nordic Jet Line at terminal C (catamarans; ☎613 7000, ⓦwww.njl.ee); Silja Line at terminal A (car ferries and catamarans; ☎611 6661, ⓦwww.silja.ee); and Tallink, also at terminal A (car ferries and catamarans; ☎640 9808, ⓦwww.hansatee.ee). The main operator for Stockholm is Tallink at terminal D (☎644 8348, ⓦwww.estline.ee), while tickets to Rostock are handled by Silja Line (see above). It's worth bearing in mind also that getting an onward connection from Helsinki to Stockholm may be quicker than going direct from Tallinn.

All domestic and international **bus routes** are served by the main bus station (Autobussijaam), 2km southeast of the Old Town at Lastekodu 46 (tram #2 from Mere pst or #4 from Pärnu mnt to the Autobussijaam stop). In summer and on weekends throughout the year it's worth booking international bus tickets in advance – as there are no agencies in the centre of town handling reservations, you'll have to trek out to the bus station itself to do this.

Train services from the Balti Jaam (Baltic Station), right on the west side of the Old Town, are more infrequent and take longer than buses – St Petersburg and Moscow are the only international destinations offered. Tickets for commuter trains to Klooga and Paldiski are sold at the Elektriraudtee counter out on the platform; tickets for all other domestic services are sold on the ground floor of the main station building, while international bookings are handled upstairs.

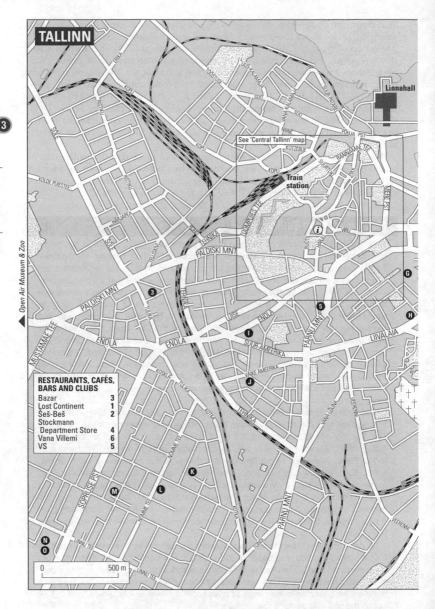

◀ Open Air Museum & Zoo

RESTAURANTS, CAFÉS, BARS AND CLUBS

Bazar	**3**
Lost Continent	**1**
Šeš-Beš	**2**
Stockmann Department Store	**4**
Vana Villemi	**6**
VS	**5**

should be validated using the on-board punches. **Taxis** are reasonably cheap (around 10EEK per kilometre, slightly more after 10pm). Most companies have a minimum charge of 25EEK, but a taxi from one point in the city centre to another should never exceed 50EEK. You'll find taxi ranks at all major entrances to the pedestrianized Old Town, although rates are often cheaper if you phone for one in advance (see p.331 for recommended taxi companies).

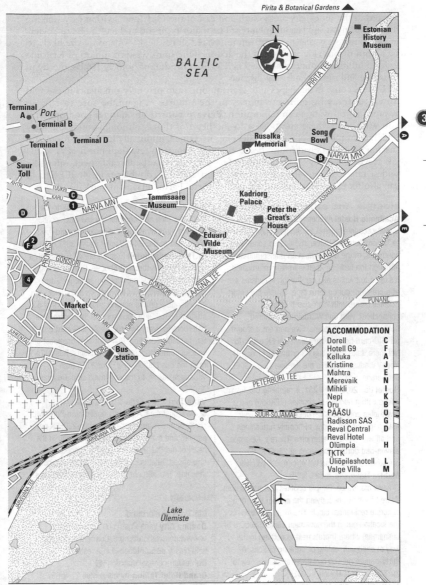

Pirita & Botanical Gardens ▲

N

BALTIC
SEA

■ Estonian
History
Museum

Terminal
A *Port*
Terminal B
Terminal C Terminal D

Suur
Toll

PIRITA TEE

Rusalka
Memorial

Song
Bowl

NARVA MNT

Tammsaare
Museum

NARVA MNT

Kadriorg
Palace

Peter the
Great's
House

LASNAMÄE

Eduard
Vilde
Museum

LAAGNA TEE

PRONKSI

GONSIORI

VILMSI

GONSIORI

LAAGNA TEE

PALDIST

PAE

VÕIDUJOOKSU

PAE/PÄRNARE

PUNANE

Market

TARTU MNT

TÜRNPU

LUBJA

LASNAMÄE

MAJAKA

MAJAKA PÕIK

PAE

Bus
station

ODRA

PETERBURI TEE

SUUR-SÕJAMÄE

JÄRVEVANA TEE

JÄRVEVANA TEE

TARTU MAANTEE

Lake
Ülemiste

ACCOMMODATION	
Dorell	C
Hotell G9	F
Kelluka	A
Kristiine	J
Mahtra	E
Merevaik	N
Mihkli	I
Nepi	K
Oru	B
PAÄSU	U
Radisson SAS	G
Reval Central	D
Reval Hotel	
Olümpia	H
TKTK	
Üliõpilashotell	L
Valge Villa	M

Accommodation

New **hotels** are opening up every month or so in Tallinn, ensuring there's no shortage of modern, high-standard accommodation. Most of the hotels in the Old Town are in the luxury bracket or just below, although there are a few isolated bargains to be had, providing you reserve in advance. Most mid-range choices are located in the inner-city areas south and east of the Old Town, within easy walking distance of most sights and amenities. The majority of the budget hotels are Soviet-era establishments that haven't been renovated since the 1980s and they're likely to be a tram or bus ride away from the action – the southwestern suburb of Kristiine is good hunting ground for these. There's also a handful of homely **B&Bs**, mostly in Kristiine and outer residential districts.

Hostels come in all shapes and sizes, ranging from privately run affairs in the Old Town to decaying concrete blocks in the suburbs – again, be sure to ring in advance if you want a central location. **Private rooms** are another good option if you want somewhere cheap close to the heart of things, although conditions vary widely – in most cases you'll be sleeping in a small, minimally furnished room and sharing your host's bathroom. *Bed & Breakfast Rasastra*, a few steps north of Viru väljak at Mere 4 (daily 9.30am–6pm; ☎661 6291, ⊛www.bedbreakfast.ee), offers the widest range of central rooms (singles from 260EEK, doubles from 460EEK) and can also fix up similar accommodation in Tartu, Pärnu, Haapsalu and Viljandi.

Hostels and student dorms

Academic Hostel Akadeemia 11 ☎620 2275, ⊛www.academichostel.ee. Student dorm attached to Tallinn Technical University, located some 5km southwest of the Old Town in an uninspiring area, although the building itself is freshly refurbished. It's open to tourists all year, though vacancies are at a premium during term time. Simple but smart doubles (some with high-speed Internet connection), with one WC/bathroom shared between every two rooms. Five percent discount for ISIC-card holders. Breakfast 35EEK extra. To get there, take trolleybus #3 or bus #E11 or #91 from Vabaduse väljak to the Keemia stop. 450EEK per person.

Hostel Uus 26 ☎641 1281. A rambling Old Town house with a handful of doubles (EEK650) and a few triples and quads (270EEK per person), all featuring a hodge-podge of homely furnishings and all with shared bathrooms. There's a cramped, eleven-bed dorm with places at 240EEK. No breakfast, but morning tea or coffee if you ask.

Mahtra Mahtra 44 ☎621 8828, ⊛www.mahtra.ee. Simple doubles and triples with shared facilities, occupying the bottom floor of a concrete residential block. The main drawback is the location out in the downbeat eastern suburb of Lasnamäe, where there's next to nothing in the way of shopping, eating or drinking options. A thirty-minute ride on bus #35 from Viru väljak to the Mahtra stop. Doubles 300EEK.

Merevaik Sõpruse 182 ☎655 3767, ⊛www.hostelmerevaik.ee. An uninspiring location, but neat singles (280EEK), doubles (340EEK) and triples (390EEK) on the second floor of a sprawling block. The furnishings have taken a bit of a battering over the years, but the place is neat and tidy. One toilet/shower for every two rooms. Breakfast 30EEK extra. Ten-percent reductions for HI and ISIC cardholders. To get there, take

trolleybus #2 or #3 from Vabaduse väljak to the Linnu tee stop and head for the red-brick school building straight ahead: the hostel is round the back, next to the *PÄÄSU* hotel (see p.308).

TKTK Üliõpilashotell Nõmme tee 47 ☎655 2679 or 655 2663, ⊛ttkhotell@hot.ee. Spartan but spic-and-span doubles and triples – some with new carpets and bathroom tiles, others with Soviet-era furnishings – on the second and third floors of a student hostel 3km southwest of the centre. One bathroom to every two rooms. An ISIC card gets a ten-percent reduction. Buy your own breakfast and snacks in the student café downstairs. Bus #17A from the bus station, or #17 or #17A from Vabaduse väljak, to the Koolimaja stop. Doubles 350EEK.

Vana Tom Väike-Karja 1 ☎631 3252, ⊛www.hostel.ee. A friendly hostel-cum-hotel with spotless three- and four-bed dorms (230EEK per person) and some doubles (550EEK), bang in the heart of the Old Town. It's justifiably popular, so ring ahead. Guests can use the kitchen and coffee machine. Ten-percent reductions for HI members.

Hotels

Old Town and around

Domina City Vana-Posti 11/13 ☎681 3900, ⊛www.dominahotels.com. Comfortable rooms with classy design touches in a restored eighteenth-century mansion. ❼

Grand Hotel Tallinn Toompuiestee 27 ☎667 7000, ⊛www.grandhotel.ee. Don't be put off by the uninspiring, functional exterior; this four-star hotel just down the hill from the Old Town offers high-standard accommodation and has super-smooth standards of service. East-facing rooms have great views of Toompea. ❼

Old House Guesthouse Uus 22 ☎641 1464, ⊛www.oldhouse.ee. Perfectly situated in the Old Town, this small and friendly six-room B&B has bright, pristine rooms, although bathrooms are shared. ❸

Old Town Maestro's Suur-Karja 10 ☎626 2000, ⓦwww.maestrohotel.ee. Snazzy en-suites with TV in a tall, narrow building squeezed into a street packed with pubs, a stone's throw from Raekoja plats. ❻

Rotermanni Mere 6A ☎668 8588, ⓦwww.rotermanni.ee. A mid-range hotel occupying a converted warehouse in the Rotermann Quarter, a five-minute walk from the Old Town. Artfully packs roominess and comfort into what seems like a tight space. All rooms with TV and shower. ❹

Rotermanni Viiking Mere 6A ☎660 1934, ⓦwww.vikinghotel.ee. In many ways a cut price version of the *Rotermanni* (see above), and located opposite. Comfortable en-suites with TV, but on the small side. ❸

Scandic Hotel Palace Vabaduse väljak 3 ☎640 7300, ⓦwww.scandic-hotels.com. A handsome inter-war building on the flanks of a lively downtown square, offering deep-carpeted, pastel-hued rooms. Pretty much faultless in the comfort and service stakes. ❼

Schlössle Pühavaimu 13/15 ☎699 7777, ⓦwww.schlossle-hotels.com. A five-star bastion of poshness and comfort in an artfully restored Old Town building. With only 23 rooms, it preserves an intimate feel. Doubles start at 4850EEK. ❽

St Petersbourg Rataskaevu 7 ☎628 6500, ⓦwww.schlossle-hotels.com. Historic nineteenth-century hotel with smart, bright rooms and a few Art Deco touches in the social areas. Only slightly less luxurious than sister-hotel *Schlössle*. Doubles from 3800EEK. ❽

The Three Sisters Pikk 71 ☎630 6300, ⓦwww.threesistershotel.com. A beautifully renovated trio of adjacent medieval merchants' houses, with plenty in the way of wooden beams, painted ceilings and exposed brickwork. The superbly equipped rooms feature bright colour schemes and modern designer furnishings to create a tasteful blend of old and new. Doubles from 3900EEK. ❽

UniqueStay Paldiski mnt 3 ☎660 0700, ⓦwww.uniquestay.com. The ideal place for devotees of modern design, featuring bright, minimally decorated rooms (each with Internet terminals and unlimited supplies of tea and coffee) – all within spitting distance of the medieval delights of the Old Town. ❺

Vana Wiru Viru 11 (entrance round the corner on Müürivahe) ☎669 1500, ⓦwww.vanawiru.ee. A spanking-new establishment in a superb location and offering top-level comforts at an affordable price. ❻

Viru Viru väljak 4 ☎630 1390, ⓦwww.viru.ee. All the big hotel comforts and conveniences make this 22-storey, Finnish-owned place on the edge of the Old Town very popular with tour groups. Noisy in the morning. ❻

East and south of the Old Town

Dorell Karu 39, entrance through a passage on Narva mnt ☎626 1200, ⓦwww.hot.ee/dorell. If you don't mind hyper-garish decor and mind-altering carpets, you could do worse than the *Dorell*, a good-value choice, ten minutes' walk from the Old Town. All rooms have TV and the cheaper ones are non-en-suite. ❷–❸

Hotell G9 Gonsiori 9 ☎626 7100, ⓦwww.hotelg9.ee. A simple place on the third floor of an office block within easy walking distance of the Old Town. Rooms are sparsely furnished, thin-carpet affairs, but all are en-suite with TV. If you're travelling as more than a twosome they can always stick extra beds in the room for a further 150EEK each. Breakfast costs an extra 50EEK in the downstairs café. ❸

Kristiine Luha 16 ☎646 4600, ⓦwww.kristiine.ee. A quiet, medium-sized place occupying two floors of a greying block around fifteen minutes' walk from the centre. The rooms are plain in the extreme, but have en-suite facilities and TV. Bus #5, #18, #36 or tram #3, #4 from Vabaduse väljak to the Luha stop. ❸

Mihkli Endla 23 ☎666 4800, ⓦwww.mihkli.ee. A mid-sized hotel only ten minutes from the centre on foot, offering smallish, sparsely furnished, but perfectly comfortable modern rooms with TV and shower. ❹

Radisson SAS Rävala pst 3 ☎669 0000, ⓦwww.radissonsas.com. Reliable standards of comfort and service in a towering modern structure. ❼

Reval Central Narva mnt 7 ☎669 0690, ⓦwww.revalhotels.com. A modern three-star with 200-plus rooms, within walking distance of the Old Town. Lacking in atmosphere, but the bright, uncluttered rooms are perfect for this price range. ❺

Reval Express Sadama 1 ☎667 8700, ⓦwww.revalhotels.com. A busy, impersonal box-hotel near the harbour that nevertheless delivers the goods: smart en-suites with TV within easy walking distance of all the sights. ❹

Reval Hotel Olümpia Liivalaia 33 ☎669 0690, ⓦwww.revalhotels.com. Glass-and-steel slab built in 1980 (when Tallinn hosted Olympic yachting events), with levels of comfort and service to justify its four-star status. The only central hotel with an indoor pool. ❼

Kristiine

Nepi Nepi 10 ☎655 1665 or 655 2254, ⓦwww.nepihotell.ee. A small and welcoming B&B with plain, brown-carpeted rooms, all with en-suite shower and TV. A trio of apartment-style rooms come with tasteful old furnishings. Bus #17 or #17A to Koolimaja, or bus #23 to Ööbiku. Breakfast is 50EEK extra. ❸

PÄÄSU Sõpruse 182 ☎654 2013, ⓦwww.infoweb.ee/paasu. Unpretentious place occupying one floor of a high school/higher education building some 3km southwest of the centre. Rooms have dated furnishings but all are clean and have TV. WC and shower shared between every two rooms. Directions as for *Merevaik* (see "Hostels" above). ❷

TKTK Üliopilashotell Nomme tee 47 ☎655 2679. A hotel attached to a student hostel some 3km southwest of the centre, offering plain but neat rooms at good rates. One bathroom for every two rooms. No breakfast. Take bus #17 or #17A from Vabaduse väljak to Koolimaja, or trolleybus #4 from the train station to Tedre. ❶

Valge Villa Kännu 26/2 ☎655 1196 or 654 2302, ⓦwww.white-villa.com. A comfortable B&B in a quiet suburban street, with a nice combination of modern interior design and traditional woody furnishings. Four cosy doubles with attic ceilings and tea/coffee-making facilities and six stylish suites with use of fridge and fireplace. Bus #17 or #17A to the Räägu stop, or trolleybus #2, #3, #4 to the Tedre stop. ❹

Northeastern suburbs

Kelluka Kelluka tee 11 ☎623 8811, ⓦwww.kelluka.ee. Quiet, pension-type place on the northeastern edge of town. Facilities include a sauna and pool – recommended if your funds stretch that far. Bus #5 from the centre to the Helmiku stop. ❸

Oru Narva mnt 120B ☎603 3300, ⓦwww.oruhotel.ee. Some 3km west of town, this peaceful, medium-sized place offers the same level of class and comforts that you'll find in the modern establishments in the Old Town – but at a slightly cheaper price. ❹

The City

The heart of Tallinn and location of most of its sights is the **Old Town** (Vanalinn), once enclosed by the city's medieval walls, significant stretches of which still exist. Above it looms **Toompea**, the hilltop stronghold of the German knights and bishops who nominally controlled the city during the Middle Ages. Beyond the medieval core, much of Tallinn is bland and uninteresting, though there are some notable exceptions, namely the park and palace at **Kadriorg** and the **Botanical Gardens** above the beach resort of **Pirita** – all located in the eastern suburbs. The **Open-air Ethnographic Museum** in Rocca al Mare is the one unmissable attraction in the western part of town.

The Old Town

Tallinn's largely pedestrianized Old Town is an enjoyable, atmospheric and ultimately addictive jumble of medieval churches, cobbled streets and gabled merchants' houses. With a street plan that comprises a confusion of curving streets and interconnecting passageways, there are few obvious itineraries to follow, although the **Raekoja plats** provides an obvious point of reference. From here, your best plan is to amble down any of the adjacent alleyways that take your fancy, emerging onto sinuous streets like **Pikk**, **Lai** and **Vene** – each of which is lined with tall, quietly imperious medieval warehouses. Must-visit attractions include the entertaining history displays at the **Tallinn City Museum** and the show-stopping medieval artworks in **St Nicholas's Church**.

Raekoja plats and around

The cobbled and gently sloping **Raekoja plats** (Town Hall Square) is as old as Tallinn itself. Surrounded by a handsome ensemble of pastel-coloured medieval houses, the square has become a living trademark of both the city and Estonia as a whole, reproduced on innumerable souvenirs and tourist posters. It is also a popular rallying point and a focus for displays of Estonian patriotic feeling: over 10,000 people packed the square in February 2002 to salute Andrus Veerpalu, the cross-country skiier who had just struck gold in the Winter Olympics at Salt Lake City, while eight months earlier it had been the site of a vast open-air reception for Tanel Padar and Dave Benton, winners of the 2001 Eurovision Song Contest – it was at this occasion that then Prime Minister Mart Laar made a since oft-quoted remark about Estonia singing its way out of the Soviet Union and into the European Union.

On the square's southern side stands an imposing reminder of the city's Hanseatic past: the fifteenth-century **Town Hall** (Tallinna raekoda), boasting an elegant arcade of Gothic arches and a delicate, slender steeple. Look out for the waterspouts in the shape of green-painted dragons just below the roof. Near the summit of the steeple you'll spy Vana Toomas (Old Thomas), a sixteenth-century weather vane in the form of a stout, spear-wielding sentry. According to legend, the real-life model for the weather vane was a local lad who excelled at the springtime "parrot-shooting" contests (which basically involved firing crossbow bolts at a painted wooden bird on top of a pole) organized by Tallinn's German-speaking elite. Unable to receive a prize owing to his low-born status, Toomas was instead rewarded with the job of town guard for life. Subsequently immortalized in copper, Toomas continues to watch over Tallinn and its citizens. Inside the Town Hall, the two main chambers – the Citizens' Hall and the Council Hall – are almost devoid of ornamentation, except for the latter's elaborately carved benches, the oldest surviving woodcarvings in the country.

Of the other old buildings lining the square, the most venerable is the **Town Council Pharmacy** (Raeapteek) in the northeastern corner; its cream-coloured facade dates from the seventeenth century, though the building is known to have existed in 1422 and may be much older. It's still a working pharmacy – which is probably a good job judging by the rather half-hearted attempt at creating a museum (Mon–Fri 9am–5pm; free) in one of its corners. If the Raeapteek leaves you underwhelmed, head for the former Town Jail (Raevangla) behind the Town Hall at Raekoja 4/6, now home to the **Museum of Photography** (Fotomuuseum; daily except Wed: March–Oct 10.30am–5.30pm; Nov–Feb 11am–5pm; 10EEK), an entertaining little photographic collection with views of Tallinn from the days when it was still known as Reval and portraits of Estonians in traditional costume (captions in English).

The Church of the Holy Ghost

Next to the Raeapteek, a small passage named Saiakang leads through to Pühavaimu tänav and one of the city's most appealing churches, the **Church of the Holy Ghost** (Pühavaimu kirik; daily 10am–2pm). A small Gothic building with stepped gables, it originally served as the Town Hall chapel before becoming the main church of Tallinn's Estonian-speaking population. In 1535, priests from the church compiled an Estonian-language Lutheran catechism, an important affirmation of identity at a time when most Estonians had been reduced to serfdom. The ornate clock set into the wall above the entrance dates from 1680 and is the oldest public timepiece in Tallinn. The slender, verdigris-coated spire was almost totally wrecked by fire in May 2002 and was craned away for a year-long period of restoration. The interior of the church – all dark-veneered wood and cream-painted walls – has an intimate beauty and contains one of the city's most significant pieces of religious art, an extraordinary triptych centred on an intricately rendered grouping of painted wooden statuettes representing the *Descent of the Holy Ghost* (1483) by the Lübeck master Berndt Notke (1430–1509).

Along Pikk tänav

The northern end of Raekoja plats sprouts a sequence of small alleyways crammed with cafés and souvenir shops. Most of them emerge onto medieval Tallinn's main thoroughfare, **Pikk tänav** ("Long Street"), cutting northeast to southwest through the town. It would have been an important link between the ecclesiastical and

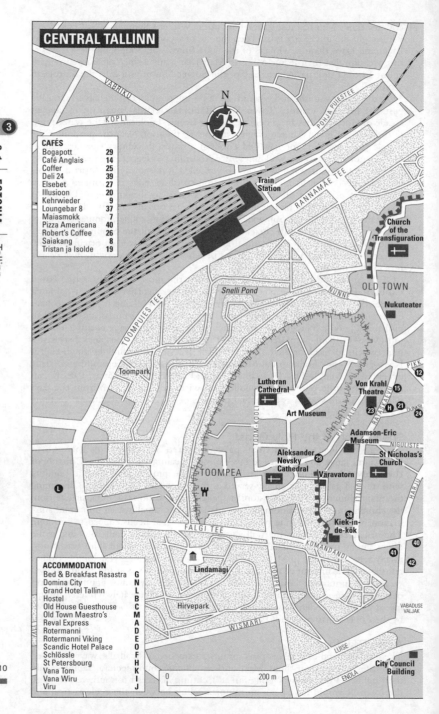

CENTRAL TALLINN

CAFÉS

Bogapott	29
Café Anglais	14
Coffer	25
Deli 24	39
Elsebet	27
Illusioon	20
Kehrwieder	9
Loungebar 8	37
Maiasmokk	7
Pizza Americana	40
Robert's Coffee	26
Saiakang	8
Tristan ja Isolde	19

ACCOMMODATION

Bed & Breakfast Rasastra	G
Domina City	N
Grand Hotel Tallinn	L
Hostel	B
Old House Guesthouse	C
Old Town Maestro's	M
Reval Express	A
Rotermanni	D
Rotermanni Viking	E
Scandic Hotel Palace	O
Schlössle	F
St Petersbourg	H
Vana Tom	K
Vana Wiru	I
Viru	J

VABRIKU

KOPLI

N

POHJA PUIESTEE

RANNAMÄE TEE

Train Station

Church of the Transfiguration

OLD TOWN

Snelli Pond

NUNNE

Nukuteater

Toompark

PIKK

12

TOOMPUIES TEE

Lutheran Cathedral

Von Krahl Theatre

15

DUNKRI

Art Museum

23

H

21

24

PIKK JALG

Adamson-Eric Museum

NIGULISTE

Aleksander Nevsky Cathedral

29

St Nicholas's Church

TOOM-KOOLI

TOOMPEA

Väravatorn

RÜÜTLI

HARJU

L

38

Kiek-in-de-kök

FALGI TEE

KOMANDANDI

41

40

42

Lindamägi

TOOMPEA

VABADUSE VÄLJAK

Hirvepark

WISMARI

LUISE

0   200 m

City Council Building

ENDLA

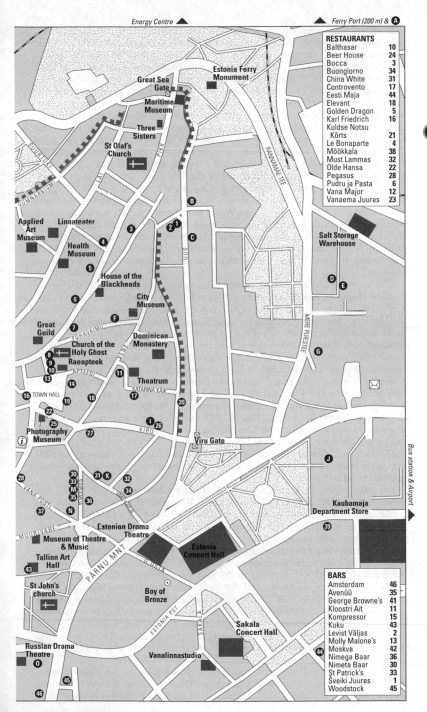

Estonia Ferry Monument

Great Sea Gate ⊠

Maritime Museum

Three Sisters

St Olaf's Church ✝

SUUR-TULI

LAI

PIKK

RANNAMÄE TEE

GÜMNAASIUMI

Applied Art Museum

Linnateater

Ⓑ

Health Museum

③
④
⑤

House of the Blackheads

City Museum

Ⓒ

UUS

Ⓓ Ⓔ

Salt Storage Warehouse

⑥

Ⓕ

Great Guild

⑦

PÜHAVAIMU

Church of the Holy Ghost ✝

Dominican Monastery

⑧
⑨
⑩
⑬

Raeapteek

VENE

APTEEGI

⑪

Theatrum

KATARINA KÄIK

⑭

TOWN HALL ⑯

⑲ ⑱

⑰

②⓪

Ⓖ

⊠

Ⓗ

MERE PUIESTEE

㉒
㉕

Photography Museum ⓘ

㉗

VIRU

Ⓘ ㉖

Viru Gate

MERE PUIESTEE

Ⓙ

㉘

VANA-POSTI

㉚ ㉛ Ⓚ ㉜
㉝ Ⓜ ㉞
㉟ ㊱

SULEVIMÄE

VIRU VÄLJAK

Ⓝ

㊲

MÜÜRIVAHE

Museum of Theatre & Music

Estonian Drama Theatre

PÄRNU MNT

ESTONIA PST

Kaubamaja Department Store ▶

㊴

Tallinn Art Hall

㊸

St John's church ✝

PÄRNU MNT

Boy of Bronze

Estonia Concert Hall

SAKALA

Sakala Concert Hall

㊹

Russian Drama Theatre Ⓞ

Vanalinnastudio

㊺

㊻

Bus station & Airport ▶

RESTAURANTS

Balthasar	10
Beer House	24
Bocca	3
Buongiorno	34
China White	31
Controvento	17
Eesti Maja	44
Elevant	18
Golden Dragon	5
Karl Friedrich	16
Kuldse Notsu Kõrts	21
Le Bonaparte	4
Mõõkkala	38
Must Lammas	32
Olde Hansa	22
Pegasus	28
Pudru ja Pasta	6
Vana Major	12
Vanaema Juures	23

BARS

Amsterdam	46
Avenüü	35
George Browne's	41
Kloostri Ait	11
Kompressor	15
Kuku	43
Levist Väljas	2
Molly Malone's	13
Moskva	42
Nimega Baar	36
Nimeta Baar	30
St Patrick's	33
Šveiki Juures	1
Woodstock	45

military buildings of Toompea and the port area, traversing the main business district on the way. Along the street's 800-metre-length lie some of the city's most important secular buildings from the Hanseatic period, kicking off with the forbidding Gothic facade of the **House of the Great Guild** (Suurgildi hoone) at Pikk 17. Completed in 1430, this provided a home for the most powerful of the city's guilds, uniting the city's German-speaking mercantile elite into an organization that effectively controlled commerce in the city. The Great Guild's doors were closed to Tallinn's petty merchants and artisans, who were instead organized into lesser institutions, such as the largely Estonian-speaking Guild of Corpus Christi. The Great Guild was the focus of many of medieval Tallinn's social events, notably the traditional springtime tournaments (participation in which was restricted to the top mercantile families), when the so-called May Count was chosen – a practice recently revived to form the centrepiece of the Old Town Days festival, although this tourist-oriented piece of pageantry now takes place in June.

The Great Guild's gloomy exterior now fronts the **Estonian History Museum** (Eesti ajaloomuuseum; daily except Wed 11am–6pm; 10EEK; ❀www.eam.ee), where the history of Estonia from the Stone Age to the eighteenth century is traced via an uninspiring and predictable array of weapons, domestic objects and jewellery. A collection of bracelets and necklaces from twelfth-century graves and a scale model of Narva in the eighteenth century do their best to enliven the proceedings.

If the appearance of their headquarters is anything to go by, the guild that occupied the **House of the Blackheads** (Mustpeade maja), Pikk 26, were a more exuberant bunch than the merchants of the Great Guild. The Renaissance facade of their building, inset with an elaborate stone portal and richly decorated door, cuts a bit of dash amid the stolidity of Pikk. Like its namesake in Rīga (see p.202), Tallinn's Brotherhood of the Blackheads was formed to accommodate visiting bachelor merchants and took the North African Saint Maurice as its patron – hence the name of the organization. Unlike in Rīga however, the Blackheads here also served a military purpose, organizing defence detachments (Blackheads fought off Russian besiegers during the Livonian Wars) and honouring visiting dignitaries with parades. Legend has it that the guild was founded to defend Tallinn during the Estonian uprising of St George's Day in 1343, though in later years it seems to have degenerated into a drinking club. The Brotherhood moved here in 1531 and stayed until 1940, when the Soviets turfed out a dwindling crew of survivors. Nowadays, the House's main first-floor hall is the venue for regular chamber concerts – attending one of these seems to be your best chance of getting to see the elegant, wood-panelled interior.

Continuing along Pikk brings you to **St Olaf's Church** (Oleviste kirik), first mentioned in 1267 and named in honour of King Olaf II of Norway, who was canonized for massacring pagans in Scandinavia. This slab-towered Gothic structure would not be particularly eye-catching, were it not for the height of its **spire**, which reaches 124m and used to be even taller. According to local legend the citizens of Tallinn wanted the church to have the highest spire in the world in order to attract passing ships and bring trade into the city. Whether Tallinn's prosperity during the Middle Ages had anything to do with the visibility of the church spire is not known, but between 1625 and 1820 the church burned down eight times as a result of lightning striking it. Occupying a niche low down on the rear exterior wall of the church is the tombstone of plague victim Johann Ballivi, an outstanding piece of fifteenth-century stone carving, featuring a deliciously macabre depiction of a decaying body surrounded by delicately rendered mourners. The chuch's interior is relatively unexceptional, the product of extensive renovation between 1829 and 1840.

Most striking of the Old Town's gabled merchants' houses are the **Three Sisters** (Kolm õde), just beyond St Olaf's Church at Pikk 71. Among the city's best-preserved Hanseatic buildings, these supremely functional buildings, with loading hatches and winch-arms set into their facades, would have been dwelling places, warehouses and offices all rolled into one. Recently, they have been converted into an upmarket hotel (see p.307) and been painted in snazzy, citrus-fruit colours, giving them the appearance of a monumental trio of ready-to-lick Gothic lollies.

Fat Margaret and the Maritime Museum

At its northern end Pikk is straddled by the **Great Sea Gate** (Suur rannavärav), a sixteenth-century arch flanked by two towers. The larger of these, the barrel-shaped **"Fat Margaret"** (Paks Margareeta), has walls 4m thick. Pressed into use as the city jail, the tower witnessed Tallinn's first outbreak of violence during the Revolution of March 1917, when striking workers joined mutineering soldiers and sailors in an assault on the prison, murdering the warders and setting the tower alight. It now houses the **Estonian Maritime Museum** (Eesti meremuuseum; Wed–Sun 10am–6pm; 25EEK; Estonian, Russian and some English captions), a diverting collection of model boats and nautical ephemera spread out over several floors. Sounding a poignant note, one of the exhibits is a scale model of the *Estonia*, the car ferry that sank midway between Tallinn and Stockholm on September 28, 1994, with the loss of 852 lives.

The area on the far side of Fat Margaret, now occupied by a road junction and a few scrappy bits of park, used to be known as the Parrot Garden in honour of the "parrot shooting" contests (see p.309) held here every spring in medieval times. Victors were presented with a silver salver, then borne in triumphal procession along Pikk to the Great Guild.

Along Lai tänav

Southwest of Fat Margaret, **Lai tänav** ("Broad Street") is another of the Old Town's set-piece thoroughfares, with rows of high-gabled merchants' houses haughtily presiding over the cobbled streets below, their cast-iron weather vanes creaking in the wind. Occupying a courtyard behind Lai 17, the **Applied Art Museum** (Tarbekunstimuuseum; Wed–Sun 11am–6pm; 20EEK) pays tribute to Estonia's strong design traditions with a well-presented collection of textiles, jewellery and ceramics; one of the highlights is the highly desirable "caveman" tea-set designed in 1937 by Adamson-Eric (see p.316), with spindly human figures chasing mammoths and other beasts around the cups and saucers. Diagonally opposite, the **Health Museum** at Lai 28 (Tervishoiu muuseum; Tues–Sat 11am–5pm; 10EEK) was clearly designed with local schoolchildren in mind, and has didactic diagrams and grisly photographs detailing the horrors that will result from unprotected sex or recreational drugs (rock and roll for some reason fails to feature).

The city walls

Just beyond the Health Museum, Suur-Kloostri strikes off westwards past the **Church of the Transfiguration** (Issanda muutlise kirik), the centrepiece of a sizeable Cistercian convent until the Reformation and given to the Orthodox Church during the reign of Peter the Great. At the end of the street, Vaike-Kloostri threads its way below one of the longest-surviving sections of Tallinn's medieval **city wall**, here featuring nine complete towers and three gates. Passing through any one of the gates and crossing the park-like expanse of Tornide väljak on the other side, provides a wonderful view back towards the towers, which look like a series of squat crimson crayons. The walls were largely constructed during the fourteenth century, then added to over the years until improvements in artillery rendered them obsolete during the eighteenth century. Citizens of medieval Tallinn were each obliged to do a stint of guard duty – one of the annual exercises required them all to gather on the walls in full armour and shake their weapons as a sign of military readiness. Once you've had your fill of turrets you can re-enter the Old Town along Nunne; or alternatively continue southwest towards the **Toompark**, a relaxing expanse of lawns and flowerbeds draped around the western slopes of the Toompea. In the middle of the park is the Snelli Pond, a W-shaped stretch of former moat that becomes a hugely popular outdoor skating rink in winter.

Along Vene: the City Museum and the Dominican Monastery

Another way of returning to the centre from Fat Margaret's end of town is to zig-zag your way west from Pikk, via the narrow streets of Sulevimägi and Olevimägi, onto Vene, another of the Old Town's main arteries, that heads south to join up with Viru. Occupying a handsomely restored merchant's house at Vene 17 is the **Tallinn City Museum** (Tallinna linnamuuseum; daily except Tues: March–Oct 10.30am–5.30pm; Nov–Feb 11am–5pm; 25EEK; ⓦ www.linnamuuseum.ee), a superbly arranged collection over three floors brought to life by the inclusion of costumed wax figures, medieval street sounds and illuminating English-language texts. A cutaway model of a sixteenth-century merchant's house reveals how these buildings once functioned, with vast cranes jutting from facades hauling merchandise to the upper storeys, where it was warehoused before being re-exported or sold in the shop space at ground level. Original furnishings and costumes feature in a display of nineteenth-century interiors, while the events of the twentieth century unfold through a collection of posters and photographs (including one of an enormous Stalin poster draped incongruously over the facade of the Town Hall), and videos document the growth of the independence movement.

Diagonally opposite the museum at Vene 16, the **Dominican Monastery** was one of the most powerful institutions in medieval Tallinn – until it was comprehensively trashed by anti-Catholic rioters in September 1524. A new church was built on the site in the mid-nineteenth century and is still the main Catholic place of worship in the city. Some of the former monastery buildings now accommodate the Dominican Monastery Museum (Dominiiklaste kloostri muuseum; mid-May to mid-Sept daily 10am–6pm; 30EEK), home to an extensive collection of medieval and Renaissance stone carving including some intricately carved fourteenth-century tombstones. Look out for a delightful relief of an angel set in a triangular frame courtesy of Arendt Passer – the doyen of sixteenth-century stone masonry who also worked on the portal of the House of the Blackheads (see p.312) and the tomb of Pontus de la Gardie in Tallinn Cathedral (p.318).

Immediately south of the monastery, a narrow alleyway known as **Katariina kaik** ("Catherine's Passage") runs round the surviving wall of the original monastery church, passing a string of craft workshops where you can observe potters, bookbinders and glaziers at work (see "Shopping"; p.330).

St Nicholas's Church

Heading south from Raekoja plats along Kullaseppa leads to a patch of raised open ground, upon which sits the imposing **St Nicholas's Church** (Niguliste kirik; Wed–Sun 10am–5pm; 35EEK; English-language pamphlets available). A three-aisled basilica fashioned from huge chunks of limestone, this was initially put up by Westphalian merchants in the thirteenth century, although most of what can be seen today dates from the fifteenth – especially the apse and the sturdy tower, built with defence in mind. Extensively restored following Soviet bombing raids at the end of World War II, it's now a **museum**, gathering together the surviving crop of Tallinn's **medieval artworks** – most of which perished in the Protestant riots of September 1524. St Nicholas's itself was saved from a thorough ransacking by the quick thinking of the warden, who – so the story goes – poured lead in the locks to prevent the raiders from gaining access. Standing out among a clutch of Gothic altarpieces is a spectacular double-winged altar by Herman Rode of Lübeck from 1481, in which scenes featuring the life of St Nicholas figure prominently, although St George also gets a look in – he's shown effortlessly skewering a dragon on one panel and getting his head chopped off in another. Standing to the left of the altar is a sixteenth-century *Crucifixion* scene by an anonymous Bruges painter, in which

Old Town, Tallinn △

the Jerusalem townscape is bestowed with the kind of medieval towers and bastions that wouldn't look out of place in a north European city like Tallinn. Over on the right, the so-called **Altar of the Blackheads** was painted for the Brotherhood by a Bruges master, who depicted robed Blackhead members kneeling in prayer on the inner sides of the wings. The central panel shows a golden-tressed Madonna flanked by Saints George and Maurice.

Occupying pride of place at the rear of the church is a largish fragment from a fifteenth-century *Dance of Death* frieze by Berndt Notke. It's an outstanding example of the genre, with skeletal figures swaying gracefully to a bagpipe ditty while cajoling a bishop, king and noblewoman to join in the fun – unsurprisingly, they look less than enthusiastic. Elsewhere around the sides of the nave lie a series of striking seventeenth-century tomb-top effigies: note the delicate floral pillow upon which rests Berndt Reinhold von Delung (died 1699), and the stiff handlebar moustache and full body armour of Hermann Neuroth (died 1641).

A side chapel near the main entrance used to hold the mummified form of Duke Charles-Eugène de Croy, who commanded the Russian army at Narva in 1701 and, electing to stand and fight rather than flee like his troops, was taken prisoner by Swedish King Charles XII. He died a year later and ended up being propped up here because nobody was prepared to pay for a decent burial (he wasn't the only one to endure this fate either: Tallinn's church wardens were notorious for demanding funeral expenses upfront). Protected from decay by dry weather, de Croy's corpse soon became an attraction, and remained on display until 1897, when the authorities finally saw fit to stick it in the ground.

The church's sonorous **organ** is put through its paces every Saturday and Sunday, with **recitals** starting at around 4 or 5pm: details of the current week's performance are posted at the entrance.

The Adamson-Eric Museum

A few steps west of the church entrance, Lühike jalg climbs uphill to Toompea (see opposite). The medieval merchant's house at no. 3 now houses the **Adamson-Eric Museum** (Tues–Sun 10am–6pm; 10EEK), charting the career of Estonian art's most talented all-rounder. Born Erich Carl Hugo Adamson, Adamson-Eric (1902–1968) drifted through various art and design schools in Tartu, Berlin and Paris before settling in Tallinn in the 1920s. He quickly garnered a reputation for producing accessible figurative paintings, while simultaneously churning out unabashedly abstract designs for tapestries, book bindings and ceramics – all showcased here to good effect. The most popular of his paintings on display here, *In Summer* (1938), is also one of his most mischievous, subverting traditional Estonian ideas of rural wholesomeness by portraying a female subject clad in national costume – but only from the waist down. Like many nonconformists of his generation, Adamson-Eric supported the Soviet Union in the 1940s (his fawning portrait of Stalin entitled *On the Coast of the Baltic Sea* is sadly not on display here), but fell out of favour with the regime in the 1950s and was banned from exhibiting until the 1960s – by which time he'd re-taught himself to paint with his left hand after a stroke had put paid to his right. Later works – Cubist designs for café murals, and rows of irregularly shaped ceramic tiles bearing primitive animal forms – show that he remained at the peak of his powers right to the last.

Along Harju to the Museum of Theatre and Music

On the eastern side of St Nicolas's Church, Harju tänav leads past a vacant lot filled with grassed-over ruins – a reminder of the night of 9 March, 1944, when the Soviet air force pummelled central Tallinn, destroying an estimated "53% of the city's living space" according to the accompanying signboard. On the opposite side of the street, the snazzy *Pegasus* eatery at Harju 1 (see "Restaurants; p.326) began life as a hip writers' and artists' café in the early 1960s and its super-cool modernist interior still survives in something approaching its original form. The café's most famous feature is the spiral staircase topped by Edgar Viies's sleek *Pegasus* – supposedly the first piece of abstract sculpture ever to appear in Soviet Estonia. Notwithstanding its small size, this graceful, three-pronged piece of aluminium is still as eloquent a statement of 1960s optimism as you'll find anywhere, and it's well worth stopping off for a drink here in order to see it.

Taking the next left brings you onto Müürivahe, a narrow street running east then north alongside what were once the city walls – chunks of medieval masonry still pepper the walls of many of the buildings around here. The **Museum of Theatre and Music** at Müürivahe 12 (Teatri-ja muusikamuuseum; Wed–Sun 10am–6pm; 15EEK) boasts publicity stills of stage stars in its stairwell and a motley collection of keyboards, music boxes and folk instruments upstairs – most striking of which is the *põispill*, a stringed instrument incorporating an animal-skin soundbox which looks like the result of an unnatural union between a cello and a bagpipe. More glamorous by half is the frilly black dress once worn by Meliza Korjus (1909–1980), the soprano who made her name singing in the Estonia Concert Hall before emigrating to Hollywood – her appearance in the 1938 film *The Great Waltz* seemed to promise great things, until a car accident brought her movie career to a premature end.

Toompea

Looming over the Old Town to the southwest is the limestone outcrop known as **Toompea**, the site of an Estonian stockade fort until the Danes took it over in 1219 and built a stone castle, later wrested from them by the Livonian Order. As the nerve centre of the Christian effort to convert the pagan Estonians, Toompea (from the German word "Domberg", meaning "Cathedral Hill") often led a separate life from the rest of Tallinn below – which was much more interested in trade than ideology. The seat of several state and religious institutions, it still stands apart from the rest of central Tallinn – a somewhat secretive lair of bureaucrats and ministers rather than the happy-go-lucky habitat of shoppers and drinkers.

The most atmospheric approach to Toompea from the Old Town is through the sturdy gate tower – built by the Livonian Order to contain the Old Town's inhabitants in times of unrest – at the foot of Pikk jalg (Long Leg). This is the cobbled continuation of Pikk, the Old Town's main street, and climbs up to Lossi plats (Castle Square), dominated by the onion-domed Russian Orthodox **Cathedral of Alexander Nevsky** (Aleksander Nevski katedraal; daily 8am–7pm). Built in 1900 to remind the local Estonians of their subservient position in the Tsarist scheme of things, this gaudy concoction has always had the slightly inappropriate appearance of an over-iced cake at a funeral feast. Inside, however, an aura of spiritual calm reigns supreme, with incense wafting over a lofty, icon-packed interior.

At the head of Lossi plats is **Toompea Castle** (Toompea loss), on the site of the original Danish fortification. The castle has been altered by every conqueror who raised their flag above it since then; these days it wears a shocking pink Baroque facade, the result of an eighteenth-century rebuild under Catherine the Great. The northern and western walls are the oldest part of the castle and include three defensive towers, the most impressive of which is the fifty-metre Tall Hermann (Pikk Hermann) at the southwestern corner, dating from 1371.

As the home to the **Riigikogu**, Estonia's Parliament, Toompea witnessed many of the events leading up to the re-establishment of Estonia's independence – most notably on May 15, 1990, when citizens gathered to defend the building against followers of the pro-Soviet Intermovement, who were attempting to storm it.

The Cathedral

From Lossi plats, Toom Kooli leads north to the **Cathedral** (Toomkirik; Tues–Sun: April–Oct 9am–5pm; Nov–March 9am–3pm; English-language leaflet 10EEK), a homely, whitewashed structure that, despite numerous rebuildings, doesn't appear to have changed much since the first stone church built by Danes on this site in 1240. Inside, set apart from the ordinary ranks of pews are glass-enclosed family boxes that would have been reserved for local notables, enabling them to keep their distance from the hoi polloi. Presiding over the pews is an ornate seventeenth-century pulpit by Christian Ackerman, who also carved many of the 107 coats of arms of noble families that adorn the white walls of the vaulted nave and choir. Stealing all the attention on the right-hand side of the main altar is the tomb of Pontus de la Gardie, the French-born mercenary who captured Narva for the Swedes in 1578, before massacring, it is said, 6000 of its inhabitants in the aftermath. The sarcophagus bears tender likenesses of Pontus and his wife, a fine piece of sculpture by local master Arendt Passer. Look out, too, for Giacomo Quarenghi's neoclassical memorial to Admiral Samuel Greigh (died 1788) halfway down the aisle, ordered by Catherine the Great as a tribute to the Scots-born seadog who commanded Russian ships in the Black Sea.

The Estonian Art Museum
Just across the square from the Toomkirik at Kiriku plats 1, a peppermint-green neo-Renaissance palace provides a temporary home for the **Estonian Art Museum** (Eesti kunstimuuseum; Wed–Sun 11am–6pm; 20EEK; ⊛www.ekm.ee), due to move to a purpose-built gallery in Kadriorg Park some time in 2005. It's hard to tell which bits of the vast collection will be on show at any given time, although the display is sure to include something by Johann Köler (1826–1899), the Viljandi-born, St Petersburg-trained society portraitist, whose stiff, Victorian-era pictures set new standards in a country where professional painters were few and far between. If Estonian art prior to World War I was a bit staid, it positively burst into life in the years immediately after it: look out for the colourful post-impressionist landscapes of Villem Ormisson and Eduard Viiralt and the incandescent, cubist-influenced canvases by the likes of Arnold Akberg, Felix Johansen-Randel and Eduard Ole. Unfortunately, the museum doesn't own any works by the greatest Estonian artist of all time, Tallinn-born Michel Sittow (1469–1525), who painted sitters as illustrious as Catherine of Aragon and Henry VII of England, and whose surviving pictures are scattered from Madrid to Moscow.

Towards Kiek-in-de-Kök
South of Lossi plats, a sloping park abuts another impressive stretch of town wall. Among the towers here is a gruff, grey blockhouse that once served as a prison for prostitutes – ironically named the Neitsitorn ("Virgins' Tower"), it's now home to one of the few café-bars popular in Soviet-era Tallinn that is still going strong today. Immediately south of the Neitsitorn is the impregnable-looking bastion known as **Kiek-in-de-Kök** (Tues–Sun: March–Oct 10.30am–5.30pm; Nov–Feb 11am–5pm; 15EEK), built in 1475 to provide a home for Toompea's main gun battery. Named in honour of a Low-German expression meaning "look in the kitchen" (the bastion's sentries could see straight into the parlours of downtown Tallinn), it now contains an entertaining, if sparse, collection of artefacts linked to the town's defences. There are suits of armour, rusty-looking weapons, and replicas of the cannon once stationed here (the originals were carted off to St Petersburg), variously nicknamed Lion, Fat Girl and Bitter Death – this last being engraved with the following cheerful rhyme:

Bitter Death is my name
Thus I travel everywhere
Killing the rich and the poor
To me, who I slay is all the same.

Immediately west of Kiek-in-de-Kök, paths climb a wooded knoll known as **Lindamägi** ("Linda's Hill") after the maiden in sculptural form who squats pensively at its summit. According to Estonian folk myth, Linda was the loving wife of Kalev and begetter of superhuman hero Kalevipoeg. On the death of Kalev, Linda laboured to build a mound of rocks in his honour – the hill known today as Toompea is said to be the result. The statue is the work of August Weizenberg (1837–1921), the cabinet maker who paid his way through art college in St Petersburg and Munich to become Estonia's first professional sculptor. Below Lindmägi to the south lies the leafy **Hirvepark**, scene of a 2000-strong gathering to mark the anniversary of the Molotov-Ribbentrop Pact on August 23, 1987, one of the first big anti-Soviet demonstrations in the Baltics.

Round the fringes of the Old Town

Fringing the Old Town are some fine nineteenth- and twentieth-century buildings, housing theatres and concert halls, offices and department stores. The main thoroughfare here is **Pärnu mnt** and its northbound extension **Mere pst**.

Vabaduse väljak

East of Kiek-in-de-Kök, Komandandi tänav slopes downhill to **Vabaduse väljak**, a large open space formerly used for parades on May Day and other Soviet holidays. Laid out in the 1920s and 1930s, the square survives as something of an architectural tribute to the achievements of the inter-war state. Hugging the southeast corner of the square, the *Gloria Palace Hotel* was the best place to stay in town during Estonia's first period of independence, and has re-emerged to become one of the more desirable tourist pieds-a-terre in the second. Standing on the same side of the square is a vivacious red-brick building built for the EKA insurance company in 1931 and now serving as the seat of Tallinn City Council; with a facade enlivened by chevrons and other zany brickwork patterns, it would look as at home in ancient Babylon as it does in the modern Baltic. More austere in appearance, but no less impressive, is the seven-storey modernist cube standing roughly opposite on the northern side of the square (and now topped by a neon advert for the Eesti Ühispank), erected by an Estonian building society in 1934 and clearly intended as a muscular statement of the republic's financial self-confidence. Also dating from the 1930s – and a major institution ever since – is the next-door **Tallinn Art Hall**, Vabaduse väljak 6 (Tallinna Kunstihoone; Wed–Sun noon–6pm; price depends on exhibition), whose high-profile exhibitions showcase the best in contemporary Estonian art.

From Vabaduse väljak to Viru väljak

Running northeast from Vabaduse väljak, Pärnu mnt and Estonia pst follow roughly parallel paths round the eastern fringes of the Old Town. Presiding over Pärnu mnt at no. 4, the eye-catching **Estonian Drama Theatre** (Eesti draamateater), built in 1910 as the city's main German-language theatre, mixes Art Nouveau with Nordic folk motifs to produce a wealth of quirky detail: roofs resemble the shingles of village huts and ancient bards in frieze-form preside over the main entrance. Behind the theatre looms the much grander, but less engaging, **Estonia Theatre and Concert Hall**, financed by public contributions and completed in 1913 to provide Tallinn's Estonian-speaking majority with a cultural institution superior to anything that the city's Germans or Russians could muster. With the Estonian Philharmonic Orchestra occupying one wing and the opera and ballet performing in the other, it's still very much the nation's cultural flagship. On the southwestern side of the Concert Hall, just across Otsa tänav, a sculpture of a nude youth – the so-called "**Boy of Bronze**" – honours the high-school pupils who fell in the post-World War I struggle for independence. When Tallinn was in danger of falling to the Bolsheviks in the winter of 1918–19, the Estonian Commander-in-Chief General Laidoner was so starved of manpower that he had no choice but to appeal to the patriotic instincts of local schoolboys: equipped with improvised uniforms and obsolete rifles, they somehow managed to save the city.

The area northwest of the Concert Hall, nowadays a grassy park leading back to Pärnu mnt, used to be the site of the **town market** (which can now be found 1.5km further east). It was here that Russian troops fired on left-wing protesters on October 16, 1905, killing 90 and wounding over 200. Four days later, an estimated 40,000 people (a staggering figure if true: it represents almost one in four of the entire city population) gathered in the market for the start of a mass funeral procession – one of the biggest anti-Tsarist demonstrations of the era. The market remained the focus of Tallinn life well into the 1920s – when British author and Tallinn resident Arthur Ransome marvelled at "pike still alive in bath-tubs" and "hunks of meat wrapped in newspaper and dripping blood and printers' ink".

Further northeast, beyond Tammsaare Park, both Pärnu mnt and Estonia pst converge at **Viru väljak**, a bustling interchange and shopping area overlooked by the huge grey slab of the **Viru Hotel**. Built in the 1970s to accommodate holidaying Finns, the Viru long enjoyed the reputation of being the most Westernized hotel in the USSR – and was the automatic honeymoon venue of choice for any Soviet couple who could afford it.

The Rotermann Quarter and the Energy Centre

Due north of Viru, Mere pst heads south towards the port area, skirting the eastern ramparts of the Old Town on the way. On the eastern side of Mere lies the so-called **Rotermann Quarter**, an area of decaying factories and warehouses established by nineteenth-century industrialist Christian Abraham Rotermann. Neglected during much of the Soviet era, it's now prime inner-city redevelopment territory – a number of bars and cafés have already moved into the big warehouses running along the side of Mere and a brace of hotels are happily installed in the alleyways just behind it. The most impressive of the quarter's buildings is the **Salt Storage Warehouse** at Ahtri 2 (Soolaadu; mid-May to Sept Wed–Fri noon–8pm, Sat & Sun 11am–6pm; Oct to mid-May Wed–Sun 11am–6pm; 50EEK; @www.arhitektuurimuuseum.ee), built by Christan Abraham's grandson, Christian Barthold Rotermann, in 1908, and renovated in the mid-1990s to serve as an exhibition space. Shared by both the Estonian Architecture and Art museums, it hosts all manner of top-notch exhibitions, often featuring visiting artists from abroad – shown to advantage in the warehouse's minimalist limestone-and-steel interior.

Towards the northern end of Mere pst, Rannamae tee and Põhja pst break off to run round the northern tip of the Old Town. Here you can either re-enter the Old Town along Pikk, or venture over to the far side of Põhja, where the old power station at no. 29 has been transformed into the **Tallinn Energy Centre** (Tallinna tehnika-ja teaduskeskus; June–Aug Mon–Fri 10am–5pm; Sept–May Mon–Sat 10am–5pm; 30EEK; @www.energiakeskus.ee). An enjoyable hands-on museum of technology, it features endless halls full of strange-looking machines – many of which you can play around on if you can make any sense of the Estonian-language instructions.

The eastern outskirts

Tallinn's eastern outskirts are dotted with a number of worthwhile attractions that could easily take up a day or two of your sightseeing time. The nearest, just 2km east of the Old Town, is the heavily wooded area of **Kadriorg Park**, with its lavishly decorated Baroque palace, built by Peter the Great. Beyond Kadriorg, the broad shoreline boulevard, Pirita tee, extends along the Bay of Tallinn, passing one of the city's better history museums at **Maaramäe Palace**, before arriving at the haunting ruins of **Pirita Convent**. Uphill from here, the luxuriant **Botanical Gardens** and the **TV Tower**, with its unbeatable views of the city, are sufficiently distant from the hubbub of central Tallinn to have the feel of a rural excursion.

Kadriorg is a ten-minute tram ride from Viru väljak, while the other destinations in eastern Tallinn are only a slightly longer bus trip from the same spot – by combining public **transport** with a bit of walking, you can link up several (conceivably all) of the attractions below in a single, day-long trip.

Kadriorg

A grassy expanse stretching for some 1.5km from southwest to northeast, generously planted with oak, chestnut and lime trees and criss-crossed with avenues, **Kadriorg** is Tallinn's favourite **park**, built, together with the **palace** at its centre, for the Russian Tsar Peter the Great. After conquering Estonia in 1711, Peter began planning the park and palace as a gift to his mistress Marta Skavronskaya. A serving girl of Lithuanian origin, Skavronskaya was taken as war booty by General Sheremetiev during one of his campaigns in Livonia and used as human currency at the Russian court – Sheremetiev gave her to Prince Menschikov, who in turn presented her to Peter in 1703. She remained the Tsar's companion thereafter, becoming Empress Catherine in 1724, hence the name of the park – Kadriorg is Estonian for "Catherine's Valley". Peter, who personally supervised the planting of the trees,

Kadriorg literary museums

The sedate streets south and west of Kadriorg are the setting for memorial museums honouring two of twentieth-century Estonia's literary giants – well worth a detour if you've a passion for Estonian culture or an interest in well-preserved inter-war interiors.

The first is the **Eduard Vilde Memorial Museum**, just south of the Kreuzwald monument at Roheline aas 3 (Edvard Vilde memoriaalmuuseum; daily 11am–6pm; 10EEK), located in the house presented to him by the government in honour of his life's work. Inspired by the naturalist novels of Emile Zola, Vilde (1865–1933) was the first Estonian novelist to write about recent Estonian history in realist, documentary style. As well as being filled with social analysis and economic statistics, his narratives were also the popular, page-turning blockbusters of their time. His most famous novel *Mahtra sõda* ("The War in Mahtra"; 1902), dealing with peasant rebellions of the 1850s, began life as a serial in the newspaper *Teataja* – readers hungry for the latest instalment would queue up outside the editorial offices on the day of publication. An opponent of the Tsarist autocracy as well as Estonia's German-speaking landowning classes, Vilde spent long periods of exile in Western Europe following the failed 1905 Revolution – first-hand experience of cosmopolitan cities like Paris and Berlin lent his writing a modern, urban edge unique for Estonian literature at the time. Not surprisingly, Vilde's battered travelling trunks are given pride of place in this charmingly reverent display of authorial heirlooms and period furnishings.

Heading west from the Vilde Museum along Koidula tänav soon brings you to the **Anton Hansen Tammsaare Memorial Museum** at Koidula 12A (A. H. Tammsaare memoriaalmuuseum; daily except Tues 11am–6pm; 10EEK), occupying the handsome timber house where this dour novelist lived for the last decade of his life. Tammsaare (1878–1940) was born into a farming family in Järvamaa, central Estonia, and went on to study law at Tartu University, although he never graduated because of poor health. His literary reputation rests primarily on the five-volume, semi-autobiographical *Tõde ja Õigus* ("Truth and Justice"), a panorama of Estonian life from the 1870s to the 1930s that still forms the staple fodder of Estonian schoolchildren. It's famous (or infamous) both for its enormously long sentences, some of which last half a page, and for an oft-quoted line from volume 2, said to sum up the mixture of doggedness and resignation that defines the Estonian character: "Work hard, sweat hard, and then love will come". Alongside manuscripts and first editions, the museum displays some charming old postcards of Tallinn (including a mesmerizing 1930s vista of a zeppelin floating over St Olaf's Church), and a startlingly life-like dummy of Tammsaare staring out of his study window.

always intended the park to be open to the public, and a stroll in Kadriorg soon became an essential fixture of the Tallinn social round. In the mid-nineteenth century, when Tallinn was one of the Russian Empire's most popular seaside resorts, Kadriorg was the place all the summer visitors gravitated towards, enjoying a constant round of what German writer J.G. Kohl called "promenades, balls, illuminations and pleasure parties".

The **main entrance** to the park is at the junction of Weizenbergi tänav and J. Poska (tram #1 or #3 from Viru väljak). Weizenbergi cuts southeastwards through the park, passing first of all a small lake bordered by formal flowerbeds and patronized by a fair number of ducks and swans. Presiding over the eastern shore of the lake is a statue of Friedrich Reinhold Kreuzwald (see p.393), the Võru doctor who kickstarted the Estonian literary renaissance by publishing *Kalevipoeg* ("The Son of Kalev"), an epic poem composed of original fragments of folk material and Tolkien-esque episodes made up by Kreuzwald himself. Before Kreuzwald's time the Estonian language had been regarded as an uncultured country dialect by the German-speaking Baltic elite, and *Kalevipoeg* was hugely influential in inspiring a new generation of native-born intellectuals to start writing in their own tongue. Round the base of the statue, plaques depicting harp-strumming bards and heroic warriors convey the required tone of myth and mystery.

From here Wizenbergi ascends gently towards **Kadriorg Palace** (Kadrioru loss), a late-Baroque residence designed by the Italian architect Niccolo Michetti to provide Empress Catherine with a comfy Baltic pad and employed as an imperial residence right up until 1918. These days the palace's opulent state rooms accommodate the **Museum of Foreign Art** (Väliskunsti muuseum; May–Sept Tues–Sun 11am–5pm; Oct–April Wed–Sun 11am–5pm; ❀www.ekm.ee; 35EEK), a genuinely impressive collection of European painting and sculpture over the centuries. The display opens on an exuberant note with Pieter Brueghel the Younger's *Wedding Feast*, followed by a room of seventeenth-century Dutch still lifes – the glistening, ready-to-eat surface of Hans van Essen's *Still Life with Lobster* being an obvious highlight. The Main Hall of the palace is an artwork in its own right, with chunky fireplaces topped by trumpet-blowing angels and two-headed eagles. A central ceiling painting illustrates the legend of Diana and Actaeon, in which the latter is transformed into a stag for having surprised Diana while bathing, and is hunted and killed by his dogs (Diana here represents the Russian Empire of Peter the Great, Actaeon the impudent and over-ambitious Swedish King Charles XII). The adjoining lime-green Banqueting Hall is in fact a large conservatory tacked on in the 1930s – packed with soft furnishings and plants, it provides a suitably sensuous environment in which to admire the aptly named *Venus of the Beautiful Buttocks*, a nineteenth-century sculpture based on a Classical Greek original. If you can tear yourself away, there follows a room full of pictures by followers of Caravaggio and a representative sample of nineteenth-century Russian realists like Ivan Shishkin and Ilya Repin – although Aleksey Bogolyubov's *Port of Tallinn* (1853) provides most in the way of local interest.

Behind the palace, an eighteenth-century **ornamental garden** is being restored to its former glory. The peach-coloured building just beyond it houses Estonia's current head of state.

Peter the Great's House

Between 1714 and 1716, Peter the Great lived in the so-called Dutch House, a small cottage about 200m uphill from Kadriorg Palace. Today this simple building harbours the **Peter the Great House Museum** (Peeter I majamuuseum; mid-May to Sept Wed–Sun 10.30am–5.30; 10EEK), comprising a hall, drawing room, dining room and bedroom decked out in the kind of utilitarian furnishings that practical-minded Peter favoured. Little in the house is original, save for a pair of slippers beside the bed, said to be the Tsar's own.

The Song Grounds and the Rusalka Memorial

Heading northeast along Mäekalda from Peter's cottage leads, after around fifteen minutes, to Narva mnt. On the other side of this busy road is the **Song Bowl** (Lauluväljak), a vast amphitheatre that has been the venue for Estonia's Song Festivals ever since its construction in the 1960s. These gatherings, featuring massed choirs thousands strong, take place every two years and have been an important form of national expression in Estonia ever since the first all-Estonia Song Festival was held in Tartu in 1869. The present structure, which can accommodate 15,000 singers (with room for a further 30,000 or so performers on the platform in front of the stage and countless thousands of spectators on the banked field beyond it), was filled to capacity for the June 1988 festival, when up to 100,000 people a night came here to express their longing for independence from Soviet rule, giving rise to the epithet "Singing Revolution". Since then the Song Grounds have hosted concerts by numerous representatives of Western urban folklore – the Rolling Stones (1998) and Depeche Mode (2001) among them. In winter, the grassy slope where spectators usually stand is transformed into an impromptu winter sports arena, with scores of kids hurling themselves down the incline on sleds, old tyres or bits of cardboard.

A tree-lined avenue runs downhill from the amphitheatre to Pirita tee, which follows the seashore. A left turn here brings you to the **Rusalka Memorial**, built in 1902 in memory of the *Rusalka*, a Russian ship that went down nine years earlier. Designed by Amandus Adamson, the leading Estonian sculptor of the day, it comprises a rocky pillar on which an angel stands on tiptoe, waving an Orthodox cross in the direction of the Gulf of Finland.

The Estonian History Museum

Turning right at the bottom of the Song Grounds access road and following the coastal Pirita tee brings you after 1km or so to a balustraded stairway leading up to the Maarjamäe Palace (Maarjamäe loss), a neo-Gothic residence built for an aide of the Tsar, Count Anatoli Orlov-Davidov, in 1873. Long considered a beauty spot on account of its position overlooking Tallinn Bay, the building now houses a branch of the **Estonian History Museum** (Eesti ajaloomuuseum; Wed–Sun: March–Oct 11am–6pm; Nov–Feb 10am–5pm; 10EEK; ⊛ www.eam.ee), covering the mid-nineteenth century onwards, and is far more interesting and imaginative than its city-centre counterpart (see p.312). The display starts with a section on urban and rural life in nineteenth-century Estonia, including a few re-created domestic interiors, before moving on to the political and social upheavals of the early twentieth century, including grainy photographs of the volunteers who fought against Bolsheviks, White Russians and Germans to win Estonian independence in the aftermath of World War I. Later sections have a display on the Molotov-Ribbentrop "secret protocols", which effectively handed the Baltic Republics to Stalin, leading into material about the fate of Estonia during World War II, and the activities of the "Forest Brothers", Estonian partisans who carried on the battle against Soviet occupation into the 1950s. Ironically, Maarjamäe Palace was earmarked as the site of a "Museum of Soviet Friendship" during the 1980s, a project which never got off the ground owing to the untimely demise of the state it was intended to celebrate. However, Evald Okas's 1987 frescoes, featuring cosmonauts, scientists, gymnasts and other symbols of communist achievement, can still be admired in the main hall.

Just beyond Maarjamäe Palace, a huge concrete needle marks the site of a Soviet-era war memorial honouring the dead of World War II – intended to symbolize the Soviet role in "liberating" Estonia in 1944–5, it has long been nicknamed "Pinocchio's Grave" by the locals.

Pirita

Two kilometres northeast of Maarjamäe, Pirita tee enters the suburb of **Pirita** (buses #1, #1A, #34 and #38 from Viru väljak), site of a huge yachting marina at the point where the Pirita River flows into the Baltic Sea. The sailing events of the 1980 Moscow Olympics were held here, which explains the presence of an ungainly concrete hotel and an under-used complex of port buildings. The main reasons to visit nowadays are the forest-backed **Pirita beach**, which stretches for some 2km on the far side of the marina and offers great views west towards Tallinn's port; and the ruins of **Pirita Convent** (Pirita klooster), which loom above the landward side of the main road. Founded in 1407 by Tallinn merchants, the convent was unusual in admitting both male and female novices, who resided in different wings under the strict rule of a single abbess. The convent was destroyed and abandoned during the Livonian Wars and all that survives now is the shell of its church, whose hugely impressive facade recalls the gabled merchants' houses of Tallinn's Old Town. Studded with tiny windows, it looks like an unearthly advent calendar.

The Botanical Gardens and the Television Tower

Just beyond Pirita Convent, buses #34 and #38 turn sharp right into Kloostrimetsa tee and begin climbing into the hilly Kloostrimets ("Convent Wood"), a peaceful area of thick pine forest and suburban cottages that seems a world away from the city. On the north side of the road tracks lead into the Forest cemetery (Metsakalmistu), Tallinn's most desirable final resting place. On the south side, just beyond the Kloostrimetsa bus stop, paths head for the **Botanical Gardens** (Botaanikaaed; Tues–Sun: May–Oct 10am–6pm; Nov–April 11am–4pm; 40EEK), a landscaped area of woodland centred on a rather wonderful palm house. With tall trees in the octagonal central hall and smaller specimens in the numerous side chambers, this lounge-like arrangement will have you jotting down ideas for your dream conservatory. There's an alpine garden and a rose garden just beyond the palm house, although you'll have to be here in late spring or summer to enjoy them at their best.

Half a kilometre further along Kloostrimetsa tee, beside the Motoklubi bus stop, a side road leads off to the **Television Tower** (Teletorn; daily noon–1am; 40EEK), where a lift whisks you to a 21st-floor observation platform with superb views back towards the church spires and port cranes of central Tallinn.

The Zoo and the Open-air Ethnographic Museum

Tallinn's western outskirts offer much less in the way of sights, the one must-see attraction here being the Estonian **Open-air Ethographic Museum**, 6km west of town in the upmarket suburb of Rocca al Mare (Italian for "Rock by the Sea") – thus christened by a merchant who built himself a mansion here during the late nineteenth century. Buses #21 and #21B make the trip here from the Baltic Station every twenty to thirty minutes.

Just before arriving in Rocca al Mare you'll pass **Tallinn Zoo** at Paldiski mnt 145 (daily: May–Sept 9am–7pm; Oct–April 9am–5pm; 40EEEK), founded in 1937 to accommodate the baby lynx won by the Estonian Riflemen's Society at the World Championships in Helsinki. There's now a much wider range of mammals on show (including, according to the English-language notes, "all the species of mountain goats living naturally within the territory of the former Soviet Union"), and a croc-filled tropical house.

The Open-air Ethnographical Museum

Arranged in a spacious wooded park overlooking the sea, the **Open-air Ethnographical Museum** at Vabaõhumuuseumi tee 12 (Eesti vabaõhumuuseum; daily: May–Aug 10am–8pm; Sept & Oct 10am–6pm; Nov–April 10am–5pm; 30EEK; ⊛ www.evm.ee) brings together over a hundred eighteenth- and nineteenth-century village buildings from different parts of the country. The exhibits illustrate how Estonian dwellings developed from single longhouses in which humans and animals lived cheek by jowl, to more sophisticated farmsteads, in which barns and other outbuildings were built to accommodate the beasts. Estonian living rooms were traditionally built around open hearths with no chimneys – the resulting fug facilitated the drying of grain and the curing of meat and fish. Until the twentieth century most Estonian houses were built from spruce or pine – except on the island of Saaremaa, where stone walls were sometimes used – as evidenced by a pair of farmsteads on display here. The museum also includes an appealing wooden church, taken from the village of Sutlepa north of Haapsalu – traditionally an area of Swedish settlement – its roof supported by swelling, cigar-shaped pillars. An additional attraction is the *Kolu Kõrts* café, which serves up traditional bean soup and beer.

If you're interested in studying the ethnography of contemporary Estonia you could do worse than catch bus #21 back into town – before making for the centre, it loops through a swathe of well-heeled suburbia northwest of Rocca al Mare, taking you past some of the most expensive real estate in the country.

Eating

Most **restaurant** menus in Tallinn feature the solid meat-and-potatoes repertoire common to many a north European country. The more expensive establishments in the Old Town pull this off with a great deal of style and variety and usually offer a range of international dishes in addition. In the more modest eateries, however, the pork chop still rules the roost. Making a welcome appearance are a growing number of (generally rather good) ethnic restaurants and plentiful pizzerias. As you'd expect, meals work out more expensive in Tallinn than elsewhere in the country – you'll rarely get away with paying less than 90–100EEK for a main course in a restaurant. However, cafés, bars and pubs often have a quite substantial menu of full meals, usually at much cheaper prices than in full-blown restaurants.

Restaurants are **open** daily until 11pm or midnight unless otherwise stated. Cafés are much more of a law unto themselves, with the more old-fashioned places closing at 6–8pm, the more fashionable joints working until 11pm or later.

Cafés and snacks

Bogapott Pikk jalg 9. A curious, quirky café on Toompea located in a ceramicists' workshop. Decent coffee and delicious homemade cakes. Till 6pm.

Café Anglais Raekoja plats 14. Excellent coffee and hot chocolate, plus a sumptuous range of salads and sweets. More expensive than average. Till 11pm.

Coffer Vanaturu Kael 8. A good place for a breakfast pastry or a pasta-based lunch, just off the main square. Till 6pm.

Deli 24 Estonia pst 1. A satisfyingly cheap salad bar and buffet, in the Lemon shopping centre just east of the Viru Gate. A good place to pick up a take-away sandwich. Open 24hr.

Elsebet Viru 2. An old-fashioned café above the *Peppersack* restaurant with a genteel atmosphere and cakes and snack dishes on the menu. Till 8pm.

Illusioon Müürivahe 50/Uus 3. A swanky, modern café squeezed into a stretch of town wall beside the Kinomaja cinema, offering good views of medieval cobbled streets through the window. A good place for coffee and cake or a more substantial meal. Till 10pm.

Kehrwieder Saiakang 1. A relaxing coffeehouse just off the main square, with low ceilings, wooden chairs and tables and a succulent range of cakes. Till midnight.

Loungebar 8 Vana-Posti 8. A designer café next to the Sõprus cinema, offering soups, pasta dishes and decent cappuccino in bright, creamy-ochre surroundings. Till midnight.

Maiasmokk Pikk 16. Tallinn's most venerable café – founded in 1864 – with a beautiful wood-panelled interior. You may have to queue for a seat, as it's hugely popular with elderly ladies taking a coffee-and-pastries break from shopping. Mon–Sat 8am–7pm, Sun 10am–6pm.

Pizza Americana Müürivahe 2. A satisfying range of deep-pan pizzas served up in antiseptic surroundings. Till 10pm.

Robert's Coffee Viru 13/15. Excellent coffee, cakes and sandwiches on the top floor of a shopping mall. Majestic views of Viru from the terrace. Till 8pm.

Saiakang Saiakang 3. An old-fashioned café serving so-so drinks and a much more palatable range of cakes, pastries and soups. Till 8pm, Sun till 6pm.

Stockmann Department Store Liivala 53. A self-service restaurant on the fifth floor with excellent sandwiches and salads. Mon–Fri till 9pm, Sat & Sun till 8pm.

Tristan ja Isolde Raekoja plats 1. A dark, poky and atmospheric café in the Town Hall with a full range of drinks and tasty salads and cakes. Till 11pm.

Restaurants

Estonian and north European cuisine

Balthasar Raekoja plats 11 ⑦ 627 6400. An elegant, formal restaurant offering a well-presented range of meaty north European fare, all liberally seasoned with the speciality ingredient of the house – garlic. Main courses in the 160EEK range.

Beer House Dunkri 5. A roomy beer hall with bench seating, cheery oom-pah music and moderately priced pork dishes. The ales (brewed on the premises) go down a treat. Till 2am at weekends.

Eesti Maja Lauteri 1. A relaxed Estonian restaurant just southeast of the Estonia Concert Hall, offering plenty of pork-based local favourites and some excellent freshwater-fish dishes, too. Main courses cost around 150EEK.

Karl Friedrich Raekoja plats 5. Fish specialities and succulent steaks in an elegant, olde-worlde interior. Some of the starters cost as much as main courses in other restaurants, but they're probably worth it. Main courses in the 140–240EEK range.

Kuldse Notsu Kõrts Dunkri 8. Estonian country dishes in a suite of rooms decked out with rustic textiles and wooden benches. Pig out on staples like roast pork, or opt for the wild boar in juniper sauce. Mains around 130EEK.

Mõõkkala Rüütli 16/18. An excellent, if a little pricey (mains 160EEK), seafood place in the cellar of what used to be the Tallinn executioner's house.

Olde Hansa Vanaturg 1. The longest-established and best of Tallinn's medieval-themed restaurants, with wooden benches set out in a sequence of atmospherically lit rooms in the Town Hall. Meaty dishes based on medieval recipes, appropriately costumed staff, and live minstrels. Main courses 160–170EEK.

Pudru ja Pasta Pikk 35. A cellar bar-restaurant with small but imaginative range of inexpensive pasta and meat-and-potato standards.

Vana Major Kinga 3. A long-standing tourist favourite in a cellar just off the main square, with cheap dishes-of-the-day and a reliable repertoire of Estonian meat-based fare.

Vanaema Juures Rataskaevu 10 ⑦ 626 9080. A cosy and elegant cellar restaurant with a country theme, serving local dishes such as pork, trout and wild boar with wine sauce. Meals average 150EEK. Reservations necessary. Till 10pm.

International cuisine

Bazar Tulika põik 3/Madara 14. A colourful Middle Eastern eatery hidden away in an area of refurbished warehouses 1.5km west of Toompea, with a wide-ranging menu and Arab-influenced background music. Fills up with a young crowd at weekends when there's a DJ.

Bocca Olevimägi 9 ⑦ 641 2610. A designer restaurant serving up expensive, but excellent, Italian cuisine to a well-heeled, fashionable crowd.

Buongiorno Müürivahe 17. A cosy cellar place turning out inexpensive soups, pasta dishes and specials at lunchtimes, more substantial Italian-flavoured fare in the evenings.

China White Väike-Karja 1 ⑦ 620 9251. A roomy Chinese restaurant on two floors with good service and presentation. Excellent all-you-can-eat buffet at lunchtime.

Controvento Vene 12 ⑦ 644 0470. A tasteful and authentic Italian restaurant in a fourteenth-century granary. Good selection of pizza and pasta dishes and a decent wine list. Main courses from around 90EEK. Reservations advised.

Elevant Vene 5. A chic Indian restaurant with mellow decor and an affordable range of dishes, including plenty of vegetarian choices.

Golden Dragon Pikk 37. A highly recommended Chinese place with a large variety of fish and vegetarian options, squeezed into a small and intimate cellar space.

Le Bonaparte Pikk 45. Top-class French cuisine in an atmospheric seventeenth-century merchant's house. As expensive as they come in Tallinn, but well worth it. Mains from 250EEK.

Must Lammas Sauna 2. A Georgian restaurant offering superbly spicy stews and grills, stylish surroundings with a few ethnic touches. Mains from 150EEK.

Pegasus Harju 1 ⑦ 631 4040. Exquisite international eats, including plenty of vegetarian choices, in a three-storey temple to 1960s modernism bang in the heart of the Old Town. The ground-floor bar attracts a hip, young after-work crowd. Mains from 220EEK, but quick-lunch soups and salads come significantly cheaper.

Šeš-Beš Gonsiori 9. Smart but affordable Azeri restaurant offering all manner of well-grilled šašlõkk (shish kebab) and some tempting salads.

Drinking

Most young Tallinn folk are enthusiastic and sociable drinkers, ensuring that the Old Town area remains lively seven nights a week. At weekends the drinking scene can be particularly raucous, with bars filling up with holidaying Finns drawn by the comparatively cheap prices and fun-seeking city-break tourists from all over Europe.

Tallinn's Old Town could have been made for drinking, its narrow, winding streets lending themselves perfectly to all manner of smoky dens and laid-back pubs. Most of them offer a full range of main meals, making it possible to hunker down for a whole evening's drinking while appeasing your hunger pangs at the same time. Many bars feature DJs and/or live bands at the weekends, making them a good alternative to the city's pay-to-enter clubs (see "Clubs and live music"; p.328). All the bars listed below are in the Old Town unless otherwise stated.

Amsterdam Pärnu mnt 16. A cosy two-room pub on the far side of Vabaduse väljak from the Old Town, featuring antique-shop furniture, unobtrusive background music, a good choice of ales and a solid menu of mid-priced eats. Till midnight.

Avenüü Suur-Karja 10. A long, narrow bar decorated to look like the outdoor terrace of a French café (hence the name) and offering a full range of meals. A civilized place to drink in the early hours if you've got the staying power. Open 24hr.

George Browne's Harju 6. A roomy "Irish pub" popular with locals and out-of-town weekenders. Fill up on spaghetti, burgers and fries if you get hungry. Live music some nights. Till 2am.

Kloostri Ait Vene 14 ⊛ www.kloostriait.ee. With its enormous open fire and intellectual crowd, this is quieter than most beer-swilling places. Also serves coffee, snacks and very cheap buffet meals. Occasional live folk music, poetry readings and jazz. Sun–Thurs till midnight, Fri & Sat till 1am.

Kompressor Rataskaevu 3. A spacious café-bar popular with a youngish crowd and famous for its Estonian pancakes – wonderfully stodgy and filling. Mon–Fri till 1am, Sat & Sun till 3am.

Kuku Vabaduse 6. During the Soviet era this was a legendary private members' club which anyone with artistic or bohemian aspirations clamoured to join. It doesn't have quite the same reputation anymore, but with its black leather sofas and intellectual clientele, it's still a one-off. Access is via the Tallinn Art Hall (see p.319) and down the steps to the right. Till midnight.

Levist Väljas Olevimägi 12. A laid-back cellar bar offering cheap drinks and strictly non-top 40 music to an engaging arty-alternative crowd. There's no sign – look for a low door with a pastiche of the Levi Jeans logo stuck to it. Till 3am.

The Lost Continent Narva mnt 19. A large, loud Australian pub 1km east of the Old Town with

lively atmosphere, pool tables, occasional live music and decent global cuisine. Till 1am.

Molly Malone's Mündi 2. A comfy pub occupying a perfect position on the shoulder of the main square – a blend of expat haunt, tourist pub and local yuppy meeting place. Frequent live music by cover bands and pub-grub menu. Till 2am.

Moskva Vabaduse väljak 10. A glass-fronted square-side café-bar with loungey design theme, cool customers and DJs at weekends. Sun–Thurs till midnight, Mon–Fri till 4am.

Nimega Baar (*The Pub with a Name*) Suur-Karja 13. Long, narrow and rather snazzy bar attracting a slightly more stylish crowd than some of the other city-centre drinking dens. DJs at weekends. Sun–Thurs till 2am, Fri & Sat till 4am.

Nimeta Baar (*The Pub with no Name*) Suur-Karja 4/6. A good place for civilized week-day drinking that hots up on the weekend. Also the best place in town to catch soccer matches on the big screen. The extensive menu includes some decent tandooris. Sun–Thurs till 2am, Fri & Sat till 4am.

St Patrick's Suur-Karja 8. A civilized central pub in a wonderful medieval building. Hearty pork-and-potatoes dishes on the menu. Till 2am.

Šveiki Juures Uus 25. An unpretentious subterranean beer hall, well off the tourist route, full of enthusiastic local drinkers. Vaguely Czech food. Till midnight.

Vana Villemi Tartu mnt 52. A welcoming, woody-furnished pub with a largely local clientele, full range of beers, and good-value Estonian food on the menu. Somewhat off the beaten track, 2km east of the Old Town, just round the corner from the bus station. Till midnight.

Von Krahli Baar Rataskaevu 10/12. A hip hangout that's always packed with a studenty crowd. The atmosphere is friendly and there's frequent live music and dancing – check the schedule on the door. Sun–Thurs till 1am, Fri & Sat till 3am.

VS Pärnu mnt 28. A hip DJ bar some 200m south of the Old Town, featuring industrial decor and restaurant-quality food (including some mouth-watering Indian dishes). Till 2am.

Woodstock Tatari 6. Two rooms of pop-art

psychedelia a few steps south of the Old Town, serving up cheap drinks and snacks to a laid-back crowd of long-hairs. Occasional live bands. Till 1am.

Entertainment

As well as offering the range of classical music and theatre that you would expect from a capital city, Tallinn is also a burgeoning nightlife centre, with clubs of all shapes and sizes offering a hedonistic menu of entertainment every night of the week – apart from Monday, when everybody takes time off to recharge their batteries.

Tickets for all events are usually obtained from the venues themselves, although the Kaubamaja Ticket Centre, Gonsiori 2, handles bookings for many of the bigger music and theatre spectacles. *Tallinn in Your Pocket* (see p.303) carries forward schedules for classical music, opera and ballet, although the *Baltic Times* is much better for weekly cinema, concert and club listings. If your language skills are up to it, the *Eesti Ekspress* magazine, which comes out every Thursday, carries exhaustive listings (under the heading *Vaba Aeg* or "Free Time", they're currently to be found at the back of the TV supplement). Major cultural **festivals** include Jazzkaar (⊛www.jazzkaar.ee), when big names in world jazz visit Tallin in April; and the **Dark Nights Film Festival** (see p.297).

Clubs and live music

Tallinn's widespread popularity as a weekend-break city has led to an explosion in the number of nightlife venues over the last few years. Mainstream discos churning out top-40 hits and techno remain the rule, although a strong upsurge in local DJ culture ensures that you'll come across all genres of dance music most nights of the week, if you know where to look. Dedicated clubbers should look out for street posters or pick up flyers in Internet cafés or record shops to get an idea of what's going on in any given week. For advance details of major DJ-led events, look up the websites of ⊛www.vibe.ee, ⊛www.spirit.ee or ⊛www.mutantdisco.com. Expect to pay 75–100EEK for **admission** to clubs and 150EEK for Friday-night events with big-name DJs.

Tallinn is never likely to become rock'n'roll capital of the universe, although you'll find a motley collection of alternative musicians, middle-of-the-road rockers and cover bands playing in clubs, or in some of the drinking venues listed on p.327. Big gigs featuring international touring bands take place at the brand-new, 10,000-capacity **Saku Suurhall**, 5km west of the centre at Paldiski mnt 104B in the suburb of Rocca al Mare (⊛www.sakusuurhall.ee; bus #21 from Baltijaam Station); and at the outdoor **Song Festival Grounds** (Lauluväljak; see p.323) near Kadriorg Park.

Bonnie & Clyde in the *Olümpia Hotel*, Liivalaia 33. Live bands usually on Saturdays and a dance floor occupied by a young, beautiful dressed-up crowd. Closed Mon.

Café Amigo beneath the *Viru Hotel*, Viru väljak 4. Heaving, but likeable, disco playing mainstream dance music for locals and tourists into the early hours. Frequent appearances by Estonian pop-rock bands. Fifty percent discount for ISIC holders.

Club Privé Harju 6 ⊛www.clubprive.ee. Lush belle époque decor and cutting-edge dance culture, with high prices and face control helping to keep out the hoi polloi. Closed Mon–Wed.

Decolte Narva mnt 24. Enjoyable disco packed

with party people getting down to anything from top-40 pop to hard-hitting house DJs.

Guitar Safari Müürivahe 22. Popular venue for live cover bands and dancing. Open daily until 3am.

Hollywood Club Vana-Posti 8 ⊛www .club-hollywood.ee. A sizeable Old Town dance club specializing in commercial techno at the weekends, more off-beat DJ styles on weeknights. Youthful, trendy and busy. Closed Sun, Mon & Tues.

Nightman Vineeri 4 ⊛www.nightman.ee. Officially a gay club, but its adventurous music policy is popular with hedonists and nonconformists of all

persuasions. Closed Sun–Thurs.
Terrarium Sadama 6 🖰www.terrarium.ee. A youthful, energetic portside warehouse doling out anything from to drum'n'bass to mainstream dance-pop. Closed Sun, Mon & Tues.

Von Krahli Baar Rataskaevu 10/12. Live music a couple of times a week and regular club nights in a welcoming, pub-like space. Bar open daily till 1am; gigs and club nights (check schedule on the door) may keep going until 3/4am.

Classical music, opera and ballet

Both the Estonian National Symphony Orchestra and the National Opera have solid reputations and attract their fair share of big-name conductors and soloists from abroad. There's also an impressive choice of chamber music on offer, much of it taking place in Tallinn's suitably atmospheric collection of medieval churches and halls; 🖰www.concert.ee is a useful website for finding out what's on in the bigger concert venues. The **box office** at the Estonia Concert Hall, Estonia pst 4 (☎614 7760), sells tickets for some, but not all, of the classical concerts around town.

Estonia Concert Hall (Estonia kontserdisaal) Estonia pst 4 ☎614 7760, 🖰www.concert.ee. Prestige venue for classical music and choral works, including performances by the Estonian National Symphony Orchestra. Box office Mon–Fri noon–7pm, Sat noon–5pm, Sun one hour before performance.
Estonia Theatre (Estonia teater) Estonia pst 4. Immediately next door to the Estonia Concert Hall, home of the National Opera (Rahvusooper; 🖰www.opera.ee), ballet and musicals. Same box office as the Estonia Concet Hall.
Estonian Music Academy (Eeesti muusikaakadeemia) Rävala 16 ☎667 5700. Chamber music several times a week.
House of the Blackheads (Mustpeademaja) Pikk 26 ☎631 31 99, 🖰www.mustpeademaja.ee. Frequent chamber music and solo recitals. Box office 1hr before performance.
Linnahall Mere 20 ☎641 2250, 🖰www.linnahall.ee. Several comfy auditoria inside

an unloved concrete cultural centre, hosting classical concerts, musicals and some of the more adult-oriented pop-rock acts. The city council wants to knock it down, although it is unlikely to close its doors just yet. Box office Mon–Sat 11am–7pm.
Sakala Centre Sakala. All-purpose hall a few steps away from the Estonia Concert Hall (see above), used for occasional musical events, notably big jazz gigs under the Jazzkaar banner (see p.297). Also main venue for the Dark Nights Film Festival (see p.330).
St Nicholas's Church (Niguliste kirik) Niguliste 3 ☎644 9911. Organ recitals at weekends – details of which are usually posted outside.
Town Hall (Raekoda) Raekoja plats 1 ☎644 08 19. Solo recitals and chamber concerts.
Väravatorn Lühike jalg 9 ☎644 0719. This is the HQ of internationally acclaimed early music ensemble Hortus Musicus – they play here once or twice a month.

Theatre

There's a great deal of top-quality **theatre** in Tallinn, but with much of it performed in the Estonian language, your best bet is to stick to major productions and concentrate on the stage-craft – or simply treat the whole experience as a social event.

Drama Theatre (Draamateater) Pärnu mnt 5 ☎644 3378, 🖰www.draamateater.ee. The country's flagship theatrical institution, offering classical drama in a wonderful building. Box office daily noon–7pm.
Linnateater Lai 23 ☎665 0800, 🖰www.linnateater.ee. Top-quality contemporary work. Box office Mon–Fri 9am–6pm, Sat 10am–6pm.
Nukuteater Lai 1 ☎667 9555, 🖰www.nukuteater.ee. Puppet theatre, with most productions kicking off at lunchtime.
Russian Drama Theatre (Vene draamateater)

Vabaduse väljak 5 ☎641 8246, 🖰www.grdt.ee. Drama from the classical Russian canon, as well as contemporary international work in Russian translation.
Theatrum Vene 14 ☎644 6889, 🖰www.theatrum .ee. Youth and student productions.
Vanalinnastuudio Sakala 3 ☎660 5051, 🖰www.vanalinnastuudio.ee. Mostly modern work in a small-sized hall. Box office Mon–Sat 11am–7pm.
Von Krahli Teater Rataskaevu 10 ☎626 9090. Modern, challenging work in a lovely old-fashioned theatre.

Cinemas

There's dwindling number of **cinemas** in central Tallinn – a trend that may continue as smaller city-centre movie theatres are replaced by modern multi-screens. Films are shown in the original language with Estonian subtitles. One event that attracts cinefiles from all over the Baltic region is the December **Dark Nights Film Festival** (Pimedate ööde festivaal; ⓦwww.poff.ee), celebrating contemporary art-house movie production.

Coca-cola plaza Hobujaama 5 ☎1182, ⓦwww.superkinod.ee. State-of-the-art multiplex with eleven screens, fizzy drinks of mass destruction and a healthy sprinkling of cafés and restaurants on the ground floor.
Kinomaja Uus 3 ☎646 4510. Art-house movies in cramped and uncomfortable surroundings.
Kosmos Pärnu mnt 45 ☎1182, ⓦwww.superkinod.ee. Mainstream Hollywood fare.
Sõprus Vana-Posti 8 ☎644 1919, ⓦwww.kino.ee. Mixture of art-house films and mainstream populist stuff.

Shopping

The streets of the Old Town are perfect for **souvenir shopping**; linen, patchwork quilts, amber jewellery, woolly jumpers and mittens are the main items on offer in a string of outlets along Pikk and Dunkri. The best place to browse for woollens is the open-air jumper market on Müürivahe, right beneath the stretch of city walls immediately north of the Viru Gate.

The main **department stores** are Tallinna Kaubamaja, Gonsiori 2 (Mon–Fri 9am–9pm, Sat 9am–8pm, Sun 10am–6pm); and Stockmann, Liivalaia 53 (Mon–Fri 9am–9pm, Sat & Sun 9am–8pm).

Souvenir and specialist shops
Galerii Vanaturu kael 3. Prints and small-scale paintings by contemporary Estonian artists and classy greetings cards.
Jardin Apteegi 3. A cosy little souvenir shop with a nice mixture of linen, wooden kitchen utensils and woollens.
Katariina Gild Vene 12/Katariina käik. An ensemble of craft workshops squeezed into Katariina käik (Catherine's Passage), where you can watch applied artists at work and peruse their wares. Experts in stained glass, ceramics, patchwork, leatherwork, millinery and jewellery all get a studio each.
Keraamika Atelje Pikk 33. Weird and wonderful ceramic creations, most of which are far too arty to qualify as simple souvenirs.
Kodukäsitöö Müürivahe 17. Handicrafts, national costume and linen.
Kuld ja Hõbeehted Pikk 27. Classy jewellery, glassware and ceramics, including repro teasets designed by Adamson-Eric (see p.316) in the 1930s.

Puupood Lai 5. Everything you ever wanted – from teaspoons to train sets – providing it's made out of wood.
Veta Pikk 4. Best of a whole line of linen shops on Pikk, selling tablecloths as well as the kind of linen clothes that you won't be ashamed to wear when you get back home.
Zizi Vene 12. Classy textiles for the home, with a few ethnographic touches.

Bookshops
Apollo Viru 23. Tallinn's biggest and brightest bookstore, offering plentiful maps, guidebooks and English-language classics in paperback.
Rahva Raamat Pärnu mnt 10. Solid selection of maps and some English-language novels.

Music shops
Lasering Pärnu mnt 38. Big selection of Estonian and international pop and rock.
Meloodia Kuninga 4. Broad range of CDs, Estonian contemporary classical composers a speciality.

Listings

Airlines Estonian Air, Vabaduse väljak 10 ☎631 3302, ⓦwww.estonian-air.ee; Finnair, Roosikrantsi 2 ☎611 0946, ⓦwww.finnair.ee; SAS, Rävala 2 ☎627 9399.

Airport (Lennujaam) 3km east of the centre; reached by bus #2 from Gonsiori. Flight information ☎605 8888.
Car rental Avis, Liivalaia 33 ☎631 5930, and at

the airport ☎605 8222, 🖱www.avis.ee; Budget,
Vabaduse väljak 10 ☎696 9158 and at the airport
☎605 8600, 🖱www.budget.ee; Hertz, at the
airport ☎605 8923, 🖱www.hertz.com; National,
at the airport ☎605 8071, 🖱www.nationalcar.ee.
Embassies and consulates Australia, Gonsiori
21 ☎650 9308, 📧mati@standard.ee; Canada,
Toom-Kooli 13 ☎627 3311, 📧canembt@zzz.ee;
Finland, Kohtu 4 ☎610 3200, 🖱www.finemb.ee;
Latvia, Tõnismägi 10 ☎646 1313; Lithuania, Uus
15 ☎631 4030; Russia, Pikk 19 ☎646 4175;
United Kingdom, Wismari 6 ☎667 4700,
🖱www.britishembassy.ee; USA, Kentmanni 20
☎668 8100, 🖱www.usemb.ee. Citizens of Ireland,
New Zealand and South Africa should ring one of
the English-speaking embassies to find out who is
currently representing their interests.
Exchange Outside banking hours, try the Monex
exchange offices in the ferry dock, or the
Kaubamaja or Stockmann department stores (all
daily 9am–8pm).
Hospital The main hospital is at Ravi 18 ☎602
7000.
Internet access Escape, Tatari 4 (25EEK per hour;
open 24hr); Kaubamaja department store, 5th floor
(20EEK for 30min; Mon–Fri 9am–9pm, Sat
9am–8pm, Sun 10am–6pm).
Laundry Sauberland, Maakri 23; Seebimull,
Liivalaia 7.
Left luggage In the basement of the bus station

(Mon–Sat 6.30am–10.20pm, Sun
7.45am–8.20pm; 4–10EEK); and at the train
station (even-numbered dates 9am–10pm; odd-
numbered dates 9am–5pm).
Libraries British Council, Vana-Posti 7.
Newspapers Some of the larger city-centre
kiosks stock English-language newspapers and
magazines; otherwise try the newsagents in the
Stockman department store, Liivalaia 53.
Pharmacies Centrally located pharmacies which
are open seven days a week include Raeapteek,
Raekoja plats 11; Tallinna Linna Apteek, Pärnu mnt
10; Tõnismäe Apteek, Tõnismägi 5. The latter has
a 24hr emergency counter (ring the buzzer).
Photo developing and supplies Filmari-Fuji,
Suur-Karja 9.
Police Pärnu mnt 11 ☎644 5266.
Post office Narva mnt 1, opposite the *Viru Hotel*
(Mon–Fri 8am–8pm, Sat 8am–6pm).
Taxis Ranks on Vabaduse väljak or just outside the
Viru gate. Otherwise call Tulika ☎612 0000 or
Linnatakso ☎644 2442.
Telephones Next to the post office on Narva mnt
1 (Mon–Fri 8am–7pm, Sat 9am–4pm).
Travel agents Baltic Tours, Pikk 31 (☎630 0400,
🖱www.bt.ee), deals in international plane tickets
and hotel reservations within Estonia. Estravel,
Suur-Karja 15 (☎626 6266, 🖱www.estravel.ee),
sells tickets for all the major ferry lines and is
agent for American Express.

Travel details

Trains

Tallinn to: Narva (4 daily; 4hr); Paldiski (7 daily;
40min); Pärnu (2 daily; 3hr); Tartu (2 daily; 3hr
30min); Viljandi (2 daily; 3hr).

Buses

Tallinn to: Haanja (2 daily; 5hr); Haapsalu (every
1hr; 1hr 50min); Kärdla (3 daily; 4hr 30min);
Kuressaare (every 2hr; 4hr 30min); Narva (hourly;
3hr 30min); Pärnu (hourly; 2hr); Tartu (every
30min; 2hr 20min); Viljandi (hourly; 2hr 30min);
Võru (12 daily; 4hr 30min).

International trains

Tallinn to: Moscow (1 daily; 14hr); St Petersburg
(3 weekly; 7hr).
International buses
Tallinn to: Berlin (1–2 daily; 30hr); Riga (5 daily;
5–6hr); St Petersburg (5 daily, 5hr); Vilnius (2 daily;
10hr).

International flights

Tallinn to: Copenhagen (2 daily; 1hr 40min);
Frankfurt (4 weekly; 2hr 40min); Helsinki (6 daily;
1hr); London (1 daily; 3hr 50min); Moscow (1
daily; 3hr); Paris (1 daily; 3hr 30min); Riga (1 daily;
1hr); St Petersburg (5 weekly; 1hr); Stockholm (5
daily; 2hr); Vilnius (2 daily; 1hr 30min).

3.2

Western Estonia

With its deeply indented coastline, archipelago of islands and hinterland of thick forest and heaths, **western Estonia** embraces many of the geographical features that are most typical of the country. Indeed many locals would maintain that it's in the region's juniper-covered heaths, quaint country towns and wave-battered shores watched over by solitary lighthouses, that the true soul of the nation ultimately lies. Although many of the coastal towns have been resorts since the nineteenth century, when the cream of the Baltic aristocracy came to bathe their weary limbs in medicinal coastal mud, much of western Estonia was treated as a sensitive border area during the Soviet period and tourism didn't

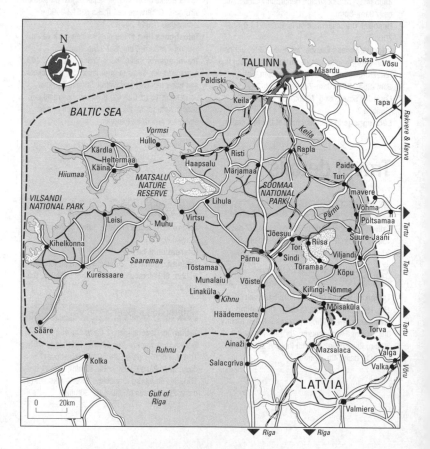

really get going again until the 1990s. Happily, the desire to develop western Estonia as a money-earning vacationland has been tempered by the realization that the region's wealth of unspoiled natural landscapes is its most valuable asset. The area also boasts a rich variety of wildlife. The heaths and forests support sizeable communities of deer, moose, elk and beaver, while fish-rich coastal inlets and lagoons provide the ideal feeding grounds for thousands of migrating birds in the spring and autumn.

The main gateway to the northwestern coast is the resort town of **Haapsalu**, an endearing mixture of belle époque gentility and contemporary chic and a convenient staging post en route to the tranquil islands of **Vormsi** and **Hiiumaa**. Immediately south of Hiiumaa, **Saaremaa** is the biggest and most popular of Estonia's islands, its enjoyably animated capital Kuressaare providing access to a beautiful hinterland of forest, heath and swamp. The southwestern coast is dominated by **Pärnu**, Estonia's one true beach resort and correspondingly abuzz with hedonistic energy on summer weekends. Inland from Pärnu, the laid-back town of **Viljandi** is one of provincial Estonia's prettiest and provides access to the beautifully desolate peat bogs of the **Soomaa National Park**.

Western Estonia is an easy area to access, with frequent **buses** speeding their way from Tallinn to the coast's principal towns, Haapsalu and Pärnu. The islands of Hiiumaa, Vormsi and Saaremaa are all served by regular **ferry** services from the mainland. In addition, express buses run from Tallinn to Hiiumaa and Saaremaa, including the ferry crossing as part of the deal. Local transport on the islands themselves, however, can be pretty scarce, and unless you have access to a car you'll need to adopt a leisurely approach to exploring the countryside.

Haapsalu and around

Straddling a three-kilometre-long thumb of land sticking out into the Baltic Sea, the family-oriented resort of **HAAPSALU** is an appealing combination of modernity and tradition: sleek, glass-fronted café-bars rub shoulders with wonky wooden houses, ranging from single-storey fishermen's cottages to the kind of grandiose neo-Gothic villas that wouldn't be out of place on an Addams Family film set. Haapsalu has been popular with holidaymakers ever since the early nineteenth century, when local doctor Carl Abraham Hunnius (1797–1851) set about publicizing the curative properties of the local mud. The town soon became a magnet for St Petersburg high society, and was attracting royalty by the end of the century – both Tsar Alexander II and son Alexander III were regular visitors. By the mid-twentieth century, Haapsalu had become a mass-market bucket-and-spade resort, although tourism was subsequently wound down by a security-conscious Soviet regime that regarded the whole of northwestern Estonia as one vast military installation. Considerably tidied up since independence, it's now increasingly popular with Estonians and Swedes. An attractive stretch of sand just west of town at Paralepa ensures Haapsalu's continuing popularity as a beach resort, while many of the bigger hotels offer the kind of mud treatments that first made the town famous.

Haapsalu is only 10km short of the Rohuküla ferry terminal serving the islands of Hiiumaa and **Vormsi**. The latter is an easy day-trip from town, as is the bird-rich nature reserve of **Matsalu** on the mainland to the south.

Arrival, information and accommodation

Buses arrive in the forecourt of the old train station on the southwestern side of town, five minutes' walk from the **tourist office** at Posti tänav 37 (mid-May to mid-Sept Mon–Fri 9am–6pm, Sat & Sun 10am–3pm; mid-Sept to mid-May Mon–Fri 9am–5pm; ☎473 3248, ⓦwww.haapsalu.ee); staff can book you into local **B&Bs** (❶–❷). Some Haapsalu **hotels** drop their prices in winter (Oct–April), and those that don't do so officially may still be open to bargaining – it always pays to ask. There's a free **tent**-pitching area just west of town in Paralepa forest and a commercial site, *Camping Piksele*, at Männiku 32 (ⓦwww.albinet.com/camping).

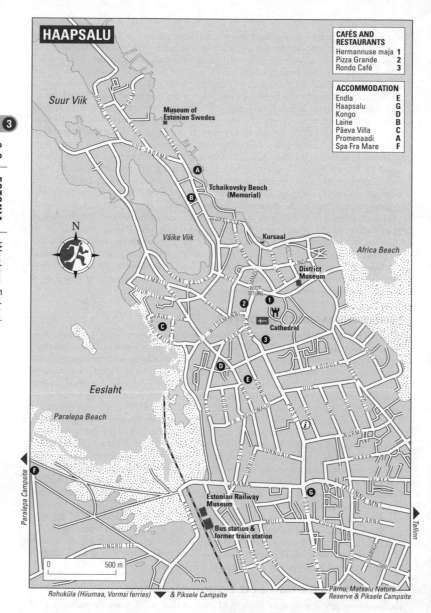

Hotels

Endla Endla 5 ☎ 473 7999, ⓦ www.hot.ee/hostelendla. An acceptable, centrally located cheapie with simply decorated rooms, shared facilities and no breakfast (but you are free to use the kitchen). Only seven doubles and two triples, so ring in advance. **①**

Haapsalu Posti 43 ☎ 473 3347, ⓔ exotrade@hot.ee. An unspectacular and slightly overpriced concrete box on a busy street, but the en-suites with TV are perfectly agreeable if the more characterful places are booked up. **⑤**

Kongo Kalda 19 ☎ 472 4800,
🌐 www.kongohotel.ee. Modern en-suites in a
building that looks like a contemporary design
showroom: expect lots of white surfaces, pale
wood and chrome. Built on the site of a bar which
was so notorious for drunken brawling during the
1960s and 1970s that it was nicknamed "Congo"
in honour of the vicious civil war then taking place
in that country. ❹
Laine Sadama 9/11 ☎ 472 4400, 🌐 www.laine.ee.
A large, Soviet-era sanatorium, a little institutional
in atmosphere, although the fully modernized en-
suites are just as comfortable as those in any
international, mid-range hotel. Mud baths and
other therapeutic treatments on site. ❹
Päeva Villa Lai 7 ☎ 473 3672,
🌐 http://paevavilla.ee. A smart, medium-sized
establishment spread over two neighbouring

houses, offering tasteful rooms with shower and
TV, all of which are different in shape and design.
Split-level suites ❺, regular rooms ❹
Promenaadi Sadama 22 ☎ 473 7250,
🌐 www.promenaadi.ee. A venerable shoreside
structure built as a private holiday villa in 1859
and extended in the 1990s. Comfortable, high-
ceilinged en-suites in the old part; rooms in the
modern wing have chic modern furnishings and
small sea-facing balconies. Free morning sauna,
and guests can rent bikes. ❹
Spa Fra Mare Ranna 2 ☎ 472 4600,
🌐 www.framare.ee. Large, low-rise complex in the
woods behind Paralepa beach, offering bright en-
suites with woody furniture and warm-colour
decor. Mud baths, aromatherapy and paraffin
treatments on site, and bike rental for guests.
Spacious top-floor suites ❺, regular rooms ❹

The Town

Haapsalu's main thoroughfare, **Posti tänav** and its extension **Karja tänav**, terminates at the northern end of town at a small market square (more of a circle, actually) known as **Rootsiturg** – "Swedish market" – a reminder of the large Swedish-
speaking population that was once concentrated in the villages north of Haapsalu.
Though settled here since the Middle Ages, the majority of Swedes fled to the
motherland in 1944 to avoid persecution by a Soviet regime that saw them as a
potentially treacherous pro-Western minority.

The Castle and Cathedral

Looming over the Rootsiturg to the southeast are the stark grey walls of Haapsalu's
combined **Castle and Cathedral**, built in the thirteenth century to serve as both
military and spiritual headquarters of the bishops of Ösel-Wiek (the German name
for Saaremaa and northwestern Estonia). The bishops were given northwestern
Estonia in the great Baltic carve-up that followed the Teutonic conquest, and they
lorded it over Haapsalu and the neighbouring islands until the combined effects of
the Livonian Wars and the Reformation sent them packing. Swashbuckling Swedish
General Jakob de la Gardie (son of Pontus de la Gardie; see p.318) bought the castle
in 1628, but it was largely destroyed by Peter the Great a century later and,
although the church was rebuilt in the 1880s the fortifications never really recovered. You can still see surviving stretches of the ten-metre-high wall that once
enclosed the **Castle Park** (Lossipark; daily 7am–9pm; free), the grassed-over
remains of the former fortress courtyard. Parts of the semi-ruined keep have been
rebuilt to accommodate the **Castle Museum** (mid–May to mid-Sept Tues–Sun
10am–6pm; 15EEK), where you can examine rusting medieval weaponry and
scramble up a section of the watchtower. More an expression of brute ecclesiastical
power than beauty, the adjoining barn-like **Cathedral** is reckoned to be the largest
single-nave church in the Baltics and has an impressively cavernous, though largely
unadorned, interior. Haapsalu's nineteenth-century tourist boom no doubt encouraged the invention of the legend of the White Lady, a medieval maid who supposedly donned male guise in order to enter the cathedral precinct and canoodle with
her priestly lover. Once discovered, she was impaled on the battlements (and/or
immured in the walls, depending on which version of the tale you like the sound of
best), bequeathing Haapsalu with a lovelorn ghost which still puts in an appearance
at one of the cathedral windows every August at full moon – although it might just
be an illusion caused by moonbeams pouring through the window onto a wall

behind. The apparition provides the perfect excuse for the good-natured ghoul-fest known as the **Days of the White Lady**, held in the castle park every summer (see opposite).

Just north of the castle, at the junction of Lossi plats and Kooli tänav, a pea-green eighteenth-century Town Hall now houses the **District Museum** (Wed–Sun: May to mid-Sept 10am–6pm; mid-Sept to April 11am–4pm; 15EEK; ◉www.muuseum.haapsalu.ee), where sepia photographs of crowded beaches reveal what a fun place pre–World War II Haapsalu must have been. There's passing mention of Ilon Wikland, the local-born Swede who went on to enjoy moderate renown as the illustrator of Astrid Lindgren's Pippi Longstocking books, and a shrine-like corner devoted to Tsarist-era mayor Gottfried von Krusenstern, who did much to promote the town's tourist profile before being shot on the main square by bolshy army deserters during the revolutionary chaos of 1917.

Africa beach and along Promenaadi

Beyond the museum lies one of the most attractive parts of Haapsalu, a web of quiet, cobbled streets lined with low-rise, nineteenth-century housing. Following these eastwards will bring you out onto **Africa beach** (Aafrika rand), so named because bathers used to coat their bodies in the medicinal black mud found in the bay. Just back from the beach you can climb the bird-watching tower for sweeping views of nearby reed beds.

From here Promenaadi winds west then north along the shore, passing the delicately carved eaves of the wooden **Kursaal** before arriving at the *Promenaadi* and *Laine* hotels, in front of which lies the stone seat known as the **Tchaikovsky Bench** (Tšaikovski pink). Placed here in 1940 to commemorate the 26-year-old composer's stay in 1867 (when he is said to have worked on parts of his first major opera, *Voyvod*), the memorial emits a light-activated blast of music whenever anyone approaches it.

The Museum of Estonian Swedes

Continuing north past the hotels eventually leads you to the **Museum of Estonian Swedes** at Sadama 32 (Rannarootsi muuseum; Wed–Sun: May–Aug 10am–6pm; Sept–April 11am–4pm; 20EEK; ◉www.aiboland.ee), which celebrates the heritage of this once-thriving community with a colourful display of richly embroidered costumes and household textiles. You can also see examples of Swedish-language newspapers once published in Haapsalu, including copies of the short-lived *Sovjet-Estland*, which appeared for a few months in 1940–41 and was so successful in selling the benefits of Soviet power that almost all of its target audience fled to Sweden when the Red Army returned in 1944. The highlight of the display is the twenty-metre-long tapestry recalling the history of the Estonian Swedes – from horn-helmeted Vikings onwards – in vivid, comic-strip style. It was made in 2002 by members of the local community who still claim Swedish ancestry and meet once a week at the museum to keep handicraft traditions alive – more of their dazzling creations are on display in a room upstairs. Berthed outside the museum is a recently completed replica of a **Jaala**, a traditional, three-sailed fishing boat from the island of Ruhnu.

The Estonian Railway Museum and Paralepa beach

Built in 1904, Haapsalu's train station, in the southwest of town, received its last passenger service in 1996, but remains an enduring monument to the Tsarist Empire's belle époque – not least because of the elegant 214-metre-long canopy above the platform, built to shelter aristocratic arrivals from the unpredictable Baltic weather. Ensconced in the former imperial waiting room, the **Estonian Railway Museum** (Wed–Sun 10am–6pm; 15EEK) harbours a modest collection of tickets, uniforms and travel posters, and there are a couple of vintage locomotives parked out the back. A ten-minute walk west of the station, the forest-fringed **Paralepa beach** is the sandiest of Haapsalu's bathing areas.

Eating, drinking and entertainment

Haapsalu has a fair scattering of places to **eat** and **drink**, mostly concentrated on Posti tänav and Karja. *Hermannuse maja*, Karja 1A, is a reasonably smart, yet relaxing, pub-restaurant serving an imaginative mixture of Estonian and international food; and the nearby *Pizza Grande*, Karja 6, dishes out better-than-average thin-crust pies in comfortable surroundings. The town's hotel restaurants are less bland than you might expect: the *Blu Holm* in the *Hotel Laine* serves up excellent fish dishes in classy, starched-tablecloth surroundings, while the café-restaurant at the *Hotel Promenaadi*, just across the road, is worth checking out for its glass-enclosed, waterfront position. *Rondo Café*, Posti 7, is the best place for pastries and cakes, and the café-bars underneath the *Haapsalu Hotel* are the liveliest spots for evening drinks.

The town offers a modest range of entertainment in summer and hosts a couple of worthwhile festivals. The **Kursaal** (open May to mid-Sept; ⓦwww.kuursaal.ee) plays host to easy-listening crooners and tame discos in season, with outdoor concerts of light classics making use of the adjacent concert bowl in good weather. International ensembles take advantage of the cathedral's excellent acoustics during the **Haapsalu Early Music Festival** in July (ⓦwww.concertogrosso.ee), while the decidedly more low-brow **Days of the White Lady** in mid-August (ⓦwww.daam.haapsalu.ee) involves live music, DJs and late-night partying in the castle park.

Vormsi

Lying 3km off the mainland, **Vormsi** (ⓦwww.vormsi.ee), about 10km by 20km in size, is a lush, green island, covered in forest, juniper heath and occasional grazing meadow. Although there's not a great deal to see on Vormsi, it's the general air of rustic calm, coupled with plentiful opportunities for walking and cycling, that makes a visit here so appealing. It was home to well over two thousand Estonian Swedes until 1944, when the vast majority packed their bags and sailed for the motherland. Although it was partially re-populated with Estonians during the Soviet period, human beings are now outnumbered by the elk, roe deer and wild boar that roam the dense woodland at the island's heart.

Ferries from the mainland arrive at the small port of **SVIBY**, within easy walking distance of the island's main settlement, **HULLO**, just 3km west. At the northern end of Hullo, the otherwise undistinguished **St Olav's Church** is worth a peek for the thicket of wheel-shaped stone grave crosses in its cemetery. The remotest place on the island and the best spot for a swim is stubby **Rumpo peninsula**, 2km southeast of Hullo, a rock-strewn stretch of shoreline backed by juniper heath and peat bog.

Two **ferries** a day make their way to Sviby from **Rohuküla**, 10km west of Haapsalu (and reached by bus #1, which runs roughly hourly); you can check timetable details on ⓦwww.laevakompanii.ee. Tanel Viks rents out bikes (130EEK a day) right on Sviby harbourfront, but they disappear fast on summer weekends – when it's a good idea to reserve in advance (☏051 78722 or 050 17579; ⓔtanvx @neti.ee), or rent one in Haapsalu and bring it with you. Haapsalu tourist office (see p.333) is the best place to get information and maps of Vormsi and may have a list of B&Bs on the island. Otherwise, *Mäe Farm*, Rumpo (April–Nov only; ☏472 6106, ⓦwww.hot.ee/streng; ❸), offers charming rooms in two outbuildings (one of which is a traditionally built log cabin), as well as bike rental and camping space.

Matsalu

Thirty kilometres due south of Haapsalu, **Matsalu Bay** is one of the biggest stop-off points for migrating birds in Europe, attracting thousands of ducks, barnacled geese, corncrakes, moorhens and mute swans every spring and autumn, as well as providing a year-round habitat for cormorants and gulls. All three sides of the bay have been under the protection of the **Matsalu Nature Reserve** (Matsalu looduskaitseala; ⓦwww.matsalu.ee) since 1957, although it's the southern shore of the bay, with its dense reed beds and grassy coastal heaths, that provides the best opportunities for getting up close to the birds.

The gateway to the area is the small provincial town of **LIHULA** (ⓦwww.lihula.ee), served by Haapsalu–Virtsu and Tallinn–Kuressaare buses. Some 3km north of here is the **Matsalu Visitors' Centre** in Penijõe Manor (mid-April to mid-Sept Sat–Thurs 8am–5pm, Fri 8am–3.30pm; ⓦwww.matsalu.ee), where you can pick up maps and take in a small museum display (same times; 10EEK) devoted to the local flora and fauna. From here you can follow tracks northwest to the birdwatching tower at **Suitsu**, 4km beyond Penijõe, where there's a good view of coastal wetlands edged by yellowy-gold reeds. Another tower can be found at **Keemu**, 6km west on the road to the village of Matsalu.

Should you wish **to stay**, the Visitors' Centre can put you in touch with the handful of B&Bs in the rustic communities near the reserve; otherwise the *Luige Villa* hotel in Lihula, Tallinna mnt 23 (☎477 8872, ⓦwww.luigevilla.ee; ❸), has well-equipped doubles, alongside more frugal four- and five-person rooms for 250–300EEK per person.

Hiiumaa

Shaped like a four-pointed star and measuring some 75km from east to west and 50km from north to south, **HIIUMAA** is Estonia's second-largest island, but also one of its most sparsely populated. The thin, sandy soil has never supported much in the way of agriculture, with the result that a great deal of the island remains covered by virgin pine forest, peat bog and shrub-covered heath – habitats favoured by elk, roe deer and wild boar. Offering just as much natural beauty as its more popular neighbour Saaremaa (see p.341), but with less tourist development, Hiiumaa makes

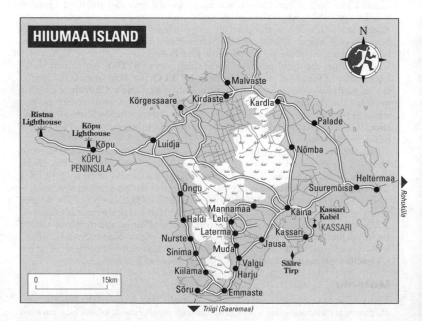

the perfect place for a rustic getaway. Along with most other facilities, the island's tourist office is located in **Kärdla** in the northern part of the island. For a heady taste of undiluted natural wilderness, head for the juniper-carpeted island of **Kassari**, linked to southern Hiiumaa by a causeway, or the wind-battered **Kõpu peninsula** at the western end of Hiiumaa.

Laevakompanii (⊛www.laevakompanii.ee) runs ferries four to six times daily from Rohuküla, just west of Haapsalu (see p.337), to the Heltermaa terminal on Hiiumaa's eastern coast. A one-way ticket costs 25EEK per person, plus 112EEK per car. Four daily Tallinn–Kärdla buses (calling at Haapsalu on the way) also make the crossing – the price of the ferry is included in your ticket. There's also a ferry service (summer only) to Sõru on Hiiumaa's southern tip from Triigi on Saaremaa, although it's operated by a small vessel that can take only a limited number of cars (expect queues at weekends) and it's not met by any buses. Eomap's 1:50 000 **plan** of Hiiumaa is the best aid to detailed exploration.

Kärdla

Sitting on the island's northeastern shoulder some 30km from Heltermaa, **KÄRDLA** may never rank among the prettiest of rural capitals, but it's Hiiumaa's only real service centre and transport hub and is a wonderfully uneventful little place in which to lie low for a few days. It's a low-rise town with plenty of timber houses and cottage gardens, most of which feature mounds of earth looking rather like air-raid shelters – but that (reassuringly perhaps) turn out to be potato cellars.

Kärdla was an important textile-producing town in the nineteenth century and the factory manager's house at the northern end of the village – known locally as the Pikk Maja or "Long House" – now holds a branch of the **Hiiumaa museum** (Mon–Fri 10am–5pm, Sat 11am–2pm; 10EEK). There's no permanent collection, but the sensitively restored rooms provide the perfect venue for seasonal art and photography displays. Five minutes' northwest of the museum lies arguably Kärdla's most attractive feature, a grassy, boulder-strewn seaside park which fills up with bathers on summer weekends.

Practicalities

Buses stop on the fringes of the centre at Keskväljak, a few steps south of the **tourist office** at Hiiu 1 (mid-April to mid-May Mon–Fri 9am–5pm, Sat 10am–2pm; mid-May to mid-Sept Mon–Fri 9am–6pm, Sat & Sun 10am–2pm; mid-Sept to mid-April Mon–Fri 10am–4pm; ☏462 2233, ⊛www.hiiumaa.ee); staff here can arrange B&B accommodation (**❶**–**❷**) in Kärdla and throughout the island. **Hotels** include *Sõnajala*, at the western end of the village on Leigri väljak (☏463 1220 or 463 1222, ✉liivi.hansen@mail.ee; **❷**–**❹**), offering simple rooms with shared facilities or comfier en-suites with TV; the *Nuutri*, a rather basic B&B just east of the main square at Nuutri 4 (☏469 8715 or 050/58896, ✉nuutri@hot.ee; **❶**); or the more stylish *Padu*, at the eastern entrance to Kärdla at Heltermaa mnt 22 (☏463 3037; **❸**), an attractive, timber-built guesthouse offering wood-panelled en-suites with TV and a small balcony.

There's a handful of unassuming **eating and drinking** venues in town. *Café Arteesia* on Keskväljak is the best place for cheap and filling meat-and-potato fare, while *Priiankru*, just north of the bus station on Sadama, has more choice and slightly higher prices. The *Rannapargu* café-bar, in a seaside park at the northern end of town, is open until the early hours at weekends. If you're simply picnicking, head for the large supermarket and food shops on the main square.

Kassari

One of the main attractions in the southern part of the island is **Kassari**, a separate land mass 8km long and 4km across, joined to the main body of Hiiumaa by a causeway. Containing some of the most unspoilt conifer-covered heathland in the region, it's compact enough to be explored on foot or bike in a day. The main jumping-off point for exploring Kassari is **KÄINA**, a small town on the Hiiumaa side of the causeway. Built around the sombre ruins of a fifteenth-century church destroyed by World War II bombing, it's otherwise pretty forgettable, but it is one of the few places on Hiiumaa served by regular bus from Kärdla, and it has a couple of decent accommodation options to boot. These include the *Liilia*, a family-run hotel just east of the bus stop at Hiiu mnt 22 (☎463 6146; ❸), which has comfy en-suites with TV, as well as a very good restaurant. One kilometre west of town in Lõokese, the *Lõokese Spa Hotel* (☎463 6107, ✆www.lookese.com; ❸–❹) is one of the swankiest places to stay on the island, offering rooms with shower and TV, outdoor swimming and paddling pools, and facilities for mud baths, aromatherapy and other spa treatments.

The road to Kassari leaves the Käina–Heltermaa road 3km east of Käina, crossing the causeway before passing after a further 3km a turn-off to the stocky, medieval **Kassari Kabel**, the only reed-roofed church in the country. A couple more kilo-metres beyond the turn-off is **KASSARI** village itself, an appealing agglomeration of timber houses and tumbledown barns nestling among thickets of juniper. Just north of the village's main street, the **Hiiumaa museum** (Mon–Fri 10am–5pm; 10EEK) offers a small but intriguing display of traditional agricultural implements and embroidered folk costumes. Beside the museum, the *Keldrimäe* guesthouse (☎469 7210; ❷) has a handful of simple rooms.

At the western end of Kassari village a signpost points the way to **Sääre Tirp**, a pebbly promontory jutting out into the sea at the southern end of the island. After 2km, the track along the promontory terminates in a car park and a path flanked by juniper bushes leads to the foot of Sääre Tirp, ending in a desolate, otherworldly shingle spit that peters out into the sea after a couple of hundred metres.

Suuremõisa

The main settlement in the eastern corner of the island is **SUUREMÕISA**, a frumpy little village 5km inland from the ferry terminal at Heltermaa and served by the Kärdla–Tallinn bus. The name literally means "Great Manor", a reference to the Baroque **manor house** built here in 1755 by Margarethe Stenbock, a descendant of the de la Gardie family (who owned most of Hiiumaa until dispossessed by the Russians in 1710). Nowadays an agricultural college, its interior is rarely accessible, although its rust-coloured exterior and extensive, unkempt grounds, open to the public, are sufficient excuse for a stop-off. In 1796, it was bought by Otto Reinhold Ludwig von Ungern-Sternberg (1744–1811), the shipping magnate and Hiiumaa landowner who became a by-word for arrogance and cruelty in nineteenth-century Estonia. In 1805, he shot one of his own captains in Suuremõisa's first-floor office, a crime for which he was deported to Siberia. Though the claims were never proven, Ungern-Sternberg was also accused of being a modern-day pirate, lighting fires on the Hiiumaa coast in order to lure ships onto the rocks so that they could be pil-laged.

The Kõpu peninsula

Five buses a day (fewer at weekends) wend their way west from Kärdla to the **Kõpu peninsula**, a rugged, rock-fringed tongue of heathland that juts out into the sea 45km or so west of town. Buses terminate at the village of Kalana, right on the tip of the peninsula, although it's worth hopping off at the village of Kõpu, 35km out of Kärdla, to see the **Kõpu lighthouse** (Kõpu tuletorn), one of the oldest continuously operating lighthouses in the world. Located on the west-ern side of the village, the lighthouse dates back to 1531 and was built at the request of the Hanseatic League to warn ships away from the Hiiu Madal sand-bank and the pirate-infested coastline. Strengthened by a quartet of bulky, angular buttresses at its base, it looks at first sight more like a Mayan temple than a piece of maritime architecture. Initially a pyre was burned at the top, but in 1845 a properly enclosed light was built. You can climb up for a view of trees and sea (admission 5EEK). Twelve kilometres beyond Kõpu lies the equally striking maroon-coloured **Ristna lighthouse**, a rocket of a building that presides over a boulder-strewn stretch of shoreline. Like many nineteenth-century lighthouses in this part of Estonia, it was built abroad (in this case in France in 1874) and reassembled here on arrival.

Saaremaa

For Estonians, the island of **Saaremaa** epitomizes the nation's natural beauty more than any other place in the country. Cloaked with pine forest, juniper heath and grasslands, its coastline girdled with tawny reed beds, it has long appealed to nature-loving, well-to-do Tallinners and increasingly attracts Scandinavian and West European tourists too. Back to nature instincts are catered for with a scattering of farmstead-based B&Bs across the island, although most accommodation is concentrated in the island's restful capital, **Kuressaare**, site of the one must-see historic attraction on the island, the impressive **Bishops' Castle**. North of Kuressaare lie some of Saaremaa's best-known sights, notably the strangely enchanting **Angla windmills** and the mysterious **Kaali meteorite crater**. On the western side of the island is the little-touristed coastal wilderness of the **Vilsandi National Park**, ideal for long- and short-range hikes. Historic churches crop up just about everywhere, with some especially fine ones at **Karja**, **Kaarma** and **Kihelkonna**.

Public transport on Saaremaa is limited, with services to most destinations leaving Kuressaare at different times on different days of the week, making timetable reading a bit of a nightmare – the Kuressaare tourist office is your best source of information. Thanks to its largely flat terrain, though, exploring the island by **bike** is also a viable option; bikes can be rented in Kuressaare (see p.344). Saaremaa is reached by taking the **ferry** (hourly in summer, every 2 hours in winter) from Virtsu on the mainland to Kuivastu on **Muhu**, a small island, 8km across from which a causeway leads to Saaremaa itself. Tickets cost 20EEK per person one-way with an extra 85EEK for a car, 30EEK for a motorbike. Several daily buses make the trip from Tallinn and Pärnu to Kuressaare – the price of the ferry is included in the ticket. Approaching from the Haapsalu direction is more awkward, although in summer there are three daily buses from Haapsalu to Virtsu, where you can change onto one of the Tallinn–Kuressare or Pärnu–Kuressare services. If you're travelling **by car**, bear in mind that there are long queues for the ferry on summer weekends – don't leave it too late in the day or you may end up stranded. Eomap's 1: 200 Tallinn, available from Kuressaare tourist office or bookshops in Tallinn, will come in useful if you intend to explore the island in any depth.

Muhu

The main launching point for Saaremaa, the island of **Muhu** is also worth visiting in its own right – swathed in pine forests and juniper thickets, it's just as attractive as its better-known island neighbour, and it seems a shame to speed right across it in the rush to get to Kuressaare. Among its draws is the village of **LIIVA**, 6km inland from the Kuivastu ferry terminal and site of the thirteenth-century **St Catherine's Church** (Katariina kirik), an angular, whitewashed building, looking fashionably modernist with its trio of steep-roofed sheds seemingly concertina-ed together.

Three kilometres beyond Liiva a minor road branches right towards **KOGUVA**, a settlement on Muhu's west coast that has been declared a "museum-village" on account of its rich stock of stone-built, reed-thatched farmhouses. Far from being museum pieces, the majority of these houses are still inhabited by local farmers – wandering the village's grassy lanes leaves you thinking how nice it would be if more Estonian villages still looked like this.

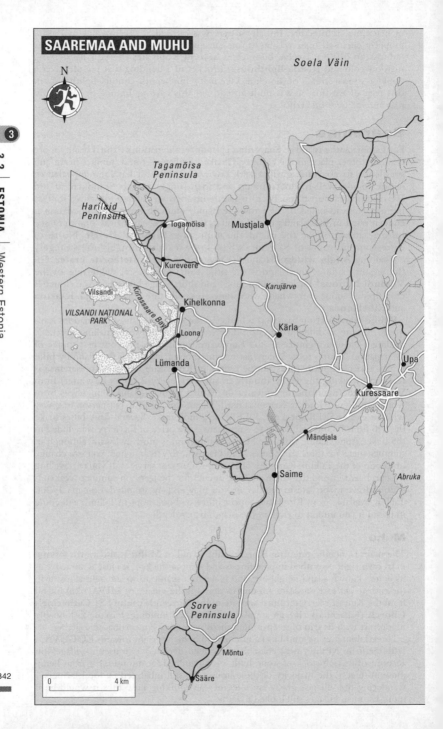

SAAREMAA AND MUHU

N

Soela Väin

Tagamõisa Peninsula

Harilaid Peninsula

● Togamõisa

● Mustjala

● Kureveere

Karujärve

Vilsandi

Kiirassaare Bay

VILSANDI NATIONAL PARK

● Kihelkonna

● Kärla

● Loona

● Lümanda

Upa

Kuressaare

● Mändjala

● Saime

Abruka

Sorve Peninsula

● Mõntu

●Sääre

0   4 km

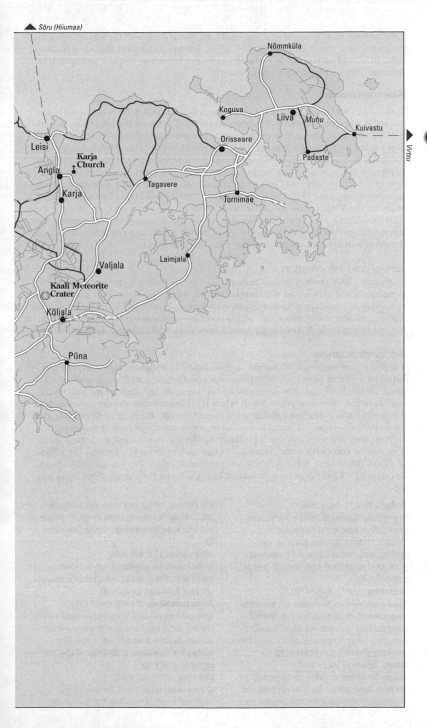

Sõru (Hiiumaa)

Nõmmküla

Koguva

Liiva · *Muhu*

Kuivastu

Orissaare

Padaste

Leisi

Karja Church ✝

Angla

Tagavere

Karja

Tornimäe

Valjala

Laimjala

Kaali Meteorite Crater

Kõljala

Piina

Virtsu

If you want **to stay** on Muhu you could do worse than head for *Pädaste Mõis*, on the coast, 6km south of Liiva (☎454 8800, ✆www.padaste.ee; ❺), a top-quality hotel in an old manor house – the decor in the luxurious doubles and split-level suites preserves a reassuringly rustic quality.

Kuressaare

Situated midway along Saaremaa's south coast, **KURESSAARE** is the island's only real town and service centre – wherever you're aiming for on the island, you're likely to pass through here at least once. Despite the presence of some Soviet-era buildings on the outskirts it's a genteel little place at heart, with a town centre that remains much as it was before World War II and a well-preserved medieval castle, as impressive as any in the Baltic region. Although it's not much of a beach resort (the best of those are some way out of town), Kuressaare can boast a health-tourism pedigree dating back to the 1840s, when the craze for mud baths first took off, and many of the local hotels still do a brisk trade in rest-cures and spa treatments. Kuressaare's growing popularity with well-to-do Estonians and West Europeans has lent a chic, cosmopolitan air to some of its newer hotels and restaurants, although the general market-town charm of the place remains intact.

Arrival and information

Kuressaare's **bus station** is conveniently located on Tallinna, the main street, five minutes' walk northwest of the **tourist office**, inside the Town Hall at Tallinna 2 (mid-May to mid-Sept daily 9am–7pm; mid-Sept to mid-May Mon–Fri 9am–5pm; ☎453 3120, ✆www.saaremaa.ee), where you buy local maps and get info on walking and biking trails. **Bikes** can be rented from Bivarix Rattapood, Tallinna 26.

Accommodation

There's a growing range of **hotels** in Kuressaare, although cheapies are outnumbered by a glut of places pitching three-star comforts to a mid-range market. It's a good idea to book ahead in summer and on weekends throughout the year. Prices tumble in the off-season (Oct–April) when it's relatively easy to pick up a bargain. The tourist office can book **B&B** accommodation (❶–❷) both in Kuressaare and on farmsteads across the island – the latter are an excellent way of savouring the local countryside, although you'll probably need your own transport to reach them. The nearest **campsite** is the *Mändjala*, 11km west of town just beyond the village of Nasva (May–Sept; ☎454 4193, ✆www.mandjala.ee); it also has accommodation in cabins (150EEK per person, including breakfast) and Kuressaare–Järve buses pass by.

Arabella Torni 12 ☎455 5885,
✆www.hot.ee/arabell. A Soviet-era residential block given a fresh lick of plaster and paint. Sparsely furnished but respectable en-suite doubles, and plenty of triples and quads (which work out at about 300EEK per person). Open May to mid-Oct. ❸
Arensburg Lossi 15 ☎452 4700,
✆www.sivainvest.ee. An elegant, but affordable, establishment whose rooms are cosy without being cramped. Furniture and fittings are mostly new and a fair proportion of standard rooms come with bathtubs rather than showers. ❹
Daissy Tallinna 15 ☎453 3669,
✆www.hot.ee/daissyhotell. A mid-sized hotel on the main street, decked out in dullish greys and browns, but rooms are generously proportioned

and those on the top floor come with atmospheric attic ceilings. Suites with sitting rooms, fireplaces and tubs in the bathroom ❻; standard en-suites ❹
Johan Kauba 13 ☎453 3036,
✆www.saaremaa.ee/johan. Small, but soothing, rooms with shower and TV, warm colour schemes and nice dark-wood furniture. ❹
Jurna turismitalu Upa küla ☎452 1919,
✆www.sarma.ee/jurna. Long, thatched-roof farm building with a handful of snug rooms, some with en-suite facilities. A restful rustic setting 6km northeast of Kuressaare in the village of Upa, just off the Leisi road. ❸
Kadri Upa küla ☎452 4633,
✆www.saaremaa.ee/mardi. Set amid juniper heath and forest, 5km northeast of town on the

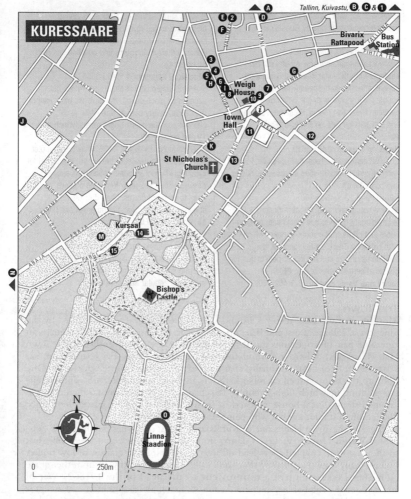

KURESSAARE

Bivarix
Rattapood

Bus Station

Weigh
House

Town
Hall

St Nicholas's
Church

Kursaal

Bishop's
Castle

Linna-
Staadion

N

0   250m

ACCOMMODATION				CAFÉS, RESTAURANTS AND BARS			
Arabella	D	Mardi	E	Budweiser Pub	4	Lokaal	7
Arensburg	L	Repo	F	Classic Kohvik	13	Maigi Juures	11
Daissy	G	Rüütli	M	Hansa	9	Monus Villem	1
Johan	H	Saaremaa		Hong Kong	3	Vaekoda	10
Jurna turismitalu	B	Valss	J	John Bull Pub	15	Vanalinna	8
Kadri	C	Staadioni	O	Kapiteni körts	5	Vanalinna	
Linnahotel	K	SÜG	A	Kass kohvik	2	Kohvipood	6
Männikäbi	N	Vanalinna	I	Kohvlk Kuursaal	14	Veskl	12

main road to Kuivastu, the *Kadri*, like the *Mardi*
below, is run by Kuressaare's Hotel and Restaurant
School. Bright, modern rooms with shower and TV,
decked out in soothing colours. **3**
Linnahotel Lasteaia 7 ☎453 1888,
✉linnahotell@kontaktid.ee. A brand-new building

in an appealing warren of alleyways just off the
main square, offering en-suites with chic, modern
furnishings and pastel colours. **4**
Männikäbi Mändjala ☎454 4100,
🌐www.saarehotell.ee. A two-storey Art Deco
pavilion 11km west of town boasting prim en-

suites with TV, with a duney beach and plenty of forested countryside nearby. Guests can rent bikes. ❸

Mardi Vallimaa 5A ☎ 452 4633, @www.saaremaa.ee/mardi. A hotel run by students from the local Hotel and Restaurant School, offering worn, sparsely furnished but clean doubles and triples, with one WC/shower shared between every two rooms. Excellent restaurant and self-service café on site (see "Eating" p.348). ❷

Repo Vallimaa 1A ☎ 453 3510, @www.saaremaa.ee/repo. A small-scale, friendly hotel offering bright, pristine rooms with shower and cable TV. ❹

Rüütli Pargi 12 ☎ 454 8100, @www.sanatoorium.ee. An ultra-modern establishment offering tidy rooms with parquet floors and citrus-fruit colours, some of which come with bathtubs. There's a full range of spa treatments on site and the indoor pool is free for guests at certain times of day. ❹

Saaremaa Valss Kastani 20 ☎ 452 7200, @www.sanatoorium.ee. Basically a cheap alternative to the *Rüütli* (see above), this big, concrete hotel-cum-sanatorium has sparsely decorated en-suite rooms and qualified spa staff on hand. ❹

Staadioni Staadioni 4 ☎ 453 3556, @www.staadionihotell.ee. Unpretentious but acceptable place next to the athletics track east of the castle. Swirly carpets and white walls characterize the clean, bright rooms, which have TV and shower. ❸

SÜG Hariduse 13 ☎ 452 4432, @www.syg.edu.ee. Ten minutes northwest of the centre, this hostel for local high-school students usually has space for tourists, either in simply furnished doubles, or four- to five-bed dorms. Shared toilets and showers. Internet room, but no breakfast. Doubles ❶, dorms 150EEK per person.

Vanalinna Kauba 8 ☎ 455 5309, @www.vanalinna.ee. Eleven-room hotel in a historic building with plenty of atmosphere, offering smallish but undeniably cosy en-suites, most with angular attic ceilings. ❹

The Town

Most life in Kuressaare revolves around an elongated central square formed by the junction of Tallinna, Lossi and Raekoja streets. On the eastern side of the square, an agreeable pair of stone lions guard the entrance to the seventeenth-century Town Hall (Raekoda), where a ground-floor **art gallery** (Tues–Fri 10am–6pm, Sat 10am–5pm; free) hosts seasonally changing exhibitions of contemporay art. One floor up, the main council chamber harbours an exuberant eighteenth-century ceiling painting in which flesh-flaunting Bacchantes enjoy an al-fresco picnic. It was salvaged from a local house, restored in Tallinn and has been displayed here since 2002, though it's not known who painted it or for whom.

Opposite the Town Hall is one of Kuressaare's oldest surviving buildings, the step-gabled **Weigh House** (Vaekoda), dating from 1633 and now a pub (see p.349). Just to the west of it, cobbled alleys lead off into an atmospheric quarter of low timber houses, many now occupied by shops and cafés. Heading southwest from the square along Lossi takes you past a **monument** to the dead of the 1918–20 War of Independence, sculpted by Amandus Adamson, Estonia's leading inter-war sculptor and recently restored to pride of place after a lengthy Soviet-era absence. Just beyond, it's impossible to miss the jaunty green domes of **St Nicholas's Church** (Nikolai kirik), an eighteenth-century Orthodox foundation serving an Estonian rather than Russian congregation – a reminder of the fact that an estimated twenty percent of Estonia's population joined the Orthodox Church when the country belonged to the Tsarist Empire. A certain Estonian sobriety of character is retained in the interior decor though – with icons set in white-painted frames, it's noticeably plainer than in Russian Orthodox churches.

Lossi continues south to the magnificent **Bishops' Castle** (Piiskopilinnus), an impressively sturdy, sandy-coloured structure built from locally quarried dolomite. The original castle was built in 1261 by Bishop German of Ösel-Wiek in order to keep the restless natives of Saaremaa in order. The castle as it stands today, surrounded by a star-shaped system of earthworks and a deep-gouged moat, dates largely from the fourteenth century and is such a well-preserved quadrangle of smooth stone that – from a distance at least – it looks more like a movie set than the real thing. Surrounding it are bastions and ramparts thrown up by Danes and Swedes in

Kuressaare Castle △

the seventeenth century, nowadays a grassy park. Used as a barracks by the Russians, the castle was restored by the Saaremaa nobility after 1904, both to serve as a symbol of provincial pride and to provide the local authorities with much-needed office space.

The labyrinthine keep now houses the **Saaremaa Regional Museum** (Saaremaa koduloomuuseum; Wed–Sun 11am–6pm; 30EEK), a didactic parade of artefacts covering the history of the island from prehistoric times to the present. Chunky chain jewellery worn by Iron Age Estonian chieftains and their molls helps to cheer up the proceedings, as do chalices and silverware once belonging to the Kuressaare bishops. There's plenty of material on Saaremaa-born worthies whom you might never have heard of otherwise, notably Tsarist-era explorers Richard Otto Mack (1825–1886), who trekked off to eastern Siberia to study plant life; and Fabian Gottlieb von Bellingshausen (1778–1852), who saw himself as the successor to Captain Cook and led a major Russian expedition to the South Seas – he's credited with being the discoverer of Antarctica, although he thought it was a small island at the time. It's also possible to view the spartan living quarters of the bishops on the ground floor and climb the watchtowers. Pikk Hermann, the eastern (and thinner) corner tower is linked to the rest of the keep only by a wooden drawbridge. In the park surrounding the castle moat you'll find the wooden **Kursaal** building, dating from 1889 and now a genteel café.

Eating

There are plenty of **cafés and restaurants** in the town centre, most of them offering a wide range of decent food at very reasonable prices. You can pick up **picnic supplies** from the Edu supermarket on the main square (daily 9am–10pm). The establishments below are open daily until 11pm or midnight unless otherwise stated.

Classic Kohvik Lossi 9. A civilized coffee-and-cakes venue with a prime high-street location. Also does cheap hot meals. Sun–Thurs till 7pm, Sat & Sun till 8pm.

Hansa Tallinna 9. An art gallery with a cosy café attached, offering the best in cakes and pastries. Succeeds in being bohemian and classy at the same time. Mon–Fri till 6pm, Sat till 3pm.

Hong Kong Kauba 14. A sizeable bar-restaurant with minimal decor and decent oriental eats. It turns into a disco after 10pm.

Kass Kohvik Vallimaa 5A. A self-service café offering dirt-cheap but excellent lunches. Part of the *Hotel Mardi* complex; the café entrance is round the side from the restaurant. Open daily 11am–3pm.

Kohvik Kuursaal in the Kursaal building in the castle park. An atmospheric place offering soup, sandwiches and fish dishes – and terrace seating. Till 10pm.

Lokaal Tallinna 11. This subterranean pub-restaurant looks like a bomb shelter and is somewhat lacking in atmosphere, but the food – hearty and simple meals based on trout, perch or pork – is good and cheap.

Maigi Juures Lossi 3. A classy cafeteria with a good salad bar and decent coffee. Till 7pm.

Vanalinna Kauba 8. The smartest restaurant in town offering a mouthwatering range of steaks and fish, stupendous desserts and an extensive choice of good wines. Above average prices, but worth the extra.

Vanalinna Kohvipood Kauba 10. The best place in town for pastries, cakes, and generous scoops of salad. Till 6pm.

Veski Pärna 19. A café-restaurant located in a windmill whose sails are lit up at night. You can choose to sit round wooden tables or vast millstones of polished granite. Standard Estonian meat-and-potatoes fare, plus a few local fish dishes.

Bars and pubs

There's a good range of drinking venues in Kuressaare, mostly cosy, convivial places that become enjoyably raucous at weekends. Don't forget to try Saaremaa-brewed beer, which packs a bit more of a punch than Saku. Bars and pubs are usually open until 11pm or midnight, later on Fridays and Saturdays.

Budweiser Pub Kauba 6. A homely pub with pool table and sport on TV, serving several international draught beers including Budweiser (the Czech

rather than the American version).

John Bull Pub Pargi 4. A lively wooden-hut pub with oodles of character – you can perch at a bar

made out of a discarded bus chassis, lounge around in a Soviet corner overlooked by Lenin portraits, or chill on an outdoor terrace overlooking the castle ramparts.
Kapiteni körts Kauba 13. A faux-rustic beer hall complete with wooden benches, fishing nets and snug alcoves.

Monus Villem Tallinna. A roomy bar with a strong local following, although it's a bit out on a limb, 500m northeast of the bus station.
Vaekoda Tallinna 3. A rather staid drinking den in the seventeenth-century Weigh House, also offering rather stylish food, featuring plenty of local fish.

Entertainment

Despite the lack of a regular theatre or concert hall, a good deal of quality culture comes to Kuressaare in the summer. A canopy-covered podium next to the Kursaal becomes a bandstand-cum-concert bowl in summer, hosting brass bands, light classics and the occasional crooner. The castle courtyard is employed to dramatic effect during the **Kuressaare Opera Days** (Kuressaare Ooperipäevad; ⓦwww.festivals.ee/kuresoop_eng.html), when two major operas – usually taken from the Estonian National Opera's regular programme in Tallinn – are performed over a long weekend at the end of July. The castle is also pressed into service during the **Kuressaare Chamber Music Days** (ⓦwww.kammerfest.ee) in August, featuring top performers from Estonia and further afield.

North of Kuressaare

There are several sights, notably the Kaali meteorite crater and the Angla windmills, strung out in the villages north of Kuressaare, many of which are on or near the Kuressaare–Leisi road and served by local buses. Lying slightly off this route, just over 10km north of Kuressaare and 5km west of the Leisi road, the small village of **KAARMA** is worth a detour for its venerable thirteenth-century **church** (Kaarma kirik), a large, red-roofed building unusual in having twin aisles. Inside is a christening stone from the same period and a pulpit supported by a wooden Joseph figure from 1450. The church's graveyard is littered with ancient stone crosses – the oldest are the so-called "sun crosses" – crosses set within a circle carved in stone.

The Kaali meteorite crater

Returning to the Kuressaare–Leisi road and heading north for 6km brings you to the turn-off for the village of **KAALI**, 2.5km further southeast, famous for the 4000-year-old **meteorite crater** on its outskirts. Signs at the entrance to the village direct you up onto the lip of the *kraater*, a 150-metre-wide pit surrounded by a huge embankment composed of the rubble thrown up on impact and now covered in mossy-trunked trees. At the base of the pit lies a murky, green pool, which ranges in depth from one to six metres, depending on rainfall. All in all, it's an eerily beautiful spot and one of the world's few easily accessible meteorite craters.

Getting to Kaali by public transport, it's a toss up between catching the Kuressaare–Leisi bus (get off at the Liiva putla stop right beside the Kaali turn-off and walk 2.5km southeast) and hopping aboard a Kuressaare–Kuivaste–Tallinn bus (get off at Kõnnu and walk 3km northwest) – either way, be sure to check return times before leaving Kuressaare. On the opposite side of the car park from the crater, the *Kaali Trahter* **café-restaurant** is a good place to stop for a breather, although it can get very busy at lunchtimes. One kilometre northeast of the crater in the village of **KÕLJALA**, the *Kõljala puhkeküla* (☎459 1255) offers **camping** and horse riding.

Angla and Karja

Around 15km north of Kaali is **ANGLA**, a village famed throughout the Baltics for its five **wooden windmills** (Angla tuulikud) standing in a much-photographed line right by the roadside. The windmills aren't open to the public, but they're mesmerizing enough to merit a stop-off – not unlike the stone heads on Easter Island, they exude an ageless dignity. Kuressaare–Leise buses pick up and drop off at the northernmost of the mills.

A right turn just past the windmills leads after 2km to the thirteenth-century **Karja Church** (Karja kirik), a plain, white structure with an unusual crucifixion carving above its side door. Inside the church are more stone carvings, depicting religious figures and scenes from village life. The village of **KARJA** itself – actually 1km south of Angla back on the main road – is the site of a particularly attractive graveyard, packed with the lovingly clipped shrubs and conifers typical of cemeteries in the region.

Western Saaremaa

Western Saaremaa is arguably the most attractive part of the island: its rugged, deeply indented coastline is backed by a sparsely populated hinterland of grasslands, juniper heath, small lakes and bogs. Many of its more beautiful stretches fall under the aegis of the **Vilsandi National Park**, founded in 1993. Named after Vilsandi island, 3km off Saaremaa's western shore, the park envelops much of the island's northwestern corner. Here, offshore islets and reed-shrouded shores provide a multitude of habitats for migrating birds, with hundreds of species – mute swans, greylag geese, oyster-catchers and Arctic terns among them – gathering in the area in spring and autumn.

The main entrance point to the park is the Visitors' Centre at **Loona**, 2.5km south of the village of **Kihelkonna**, an easy bus ride from Kuressaare. The north-western extremities of the park on the **Harilaid peninsula** offer most in the way of desolate beauty, although you'll need your own transport to explore this area.

Viki, Kihelkonna and Loona

The road west from Kuressaare forges through a landscape of arable land and forest before arriving after some 30km at the village of **VIKI**, home to the **Mihkli Farm Museum** (mid-April to Sept daily 10am–6pm; 15EEK), a re-creation of a typical nineteenth-century Saaremaa farmstead. With a windmill in full working order and a small cluster of thatch-roofed farmhouses smothered in moss, it's as delightful a taste of traditional Saaremaa life as you'll get. From here it's only 5km further to **KIHELKONNA**, a bucolic village draped around a dazzlingly whitewashed **parish church**. Dating from the 1260s, it's one of the oldest on the island, although its dominant feature – a sky-rocketing steeple, for a time also a lighthouse – was only added in 1897. Crowning a hillock 200m south of the church is a squat, grey building that looks like a cross between a cow shed and a gun emplacement – it's actually the church's seventeenth-century belfry.

Thirty-five minutes' walk south of Kihelkonna on the Lümanda road, a signed right turn leads to Loona manor (Loona mõis), a nineteenth-century gentry farmstead housing the **Vilsandi National Park Visitors' Centre** (Mon–Fri 9am–5pm; ☎454 6704), where you can buy maps and pick up advice on where to walk. The park comprises over 150 uninhabited offshore islets favoured by local birdlife, as well as a narrow coastal belt criss-crossed by – largely unmarked – dirt roads. The quickest way to get a taste of the area is to follow forest paths due west of Loona, emerging after fifteen minutes onto the reed-fringed Kiirassaare Bay (Kiirassaare laht), which offers fleeting glimpses of rocky offshore islands. From here you can turn northeast back to Kihelkonna (20min), or improvise your own itinerary by following the coast southwest through a wonderfully tranquil region characterized by pine woods, grassland and swamp.

The best place **to stay** in the Kihelkonna–Loona region is the National Park Visitors' Centre itself, which has a handful of tastefully decorated en-suite rooms (May–Sept only; ☎454 6704; ❸). Somewhat more frugal is the *Kihelkonna Parsonage* (Pastoraadi Oomaja; ☎454 6558; ❶) next to the church, offering four rooms with shared facilities. There's a well-stocked food shop in Kihelkonna diagonally across from the bus stop.

Towards the Harilaid peninsula

North of Kihelkonna the national park boundary continues to follow Saaremaa's west coast, ballooning out after some 20km to envelop the **Harilaid peninsula**, a compact thumb of land offering some of the island's most strikingly stark scenery, characterized by stony ground with a sparse covering of waist-high junipers. The easiest way to get here from Kihelkonna is to follow the northbound Tagamõisa road and take a left turn onto a dirt road 5km north of the village of Kureveere. This passes through the once-flourishing settlement of Kõruse, depopulated after World War II when the Soviets turned the area into a military zone and now a virtual ghost village. Carrying on, you arrive at a sandy neck of land that joins the main body of Saaremaa to the Harilaid peninsula – Harilaid was a separate island until the narrow channel between it and Saaremaa silted up in the seventeenth century. This is as far as cars can go; a national park information board bears details of hiking trails around the peninsula – the complete circuit amounts to about 12km, but even a short walk will suffice to give you an idea of Harilaid's other-worldly beauty. The centre of the peninsula is thick with pines and junipers, ringed by a belt of steppe-like grassland, which in turn gives way to a part-sandy, part-pebbly shore-line supporting a stubborn covering of mosses and heathers. It'll take you about an hour to walk up the eastern side of the peninsula to the northern tip, just beyond which lies the slender, black-and-white-striped Kiipsaare lighthouse, built in 1933 and no longer in use – with its foundations battered by the sea, it's now listing dramatically to one side.

Pärnu

Sprawled around the estuary of the Pärnu River, **PÄRNU** rejoices in the title of "Estonia's Summer Capital", a not unreasonable description considering that one in four Estonians visit the town at least once during the holiday season. The resort's main asset is its seven-kilometre-long beach, packed with sunbathers in July and August and a popular place for a walk all year round. While there are plenty of beach-side bars to keep the party-hard hedonists satisfied, Pärnu itself preserves a small-town gentility, its avenues lined with lime trees and an appealing mixture of traditional wooden houses and Bauhaus-inspired inter-war villas. The town also enjoys a rich cultural life: its prestigious theatre and a new state-of-the-art concert hall mean that Pärnu is one of the few places outside Tallinn and Tartu where you can enjoy top-quality drama and music all year round.

It has to be said that the town has few sights as such; most visitors come to soak up the summer atmosphere, and with regular bus connections to Tallinn, Tartu and Rīga, it's a convenient place in which to rest up for a few days if you're in the middle of a Baltic tour. The rustic charms of **Kihnu island** (see p.357) and the desolate, boggy beauty of the **Soomaa National Park** (p.358) provide the main targets for out-of-town day-trips.

Arrival and information

The town's **bus station** is on Pikk at the northeastern edge of the Old Town (the information and ticket office is round the corner at Ringi 3), while the **train station** is a rather inconvenient 5km east of the centre at Riia mnt 116, though with only two trains a day to and from Tallinn, it's unlikely to feature in your travel plans. Pärnu's small **airport**, 5km northwest of the centre just off the Tallinn road, handles services to and from Kuressaare, Kihnu and Ruhnu (information on ☎447 5001 or 447 5007, ✆www.airlivonia.ee); bus #23 connects it with town.

The **tourist office** at Rüütli 16 (June–Aug Mon–Sat 9am–6pm, Sun 10am–3pm; May–Sept Mon–Fri 9am–5pm; ☎447 3000, ✆www.parnu.ee) hands out helpful advice and has plenty of English-language brochures at hand. The booklet-sized *Pärnu In Your Pocket*, available from news kiosks for 25EEK, is a useful source of local listings information, updated annually. You can log onto the

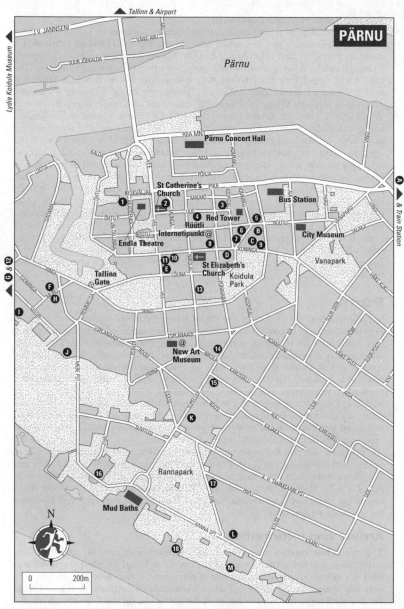

PÄRNU

Pärnu

Tallinn & Airport

J.V. JANNSENI

VÄIKE-ABRU

SUUR-JÕEKALDA

Lydia Koidula Museum

RIIA MNT

Pärnu Concert Hall

AIDA

PÕHJA

KALDA

KESKVÄLJAK

St Catherine's Church

MALMÖ

PIKK

Bus Station

ÕHTU P.

Red Tower

** Rüütli Internetipunkt @**

Endla Theatre

RÜÜTLI

City Museum

Vanapark

Tallinn Gate

St Elizabeth's Church

Koidula Park

RINGI

ESPLANAADI

ESPLANAADI

New Art Museum

NIKOLAI

KARUSSELLI

A. ADAMSONI

SUVITUSE

K

Rannapark

A.H. TAMMSAARE PST

Mud Baths

RANNA SPJ

N

0   200m

Internet at the Chaplin Centre, Esplanaadi 10 (open 24hr; 30EEK an hour); and the Rüütli Internetipunkt, Rüütli 25 (Mon–Fri 10am–9pm, Sat & Sun 10am–6pm).

Accommodation

The tourist office can provide accommodation price lists, but won't make bookings on your behalf. **Private rooms** (❶–❷) are available from Tanni Vakoma Majutusbüroo, a block east of the bus station at Hommiku 5 (☎443 1070, ✉tanni@online.ee). The best **campsite** is *Konse Holiday Village* (☎053/435092, ⊛www.konse.ee), 1.5km northeast of the centre at Suur-Jõe 44A, on the banks of the Pärnu River; it has clean, modern facilities, tent and caravan pitches (100EEK) and two- to four-person cabins (150EEK per person), and you can get breakfast in the on-site café.

Of the two **hostels** in town, the central *Lõuna*, Lõuna 2 (☎443 0943, ⊛www.hot.ee/hostellouna), has beds for 200–250EEK in a variety of triples, quads and dorms and is preferable to the *Spordiselts Kalev*, next to the stadium at Ranna pst 2 (☎442 5799; ❷), which, though it can offer self-contained singles (300EEK) and doubles, has grubby shared facilities.

Most of the town's **hotels** are located in the grid of streets between the Kesklinn and the beach. They're packed in July and August, so always reserve ahead if possible. Hotel prices drop by about 25–40 percent in the low season (Oct–April).

Ammende Villa Mere pst 7 ☎447 3888, ⊛www.ammende.ee. A gorgeously restored Art Nouveau villa built for the Pärnu magnate Herman Ammende in 1905 and opened as a hotel in 1999. All rooms boast exhaustively researched repro decor and there are opulent sitting rooms and restaurant areas on the ground floor. You can also stay in the less luxurious, but still eminently comfy, rooms in an annexe which used to serve as the gardener's house, and still use the main building's facilities. ❺–❼

Bristol Rüütli 45 ☎443 1450, ✉victoria@hot.ee. A downtown hotel on the main street offering pleasant en-suites with TV, although the lime-green colour scheme takes a little getting used to. ❺

Delfine Supeluse 22 ☎442 6900, ⊛www.delfine.ee. Prim, pastel-coloured rooms in a medium-sized, informal establishment. ❹

Koidula Park Hotell Kuninga 38 ☎447 7030, ⊛www.koidulaparkhotell.ee. A lusciously restored wooden villa, although the en-suite rooms – woody floors apart – are swishly modern in style. ❹

Laine Laine 6A ☎443 9111, ⊛www.gh-laine.ee. The drab exterior and unexciting location, 2km southeast of the centre, shouldn't necessarily put you off: the sparsely furnished rooms all come with en-suite shower and are good value. ❷

Lootos Muru 1 ☎443 1030. Small but quite chic TV-equipped en-suites, with distressed-wood furniture in a medium-sized modern building. ❹

Maritime Seedri 4 ☎447 8910, ⊛www.pergohotels.ee. A low pavilion beside the beachside park with small but tidy en-suites with modern pine furniture, TV, and warm, orangey colour schemes. ❹

Rannahotel Ranna pst 5 ☎443 2950, ⊛www.scandic-hotels.com. A cool, grey Bauhaus-inspired structure dating from 1937, located right on the beach. Rooms are smallish, but prim and proper, with TV, telephone and en-suite shower. ❺

Vesiroos Esplanaadi 42A ☎443 0940, ⊛www.hot.ee/pina. A functional concrete building, with sparsely furnished, but acceptable, en-suites with TV, and a small outdoor pool. ❹

Victoria Kuninga 25 ☎444 3412, ⊛www.hot.ee/victoria. An attractive town house just off the main street, run by the same company as the *Bristol* but offering slightly plusher rooms – salmony-pink en-suites with TV. The ground-floor *Café Grand* oozes olde-worlde charm. ❹

Villa Marleen Seedri 13/15 ☎442 9288. Five-room guesthouse a couple of minutes' walk from the beach offering simple, neat rooms with TV and fridge. Some rooms with shared facilities, others en-suite. ❹

The Town

With most of Pärnu laid out in neat grids, it's a fairly easy place to find your way around. The main thoroughfare is **Rüütli**, a pedestrianized shopping street running from east to west and featuring a fair sprinkling of attractive two-storey wooden houses. Occupying a rather more staid brick building near Rüütli's eastern end at no. 53, the **City Museum** (Linnamuuseum; Tues–Fri 11am–6pm, Sat 11am–5pm; 30EEK; ⊛www.pernau.ee) houses some of Estonia's oldest archeological finds, many of which originated in an 11,000-year-old Neolithic settlement unearthed near the village of Sindi just inland – among the pottery fragments, look out for a small human form carved from animal horn. After this promising start the collection deteriorates into a rather colourless and badly labelled trot through local history, only marginally brightened up by costumes, mittens and models of the ships constructed in the Pärnu boatyards.

Two blocks west of the museum, just off Rüütli on Hommiku, is the **Red Tower** (Punane torn), a fifteenth-century remnant of the medieval city walls and the oldest surviving building in town. Despite its name, this squat, unassuming cylinder is actually white – only the roof tiles are red – and it now houses an antique shop.

Pühavaimu, a few blocks to the west, has a pair of respectable-looking seventeenth-century houses near the junction with Malmö, one in lemon-yellow, the other in washed-out green with a large gabled vestibule. Moving west from Pühavaimu along Uus, you come to **St Catherine's Church** (Ekateriina kirik), built during the reign of Catherine the Great, and dedicated to her namesake by way of tribute. Encrusted with sea-green domes and pinnacles topped by wrought-iron crosses, it's undoubtedly one of the most delicious Baroque buildings in the country and has an icon-rich interior. Immediately west of the church lies a flag-stoned plaza dominated by the **Endla Theatre**, a fairly functional piece of 1960s architecture built to replace the original theatre building, erected in 1911 and feted throughout northern Europe as an Art Nouveau masterpiece until bombed to smithereens in World War II – you'll see photographs of it in history museums both here and in Tallinn (notably at the Maarjamäe Palace; see p.323). One of the most talked-about pieces of architecture in today's Estonia is the coquettishly curvy **Pärnu Concert Hall** (Pärnu kontserdimaja), dunked between greying blocks just northeast of the Endla Theatre at Aida 4. Opened in 2002, this vast, glass-and-steel hat box of a building accommodates a state-of-the-art 1000-seat auditorium for top-notch music and drama, and also finds room for the **City Art Gallery** (Linnagalerii; Tues–Fri noon–7pm, Sat noon–5pm), where you can catch high-profile exhibitions by contemporary Estonian artists.

From the Tallinn Gate to the beach

South of the Endla Theatre, Vee runs down to Kuninga, the western end of which is marked by the seventeenth-century **Tallinn Gate** (Tallinna värav), a rather elegant relic of the Swedish occupation, set into the remains of the city ramparts and now home to a quaint bar (see p.357). To see the gate at its best, head into the park on its other side: from here, with its massive gable and decorative pillars, it looks more like a Baroque chapel. Heading east along Kuninga leads to eighteenth-century **St Elizabeth's Church** (Eliisabeti kirik; Mon–Fri 10am–2pm), boasting a maroon and ochre Baroque exterior and plain, wood-panelled interior. As well as being the principal Protestant place of worship in the city, it's also home to a famously sonorous organ, put through its paces at weekend concerts. From here, Nikolai leads south to Esplanaadi, where a headless statue of Lenin stands watch over the entrance to an office block that once served as the headquarters of the Pärnu communist party. Taken over by local artists in the immediate post-independence period, it was briefly re-named the Charlie Chaplin House (no longer its official moniker, but still very much in colloquial use) before becoming the **Pärnu New Art Museum** (Pärnu uue kunsti muuseum; daily 9am–9pm; 20EEK; ⊛www.chaplin.ee). Its collection of twentieth-century Estonian paintings is complemented by contemporary works donated by international artists, including Yoko Ono.

Beyond the art museum Nikolai bends east to join Supeluse, which runs southwest through suburbia then parkland before arriving at the beach area after about ten minutes. Marking the southern end of Supeluse are the colonnaded **Pärnu Mud-Baths** (Pärnu mudaravila), a bombastic piece of neoclassicism that couldn't be more different from its contemporary, the inter-war **Rannahotel**, 400m to the east at Ranna 5, a cream-coloured ocean liner of a building that has become something of an icon of Estonian modernism. Both buildings gaze out onto Pärnu's glorious white-sand **beach**, thick with sunbathers on summer weekends. To escape the crowds make for the dunes east of the Mud Baths, but if you want to mingle with the masses head in the opposite direction, where you'll find a stretch of open sand backed by kiosks, bars, cafés and ice-cream stalls.

The Lydia Koidula Museum

The grid of post-war suburban buildings stretching north of the Pärnu River is as unexciting as you would expect, and there's not much point in venturing out here unless you're keen to peruse the literary mementos on display at the **museum** honouring nineteenth-century poet **Lydia Koidula** (see box overleaf), a ten-minute hop over the river from the city centre at J.V. Jannseni 37 (Wed–Sun 10am–7pm; 15EEK). Occupying the building where her father Johann Voldemar Jannsen ran a primary school from 1857 to 1863, Koidula is remembered through a modest collection of family photographs and rooms, including a re-creation of the bedroom (in the Russian town of Kronstadt) where Koidula breathed her last in 1886. The curator will probably put on a tape of Koidula-penned songs, including *Mu Isamaa* ("My Fatherland"), the patriotic ditty that became an unofficial national anthem during the Soviet period.

Eating and drinking

Pärnu has a respectable spread of cafés, restaurants and bars serving up a wide range of food and drink. While most cafés close by mid-evening, restaurants and bars are open until 11pm or midnight. All are open daily unless otherwise stated.

Snack bars and restaurants

Kadri Kohvik Puhavaimu 13. Down-to-earth and cheap, this central bakery-cum-café specializes in *pirukas* – little pies stuffed with cheese, meat or mushroom. Mon–Fri till 7pm, Sat till 5pm, Sun till 3pm.

Kohvik Georg Rüütli 43. An inexpensive, but civilized, self-service restaurant patronized by downtown shoppers, good for either a quick coffee-and-cake break or a more filling snack. Till 7.30pm.

Mõnus Margarita Akadeemia 5. A reasonably priced Tex-Mex restaurant with Aztec-inspired paintings and ethnic rugs on the walls, and decent – if not exactly explosively spicy – food.

Munga Munga 9. A refined and intimate café housed in a wooden, nineteenth-century town house decked out in rather posh period furnishings. A range of food is served, from soups to full meals, although expect to pay restaurant prices. Till 11pm.

Pappa Pizza Kuninga 34. Thin-crust pies in plain surroundings – good for a quick fill-up rather than a candle-lit dinner.

Postipoiss Vee 12. A Russian-themed eatery with rustic decor, long wooden tables and waiting-staff in an amateur dramatist's idea of folk costume.

Excellent light meals such as *pelmeni* (Slavic ravioli) or *bliny* (pancakes) with caviar, as well as mainstream north European meat dishes. Fills up with late-night diners and drinkers at weekends, when you can expect live entertainment in crooner-meets-electronic-keyboard style. Till 2am at weekends.

Seegi Maja Hospidali 1. In an impeccably restored seventeenth-century house, this is probably the best place in town for expertly prepared meat and fish dishes, but it's not overly formal and prices are moderate, too.

Steffani Nikolai 24. A big choice of pizzas and salads and generous pasta dishes, too. Prices are slightly higher than in other, fast-food pizza joints, but probably justified.

Bars and pubs

Jazz Café Ringi 11. A small, minimally decorated, but soothing, space just off Rüütli, with a good range of international cuisine and chilled-out background sounds.

Lehe Lehe 5. A funky café-bar decorated to look like an aquarium, within striking distance of the beach. Does good lunchtime food.

Lonkava konna kõrts Supeluse 14. A rambling ale house done up to look like a country barn. Live

Estonia's leading poet of the nineteenth century was born Lydia Emilie Florentine Jannsen in Vändra, where her father, Johann Voldemar Jannsen, was the village schoolteacher. The family moved to Pärnu in 1850, where Lydia was lucky enough to be among the handful of Estonians admitted to the prestigious German-language Pärnu School for Girls,

In 1857, her father launched the first-ever Estonian-language weekly, *Perno Postimees* ("Pärnu Courier"), which aimed to spread literacy among the local peasantry – it was just about the only non-religious reading material they had access to at the time. Koidula was roped in to help with the paper's preparation and ended up writing much of it herself, a role she continued when Jannsen moved to Tartu in 1863 to found the *Eesti Postimees* ("Estonian Courier") – a publication that bound together the nascent Estonian intelligentsia and transformed Jannsen into a pivotal figure in the national movement. A self-taught country boy of limited literary abilities, Jannsen was from the outset outshone as a writer and editor by his daughter, but her contribution to the paper had to remain in the background – nineteenth-century Estonia was not the kind of place where well-brought-up young ladies embarked on literary careers. When Koidula's first collections of lyric poems were published anonymously – *Vainolilled* ("Meadow Flowers") in 1866 and *Emajõe Ööbik* ("Emajõgi Nightingale") in 1867 – Jannsen himself published reviews of them without knowing the identity of the author. Regular visitors to the Jannsen family home were in no doubt about Lydia's literary potential, however. One of them, Karl Robert Jakobson (see p.361) gave her the pseudonym "Koidula" (literally "of the dawn") so that he could include some of her poems in an Estonian-language primer. Koidula's greatest admirer at this time was Friedrich Reinhold Kreuzwald, compiler of the Estonian folk epic *Kalevipoeg* (see p.393), and with whom Koidula started to correspond in 1867. The epistolary relationship between the intelligent, witty Koidula and a man forty years her senior quickly became a mutual intellectual obsession. Kreuzwald finally invited Koidula to visit his home in Võru in June 1868, but the trip was cut prematurely short owing to the hostility of Kreuzwald's wife, who feared that her husband was becoming besotted with his protégée.

Thanks to her father, Koidula remained at the centre of Estonian cultural life, helping him set up the Vanemuine Society (the first Estonian-language drama group), and assisting in the organization of the first-ever All-Estonian Song Festival in Tartu in 1869. Her patriotic poem *Mu Isamaa* ("My Fatherland"), set to music by a Tartu choirmaster for the occasion, has been a prime ingredient of song festivals ever since – during the Soviet period, audiences insisted in closing festivals with a rousing rendition of the song, regardless of whether it had been included in the official programme or not.

The small size of the nineteenth-century Estonian reading public meant that it was well-nigh impossible for any writer to make a living without recourse to another profession. The only career options open to Koidula were either marriage and domesticity, or a life of spinsterhood helping her father out behind the scenes. Koidula finally settled for marriage and set up home with a stolid Latvian doctor, Eduard Michelson, in 1873. Michelson took Koidula to live in Russian-speaking Kronštadt, a Tsarist naval base in the Gulf of Finland, where the couple had four children (two of whom died in infancy). Although Koidula continued to write poems, her contacts with Estonian literary circles were effectively severed, and her early death from cancer prevented her from fully enjoying the acclaim generated by her works. Koidula exerted a huge influence over subsequent generations – not least because she demonstrated that the Estonian language was versatile and lyrical enough to challenge the cultural predominance of German – and there's hardly an Estonian alive today who can't recite at least a few of her poems by heart.

cover bands at weekends when it's open till 2am.

Tallinna Värav Kuninga 1. An atmospheric, if surprisingly staid, bar located in the top storey of the Tallinn Gate (see p.354) – a bit like having a drink in the converted attic of an old-fashioned neighbour. The outdoor terrace is more fun.

Väike Klaus Supeluse 3. A roomy, civilized pub that functions pretty well either as a drinking den or a dining venue, with a full menu of meat-and-potato standards and lunchtime soups and sandwiches. Till 2am at weekends.

Veerev Õlu Uus 3A. An enjoyably unpretentious wooden-bench bar attracting a nice mixture of holidaymakers and garrulous locals.

Viies Villem Kuninga 11. A roomy basement pub that rounds up an enthusiastic cross-section of drinkers most nights of the week. Decent salads and main meat courses. Till 2am at weekends.

Entertainment

Pärnu is a thriving cultural centre, with concerts and plays all year round. The Endla Theatre, Keskväljak 1 (☎443 0691, ⊛www.endla.ee), hosts top-quality **theatre and dance** performances, while the Pärnu Concert Hall, Aida 4 (Pärnu kontserdimaja; ☎445 5800, ⊛www.concert.ee), provides the perfect venue for chamber **concerts** and major classical-music events – the Estonian National Symphony Orchestra plays here a couple of times a month. Regular organ recitals are given at St Elizabeth's Church.

Annual events attracting top-class international participants include the **Pärnu Days of Contemporary Music** (Pärnu Nüüdismuusika Päevad; ⊛www.ooper .parnu.ee) in mid-January; the **David Oistrakh Festival** (⊛www.ooper.parnu.ee) in the first half of July, featuring plenty of star conductors and soloists; and the **Festival of Documentary and Anthropological Film** (⊛www.chaplin.ee), also in July.

For clubbers, *Mirage*, Rüütli 40, is a year-round, seven-days-a-week **disco** as well as a convenient late-night drinking joint, while the beachfront *Sunset Club*, Ranna pst 3 (⊛www.sunsetclub.ee), attracts a trendier, party-animal crowd. The *Kursaal*, Mere 22 (⊛www.parnukuursaal.ee), hosts live music and club events, including DJs from Tartu's *Club Tallinn* (see p.389), which sets up camp here in July and August.

Kihnu

Forty-five kilometres southwest of Pärnu, the mellow island of **Kihnu**, just 7km long and 3.5km across, offers an enticing three-way mixture of pine forest, juniper heath and pasture. The island supported a population of 1200 until the end of World War II, when a third fled to the West, and the seafaring activities of those who remained were severely curtailed by the security-conscious Soviet authorities. These days, only some 600 souls live on Kihnu and many of the older female residents still wear traditional costume, especially the highly distinctive red-tassled headscarves, and red-green-and-yellow striped skirts.

The island is compact enough to explore on a day-trip from Pärnu, although you can stay in one of a handful of farmhouse **B&Bs** (booked in advance through Kihnurand; ☎446 9924) if you feel like truly unwinding. Kihnu is served by two daily **ferries** in summer from the port of Munalaiu, 40km west of Pärnu (Pärnu–Tõstamaa buses pick up and drop off by the harbour). In addition, there are two to three daily flights from Pärnu to Kihnu, operated by Air Livonia (☎447 5007, ⊛www.airlivonia.ee); expect to pay 120EEK each way.

Two kilometres west of the ferry harbour, Kihnu's main settlement of **LINAKÜLA** huddles around a plain parish church that began as Lutheran when it was first built in the eighteenth century, but became Orthodox in 1858 after the mass conversion of most of the islanders – they switched faiths in order to take up a tempting offer of free land promised by crafty Tsarist bureaucrats. The church graveyard is the last resting place of Kihnu Jõnn, a much-travelled merchant seaman who came to symbolize the sea-roving lifestyle of the average Kihnu male, for whom years of hard graft at sea – punctuated by intermittent bouts of drinking and fighting – was the norm. Jõnn was drowned off the coast of Denmark, where he was buried in 1913, only to be re-interred here in Kihnu eight decades later. A small museum just opposite the church contains several sprightly canvases by self-taught local painter Jaan Oad (1899–1984), whose pictures of pre-World War II fisherfolk at work and play exude a vitality that seems largely absent in the laid-back Kihnu of today.

Soomaa National Park

Extending across the flatlands some 20km due east of Pärnu, the **Soomaa National Park** (Soomaa rahvuspark; ⊛ www.soomaa.ee) was established in 1994 to protect a patchwork of grassland, peat bog and riverine forest – the perfect habitat for elk, beavers, buzzards and grouse. The whole area is susceptible to flooding during the spring thaw, when roads in the centre of the park may become impassable – especially around the village of Riisa, where the Raudra, Lemmjõgi and Halliste rivers meet. Given Soomaa's generally soggy nature it's not surprising to discover that it's the traditional home of the *haabja*, a canoe carved from a single trunk of aspen, and propelled by an enormous paddle, rather like a punt. *Haabjas* are still made in the area and a handful of local tour operators organize guided *haabja* excursions along Soomaa's waterways – although canoes and kayaks are more common. If you prefer to stick to dry land there are plenty of marked trails offering a flavour of the park's bogscapes and forest belts.

You'll need your own **transport** to get to the park, easily accessed by road from either Pärnu or the inland town of Viljandi (see opposite). Tourist offices in both places can provide **information**, although the one in Viljandi seems to be more clued up about accommodation and **canoe trips**. The best of the local canoe outfits is Sarrisoo Kanuukeskus, based on the Navesti River in the heart of the park (☎ 050/61896); they can organize guided hikes, horse-and-trap trips and canoe excursions (from 350EEK for one day, 500EEK for two days with one night in a tent). If you're approaching the area from Viljandi, Soo ja Raba, Väike 11, Viljandi (☎ 051/06029 or 056/633568, ⊛ www.kanuumatkadsoomaal.ee), also organizes canoe trips in the park and may pick you up in Viljandi if you don't have your own car.

Regio's invaluable 1:100 000 *Soomaa jõed/Rivers of Soomaa* **map** can be obtained from Viljandi's tourist office or from bookshops in Tallinn, Tartu and Pärnu. A day-trip will do to get a flavour of the park, although there's a smattering of accommodation around if you fancy a longer stay.

Into the park

The best way to reach the park from Pärnu is to head 35km northeast as far as the village of **JÕESUU**, where the River Navesti flows into the broader Pärnu. From here you can choose between the Kaansoo road, which follows the northern bank of the Navesti before arriving at the Sarrisoo Kanuukeskus (see above) after 6km, or the Tipu road, which heads south through the centre of the park. This latter route gives you a good first taste of Soomaa's archetypal bog-scape in the shape of the **Riisa Bog Trail**, signed off the road to the left after 7km. A boardwalk leads across the peaty soil, which supports a surprisingly diverse range of vegetation, its carpet of lichens, grasses and heathers punctuated by slender birches and stunted conifers. Three kilometres south, *Riisa Ranch* on the south side of **RIISA** village (☎ 447 4804 and 053/944855, ⊛ www.riisarantso.ee) primarily organizes horse-riding trips, but also rents out simple rooms (❶).

Some 4km south of Riisa is **TÕRAMAA** (a road junction rather than a full-blown settlement) and the **National Park Visitors' Centre** (summer daily 10am–6pm; winter Wed–Sun 10am–4pm; ☎ 043/57164, ⊛ www.soomaa.ee), which has English-language leaflets on what to see in the park, a small exhibition devoted to conservation issues and a handful of **rooms** (❷). The centre marks the start of a short **Beaver Trail** (Koprarada), which leads along the banks of the Tõramaa stream, passing enthusiastically gnawed tree trunks and branch-built dams. The minor road running east from the Visitors' Centre brings you after 3km to the **Lemmjõe Keelemets**, a short, but fascinating, marked trail through the riverine forest on the north side of the road.

South of the Visitors' Centre the road runs along the western edge of the Öördi bog before veering east towards Viljandi. Twenty kilometres out from the Visitor's Centre, just beyond the village of **IIA**, a dirt road heads north towards Lake Öördi (Öördi järv), where there's a two-kilometre boardwalk path through a serene environment of squelchy mosses, speckled red with cranberries in the autumn. Back in Iia and heading east, it's only 5km to **KÕPU**, where you can pick up the main road to Viljandi.

Viljandi and around

Roughly midway between Pärnu and Tartu, **VILJANDI** is one of the more pleasant provincial centres in the country, a pleasingly low-rise jumble of houses draped around the northwestern end of the five-kilometre-long, boomerang-shaped Lake Viljandi (Viljandi järv). The grizzled, park-shrouded ruins of a once-mighty castle bear witness to the town's erstwhile importance as a staging post on the Rīga–Novgorod trade route, although it's the sizeable stock of early twentieth century architecture – handsome red-brick buildings and prim timber cottages – that gives the modern-day town centre its flavour. The town is at its busiest during the **Viljandi Folk Festival** in July (Viljandi pärimuusika festival; ⊛www.folk.ee), when ensembles from all over Estonia perform in the castle grounds.

Arrival, information and accommodation

Viljandi's **bus station** is at the junction of Tallinna and Uus, a ten-minute walk north of the **tourist office** at Tallinna 2B (May–Aug Mon–Fri 9am–6pm, Sat & Sun 10am–3pm; Sept–April Mon–Fri 10am–5pm, Sat 10am–2pm; ☏433 3755, ⊛www.viljandimaa.ee), which has free town plans and information about the Viljandi region – notably the Soomaa National Park (see opposite).

There's a handful of decent **hotels** and **B&Bs** in Viljandi itself, and the tourist office can provide details of rural accommodation in local villages – they'll call them on your behalf if the owners don't speak English.

Alice Jakobsoni 55 ☏434 7616, ⊛www.matti.ee/~alice. A six-room B&B in a Bauhaus-influenced suburban house, a ten-minute walk east of the bus station. Bright en-suites with TV and parquet floors. ❸
Centrum Tallinna 24 ☏435 1100, ⊛www.centrum.ee. Comfortable business-oriented en-suites with TV, occupying a glass-fronted shopping centre-cum-office block opposite the bus station. ❹
Grand Hotel Viljandi Tartu 11 ☏435 5800, ⊛www.ghv.ee. The top place to stay in town, occupying a superbly central Art Deco building, which, doom-grey colour scheme aside, still manages to impress. Stylish rooms with all the comforts. ❺

Oma Kodu Väike 6 ☏435 5755, ⊛www.omakodu.ee. Tastefully renovated block occupying the high ground just east of the centre. Rooms (all with shower and TV) are simply furnished, but homely, and there are some family-sized suites with kitchenette – most rooms on the southeastern side come with views of the lake. ❸
Peetrimõisa Villa Pirni 4 ☏434 3000, ⊛www.hot.ee/peetrimoisavilla. Smartish B&B out in northeastern suburbs, fifteen minutes' walk beyond the bus station. Whoever decorated the rooms seems to have suffered from wild mood swings – choose between garish pink ones or more subdued blues. ❸

The Town

The most obvious place to start exploring Viljandi is the tree-shaded expanse of **Castle Hill** (Lossimäed), at the southern end of Tallinna and its extension Tasuja pst. Built by the Livonian Order in the thirteenth century, the castle was one of the

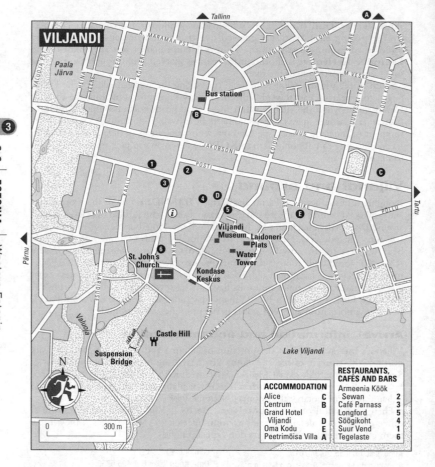

VILJANDI

Bus station

Viljandi
Museum
Laidoneri
Plats
Water
Tower
St. John's
Church
Kondase
Keskus

Castle Hill
Suspension
Bridge

Lake Viljandi

*Paala
Järva*

N

0   300 m

ACCOMMODATION		RESTAURANTS, CAFÉS AND BARS	
Alice	C	Armeenia Köök	
Centrum	B	Sewan	2
Grand Hotel		Café Parnass	3
Viljandi	D	Longford	5
Oma Kodu	E	Söögikoht	4
Peetrimõisa Villa	A	Suur Vend	1
		Tegelaste	6

most important strongholds in southern Estonia until the 1620s, when Swedish siege guns blasted it into a state beyond repair. Nowadays a few jagged sections of wall are all that remain of the castle keep, although there's a sweeping view of the lake from the grassed-over ramparts. Immediately west of the ruins, a stretch of the former moat is spanned by a dainty, pedestrian-only **suspension bridge**, built in 1931 by public-spirited aristocrat Karl von Mensenkampff and nowadays a much-photographed civic trademark.

Immediately north of the castle, a tangle of cobbled alleyways behind the white-washed **St John's Church** provides the setting for one of the country's more in-your-face art museums, the **Kondase Keskus** at Pikk 26 (Wed–Sun 10am–5pm; 15EEK). It's primarily devoted to self-taught local painter Paul Kondas (1900–1985), the outwardly conventional primary school teacher who seemed to escape into a psychedelic dream world whenever he put brush to canvas. Kondas clearly believed that a wild zest for living lay behind the outwardly calm, unex-citable nature of the Estonian national character and his pictures of St John's Eve celebrations and summer bathing trips are filled with uninhibited dancing, nudity and mischief. There's a handful of works by other Estonian naive artists on display here, notably Jaan Oad, whose pictures of boozing fishermen and partying peasants represent an affectionate look at life on his native island of Kihnu (see 357).

A block north at Laidoneri plats 10, **Viljandi Museum** (Wed–Sun 10–am–5pm; 20EEK) offers a neatly arranged display of peasant interiors, local costumes and an impressive model of the castle as it looked in the thirteenth century, revealing a system of outer walls and defensive ditches that would stretch halfway to Viljandi bus station were it still in existence today. Upstairs, an impressive horde of local oddities includes the ceremonial horsehair-plumed helmets once worn by the Viljandi fire brigade and unintentionally absurd Soviet-era dioramas showing socialist farming methods – one of which showcases the (nowadays much ridiculed) attempts to cultivate maize in Estonia in the 1960s.

Immediately east of the museum, the well-tended lawns of Laidoneri plats bask beneath a thirty-metre-high **Water Tower** (May–Sept daily 11am–6pm; 10EEK), built in 1911 when the town was plumbed into the public water supply for the first time. Looking like a huge octagonal tree house perched atop a factory chimney, it contains photographs of Viljandi past and present. Somewhat dwarfed by this structure is the square's other main focus, a statue of the locally born portrait painter **Johann Köler** (1826–1899), who was educated (and subsequently became a teacher) at the St Petersburg Academy. Passionately committed to the national cause, Köler was the most prominent of the so-called "St Petersburg Patriots", expat Estonians who lobbied the Tsarist authorities for sweeping social reforms in their homeland.

North of Laidoneri plats, the junction of Lossi and Tartu provides downtown Viljandi with a sort of centre, a small plaza extending around a statue of schoolteacher and nationalist firebrand **Karl Robert Jakobson** (1842–1882). Overcoming years of obstruction by the local Baltic barons, Jakobson founded the Estonian-language newspaper *Sakala* in Viljandi in 1878. The paper's anti-clerical, anti-German stance represented a complete break with the older generation of Estonian activists, grouped around Johann Voldemar Jannsen's cautiously patriotic *Postimees* (see p.356), an organ which Jakobson believed was funded by German aristocrats. *Sakala* continues to be published in Viljandi, still bearing the ornate masthead it had in Jakobson's time. Heading east along Tartu brings you down to tranquil, sandy-shored Lake Viljandi (Viljandi järv), where there's a beachside café and a place to rent pedaloes. A round-trip run, known as the **Lake Viljandi Race** (Viljandi järve jooks), has been held here on May Day every year since 1928 and is one of the major events in the Estonian cross-country calendar – names of past winners are engraved on a row of stone blocks running along the waterside Ranna pst.

Eating and drinking

There are plenty of **eating** opportunities in and around the town centre. Local shoppers in search of a bite throng to the *Söögikoht* at Tartu 8A, a sparsely decorated café renowned for its cheap but tasty doughnuts and pastries. You'll get plusher seating and a wider range of daytime eats at *Café Parnass*, inside the Kulturimaja ("House of Culture") at Tallinna 5, while the nearby *Armeenia Köök Sewan*, just off Tallinna north of the tourist office, serves up expertly grilled kebabs in an outdoor yard. *Tegelaste*, near the approach to the castle at Pikk 2B, is a more mainstream restaurant, offering a broad spread of Estonian meat dishes, with plenty of chicken and fish choices thrown in. You can also eat at **drinking** venues like *Longford*, Tartu 14, decked out in antique-shop junk and with plenty of pork and trout on the menu, though it's probably eclipsed in the pub stakes by the *Suur Vend*, Turu 4, which has more variety in the food department and is ideally suited to either a relaxing daytime meal or a more animated evening guzzle-fest.

Travel details

Trains

Pärnu to: Tallinn (2 daily; 3–3hr 20min).

Buses

Haapsalu to: Kärdla (Mon–Fri 4 daily, Sat & Sun 3 daily; 2hr); Tallinn (hourly; 1hr 50min); Virtsu (2–3 daily; 1hr 30min).

Kärdla to: Haapsalu (Mon–Fri 4 daily, Sat & Sun 3 daily; 2hr); Tallinn (Mon–Fri 4 daily, Sat & Sun 3 daily; 4hr 30min).

Kuressaare to: Karujärv (summer: Mon–Fri 1 daily; Sat & Sun 2 daily; winter: 1 daily; 25min); Kihelkonna (5 daily; 50min); Leisi (Mon–Fri 5 daily, Sat & Sun 4 daily; 1hr 10min); Tallinn (7 daily; 4hr 30min); Tartu (July & Aug 5 daily, Sept–June 3 daily; 6hr); Undva (2 daily; 1hr).

Pärnu to: Kuressaare (3 daily; 3hr); Tallinn (hourly; 2hr); Tartu (hourly; 2hr 45min–3hr 45min).

Viljandi to: Tartu (8 daily;1–1hr 20min).

Ferries

Munalaiu to: Kihnu (2 daily; 2hr).

Rohuküla to: Heltermaa (Hiiumaa; Mon–Fri 8 daily, Sat 4 daily, Sun 6 daily;1hr 30min); Sviby (2 daily; 50min).

Triigi to: Sõru (2 daily).

Virtsu to: Kuivastu (for Muhu and Saaremaa; summer 14 daily, winter 8–10 daily; 35min).

Flights

Pärnu to: Kihnu (daily; 15min); Kuressaare (2 weekly; 55min); Ruhnu (2 weekly; 25min).

Tallinn to: Kärdla (Mon–Fri 2 daily; 40min); Kuressaare (Mon–Fri 1 daily; 55min).

International buses

Pärnu to: Rīga (5 daily; 3hr 20min); Vilnius (1 daily; 8hr 45min).

3.3

Eastern Estonia

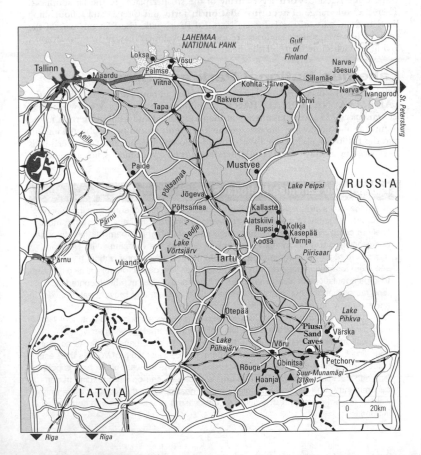

E astern Estonia may not attract as many visitors as the island-scattered west coast, but it offers just as much in terms of variety. While some of the countryside is typical of Estonia in general – forests of pine and birch alternating with arable land and patches of bog – it also possesses a range of landscapes less commonly found in the Baltics, notably the rippling hills of the southeast, the broad freshwater expanse of **Lake Peipsi** and the boulder-strewn beaches of the northeast coast. Long stretches of the last fall within the boundaries of the **Lahemaa National Park**, a vast area of primeval woodland, reed-shrouded coast and well-preserved fishing villages; just 50km east of Tallinn, it's one of the most accessible areas of natural wilderness in the country.

The landscape east of Lahemaa is brutally different, characterized by the dour mining towns and cone-shaped slag heaps of Estonia's oil-shale industry, and there's little of interest until you arrive at **Narva**, a historical fortress town right on the border with Russia and inhabited, unsurprisingly, by a large number of Russian-speakers. Though somewhat blighted by post-war architecture, it's nevertheless a good base from which to explore the sweeping, sandy beaches at **Narva-Jõesuu** and the Stalinist-era toy-town architecture of **Sillamäe**.

The southeast is dominated by **Tartu**, Estonia's second city and a historic university town that manages to combine nineteenth-century gentility with raw, student-fuelled energy. The one place outside Tallinn that has a sufficient menu of urban sights to keep you going for several days, it's also a good base from which to explore the lakes and rolling hills of the far south, with **Suur Munamägi**, the highest point in the Baltics, and the winter sports resort of **Otepää**, both within easy striking distance. Bearing witness to the cultural and racial diversity of Estonia, Russian **Old Believers** continue to inhabit bucolic fishing settlements along the western shores of Lake Peipsi, while surviving communities of **Setu** – an Estonian people with a distinct folk culture – still live in the scattered villages of the extreme southeast.

Getting around the region is fairly straightforward, with buses from Tallinn and Tartu serving almost all the places mentioned in this chapter. In addition, the market town of **Rakvere** is a useful transport hub for the Lahemaa National Park, while calm, lakeside **Võru** serves many of the smaller places in the far southeast. There's a wide range of **accommodation** in Tartu and Otepää and a flourishing B&B trade in parts of the Lahemaa National Park – elsewhere in this part of the country, however, tourist facilities are less well developed than in western Estonia, giving it much more of an off-the-beaten-track feel.

Lahemaa National Park and around

Extending over a deeply indented stretch of coastline an hour's drive east of Tallinn, the **LAHEMAA NATIONAL PARK** (Lahemaa rahvuspark; ⓦ www.lahemaa .ee) embraces 725 square kilometres of the most varied and beautiful terrain in the country. Its most distinctive features are the four evenly spaced peninsulas sticking out into the Baltic Sea, each fringed with custard-coloured beaches and tawny reed beds and backed by a sandy coastal plain generously carpeted with mosses, lichens, pine and

Fauna in the Lahemaa National Park

Given the park's array of unspoiled natural landscapes, it's not surprising that it sup-ports a rich variety of wildlife. The four-legged denizens of Lahemaa you're most likely to catch sight of are roe deer, large numbers of which roam the forests and occasionally graze on farmland, especially early in the morning. Wild boar and moose are slightly less common and stick to the forests in winter, although you may see them foraging in open countryside in summer. The park's forests are also home to large populations of hares, martens and foxes and a small number (counted in the tens rather than the hundreds) of badgers, lynx, wolves, and brown bear. Beavers are extremely secretive, but signs of their industry are everywhere: dams can be seen beside the Beaver Trail at Oandu (see p.371) and elsewhere, and what look like clumsily felled tree trunks are a sure sign of their nocturnal gnawing activities.

As well as the resident songbirds thronging the forests, Lahemaa hosts several migrating bird species in spring and autumn. Eru Bay just west of Võsu is the best place for migrating waterfowl; while Kahala Lake in the far west of the park is pop-ular with ducks and grebes. White storks and cranes can be seen feeding in agri-cultural land from May onwards, black storks nest deep in the forest and are only sighted on rare occasions. The fields around Käsmu Bay are thick with corncrakes in June.

LAHEMAA NATIONAL PARK

spruce. Five to ten kilometres inland lies a limestone plateau covered with juniper heath, peat bog, forests of alder, ash and elm and patches of farmland mainly given over to potatoes and rye. Dividing the plain from the plateau is the limestone escarpment known as the **North Estonian Glint**, which runs from east to west through the middle of the park – although it's so smothered by soil and vegetation that it looks more like a gentle slope than a cliff and in some parts of the park is hardly visible at all. A more conspicuous geological phenomenon than the Glint is the profusion of so-called **erratic boulders**, isolated lumps of rock strewn all over this part of Estonia by retreating glaciers some 12,000 years ago.

After World War II the whole of this coast became a high-security border area that non-residents needed a permit to enter, a policy that ironically helped to preserve the natural landscape by stifling economic activity. However, the Soviet military establishment remained suspicious of Estonian environmentalists, which makes it all the more surprising that the authorities sanctioned the creation of the Lahemaa National Park – the USSR's first – in 1971. The national park ethos, in which the preservation of nature was given a higher moral value than the furtherance of communism or any other ideology, immediately turned Lahemaa into a cult destination with Estonian intellectuals. Official permits to enter the park were still required, however, and strings had to be pulled in order to secure some of the park's meagre stock of accommodation. Foreign groups were admitted only after 1986 and were not allowed to stay overnight. Nowadays, tourist facilities are plentiful and Lahemaa is one of the most popular destinations in the country, often besieged by tour buses on summer weekends.

Many of the park's most exciting **natural features** can be accessed by marked paths, ranging from deep-forest hikes long enough to satisfy the seasoned walker to well-designed study trails (often with signboards en route detailing the flora and fauna you're likely to see), taking only an hour or two to complete. Restored palace complexes at **Palmse** and **Sagadi**, in the southeast of the park, provide an insight into the feudal manor-house culture of the German barons who once held sway over the region, while another attraction are the charmingly under-commercialized beach resorts of **Võsu** and **Käsmu**.

If you want to explore the park in depth it's worth getting hold of Regio's 1:60 000 *Lahemaa Rahvuspark* **map**; it comes in Estonian, English and Russian versions and you can pick it up from bookshops in Tallinn and at the National Park Visitors' Centre in Palmse (see p.368).

Park practicalities

Most Lahemaa-bound tourist traffic approaches from the west along the Tallinn–Narva highway (which forms the park's southern boundary for a lengthy stretch) before arriving at Viitna, a major crossroads from which the road to Palmse, Võsu and Käsmu branches off to the north. In the account below we've chosen to cover this main route first, before fanning out to explore outlying areas of the park – although any number of alternative itineraries are viable.

The main source of **information** is the National Park Visitors' Centre in the inland village of **Palmse** (see p.368), and if you're travelling by car then this should be one of your first ports of call. If you're dependent on public transport it makes more sense to aim instead for the seaside villages of Võsu and Käsmu, which offer much more in the way of accommodation and bus connections – you can always hike or hitch to Palmse once you get settled in.

Käsmu is certainly the best base if you want a range of hiking possibilities right on your doorstep, with a number of local trails ranging in duration from forty minutes to four hours. Staying in Võsu or elsewhere in the park, you'll still be able to see a great deal on foot, providing you don't mind tramping 20–30km a day. Otherwise, you'll need a car or bike to access all the main areas of interest. Võsu is the one settlement in the park that has a decent number of food and drink shops.

If you do come to Lahemaa by car, remember to leave nothing of value inside it wherever you park – it has been known for thieves from nearby towns to descend on the area in summer to rob vehicles while their owners are hiking in the woods.

Public transport to the park

From Tallinn bus station there are three daily services to Võsu (some of which terminate at Altja, a useful name to look for on timetables and destination boards) and one to Käsmu. There are also four daily buses **from Tallinn train station** to Viinistu in the western part of the park, although this is less useful as a base from which to explore. Võsu and Viinistu are do-able as a **day-trip** from Tallinn.

If you're approaching Lahemaa **from Narva or Tartu**, make first for the town of **Rakvere** (see p.371), just outside the park. From Võsu you can catch connecting servic-es to Võsu and Käsmu providing you don't arrive too late in the afternoon (aim to arrive before 4pm). There's also a bus from Rakvere to Palmse, but only four days a week. See "Travel details" on p.399 for more detailed bus information.

Accommodation

Small **hotels** and **B&Bs** are scattered throughout the park, with the biggest con-centration in and around Käsmu. Beware, however, that summer weekends are often booked up months in advance. Most establishments claim to be open all year round, although in practice the smaller B&Bs turn away individuals or small groups of visitors in the October–April period – they can't afford to turn on the heating unless they have a houseful. In summer, **hostel**-style accommodation is available in Võsu, Käsmu, Palmse and Sagadi. There's also a network of free **campsites** (May–Sept) run by the national park, in which firewood is provided (so that campers don't go around cutting their own), but little in the way of other facilities – although there may be a couple of dry toilets on hand. The sites are nicely spaced out so that hikers can feasibly walk from one to another in the course of a day.

Viru Bog

Approaching Lahemaa from the Tallinn direction, the first of the park's set-piece attractions you come across is **Viru Bog** (Viru raba), an area of peat bog, just over 2km square, created over a period of 10,000 years by decaying mosses, about 50km out from the capital. It's just north of the Tallinn–Narva highway – take the Loksa turn-off and look for a sign indicating the **Viru Bog Nature Trail** (Viru raba õpperada) on your right after about 1km. A 3.5-kilometre wooden walkway curves northeast across the bog, providing an excellent vantage point over this strange landscape of grey-brown lichens and stunted conifers, with pine-covered dunes just visible to the northwest. Late May to early June is the best time to visit, when stretches of the bog are covered in wild flowers.

Viitna

Twenty-two kilometres beyond the Loksa turn-off, **VIITNA** has served as an important rest-stop on the Tallinn–Narva road since medieval times, and is still the place where most people break for a breather before turning north towards Palmse and the central area of the park. Viitna's enduring popularity is in large part due to the presence of the *Viitna kõrts* **tavern**, built in imitation of an eighteenth-century coaching inn and boasting an atmospheric timbered interior – the perfect place to fill up on pork and freshwater fish dishes. Immediately south of the tavern, a 2.5-kilometre-long nature trail skirts **Great Viitna Lake** (Viitna suurjärv or Viitna pikkjärv), a glacier-gouged finger of water formed by retreating ice some 11, 500 years ago. Fringed by pine forest, it's a supremely restful spot.

Should you wish **to stay** in Viitna, head for the *Viitna Holiday Centre* (☎329 3651; ❶), down a side road 500m east of the main crossroads, offering spartan dou-bles with shared facilities in pleasant wooded surroundings.

Palmse and around

Six kilometres north of Viitna, the village of **PALMSE**, home to the park's Visitor Centre (see below), began life as a Cistercian convent before being bought in 1677 by the von Pahlens, a leading family of Baltic barons who stayed here until they were booted out by the land reform of 1919. The eighteenth-century complex of manorial buildings, bequeathed by the Pahlens, subsequently served as a barracks, then a childrens' holiday camp, before the Lahemaa National Park authorities set up their HQ here in 1972 and began painstakingly restoring the place. It's now an impressive ensemble of brightly painted cream and pale-blue buildings grouped around a central courtyard, bounded by fruit orchards and landscaped parkland. Inside the courtyard, a balustraded staircase sweeps up to the doors of the neoclassical **Manor House** (May–Sept daily 10am–7pm; Oct–April Mon–Fri 10am–3pm; 20EEK), filled with antique furniture from all over Estonia and sepia photographs of the estate as it was in the Pahlens' time. Outside, an old creamery (July & Aug only: same times as above) contains an exhibition of sleds and coaches, and beyond this lies a conservatory filled with palms and cacti. Lawns slope down towards a small lake, on the far side of which lies a wooded park crisscrossed by paths.

You'll find the **National Park Visitors' Centre** (May–Aug daily 9am–7pm; Sept daily 9am–5pm; Oct–April Mon–Fri 9am–5pm; ☎329 5555, ✉info@lahemaa.ee), in a former coach house at the entrance to the manor courtyard. It's well stocked with maps and English-language leaflets describing various trails. Some of the swishest accommodation in the park is to be found right next door to the Visitors' Centre in the *Palmse* **hotel** (☎322 3626, ⓦwww.phpalmse.ee; ❹), an old vodka distillery converted into bright, feel-good en-suites with chunky wooden furniture. There's also a good café-restaurant on site, and guests can rent bikes for 150EEK per day. Right at the other end of the scale, about 1.5km southeast of the manor, overlooking a lake just off the road to Sagadi, the *Ojaäärse matkamaja* **hostel** (☎323 4108) offers basic bunk accommodation in cramped, but clean, dorms for 150–200EEK per person, and has tent space out the back (55EEK).

Võsu

Strung out along the southern shores of Käsmu Bay (Käsmu laht), 8km north of Palmse, the village of **VÕSU** has been a holiday resort ever since the late nineteenth century, when its pine-fringed beach was discovered by the St Petersburg intelligentsia. It's a pretty uneventful little place, but serves as a good base for further exploration: within striking distance lies wood-shrouded Oandu (see p.371) and the appealing fishing village of Altja (p.370), both reached via a ten-kilometre-long forest trail starting at the southern entrance to Võsu, while the Käsmu peninsula, strewn with erratic boulders, is only 8km to the northwest.

Võsu is over 2km long from east to west, and **accommodation** in the settlement is scattered accordingly: beginning at the eastern end (where the road from Palmse enters the village), the *Võsu-Viiking*, Karja 9 (☎323 8521; ❷), offers prim rooms with grey-brown decor, most of which come with en-suite shower and TV; while the *Männisalu Hostel*, signed off the main road at Lääne 13 (☎323 8320, ⓦwww.mannisalu.ee; ❷; May–Sept only), musters a few sparsely furnished doubles, as well as dorm accommodation in quads (200EEK per person), with breakfast included. At the western end of the village, the smart *Rannaliiv*, Aia 5 (☎323 8456, ⓦwww.rannaliiv.ee; ❷), boasts stylish doubles with wooden furnishings, shower and TV. In the back streets just behind it, *Hostell Sinikorall*, Metsa 3 (☎323 8455, ⓦwww.sinikorall.ee; ❶; May–Sept only), has a handful of doubles with shared facilities and twenty places in four-bed dorms for 120EEK per person, although breakfast costs extra. *Camping Lepispea*, 2km west of the centre on the Käsmu road (late May to late Sept; ☎324 4665, ⓦwww.hot.ee/lepispeale), is one of the best-equipped sites in the country, with clean toilet blocks and electricity points for caravans.

For **eating** and **drinking**, try the *Grillbaar*, a pub-restaurant midway through the village on the main street, where you can get a decent range of pork and chicken dishes. The *Võsu Pagariäri* bakery, near the eastern entrance to the village, is the place to stop off for cakes, pastries and pancakes.

Käsmu

People tend to speak in superlatives about **KÄSMU**, an appealing ensemble of pastel-coloured houses and neat gardens that seems to meet everyone's expectations of what a traditional Estonian village ought to look like. The place owes its prosperous, white-picket-fence appearance to a brief period in the seafaring limelight in the decades before World War I, when Käsmu Bay – not as prone to thick ice as some of the other spots along the northern coast – became a popular winter anchorage for sailing ships. A maritime school was opened in 1884, many of whose graduates chose to settle down in the village once their ocean-going days were over, earning Käsmu the nickname of "Captains' Village". The development of deep-hulled steamships put paid to Käsmu's importance, however, and it's now a pleasantly low-key, summer-holiday village, offering plenty of B&B accommodation and excellent walking opportunities in the forests of the Käsmu peninsula.

Käsmu's maritime heritage is remembered in a small, private **museum** (open whenever the owner's family is around – usually most of the day), signed off the main street midway through the village. There's an atmospheric, pre-World War I living room containing the furniture of the owner's grandfather, while elsewhere are displays of bits of old boats, fishing tackle and baskets made from birch-bark – some of them look more like modern art installations than historical artefacts. Just inland from the museum, the **parish church** is renowned for the charm of its graveyard, planted with a kaleidoscopic array of flowers every spring.

At the northern end of Käsmu village a path leads to the tip of the Käsmu peninsula, where you can gaze at a chain of erratic boulders stretching away towards the uninhabited island of Kuradisaare. From here a path leads along the rock-strewn northern and western coasts of the peninsula, before looping back to Käsmu village through dense forest – a scenic circuit of about 14km in all. For a shorter woodland walk – or simply to cut a huge corner off the main circuit – head west from the village along the track that starts roughly opposite the *Lainela Holiday Village* (see below). This soon lands you in the midst of the so-called **Stone Plantation** (Kivikülv), a vast, eerie expanse of moss-covered erratic boulders sheltered by pines.

Accommodation

Accommodation in Käsmu is provided by a string of B&Bs on the main street. Most of these also allow you to pitch a tent in the garden for around 50EEK, although they'll turn campers away if things get too busy. A good fallback is the free national park **campsite** on the shores of Käsmu järv, a forest-shrouded lake about an hour's walk southwest of the village. There's a simple café at the *Lainela Puhkeküla* (see below).

Lainela Puhkeküla (Lainela Holiday Village) Neeme 70 ☎323 8133, ✉suved@hot.ee. A former childrens' holiday camp now open to all-comers, with seven hostel-like halls offering sparsely furnished two- and three-bed rooms, with showers and WC in the corridor. Despite its 100-bed capacity it's still likely to be packed with groups in summer. Open May–Sept. ❶

Merekalda Neeme 2 ☎323 8451, ❦www.merekalda.ee. A plush B&B at the southern end of the village, right on the shore, with en-suite rooms in the main family house or in the annexe across the lawn. ❸

Rannamännid Neeme 31 ☎323 8329. A smart B&B midway along the main street offering eight sunny rooms, some en-suite, others with shared facilities. Top-floor rooms with sloping ceilings are particularly atmospheric. Half-board arrangements are well worth the extra few kroon. ❷

Uustalu Neeme 78A ☎325 2956. A cosy B&B near the northern tip of the peninsula with snug en-suite rooms. ❷

Vahtra Laane 9 ☎325 2917. Friendly household behind the parish church with a family-sized apartment sleeping four (700EEK), and four simple, but snug, doubles with shared facilities. ❷

West of Käsmu Bay: the Pärispea peninsula

West of Käsmu Bay, roads from Võsu work their way along the southern shore of Eru Bay (Eru laht) before heading north onto the **Pärispea peninsula**, another inviting area of desolate, boulder-strewn beauty. You really need a car to explore this area, as public transport is negligeable and settlements are far-flung.

As you head up the east coast you'll pass lots of reed beds, a paradise for migrating birds in late spring, especially mute swans, mallards and barnacled geese. The first village of any interest is **VIINISTU**, squatting on the northeastern corner of the peninsula. During the inter-war years Viinistu was known throughout Estonia as the "Village of the Spirit Kings" (*Piiritusekuningate Küla*) on account of the huge profits made from smuggling vodka to Finland. After World War II, a sizeable fishing fleet was based here until that industry went into decline, and large parts of the port-side canning factory have now been transformed into the **Viinistu Art Gallery** (Viinistu kunstimuuseum; daily 11am–6pm; 25EEK). Based on the private collection of Jan Manetski, a Viinistu native who made it big in Sweden, the gallery provides a definitive overview of Estonian art from the early twentieth century onwards, kicking off with one of the most frequently reproduced paintings in the country, Aleksander Vardi's impressionistic view of Paris's Boulevard Clichy. There are some inter-war graphics of North African tribesmen by the much-travelled, inter-war artist Eduard Viiralt, and a whole room devoted to the often unsettling conceptual creations of the post-1991 generation – look out for the pieces of cardboard daubed with paint on the afternoon of September 11, 2001 by Raul Kurvitz (who was staying in New York at the time). Two adjacent water towers provide the perfect place for temporary exhibitions, mostly devoted to new works by Estonian artists. The gallery runs a small **hotel** in an adjacent building, offering simple but pristine doubles with shower (☎608 6422 & 051/257270; ❷). On the landward side of the gallery, *Viinistu Kõrts*, in an old, whitewashed house, is a cheery place to fill up on fried fish and beer.

The western side of the peninsula is characterized by a string of former Soviet military settlements, beginning with **PÄRISPEA** in the northwest, built to serve a radar installation on the headland, 2km to the northeast. A track runs past abandoned barracks to reach the headland, where an earthen mound (the erstwhile perch of the biggest of the eight radar dishes once sited here) provides a superb vantage point from which to survey a chain of sea-splashed erratic boulders strung out to the north. The free national park **campsite** just below the mound is very popular on summer weekends.

Three kilometres south of Pärispea, **SUURPEA** once boasted an institute dedicated to making Soviet submarines invisible to sonar, but its sparsely inhabited concrete apartment blocks nowadays have a ghost-town look about them. More animated, but probably less interesting for the visitor, is **LOKSA** 8km further south, a gritty shipbuilding town occupying an isolated pocket of non-national park territory.

East of Käsmu Bay

The road east out of Võsu skirts the northern fringes of Oandu forest and leads to **ALTJA**, a charming fishing village with timber buildings, 15km away. For walkers, there's a more direct, ten-kilometre path through the forest, starting at the southern end of Võsu and emerging near the Oandu nature trails described below. Altja's main landmark is an enormous **wooden swing** at the eastern end of the village. Before World War II, every Estonian village would have had one of these: they provided a summer-evening social focus where local youth would gather in the days before bus shelters were invented. Beyond the swing there's a short stretch of sandy beach and an ensemble of fishermen's cottages and net sheds, many sporting recently restored thatched roofs. If you want **to stay** in a traditional log-built building, head for *Toomarahva B&B*, right by the village's main road (☎325 2511, ⓔtoomarahva@hot.ee; ❷); it has two cosy doubles sharing a bathroom, plus there's tent space in the garden, and guests can rent bikes for 150EEK a day. Built in the style of a nineteenth-century village tavern, *Altja Kõrts*, close by the swing, does a good line in local fish.

Oandu

Beyond Altja the road climbs uphill to the south, passing after 1.5km the start of the **Oandu Beaver Trail** (Koprarada) on the left side of the road, a 1.7-kilometre circuit which passes several beaver dams, and no doubt you'll also see tree trunks bearing fresh gnaw marks. Just under 1km north of the Beaver Trail, **OANDU** itself is no more than a couple of scattered farmsteads in the forest. Signs on the right-hand side of the road mark the start of the **Oandu Forest Nature Trail** (Oandu loodusmetsa rada), a circular, 4.7-kilometre path designed to give you a taste of the park's varied forest landscape: a mixture of evergreen and deciduous trees drawing a dark green canopy over a woodland floor covered in mosses and ferns. Here and there, scarred tree-trunks bear witness to the activities of itchy-scratchy moose and bark-nibbling bears. If you're camping, you could head for the free national park **campsite** just north of the Oandu Forest Nature Trail, right beside the road and overlooking a small lake.

Sagadi

Three kilometres beyond Oandu lies **Sagadi Manor** (Sagadi mõis), a handsome ensemble of cherry-and-cream buildings lying behind a low, brick wall. It was built for the von Fock family in the mid-eighteenth century and is now the regional HQ of the Estonian Forestry Commission. Presiding over a large, oblong courtyard, the Manor House (May–Sept daily 11am–6pm; closed rest of year; 20EEK; combined ticket including Forestry Museum 30EEK) harbours an attractively arranged collection of period furniture and paintings, beginning in the central hall with a curious canvas by an unknown artist of a dog and cat fighting over a chicken. As in most Baltic aristocratic homes of the late eighteenth century, the lady of the house lived in one wing of the building, while the master lived in another – it's easy to see which wing is which in Sagadi, with businesslike green hues dominating the decor in one half of the house and shades of pink and purple holding sway elsewhere. Occupying outbuildings on one side of the courtyard, the **Forestry Museum** (Metsamuuseum; same times and prices) is mainly intended for schoolchildren, with a didactic display of stuffed woodland animals and a thorough rundown of all the types of tree found in Estonia.

Sharing the same building as the Forestry Museum, the *Sagadi* **hotel** (☏325 8888, ⓦwww.sagadi.ee; ❹) offers comfortable, en-suite rooms with TV, most featuring attic ceilings and decorative half-moon windows. Occupying the former bailiff's house on the opposite side of the courtyard, the impressively high-ceilinged quarters at Sagadi **hostel** (☏325 8888) are sparsely furnished, but comfortable, with beds costing 130EEK per person in a crowded dorm, 200EEK per person in a triple (breakfast isn't included, but you can buy it in the hotel café). Hostel and hotel guests can rent **bikes** for 150EEK a day.

Rakvere

Situated some 27km beyond the southeastern border of the park, just off the Tallinn–Narva highway, is the laid-back, largely unindustrial town of **RAKVERE**. The dominant feature of the town centre is a long, grassy ridge topped by the grizzled grey ruins of **Rakvere Castle** (Rakvere linnus; May–Sept daily 11am–7pm; 10EEK), built by the Danes in 1220 and expanded by the Livonian Order when they took over in 1346. A restored tower contains a display of archeological oddments, and you can walk a short section of the battlements. Just north of the castle is an enormous, golden-horned statue of an aurochs (a now extinct breed of cattle) placed here in 2002 in honour of the beasts that long ago roamed the plain below.

Downhill from the aurochs, the high-profile temporary exhibitions on Estonian historical themes at the **Rakvere Museum** at Tallinna 3 (Tues–Sat 11am–5pm; 5EEK) are usually pretty worthwhile. Heading from Tallinna along the eastern flanks of the castle hill, **Pikk** is the most atmospheric of Rakvere's streets, with a largely low-rise jumble of pre–World War I buildings. Occupying one of these at Pikk 50 is the **Museum of the Rakvere Citizen** (Rakvere linnakodaniku majamuuseum; Wed–Sat 11am–5pm; 5EEK), which preserves a neat nineteenth-century interior, complete with a welcoming samovar on the sideboard, and all sorts of charming period crockery, including a butter dish in the form of a bundle of asparagus.

Rakvere's **bus station** is ten minutes' walk southeast of the centre on Laada, just beyond a brochure-stocked **tourist office** at Laada 14 (Mon–Fri 9am–5pm; ☎324 2734, ⓔrakvere@visitestonia.com). The cosiest of the town's **hotels** is the *Katariina Külalistemaja* at Pikk 3 (☎322 3943, ⓦwww.katariina.ee; ❸), which has en-suite rooms in soothing pastel colours, while the *Rakvere Theatre* (☎329 5420, ⓦwww.rakvereteater.ee; ❶), just behind the museum, offers a handful of rustic, wooden-floored rooms, the more expensive ones with en-suite bathrooms. For **eating**, *Wiru Kohvik*, at the junction of Tallinna and Laada, is the place for cheap cafeteria stodge, while *Berliini Trahter*, occupying an old brick building at Lai 15, does a wider range of pork-and-potato staples. The *English Pub Old Victoria*, Tallinna 27, has a charming **beer garden**.

Narva and around

"For sheer romantic medievalism **NARVA** ranks even above Tallinn," wrote Ronald Seth in 1939, unaware that this atmospheric city of cobbled streets was about to be pummelled to oblivion by German–Soviet artillery battles. Subsequently smothered by the greyest grid of residential blocks you're likely to see in the Baltics, Estonia's third-largest city now feels rather like an ungainly suburb serving a centre that has mysteriously gone missing.

It's hardly surprising that this oft-disputed border town has ended up looking like a history-scarred mish-mash. Founded by the Danes in 1229 and bequeathed to the Livonian Order a century later, the city, straddling both banks of the Narva River, marked for centuries the frontier between the Teutonic-ruled western Baltic and the emerging Russian state to the east. The building of Narva Castle on the western side of the river was soon followed by the construction of Ivangorod (built by Ivan III of Muscovy in 1492) on the opposite bank; the two strongholds continue to glower across the water at each other to this day. Gaining in mercantile as well as strategic importance, Narva was repeatedly fought over by Russians and Swedes from the mid-sixteenth century onwards, Peter the Great's successful assault of May 1704 finally settling the issue. Under Tsarist rule Narva flourished as a port and became a world-famous centre for the textile industry with the founding of the Kreenholm cotton mill in 1857.

Today, Narva is still an important manufacturing centre, although economic activity has slumped since the collapse of communism, and nowadays the city is more famous for high levels of unemployment and drug abuse than for any industrial achievements. Narva's problems aren't helped by the fact that over ninety percent of its inhabitants are Russian-speaking, providing the Estonian establishment with a convenient excuse to turn its back on the city. Even Narva's position on the main Tallinn–St Petersburg highway fails to bring much in the way of tourism or prosperity, with most travellers speeding straight through town without bothering to stop off.

It would be a mistake to discount Narva entirely, however. Its **castle** is still a truly impressive sight and the proximity of the Stalin-era model town of **Sillamäe** and the beach resort of **Narva-Jõesuu**, easily seen on a side trip, are sufficient to justify a stay of a day or two.

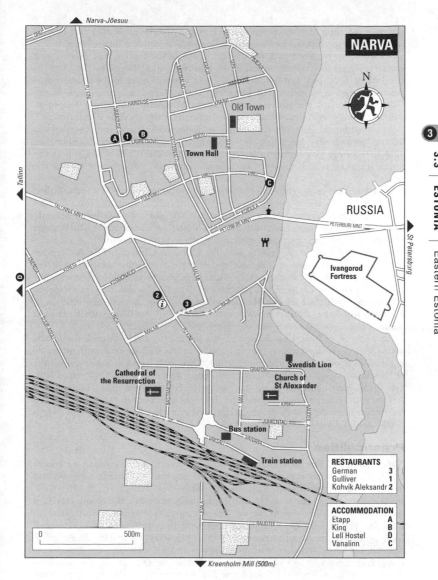

Narva-Jõesuu

NARVA

N

Old Town

Town Hall

RUSSIA

St Petersburg

PETERBURI MNT

**Ivangorod
Fortress**

**Cathedral of
the Resurrection**

Swedish Lion

**Church of
St Alexander**

KIRIKU

Bus station

Train station

RESTAURANTS	
German	3
Gulliver	1
Kohvik Aleksandr	2

ACCOMMODATION	
Etapp	A
King	B
Lell Hostel	D
Vanalinn	C

0   500m

Kreenholm Mill (500m)

The Town

Narva's main point of reference is the **border post** serving the bridge over the
Narva River, the approach road to which cuts right across what remains of the city
centre. There's usually a good deal of pedestrian traffic crossing the frontier, with
Narva folk visiting family and friends on the Ivangorod side of the river. Just north
of the border post lies what was once Narva's Old Town; there's little of real vintage
left now save for the reconstructed **Town Hall** (Raekoda), striking a forlorn pose
on one side of an otherwise desolate Raekoja plats. Built by Georg Teuffel of
Lübeck in 1668–74, the Town Hall is a salmon-coloured, spire-topped structure, the

outstanding feature of which is the ornate Baroque portal with Narva's coat of arms (a pair of fish) surrounded by allegories of Justice, Wisdom and Temperance.

Occupying a riverfront park on the south side of the border post, Narva's one great surviving medieval monument is the **Castle** (Linnus), begun by the Danes in the thirteenth century and expanded by the Livonian Order in the fourteenth – when its huge main tower, Tall Hermann (Pika Hermanni torn), took shape. Occupying much of the tower today is **Narva Museum** (Wed–Sun 10am–6pm; 30EEK), a rambling collection of armour, cannonballs and muskets which demands to be visited for the drama of its setting – an atmospheric succession of stone-built halls and passageways. Ascending through exhibition galleries inside Tall Hermann ultimately brings you out onto an enclosed walkway just below the top of the tower, affording superb views of Ivangorod fortress on the opposite side of the river.

The main focus of the riverside park stretching south of the castle is the so-called **Swedish Lion**, a modern replica of a 1936 memorial commemorating Charles XII's victory over Narva's Russian besiegers in 1701, when the Swedes audaciously used a driving snowstorm as cover for their attack. As an implicitly anti-Russian monument, the Lion is just about tolerated by the locals. Further south lie a handful of architectural oddities, beginning with the Lutheran **Church of St Alexander** (Aleksandrikirik) between Grafovi and Kiriku, a curious rotunda built for Kreenholm cotton-mill workers in 1884 and largely gutted in 1944 – restoration is currently underway. About 200m due west of here, the roughly contemporaneous **Orthodox Cathedral of the Resurrection** (Õigeusu Ülestõusmise kirik) is in much better shape, an impressive barrel of red brick bursting with Byzantine domes.

Just southeast of here, a footbridge crosses the railway tracks towards the south-bound Joala tänav, lined with moderately well-preserved Stalin-era apartment buildings rich in neoclassical mouldings. Further down Joala lie some impressive workers' housing projects of the pre-Soviet era, huge slabs of red brick encrusted with neo-Gothic detail, built to house workers at the **Kreenholm mill**. The mill itself sprawls at the southern end of Joala, the three vast towers of its facade mounting a confident nineteenth-century challenge to the medieval battlements of Narva Castle and Ivangorod just downstream.

Practicalities

Narva's **train** and **bus stations** are just off the southern end of Puškini, the boulevard that runs roughly north–south through the city centre, taking in a friendly and helpful **tourist office** at Puškini 13 (Mon–Fri 9am–5pm; ☎356 0184, ⓦwww.narva.ee) on the way. The most reasonably priced of the town's **hotels** is the *Vanalinn*, occupying one of Narva's few surviving seventeenth-century houses at Koidula 6 (☎357 3253; ❷), with dowdy, but perfectly comfortable, en-suite rooms. More upmarket, the *King*, Lavretsovi 9 (☎357 2404, ⓦwww.hotelking.ee; ❸), offers cosy, almost rustic-styled rooms, with shower and TV, although the brand-new *Etapp*, Lavretsovi 5 (☎359 1333, ⓔetapphotell@hot.ee; ❸), just about shades it in the comfort stakes. There's a **hostel**, the *Lell*, in a greying block, twenty minutes' walk west of the centre at Partisani 7 (☎354 9009, ⓔlell77@hot.ee), with two- and three-bed rooms from 200EEK per person.

Narva isn't exactly overflowing with decent places to **eat** and **drink**. Your best bets for eats include *Kohvik Aleksandr*, Puškini 13, a calming and civilized place in which to relax over coffee and cakes or more substantial snacks. Alternatively, try *German*, Puškini 10 (entrance round the corner on Malmi), a pub-like subterranean space with a full menu of satisfying meat-and-two-veg main courses, or the restaurant of the *King* hotel, with a wider range of dishes and a slightly smarter clientele. For drinks, head for *Gulliver*, Lavretsovi 7, a cosy café-bar serving up cheap and tasty Wiru beer.

Narva-Jõesuu

The road leading northwest out of Narva runs along the left bank of the Narva River, passing a string of German and Soviet military cemeteries – a reminder of just how fiercely the region was fought over in 1944. After some 13km, the road winds up in the beachside settlement of **NARVA-JÕESUU**, a four-kilometre-long line of holiday homes and concrete hotels sheltered by pines. One of the most glamorous watering holes in the Baltic during its pre-World War I heyday, Narva-Jõesuu now has the half-abandoned air of so many post-Soviet resorts. A central spa park complete with swan-patrolled lake and bandstand serves as a reminder of past glories, as does the neighbouring Kursaal, now falling into ruin, where the cream of St Petersburg high society used to congregate for concerts and balls. The sandy beach is as good as they come, however, and the general peacefulness of the place makes Narva-Jõesuu a more restful place to stay than Narva.

Narva-Jõesuu is easily reached from central Narva by catching municipal **bus** #31 or #31R from outside the post office on Puškini (every 20–30min). Privately operated minibuses run the same route, but don't keep to a regular timetable. Of the high-rise **hotels**, one of the most basic is the beachside *Mereranna* (☎357 2827; ❶) which hasn't changed much since Soviet times; you'll get more in the way of creature comforts at the *Liivarand* at the western end of the resort (☎357 7391, ⓔliivarand@hot.ee; ❷), where you can choose between standard en-suite doubles with frumpy decor, or slightly plusher "business class" rooms with TV. Hidden away in back streets near the *Liivarand*, the more intimate and cosy *Kulalistemaja Valentina* (☎357 7468; ❷) offers swanky B&B accommodation.

Sillamäe

Twenty-five kilometres west of Narva and served by hourly buses, the seaside town of **SILLAMÄE** is a living memorial to the showpiece architecture of the late Stalinist period, its elegantly proportioned apartment blocks combining neo-Egyptian pilasters and scallop-shell lunettes with hammers, sickles and facade-topping, five-pointed stars. The model town's inhabitants were almost all employed in the local uranium mine, built by prison labour in 1948. The mine fed the USSR's nuclear energy programme and was closed down by the Estonian government in 1991. The mine's environmental legacy constitutes a considerable headache for the authorities, with a waste pond just west of town bleeding radioactive material into both sea and soil – an EU-funded clean-up operation is under way. Neat-and-tidy Sillamäe itself is an enchanting urban relic and well worth a trip from Narva to see.

From the **bus station** on the edge of town a tree-lined boulevard takes you past manicured parks to the set-piece **main square**, where a statue of a bare-torsoed miner juggles a confusion of hoops and balls – signifying, presumably, molecules orbiting the nucleus of an atom. Opposite the statue, a mock-medieval Town Hall sprouts an incongruous-looking church spire, while the nearby House of Culture flaunts the kinds of colonnades and pediments you'd expect to see on a Graeco–Roman temple. From the House of Culture, a mauve-and-turquoise staircase leads down to the stately apartment buildings of Mere pst, at the far end of which you'll find a shingle seashore – the brown-coloured headland over to the west is where most of the mining took place.

If you're looking for somewhere to **stay**, head for the recently renovated *Hotel Krunk* on the main square (☎392 9030, ⓦwww.krunk.ee; ❷), which offers attractive en-suites and also has a **restaurant**.

Tartu

Perched on the banks of the River Emajõgi, the tranquil, leafy city of **TARTU** is the undisputed intellectual capital of the country, home to a 370-year-old university, which, during its nineteenth-century heyday, was the most prestigious seat of

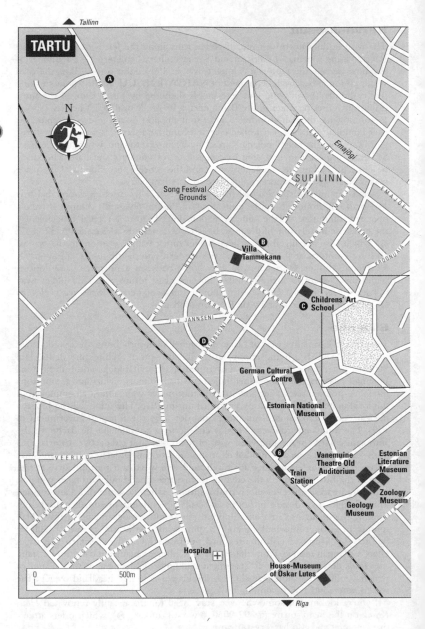

learning in the Baltics. Many of the city centre's solid neoclassical buildings date from the university's greatest period of expansion in the early 1800s, and the academic world remains absolutely central to the city's character – one fifth of Tartu's population of 100,000 is reckoned to be made up of students, researchers, or their egg-headed supervisors. Tartu has long been considered the natural home of the nation's educated elite (ambitious Estonians still choose to study here in preference

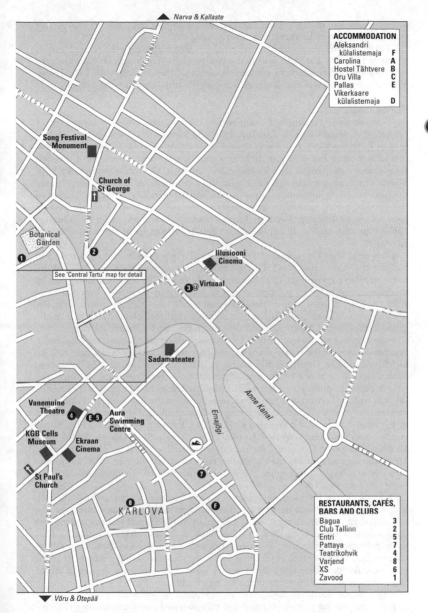

ACCOMMODATION

Aleksandri külalistemaja	**F**
Carolina	**A**
Hostel Tähtvere	**B**
Oru Villa	**C**
Pallas	**E**
Vikerkaare külalistemaja	**D**

See 'Central Tartu' map for detail

RESTAURANTS, CAFÉS, BARS AND CLUBS

Bagua	3
Club Tallinn	2
Entri	5
Pattaya	7
Teatrikohvik	4
Varjend	8
XS	6
Zavood	1

to the capital), and the city's tangible sense of superiority over Tallinn is bolstered by the fact that it's one of the most truly Estonian urban centres in the country – it was spared mass immigration from other parts of the Soviet Union, with the result that less than 25 percent of today's population count Russian as their first language. Filled with national self-importance though it is, Tartu retains an easy-to-get-to-know, small-town feel – and as a hotbed of traditional student activities such as lounging around, discussing the meaning of life or just drinking, it's the perfect place in which to make contacts, or simply hang out.

A couple of days are enough to take in Tartu's sights, although the relaxed atmosphere of its parks and pubs will make you want to stay longer. It's certainly an excellent base from which to explore the south of the country, with Lake Peipsi, Võrumaa, Setumaa and even Viljandi (see p.359) within easy day-trip range.

Some history

An Estonian hilltop stronghold conquered by the Livonian Order in the thirteenth century, then fought over by Russians, Poles and Swedes in the sixteenth – the history of Tartu (or Dorpat as it was known until 1918) would be much the same as that of any other Estonian provincial city were it not for the decision of Swedish King Gustav Adolphus to found a university here in 1632. With government jobs in Swedish Livonia open only to those who had a degree from Tartu, it soon became the only academic institution in the region worth attending. The early history of the university was somewhat chequered, largely owing to Tartu's proximity to a zone of almost constant Swedish-Russian warfare: it was evacuated to Tallinn in 1656, didn't function at all between 1665 and 1690, and spent ten years in Pärnu after 1699.

When Peter the Great captured Tartu in 1708, he deported its leading citizens and had the city walls demolished. The townsfolk were allowed back in 1714, but the university had to wait until 1802 before it could resume its activities. Energized by the prospect of having a prestigious seat of learning in their own back yard, the Baltic nobility poured money into the university's wholesale reconstruction, the resulting rash of assembly halls, libraries and lecture theatres lending Tartu a distinguished, neoclassical appearance, still very much the city's hallmark today.

Despite being an almost wholly German-speaking institution, the university became an important centre for research into indigenous Estonian culture. The Gelehrte Estnische Gesellschaft (Estonian Learned Society), founded by Tartu professors in 1837, was one of the first organizations to treat the local language as a serious object of study. Those Estonians lucky enough to be admitted to the university still had to Germanize their names in order to be socially accepted, but as the nineteenth century progressed Tartu nevertheless established itself as a major centre of Estonian – and not just German or Russian – learning. It's no coincidence that cultural activist Johann Voldemar Jannsen chose Tartu as the place to publish *Eesti Postimees* ("Estonian Courier"), the nation's first genuinely influential newspaper, in 1863. Jannsen also founded the Vanemuine cultural society here in 1868 (an institution that is still going strong; see p.378), and organized the first-ever All-Estonian Song Festival a year later.

This upsurge in Estonian consciousness coincided with a period of creeping Russification throughout the empire. Russian superseded German to become the sole language of instruction at Tartu University in 1889, and the town itself was renamed Yuryev four years later. In other respects the university remained a relatively progressive institution by Tsarist standards: women were allowed to follow courses (but not sit exams) from 1905 and were admitted as full students in 1915. Jews were not descriminated against as they were elsewhere – on the eve of World War I they made up 23 percent of the student body.

During World War I, the university was evacuated to Voronezh – where many of its Russian-speaking professors stayed and later founded a new university, still thriving today. Back in Tartu, a university largely cleansed of Russian and German influences was re-opened in December 1919, the city strengthening its position as the nation's intellectual capital. Appropriately, Tartu was at the centre of opposition to Soviet rule after June 1940, with medical students turning the university's Health Care Society into a front for subversive activities. On July 10, 1941, the society's members led a city-wide revolt against the Soviets, aiming to establish an independent Estonian administration prior to the arrival of the Germans. The latter were unimpressed, closing the university down and planning its rebirth as an elite academy serving the Nazi province of Estland.

After 1945, a revitalized university preserved its pre-eminence in Estonian academic life, but found it difficult to retain international contacts, not least because the presence of a Soviet bomber squadron at Tartu airport rendered the city virtually off-limits to foreigners. Since the regaining of independence, however, the university has lost no time in rejoining the international academic mainstream, with increasing numbers of foreign students and visting lecturers turning it into a more cosmopolitan place than its founder ever imagined.

Arrival, information and getting around

Major points of arrival are conveniently located on the western side of the river. Tartu's **bus station** is ten minutes' walk east of the centre at Turu 2. The delapidated **train station** 1.5km west of the centre looks more like a haunted house than a transport terminal – the ticket office opens about thirty minutes prior to each departure, but there are no other facilities.

Tartu's **tourist office** at Raekoja plats 14 (Mon–Fri 9am–5pm, Sat 10am–3pm; ☎744 2111; ⓦwww.tartu.ee) is an extraordinarily efficient source of information on just about everything in Tartu and the surrounding region. With almost everything of sightseeing interest within walking distance of the city centre, you're unlikely to make use of Tartu's municipal **bus** network unless you're staying in the suburbs. Flat-fare tickets cost 8EEK from kiosks (or 10EEK from the driver) and must be inserted into the ticket-punch machines on board. **Taxi** ranks can be found at the bus station and at the junction of Raekoja plats and Turu; otherwise call Tartu Taksopark (☎742 2222) or Linna Takso (☎736 6666).

Accommodation

There's no shortage of good-quality accommodation in the city centre, although most of it is geared towards foreign businessmen and prices are creeping up. There are a few mid-range choices in the centre and a scattering of cheaper **hotels** and family-run **guesthouses** in the suburbs, although you're well advised to reserve in advance if you're looking for a bargain.

In addition to the hotels and guesthouses listed below, a number of private households in Tartu's suburbs offer **B&B** in the 400–500EEK range, although few of the hosts speak English: you're best off asking the tourist office (see above) about these and asking them to book for you.

Central Tartu
Barclay Ülikooli 8 ☎744 7100, ⓦwww.barclay.ee. Housed in a handsome Art Nouveau office block that once served as the regional HQ of the Soviet army, the *Barclay* is well worth the money if you get one of the east-facing rooms overlooking a leafy square. If you're prepared to hand over the readies go for one of the suites with private sauna. ❻–❼

Draakon Raekoja plats ☎744 2045, ⓦwww.draakon.ee. Tartu's most expensive hotel occupies prime position on the main square and boasts thick carpets and quality furniture. However, standard doubles come with straightforward showers instead of bathtubs – if you want one of those, you'll have to pay a little extra for a "de luxe" room or a suite. ❻–❼

London Rüütli 9 ☎730 5555, ⓦwww.londonhotel.ee. The only hotel in Tartu to have a water feature in the lobby offers smallish but supremely snazzy en-suites with Sat-TV, each furnished in a style that wouldn't look out of place in the coolest of design magazines. De-luxe doubles are slightly bigger than regular rooms and have bathtubs, while suites come with private sauna. The (nowadays disappointingly well-behaved) café-restaurant was a prime hangout of drunkard-intellectuals in the inter-war years. ❻–❼

Oru Villa Oru 1 ☎742 2894, ⓦhttp://oruvilla.ee. Seven-room hotel in the leafy shadow of Toomemägi, housed in the former home of Professor Ants Piip, one of the inter-war state's foreign ministers. Pastel-coloured rooms have TV, tea/coffee-making facilities, and en-suite showers in most cases – the cheaper ones share bathrooms in the hallway. No-smoking throughout. ❹

CENTRAL TARTU

Map labels: Bus station; Kaubamaja department store; Tartu City Museum; Market; Emajõgi; Art Museum; Town Hall; Puppet Film Gallery; St John's Church; Maxgame; Museum of the Nineteenth Century Citizen; University Main Building; Observatory; Angel's Bridge; Toy Museum; University History Museum; Sacrifice Stone; Kissing Hill; Cathedral; Devil's Bridge; Anatomical Theatre; Methodist Church; Zum Zum; TOOMEMÄGI

Street labels: NARVA MNT; RAATUSE; ROOSI; VASKA; KROOSI; FORTUUNA; VABADUSE PST; KOMPANII; GILDI; RÜÜTLI; MAGASINI; LAI; KROONUAIA; JAKOBI; JAANI; MUNGA; LOSSI; ÜLIKOOLI; KÜÜNI; KÜÜTRI; KOIDU; PIKK; SOOLA; HIIA; VANEMUISE; TÄHTVERE; VALLIKRAAVI; K.E.V. BAERI; LUTSU; KLOOSTRI; TARTU MNT

0 100 m

Pallas Riia 4 ☎730 1200, ⓦwww.pallas.ee. On the fourth floor of a glass-and-concrete shopping centre (but named after the Pallas School of Fine Arts, which stood on this spot until destroyed in 1944). There's a refreshing, non-chintzy modernity about the furnishings in the standard rooms, and the suites are decked out in massive reproductions of inter-war works of art. Rooms on the northern side have floor-to-ceiling windows and great views of town. ❺

Park Hotel Vallikraavi 23 ☎742 7000, ⓦwww.parkhotell.ee. Set amid trees on the western side of Toomemägi, this white-cube modernist building dating from the 1930s is beginning to show its age, but the parquet floors and pastel decor are soothing enough. The cheaper rooms come with WC and a wash basin, pricier ones boast en-suite shower and TV. ❷–❹

Tampere maja Jaani 4 ☎738 6300, ⓦwww.tamperemaja.ee. A historic town house refurbished with money from the city of Tampere in Finland to serve as a cultural centre and guesthouse. Two four-bed family rooms and a handful of doubles with en-suite shower and TV – all kitted out with wooden floors, muted colours and tasteful fabrics. ❹

Tartu Soola 3 ☎731 4300, ⓦwww.tartuhotell.ee. A Soviet-era concrete slab just beyond the bus station, offering recently renovated prim en-suites. Less atmospheric than other downtown choices. ❹

Uppsala maja Jaani 7 ☎736 1535, ⓦwww.uppsalamaja.ee. Located in a lusciously restored eighteenth-century house – one of the oldest surviving dwellings in Tartu – intended primarily for visiting academics from Uppsala University, but open to all-comers providing there's space. Only five rooms though, so book ahead. ❹

The suburbs

Aleksandri külalistemaja Aleksandri 42 ☎736 6659, ⓦwww.hot.ee/aleksandri. A renovated nineteenth-century red-brick building on the fringes of the suburban Karlova district, fifteen minutes' walk southeast of the centre. Rooms are sparsely furnished but bright and shipshape – all have TV and all but two come with en-suite WC and shower. Plenty of good-value triples and quads if you're travelling as a family or small group. ❸

Carolina Kreuzwaldi 15 ☎742 2070, ⓔcarolina@hot.ee. A comfy guesthouse 4km north of the centre (you'll see it on the left as you enter town from the Tallinn direction), harbouring a homely warren of odd-shaped rooms, all with en-suite shower and TV. Rooms are no smoking throughout. To get there from the centre, take bus #6 from opposite the Kaubamaja department store to the Teemeistri stop. ❸

Hostel Tähtvere Laulupeo 19 ☎742 1708 or 421 364. A timeworn, but welcoming, guesthouse 1km northwest of the centre, with six rooms, all different – they range from a cramped and musty triple to a palatial double with sofas and a fireplace. Perfectly comfy if you don't mind chipped furniture and colour-clash carpets. No breakfast, but the staff will provide morning tea or coffee if you ask nicely. ❶

Vikerkaare külalistemaja Vikerkaare 40 ☎742 1190, ⓦwww.hot.ee/tdc. A fair-sized B&B in the peaceful Tähtvere suburb, 15–20 minutes' walk northwest of the centre. Smallish but exceedingly comfy rooms, all with shower and TV. Double with private sauna ❸, regular rooms ❷

The City

Tartu's main point of reference is the Emajõgi River, which winds lazily through the city from northwest to southeast. The largely pedestrianized historic centre, centred on the attractive **Raekoja plats**, lies on the west bank of the Emajõgi, while many of the set-piece **university** buildings are just uphill from here on **Toomemägi** ("Cathedral Hill"), a wonderfully leafy area bordered by atmospheric nineteenth-century suburbs.

The Raekoja plats

Tartu's focal point is its **Raekoja plats** ("Town Hall Square"), paved with lumpy cobblestones and surrounded by prim neoclassical buildings, the most eye-catching of which is the lilac-and-orange **Town Hall** (Raekoda) at the head of the square. It was designed in the 1780s by Rostock builder J.H.B. Walter, whose brief was to give the town a European flavour; he duly obliged with this Dutch-influenced edifice. The bell tower emits a shrill music-box-like ditty on the hour – until about 10pm, after which it reverts to discreet bonging sounds.

Directly in front of the Town Hall stands a fountain topped by a three-metre-high statue of a young couple kissing under an umbrella. Unveiled in 1998 to provide

Tartu with a millennial marker, it was immediately criticized for spoiling the eighteenth-century character of the square – pictures of the statue have nevertheless found their way onto most of the mugs and T-shirts sold by nearby souvenir shops.

At the eastern end of the square, the house at no. 18, leaning crookedly to one side (owing to a shifting of the water table), was originally the pied-a-terre of Mikhail **Barclay de Tolly** (1761–1818), a Livonian baron of Scottish descent and one of Tsar Alexander I's top generals during the Napoleonic Wars. Roundly criticized by St Petersburg society for his strategy of retreating before Napoleon's advance in 1812, Barclay de Tolly was vindicated when the French ran out of steam, fleeing homewards with the onset of winter. De Tolly's country estate was some 70km southwest of Tartu in Jõegeveste – where his mausoleum can still be seen. His house here in Tartu now accommodates the **Tartu Art Museum** (Tartu kunstimuuseum; Wed–Sun 11am–6pm; 10EEK, free on Fri; ✆www.tartmus.ee), a vast collection embracing works by just about any Estonian ever to pick up a paintbrush. The collection is regularly shifted around in order to accommodate temporary themed exhibitions and it's impossible to predict what will be on display at any given time.

South of Raekoja plats

South of Raekoja plats, pedestrianized Küüni heads past a zone of modern shops, passing first through a garden graced with a bust of Barclay de Tolly. Behind him loom the gothic-looking gables of an Art Nouveau office block, now occupied by the *Barclay Hotel* (see p.379). Immediately south of the hotel on the corner of Vallikraavi (just outside the *Wilde Irish Pub*; see p.388) is one of the most popular pieces of sculpture in Tartu, showing **Oscar Wilde** and his Estonian near-contemporary **Eduard Vilde** (see p.321) engaged in earnest conversation – although one wonders what the straight-laced Vilde would have made of the high priest of camp had the pair ever met in real life. As well as being a rather obvious play on the similarity of the two writers' names, the ensemble also points up the fact that Vilde – who led a bohemian existence in Paris and Berlin in the years before World War I – is the only Estonian cultural figure who can compete with the aura of celebrity decadence cultivated by Wilde.

A few steps further south, in an alley between Küüni and Ülikooli at Kaupmehe 6, the **Puppet Film Gallery** (Filminukkude galerii; Wed–Sun 11am–6pm; 10EEK) celebrates the achievements of Nukufilm, the Tallinn-based animation studio established in 1957 and famed for its use of puppets. The small, but captivating, display includes several superbly modelled stage sets, including a deliciously chaotic bar scene used in Riho Unt's 1997 film *Back to Europe*. If you arrive during a quiet spell, the curator may well show you examples of the studio's output on video.

North of Raekoja plats

North of Raekoja plats, Ülikooli runs past the colonnaded facade of **Tartu University Main Building** (Tartu ülikooli peahoone), a cool, lemon-and-meringue-coloured confection designed by J.W. Krause, the architect who presided over the expansion of the university once the Tsarist authorities permitted its reopening in 1802. Pass through the unassuming main doorway and head left towards the south wing to find the **Tartu University Art Museum** (Tartu ülikooli kunstmuuseum; Mon–Fri 11am–5pm; 8EEK), where plaster replicas of ancient artworks throng a suite of galleries decked out in imperial Roman style. Familiar Classical-era friends like the *Discus Thrower*, the *Belvedere Apollo* and the *Venus de Milo* are joined by comparatively less well-known characters such as the *Suicidal Celt,* here portrayed plunging a dagger into his throat.

The art museum sells tickets for two remaining public attractions in the university building: the first, the **Assembly Hall** (Aula; Mon–Fri 11am–5pm; 10EEK), turns out however to be just a big, grey–white function room, and the decision to open it up to the public seems more like a statement of the university's preening self-regard than anything else. Considerably more interesting is the **Lock-up** (Kartster; Mon–Fri 11am–4.30pm; 5EEK), located up in the attic of the south wing, where badly behaved students had to endure a few days of solitary confinement. According to the exhaustive list of offences pinned to the wall, you could get three days here for being rowdy in the streets – were such punishments still in force today, half the university would be cooped up here seven days a week.

North of the University Main Building, the corner of Ülikooli and Gildi is graced by a modern **statue of Jan Tõnisson** (1869–1942), who was Estonia's prime minister for a brief spell and long-serving editor of the Tartu newspaper *Postimees*. As the most respected organ in the country, *Postimees* traditionally symbolized Tartu's pre-eminence over Tallinn in the field of journalism as well as in that of academia – until the paper's head office finally moved to the capital in the mid-1990s.

Along Ülikooli and Jaani

Continuing along **Ülikooli** and its extension, **Jaani**, you soon come to the red-brick bulk of the Gothic **St John's Church** (Jaani kirik), founded in 1330, bombed out in 1944 and left half-ruined until 1989, when the restorers moved in and added a new spire. The building is still inaccessible, but from the street you can admire the gallery of terracotta heads arranged in niches around the main entrance. Placed here some time in the fourteenth century, they portray mostly medieval archetypes – nobles, tradesmen, peasants and so on – and were no doubt modelled on Tartu folk of the time.

Diagonally opposite the church, the **Museum of the Nineteenth-Century Citizen** at Jaani 16 (19. sajandi Tartu linnakodaniku muuseum; Wed–Sun: April–Sept 11am–6pm; Oct–March 10am–3pm; 10EEK) features the kind of furnishings and textiles that would have graced the dwelling of a middle-ranking merchant family. With a kitchen lit by candlelight and a grandfather clock ticking away in the background, it's a charming period piece.

The Botanical Garden

Following Jaani to the end and turning right into Lai soon brings you to the **Botanical Garden** at no. 38 (Botanikaaed; daily: summer 7am–9pm; winter 7am–7pm; free). Tropical and subtropical plants are packed into the central Palm House (Palmimaja; daily 10am–5pm; 10EEK), behind which lies a small, but enormously varied, display of outdoor plants, occupying what's left of a defensive earthwork built to protect the northeastern corner of the (now disappeared) town wall. The most striking of the sculptures littering the garden is an imperious-looking Lithuanian fertility spirit carved from a tree trunk, presented to Tartu by Vilnius University in 1982.

Toomemägi

From behind the Town Hall, Lossi tänav climbs **Toomemägi** ("Cathedral Hill"), site of a fortress and a cathedral during the Middle Ages, both of which were abandoned after damage in the Livonian Wars. The area was left derelict until the refounding of the university in 1802, when it was chosen as the site of several key academic buildings and generously planted with the trees that make it such a marvellously relaxing spot today.

Presiding over the bottom end of Lossi is a bust of Russian medical hero **Nikolai Pirogov**, who taught at Tartu in the 1840s and went on to become a pioneer in modern surgical technique. A kind of Florence Nightingale with hairy whiskers, Pirogov introduced new standards of cleanliness and organization to Tsarist military hospitals during the Crimean war, and hordes of high-born Russian ladies thronged to Sevastopol to join his nursing staff. The steeply banked park behind the bust is a favourite place for lounging around in summer – especially with students who, suitably armed with take-out beers, turn the area into a vast outdoor bar.

From here, Lossi heads uphill beneath Angel's Bridge (Inglisild), a brightly painted wooden structure dating from the nineteenth century – carry on over the brow of the hill and you'll pass under its counterpart on the other side, the Devil's Bridge. Heading right at the brow will bring you face to face with the stark, skeletal remains of the red-brick **Cathedral** (Toomkirik), built by the Knights of the Sword during the thirteenth century. Although Tartu became a thoroughly Protestant city in the 1520s, the Poles returned the cathedral to the Catholic fold when they took control of Tartu in 1582, and the building's destruction by fire in 1624 – the result of sparks flying from a Midsummer Night's bonfire – was seen by many contemporaries as a sign of divine displeasure. It was J.W. Krause, the architect in charge of the redevelopment of Toomemägi at the beginning of the nineteenth century, who hit on the idea of leaving the bulk of the cathedral as a romantic ruin, while rebuilding the choir to serve as the university library – the charmingly lop-sided results of which can be seen today.

Since 1979, the library has served as the **University History Museum** (Wed–Sun 11am–5pm; 10EEK), a three-floor collection beginning (at the top) with portraits of the university's first rectors and a diorama of a seventeenth-century anatomical theatre, in which intestines hang from the table like a string of butcher's best sausages. On the floor below, a stuffy display of professors through the ages is enlivened by the re-created physics lab of Rector Georg Friedrich Parrot (1765–1852), where a host of beautifully crafted instruments includes an electrostatic generator constructed from Karelian birchwood and turquoise glass tubes. On the same floor, one hall is preserved as it was in the nineteenth century, with rows of musty books and an unlabelled dummy of what looks suspiciously like the library's founder, Professor J.K.S Morgenstern, who also established the University Art Museum (see p.382). Nearby are the sabres and flags brandished by nineteenth-century student fraternities – predominantly German-speaking affairs until 1870, when the first Estonian student association emerged. All the fraternities had tricolour banners, and in 1884 the Estonians chose a blue, black and white colour scheme (by this time it was the only combination left), subsequently adopted as Estonia's national flag. Despite being banned during the Soviet period, fraternities are once again a central feature of university life, not least because of the networking opportunities that membership (by invitation only) affords.

Toomemägi's main landmark north of the museum is a monument to one of Tartu University's most famous alumni, **Karl Ernst von Baer** (1792–1876), whose pioneering work in the field of embryology was credited by Charles Darwin as being a major step towards the development of evolutionary theory. Looking west from here it's easy to miss the so-called **Sacrifice Stone** (Ohvrikivi), an unobtrusive lump of rock where pre-Christian Estonians would place offerings to the departed and where present-day students come to burn their exam papers. Behind it rises a knoll known as **Musumägi** or "Kissing Hill", possibly because the path leading up it is barely wide enough to allow two people to walk side by side without rubbing up against each other.

Just east of here, paths descend towards the **Toy Museum** at Lai 1 (Mänguasjamuuseum; Wed–Sun 11am–6pm; 10EEK; ⊛www.mm.ee), an entertaining jumble of playthings through the ages, including the inevitable display of dolls from around the world and a model train set.

From the Anatomical Theatre to the Methodist Church

Returning to Angels Bridge and heading for the southern end of Toomemägi brings you face to face with the impressive, barrel-shaped **Anatomical Theatre**, designed by J.W. Krause in 1803. In many ways the university's trademark – medicine was always one of the most prestigious subjects taught here (and still is) – the building was in use as an anatomical theatre right up until 1999 and is currently being restored. Pondering the parkscape just in front of the theatre is a bust of **Friedrich Robert Faehlmann** (1798–1850), the Germanized Estonian who played a leading role in the founding of the Estonian Learned Society (see p.378), and whose enthusiasm for collecting old folk tales inspired F. R. Kreuzwald (see p.393) to compile Estonia's epic, *Kalevipoeg*. A short distance further south, a building that looks like a decapitated windmill turns out to be the **University Observatory**, also designed by the ubiquitous Krause. Best known among the astronomers who came to ogle celestial bodies here was F.W. Struve (1793–1864), one of the first scientists to accurately measure the distances of various stars from the earth – he's celebrated by an angular concrete monument out front.

The sunken street of **Vallikraavi** coils its way around the southern end of Toomemägi, presenting a choice of itineraries: either back towards the *Wilde Pub* (see p.388), or uphill and west past a brand-new **Methodist Church** (Metodisti kirik). With its angular belfry clad in copper-coloured strips and minimalist interior decor (the altar would do quite nicely as a desk in an ultra-cool office), the church is as popular with devotees of modern design as it is with the Christian faithful.

South of Toomemägi

Beyond the Methodist Church, Vallikraavi curves south and comes out on Kuperjanovi. Here, at no. 9, is the **Estonian National Museum** (Eesti rahvamuuseum; Wed–Sun 11am–6pm; 20EEK, free on Fri; ✪www.erm.ee), offering an exemplary overview of the nation's ethnography, with some imaginatively re-created farmhouse interiors, good English labelling and a comprehensive display of folk costume from all over the country. Rakes the size of small trees serve as a reminder of how haymaking and preparation of winter fodder was a matter of life and death to the average Estonian farmstead, while a sizeable collection of carved, wooden beer tankards introduce a section on village feasts and holidays. There's an astounding array of other handicrafts, including hand-woven textiles that look far more exotic than the bland, linen tablecloths sold in the Estonian souvenir shops of today. As if in deliberate counterpoint to the natural creativity of the Estonian peasant, a re-created living room from 1978 is filled with the dull-brown furniture that was standard issue in the Soviet Union.

A short detour north of the museum along Kastani will take you past some evocatively shabby, nineteenth-century buildings, including a palatial-looking wooden apartment house at no. 17, with intricately carved door and window frames. Part fairytale cottage and part medieval fortress, the building on the corner of Kastani and Näituse once served as the headquarters of the Neobaltia student fraternity (dissolved when the Baltic Germans were repatriated in 1940) and now houses a **German Cultural Centre** – German artists sometimes exhibit in the small gallery inside (Mon–Fri 9am–5pm).

Heading south and west from the National Museum along Kastani then Tiigi brings you out onto a leafy square centred on a smooth granite statue of **Jakob Hurt** (1839–1907), whose mania for transcribing village songs and collecting traditional artefacts inspired a new appreciation of folk culture among educated nineteenth-century Estonians – and provided the impetus for the establishment of the National Museum in 1905. A trio of less-than-gripping museums lurks in the university buildings along Vanemuise tänav on the southern side of the square: the **Estonian Literature Museum** at no. 44 (Eesti kirjandus muuseum; Mon–Fri 9am–5pm; free), whose changing exhibitions on great writers and their works are usually labelled in Estonian only; the **Zoology Museum** at no. 46 (Wed–Sun 10am–4pm; 5EEK); and the **Geology Museum** in the same building (same times and prices).

The KGB Cells Museum

Considerably more compelling is the **KGB Cells Museum** one block south at Riia 15B (KGB kongid; Tues–Sat 11am–4pm; 5EEK), where the so-called "Grey

House" (Hallis majas) served as the regional headquarters of the Soviet secret police. As well as preserving the basement cells in their original state, the museum offers a history lesson in Soviet methods of control. Any lack of English-language labelling is more than made up for by the narrative power of the grainy photographs on display, recalling the deportations of 1941 and 1949, as well as the gruelling conditions of life in Siberia experienced by the victims. Most poignant of all are the pictures of idealistic schoolchildren who joined secret patriotic organizations like the Tartu-based Blue-Black-and-White (named after the colours of the Estonian flag), only to be confined in the cells here before being sent to work camps in the east.

Riia mnt and Karlova

Another 400m southwest along Riia, the red-brick **St Paul's Church** (Paulusekirik) is a highly individual piece of Estonian inter-war architecture, its central tower resembling a bloated Egyptian obelisk thrust skywards by rocket boosters. Continuing along Riia for another five minutes brings you to the **House Museum of Oskar Luts**, Riia 38 (Oskar Lutsu majamuuseum; Wed–Sat 11am–5pm, Sun 1–5pm; 15EEK), celebrating the Tartu-trained pharmacist and author (1887–1953), best known for the semi-autobiographical *Kevade* ("Spring"), a classic account of growing up in the Estonian countryside. The house where he lived from 1918 until his death is packed with inter-war furnishings, old photographs of Tartu and the hideous-looking puppets used in animated films based on Luts's childrens' story "Forest Fairytale". Luts was one of the pillars of the inter-war literary establishment and a 1937 newsreel (the curator will probably run the video) shows the great and the good flocking to his fiftieth birthday party.

Returning back to town along Riia, it's worth making a southward detour along streets like Tähe or Kalevi into the suburb of **Karlova**, famous for the handsome array of nineteenth-century wooden houses that still line its streets. Some of the best are to be found 750m southeast of Riia along Tolstoi.

Northwest of the centre

There's enough interesting architecture in the northwestern suburbs of Tartu to justify a brief stroll up **Jakobi**, the street which connects the city centre with a plateau of residential streets above. The **Childrens' Art School** at Jakobi 32 is a wonderful example of a pre-World-War-I timber mansion, with a fanciful medieval-style central tower and lovingly carved door and window frames. Jakobi's extension, Kreuzwaldi, enters **Tahtvere**, an elite suburb built for university professors in the 1920s and packed with the kind of Bauhaus-influenced houses that were all the rage with the inter-war Estonian middle class. The best known of these is the white-cube **Villa Tammekann** at Kreuzwaldi 6, designed by Alvar Aalto in 1932 and now occupied by a university research institute. From here it's only a ten-minute walk to the **Song Festival Grounds** (Laululava), on the very edge of Tartu, where a stage capable of accommodating 10,000 singers shelters under a boldly contemporary sea-shell canopy, built in 1994. Built to symbolize Tartu's place in Estonian choral culture (it was here that the first ever national song festival was held; see p.387), it's nowadays the venue for pop concerts and musicals, as well as strictly folk-singing performances. Moving on, you can either dally in the adjacent amusement park, or return to the centre via the streets of **Supilinn** immediately to the east, a ramshackle residential area of old wooden houses and vegetable plots. Thoroughfares such as Oa ("Bean street), Kartuli ("Potato street") and Herne ("Pea street") help explain how the suburb got its name – "Soup Town".

Across the river

At the eastern end of Raekoja plats, pedestrian traffic bustles across the River Emajõgi by means of a small bridge built in modest commemoration of the so-called Stone Bridge, an elegant eighteenth-century structure and a symbol of the city until the retreating Red Army destroyed it in 1941. A five-minute walk through parkland on the opposite bank takes you to the **Tartu City Museum** at Narva mnt 23 (Tartu linnamuuseum; Tues–Sun 11am–6pm; 20EEK; ⓦwww .tartu.ee/linnamuuseum), an easy-on-the-eye display of furniture, prints and porcelain in a lusciously restored eighteenth-century mansion. Highlights include a round table of truly Arthurian proportions, around which the Estonian–Soviet Peace Treaty was signed on February 2, 1920, and a fascinating model of Tartu as it was in 1940 – free of the Soviet-era tower blocks that now clutter the suburbs.

A ten-minute walk northeast along Narva mnt is the **Church of St George** (Jüri kirik), the most delightful of Tartu's Orthodox places of worship. Like Barclay de Tolly's house, it has a slightly crooked appearance owing to shifting foundations and, resplendent in a bright-pink paint job, it looks rather like a wobbly cake. Just beyond, at the junction of Narva mnt and Puiestee, a monument marks the spot where the very first **All-Estonian Song Festival** took place in 1869. Featuring a row of dismembered heads squashed beneath a hunk of granite, it looks less celebratory than its creators intended. The festival, largely put together by newspaper editor Johann Voldemar Jannsen and his daughter, the poet Lydia Koidula (see p.356), was a huge undertaking, bringing together 46 choirs, 5 brass bands, 800 singers and an audience of 15,000. Koidula wrote the patriotic hymn *Mu Isamaa* ("My Fatherland"; closely based on the Finnish patriotic song Maame) especially for the festival and it subsequently became Estonia's national anthem.

Eating and drinking

There's a plethora of places to **eat** in Tartu and it's a tribute to the cosmopolitan nature of the place that plenty of ethnic and vegetarian fare exists alongside the usual north European porky favourites. As you would expect from a university town, there are **pubs and bars** in abundance, many of which offer a full menu of main-course food. Restaurants are usually **open** daily until 11pm, bars and pubs till midnight Sunday to Thursday and 2 or 3am on Friday and Saturday.

You can pick up **picnic supplies** from the covered market at Riia 1 or the supermarket inside the Kaubamaja department store, Riia 2 (Mon–Fri 7am–10pm, Sat 7am–8pm, Sun 9am–5pm).

Cafés

Bistroc Raekoja plats 9. Basic, but reliable, source of *karbonaad* and other pork-chop staples, alongside some daintier salads and open sandwiches. Mon–Sat till 6pm, Sun till 5pm.

Café Werner Ülikooli 11. The kind of genteel coffee-and-cakes venue your grandmother would like (the quarrelsome intellectuals who thronged the place in Soviet times having moved on). Courtyard seating out the back. Till 9pm.

Café Wilde Vallikraavi 4. A roomy, relaxing place doling out the best coffee in town, a good choice of teas and delicious cakes. Till 9pm.

Kondiitriäri Pere Leib Rüütli 5. An all-pervading smell of coffee and freshly baked nibbles makes this one of the best places in the centre to sit down for a day-time breather. Croissants and pastries for breakfast, scrumptious cakes for later. Mon–Fri till 7pm, Sat till 5pm, Sun till 4pm.

Rotundi kohvik Toomemägi. A summer-only café in a cosy octagonal pavilion, with outdoor seating beneath the trees of Toomemägi. Till 5pm.

Teatrikohvik Vanemuise 6. A roomy establishment inside the Vanemuine theatre and concert hall offering a full range of drinks, as well as reasonably cheap salads and meat-and-potatoes main courses. Relatively staid during the daytime, it turns into a hip bar with DJs on weekend evenings. Till 11pm.

Ülikooli kohvik Ülikooli 20. A student café with cheap and tasty canteen food. Located in a suite of lovingly restored rooms in a historic house, next door to the main university building. Till 5pm.

Restaurants

Atlantis Narva mnt 2. Civilized but not over-expensive dining in a curved, glass-fronted building overlooking the river. You'll get the same pork, chicken and beef as elsewhere, but with a bit more stylish service and presentation.

Bagua Pikk 40. An informal eatery with Chinese menu in one half, Thai in the other. Sufficiently spicy and exotic to make a trip over the river worthwhile.

China Garden Raekoja 3. A moody red cellar offering up a familiar range of Chinese dishes, cooked in a not-exactly-authentic way, but tasty and satisfying nonetheless. And there is a garden (well, a yard at least) for al-fresco dining in summer.

Dolce Vita Kompanii 10. Quick, reasonably priced pizzas served up in surroundings more comfortable than the usual fast-food places. Appealing soups and salads too.

Entri Riia 4. A stylish café-restaurant whose interior manages to combine futuristic design and 1950s retro at the same time. The meat-and-potatoes fare is reliable if not spectacular, and the place fills up with fashionable young drinkers at weekends.

Gruusia Saatkond Rüütli 8. Refined and relaxing, the "Georgian Embassy" grills a decent shish kebab as well as offering satisfyingly exotic stews flavoured with walnuts, plums or peppers. Dishes like *lobia* (bean stew) or *hachapuri* (Georgian bread and melted cheese) make a good lunch.

Pronto Pizzeria Küütri 3. Serving up thin-crust pies with non-Italian ingredients, this is a conveniently central, cost-effective stomach filler rather than one for the cognoscenti. Take-out service available.

Püssirohu Kelder Lossi 28. Housed in a cavernous, red-brick armoury built under Peter the Great, *Püssirohu Kelder* is a suitably atmospheric place in which to swill beer at big wooden tables and tuck into platefuls of pork and sauerkraut. A wide choice of traditional Estonian dishes, and none too expensive.

Taverna Raekoja 20. A cosy basement restaurant with an Italian flavour – the regular repertoire of porky Estonian fare augmented by a good range of pizzas, and a few pasta choices.

Tsink Plekk Pang Küütri 6. Tasty Chinese-influenced food and enormous pots of tea in wonderfully relaxed, loungey surroundings. Also a good place for a drink, with DJs providing the entertainment at weekends.

Bars and pubs

Illegaard Ülikooli 5. A snazzy subterranean hideaway which used to be a private members' club and preserves an intimate feel. Jazzy background music and occasional live gigs.

Krooks Jakobi 34. A laid-back, red-brick bar decked out in an engaging clutter of rock album covers and beer-related bric-a-brac. Salads, beer snacks and a couple of daily specials on the menu. Usually open later than the other bars in the centre.

Ristiisa Pubi Küüni 7. A roomy city-centre boozing venue with a 1920s speakeasy theme, attracting a cross-section of Tartu society. Full menu of food.

Wilde Irish Pub Vallikraavi 4. A comfortable, welcoming place a floor above the café of the same name, attracting sizeable contingents of students, academics, yuppies and expats. Middle-class Tartu at play.

Zavood Lai 30. A studenty bar near the Botanical Garden with post-industrial decor, late opening hours, and eccentric indie sounds on the CD player.

Nightlife and entertainment

Tartu's main **theatre** and **concert** venue, the Vanemuine, Vanemuise 6 (box office Mon–Sat 10am–7pm; ☎744 0165, ⓦwww.vanemuine.ee), is one of the most prestigious in the country, presenting top-quality drama, classical music, opera and dance performed by top acts from Tallinn or abroad – either in the comfortable modern main building, or in the smaller but equally stylish nineteenth-century auditorium just uphill at Vanemuise 45A. A range of broadly contemporary theatre and dance performances also takes take place in the modern auditorium of the riverside Sadamateater, Soola 5B (box office Mon–Sat noon–5pm & 1hr before performance; ☎744 1138). Big productions of an operatic or musical nature are staged at the Song Festival Grounds in summer – you'll find posters advertising these extravaganzas hard to avoid.

Tartu is rather poorly served with **cinemas**, with Illusiooni, Raatuse 97, and the two-screen Ekraan, Riia 14 (ⓦwww.kosmos.ee), ensuring that there's a mind-boggling choice of three mainstream releases in town at any given time.

Clubs

The venues listed below are usually open from Wednesday to Saturday. Themed club nights and DJ evenings also take place at *Teatrikohvik* (see "Cafés" p.387), *Tsink Plekk Pang* (see "Restaurants" above), and the Sadamateater (see above).

The University Spring Days and other annual events

The best-known and probably most enjoyable of Tartu's annual events is the **University Spring Days** (Ülikooli kevadpaevad), a five-day fiesta straddling May 1, when the town is transformed into a vast open-air student party. Highlights include a fund-raising rubber-boat regatta on the Emajõgi River, and the night of May 1 itself, when the town's pubs are allowed (nay, expected) to stay open all night.

Other festivals include the **Soup City Days** (Supilinna päevad), when open-air concerts are organized in the suburb of Supilinn (see p.386) over the last weekend of April; and the **International Dance Festival** (Rahvusvaheslisel tantsufestival) in late May/early June. Rather than a specific event, the **Tartu Summer Music Festival** is the general banner under which a broad range of classical and jazz concerts take place from early June through to late August.

Atlantis Narva mnt 2 ⓦwww.atlantis.ee. A riverside disco of many years' standing, packing in a youngish, hedonistic crowd.

Club Tallinn Narva mnt 27 ⓦwww.club-tallinn.ee. Main gathering point for the more style-conscious music freaks, offering a variety of cutting-edge sounds and the best in the way of big-name DJs. A short hop across the river from the old town.

Pattaya Turu 21 ⓦwww.pattaya.ee. Enjoyable mish-mash of top-40, techno and latino material in this swish club just south of the bus station. More dress-code-obsessed than the other places, but not discouragingly exclusive by any means.

Varjend Pargi ⓦwww.varjend.ee. Hard-edged dance music and live bands in a graffiti-covered bunker in the Karlova district – check posters before setting out.

XS Vaksali 21 ⓦwww.xs.ee. Mainstream disco, techno and hip-hop in popular club opposite the train station.

Listings

Bicycle rental Jalgratas, Laulupeo 19 ☏742 1731; Velospets, Riia 130 ☏738 0406, ⓦwww.velospets.ee.

Books For the biggest range of maps, local guidebooks and English-language paperbacks, head for Apollo, Küüni 1; or Tartu Ülikooli Raamatupood (Tartu University Bookshop), Ülikooli 11.

Ferry trips Tartu Sadam, Soola 5 (☏734 0026, ⓦwww.transcom.ee/tartusadam) organizes short cruises on the Emajõgi, as well as longer excursions to the island of Piirissaar on Lake Peipsi.

Hospital The main city hospital is at Puusepa tee, 2km southwest of the centre (for an ambulance call ☏112).

Internet Maxgame, Rüütli 21; Virtuaal Pikk 40; Zum Zum, Küüni 2.

Left luggage At the bus station (Mon–Sat 6am–3pm & 3.30–9pm; Sun 7am–3pm &

3.30–9pm).

Pharmacy Raekoja apteek, Town Hall, Raekoja plats (24hr).

Police Raekoja plats 7. In emergencies ring ☏112.

Post office Vanemuise 7 (Mon–Fri 7am–7pm, Sat 9am–4pm).

Ski equipment rental To get kitted out before heading for the slopes of Otepää (see p.390), try Surfar, Baeri 1 ☏744 1359.

Swimming Aura, just beyond the bus station at Turu 14, is a massively popular indoor complex with fifty-metre pool, paddling sections and water slides. For outdoor bathing, the beach at the Anne Canal, just across the river from the city centre at the southeastern end of Pikk, is nowhere near as nice as the stretch of the River Emajõgi northwest of town, reached by walking along Ujula from the Kroonuaia bridge.

South of Tartu

South of Tartu lies the one genuinely hilly region in the whole of Estonia, a glacier-sculpted landscape of smooth, dome-shaped heights and lake-filled depressions that stretches all the way to the Latvian border. With few summits exceeding 300m above sea level there's little for ambitious hillwalkers to get excited about, but it's a visually arresting area all the same, with swathes of pine forest, deciduous woodland, arable land and pasture combining to produce a crowded palette of greens.

The principal destination in this part of the country is **Otepää**, a small town set among rippling hills that becomes an important centre for both downhill and cross-country skiing in winter. Further south, the larger, but equally laid-back, town of **Võru** offers a couple of worthwhile museums, but is really a staging-post en route to attractive villages lying in the folds of the hills, like Haanja and Rõuge.

Otepää

Forty-five kilometres southwest of Tartu and reached by regular bus, the country town of **OTEPÄÄ** is the best place to see this lakes-and-hillocks landscape at its best – something that has been recognized by generations of urban Estonians, for whom it has been a favourite holiday retreat ever since the inter-war years. The mellow beauty of the surroundings – enhanced by the presence of Lake Pühajärv just 3km south of town – has helped turn it into the most popular inland summer resort in the country, and there's a correspondingly wide choice of accommodation in and around town. As the only place in Estonia possessing a sufficient number of slopes to make downhill skiing worth bothering with, it's also an increasingly popular venue for winter week-enders, when Otepää's pubs and hotel bars take on a new lease of life.

The town is full to bursting for the **Tartu Marathon** (Ⓦ www.tartumaraton.ee), a cross-country skiing race that takes place on the first or second Sunday in February, starting at the Otepää ski stadium and winding up 63km later in the town of Elva, southwest of Tartu. The same course is pressed into service for the Tartu Cycle Marathon in mid-September.

Otepää's **bus station** is right behind the Town Hall, inside which you'll find a helpful **tourist office** (Mon–Fri 9am–5pm, Sat 10am–3pm; ☏765 5364, Ⓔ otepaa@visitestonia.com), well stocked with local maps and brochures.

Accommodation

There's a handsome choice of **hotels** in Otepää and the surrounding region, and the tourist office can book you into local **B&Bs** (❶–❷), either in town or in the neighbouring countryside. The price codes listed below refer to the room rates charged during Otepää's two high seasons (Jan–Feb, July–Aug). Some hotels officially drop their prices outside these periods, and others may well be open to bargaining – especially if you're travelling midweek.

Bernhard Kolga 22A ☏766 9600, Ⓦ www.bernhard.ee. A classy place 3km southeast of town and a short walk from Lake Pühajärv, offering balconied en-suite rooms decked out in warm reds and browns. Indoor pool, and free morning sauna. ❹

Kesklinna Hostel Lipuväljak 11 ☏765 5993 or 55095. Despite the "hostel" tag, this place on the main street offers smart modern rooms with furniture-showroom fittings, TV and shower. Lack of breakfast is the only drawback. ❸

Kuutsemäe Puhkekeskus Arula village ☏766 9007, Ⓦ www.kuutsemae.ee. Holiday centre 11km southwest of Otepää, in close proximity to several downhill runs. Four- to six-person self-catering cottages (2400EEK/night) and double rooms in the main guesthouse. Summer ❶; winter ❸.

Pühajärve Pühajärve ☏766 5500, Ⓔ pjpk@pjpk.ee, Ⓦ www.pyhajarve.com. A classic inter-war hotel with modern annexes tacked on either side, offering a superb lakeshore position and a variety of on-site spa facilities. Rooms are done out in pleasant pastel colours with chic Nordic-style furnishings. Doubles with private sauna ❹, regular en-suites ❸

Scandic Hotel Karupesa Tehvandi 1A ☏766 1500, Ⓦ www.scandic-hotels.com. Medium-sized hotel with all the creature comforts, a five-minute walk south of the town centre. Some rooms come with views towards Linnamägi and the parish church. ❹

Setanta Nüpli ☏766 8200, Ⓦ www.setanta.ee. A nine-room B&B above a popular pub of the same name, perched above the Pühajärv shore – perfect if you want a lakeside location and don't mind staying up as late as the bar patrons downstairs. Rooms come with woody furnishings and en-suite shower – prices depend on whether they look out towards the lake or not. ❸

Tehvandi Nüpli ☏766 9500, Ⓦ www.tehvandi.ee. Cosy en-suite rooms in a winter sports training centre – a concrete horseshoe that looks like a missile siloh, right beside the cross-country skiing tracks. ❷

The Town

Otepää's ridge-top town centre looks out towards a series of pudding-shaped hills. The first of these to the east is crowned by the **parish church**, a dainty Baroque edifice whose exterior is decorated with plaques recalling the one historical event for which Otepää is famous: on June 4, 1884 members of Tartu University's Estonian student fraternity came here to consecrate the blue-black-and-white tricolour they had chosen as their banner. Obligingly stitched together by fraternity members' wives and girlfriends, the tricolor was subsequently adopted as the Estonian state flag and Otepää has been enshrined as a low-key patriotic pilgrimage centre ever since. Opposite the church's main door, a memorial honouring those who fell in the 1918–20 War of Independence shares the history of many similar monuments up and down the country – erected in 1928, it was removed by the Soviets in 1950, only to be restored to its rightful place in 1989.

Five hundred metres due south of the parish church, paths curl their way towards the summit of **Linnamägi**, a low wooded hill which served Iron Age Estonian chieftains as a natural stronghold until German crusading knights expelled them from it in the thirteenth century. Apart from a few stretches of reconstructed wall there's nothing much to see here now, but the bare hilltop offers excellent views back towards the church and the rippling hills to the south, where you'll see the summit of Otepää's ski-jump ramp poking up above the trees.

Lake Pühajärv

From the centre of Otepää it's an easy thirty-minute walk to the northern shore of **Lake Pühajärv** the journey is also made by about twelve daily buses (destination Kariku or Valga), which drop off beside the *Pühajärve* hotel. About 3km from north to south and 1km across, this serene stretch of water occupies an important place in Estonian folklore – according to legend, it was formed by the tears of a mother grieving for five sons killed in battle and its waters have had healing powers ever since – especially if drunk on Midsummer's Eve. Most visitors only get as far as the northern end of the lake, where there's a sizeable sandy beach, pedaloes for rent and a couple of waterfront cafés. To get away from the throng it's well worth exploring the thirteen-kilometre-long hiking route that follows the lake's heavily indented shoreline (partly on asphalt road, partly off-road), passing through an enthralling landscape of coastal meadows and golden-brown reed beds. You'll probably catch sight of plenty of grebes and ducks on the way, with sandpipers, kingfishers and herons occasionally making an appearance towards the quieter, southern end of the lake.

For one weekend in mid-July the northern shores of Pühajärv play host to the **Beach Party**, Estonia's biggest pop/rock festival, when bands and DJs perform to up to 20,000 revellers, many of whom pitch tents in the lakeside camp grounds specially set aside for the occasion.

Skiing around Otepää

The main **downhill skiing** areas around Otepää are at Väike Munamägi, 3km southeast of the town centre, and Kuutsemäe, 11km southwest. At both places you'll find an undemanding range of 150- to 250-metre-long slopes served by simple drag lifts and kiosks renting out gear. In addition, there's an impressive network of **cross-country skiing** routes in the area, many of them fanning out from the Winter Sports Stadium on the southeastern outskirts of town.

Eating and drinking

The most central place for an inexpensive **meal** is *Raekohvik*, behind the Town Hall, dishing out pastries, salads and simple main meals until 7pm. *Oti Pubi*, occupying a glass-fronted cylinder right by the bus station, does reliable cheap set lunches as well as more substantial main meals, while *Hermanni*, diagonally opposite the

Town Hall on Lipuväljak, offers more of the same in an enjoyable pub-like interior plastered with ski memorabilia. Slightly further afield, *Setanta*, on the eastern shore of Pühajärv, is a roomy wooden-floor pub with a big verandah overlooking the lake and serves a good choice of pork- and fish-based dishes.

Võru

Ranged along the eastern shores of Lake Tamula, the quiet provincial town of **VÕRU** is of relatively recent origin – it was founded by decree of Catherine the Great in 1784 – which helps to explain its neat, grid-plan appearance. The long, straight strip of Jüri tänav runs through the centre, separating the modern, concrete parts of town to the northeast from an altogether more charming neighbourhood of timber houses to the southwest. Heading into the latter along Katariina brings you to the **Võru District Museum** at no. 11 (Võrumaa muuseum; Wed–Sun 11am–6pm; 10EEK), a fairly traditional display accompanied by Estonian- and Russian-language labelling. The most venerable item in the collection is the skull of a Stone Age woman, thought to date from the 4th millennium BC, making it the oldest human remain yet found in Estonia. There's also a history of the Võru region as told through old photographs, domestic knick-knacks and an at times eccentric choice of artefacts: a display case devoted to the political confusion that followed World War I contains the visiting card of local Bolshevik leader Oskar Leegen and the noose used by German occupying forces to hang him. Inter-war agricultural life is illustrated by the inclusion of a machine that looks like an enormous meat grinder – it's actually a hand-operated contraption for separating the milk from the cream.

At the bottom of Katariina turn left into Kreuzwaldi and after ten minutes you come to the **F.R. Kreuzwald Memorial Museum** at no. 31 (F.R. Kreuzwaldi memoriaalmuuseum; Wed–Sun 11am–6pm; 10EEK), occupying the property where the author of Estonia's national epic, *Kalevipoeg* ("Son of Kalev"), practised as a doctor from 1833 until his retirement in 1877. The exhibition opens with a stolid, text-based survey of Kreuzwald's life, and it's something of a relief to move on to the barn in the courtyard, where works of art inspired by his writings are displayed – look out for Kristjan Raud's celebrated illustrations for the inter-war editions of *Kalevipoeg*. Finally, visitors are ushered into the house that also contained Kreuzwald's waiting room, surgery and library. An inkpot in the form of a dragon is the only artefact on display that Kreuzwald actually owned, but the period furnishings convey a strong flavour of nineteenth-century small-town life.

Southwest of here, streets slope down to the sandy shores of **Tamula järv Lake**, a popular year-round strolling area, with a sandy beach and good views of the low green hills to the southwest. Built to celebrate the millennium, the ultra-modern footbridge at the beach's northern end leads over towards a reed-shrouded park.

Practicalities

Võru's **bus station** is on the northeastern side of town, about five minutes' walk downhill from the main Jüri tänav. The **tourist office**, on the southwestern side of Jüri at Tartu 31 (Mon–Fri 9am–5pm; ☎782 1881, ⊛www.werro.ee), has plenty of local brochures and can help find **B&B accommodation** in the villages south of town. As for **hotels** in Võru, the best is the *Tamula*, right on the beach at Vee 4 (☎783 0430, ⊛www.tamula.ee; ❹), offering swish, bright en-suites with TV in a stylish, modern building; try and get one of the rooms facing the lake if you can. Less expensive is the *Hermes*, occupying a grubby-looking tower block at Jüri 32A (☎782 1326, ⊛www.hot.ee/hermes; ❶–❷), but offering comfortable, if simply furnished, rooms, either with shared facilities or with shower and TV. A less central, but pleasant, option is the pine-shrouded *Kubija*, 5km southeast of town at Männiku 43A (☎782 2341, ⊛www.kubija.ee; ❸), which has recently renovated rooms with shower and TV and also allows **camping** in the grounds.

F. R. Kreuzwald 1803–1882

"And what is wrong if an Estonian learns the German language and becomes a learned man, as long as he remains true to his people in his heart... I have been fortunate because it has been so with me and I am really proud that I can call myself an Estonian"

F.R. Kreuzwald

Throughout the nineteenth century, many ambitious Estonians had turned their backs on their native heritage, regarding it as a mark of peasant backwardness from which they had been lucky to escape. By providing Estonians with a literary heritage they could be proud of, Friedrich Reinhold Kreuzwald was one of the first to buck this trend.

Kreuzwald was born to a family of Estonian serfs in Jõepere near Rakvere. After doing well at school he was groomed to become one of the first instructors at an Estonian-language teacher-training college. The college never got off the ground, however, and Kreuzwald became a private tutor in Tallinn, then St Petersburg, saving enough money to enter Tartu University as a student of medicine in 1826. Receiving a Physician's License Third Class (insufficient to become a doctor to gentlefolk) he set up a modest practice in Võru in 1833.

Kreuzwald's enthusiasm for indigenous folklore had been nurtured through contact with other young intellectuals at Tartu University, notably Friedrich Robert Faehlmann, who set up the Estonian Learned Society in 1838. Inspired by the example of Elias Lönnrot, who had created a Finnish national epic in the 1830s by bundling together traditional folk tales to to form the heroic tale known as the *Kalevala*, Faehlmann came up with the idea of collecting indigenous Estonian material to the same end. The project was enthusiastically taken up by Kreuzwald, and *Kalevipoeg* ("Son of Kalev") was the result.

Published as a series of booklets In Tartu between 1857 and 1859, *Kalevipoeg* immediately made Kreuzwald's reputation and has enjoyed an almost sacred position in Estonian culture ever since. It was initially believed that *Kalevipoeg* was a compilation of genuine folk tales and it only emerged later that Kreuzwald had made most of the story up – by which time Estonian intellectuals had already embraced the epic and were unwilling to question its value.

Despite the success of *Kalevipoeg* among educated Estonians, Kreuzwald never earned much from writing it and came to resent contemporaries like Johann Woldemar Jannsen (editor of *Postimees*; see p.356), who managed to make a living from journalism, while the great intellectual Kreutzwald continued to languish as a country doctor in Võru. Despite remaining aloof from the emerging cultural scene in Tartu and Tallinn, Kreuzwald exerted a strong influence over young, educated Estonians – not least Jannsen's poetry-writing daughter Lydia Koidula. Koidula saw the author of *Kalevipoeg* as her mentor, while Kreuzwald regarded Koidula as an intriguing prodigy who looked set to continue the literary upsurge his own work had started. The pair exchanged over ninety letters from 1867 onwards, a touchingly intimate correspondence full of mutual intellectual admiration. When Koidula married Eduard Michelson – a Latvian doctor who didn't speak Estonian – in 1873, Kreuzwald regarded it as a betrayal of her cultural mission, and never wrote to her again.

As far as **eating** and **drinking** are concerned, *Paula*, Jüri 20, may not look much from the outside, but is one of the best places in town for pastries and cakes. *Katariina*, diagonally opposite Võru Museum at Katariina 4, is a cheap but rather basic pizzeria; for a filling sit-down meal you'd do better to head for *Õlle Nr. 17*, Jüri 17, a wonderfully relaxing pub with a wide choice of meat and fish. *Hundijalg*, Jüri 18B, isn't nearly as atmospheric, but serves up decent salads and cheap dishes of the day. The **Võru Folklore Festival** (@www.werro.ee/folkloor) attracts a variety of Estonian and international ensembles for three days of parades, dancing and concerts in mid-July.

Suur Munamägi and around

Twelve kilometres south of Võru, the wooded dome of **Suur-Munamägi** ("Great Egg Hill") would barely register as a bump in most other European countries, but at 318m above sea level it's the highest point in the Baltic States – and a popular focus for Estonian day-trippers. The surrounding landscape of farmsteads, humpbacked hills and forests is as attractive as any in the region, and the country lanes are perfect for cycle rides and undemanding hikes. There's a lot of off-the-beaten-track **B&B** accommodation in the area if you want to stay – it's best to ask the tourist offices in Võru (see p.392) or Rõuge (see below) to reserve a place for you, as knowledge of English is patchy. Regular **buses** make their way from Võru to **HAANJA**, an uneventful village, 1km north of the hill. There's also one daily bus to Haanja from Tallinn (passing through Tartu on the way), which arrives in the early afternoon and heads back again after about ninety minutes – giving you ample time to clamber up Suur-Munamägi and down again.

The path to Suur-Munamägi's summit heads uphill about 1km south of Haanja, starting from a roadside monument recording an episode from the War of Independence, when a clash with Bolsheviks on 20, March 1919, left seven Estonians dead. It takes only five minutes to reach the fir-tree-carpeted hilltop, where an Art Deco Viewing Tower (Vaatetorn; May–Sept daily 10am–8pm; Oct Sat & Sun 10am–5pm; Nov–April Sat & Sun noon–3pm; 10EEK), built in 1939, offers a superb panorama of the surrounding countryside.

Rõuge

Nine kilometres west of Haanja, **RÕUGE** is famous for being one of Estonia's most picturesque villages, its buildings scattered haphazardly around the shores of Rõuge Suurjärv Lake – which, at 38m, is the deepest in the country. Behind the whitewashed, eighteenth-century church stretches the 300-metre-long Ööbikuorg ("Valley of Nightingales", so-called because it's a favourite nesting area of the birds in spring), an eerily self-contained, steep-sided vale that seems a world away from the flatlands that make up most of Estonia. The **tourist office**, occupying a timber hut at Haanja mnt 1 (☎785 9245, ⊛www.hot.ee/rauge, ✉raugeinfo@hot.ee), can fix you up with farmhouse accommodation; otherwise try *Suurjärve Külalistemaja*, a tastefully renovated farmstead at Metsa 5 (☎785 9273, ⊛www.hot.ee/maremajutus; ❶–❸), offering simply decorated rooms with shared facilities, as well as more modern en-suites, and a log-built smoke sauna in the garden. If you've got your own transport, you can choose from plenty of B&Bs within a short drive of Rõuge, including the *Lätte Turismitalu*, 5km northwest near Nursi village (☎786 0706; ❷), with rustic rooms in the main house or its two annexes, right beside Kahvila Lake; and the *Kanarbiku Turismitalu*, 4km west (☎785 9373, ⊛www.hot.ee/aretalu; ❷), offering rooms in a snug farmhouse and camping in the garden (30EEK per person).

Lake Peipsi

Thirty kilometres east of Tartu, **Lake Peipsi**, measuring 3555 square kilometres, forms a large stretch of Estonia's border with Russia. Despite ranking as the fifth-biggest lake in Europe, Lake Peipsi is a low-key area of sleepy fishing settlements, thick reed beds and quiet, sandy beaches, offering little in the way of tourist facilities. If you have a taste for simple rusticity, however, you'll find a visit here rewarding, not least because of Lake Peipsi's ethnographic peculiarities. Many of the shoreline villages are home to members of the Russian Orthodox sect of **Old Believers**, who came here in the early eighteenth century to escape persecution at home and settled down to catch fish and grow onions. Renowned for their surviving stock of

The Old Believers

The origins of the Old Believers – or *Staroviertsii* as they are known in Russian – lie in the liturgical reforms introduced into the Russian Orthodox Church by Nikon, the mid-seventeenth-century patriarch of Moscow. Faced with the task of systematizing the divergent liturgical texts and practices then in use in the national church, Nikon opted to comply with the dominant Greek practices of the time, such as the use of three fingers instead of two when making the sign of the cross and the use of Greek ecclesiastical dress. Priests who opposed the reforms were removed from office, but many of their congregations persisted with the old practices and were dubbed "Old Believers" by a church hierarchy eager to see them marginalized. Peter the Great was particularly keen to get rid of them and it was under his rule that groups of Old Believers moved to Lake Peipsi – and other areas on the western fringes of the empire – in the hope that here at least they would be left alone to practise their religion as they wished. In liturgical matters, the Old Believers are egalitarian, rejecting the ecclesiastical hierarchy of conventional Orthodoxy, choosing clergy from among the local community rather than relying on a priesthood. Services are conducted in Old Church Slavonic – the medieval tongue into which the scriptures were originally translated – rather than in modern Russian.

An estimated 15,000 Old Believers still live in Estonia, most of whom remain in the Lake Peipsi region. Strict adherence to their beliefs has traditionally prevented them from being assimilated by post-World-War-II Russian migrants, although their numbers are now in decline – largely owing to the migration of the young to the towns and their intermarriage with other groups.

wooden houses and timber churches, Old Believer settlements like Nina, Kasepää, Varnja, and most of all **Kolkja**, exude an untroubled tranquillity that probably hasn't changed much since the community first arrived.

Lake Peipsi is easy to **access from Tartu**: the main road passes through **Kallaste**, the chief settlement and service centre on the central part of the lake, before wheeling north towards Narva (see p.372). The principal Old Believer villages are a short detour away from this route, but a handful of Kallaste-bound buses pass through Kolkja en route.

About 35km out from Tartu, the Kallaste-bound road passes through the village of **KOOSA**, where an eastbound turn-off leads to a string of Old Believer villages occupying a reedy stretch of the Lake Peipsi shoreline. The first of these is **VARNJA**, a largely nondescript huddle of houses grouped around a church with a tower shaped like a spear. **KASEPÄÄ**, 3km up the shore to the north, is more picturesque, its jauntily pea-green church surrounded by a thicket of graveyard crosses. The northern end of Kasepää runs imperceptibly into **KOLKJA**, a four-kilometre shoreline stretch of brightly painted wooden houses, most of which are surrounded by neat onion plots. Set back from the shore in the modern part of the village, the **Museum of Old Believers** (☎745 3431; donation requested) occupies a back room of the village school. Unfortunately, it's only open if you phone in advance, and the curator doesn't speak English, though staff at Tartu tourist office (see p.379) will arrange things for you if you ask. Inside lies an incandescent display of beautifully embroidered traditional costumes, including some especially attractive pink caftans – which turn out to be burial shrouds. There's a cabinet full of liturgical books in Old Church Slavonic – a handful of local schoolchildren still receive lessons in the language.

There's nowhere **to stay** in Kolkja, but the *Kala-ja Sibula* **restaurant**, midway between the museum and the lakeshore, serves up *sudak* (pike-perch) and other local fish, often garnished with sauces featuring the local onions.

On to Kallaste

Back on the main Tartu–Kallaste road, 4km beyond Koosa, the village of **RUPSI**, 4km northeast of Koosa, provides an attractive setting for the **Museum of Juhan Liiv** (Wed–Sun 9am–5pm), in a timber farmstead just beside the main road. The author of some notoriously dour and depressing verse, Liiv (1864–1913) eventually died of pneumonia after being turfed off a train to Warsaw for travelling without a ticket – he was suffering from the delusion that he was descended from the Polish royal family at the time. As well as facsimile manuscripts and first editions, there's a pleasing array of rustic nineteenth-century furnishings inside. Five kilometres up the road from Rupsi, the village of **ALATSKIVI**, served by Tartu–Kallaste buses, is worth a brief stop on account of its dreamily neo-medieval **Manor House**, built by Baron Arved von Nolckens in the 1880s and said to be modelled on Balmoral – hence the pointy-headed turrets. The interior is currently being restored and will be open to visitors at some point in the future. For restful **B&B** accommodation, try *Hirveaia*, near the Manor House at Hirveaia 4 (☎745 3837; ❷) – they also have a few rooms in the village of Nina, 4km east on the shores of the lake.

Kallaste

Beyond Alatskivi the road runs parallel to the lakeshore, passing through the western suburbs of **KALLASTE** before speeding north towards Narva. The main fishing port on this part of the lake, Kallaste looks disconcertingly like a grey, industrial settlement at first sight, although there's something of an old quarter on the south side of town, where you'll find a knot of cobbled alleyways edged with one-storey timber houses and a hilltop cemetery overlooking the lake. Kallaste's main attraction for local holidaymakers, though, is its superb sandy beach, backed by brooding sandstone cliffs. There's a pair of supermarkets in the town centre, and a couple of beachside bars open up in summer to cater for trippers.

Piirisaar

Lying off the shores of Lake Peipsi, some 40km due east of Tartu, **Piirisaar** is a small, marshy island (only 3.5km across at its widest), whose inhabitants, like those of Kolkja, earn a living from fishing and growing onions. A mixture of Estonian Lutherans and Russian Old Believers, they're scattered among three small villages, Piiri, Tooni and Saare – each characterized by oblong timber houses and quiet, grassed-over streets. It's a marvellous place for a rustic ramble and draws its fair share of bird-watchers in spring – the island is an important staging post for migrating birds, especially mute swans and white-tailed eagles.

From mid-May to mid-September there are a number of ways of reaching Piirisaar: by hydrofoil from Tartu (Fri, Sat & Sun; note that the Friday service comes straight back without giving you time to look around) and from Värska Sanatorium outside Värska (see opposite; Sat only). Details of these services can be obtained from Tartu Sadam, Soola 5 (☎734 0026, ⊛www.transcom.ee/tartusadam).

Setumaa

East of Võru, rolling hills give way to a more gently undulating landscape, with broad pastures and arable land broken up by occasional wedges of forest. This southeastern corner of the country is known as **Setumaa** or "land of the Setu" – a branch of the Estonian nation that has preserved distinctive ethnographical features and an archaic dialect. The historic isolation of the **Setu** from the rest of the country owes much to the fact that the region was under the jurisdiction of the Russian principalities of Pskov and Novgorod during the Middle Ages and, unlike the rest of Estonia, was Christianized by the eastern Orthodox Church.

The grammar and pronunciation of the Setu dialect is sufficiently close to that of the nearby Võru region for local linguists to group the two together, claiming the existence of a Võro-Seto language which is distinct from modern Estonian. Although Võro-Seto is yet to be officially recognized, Estonian society is much more tolerant towards this kind of regional particularism than it was during the Soviet period – when cultural and linguistic unity was considered essential to the nation's survival. Indeed, the Setu region is increasingly seen as a source of ethnographic riches, not least because of the survival of archaic **folk singing** techniques that have died out elsewhere. Often featuring partly improvised epic narratives, Setu songs or Leelos are usually sung by a group of five or six women, one of whom sings a semitone higher than the others – producing a discordant polyphony which once heard is never forgotten. Traditional Setu dress is also distinctive, with dark red the dominant colour, augmented by plenty of heavy, metal jewellery – notably the vast metal breast plates worn by unmarried women.

What makes the Setu heritage particularly precious to present-day Estonia is the fact that of the twelve *nulks*, or tribal units, into which Setumaa is divided, four lie across the border in the Russian Federation – a division made all the more galling by the knowledge that they were all part of Estonia until the Soviets arbitrarily redrew the frontier in 1940. Setumaa's main market centre, **Petchory** (Petseri in Estonian), now lies 3km on the wrong side of the border, leaving the Estonian Setu without an urban focus. Nowadays, the main centres of Setu culture are the villages of **Obinitsa** (served by regular buses from Võru) and **Värska** (reached by bus from Tartu) – if only because both places possess museums and singing groups, keeping the local folklore alive.

Värska

Ninety kilometres southeast of Tartu, **VÄRSKA** is a pleasant, forest-shrouded village on the southwestern shores of Lake Pihkva, a southern extension of Lake Peipsi. Set in an attractive reedy landscape frequented by herons and other waterfowl, it's a relatively undramatic place, its only real sight being the rather charming **Setu Village Museum** (Setu talu muuseum; Mon–Fri 10am–4pm; 10EEK) set amid birch trees a 25-minute walk south of the village along the Säätse road. The museum is basically a recreation of an extended Setu family's farmstead, consisting of a log-built ensemble of reed-thatched buildings around a common yard. The granary, barns, mill and smithy are filled with the simple tools that would have characterized nineteenth-century farm work, while the interior of the main farmhouse is brought to life by a display of bright-red textiles.

Värska's **tourist office**, on the main street at Pikk 12 (Mon–Fri 9am–5pm; ☎796 4782, ✉varska@visitestonia.com), can advise on local **B&B** possibilities. Other options include **Hirvemäe Holiday Centre**, Silla 2A (☎797 6114, ⓦwww .hirvemae.ee; ❷), offering modern en-suites with pine furnishings and attic ceilings. You can **camp** in the grounds for 50EEK per tent plus 25EEK per vehicle. Three kilometres north of town, the Värska Sanatoorium (☎796 4666, ⓦwww.spavarska.ee; ❷) offers prim en-suites and a range of spa treatments good for respiratory complaints, arthritis and gastric ulcers. The café of the *Hirvemäe Holiday Centre* is the best place to **eat**, although it closes at 4 or 5pm out of season. The quay outside Värska Sanatoorium is the departure point for weekend hydrofoil **trips to the island of Piirisaar** (see opposite).

Obinitsa

Twenty kilometres southwest of Värska and 25km east of Võru lies the quiet agricultural settlement of **OBINITSA**. Buses from Võru pick up and drop off just south of the staggered central crossroads, where a signed alley leads east to the **Setu Heritage Museum** (Seto muuseumitarõ; May–Sept Tues–Sun 11am–5pm; Oct–April Mon–Fri 10am–4pm; 10EEK), housed in a traditional timber building. Inside is a re-creation of a typical Setu home, including a living room with a special corner set aside for icons, and a gorgeous display of handicrafts featuring some

Setu women △

intricately embroidered folk costumes. There's also a small **tourist office** inside the museum (same times; ☎785 4190, ❻www.hot.ee/setotour).

Continuing east from here brings you after five minutes to an artificial lake with a beach. Overlooking the lake from its unmissable hillside position is the granite statue of the **Setu Song-Mother** (Setu Lauluimä), a stylized tribute to the female singers who have kept the tradition of epic narrative songs alive. Scattered in the grass around the statue are boulders engraved with the names of individual performers who were bestowed with the honorific title of Lauluimä during their lifetime, notably Miko Ode, Irõ Matrina, and Hilane Taarka (1856–1933), who did more than most to preserve Setu traditions into the modern age. About 500m north of the central crossroads is Obinitsa's wooden **church**, built in 1905 and largely destroyed after World War II, but returned to use in the early 1950s, when the communist authorities turned a blind eye to its reconstruction. **Transfiguration Day** (Paasapäev) on August 19 is one of the biggest feast days in Setumaa: thousands of Orthodox descend on Obinitsa church to commemorate the dead and local families tuck into picnics on top of their ancestors' graves in the adjoining cemetery.

Piusa Sand Caves

Five kilometres north of Obinitsa, the **Piusa Sand Caves** are one of the country's more offbeat tourist attractions. They're relatively easy to find: the road north from Obinitsa church forges through an entrancing landscape of farmland, forest and farmsteads before passing over the Piusa River and under the railway tracks, just beyond which a sign on the right reading "Piusa koopad" directs you to the caves themselves. The caves (really a single chamber rather than a network of caverns) were excavated between 1922 and 1970 to extract sand for use in the glassmaking industry. The area became a protected nature reserve in 1999, largely owing to the caves' importance as a habitat for bats – the creatures have flourished since the end of mining activities and Piusa now harbours one of the biggest colonies in the Baltics. You're free to enter the excavations at any time, although some sections are boarded off for fear of cave-ins. Inside, there's not a great deal to see or explore, but it's a marvellously atmospheric place, its rows of sand-carved arches bringing to mind some kind of abandoned subterranean cathedral. The section nearest the entrance is hauntingly illuminated by daylight leaking in from outside; if you want to venture further in you'll need to bring a torch. Round the back of the caves, paths lead around the edges of the Piusa Sandpit (Piusa liivakarjäär), a Sahara-like expanse of sand edged by rare grasses and shrubs.

Travel details

Trains

Tallinn to: Tartu (2 daily; 3hr 30min).

Buses

Narva to: Narva-Jõesuu (every 20–30min; 20min); Otepää (2 daily; 4hr 30min); Rakvere (7 daily; 2hr 20min); Sillamäe (hourly; 30–40min); Tartu (11 daily; 2hr 50min–3hr 35min).

Otepää to: Narva (2 daily; 4hr 30min); Põlva (1 daily; 1hr 10min); Tallinn (2 daily; 3hr 30min); Tartu (10 daily; 1hr 10min–2hr); Võru (3 daily; 1hr 10min).

Rakvere to: Käsmu (Mon–Fri 4 daily, Sat 3 daily, Sun 2 daily; 1hr 15min); Narva (7 daily; 2hr 20min); Palmse (Mon, Wed, Fri & Sun 1 daily; 40min); Võsu (Mon–Fri 4 daily, Sat 3 daily, Sun 2 daily; 1hr).

Tallinn to: Altja (2 daily; 1hr 35min); Haanja (1 daily; 4hr); Käsmu (1 daily; 1hr 30min); Tartu (every 30min; 2hr 20min–3hr); Võsu (Mon–Thurs & Sat 3 daily, Fri & Sun 4 daily; 1hr 15min).

Tartu to: Haanja (2 daily; 1hr 30min); Kallaste (Mon–Fri 5 daily, Sat & Sun 3 daily; 1hr 20min–1hr 50min); Käsmu (mid-May to mid-Sept 1 daily; 2hr 50min); Kolkja (Mon–Fri 4 daily, Sat 1 daily; Sun 2 daily, 1hr 20min); Kuressaare (July & Aug 5 daily,

Sept–June 3 daily; 6hr); Narva (11 daily; 2hr 50min–3hr 35min); Narva-Jõesuu (2 daily; 3hr 30min); Otepää (10 daily; 1hr 10min–2hr); Põlva (10 daily; 40min); Rakvere (8 daily; 2hr 10min–3hr); Rapina (4 daily; 1hr 15min); Rõuge (2 daily; 2hr); Sillamäe (3 daily; 2hr 30min); Tallinn (every 30min; 2hr 20min–3hr); Värska (3 daily; 2hr); Viljandi (8 daily;1hr–1hr 20min); Võru (every 30min–1hr; 1hr 20min); Võsu (mid-May to mid-Sept 1 daily; 2hr 40min).

Võru to: Haanja (5 daily; 25min); Obinitsa (Mon–Sat 4 daily; Sun 3 daily; 40min–1hr 30min); Otepää (3 daily; 1hr 10min); Põlva (10 daily; 40min); Rõuge (Mon–Fri 8 daily; Sat & Sun 5 daily; 25min); Tartu (every 30min–1hr; 1hr 20min).

International buses

Narva to: St Petersburg (7 daily; 3hr).
Tartu to: Moscow (4 weekly; 14hr); St Petersburg (2 daily; 6hr).

Contexts

Contexts

History

H istory is a serious business in a region that has seen more than its fair share of conquests, foreign occupations and hard-fought independence struggles. While there is much that all three Baltic States have in common – most notably the shared experience of Tsarist rule in the nineteenth century and Soviet occupation in the twentieth – there are equally long periods when Estonians, Latvians and Lithuanians have pursued widely diverging destinies. The very expression "Baltic States" is itself merely a convenient geographical label of twentieth-century invention – under the surface of which lie three emphatically different cultures.

Lithuania

It's far from certain who the original human inhabitants of Lithuania were, and the history of the region doesn't really begin until around 2000 BC, when the **Baltic tribes** – the ancestors of today's Lithuanians and Latvians – migrated to the Baltic seaboard from their original home somewhere in west-central Russia. These tribes originally lived in loose, clan-based units closely related by language, speaking a unique and ancient group of Indo-European dialects distinct from the Slav tongues of their near neighbours – indeed contemporary Lithuanian is said to be the closest of all living languages to Sanskrit. They also had a common religion, involving a pantheon of gods, of which Perkūnas (the thunder god) and Laima (Fortune) were among the most prominent. There was also much nature-worship, with trees, lakes and glades accorded a sacred importance.

Protected by belts of forest and swamp, the early Lithuanians lived largely undisturbed by events elsewhere in Europe, preserving a village-based, iron-age lifestyle, without a written language, untill well into the Middle Ages. In the twelfth century, Lithuanian society came under increasing pressure from their German and Slav neighbours, and tribes in eastern Lithuania began to unite into something resembling a centralized state, with the fortresses of Kernavė, Trakai and **Vilnius** serving as its main strongholds. The absence of defendable frontiers meant that the nascent Lithuanian state could only ensure security by expanding, leading to the emergence of a highly mobile military machine which soon imposed its rule on Slav lands to the south and east.

The western Lithuanians (known as **Žemaitijans** and speaking a slightly different dialect, they were long considered to be a nation in their own right) were still divided into small tribes at this time, although they somehow managed to come together in inflicting a crushing defeat on Rīga-based crusaders the Brotherhood of the Sword at the **Battle of Saulė** in 1236. Other tribes closely related to the Lithuanians fared less well: the **Yotvingians** to the southwest and the **Prussians** to the west either died out or were assimilated by more powerful neighbours, although the name of Prussia was subsequently adopted by that region's German conquerors.

The rise of the medieval state

Little is known of Lithuania's rulers until the emergence of **Mindaugas** in the mid-thirteenth century, a powerful chieftain who had become master of the state by the 1240s and accepted Christianity in the hope of winning recognition from Western rulers. He was crowned King of Lithuania by a papal representative in 1253, only to be murdered ten years later by nobles eager to preserve Lithuania's pagan culture.

Lithuania's status as the last pagan state in Europe increasingly attracted the attention of Germany's crusading orders, with the Teutonic Knights raiding the country from the west and the Livonian Order mounting frequent attacks from the north. Many Western European knights volunteered to serve in these campaigns – Lithuania is mentioned by Geoffrey Chaucer as being one of the places where the Knight of Canterbury Tales fame saw action.

The experience of constant warfare against the crusaders helped forge Lithuania into a major military power. Prevented from making territorial acquisitions in the west, fourteenth-century ruler **Gediminas** (1271–1341) extended Lithuanian rule eastwards into Russia and Ukraine. Slav chieftains from the conquered territories were co-opted into the Lithuanian ruling elite, and a Slav dialect close to modern Belarussian became the official language used in court documents – the Lithuanians themselves still didn't have a written form of their own tongue.

Jogaila and Vytautas

By the late fourteenth century, Lithuania was a vast multinational empire, which, despite being demonized by Western propagandists for its continuing pagan sympathies, was an increasingly important player in central European affairs. When King of Poland Louis of Anjou died without a male heir in September 1382, Polish nobles offered the hand of his daughter **Jadwiga** to Gediminas's grandson and current Lithuanian ruler **Jogaila** – henceforth known to history by the Polonized form of his name, Jagiełło. The Poles hoped that the marriage would provide them with a key ally in their struggles against the German orders and facilitate a joint Lithuanian-Polish programme of expansion into Eastern Europe into the bargain. Jogaila jumped at the chance to internationalize his power base, forging a dynastic link between Lithuania and Poland that would endure for the next four centuries. Jogaila's part of the deal was to promise the **Christian conversion** of his country, bringing down the curtain on Europe's longest-enduring pagan culture.

The marriage took place in 1389, after which Jogaila was crowned King of Poland and went on to spend most of his time in Kraków. A large part of the Lithuanian nobility saw Jogaila as a traitor who had sold out to the Poles and supported a rebellion by his cousin **Vytautas** in 1392. Unable to control events in Lithuania, and fearful that his newly won inheritance might soon disintegrate, Jogaila offered Vytautas the position of **Grand Duke** of Lithuania, on condition that Lithuania would pass to Jogaila or his heirs after Vytautas's death. On 15 July, 1410, Jogaila and Vytautas together led Polish-Lithuanian forces to victory at **Žalgiris** (called Grünwald in Poland; Tannenberg in Germany), a battle which destroyed the Teutonic Order as an effective military power. Vytautas went on to rule Lithuania as a virtually autonomous sovereign – a situation which suited Jogaila, because it demonstrated to the Polish nobles that Lithuania was still a powerful state with a will of its own. It was under Vytautas that Lithuania achieved its greatest territorial exent, stretching from the Baltic in the north to the Black Sea in the south – not surprisingly, Grand Duke Vytautas "the Great" has always been a bigger national hero in Lithuania than Jogaila.

The sixteenth and seventeenth centuries

After Jogaila's death, his descendants continued to rule in Poland while Lithuania remained an autonomous Grand Duchy. Sometimes the King of Poland appointed himself Grand Duke of Lithuania; at others he would award the title to a trusted son or cousin. Although technically separate from Poland, Lithuania was soon drawn into the Polish cultural orbit. The Polish language was the main vehicle by which Catholic ritual and Renaissance culture arrived in Lithuania, and by the sixteenth century almost all of the Lithuanian nobility was **Polish-speaking**. Leading magnates retained a sense of regional patriotism, however, and the defence of Lithuania's special status vis-a-vis the Polish crown remained a popular rallying cry.

By the mid-sixteenth century, Lithuania's eastern borders were increasingly threatened by an aggressively expansionist Russia. Fearful that their Polish counterparts would abandon Lithuania rather than assist in its defence, the Lithuanian nobles allowed themselves to be rushed into a more formal union between the two states. In 1569, the agreement known as the **Union of Lublin** created the so-called **Polish-Lithuanian Commonwealth**, in which the Grand Duchy retained certain self governing rights but lost its wholly autonomous status.

The Grand Duchy's position on the eastern fringes of a large state centred on Warsaw didn't leave it immune to intellectual currents coming from the rest of Europe. Although the **Reformation** arrived here somewhat later then elsewhere, an estimated sixty percent of the aristocracy had turned Protestant by the late 1500s, and the gradual re-Catholicization of the country was carried out without recourse to violence. The atmosphere of religious debate occasioned the first attempts at Lithuanian publishing, with Protestant nobles sponsoring the production of native-language prayer books and Counter-Reformers responding with texts of their own.

Among the beneficiaries of the Grand Duchy's reputation for cultural and religious tolerance were the **Jews**. Present in Lithuania ever since the Middle Ages, their numbers increased massively in the sixteenth century owing to an influx of Yiddish-speaking Jews from Germany. They soon became the dominant ethnic group in many provincial towns, with Vilnius serving as their spiritual and cultural capital.

Lithuania under the Tsars

Having taken control of most of Estonia and Latvia in the **Great Northern War** of 1700–21, Russia exerted an increasing amount of influence in the affairs of the Commonwealth and installed a succession of weak kings on the Polish throne before deciding to do away with the country altogether. Russia, Austria and Prussia progressively helped themselves to more and more of the Commonwealth until wiping it off the map once and for all in the so-called **Third Partition of Poland** in 1795. The Grand Duchy of Lithuania was formally absorbed into Tsarist Russia and, carved up into lesser administrative units, ceased to exist as a territorial entity.

With Lithuania's aristocracy and intelligentsia thoroughly Polonized, any aspirations to independence were invariably tied to the idea of a resurrection of the Polish-Lithuanian Commonwealth. Lithuanian landowners, priests and peasants took an enthusiastic part in the **Polish Uprising of 1830**, liberating much of the countryside, until Tsarist troops arrived to restore order. Lithuanian participation in the **Polish Uprising of 1863** was even more widespread, provoking a brutal crackdown engineered by new governor-general Mikhail "the hangman" Muravyev. Muravyev's response to the threat of Polish-Lithuanian patriotism was to embark on a wholesale programme of **Russification**. Russian became the language of instruction in all but a handful of schools, and a ban on the printing of books in any script other than cyrillic effectively put paid to any Lithuanian-language publishing.

The 1863 Uprising was the last occasion on which Lithuanians and Poles fought side by side for the restitution of a common state. A new generation of educated Lithuanians increasingly saw the dominance of Polish culture as a barrier to national self-realization. The main ideologue behind this new course was **Jonas Basanavičius** (1851–1927), who encouraged research into traditional folk culture and promoted fresh study of Lithuania's period of medieval greatness. From 1883 onwards many of these ideas found expression in the magazine *Aušra* (Dawn), printed over the border in Germany and smuggled into Tsarist Russia by a dedicated underground team of *knygnešiai* or "**book-bearers**". In 1904, the forty-year ban on printing Lithuanian in the latin alphabet was rescinded, leading to a flowering of indigenous-language culture.

World War I

Lithuania represented a key line of defence for Tsarist armies on the outbreak of **World War I** in 1914, but within a year the whole country had been overrun by the Germans. The collapse of the Tsarist regime in 1917 persuaded Lithuanian national leaders that the time had come to make some kind of pro-independence statement, although they were extremely wary of upsetting either their German occupiers or the Western powers. In December 1917, the recently formed Lithuanian **Taryba** or Council declared Lithuania an independent state under the protection of Germany. On February 16, 1918, they reissued the declaration, this time cutting any explicit reference to the Germans. The Germans quietly ignored both declarations and the Taryba was left in limbo until November 1918, when Germany's unexpected collapse left surprised Lithuanian leaders in command of a newly independent country.

The inter-war years

It had always been assumed that the Lithuanian state would be centred on the old ducal capital **Vilnius**, an ethnically mixed city that was also claimed by Lithuania's neighbours. After an inconclusive three-way tug of war between Poles, Lithuanians and Bolsheviks, the city was finally seized by Polish General Żeligowski in 1920. The Lithuanian government took up residence in **Kaunas** instead, but refused to recognize the loss of Vilnius, declaring Kaunas to be only the "provisional capital" and freezing relations with Poland as a sign of their displeasure. Having failed to prevent the Polish seizure of Vilnius, the international community turned a blind eye when the Lithuanians themselves grabbed the German-speaking port city of **Memel** (**Klaipėda** in Lithuanian) in 1923.

The emerging nation's attempts to build a viable democracy were short-lived. In 1926, a left-of-centre government signed a treaty of friendship with the Soviet Union, enraging right-wing nationalists and encouraging the authoritarian-minded President **Antanas Smetona** to suspend parliament. A decade and a half of benign dictatorship followed, with the main opposition coming from radical right-wing groups such as Iron Wolf (Geležinis Vilkas), which peddled a modish mixture of anti-liberal, anti-Semitic ideas. On the international stage, Lithuania was the most isolated of all the Baltic States, distrustful of neighbours like Poland and Soviet Russia and in dispute with Germany over the status of Klaipėda – when Hitler reoccupied the city in March 1939, the Lithuanians had no choice but to meekly stand aside.

World War II

Lithuania was in no position to offer resistance when the **Soviet Union**, having grabbed the eastern half of Poland in autumn 1939, moved to occupy all three Baltic States in June 1940. Managed elections produced a pro-Soviet Lithuanian parliament which voted for immediate incorporation into the USSR. With the threat of war with Nazi Germany looming, the Soviet Union tightened its grip on Lithuania with the **deportation** of a randomly chosen cross-section of its citizens to Siberia in June 1941.

The Germans launched **Operation Barbarossa** against the Soviet Union on June 22, 1941, overrunning Lithuania within days. Almost immediately, a murderous campaign of terror was launched against the country's 240,000-strong Jewish population. Special units known as Einsatzgruppen were sent to the Baltic to "deal" with the "Jewish problem" – thousands of Lithuania's Jews were taken to forest clearings and shot within weeks of the Nazi occupation. Many Lithuanians participated enthusiastically in round-ups and killings – it was widely believed that Jews were more likely than Lithuanians to harbour communist sympathies and therefore had to pay for the Soviet occupation of 1940–41. **Ghettos** were established in the cities of Vilnius, Kaunas and Šiauliai, where a semblance of Jewish life continued until summer 1943, when SS leader Heinrich Himmler ordered their closure. By September of the same year the Lithuanian ghettos had been cleared, and their inhabitants were either shot straight away or marched off to concentration camps in Poland and the Reich. About ninety percent of Lithuania's Jewish population was wiped out during the Holocaust, and many of the survivors emigrated to Israel or the USA after the war. There are currently around 5000 Jews left in the country, most of whom live in Vilnius.

From occupation to independence

With the Red Army's advance into Lithuania in 1944, resistance to Soviet rule started up almost immediately, with various partisan groups joining forces to form the movement subsequently known as the **Forest Brothers**. Despite the KGB's success in infiltrating the organization, armed resistance continued for almost a decade, finally petering out after the arrest and execution of the Brothers' most senior leader, Jonas Žemaitis, in 1953. Meanwhile, in March 1949, another round of **mass deportations** had deprived Lithuania of much of its intelligentsia. The **Church** continued to provide a limited outlet for anti-Soviet sentiment, most notably in the person of Bishop Sladkievičius, who, despite being exiled to a rural village in 1959, organized the production and distribution of the underground dissident journal *Chronicle of the Lithuanian Catholic Church*. Sladkevičius later became archbishop of Kaunas and was made a cardinal by the pope in 1988.

The post-war political scene was dominated by **Antanas Sniečkus**, a trusted servant of Moscow who presided over a purge of "national communists" in 1959. A political thaw in the mid- to late-1960s led to a modest cultural revival, although Lithuanians had to wait until the Glasnost era of the 1980s before outright political dissent was allowed into the open. The first **anti-Soviet demonstration** in Lithuania, held on August 23, 1987, to demand the publication of the Molotov-Ribbentrop Pact (the secret Nazi-Soviet agreement which sealed the fate of the Baltic States in 1939), only attracted a crowd of a few hundred. Within a year, however, the opposition had mushroomed into a mass movement, with the openly pro-independence **Sąjūdis** ("Movement") organization holding its first congress in October 1988. The same year saw the Lithuanian Communist Party elect a new leader, Algirdas Brazauskas, who began to offer cautious support to the independence movement.

Elections to the Lithuanian Supreme Soviet in February 1990, produced a majority for the Sąjūdis camp, with professor of music **Vytautas Landsbergis** becoming its chairman. Landsbergis declared Lithuania's independence from the Soviet Union on March 11, 1990, the first Soviet republic to do so. The Kremlin responded with an economic blockade of Lithuania that led to severe shortages of food and fuel. Egged on by hardliners in Moscow, Mikhail Gorbachev authorized a military **clampdown** in January, 1991, which began with an attack on Vilnius TV Tower by Soviet tanks. After the deaths of thirteen unarmed demonstrators (a further five hundred were injured) the operation was called off by a Soviet leadership fearful of causing a bloodbath. Kremlin hardliners remained eager to teach Lithuania a lesson, and on July 31, 1991, a special forces' detachment attacked a frontier post at Medininkai on the Lithuanian–Belarussian border, killing seven Lithuanian border guards in the process. With the failure of the anti-Gorbachev Moscow coup of August the same year, however, Soviet power quickly evaporated, leaving Lithuania suddenly, and joyously, independent.

The political present

Although the nationalist-conservative Landsbergis remained the dominant figure in parliament during the first ten years of independence, he surprisingly lost the first presidential elections of 1992 to former communist and born-again Social Democrat **Algirdas Brazauskas**. Brazauskas was on hand to welcome Pope John Paul II to Lithuania in September 1993, the pontiff's visit serving as a powerful symbol of the country's break with the communist past.

The Conservative Party of Landsbergis provided much of the ideological impetus behind the wholesale switch to **free-market economics** that transformed Lithuania in the 1990s. The change was not without negative consequences, however, with the collapse of loss-making industries, rising unemployment and declining living standards for the majority. Widespread popular disillusionment led to big losses for the Conservatives in the elections of October 2000. The Social Democrats of Brazauskas (back in parliament after losing the presidency to Valdas Adamkus in 1998) became the largest party in parliament, although the balance of power was held by a relatively new group of pragmatic, centre-right parties – notably Arturas Palauskas's Social Liberals and Rolandas Paksas's Liberal Union – whose popularity was based on the personal charisma of their leaders rather than any coherent ideology. All parties cultivated the support of business cliques in order to bolster their campaign funds, leading to renewed voter cynicism about the impartiality of Lithuania's leaders as far as economic policy was concerned. The sale of major oil and gas companies to international conglomerates – many backed by major Russian concerns like Lukoil and Gazprom – has led to renewed fears of Russian economic penetration of Lithuania in particular and the Baltic region as a whole.

The pro-Western orientation of the country's foreign policy has never been in doubt, however, with successive administrations championing the cause of Lithuanian entry into NATO and the EU. President Adamkus, a well-respected figure on the international stage, played a key role in successfully guiding

Lithuania towards acceptance by both organizations. It therefore came as something of a shock when Adamkus lost the presidential elections of 2003 to **Rolandas Paksas** – a populist who employed anti-EU rhetoric to win the support of farmers fearful of European agricultural competition. A referendum on **EU membership** in May 2003, produced a huge majority in favour, however, signalling genuine popular excitement – the result symbolized for many Lithuanians their extraordinary voyage from Soviet satellite to modern European state. Within a year, Paksas himself had been engulfed in scandal following allegations about his links with organized crime, making his hold on the presidency increasingly tenuous.

Latvia

Along with the ancestors of the Lithuanians, the forebears of today's Latvians moved into the Baltic seaboard from western Russia from around 2000 BC onwards. They soon coalesced into a handful of regionally based tribal units, with the Curonians (Kurši) in the west, the Zemgalians (Zemgaļi) in central Latvia, and the Selonians (Sēļi) and Latgalians (Latgaļi) further east. Initially they had to share northern and central Latvia with remaining pockets of Livs, a Finno-Ugric people closely related to the Estonians, who lived around the Gulf of Rīga. None of these tribes had unified state structures based on capital cities, living instead in a network of loosely allied rural communities defended by stockade forts.

The Baltic Crusades

The pagan Latvians remained wholly outside the orbit of Western Europe until the twelfth century, when ambitious German clerics conceived the idea of converting the Baltic peoples to Christianity. First to make the arduous trip to Latvia's shores was Father Meinhard of Holstein, who built a church at Uexküll (Ikšķile) on the banks of the Daugava, east of present-day Rīga, and persuaded the pope to declare him Bishop of Uexküll in 1188.

Although Meinhard died soon afterwards and his followers were chased off by hostile locals, the publicity generated by his enterprise encouraged Pope Innocent III to declare a full-scale **crusade** against the Baltic pagans in 1198. Three years later the Bremen-based ecclesiastic, Albert of Buxhoeveden, led a fleet of ships to the mouth of the Daugava River and chose Rīga (formerly a Liv fishing village) as the site of his projected crusader capital. Albert's retinue of idealistic Christian knights and plunder-hungry freebooters formed themselves into the **Brotherhood of the Sword**, a military-religious organization, that (initially at least) enforced a strict, almost monastic code of behaviour on its members. The Brotherhood advanced from Rīga, conquering the Latvian communities one by one and confiscating their land – subsequently divided up between the Brotherhood's members. The social order established by the Brotherhood, in which a German feudal aristocracy ruled over a Latvian-speaking peasant majority, was to remain in place for the next seven centuries.

The Brotherhood didn't have things all their own way, encountering stiff resistance from the Zemgaļi and failing to extend their crusade south towards Lithuania as planned. Defeated by a combined Zemgalian-Lithuanian army near Šiaulai in 1236, the Brotherhood lost so many knights that it no longer had the numerical strength to carry on as a crusading organization. Its surviving members merged with the Prussian-based German Order to form a new grouping, the **Livonian Order**, which consolidated its rule over the Latvian lands, expanded northwards into Estonia, and established the Livonian Confederation – to remain the dominant political force in the region for over three hundred years.

The archbishop of Rīga served as the Confederation's titular head, although he presided over a far from unified body politic: the Livonian Order and the Church were both major landowners and tended to be competitors for temporal power rather than spiritual partners, while the mercantile city of Rīga enjoyed privileges that increasingly made it hostile to both.

The end of the Livonian Order

It was the townsfolk of Rīga who spearheaded support for the **Reformation** in the early sixteenth century, seeing the new creed as a useful way of avoiding the financial demands made on them by the Catholic Church authorities. The Reformation also had unforeseen benefits for Latvian culture, with rural aristocrats funding vernacular translations of the gospels in order to popularize the new faith among their serfs.

The Reformation eroded the ideological certainties that had underpinned the crusading effort in the Baltic and a dissent-riven Livonian Order was incapable of defending its territories against ambitious neighbours. The region was devastated by the **Livonian Wars** of 1558–83, a three-way struggle involving Sweden, Russia and the Polish-Lithuanian Commonwealth. The Livonian Order was dissolved in 1562 by its last grand master, Gottfried Kettler, who appointed himself secular duke of Courland (see p.232) and placed himself under the protection of the Polish-Lithuanian crown – which also gained control of Latgale in the southeast. With Rīga and the northeast falling to the Swedes in 1621, the Latvian lands were effectively divided between two rival empires.

Latvia remained a target for Russian territorial ambitions, too, however, and in the **Great Northern War** (1700–21) Peter the Great kicked the Swedes out of the east and dragged the Polish-controlled west into the Russian sphere of influence. Full Russian control of Latvia was confirmed in 1795, when the so-called Third Partition finished off what was left of the Polish-Lithuanian state.

The Latvian National Revival

Despite these changes in sovereignty, little changed for the Latvians themselves, the vast majority of whom continued to work on the land, largely owned by a German-speaking aristocracy. It was only in the mid-nineteenth century that a Latvian middle class began to emerge in Rīga and other towns, eager to develop indigenous language and culture. The Baltic Germans continued to regard the Latvians as second-class citizens who had to either abandon their culture or stay on the farm – an attitude best summed up by Rīga newspaper editor Gustav Keuchel, who declared that, "to be both Latvian and educated is an impossibility".

Unsurprisingly, a rising generation of Latvian patriots increasingly saw German-language culture as an instrument of oppression that could only be overcome by encouraging the more widespread use of Latvian. The leader of these so-called **New Latvians** (Jaunlatvieši) was **Krišjānis Valdemars** (1825–1891), who founded the first Latvian newspaper, *Pēterburgas avīzes* ("St Petersburg News"), in 1862 and helped set up a series of Latvian naval colleges that, it was hoped, would create an indigenous technocratic elite. Encouraged by Valdemars, **Krišjānis Barons** (1835–1923) embarked on the collection of folkloric materials in order to provide the Latvians with a sense of their own cultural history, in the process building up a remarkable archive of over one million *dainas* – four-line folk songs passed from one generation to the next, but never previously written down.

The New Latvians had always assumed that the Tsarist bureaucracy was their most likely ally in the struggle against the Baltic Germans – a delusion that it took the turmoil of the **1905 Revolution** to dispel. A pro-democracy uprising that spread from St Petersburg across the Russian Empire, the revolution was followed by a mercilessly authoritarian crackdown, and in Latvia a whole generation of nationalist activists were exiled or imprisoned.

War and independence

The outbreak of **World War I** in 1914 pushed national aspirations further into the background, and with the Russian Revolution leading to the eastern front's wholesale collapse in 1918, Latvia fell to the Germans – who set about turning it into a protectorate of the Reich. However, Germany surrendered to the Western allies in November 1918 and a hastily convened Latvian National Council rushed to seize the initiative, meeting in Rīga's Russian Theatre (now the National Theatre) on November 18, 1918 to declare Latvia's independence. Lawyer and Agrarian Party leader Karlis Ulmanis was appointed head of government and was to remain at the apex of Latvian politics for the next twenty years. Ulmanis's freedom of manoeuvre was limited by the fact that German troops were still in control of Latvia and had no intention of withdrawing. Indeed the British and French – neither of whom could spare the troops to garrison Latvia themselves – wanted the Germans to stay put in order to defend the region from Bolshevik Russia. In the event, both the Latvians and the Germans ended up fleeing Rīga in the face of the Bolsheviks, who captured the city on January 3, 1919, and established a Latvian Soviet Republic under veteran left-wing activist, Pēteris Stučka.

Ulmanis and his government took refuge in the port city of Liepāja, where they remained virtual pawns of a more powerful German force led by the charismatic General Rudiger von der Goltz. Supported by the local aristocracy, von der Goltz dreamed of turning Latvia into a German-dominated statelet that would both stem the tide of Bolshevism and put the indigenous population in their place. The Ulmanis government formed a fledgling Latvian army (under Colonel Oskars Kalpaks) as a counterweight to von der Goltz's Germans, but this didn't prevent the latter from trying to depose Ulmanis in favour of a more malleable puppet in April 1919. Ulmanis was saved by the British, who installed him on a ship in Liepāja harbour and began delivering arms and supplies to his men. The Germans threw the Bolsheviks out of Rīga in May, but were themselves compelled to leave by a combined force of Estonians and Latvians – backed up by British and French warships. The British arranged for Ulmanis's return to Rīga in July, and after the failure of another German attack on the capital in October, the independent state of Latvia looked secure. The Bolsheviks, who still occupied parts of southeastern Latvia, were beaten off in the winter war of 1919–20 and the Latvian-Soviet treaty signed on August 11, 1920, officially ended hostilities.

The inter-war period

Inter-war Latvian politics were characterized by the proliferation of small parties and a succession of short-lived coalition governments – although the presence of the Farmers' Union (and their leader Karlis Ulmanis) in all cabinets ensured a degree of continuity. During the 1920s, Latvia won export markets both for its dairy products and the consumer goods made by Rīga's VEF electronics factory, but a period of steadily rising living standards was cut short by the onset of the **Great Depression** after 1929. The ensuing economic slowdown led to widespread disillusionment with parliamentary politics and the emergence of anti-democratic (and often anti-Semitic) right-wing groups, such as **Perkonkrusts** (Thunder Cross), persuaded Prime Minister Ulmanis to declare a **state of emergency** on March 16, 1934. Fearing that a return to democracy would render the country ungovernable, Ulmanis appointed himself president in 1936 and proceeded to dismantle Latvia's liberal institutions, presiding over the construction of a corporatist state based on Mussolini's Italian model.

World War II

With the rise of Nazi Germany and consolidation of communist rule in Russia, the fragility of Latvian independence became increasingly apparent as the 1930s wore on. With the signing of the **Molotov-Ribbentrop Pact** on August 23, 1939, Germany and the USSR agreed to the establishment of spheres of influence in north-central Europe. Along with the other Baltic States, Latvia was designated part of the Soviet sphere. Latvia was forced to sign a mutual assistance pact with the USSR in October 1939, a prelude to the wholesale military occupation of the country on **June 17, 1940**. Deciding that armed resistance would be futile, President Ulmanis advised the nation to stay calm and adopt a wait-and-see approach, famously announcing in a live radio broadcast, "I'm staying where I am, and I want you to stay where you are." In the event, the Soviet invaders simply sidestepped Latvia's timorous political elite and did as they pleased; Stalin's trusted sidekick, Andrey Vishinsky, arrived in Rīga to oversee the country's painless incorporation into the Soviet Union. Under his guidance, stage-managed elections were held in July (most anti-Soviet candidates were barred from competing), and the resulting parliament, packed with Soviet puppets, voted to join the USSR. Ulmanis himself was exiled to Siberia, where he died in September 1942.

As the likelihood of war between the Soviet Union and Germany drew near, Stalin decided to tighten his grip on Latvia by **deporting** a large part of the country's intelligentsia to Siberia, and an estimated 16,000 people were rounded up and shipped east on the night of June 13–14, 1941.

The **German army** began its invasion of the Soviet Union on June 22, 1941, and were in total control of Latvia two weeks later. Although most Latvians initially greeted the Germans as liberators, they were soon disappointed by the realities of occupation, with Latvia becoming a marginal province in the new Nazi protectorate of Ostland. Special units arrived almost immediately to deal with Latvia's Jewish population, murdering an estimated 30,000 in the first six months of the war and a further 40,000 by 1945. The Germans were assisted in their butchery by a 12,000-strong Latvian auxiliary force led by local police chief **Viktors Arājs** – later sentenced to life imprisonment for war crimes after being unmasked in Germany in 1979.

Fears that Germany might lose the war and leave Latvia to the mercies of the Soviet Union encouraged more Latvians to sign up to the Nazi cause. A **Latvian Legion** was formed as an auxiliary to the SS in 1943 and led Latvia's defence against the advancing Red Army a year later. Rīga itself fell to the Soviets in October 1944 – thousands of Latvians were immediately conscripted into the Red Army and sent to fight their own countrymen in the Legion, who were still holding out in the northwest. As the war neared its end, as many as 200,000 Latvians **fled the country**, preferring life in West European refugee camps to the future offered by the Soviet Union.

Latvia under the Soviets

Resistance to the re-imposition of communist rule was initially encouraged by the erroneous belief that the Western powers would sooner or later come to Latvia's aid. In the immediate post-war years as many as 20,000 Latvians took to the countryside to join the anti-Soviet partisan movement known as the **Forest Brothers**. The Soviet security services responded by creating bogus partisan units of their own and using them to lure the real Forest Brothers into the open. The Soviet grip on the country was confirmed by a new wave of **deportations**, which saw the transport of over 43,000 Latvians to work camps in Siberia and beyond in March 1949.

Loyal Moscow-trained communists were imported to run the local party, and tens of thousands of workers were encouraged to emigrate to Latvia from other parts of the USSR in order to render the republic less ethnically homogenous. The death of Stalin in 1953 led to a gradual relaxation of ideological controls, but outright opposition to official Kremlin policy remained off the agenda. When leading Latvian communists **Berklavs** and **Krūmiņš** began to openly voice misgivings about the ongoing Russian emigration into Latvia, they were thrown out of the party by a specially convened central committee plenum in 1959 – Berklavs himself was exiled to Russia.

Denied political expression, patriotic Latvians threw their energies into the **cultural sphere**. In the 1970s and 1980s, folklore groups and choral societies blossomed: music was one of the few areas of Latvian life in which national sentiment could be expressed without provoking a clampdown by the Soviet state.

Latvians also prided themselves on being more culturally liberated than their conservative Soviet counterparts, and it's no surprise that the Soviet Union's first (and last) sex manual – psychotherapist Jānis Zālītis's *In The Name of Love* – was published here in 1981. After selling 100,000 copies it was banned by party officials, scandalized by the explicit illustrations – a picture-free second edition went on to shift another 75,000 units.

The road to independence

The appointment of the reformist **Mikhail Gorbachev** as General Secretary of the Soviet Communist Party in 1985 began a gradual erosion of ideological certainties throughout the USSR. Latvian intellectuals were suddenly able to discuss subjects that had been taboo for years – notably the highly illegal nature of the Soviet Union's initial occupation of Latvia in 1940. In autumn 1988, Latvian communists tried to take control of the growing tide of anti-Soviet feeling by forming a **Popular Front** with themselves at the helm – they were soon outmanoeuvred by more genuine patriots. Swiftly growing into a broad-based mass organization, the increasingly confident Front called for the full restoration of Latvian independence in October 1989. Relatively **free elections** to the Latvian Supreme Soviet in March 1990 produced a pro-independence majority which immediately issued a Declaration of Restored Independence and announced the restoration of the 1922 Latvian Constitution.

Although many of Latvia's communists swung behind the independence drive, a pro-Moscow faction under Alfrēds Rubiks took control of the party in

May 1990, and kicked pro-independence members out. Exploiting the fears of a sizeable ethnic Russian population made anxious by the implications of Latvian independence, the pro-Moscow lobby also launched a mass organization called **Interfront**, which attempted to storm the Supreme Soviet on May 14.

For the next nine months Latvia drifted in a strange limbo between independence and Soviet rule, with most people waiting on the outcome of the power struggle between Gorbachev, reformists and hardliners then unfolding in Moscow. In **January 1991,** Gorbachev sided with the hardliners, launching a military operation to seize key installations in the Lithuanian capital Vilnius. Fearing that the same would happen in Rīga, Latvians converged on the capital to mount a 700,000-strong pro-independence demonstration on January 13. Many of the participants stayed on to man barricades hastily erected around the Supreme Soviet, Telephone Exchange and TV Tower. On January 20, Soviet special forces attempted to gain control of the Latvian Interior Ministry, gunning down five innocents in the process (see p.207). Stung by criticism from the international community, Gorbachev abandoned plans for a further Baltic crackdown and another period of uneasy stand-off ensued. When conservative communists tried to unseat Gorbachev in the **Moscow Coup** of August 1991, only to surrender power several days later, the Soviet Union entered its death throes. Latvia re-iterated its independence declaration later the same month and international recognition soon followed.

Independent Latvia

The main issue facing Latvia's post-independence rulers was the question of how best to deal with the country's sizeable **non-Latvian population**. Of a population of 2.5 million, as many as forty percent were Russian-speaking – a direct result of the resettlement policies pursued by the Soviet regime. Latvian nationalists argued that full **citizenship** should only be granted to those descended from the pre-1945 population, attracting fierce criticism from an international community keen to promote a non-ethnic approach to civic rights. Latvian demographic angst was compounded by the fact that the country had one of the lowest birth rates in Europe and was therefore most unlikely to breed its way out of a population crisis. In the end, the Latvian government opted to bestow citizenship on post-1945 immigrants who had a "basic proficiency" in the Latvian language, while the European Union helped to fund language-study opportunities for those who wanted to qualify. Those who remained non-citizens retained the right to reside in Latvia, but couldn't vote and were barred from civil service jobs. In the early 1990s, there were an estimated 750,000 non-citizens in Latvia, a number that has now fallen to just over 500,000 – although this is due as much to outward migration and natural death as to any real improvement in language learning.

The other main theme of domestic politics has been the transformation of a dysfunctional state-run economy into a free, consumer-driven market. This has been achieved at miraculous speed, but at great social cost, with a minority making big bucks from the transition to pure and unfettered **capitalism**, while the majority eke a living on meagre wages. The failure of successive governments to battle post-independence corruption and raise living standards for all has produced a fluid political landscape in which few parties can count on consistent mass support. Stars of the 1999 elections were Latvias ceļš ("Latvia's Way"), a group of technocrats promising a media-friendly mixture of business competence and anti-corruption drives; in 2003, they were swept aside by

Jaunais laiks ("New Times"), another newly constituted party pledging much the same thing. What all Latvian parties have agreed upon is the need to integrate the country into international structures such as **NATO** and the **EU**, not least because membership of both organizations will help protect the country from any future resurgence of Russian influence. Until recently, the prospect of joining the EU enjoyed little popular enthusiasm, largely owing to fears that a small country like Latvia would be unable to protect its interests in a huge supra-national organization. In the end, there was a surprisingly high turn-out for the **referendum on EU membership** held in September 2003, with 67 percent voting in favour – thus paving the way for the country's official acceptance in May 2004.

Estonia

The history of Estonia begins in the tenth millennium BC at the close of the last ice age, when the retreat of the glaciers finally made the region fit for human habitation. It's not known who first settled the area, but by 3000 BC they had been either assimilated or displaced by the ancestors of today's Estonians, a **Finno-Ugric** people closely related to the Finns – and more distantly, the Hungarians. The Estonians, together with related Finno-Ugric tribes such as the Livs (see p.240) originally occupied a much larger territory than they do today, but were pushed back by the arrival of the Baltic peoples (forerunners of today's Lithuanians and Latvians) after 2000 BC – and Estonia has been a more-or-less stable ethnic unit ever since.

The early Estonians were farmers and fishermen, practising an animist religion of which little is known. There weren't really any villages or towns until the tenth century, when a tribal society emerged, presided over by chieftains ruling from stockade forts.

The Christian conquest of Estonia

Contacts with the outside world were limited until the tenth century, when the Vikings established trading posts on the northern coast and the emerging Russian towns of Pskov and Novgorod began sending mercantile and military missions to the southeast. In the early thirteenth century, land-hungry Western rulers persuaded the pope to authorize a crusade against the pagan peoples of the Baltic region, and with the German-based **Brotherhood of the Sword** (subsequently the Livonian Order) given free reign to invade what is now Latvia, rights to northern Estonia were granted to **King Valdemar II of Denmark**. Valdemar sent an army in 1219, founded the fortress town of Tallinn to serve as a base for future expansion and went on to build castles at Rakvere and Narva. Meanwhile, the Brotherhood of the Sword, well established in Rīga since 1201 and eager to prevent the Danes from becoming the dominant power in the region, expanded into Estonia from the south.

Although the Estonians put up fierce resistance, they were no match for their heavily armed, technically superior adversaries, and by the 1230s the Danes and the Brotherhood had succesfully carved up the country betwen them. The locals were forcibly **converted to Christianity** and their land divided up among a new ruling class of knights and bishops. While towns like Tallinn and Tartu filled up with German-speaking immigrants drawn by the region's mercantile potential, the Estonians themselves remained on the land, obliged as serfs to work on the feudal estates carved out by their conquerors – a situation which was to remain largely unchanged until the nineteenth century.

Feudal exactions in the Danish-controlled north provoked the so-called **St George's Night Uprising** of 1343, when Estonian peasants went on a rampage of violence, massacring landowners and burning monks in their monasteries. Worried by the cost of pacifying the countryside, the Danes sold all their possessions in northern Estonia four years later to the Brotherhood of the Sword's successor organization, the **Livonian Order**, for 19,000 silver marks. A geographical distinction between the southern and northern halves of the country remained: the south, together with northwestern Latvia, was known as Livland ("Livonia") and tended to look towards Rīga as its principal city; while the north, centred on Tallinn, was termed Estland ("Estonia") – a name which, centuries later, was to be applied to the whole country.

Under the Order, the gulf separating Estonian peasants from German-speaking landowners and priests grew wider. The towns in particular remained oases of German culture – even in the cosmopolitan port city of Tallinn, which attracted a growing Estonian community of domestic servants, boatmen and artisans from the fifteenth century onwards, total absorption into the German-language community was the prerequisite for social advancement.

Swedes and Russians

Estonian society under the Livonian Order was characterized by a slow-burning power struggle between the landed gentry, townsfolk and the Church. In the early sixteenth century, the cause of the **Reformation** (and especially its attack on ecclesiastical privilege and corruption) was enthusiastically taken up by aristocrats and burghers alike, transforming Estonia from a Catholic country into a bastion of Lutheranism almost overnight. Founded on medieval crusading ideals, the Order itself lost its raison d'être, producing a power vacuum eagerly exploited by neighbouring powers. In 1556, the **Swedes** captured Tallinn, using it as a base from which to expand across the whole of Estonia and northern Latvia. When the Russians invaded Estonia in 1558, the locals were glad of Swedish protection. The Swedes enlisted Polish support to throw the Russians back, beating them outside the Latvian town of Cēsis in 1578 and forcing them eastwards and capturing Narva later the same year. In 1595, the Treaty of Tensina confirmed Swedish control over the whole of Estonia.

Estonians still refer to the seventeenth century as the "**Good Swedish Times**". Although the power of the German magnates remained largely intact, Swedish rule brought a degree of justice to rural courts (torture was outlawed in 1686) and extended primary education to an increasing number of rural towns. Local government was placed in the hands of a new breed of competent, enlightened administrators – most of whom were graduates of the newly established Tartu University, founded by Swedish King Gustav Adolphus in 1632.

This comparative golden age came to an end with the **Great Northern War** (1700–21), a titanic struggle between Swedes and Russians which laid waste to large parts of Estonia, left Tallinn and Tartu in ruins, and made Russian Tsar Peter the Great the undisputed master of the Baltic. Having incorporated Estonia and Livonia into his empire, Peter won the support of the German magnates by reconfirming their privileges and offering them top jobs in the imperial administration. Manorial estates flourished, encouraging their owners to build ever grander manor houses (such as those at Palmse and Sagadi; see pp.368 & 371), although conditions failed to improve for the Estonian peasants, for whom eighteenth-century feudalism increasingly came to resemble a system of forced labour. The abolition of serfdom (in Estonia in 1816, Livonia in 1819) actually led to impoverishment for many peasants, who, cut loose by the big manorial estates that once supported them, ended up working as seasonal labourers for meagre wages.

The Estonian National Awakening

At the start of the nineteenth century, there was little in the way of an Estonian national consciousness. Even those Estonians who had escaped from the countryside to make a career in the towns had thoroughly Germanized themselves in order to do it. However, an increasing number of enlightened Baltic Germans were becoming interested in Estonian language and folklore. The **Estonian Learned Society**, founded by Germans attached to Tartu University in 1838, promoted the study of local culture and soon welcomed educated Estonians into its ranks. One of these, **Friedrich Reinhold Kreutzwald**, used traditional folk-tale fragments as the inspiration behind his epic poem *Kalevipoeg* ("Son of Kalev"; 1857), the first large-scale piece of narrative fiction to be written in the Estonian language. Estonian journalism was taking off too, with **Johann Voldemar Jannsen** publishing the weekly *Pärnu Postimees* ("Pärnu Courier") from 1857, then moving to Tartu in 1863 to found the (still-flourishing) daily *Eesti Postimees*. It was Jannsen who organized the first-ever **All-Estonian Song Festival** in Tartu in 1869.

The Russian authorities increasingly came to see Estonian-German struggles as an inconvenience and by the 1890s had begun a programme of **Russification** in a belated attempt to build a pan-national sense of Tsarist patriotism. Use of Russian was imposed on the (previously German-speaking) University of Tartu and the ensuing disruption led to a fall in academic standards. The chief result of the Russification campaign was to radicalize the Estonian national movement. Local intellectuals who had previously seen the Tsarist bureaucracy as a potential ally against the Baltic Germans now realized that they had to challenge both at the same time.

In 1904, Estonian parties won a majority of the seats on Tallinn City Council, with Tartu-educated lawyer **Konstantin Päts** (1874–1956) becoming vice-mayor – form dictated that the post of mayor itself go to a Russian. Estonians enthusiastically supported the anti-Tsarist **Revolution of 1905** in the hope that it would result in further constitutional reforms; its failure was a serious setback – most national leaders were forced into exile (including Päts, who was condemned to death in absentia) before an amnesty in 1910 allowed them to return.

World War I and the Estonian War of Independence

With the outbreak of **World War I** in 1914, the outlook for the Estonian national movement was pretty bleak. Hopes were revived, however, when the **Russian Revolution** of February 1917 delivered the sudden collapse of the Tsarist system. The Estonian representative in Petrograd, Jan Tõnisson, persuaded the new regime to grant Estonia a good measure of autonomy, and an **Estonian Assembly** was established in Tallinn to take over administrative duties. November 1917 saw the Bolsheviks win power in Russia; they won control of Tallinn, too, in early 1918, but soon evacuated the city, leaving the coast clear for a newly constituted Estonian government under the leadership of Päts to declare **Estonian independence** on February 24. Encouraged by the Bolshevik withdrawal, the German army marched into town the next day and had Päts arrested. When Germany surrendered to the Western allies on November 11, 1918, Päts quickly reassumed control, declaring Estonian independence again on November 18. Resurgent Bolsheviks occupied Narva and Tartu, but were prevented from capturing Tallinn by a swiftly assembled defence force that included teenage schoolboys. With former Tsarist officer **General Laidoner** at the helm, Estonia's nascent army soon developed into an efficient, highly motivated unit. Supplied with arms by the British and supported by volunteers from Finland (drawn to Estonia by the close ethnic ties between the two nations), Laidoner swiftly rolled the Bolsheviks back, forcing them to accept peace terms by autumn 1919.

At the same time, the Estonians had to counter the threat of a Baltic-German army under General von der Golz advancing towards their southern borders from Rīga. In June 1919, Estonian troops, accompanied by Latvian volunteers, marched into northern Latvia, defeated the Germans at the **Battle of Cēsis** and chased them all the way back to Rīga before signing an armistice and returning home.

The inter-war years

The Constituent Assembly elected in April 1919, opted for an idealistic constitutional model, establishing a single-chamber parliament (Riigikogu) to be presided over by a head of state (Riigivanem or "State Elder") who combined the duties of prime minster and president. Estonian democracy never functioned as perfectly as had been intended, however, and left-wing coup attempts in 1924 led to the outlawing of the communist party and the execution of its leaders. The 1920s were good years for agriculture (Estonian tinned pork was a big hit in the UK), but post-independence prosperity was brought to an end by the Great Depression after 1929. Many of those who had fought in the 1918–19 War of Independence were now disillusioned with an Estonian state unable to provide them with the jobs and rising living standards they'd expected and voiced their discontent by joining the **VAPS** – a fascistic pressure group which called for the imposition of authoritarian rule. Konstantin Päts sidestepped the appeal of VAPS by carrying out an authoritarian coup of his own: parliamentary parties were banned in 1934 and the Fatherland Front (Isamaaaliit) was created to provide the country with a single, guiding ideological force. Päts appointed himself president and set about transforming Estonia into a corporatist state similar to Mussolini's Italy, although World War II intervened before his reforms bore fruit.

World War II

As a small state lying between powerful neighbours, Estonia never had much room for manoeuvre and her fate was sealed by the **Molotov–Ribbentrop Pact** of August 1939, a secret agreement between Germany and the USSR which placed the Baltic States firmly within the Soviet sphere of influence. Eager to press the advantage, the Soviets insisted on establishing military bases in Estonia in October 1939, going on to occupy the country outright in **June 1940**. Fixed elections produced a pro-Soviet parliament, which obediently declared Estonia's accession to the USSR. Hostility to the new order was widespread; the Soviet authorities tried to break the back of Estonian opposition by organizing mass **deportations** – on June 14, 1941, as many as 10,000 Estonians of all social classes were bundled into cattle trucks bound for the east.

Many young Estonians took to the forests at this time, fearing that further round-ups were on the cards. They formed partisan groups that helped kick the Red Army out when **Nazi Germany** declared war on the Soviet Union on June 22. Any hopes that the Germans would behave like liberators were soon disappointed, however, with the country being incorporated into the new protectorate of Ostland – which, ironically, fell under the aegis of the Tallinn-born Nazi Alfred Rosenberg, leading ideologue of Aryan superiority and no great friend of the Estonians.

The second Soviet occupation

By September 1944, the Germans had been thrown out of Estonia by the advancing Red Army and the country once more became part of the USSR. If anything, the **second Soviet occupation** was even harsher than the first: a hard core of Moscow-trained activists was brought in to run the local communist party and a second wave of **deportations** in March 1949, removed as many as 20,000 Estonians (2.5 percent of the total Estonian population) to camps in the east. Women, children and the elderly made up ninety percent of the total – suggesting that deportees were arbitrarily chosen to fulfil a predetermined quota rather than being punished for any specific anti-Soviet beliefs. The bulk of deportees came from the countryside, leading to a collapse in agricultural production, only made worse by forced collectivization.

Thousands of young Estonians joined the anti-Soviet partisan movement known as the **Forest Brothers**, believing that the Western powers were bound to declare war on the USSR sooner or later. The British secret services trained Estonian exiles in London before shipping them across the Baltic Sea to join the Brothers, unaware that their movements had already been betrayed to the KGB by London-based moles. The movement had petered out by the early 1950s, by which time it was clear that no further help from the West was forthcoming. Amnesties in 1956–57 encouraged most surviving partisans to give themselves up, although the last known Forest Brother, August Stubbe, survived until September 1978, when he committed suicide to avoid capture by the KGB. Other pockets of **anti-Soviet resistance** included the Underground Committee of the Young Partisans of Estonia, who hoisted the Estonian tricolor from a church in Viljandi in 1954; and the Blue-Black-and-Whites, a group of idealistic high-school students who blew up a Soviet statue in Tartu in 1956.

Towards the "Singing Revolution"

Communist discipline was relaxed slightly during the post-Stalin thaw of the late 1950s, but expressions of Estonian patriotism were still viewed with displeasure by the party hierarchy. Things didn't really change much until the mid-1980s, when the policy of **Glasnost** ("Openness") initiated by Kremlin leader Mikhail Gorbachev gradually released long-repressed feelings of national resentment and outrage.

The first signs of change in Estonia came on August 23, 1987, when 2000 protesters met in Tallinn's Hirvepark to mark the anniversary of the Molotov-Ribbentrop Pact, followed by a 3000-strong demonstration in February 1988, to commemorate the anniversary of Estonia's 1918 declaration of independence. In April 1988, Tartu University history professor Edgar Savisaar called for the formation of a **Popular Front** during a TV phone-in, launching a mass popular movement at a single stroke. In September of the same year, over 250,000 Estonians converged on Tallinn's Song Grounds to hear a string of speakers demand the country's independence from the USSR. TV pictures of singing, flag-waving crowds were beamed around the world and the Baltic push for independence has been known as the "**Singing Revolution**" ever since. On August 23, 1989, the fiftieth anniversary of the Molotov-Ribbentrop Pact was marked in all three Baltic nations with over 200,000 people joining hands to form a **human chain** from Tallinn to Vilnius.

Now controlled by Popular Front members and pro-independence communists, the Estonian Supreme Soviet adopted a cautious approach, pressing for increased autonomy rather than outright secession from the union. Despite abortive attempts to crush the independence movements in Lithuania and Latvia in January 1991, the Soviet regime held back from launching a similar crackdown in Estonia. In March 1991, the Estonians felt confident enough to hold a **referendum** on full independence from the USSR, with 65 percent voting in favour. With the **Moscow Coup** of August 1991 threatening a return to the bad old days of hardline rule, the Estonian Supreme Soviet swiftly convened to make a full **declaration of independence**. On the collapse of the coup, international recognition of Estonian independence quickly followed.

From independence to the present

In September 1992, Estonia's first fully free elections in over sixty years were won by the right-of-centre Fatherland Party, whose youthful leader **Mart Laar** became prime minister. Despite numerous political realignments in the years that followed, the tone of post-independence politics has remained essentially the same, with a succession of cabinets – usually staffed by young technocrats untainted by involvement in Soviet politics – pursuing unabashedly free-market policies.

Throughout the 1990s, privatization of state-run enterprises and the emergence of a brash, new business culture opened the door to corruption and organized crime. The Estonian public expressed their distaste for this by using the 2003 elections to vote in a new government headed by **Res publica** – a typically post-modern, ideologically vague party promising managerial competence and moral government.

Estonia's first post-independence president, former Siberian deportee **Lennart Meri**, was a largely ceremonial figure at home – but the dignity and charm he deployed on the international stage helped to reaffirm Estonia's position in the world. In 2001, he was replaced by **Arnold Rüütel**, a former leader of the Estonian Communist Party who had chosen to swim with the patriotic tide in the late 1980s.

In many ways, the election of Rüütel symbolized a reconciliation between the strident Estonia-for-the-Estonians nationalism of the early 1990s and a more pragmatic approach to the country's Soviet heritage, most notably the presence of a large number of Russian-speakers on Estonian territory. Before the Soviet occupation, Estonia had been one of the most ethnically homogenous nations in Europe. After 1945, however, **Russian-speaking immigrants** from all over the USSR had been encouraged to move to Estonia – both to provide an industrial workforce and to engineer a new, less wholly Estonian, demographic profile. By 1990, Russian-speakers constituted about thirty percent of the population, concentrated especially in Tallinn, Narva and the oil-shale mining towns of the northeast. The introduction of a **citizenship law** that required non-Estonians to take a language test resulted in the exclusion of almost all of the non-Estonian population. Although many Russian-speakers have since passed the test, just over 200,000 so-called "non-citizens" remain in the country – allowed to live and work in Estonia, they are denied Estonian passports and remain poorly integrated into national life. Schools in areas of Russian settlement still use Russian as the main working language, although there are plans to enforce the use of Estonian in all schools by 2007. Whether this policy is achievable (currently there simply aren't enough Estonian-speaking teachers to go round) remains the subject of much debate.

In general, Estonia's "non-citizens" are becoming more enthusiastic about normalizing their status: the prospect of **EU membership** – and the attendant freedoms to travel and work abroad – have made Estonian passports increasingly worth having. The Estonians themselves voted overwhelmingly to join the EU in the **referendum of September 2003**, paving the way to full membership in May 2004.

Baltic folk music

The characteristic Baltic singing festivals – hugely popular events – played a major role in expressing the national identities of Estonia, Latvia and Lithuania during their move to independence. Now there are increasing signs of interest in their other musical traditions, many of which draw on ancient ways of making and hearing music.

Despite the considerable national and regional differences between (and within) the three countries, they share in the continuity of culture around the Baltic (including Finland and the Russian Baltic areas), reaching back thousands of years. All have folk song-poetry of the **runo-song** type and they have in common several traditional instruments, notably **Baltic psalteries** variously called kantele, kannel, kokles or kanklės. As a result of historical domination, however, the Baltic States manifest Germanic and Slavic cultural traits not found in Finland.

Though the inevitable changes in village life have meant that the context of much song and dance has disappeared, there's still a great deal to be found in living memory. In the 1960s, folklore movements sprang up, encouraging field trips to the villages and performances by urban enthusiasts: these attempted to reflect still-living musical traditions rather than the idealized, classically harmonized, folk-costumed approach of the Soviet-style ensembles.

Now there is the freedom for individual expression, but though the economies are growing, incomes are small and there's little money available for CD recording or high-powered staging. Baltic roots music remains relatively low-profile and uncommercial.

Lithuania

The largest Baltic state has a notably rich variety of folk forms, including layered **polyphonic music**, sung or played on reed instruments, flutes and – in common with its neighbours to the north – Baltic zithers.

Song

Thousands of Lithuanian traditional songs – **dainos** – have been collected. They deal with every aspect of life, and wedding and love songs feature particularly prominently. Some would be passed on as well-known songs, but others, such as lullabies, would be varied or improvised to suit the occasion. In the early twentieth century many women – predominantly the creators and carriers of songs – had repertoires of a hundred or more.

Singing can be solo or in a group, in unison or in parallel chords of thirds, fourths or fifths. Aukštaitija, Lithuania's northeastern region, has a distinctive and well-known tradition of polyphonic songs, **sutartinės**, whose melody and form are also transferred to instrumental music. They are duophonic – two voices, or groups of voices in harmony. In the case of **dvejinės** (by twos) and **keturinės** (by fours) two harmonizing lines are sung together, then they stop and are replaced by a second group of singers and two different harmonizations, while in **trejinės** three parts overlap, two at a time, as in a canon. The word stresses create a syncopating internal rhythm.

Instruments

There is a relatively large range of Lithuanian traditional instruments. The basic form of the Lithuanian version of Baltic zither, the **kanklės**, differs regionally in playing style and in the number of strings, which can be anywhere between five and twelve. The repertoire of the traditional kanklės consisted of old-style material such as sutartinės and more modern dance tunes such as polkas, waltzes and quadrilles. A "concert series" of large, many-stringed box kanklės was devised for the Soviet-style ensembles.

Whereas previously, the old round dances (*rateliai*) were traditionally accompanied by singing only, during the nineteenth and twentieth centuries instrumental ensembles commonly played the newer dance forms. Instrumental groups playing kanklės and lamzdeliai (wooden or bark whistles) existed as far back as the sixteenth century. Later, the fiddle and three-stringed bass basetle joined them, and in the nineteenth and early twentieth centuries accordions, bandoneons, concertinas, Petersburg accordions and harmonicas, mandolins, balalaikas, guitars, modern clarinets and cornets. During the Soviet era, dressed-up ensembles emerged using box kanklės and birbynės (folk clarinets – they used the developed form which is a mellow-sounding thick tube with a cowhorn bell). These groups actually made quite a pleasant sound, not so different from a disciplined village band, but they were often used, to the annoyance of those searching out the "real thing", in classically influenced arrangements to accompany choral singing of harmonized and denatured so-called sutartinės with all their dissonances smoothed out.

In the northeast, tunes of the sutartinė type were played on skudučiai – rather like dismantled pan-pipes, played by a group of men. The same type of tune was played by five-piece sets of birch-bark-bound wooden trumpets (ragai), or alternatively, by pairs of the straighter, longer daudytės; each of the latter could produce up to five natural harmonics, so only two daudytės were needed for a set.

Other wind instruments include švilpas (overtone whistle), goat-horns, and sekminiu ragelis (a single-drone bagpipe). Percussion instruments include tabalas (a flat piece of wood hung and hit like a gong) and drums. An unusual stringed instrument is the pūslinė – a musical bow with an inflated pig's bladder resonator containing a rattling handful of dried peas.

Performers

As the social structure changed, and Sovietization altered Lithuanian society from the outside, the old ways of music lost much of their role. Tradition moved to post-traditional, or "secondary folklore", with material collected from those who remembered the old ways converted to a form considered suitable for performance to an audience.

The first Lithuanian folklore ensembles were formed around the beginning of the twentieth century. One of them, formed in 1906 and still existing, is the **Skriaudžiai kanklės ensemble**. Subsequently, ethnographic plays such as **The Kupiskenai Wedding** were staged. While these tried to reflect genuine village life, concert ensembles worked on the premise that the rough old folk songs needed sprucing up.

A choral movement gathered momentum, resulting in the huge song festivals, **Dainu Sventes**. The first of these was held in 1924, and then every five years during the Soviet period. As well as choirs, professional concert folk ensembles such as **Lietuva**, formed in 1940, appeared at such events.

"Modernized" folk instruments were created, and traditional dress was formalized into national costume.

While this was an acceptable form of national expression within the Soviet regime, a back-to-the-villages folklore movement began during the 1960s, spurred on later in the decade by the Prague Spring events in Czechoslovakia. Rasa (the summer solstice) and other Baltic pagan events were publicly celebrated despite persecution by the KGB. **Folklore ensembles** sprang up in towns and cities, and the village musicians from whom they collected formed performing units themselves, usually known as "ethnographic ensembles". There were folklore camps and competitions. The first republic-wide ensemble competition Ant mario krantelio ("On the Sea Shore") occurred in the 1980s at Rumsiskes, attracting a thousand contestants. The annual Skamba skamba kankliai in Vilnius's Old Town began in 1975, and Kaunas hosted Atataria trimitai. The first **Baltica** International Folklore Festival, which moves between the Baltic States each year, took place in 1987 in Vilnius.

The current undisputed doyenne of Lithuanian folk singing is **Veronika Povilionienė**, a native of the Dzūkija region who has been the nation's outstanding performer of unaccompanied female narrative songs ever since her student days in the late 1960s. Having championed the role of folk music as a rallying point for anti-Soviet intellectuals during the Soviet period, she has since become something of a national treasure. Her repertoire consists mostly of traditional material from all over the country, although she's also made several excursions into crossover territory – the 1993 album *Povilionienė/Vyšniauskas* (recorded with jazz saxophonist Petras Vyšniauskas) is one of the most startling exercises in fusion to come out of the Baltics, although it's hard to get hold of nowadays.

The main problem for Lithuanian roots music since independence has been the lack of record-industry support, although things seem to be changing with the emergence of Juosta Records, the designated folk off-shoot of mainstream label Muzikos bomba (🌐www.bomba.lt). Juosta is in the process of releasing a whole raft of regional compilations, as well as outstanding individual albums by leading interpreter of Žemaitijan song Loreta Mukaitė; and archive material by X Ženklas, an enigmatic group of post-folk, post-rock instrumentalists active in the early 1990s. One other adventurous label to look out for is Dangus (🌐www.dangus.net), whose releases range from the archly archaic chanting of neo-pagan priests Kūlgrinda to the cacophonous twenty-first-century folk-metal of Notanga.

Latvia

The land of amber has more Baltic zithers, drone-based singing, and a large body of traditional song-poetry – **dainas** – with strong pre-Christian symbolism and a lack of heroes.

The daina

The Latvian **daina** is a short song of just one or two stanzas, one or two lines long, without rhyme, and largely in the same four-footed trochaic metre as runo-songs. *Dainas* feature mythological subjects and most aspects of village life, but the stories and heroic exploits described in many countries' folksongs are notably absent.

The sun is a dominant image, often personified as **Saule**, and her daily course across the sky and through the year is linked metaphorically with human life. While the sun is female, **Mēness**, the moon, is male, and a frequent song theme is courtship between them or other celestial figures such as the twin sons of Dievs (God) and the daughter of the sun. The solstices were traditional occasions for celebration – in particular **Jāņi** (midsummer) – whose central figure was Janis, the archetypal vigorous, potent male with strong phallic associations. As the *ligotne* (midsummer song) "Jāņa Daudzinajums" describes him:

> *Oh Jānis, the son of Dievs,*
> *what an erect steed you have*
>
> *The spurs are glittering through forests,*
> *the hat above trees*
>
> *Jānis was riding all the year*
> *and has arrived on the Jāņi eve;*
>
> *Sister, go and open the gate, and let Jānis in*

(Translation by Valdis Muktupāvels)

The major collection of *dainas* was made by **Krišjānis Barons** (1835–1923); the six volumes of his *Latvju Dainas* were published between 1894 and 1915, and contain about 300,000 texts.

In keeping with other regions of the Baltics, newer song forms spread during the nineteenth century, when chordal, fixed-scale instruments – such as the accordion – arrived. Thus **zinge** is a singing style with a strong German influence. The older forms remained, however: **dziesma** means a song having a definite melody, while **balss** means "voice" or "speech" and has no clearly defined melody, changing with the rhythm of the words. Balss was the style used in calendar celebrations as well as during work. It usually follows a three-voice form: the leader sings a couple of stanzas of a *daina*, then the others repeat them. In some regions these repetitions are sung over a vocal drone – a distinctive feature not found elsewhere in the Baltics but still a living tradition in some parts of Latvia.

Kokles and citara

For village dance music and song tunes (*sadzīves* music), the traditional Latvian instruments include bagpipe, goat horn, whistles and rattle-stick, and more recently fiddle and various accordions. But as elsewhere in the Baltic, it is the zither that is dominant.

The Latvian Baltic zither is called the **kokle** or **kokles**, and in its traditional form it has between five and twelve strings. It is seen as a national symbol, and as elsewhere in the Baltics larger, box-built instruments were developed for use in Soviet-style folkloric ensembles. These, fitted with screw-in legs and often ornamented with a central jewel of the locally abundant amber, are attractive in appearance and ensemble sound, but not very responsive as instruments, with musicians displaying a rather stiff playing style based on a Western classical approach.

Renewed interest in the traditional, smaller carved kokles began during the folklore movement of the 1970s. The instrument survived in the living tradition of only a few areas: the Catholic enclaves of Kurzeme in western Latvia and Latgale in the east. The strongest influence in this revival was **Jānis**

Porikis, who made a couple of hundred kokles and organized workshops and performances. **Valdis Muktupāvels**, Latvia's leading player, learned the style of the Suiti region from Porikis, and has gone on to champion the instrument.

Muktupāvels normally plays a nine-string kokles of the type found in eastern Latvia – with a "wing" extension of the soundboard beyond the soundbox and pegs. Drones occur in Latvian singing, and it's usual to tune the lowest string of a kokles to a drone a fourth below the key note. There are several regional playing styles involving plucking or strumming and damping, including – as in some Estonian styles – that of resting the fingers of the left hand on the soundboard between the strings and moving them from side to side, damping sets of strings alternately to leave the rest ringing as chords while strumming with the other hand.

In North America the small kokles has become the main instrument of Latvian-American cultural groups. While in Latvia there's no dominant design – the instruments were homemade and each maker-player put in individual features – most of these American kokles are of a single pattern, wingless and with almost identical soundboard decoration, probably because buyers from the handful of North American makers want an instrument identical to the one they've seen played at Latvian-American gatherings.

A wide variety of interesting designs of **citara** (chord-zither) are still in use in Latvia. Most have large numbers of strings, some or all of which are tuned as ready-made chords. These are not principally related to Baltic psalteries but rather to the mostly German factory-made chord-zithers and autoharps sold since the nineteenth century across Europe and North America. Individual Baltic makers have made ingenious modifications, some resulting in very big instruments and a few that are cylinder-shaped. There are also hybrid forms between citara and kokles, known as **citarkokles**.

In the eastern province of Latgale, **hammered dulcimers** have been played since the early nineteenth century, a borrowing from nearby Belarus.

Performers

The core of musicians working with real traditional music across the divide from Soviet to post-Soviet Latvia, rejecting Soviet-approved folkloric decorativeness, has been very small in number. Today's best-known group is **Iļģi**, which since its formation way back in 1981 has progressed from an acoustic sound to more of a folk-rock approach. Iļģi's Ilga Reizniece and Māris Muktupāvels also provide the main folk component of pop-charting Latvian rock band **Jauns Mēness** (New Moon). Jauns Mēness leader **Ainars Mielavs** and his Upe record label are taking a prime role in the development and popularization of new Latvian tradition-rooted music at home and abroad.

Valdis Muktupāvels, elder brother of Iļģi and Jauns Mēness's Māris, is a leading bagpiper and kokles player and the key authority on Latvian ethnomusicology. **Grodi** and **Rasa**, of which Valdis is a member, both formed in the late 1980s as Soviet rule was crumbling. He describes the music they and the other roots-revival bands make as "post-traditional". Also significant is **Auri** (formed in 1991 and led by Māris Jansons). Now that things have got moving, not just in Latvian roots music, but also in the country's pop, rock, jazz and techno scene, new names and fresh ideas are emerging, including the all-female group **Laiksne** and singer and kokles player **Biruta Ozoliņa**.

Estonia

Estonia's traditional culture, while distinct, has strong links with that of the linguistically and geographically close Finland, with **runo-songs** and its own variants of **Baltic zither**.

Runo-song

Estonian runo-song has the same basic form as the Finnish variety to which it is related: the line has eight beats, the melody rarely spans more than the first five notes of a diatonic scale and its short phrases tend to use descending patterns.

A large number of runo-song texts have been collected, largely from women, and thus offering a female point of view. They cover most aspects of life, including work, rituals, spells, ballads and mythical stories, and tend to a stoic sadness, or wry observation of life's realities, rather than extreme expressions of joy or love. The more ornamented **swing-songs** were sung while sitting on the big communal village swing whose movement made its own rhythmic demands.

Estonia's national epic **Kalevipoeg**, by folklorist **F. Reinhold Kreutzwald** (1803–1882), was published in the 1860s, paralleling folklorist Elias Lonnröt's creation from runo-song sources of Finland's *Kalevala*, first published in 1835. **Armas Launis**'s collection of melodies of the runo-songs from which *Kalevipoeg* had been constructed was published in 1930.

By the early twentieth century, runo-song was largely overtaken by more European forms of rhyming folksong with wider-spanning tunes and sometimes instrumental accompaniment. Nevertheless, it survived in a few areas – notably in Setumaa, which straddles Estonia's Russian border, and also on the island of Kihnu and among Estonian-resident members of Ingria's repeatedly displaced population.

Setu song

The songs of the **Setu people** have considerably influenced contemporary roots singers, both in Estonia and in Finland. There's been a recent revival in Setu culture and the speaking of its dialect. Several villages, such as Värska (see p.397), Kosselka, Helbi, Obinitsa (see p.397) and Uusvada have established women's vocal groups that perform songs traditionally sung and danced while working or at social events, particularly the three-day wedding celebration. The eight-syllable runo pattern of these songs is often interrupted by extra syllables and refrains, and unlike other Estonian vocal traditions, they are sung polyphonically, the other singers taking the leader's line (the *torrõ*) and adding a lower part (the second *torrõ*), and a higher, penetrating single voice (the *killõ*) which often uses just two or three notes.

Kannels and zithers

The old pastoral wind instruments such as animal horns, wooden birch-bark-bound trumpet, willow overtone whistle and bagpipe have lost their traditional herding context, but are used to some extent by present-day, folk-rooted musicians. The fiddle, the ever-popular accordion and the long-bellowed concertina are used in the playing of couple-dance tunes, the most prevalent form of which is the **polka**.

Discography

General Baltics compilations
Voix des pays Baltes – Chants traditionnels de Lettonie, Lituanie, Estonie (Inedit, France). Field recordings from all three Baltic countries going back as far as the 1930s, including calendar songs, work songs and Lithuanian sutartinės.

Estonia compilations
Estonia: Olden Tunes (Ocora, France). 26 tracks, mostly recorded by Estonian national radio, of performers, solo and in groups, using traditional instruments; kannel, torupill (bagpipe), karjapasun (herder's horn), roopill (reed pipe) and vilepill (willow whistle), with some archive recordings from as early as 1912.

Estonian Traditional Music 2001 (Viljandi Folk Music Festival, Estonia). Recordings by many of the young Estonian groups playing at the country's biggest folk festival in 2001.

Setu Songs (Mipu, Finland). Setu women's singing groups from the villages of Helbi, Kosselka, Obinitsa, Uusvada, Meremäe and the Leiko group from Värska, recorded in situ and in Helsinki.

Estonia artists
Veljo Tormis *Forgotten Peoples* (ECM, Germany). Critically acclaimed double CD of six compositions by Veljo Tormis, an influential composer of choral arrangements of Estonian folk songs based on the music of Livonian, Votic, Izhorian and Karelian Finno-Ugric peoples, here sung by the Estonian Philharmonic Chamber Choir.

Kirile Loo *Saatus (Fate)* (Erdenklang, Germany; Alula, US). Runo-song-based material sung by north-Estonian Kirile Loo in sparse, atmospheric settings with traditional instruments (kannel, bagpipe, reed-pipe, straw whistle, Jew's harp) plus keyboards and guitar, arranged by Peeter Vähi.

Lullabies for Husbands (Erdenklang, Germany). Kirile Loo's excellent 1999 album, with more developments of traditional lyrics and melodic forms, in collaboration with Tiit Kikas, who plays all the instruments, acoustic and electronic.

Latvia compilations
Beyond the River: Seasonal Songs of Latvia (EMI Hemisphere, UK). A credible and widely available introduction to the leading contemporary Latvian roots groups. 17 tracks of Auri, Iļģi, Grodi and Rasa.

Dūdas Latvijā – Latvian Bagpipes (Upe, Latvia). A collection featuring seven bagpipers, including Valdis and Māris Muktupāvels.

Music From Latvia (Cooking Vinyl/Upe, UK/Latvia). Also released by Upe itself as *A Touch Of Latvian Folk Music* (Upe, Latvia). A compilation from Upe, the label that has made most of the recent releases of Latvian roots music. Features tracks from Iļģi, Uģis Prauliņš, Biruta Ozoliņa, Laiksne, Vilki, Ainars Mielavs and more. (Upe records are available from its online store at ⊛www.upe.parks.lv.)

Latvia artists
Iļģi *Saules Meita* (Upe, Latvia). This leading Latvian band explores traditional repertoire and creates new material using largely traditional instrumentation. Their 1998 album saw a move to a more electrified approach, and some line-up changes, but still with strong attachment to traditional styles and instruments.

Kaza Kāpa Debesīs (Upe, Latvia). This recording was released in 2003, after extensive tours abroad, including in the USA, and it reflects the band's new perspectives in an ever more hefty sound that, while drawing on some rock rhythm-section universals, nevertheless very effectively punches home the distinctiveness of Latvian musical forms.

Jauns Mēness *Dzivotajs* (Upe, Latvia). Meaning "New Moon", this influential rock band, pop-charting during the 1990s, plays original material but with traditional music aspects. The group's most recent (1998) album has a mainstream rock approach, spiced by lead singer's Aigars Voitiskis's mandolin and the traditional instruments of Iģļi's Ilga Reizniece and Māris Muktupāvels.

Uģis Prauliņš *Paganu Gadagramata* (Upe, Latvia). Programmer, producer, singer, keyboard, kokles and flute player Prauliņš combines traditional music with current studio technology. The material on this CD is from the folksong collections of Emilis Melngailis, in very sympathetic atmospheric settings. It features Jauns Mēness guitarist Gints Sola and the voices and traditional instruments of Ilga Reizniece and Māris Muktupāvels. Released in 1999, it was an impressive start to the "Latvian Folk Music Collection" from Ainars Mielavs' Upe label.

Rasa Ensemble *Latvia: Music of Solar Rites* (Inedit, France). Traditional songs, both polyphonic (with vocal drones) and monophonic, for summer and winter solstices, weddings, funerals, working and drinking, plus instrumentals including a kokles solo and dance music.

Valdis Muktupāvels *Kokles* (Upe, Latvia). A double CD, one of traditional tunes, the other of Muktupāvels' own compositions for kokles. A prime mover in maintaining and reviving Latvian traditional music during the difficult Soviet days and carrying it through to the new Latvia, Muktupāvels is a player of kokles and bagpipes, singer, and highly regarded ethnomusicologist.

Biruta Ozoliņa *Balta eimu* (Upe, Latvia). A superb collection of sparsely arranged, heart-stoppingly haunting, traditional songs delivered in Latgale dialect by long-established singer Biruta Ozoliņa. Her second album *Sirdsgriezi* (Upe), includes instrumental backing from jazz bass and electric piano, and is disappointingly coffee-table in comparison.

Tulli Lum *Tulli Lum* (Viljandi Folk Music Festival, Estonia). A live album recorded at the Viljandi Folk Music Festival by this Estonian-based band. The vocals to their folk-rock-jazz are in Livonian, the almost disappeared Finno-Ugric language that survives only in coastal Latvia; indeed it's now spoken only by the Stalte family, of which Tulli Lum lead singer Julgi Stalte is a member.

Lithuania compilations

Lithuanian Folk Music (33 Records, Lithuania). 46 recordings from 1930s to 1980s of work, ritual, wedding, nature, children's, historical and war songs, and instrumental music – with extensive English notes.

Lituanie: Le Pays Des Chansons (Ocora, France). Excellent, varied collection of 35 traditional songs and instrumentals, including horn, kanklės and sutartinės, recorded for Lithuanian Radio between 1958 and 1990. Notes in French and English.

Lithuanian Folk Dreams (Sutaras/Kuku, Lithuania). Compilation of recordings on the Kuku label, including Atalyja, Veronika Povilionienę, Sutaras, the Keisto folklore group and others. (CDs on the Kukū label and most other Lithuanian folk music recordings can be bought online from http://www.sutaras.lt.)

Lithuanian Traditional Music: Sutartinės *(Lithuanian Polyphonic Songs)* (TNS, Lithuania). 39 wedding, work, dance, spinning, war, family songs from four regions of Lithuania, in field recordings from 1911 onwards, with extensive booklet notes.

continued overleaf

Lithuanian artists

Atalyja *Atalyja* (Sutaras/Kuku, Lithuania). Powerful and fresh 2001 debut release by a ten-member band of new developments based on seasonal songs and sutartinės. The melodies are very narrow in compass, virtually never straying outside a repeated short sequence made from the first five notes, often fewer, of a minor scale, but they develop them by floating the grainy vocals over bass guitar patterns, adding the textures of the traditional instruments.

Veronika Povilionienė *Vai Ant Kalno* (Sutaras/Kuku, Lithuania). Compilation of recordings by a singer long highly regarded in Lithuania for her serene, rich-toned voice. The songs were recorded from 1986 and 2000, some unaccompanied except for the sounds of the forest where they were recorded, others involving unexpected and wonderfully eccentric collisions with rock, jazz and avant-garde.

Jievaras *Jievaras* (Sutaras/Kuku, Lithuania). Re-release on CD of a 1988 recording. Founded in 1979, this folk band sings songs they have collected around the country, accompanying them with traditional instruments including bagpipe, cymbals, kanklės, lamzdeliai, ragai, skuduciai and harmonica.

Sutaras *Radijo Bangomis – On The Radio* (Sutaras/Kuku, Lithuania). A live radio concert recorded in 2003 and consisting of 28 tracks of dance tunes and songs. Formed in 1988 and led by Antanas Fokas, the group specializes in reviving ancient instruments and repertoire. It has made six albums to date and been a training ground for a stream of musicians.

Polkas also feature, together with older music, in the repertoire of the **kannel**, the Estonian version of the Baltic psaltery, which, though it tends to have six strings rather than five, is of the same basic design as Finland's kantele – a carved, wedge-shaped box, with strings passing direct from pegs to a single attaching bar. Players died out during the twentieth century, but the instrument itself survived (if only to hang on the wall) amongst the many exiles in North America – where the small kannel has had something of a revival. In Estonia itself, the formation of Soviet-style folkloric ensembles involved the creation of an "orchestral series" of bigger chromatic box-kannels. However, visits from contemporary Finnish kantele-players such as Hannu Saha and Antti Kettunen have helped to stimulate new interest in small kannels.

Setumaa has its own form of kannel, usually with a soundboard extended wing-like beyond the box, rather like those found in eastern Latvia and parts of western Russia. This form is increasingly used, for example by Finnish kantele virtuoso Timo Väänänen. Leading Estonian kannel players include **Tuule Kann** and multi-instrumental ethnomusicologist **Igor Tõnurist**.

In Estonia, as in Latvia and Lithuania, folk players of a wide and ingenious range of **board-zither** or **chord-zither** can be found. These aren't true kannels/kanteles, but are closer in design to the zithers, autoharps and other domestic multi-stringed instruments made largely in German factories and sold across northern Europe and North America. The bowed lyre, **hiiu-kannel** (called a **jouhikko** in Finnish) was played until the twentieth century in the Swedish enclaves of Estonian islands (relics of Sweden's fifty-year rule over Estonia from 1660 until 1710), particularly Runö, and is finding a role again today in some of the modern folk bands.

Ensembles and festivals

During the 1960s, instructions were sent by Moscow to cultural organizers throughout the Soviet Union that supervised manifestations of genuine, living folk culture were to be encouraged, to demonstrate the government's support for the needs and expressions of the masses. In the Baltics, reluctant members of these "masses" were researching these same living cultures, not in response to Moscow's wishes but in order to explore the distinctiveness of their own culture.

Performing ensembles fell into two groups: "ethnographic" – which came from a particular area and specialized in local forms – and "folkloric" – which drew on the whole country's traditions. The first of the "ethnographic" type to appear in the more liberal climate of the 1960s was the Setu choir **Leiko** from Värska, formed in 1964. Of the "folkloric" type, **Leigarid** (formed in 1969 to entertain tourists at Tallinn Open-air Ethnographic Museum) soon turned away from the colourful folkloric spectacle approach towards a more authentic style rooted in village traditions. Regional ethnographic performance groups were formed, too, as were young city-based ensembles such as **Leegajus** (led by **Igor Tõnurist**) and **Hellero**.

In 1985, the conference of CIOFF (Conseil International des Organisations de Festivals de Folklore et d'Arts Traditionelles) was held in Estonia, and in 1986 the **Viru säru** folk festival took place in Palmse. The **Baltica** festival, which moves each year to a different Baltic state, began in 1987, and Tallinn first hosted it in 1989. These growing performance opportunities stimulated more groups and further cultural developments, including the opening of a folk music department at the Cultural College in **Viljandi** in 1990.

More fuel for revival, or for continuation of the traditional music in different "post-traditional" circumstances, had been provided by the publication between 1956 and 1965 of the five volumes of **Eesti Rahvalaule Viisidega** ("Estonian Folk Songs with Notations") edited by **Herbert Tampere**, who had been working on and publishing folk music since the 1930s. In 1969 appeared the first book of the eight-volume anthology of Estonian folk-song texts, *Eesti Rahvalaulud*. The first anthology of recordings on LP, **Eesti Rahvalaule ja Pillilugusid** ("Estonian Folk Songs and Instrumental Music"), was released in 1967 and a second followed in 1970.

Contemporary composers and musicians have gone to work on traditional sources. The choral folk and runo-song arrangements of composer **Veljo Tormis** became popular, having influence as far away as the Estonian community in Australia where the choir **Kiri-uu** added avant-gardist synths and samples to their own choral performances using many of Tormis's arrangements. Kiri-uu nowadays is no longer a choir, but a vocal and technology duo comprising **Olev Muska** and **Coralie Joyce**.

Singer **Kirile Loo** combines traditional runo-song influences and modern sensibilities. After two albums she has recently begun to take these approaches into live performance with a band fusing samples and traditional instruments.

Finally, and although not rooted in traditional music, a major Estonian contribution to modern music is the instrumental and choral work of one of the twentieth century's major composers and musical innovators, **Arvo Pärt**.

It is still a little early for Estonian roots performers to be making an impression on the world music touring and festival circuit, but at home the scene is growing. The annual **Viljandi** folk festival at the end of July attracts a young audience to see a variety of roots bands, and whether it's in Estonia, Latvia or Lithuania there's a substantial list of Estonian performers on the bill of **Baltica**.

Written and researched by Andrew Cronshaw

Books

P lenty of books were written about the Baltic States during the collapse of the Soviet Union and its aftermath, and if a brief grounding in the region's history and politics is what you're after, there's a good deal to choose from. Other aspects of Baltic culture are much less visible in the bookshops and many of the most perceptive accounts of travel in the area were produced by nineteenth- and early twentieth-century writers whose works are nowadays hard to find. A number of non-Baltic writers have used the Baltic States as a background for their fiction, but – curiously, and rather depressingly – the rich traditions of Lithuanian, Latvian and Estonian literature are almost invisible in English-speaking countries, with Estonia's grand old man of letters Jaan Kross the only novelist who regularly gets translated. Titles marked with a book symbol are particularly recommended. The abbreviation "o/p" means "out of print".

General Baltics

History and politics

Eric Christiansen *The Northern Crusades*. Definitive account of the thirteenth-century conquest of Estonia and Latvia by German-speaking knights and priests. The mixture of missionary zeal and near-genocidal savagery that characterized the times comes in for thought-provoking scrutiny.

John Hiden and Patrick Salmon *The Baltic States and Europe*. Excellent introduction to the main themes of Baltic history, concentrating on the twentieth century.

David Kirby *The Baltic World. Vol. I 1492–1772; vol II 1772–1993*. General, wide-screen history examining long-term German, Swedish and Russian interests in the region, as well as the fates of the Baltic peoples themselves.

★ **Anatol Lieven** *Baltic Revolution*. Witty, erudite and endlessly stimulating book which successfully mixes history, reportage and where-do-the-Baltics-go-from-here analysis, written by the journalist-descen-dant of a long line of Latvian aristocrats.

R.J. Misiunas & R. Taagepera *The Baltic States: Years of Dependence, 1940–1980*. Baltic society and politics under Soviet occupation, Nazi occupation and Soviet occupation again, examined by a pair of leading scholars.

Georg von Rauch *The Baltic States: Years of Independence, 1917–1940* (o/p). The definitive work on the inter-war period, covering the intrigues of internal politics, as well as the growing threats posed to the three Baltic States by outside powers, notably the Soviet Union.

Clare Thomson *The Singing Revolution*. The main events of the late 1980s and early 1980s, presented with involving immediacy by a journalist who was there at the time.

Various *The Anti-Soviet Resistance in the Baltic States* (Lithuania, Genocide and Resistance Research Centre).

Stimulating and readable series of articles written by historians from all three Baltic States (including erstwhile Estonian Prime Minister Mart Laar), investigating the rise and fall of the partisan movements that attempted to resist Soviet power in the decade 1945–55.

Memoirs and travel

Walter Duranty *I Write as I Please* (o/p). Rollicking war-correspondent memoirs from an eye-witness to the Latvian and Estonian wars of independence. If you want to know what conflict-scarred cities like Tallinn and Rīga were like in 1919, this is a good start.

J.G. Kohl *Russia* (o/p). Indefatigable German guide-book writer who ventured all over Europe in the 1830s and 1840s and wrote vast, best-selling tomes about his travels. This one covers much of the Tsarist Empire, including an account of a journey through Latvia and Estonia that remains an important source on the semi-feudal, manorial culture that prevailed in the countryside at the time.

E. Alexander Powell *Undiscovered Europe* (o/p). An American journalist who visited Lithuania, Latvia and Estonia in the 1930s, Powell is a sympathetic and well-informed observer who offers the occasional insightful nugget.

Owen Rutter *The New Baltic States and their Future* (o/p). Travelling through the Baltic in the early 1920s, Rutter never quite got to grips with the region and comes across as a bit of a bumbler. The resulting text is pooterish in the extreme, but remains a wonderful source of local colour from a time when few other foreigners were travelling in the area.

Literature about the Baltic States

Johannes Bobrowski *Shadow Lands*. One of Germany's greatest twentieth-century poets, Bobrowski grew up in an East Prussian town shaped by German, Lithuanian, Polish and Jewish influences, only to see this cosmopolitan world destroyed during World War II. Feelings of cultural loss (and German guilt) fill his poems – of which this volume is a beautifully translated selection.

Stephan Collishaw *The Last Girl*. Eminently readable offering in which an elderly Lithuanian poet stalks the streets of post-Soviet Vilnius, haunted by memories of wartime betrayal. The atmosphere of Lithuania in the 1990s is authentically rendered.

Jonathan Franzen *The Corrections*. Award-winning novel about contemporary America and its discontents, centring on a mid-western couple and their far-flung offspring – one of whom ends up in the Lithuanian capital in the early 1990s. The Vilnius portrayed by Franzen – a post-communist wild east characterized by organized crime and pollution – is rather different from the one that exists today. Unsurprisingly, the book became notorious in Lithuania itself, where Franzen is considered persona non grata.

Tadeusz Konwicki *Bohin Manor*. Elegaic novel set among the Polish-Lithuanian gentry in the wake of the 1863 anti-Tsarist upris-

433

ing, written by one of Poland's leading twentieth-century novelists – himself a native of the Vilnius region. Capturing wonderfully the tone of manor-house life in the Lithuanian backwoods, this is a knowing attempt to update *Pan Tadeusz* (see below) for a modern audience.

Henning Mankell *The Dogs of Riga*. World-weary Swedish cop Kurt Wallender heads for Rīga looking for help in solving a murder case. Set in 1990, with Latvia in an uneasy limbo between communism and independence, this book paints a convincing picture of the paranoia and uncertainty of the times.

Adam Mickiewicz *Pan Tadeusz*. Poland's national epic, a poem of Homeric proportions describing the ructions and reconciliations of a Polish-Lithuanian gentry family on the eve of Napoleon's invasion of the Tsarist Empire.

★ **Czesław Miłosz** *The Issa Valley*. Wonderfully lyrical, semi-autobiographical account of a post-World War I boyhood spent in the Lithuanian countryside by Nobel Prize-winning Miłosz. The Issa of the title is based on the real-life River Nevėžis, north of Kaunas.

★ **Denise Neuhaus** *The Christening*. Spellbinding novel about the fates of three Estonian women split between Stockholm and Tallinn in the 1970s and 80s. Combining elements of family saga

and political thriller, its depiction of life in the last decades of Soviet Estonia is totally believable.

William Palmer *The Good Republic*. Well-written, intelligent and thought-provoking novel about a London-based emigre returning to the unnamed Baltic state of his birth (an artistic amalgam of Estonia and Latvia), to be confronted by the ghosts of his politically ambiguous past.

Anthony Powell *Venusberg* (o/p). An inter-war novel involving a junior English diplomat who is posted to an East European capital – clearly based on a mixture of Tallinn and Rīga – where he falls in with a bunch of tedious expats and ridiculously Ruritanian locals who spend most of their time going to each others' self-congratulatory parties. A whimsically intriguing period piece, but hardly Powell's best.

Marguerite Yourcenar *Coup de Grace* (o/p). Sombre meditation on fate and responsibility set during the Latvian War of Independence, with a Baltic German officer discovering that his childhood sweetheart is fighting on the opposite side.

Ed Carey. *Alva & Irva*. Fantasmagorical modern fable focussing on the adventures of two girls in the mythical city of Entralla, loosely based on the Lithuanian capital Vilnius. Dark, quirky, mesmeric stuff.

Lithuania

History, politics and travel

E. J. Harrison *Lithuania Past and Present* (o/p). Harrison was British vice-consul in Vilnius in the wake of World War I, left it just as the Poles took over and returned as a newspa-

per correspondent. Eye-witness accounts of a turbulent period are mixed with satisfying chunks of history, cultural commentary and travelogue.

Czesław Miłosz *Native Realm* (o/p). Born in Lithuania to Polish parents, Miłosz's meditative autobiography is especially illuminating on the Polish-Lithuanian relationship in particular, and East European culture in general. The same author's *Beginning with my Streets* (o/p) is a wide-ranging collection of essays, including some invigorating pieces about Vilnius, where the poet attended high school and university.

S.C. Rowell *Lithuania Ascending*. Few documentary sources reveal the exact processes by which Lithuania rose from being a tribal statelet to a huge empire stretching from the Baltic to the Black Sea, but Rowell has done a remarkable job in sifting the available evidence – and this ground-breaking analysis of thirteenth century power politics is the result. One for the medievalist rather than the general reader.

Alfred Eric Senn *Lithuania Awakening* (o/p). Account of the rise of Sąjūdis and the push towards freedom, written with eye-witness freshness by an American academic who was there for most of the events described.

V. Stanley Vardys and Judith B. Sedaitis *Lithuania the Rebel Nation*. Good overview of twentieth-century history and a blow-by-blow account of the drive to independence. Eager to nail Western darling Gorbachev for his part in the anti-democratic crackdown of January 1991.

Various authors *Lithuania: past, culture, present*. Published in Lithuania by Baltos Lankos and sold in most bookshops in central Vilnius, this is one coffee-table book which you will actually read and treasure. Intelligent, readable essays on key aspects of Lithuanian identity, accompanied by a wonderful selection of photographs.

Tomas Venclova *Vilnius*. Best of the locally produced guides to the city, with solid descriptions of its principal monuments, a handsome set of illustrations, and a suitably lyrical introduction by the US-based Lithuanian poet. Available from most bookshops in Vilnius.

Literature

Sigitas Geda *Biopsy of Winter*. Arrow-sharp shards of verse from one of the country's leading literati, deftly translated by American poet Kerry Shawn Keys. Published by Vaga and available from their bookshop in Vilnius.

Jonas Mekas *There is no Ithaca*. Collection of poems by the Lithuanian-born, New-York-based writer and avant-garde film-maker. Contains *Idylls of Semeniskiai*, a lyrical evocation of Lithuanian village life. Parallel English-Lithuanian texts.

Kornelijus Platelis *Snare for the Wind*. Varied, career-spanning selection from one of Lithuania's most respected contemporary poets. Available from Vaga and other big bookshops in Vilnius.

Balys Sruoga *Forest of the Gods*. Powerful, concentration-camp memoirs from a poet and playwright who was imprisoned in Stutthof towards the end of World War II. Available in Vilnius bookshops.

Lithuanian-Jewish history and memoirs

Lucy S. Dawidowicz *From That Place and Time* (o/p). American academic Dawidowicz went to study at Vilnius's YIVO (Yiddish Institute) as a young graduate in 1938 and wrote this memoir as a nostalgic tribute to the city. The same author's *The War Against the European Jews* is one of the best overall histories of the Holocaust.

Waldemar Ginsburg *And Kovno Wept.* Gripping, unforgettable account of ghetto life in Kaunas (Kovno to its Jewish inhabitants), written by a survivor.

Dan Jacobson *Heshel's Kingdom.* Hugely involving account of a voyage through Lithuania inspired by memories of Jacobson's grandfather Heshel, who had been a rabbi in the west-Lithuanian town of Varniai. This is a wistful, elegiac book with thought-provoking things to say about contemporary Lithuania's ambiguous relationship with its multicultural past.

Howard Jacobson *Roots Schmoots.* Both humorous travelogue and identity-seeking enquiry, this book ends up in the southern Lithuanian town of Lazdijai – the home town of Jacobson's great grandparents. Lithuania and its capital sound pretty grim the way Jacobson describes it, but then he was travelling in the post-Soviet early 1990s.

Herman Kruk *The Last Days of the Jerusalem of Lithuania.* Chronicle of Vilnius's wartime ghetto, scribbled down nightly by Kruk, who dedicated himself to documenting a culture he knew was being snuffed out. Enormously valuable as a social document, this also makes for gut-wrenching reading.

⭐ **Hillel Levine** *In Search of Sugihara.* Well researched and engagingly written biography of the diplomat frequently dubbed the "Japanese Schindler". Levine clearly likes his subject, and yet his determination to portray him as a complex, often flawed human being has earned the enmity of the Sugihara family.

William W. Mishell *Kaddish for Kovno.* The story of Kaunas's Jewish community, with a sensitive overview of Lithuanian-Jewish relations over the centuries, and an unflinching narrative of the Nazi occupation.

Avraham Tory *Surviving the Holocaust: Kovno Ghetto Diary.* Harrowing tale of survival in World War II Kaunas, written by the deputy secretary of the ghetto council. Retained as a personal memoir by Tory, the manuscript was dusted off in 1982, when the author was called to testify against Kazys Palciauskas, the city's wartime mayor.

Lithuanian-Jewish literature

Chaim Grade *My Mothers Sabbath Days* (o/p). Outstanding prose from one of Vilnius's best Yiddish-language writers. The first half of this book consists of quirky short-story snapshots of life in Jewish Vilnius on the eve of World War II; the second is harrowing autobiography, with Grade escaping the Nazi invasion while his wife chooses to stay in the Vilnius ghetto.

Menke Katz *Burning Village.* Powerful cycle of poems set on the eve of World War II in the author's native Michalishek, a Jewish village in the Lithuanian-Belarussian borderlands.

Avram Sutzkever *Selected Poetry and Prose*. Leading light of the Yung Vilne movement, who escaped from the Vilnius ghetto and lived as a partisan in the forest before emigrating to Israel after the war. Lots of electrifying verse and experimental prose poems about Vilnius and the war, highly charged with imagery and nostalgia.

Latvia

History, politics, travel and memoirs

Lucy Addison *Letters from Latvia* (o/p). Addison was an Anglo-Latvian who chose to stay in Latvia throughout World War II and the Soviet occupation, recording the madness of war and political repression from the sanctuary of a wooden cottage in Jūrmala. Collected and published posthumously by a granddaughter, these letters are both gripping historical narrative and a touching read.

Peggie Benton *Baltic Countdown* (o/p). Recollections of Rīga in the late Thirties, written by the wife of a British diplomat. From beach holidays in Jūrmala to the arrival of Soviet tanks in 1940, this is an enjoyable slice of Englishwoman-abroad writing.

★ **Modris Eksteins** *Walking Since Daybreak*. Mixing family memoir with a general history of Latvia's tragic twentieth century, this is beautifully written, totally engrossing stuff. If you only ever buy one book about Latvia, choose this one.

Silvija Grosa *Art Nouveau in Rīga*. With a good balance of glossy photos and informative texts, this is the best of many books about the Latvian capital's dominant architectural style. Published by Jumava and available from most big bookshops in Rīga.

Andris Kolbergs *The Story of Rīga*. Pocket-sized guide to the capital in three separate volumes (covering the Old Town, Parks and Boulevards of the Centre, and the Suburbs). Readable, full of anecdote, and with good pictures too. Published by Jāņa Sēta, Latvia.

Andrejs Plakans *The Latvians*. Reliable introduction to Latvian history.

George Popoff *City of the Red Plague* (o/p). Memoirs of life in Bolshevik-ruled Rīga during the first months of 1919. A winter of disease, starvation and political terror is recounted in wide-eyed style by a scandalized Popoff – an impressionable Red-hating misogynist who believed that the commies had recruited street prostitutes to command their firing squads.

Ernst von Salomon *The Outlaws* (o/p). Combat reminiscences of a young volunteer who headed for Latvia to join up with General von der Goltz's Baltic-German army in 1919. Characterized by nationalist euphoria, love of comradeship and bloodlust, it's a disturbing document.

Stephen Tallents *Man and Boy* (o/p). Lively, self-deprecating autobiography of the man who led the British mission to Latvia in 1919–20, serving (albeit briefly) as governor of Rīga. For a full account of what went on during those war-town years, there is no better starting point.

Literature

★ **Alberts Bels** *The Cage* (o/p). Beginning like a hard-boiled detective story and ending as a disturbingly surreal fable, this is an outstanding piece of contemporary fiction – and one of the few morsels of Latvian literature that's available in English. A subtle critique of the Soviet system (it first appeared in 1971), it's a profound enough read to outlive the society that shaped it.

Various *All Birds Know This*. Well-translated and representative anthology of contemporary Latvian poets, including formidable national literary figures like Vesma Belševica and Imants Ziedonis. Available from the bigger Rīga bookshops.

Estonia

History and politics

E. Nodel *Estonia: Nation on the Anvil* (o/p). A handy introduction to Estonian politics and culture, from the earliest times to the Soviet occupation.

Madli Puhvel *Symbol of Dawn*. Well-researched biography of Estonia's leading nineteenth-century poetess, Lydia Koidula, written in accessible style by an American-Estonian academic. A good source of background on the formation of nineteenth-century society and culture. Available in big bookshops in

Tallinn and Tartu.

Toivo U. Raun *Estonia and the Estonians*. Best of the general histories, covering the main themes of Estonian society and politics from the earliest times up to 1991, in readable style.

Rein Taagepera *Estonia: Return to Independence*. A useful addition to the above titles, this provides plenty of detailed analysis on the fall of the Soviet Union and the political landscape of the 1990s.

Travel and memoirs

Tania Alexander *A Little of All of These* (o/p). Memories of a childhood spent on an Estonian country estate during the inter-war years, among a cosmopolitan bunch of Russo-German aristocrats.

Arthur Ransome *Racundra's First Cruise* (o/p). The author of children's classic *Swallows and Amazons* spent the summer of 1922 sailing from Rīga to Tallinn, stopping off at sundry Estonian ports and islands on the way. If you know your sextant

from your spinnaker, this is an absorbing read.

Elizabeth Rigby *Letters from the Shores of the Baltic* (o/p). Account of a sojourn on a baronial estate in Estonia in the 1840s, full of domestic detail and a best-seller in its day, written by a formidable woman of letters who noted elsewhere that "well-read, solid-thinking, early-rising, sketch-loving, light-footed, trim-waisted, straw-hatted" Englishwomen always made the best travel writers.

Ronald Seth *Baltic Corner: Travels in Estonia* (o/p). Engaging, if low-key, memoirs of an English teacher in inter-war Estonia. Some good stuff on daily life in the Tallinn of the 1930s, and lively descriptions of trips to Narva and Petseri monastery – the latter a Setu shrine which was then part of Estonia, but subsequently awarded to Russia by post–World War II border changes.

Literature

★ *ELM (Estonian Literary Magazine)*. Quarterly magazine published by the Estonian Institute and available from Tallinn bookstores, featuring contemporary poetry and prose in English translation, and a round-up of literary news. Find out more on ⓦwww.einst.ee/literary.

★ **Jaan Kaplinski** *The Same Sea in us All* and *The Wandering Border*. Two collections from Estonia's leading contemporary poet, whose verse is imbued with an almost spiritual appreciation of nature. You can read more of his poems on ⓦhttp://jaan.kaplinski.com.

★ **Jaan Kross** *The Czar's Madman*. First published in Estonia in 1978, the best-known work from the country's greatest living prose writer functions both as a rich historical novel and subtle allegory of life in Brezhnev's USSR – which makes it all the more remarkable that it ever got past the censor. The kernel of the story involves a nineteenth-century Baltic German aristocrat who is locked up in the mad house for daring to criticize the Tsar, with the stoical, self-denying lives of rural Estonians providing the intricate background weave. Kross's most recent work to be translated into English, *Treading Air*, is a richly textured guide to twentieth-century Estonia in the form of a civil servant's life story, and comes with an invaluable introduction to Kross's life and times by translator Eric Dickens. *Professor Martens' Departure*, in which a nineteenth-century Estonian advisor to the Tsar looks back on his life, is an altogether less penetrable meditation on the Estonian-Russian relationship.

Language

Language

Lithuanian

Lithuanian is an Indo-European language belonging to the Baltic family, of which Latvian is the only other surviving member – other Baltic peoples such as the Prussians and the Yotvingians having died out in the Middle Ages. It's thought that the vocabulary and grammar of Lithuanian have changed little over the centuries, leading some linguists to argue that it is closer to ancient Sanskrit than any other living language. Few Lithuanian words bear much resemblance to those you may have encountered elsewhere in Europe, lending the language an exotic aura – and although it's a difficult language to pick up at first, it soon becomes addictive. If you are interested in learning, then *Colloquial Lithuanian* published by Routledge is the best of the available self-study courses. Once you get to Vilnius, a range of Lithuanian-produced textbooks aimed at foreign students are available from bigger bookshops.

There are two **genders** in Lithuanian – masculine and feminine. Masculine nouns almost always end with -s, feminine nouns usually with -a or -ė. Even foreign names are made to fit in with Lithuanian rules, as you will see from local newspaper references to figures as diverse as Georgeas Bushas and Saddamas Husseinas. Plurals are formed by adding -ai or -iai to masculine nouns; -s to feminine ones. It's also worth bearing in mind that there are six noun **cases** in Lithuanian, ensuring that each noun changes its ending according to which part of the sentence it occupies: thus "į Vilnių" means "to Vilnius", "iš Vilniaus" "from Vilnius", and "Vilniuje" "in Vilnius".

Pronunciation

Pronunciation is not as difficult as it first appears. Every word is spoken exactly as it's written, and each letter represents an individual sound. Most letters are pronounced as they are in English, with the following exceptions:

a "a" as in clap
ą originally a nasal vowel; nowadays pronounced in much the same way as "a"
c "ts" as in cats
č "ch" as in church
e usually pronounced like "e" as in bet, but in some words resembles the "ai" in fair
ė like French "é" in café
ę "e" as in bet
i "i" as in hit

į "i" as in hit
j "y" as in yesterday
š "sh" as in shut
u "u" as in put
ū "oo" as in fool
ų "u" as in put
y "i" as in hit
ž "s" as in pleasure

Lithuanian words and phrases

Basics

Do you speak English?	**Ar Jūs kalbate angliškai?**	Goodbye	**Viso gero**
I don't understand	**Nesuprantu**	Bye!	**Ate!**
Yes	**Taip**	See you!	**Iki!**
No	**Ne**	How are you?	**Kaip gyveni?**
Please	**Prašau, prašom**		**/Kaip sekasi?**
Thank you	**Ačiū**	Fine, thanks	**Ačiū, gerai**
OK	**Gerai**	What is your name?	**Koks tavo vardas?/**
Excuse me/sorry	**Atsiprašau**		**Kuo tu vardu?**
Hi!	**Labas!, Sveikas**	My name is...	**Mano vardas...**
	(m)/sveika (f)!	Today	**Šiandien**
Hello/Good day	**Laba diena**	Yesterday	**Vakar**
Good morning	**Labas rytas**	Tomorrow	**Rytoj**
Good evening	**Labas vakaras**	In the morning	**Rytą**
Goodnight	**Labanakt**	In the afternoon	**Popiet**
		In the evening	**Vakare**

Some signs

Entrance	**Įejimas**	Market	**Turgus**
Exit	**Įšejimas**	Hospital	**Ligoninė**
Arrival	**Atvykimas**	Pharmacy	**Vaistinė**
Departure	**Išvykimas**	Toilet	**Tualetas**
Open	**Atidaryta**	No Smoking	**Nerūkyti/Nerūkoma**
Closed	**Uždaryta**		

Questions and directions

Where is...?	**Kur yra..?**	Straight on	**Tiesiai**
When?	**Kada?**	Train/bus/boat/	**Traukinys/**
What?	**Kas?**	ferry/bicycle	**autobusas/laivas/**
Now	**Dabar**		**keltas/dviratis**
Early, earlier	**Anksti, ankščiau**	Ticket/ticket office	**Bilietas/bilietų kasa**
Late, later	**Vėlu, vėliau**	A ticket to... please	**Prašom, vieną**
What time is it?	**Kiek valandų/**		**bilietą į...**
	Kelinta valanda?	Single	**Į vieną pusę**
Big/small	**Didelis/mažas**	Return/round-trip	**Pirmyn ir atgal**
Cheap/expensive	**Pigus/brangus**	I'd like...	**Norečiau**
Hot/cold	**Karštas/šaltas**	Single room	**Vienutė**
Near/far	**Arti/toli**	Double room	**Kambarys dviems**
Good/bad	**Geras/blogas**	How much is it?	**Kiek kainuoja?**
More/less	**Daugiau/mažiau**	Do you have anything	**Ar tūrite ką nors**
Left/right	**Kairė/dešinė**	cheaper?	**pigiau?**

Numbers

1	vienas (m), viena (f)	16	šešiolika
2	du (m), dvi (f)	17	septyniolika
3	trys	18	aštuoniolika
4	keturi (m), keturios (f)	19	devyniolika
5	penki (m), penkios (f)	20	dvidešimt
6	šeši (m), šešios (f)	30	trisdešimt
7	septyni (m), septynios (f)	40	keturiasdešimt
8	aštuoni (m), aštuonios (f)	50	penkiasdešimt
9	devyni (m), devynios (f)	60	šešiasdešimt
10	dešimt	70	septyniasdešimt
11	vienuolika	80	aštuoniasdešimt
12	dvylika	90	devyniasdešimt
13	trylika	100	šimtas
14	keturiolika	200	du šimtai
15	penkiolika	1000	tūkstantis

Days and months

Monday	Pirmadienis	April	Balandis
Tuesday	Antradienis	May	Gegužė
Wednesday	Trečiadenis	June	Birželis
Thursday	Ketvirtadienis	July	Liepa
Friday	Penktadienis	August	Rugpjūtis
Saturday	Šestadienis	September	Rugsėjis
Sunday	Sekmadienis	October	Spalis
January	Sausis	November	Lapkritis
February	Vasaris	December	Gruodis
March	Kovas		

Countries

Belarus	Baltarusija	Lithuania	Lietuva
Estonia	Estija	Poland	Lenkija
Finland	Suomija	Russia	Rusija
Germany	Vokietija	Sweden	Švedija
Latvia	Latvija		

Food and drink terms

Basic words and phrases

The menu, please	Prašom, meniu
A coffee, please	Prašom, kavos
Two beers please	Prašom, du alaus
I am a vegetarian	Aš vegetaras (m), vegetarė (f)

Do you have anything without meat?	Ar yra kas nors be mėsos?
Cheers!	Į sveikatą!
Bon appetit!	Skanaus!
The bill, please	Prašom, sąskaitą

445

Essentials

Cukrus	Sugar
Druska	Salt
Duona	Bread
Grietinė	Sour cream
Kiaušiniai	Eggs
Medus	Honey
Padažas	Sauce
Pienas	Milk
Pipirai	Pepper
Sriuba	Soup
Sūris	Cheese
Sviestas	Butter

Lithuanian staples

Blynai	Pancakes
Bulvių blynai	Potato pancakes
Bulvių plokštainis	Baked slab of potato
Cepelinai	Zeppelin-shaped potato parcels stuffed with meat
Didžkukuliai	see "cepelinai"
Kibinas	Meat pasty
Koldūnai	Ravioli-like parcels with meat stuffing
Kugelis	see "bulvių plokštainis"
Šaltibarščiai	Cold beetroot soup
Vedarai	Pig intestine stuffed with potato

Meat (*Mėsa*)

Dešra	Thick, salami-like sausage
Dešrelė	Frankfurter-like sausage
Jautiena	Beef
Kalakutiena	Turkey
Karbonadas	Pork chop
Kepsnys	Fried or roast cut of meat
Kumpis	Ham
Kiauliena	Pork
Vištiena	Chicken

Fish (*žuvis*)

Lašiša	Salmon
Menkė	Cod
Rukyta žuvis	Smoked fish
Unguris	Eel
Upėtakis	Trout

Vegetables (*daržovės*)

Agurkas	Cucumber
Bulvės	Potato
Česnakas	Garlic
Grybai	Mushrooms
Kopūstas	Cabbage
Moliūgas	Pumpkin
Morkos	Carrots
Pomidoras	Tomato
Pupelės	Beans
Svogūnas	Onion
Žirniai	Peas

Fruit (*vaisiai*)

Apelsinas	Orange
Avietės	Raspberries
Braškės	Strawberries
Citrina	Lemon
Kriaušė	Pear
Obuolys	Apple
Slyva	Plumb
Vyšnia	Cherry

Desserts (*desertai*)

Ledai	Ice cream
Pyragaitis	Small cake
Pyragas	Cake or pudding
Riešutai	Nuts
Tortas	Cake
Uogienė	Jam

Drinks (*gerimai*)

Alus	Beer
Arbata	Tea
Degtinė	Vodka
Kava	Coffee
Sultys	Juice
Vanduo	Water
Vynas	Wine

Glossary

Aikštė	Square	Naujamiestis	New town
Autobusų stotelė	Bus stop	Parkas	Park
Autobusų stotis	Bus station	Paštas	Post office
Bankas	Bank	Piliakalnis	(Iron Age) castle
Bažnyčia	Church		mound
Dviračių takas	Cycle path	Pilis	Castle
Ežeras	Lake	Rotušė	Town Hall
Gatvė	Street	Sodas	Garden
Giria	Forest	Senamiestis	Old Town
Kaimas	Village	Stotis	Station
Kalnas	Hill	Takas	Path
Katedra	Cathedral	Tiltas	Bridge
Kopa	Dune	Turgus	Market
Ligoninė	Hospital	Upė	River
Miestas	Town	Vaistinė	Pharmacy
Miškas	Forest	Vienuolynas	Abbey
Muziejus	Museum		

Latvian

A long with Lithuanian, Latvian is a member of the Baltic family of languages and in terms of grammar and basic vocabulary is very close to its southerly neighbour. There, however, the similarity ends: unlike the staccato, almost Mediterranean-sounding delivery of Lithuanian, Latvian has a melodic, rolling quality that sounds closer to Scandinavia than the European mainland. The stress always falls on the first syllable of the word (the only exception to this rule being "paldies", meaning "thank you"); accented vowels are pronounced in a long, drawled-out way; and unaccented vowels are clipped back in everyday speech to the extent that you can't always hear that they're there at all. *Colloquial Latvian* (Routledge) is a good place to start if you're learning, although it's less fun than the excellent *Palīgā!* series of textbooks published by Latvian television (and available from the Zvaigzne bookshop; see p.226) – although they're intended for Russian-speakers and don't have any instructions in English.

Pronunciation

Aside from a few tricky consonants not found in English, Latvian pronunciation is pretty straightforward, providing you pay attention to the vowel sounds below.

a "a" as in clap
ā "a" as in hard
c "ts" as in cats
č ch as in church
e usually pronounced like "e" as in bet, but in some words resembles the "aa" in aah
ē like French "é" in café, but in some words resembles the "aa" in aah
ģ somewhere between the "d" in endure and the "j" in jeep
i "i" as in hit
ī "ee" as in green

j "y" as in yesterday
ķ t"" as in future
ļ rolled combination of "l" and "y"; like the final "l" and initial "y" of "cool yule" pronounced together.
ņ "n" as in new
o "wo" as in water
š "sh" as in shut
u "u" as in put
ū "oo" as in fool
ž "s" as in pleasure

Latvian words and phrases

Basics

Do you speak English?	**Vai Jūs runājat angliski?**	Good evening	**Labvakar**
Yes	**Jā**	Good night	**Ar labu nakti**
No	**Nē**	Goodbye	**Uz redzēšanos**
I don't understand	**Es nesaprotu**	Bye!	**Atā!**
Please	**Lūdzu**	What is your name?	**Kā Jūs sauc?** (formal);
Thank you	**Paldies**		**kā tevi sauc?**
OK	**Labi**		(informal)
Excuse me/Sorry	**Atvainojiet/Piedodiet**	My name is...	**Mani sauc...**
Hi!	**Sveiks!** (sing);	Today	**Šodien**
	sveiki! (pl); **čau!**	Yesterday	**Vakar**
Hello/Good day	**Labdien**	Tomorrow	**Rīt**
Welcome	**Esiet sveicināti**	In the morning	**Rītā**
Good morning	**Labrīt**	In the afternoon	**Pēcpusdienā**
		In the evening	**Vakarā**

Some signs

Entrance	**Ieeja**	Open	**Atvērts**
Exit	**Izeja**	Closed	**Slēgts**
Arrival	**Pienākšana, pienāk**	Toilet	**Tualete**
Departure	**Atiešana, atiet**	No Smoking	**Smēķēt aizliegts!**

Questions and directions

Where?	**Kur?**	Hot	**Karsts**
Where is..?	**Kur atrodas..?**	Cold	**Auksts**
When?	**Kad?**	Here	**Šeit**
What?	**Kas?**	There	**Tur**
Why?	**Kāpēc?**	Left	**Pa kreisi**
Where is the railway station?	**Kur ir dzelceļa staoija?**	Right	**Pa labi**
		Straight on	**Taisni**
Train/bus/bicycle	**Vilciens/autobuss/ velosipēds**	Near/far	**Tuvu/tālu**
		Ticket/ticket office	**Biļete/biļešu kase**
How much?	**Cik?**	Train/bus station/ bus stop	**Stacija/autoosta/ pietura**
How much does it cost?	**Cik tas maksā?**	To Rīga	**Uz Rīgu**
I'd like	**...Es vēlos...**	To Ventspils	**Uz Ventspili**
Cheap	**Lēts**	Now	**Tagad**
Expensive	**Dārgs**	Early, earlier	**Agri, agrāk**
Good	**Labs**	Late, later	**Vēlu, vēlāk**
Bad	**Slikts**	What time is it?	**Cik ir pulkstenis?**

Countries

Belarus	**Baltakrievija**	Lithuania	**Lietuva**
Estonia	**Igaunija**	Poland	**Polija**
Finland	**Somija**	Russia	**Krievija**
Germany	**Vācija**	Sweden	**Zviedrija**
Latvia	**Latvija**		

Numbers

1	**viens** (m); **viena** (f)		16	**sešpadsmit**
2	**divi** (m); **divas** (f)		17	**septiņpadsmit**
3	**trīs**		18	**astoņpadsmit**
4	**četri**		19	**deviņpadsmit**
5	**pieci**		20	**divdesmit**
6	**seši**		30	**trīsdesmit**
7	**septiņi**		40	**četrdesmit**
8	**astoņi**		50	**piecdesmit**
9	**deviņi**		60	**sešdesmit**
10	**desmit**		70	**septiņdesmit**
11	**vienpadsmit**		80	**astoņdesmit**
12	**divpadsmit**		90	**deviņdesmit**
13	**trīspadsmit**		100	**simts**
14	**četrpadsmit**		200	**divi simti**
15	**piecpadsmit**		1000	**tūkstotis**

Days and months

Monday	**Pirmdiena**	April	**Aprīlis**
Tuesday	**Otrdiena**	May	**Maijs**
Wednesday	**Trešdiena**	June	**Jūnijs**
Thursday	**Ceturtdiena**	July	**Jūlijs**
Friday	**Piektdiena**	August	**Augusts**
Saturday	**Sestdiena**	September	**Septembris**
Sunday	**Svētdiena**	October	**Oktobris**
January	**Janvāris**	November	**Novembris**
February	**Februāris**	December	**Decembris**
March	**Marts**		

Food and drink terms

Essentials

Cukurs	Sugar	**Rupjmaize**	Rye bread
Krējums	Sour cream	**Sāls**	Salt
Maize	Bread	**Siers**	Cheese
Merce	Sauce	**Soļanka**	Meat-and-vegetable broth
Olas	Eggs	**Sviests**	Butter
Pipari	Pepper	**Zupa**	Soup

Latvian staples

Cūkas galerts	Pork in aspic
Pelēkie zirņi	Peas with bacon
Pelmeņi	Dough parcels with meat stuffing
Pīrāgs/pīrādziņš	Doughy pasty stuffed with bacon and/or cabbage
Rasols	Salad consisting of chopped meat and vegetables dressed in sour cream
Zirņu pikas	Mashed pea balls with bacon

Meat (gaļa)

Cālīšu gaļa	Chicken
Cūkas gaļa	Pork
Desa	Sausage
Karbonāde	Pork chop
Liellopu gaļa	Beef
Teļu gaļa	Veal
Žāvēta desa	Smoked sausage

Fish (zivs)

Forele	Trout
Lasis	Salmon
Siļķe	Herring
Šprotes	Sprats
Tuncis	Tuna
Zandarts	Pike-perch
Zutis	Eel

Vegetables (dārzeņi)

Burkāni	Carrots
Gurķi	Cucumbers
Kartupeļi	Potatoes
Kāposti	Cabbage
Ķiploks	Garlic
Loki	Spring onions
Salāti	Lettuce
Sēnes	Mushrooms
Sīpoli	Onions
Skābie kāposti	Sauerkraut
Skābie gurķi	Pickled gherkins
Tomāti	Tomatoes

Desserts and fruit

Ābols	Apple
Apelsīns	Orange
Biezpiens	Curd cheese
Kūka	Cake
Ķīselis	Sweet porridge with fruit
Pankūkas	Pancake
Pudiņš	Pudding
Rieksti	Nuts
Saldējums	Ice cream
Torte	Gateau

Drinks (dzerieni)

Alus	Beer
Balzāms	Balsam – gloppy black liqueur
Degvīns	Vodka
Kafija	Coffee
Karstvīns	Mulled wine
Piens	Milk
Sula	Juice
Šņabis	Vodka
Tēja	Tea
Ūdens	Water
Vīns	Wine

Glossary

Aptieka	Pharmacy
Banka	Bank
Baznīca	Church
Darzs	Garden
Dome	Cathedral
Ezers	Lake
Iela	Street
Laukums	Square
Mežs	Forest
Muiža	Manor house
Muzejs	Museum
Parks	Park
Pasts	Post office
Pils	Castle
Pilskalns	(Iron Age) castle mound
Purvs	Bog
Sala	Island
Slimnīca	Hospital
Tilts	Bridge
Tirgus	Market
Upe	River

Estonian

stonian belongs to the Finno-Ugric family of languages; it's closely related to Finnish and somewhat more distantly to Hungarian. Despite the importance of Germans, Swedes and Slavs in Estonia's history, the language itself has remained remarkably free of foreign-influenced words, and its relative purity is regarded by the locals as a powerful symbol of their own ability to survive hundreds of years of foreign domination with their culture unscathed. Bearing little relation to any Indo-European language, Estonian is a difficult language for outsiders to master. Although it has no masculine or feminine gender, the situation is complicated by the existence of fourteen noun cases, which take the form of a fiendishly difficult-to-learn set of suffixes. "Tallinna" ("Tallin's"), "Tallinas" ("in Tallinn"), "Tallinast" ("from Tallinn") are just three examples of the way the system works.

If you wish to investigate further, *Colloquial Estonian* (Routledge) makes an admirable attempt to render this notoriously impenetrable language both fun and accessible.

Pronunciation

In Estonian, words are pronounced exactly as they're written, with the stress almost always falling on the first syllable. Estonian consonants are pronounced pretty much as they are in English, and it's only really the vowels, listed below that require particular attention. If you're leafing through an Estonian dictionary, bear in mind that the vowels õ, ä, ö and ü usually come at the end of the alphabet, just after z.

a "a" as in attitude
aa "a" as in cart
ä midway between the "a" in hat and "e" in met
e "e" as in met
ee "é" as in café
j "y" as in yellow
o "o" as in dog
oo "o" as in port

ö the same as German ö; a combination of o and e that sounds like the "u" in fur
õ no equivalent in English; midway between the "ur" in fur and the "i" in sit
š "sh" as in shiny
u "oo" as in fool
ü the same as German "ü"; a combination of u and e that sounds like the French "u" in "sur"

Estonian words and phrases

Basics

Do you speak English?	**Kas te räägite inglise keelt?**	Bye!	**Hüvasti!**
Yes	**Jah**	How are you?	**Kuidas sa elad?**
No	**Ei**	Fine thanks	**Tänan, hästi**
I don't understand	**Ma ei saa aru**	What is your name?	**Kuidas sinu nimi on?**
Please	**Palun**	My name is...	**Minu nimi on...**
Thank you	**Tänan/aitäh**	Yesterday	**Eile**
Excuse me	**Vabandage**	Today	**Täna**
Hello	**Tere**	Tomorrow	**Homme**
Good morning	**Tere hommikust**	In the morning	**Hommikul**
Good evening	**Head õhtust**	In the afternoon	**Pärastlõunat**
Goodnight	**Head ööd**	In the evening	**Õhtul**
Goodbye	**Nägemiseni/ nägemist**		

Some signs

Entrance	**Sissepääs**	Open	**Avatud**
Exit	**Väljapääs**	Closed	**Suletud**
Arrival	**Saabumine**	Toilet	**Tualett**
Departure	**Väljumine**	No Smoking	**Mitte suitsetada!**

Questions and directions

Where is..?	**Kus on..?**	Expensive	**Kulukas**
When?	**Millal?**	Good	**Hea**
What?	**Mis?**	Bad	**Halb/paha**
Why?	**Miks?**	Here	**Siin**
Train/bus/ferry/bicycle	**Rong/buss/laev/ jalgratas**	There	**Seal**
How much?	**Kui palju?**	Left	**Vasak**
How much does this cost?	**Kui palju see maksab?**	Right	**Parem**
I'd like...	**Ma soovin...**	Straight on	**Otse**
Cheap	**Odav**	Ticket/ticket office	**Pilet/piletikassa**
		Train station	**Jaam, vaksal**
		Bus station/bus stop	**Bussijaam/peatus**

Days and months

Monday	**Esmaspäev**	January	**Jaanuar**
Tuesday	**Teisipäev**	February	**Veebruar**
Wednesday	**Kolmapäev**	March	**Märts**
Thursday	**Neljapäev**	April	**Aprill**
Friday	**Reede**	May	**Mai**
Saturday	**Laupäev**	June	**Juuni**
Sunday	**Pühapäev**	July	**Juuli**

August	**August**	November	**November**
September	**September**	December	**Detsember**
October	**Oktoober**		

Numbers

1	**üks**	16	**kuusteist**
2	**kaks**	17	**seitseteist**
3	**kolm**	18	**kaheksateist**
4	**neli**	19	**üheksateist**
5	**viis**	20	**kakskümmend**
6	**kuus**	30	**kolmkümmend**
7	**seitse**	40	**nelikümmend**
8	**kaheksa**	50	**viiskümmend**
9	**üheksa**	60	**kuustkümmend**
10	**kümme**	70	**seitsekümmend**
11	**üksteist**	80	**kaheksakümmend**
12	**kaksteist**	90	**üheksakümmend**
13	**kolmteist**	100	**sada**
14	**neliteist**	200	**kaksada**
15	**viisteist**	1000	**tuhat**

Some countries

Estonia	**Eesti**	Germany	**Saksamaa**
Latvia	**Läti**	Finland	**Soome**
Lithuania	**Leedu**	Belarus	**Valgevene**
Poland	**Poola**	Russia	**Venemaa**
Sweden	**Rootsi**		

Food and drink

Basic words and phrases

Menüü/toidukaart	Menu
Hommikueine	Breakfast
Lõuna	Lunch
Head isu	Bon appetit
Terviseks	Cheers!
Arve	Bill

Essentials

Eelroad	Starters
Juust	Cheese
...kastmes	In ... sauce
Kaste	Sauce
Leib	(Brown) bread
Päevapraad	Dish of the day
Pipar	Pepper
Roog	Dish, course

Sai	(White) bread
Sool	Salt
Suhkur	Sugar
Või	Butter
Vorm	Stew

Snacks and starters

Kartulisalat	Potato salad
Pannkook	Pancake
Pelmeenid	Pelmeny
Pirukas	Dough parcel stuffed with cabbage and bacon
Salat	Salad
Sült	Cold meat in jelly
Supp	Soup

Meat (*liha*)

Kana	Chicken
Kanapraad	Roast chicken
Karbonaad	Pork chop in batter
Lammas	Lamb
Peekon	Bacon
Šašlõkk	Shish kebab
Sealiha	Pork
Seapraad	Roast pork
Sink	Ham
Šnitsel	Schnitzel (usually veal, but can be pork or chicken)
Verivorst	Blood sausage, black pudding

Fish (*kala*) and seafood (*mereannid*)

Haug	Pike
Krevet	Shrimp
Makra	Crab
Räim	Baltic herring
Sprott	Sprat
Tuunikala	Tuna

Vegetables (*köögivili*)

Ahjukartulid	Roast potatoes
Hapukapsas	Sauerkraut
Hapukurk	Pickled gherkin
Hernes	Pea
Kartulid	Potatoes
Küüslauk	Garlic
Mädarõigas	Horseradish
Porgand	Carrot
Sibul	Onion
Tomat	Tomato

Desserts (*desserdid*)

Jäätis	Ice cream
Juustukook	Cheesecake
Kook	Cake
Piparkook	Gingerbread
Saiake	Bun
Šokolaadikook	Chocolate cake

Fruit (*puuvili*)

Apelsin	Orange
Õun	Apple
Pirn	Pear
Ploom	Plum
Vaarikas	Raspberry

Drinks (*joogid*)

Höögvein	Mulled wine
Kohv	Coffee
Mahl	Juice
Õlu	Beer
Piim	Milk
Vesi	Water
Vein	Wine
Viin	Vodka

Glossary

Aed	Garden
Apteek	Pharmacy
Järv	Lake
Jõgi	River
Kauplus	Shop
Kesklinn	Town centre
Kirik	Church
Laht	Gulf
Linn	Town
Linnus	Castle
Loss	Castle
Maantee	Road
Mägi	Hill
Mõis	Manor house
Muuseum	Museum
Pakihõid	Left-luggage office
Pank	Bank
Pood	Shop
Postkontor	Post office
Raba	Bog
Saar	Island
Saatkond	Embassy
Sild	Bridge
Soo	Bog
Supelrand	Beach
Tänav	Street
Toidupood	Food shop
Toomkirik	Cathedral
Turg	Market
Tuulik	Windmill
Väljak	Square

Index

and small print

A Rough Guide to Rough Guides

In the summer of 1981, Mark Ellingham, a recent graduate from Bristol University, was travelling round Greece and couldn't find a guidebook that really met his needs. On the one hand there were the student guides, insistent on saving every last cent, and on the other the heavyweight cultural tomes whose authors seemed to have spent more time in a research library than lounging away the afternoon at a taverna or on the beach.

In a bid to avoid getting a job, Mark and a small group of writers set about creating their own guidebook. It was a guide to Greece that aimed to combine a journalistic approach to description with a thoroughly practical approach to travellers' needs – a guide that would incorporate culture, history and contemporary insights with a critical edge, together with up-to-date, value-for-money listings. Back in London, Mark and the team finished their Rough Guide, as they called it, and talked Routledge into publishing the book.

That first *Rough Guide to Greece*, published in 1982, was a student scheme that became a publishing phenomenon. The immediate success of the book – with numerous reprints and a Thomas Cook prize shortlisting – spawned a series that rapidly covered dozens of destinations. Rough Guides had a ready market among low-budget backpackers, but soon also acquired a much broader and older readership that relished Rough Guides' wit and inquisitiveness as much as their enthusiastic, critical approach. Everyone wants value for money, but not at any price.

Rough Guides soon began supplementing the "rougher" information about hostels and low-budget listings with the kind of detail on restaurants and quality hotels that independent-minded visitors on any budget might expect, whether on business in New York or trekking in Thailand.

These days the guides – distributed worldwide by the Penguin group – offer recommendations from shoestring to luxury and cover more than 200 destinations around the globe, including almost every country in the Americas and Europe, more than half of Africa and most of Asia and Australasia. Our ever-growing team of authors and photographers is spread all over the world, particularly in Europe, the USA and Australia.

In 1994, we published the *Rough Guide to World Music* and *Rough Guide to Classical Music*; and a year later the *Rough Guide to the Internet*. All three books have become benchmark titles in their fields – which encouraged us to expand into other areas of publishing, mainly around popular culture. Rough Guides now publish:

- Travel guides to more than 200 worldwide destinations
- Dictionary phrasebooks to 22 major languages
- History guides ranging from Ireland to Islam
- Maps printed on rip-proof and waterproof Polyart™ paper
- Music guides running the gamut from Opera to Elvis
- Restaurant guides to London, New York and San Francisco
- Reference books on topics as diverse as the Weather and Shakespeare
- Sports guides from Formula 1 to Man Utd
- Pop culture books from *Lord of the Rings* to Cult TV
- World Music CDs in association with World Music Network

Visit **www.roughguides.com** to see our latest publications.

SMALL PRINT

Rough Guide Credits

Text editor: Ruth Blackmore
Layout: Katie Pringle
Cartography: Katie Lloyd-Jones, Manish
Chandra, Rajesh Chhibber, Jai Prakesh
Mishra, Ashutosh Bharti, Rajesh Mishra,
Animesh Pathak
Picture research: Jo Mee
Proofreader: Jo Mead

....

Editorial: London Martin Dunford, Kate
Berens, Helena Smith, Claire Saunders, Geoff
Howard, Gavin Thomas, Polly Thomas,
Richard Lim, Lucy Ratcliffe, Clifton Wilkinson,
Alison Murchie, Fran Sandham, Sally Schafer,
Alexander Mark Rogers, Karoline Densley,
Andy Turner, Ella O'Donnell, Keith Drew,
Andrew Lockett, Joe Staines, Duncan Clark,
Peter Buckley, Matthew Milton; **New York**
Andrew Rosenberg, Richard Koss, Yuki
Takagaki, Hunter Slaton, Chris Barsanti,
Thomas Kohnstamm, Steven Horak
Design & Layout: London Helen Prior, Dan
May, Diana Jarvis; **Delhi** Madhulita
Mohapatra, Umesh Aggarwal, Ajay Verma

Production: Julia Bovis, John McKay,
Sophie Hewat, Michelle Bhatia
Cartography: London Maxine Repath, Ed
Wright, Katie Lloyd-Jones; **Delhi** Manish
Chandra, Rajesh Chhibber, Jai Prakesh
Mishra, Ashutosh Bharti, Rajesh Mishra,
Animesh Pathak
Cover art direction: Louise Boulton
Picture research: Sharon Martins, Mark
Thomas, Jj Luck
Online: New York Jennifer Gold, Cree
Lawson, Suzanne Welles; **Delhi** Manik
Chauhan, Amarjyoti Dutta, Narender Kumar
Marketing & Publicity: London Richard
Trillo, Niki Smith, David Wearn, Chloë
Roberts, Demelza Dallow, Kristina Pentland;
New York Geoff Colquitt, David Wechsler,
Megan Kennedy
Finance: Gary Singh
Manager India: Punita Singh
Series editor: Mark Ellingham
PA to Managing Director: Julie Sanderson
Managing Director: Kevin Fitzgerald

Publishing Information

This first edition published April 2004 by **Rough
Guides Ltd**,
80 Strand, London WC2R 0RL.
345 Hudson St, 4th Floor,
New York, NY 10014, USA.
Distributed by the Penguin Group
Penguin Books Ltd,
80 Strand, London WC2R 0RL
Penguin Putnam, Inc.
375 Hudson Street, NY 10014, USA
Penguin Books Australia Ltd,
487 Maroondah Highway, PO Box 257,
Ringwood, Victoria 3134, Australia
Penguin Books Canada Ltd,
10 Alcorn Avenue, Toronto, Ontario,
Canada M4V 1E4
Penguin Books (NZ) Ltd,
182–190 Wairau Road, Auckland 10,
New Zealand
Typeset in Bembo and Helvetica to an original
design by Henry Iles.

Printed and bound in China

© Jonathan Bousfield

No part of this book may be reproduced in any
form without permission from the publisher
except for the quotation of brief passages in
reviews.

480pp includes index
A catalogue record for this book is available from
the British Library

ISBN 1-85828-840-1

3   5   7   9   8   6   4

Help us update

We've gone to a lot of effort to ensure that the first edition of **The Rough Guide to the Baltic States** is accurate and up-to-date. However, things change – places get "discovered", opening hours are notoriously fickle, restaurants and rooms raise prices or lower standards. If you feel we've got it wrong or left something out, we'd like to know, and if you can remember the address, the price, the time, the phone number, so much the better.

We'll credit all contributions, and send a copy of the next edition (or any other Rough Guide if you prefer) for the best letters. Everyone who writes to us and isn't already a subscriber will receive a copy of our full-colour thrice-yearly newsletter. Please mark letters: **"Rough Guide Baltic States Update"** and send to: Rough Guides, 80 Strand, London WC2R 0RL, or Rough Guides, 4th Floor, 345 Hudson St, New York, NY 10014. Or send an email to **mail@roughguides.com**

Have your questions answered and tell others about your trip at **www.roughguides.atinfopop.com**

Acknowledgements

Jonathan Bousfield would like to thank Nijolė Beliukevičienė, Rita Bidvaitė, Liz & David Bousfield, Tomas Butkus, Janis Daugavietis, Dr Green, Jānis Elsbergs, Gunilla Forsen, Paul Jaskunas, Dovid Katz, Kerry Shawn Keys, Kaie Kotov, Anne Kurepalu, Kalevi Kull, Tiina Laats, Lidija Lukšytė, Ints Mednis, Elo Mets, Ainars Mielavs, Līga Miesniece, Märt Milter, Kristina Ojamaa, Lelda Ozola, Darius James Ross, Uldis Rudaks, Vilnis Skuja, Sergej Timofeev, Vladimir Tarasov, Uldis Tirons, Ugnis at Dangus, Zinta Uskalis, Irena Veisaitė, Audra Žukaitytė, the good samaritans of Stabu iela, and most of all Violeta without whom chapters 1 to 4 would simply not have been the same.

Thanks are also due to Martin Dunford and Kate Berens for keeping the project on track, and Ruth Blackmore for an editorial input which went above and beyond the call.

Both author and editor would like to thank Katie Pringle for typesetting; Katie Lloyd-Jones, Manish Chandra, Jai Prakash Mishra, Rajesh Chhibber, Ashutosh Ranjan Bharti, Rajesh Kumar Mishra and Animesh Kumar Pathak for maps; Jo Mead for proofreading; and Joe Mee for picture research.

Photo Credits

Cover credits
Main front Trakai Castle, Lithuania © Robert Harding
Small front top picture stained glass, near Tallinn © Robert Harding
Small front lower picture Muhu Island Estonia © Robert Harding
Small front top picture houses, Latvia © Getty
Back lower picture Latvia © Corbis

Colour introduction
Stocky horse pulling hay cart © David Forman/Eye Ubiquitous
White church, Kihelkonna © J. Bousfield
Wooden sculpture of local mythical figure © INNA Agency Lithuania
Fishermen's cottage, Nida © J. Bousfield
Folk Festival, Tallinn, Estonia © Gregory Wrona
Song Festival, Tallinn, Estonia © T. Noorits/Trip
Stork's nest on a farm near Smiltynė, Latvia © Edward Parker/Hutchison
Fishing through ice, Liepāja, Latvia, © B. Turner/Trip
Bog forest in autumn, Endla, Estonia © T. Noorits/Trip
Folk dancers at Midsummer Festival, Liepāja, Latvia © V. Kolpakov/Trip
Old Cemetery in the south of Estonia © Tiit Veermae/All Over Press Baltic
Brown bear in water © T. Noorits/Trip
Lady selling marmalade, Rīga Central Market, Latvia © David Potter/Axiom
Meadow flowers, Latgale, Latvia © Niall Benvie/Corbis

Things not to miss

1. Trakai Castle, Lithuania © J. Bousfield
2. Pažaislis Monastery, Kaunas, Lithuania © J. Bousfield
3. Piusa sand caves © J. Bousfield
4. Water tourists in a raft on the river, Gauja National Park, Latvia © EPA
5. The beach and huge dunes at Nida, Lithuania © Nick Haslam/Hutchison
6. Skamba Skamba Kankliai folk festival, Vilnius, Lithuania © J. Bousfield
7. Walker in a bog forest in autumn © T. Noorits/Trip
8. Āraiši lake village © Normunds Mezins/AFI/EPA Photo
9. Statue of Lenin, Gruto parkas, Lithuania © Magali Delporte/Axiom
10. Cepelinai-eating competition © INNA Agency, Lithuania
11. Biķernieki Forest Holocaust Memorial, Latvia © J. Bousfield
12. Lakes, Harilaid Peninsula, Vilsandi National Park, Estonia © T. Noorits/Trip
13. Art Nouveau building, 106 Elizabetes, Rīga, Latvia © K. McLaren/Trip
14. Pedvāle open air museum, Latvia © J. Bousfield
15. Madonna of the Gate of Dawn, Vilnius © J. Bousfield
16. A Latvian woman wearing traditional clothes pulls a Yule log (bļuks) during the celebration of the national winter fest at the Latvian Open-Air Ethnographic Museum in Rīga © AFI/EPA Photo
17. St. Anne's Church, Vilnius, Lithuania © K. McLaren/Trip
18. Wild horses at Pape, Latvia © Aigars Jansons/AFI/EPA Photo
19. Old farmhouse, Open-Air Ethnographic Museum, Rīga, Latvia © M.Jenkin/Trip
20. Beer being sold from a restaurant, Tallinn, Estonia © Gregory Wrona
21. Town Hall Square, Tallinn, Estonia © Gregory Wrona
22. Bottles of Rīgas Melnais Balsams © Elmars Rudzitis/AFI/EPA Photo
23. Selling hand-picked mushrooms and berries in an open-air market, Tallinn, Estonia © J. Greenberg/Trip
24. Aglona Basilica, an important pilgrimage site, Latgale, Latvia © J. Sweeney/Trip
25. Eratic boulders, Käsmu Village, Lahemaa National Park © T. Noorits/Trip
26. Hill of Crosses, Siauliai, Lithuania © E. Simanor/Axiom
27. Exterior view of The Three Brothers, The Oldest Houses in Rīga, Latvia © James Davis Worldwide
28. The Beech, Pärnu, Estonia © K. Gillham/Robert Harding
29. Windmills and haystacks, Angla, Saaremaa Island, Estonia © Nick Haslam/Hutchison
30. Town Hall Square (Raekoja Plats) and university building, Tartu, Estonia © T. Noorits/Trip

Black and white photos

Hill of crosses, Siauliai, Lithuania © Brian Harris/Axiom
The neo-gothic cathedral, Vilnius, Lithuania © Gregory Wrona
Uzgavenes masks © INNA Agency, Lithuania
Straw sculpture depicting local myth © INNA Agency Lithuania
Gauja River valley, Sigulda, Latvia © John Dakers/Eye Ubiquitous
River Daugava, Rīga, Latvia © J. Bousfield

Mežotne Palace interior © J. Bousfield
Russian Orthodox Church, Liepāja, Latvia © B. Turner/Trip
Boulder-strewn coastline, Vilsandi Island, Estonia © T. Noorits/Trip
Old houses, Tallinn, Estonia © Ian Cook/Axiom
Kuressaare Castle © J. Bousfield
Setu women celebrate one of their national holidays © Tiit Veermae/All Over Press Baltic

Index

Map entries are in colour

V

Rough Guides travel...

UK & Ireland
Britain
Devon & Cornwall
Dublin
Edinburgh
England
Ireland
Lake District
London
London mini guide
London Restaurants
London & SE England,
  Walks in
Scotland
Scottish Highlands &
  Islands
Wales

Europe
Algarve
Amsterdam
Andalucía
Austria
Baltic States
Barcelona
Belgium & Luxembourg
Berlin
Brittany & Normandy
Bruges & Ghent
Brussels
Budapest
Bulgaria
Copenhagen
Corfu
Corsica
Costa Brava
Crete
Croatia
Cyprus
Czech & Slovak
  Republics
Dodecanese & East
  Aegean
Dordogne & The Lot
Europe
First-Time Europe
Florence
France

Germany
Greece
Greek Islands
Hungary
Ibiza & Formentera
Iceland
Ionian Islands
Italy
Languedoc & Roussillon
Lisbon
The Loire
Madeira
Madrid
Mallorca
Malta & Gozo
Menorca
Moscow
Netherlands
Norway
Paris
Paris Mini Guide
Poland
Portugal
Prague
Provence & the Côte
  d'Azur
Pyrenees
Romania
Rome
Sardinia
Scandinavia
Sicily
Slovenia
Spain
St Petersburg
Sweden
Switzerland
Tenerife & La Gomera
Turkey
Tuscany & Umbria
Venice & The Veneto
Vienna

Asia
Bali & Lombok
Bangkok
Beijing

Cambodia
China
First-Time Asia
Goa
Hong Kong & Macau
India
Indonesia
Japan
Laos
Malaysia, Singapore &
  Brunei
Nepal
Philippines
Singapore
South India
Southeast Asia
Thailand
Thailand Beaches &
  Islands
Tokyo
Vietnam

Australasia
Australia
Gay & Lesbian Australia
Melbourne
New Zealand
Sydney

North America
Alaska
Baltic States
Big Island of Hawaii
Boston
California
Canada
Chicago
Florida
Grand Canyon
Hawaii
Honolulu
Las Vegas
Los Angeles
Maui
Miami & the Florida
  Keys
Montréal

New England
New Orleans
New York City
New York City Mini
  Guide
New York Restaurants
Pacific Northwest
Rocky Mountains
San Francisco
San Francisco
  Restaurants
Seattle
Skiing & Snowboarding
  in North America
Southwest USA
Toronto
USA
Vancouver
Washington DC
Yosemite

Caribbean
& Latin America
Antigua & Barbuda
Argentina
Bahamas
Barbados
Belize
Bolivia
Brazil
Caribbean
Central America
Chile
Costa Rica
Cuba
Dominican Republic
Ecuador
First-Time Latin
  America
Guatemala
Jamaica
Maya World
Mexico
Peru
St Lucia
South America
Trinidad & Tobago

Rough Guides are available from good bookstores worldwide. New titles are published every month. Check www.roughguides.com for the latest news.

...music & reference

Africa & Middle East
Cape Town
Egypt
The Gambia
Jerusalem
Jordan
Kenya
Morocco
South Africa, Lesotho
  & Swaziland
Syria
Tanzania
Tunisia
West Africa
Zanzibar
Zimbabwe

Travel Theme guides
First-Time Around the
  World
First-Time Asia
First-Time Europe
First-Time Latin
  America
Gay & Lesbian
  Australia
Skiing & Snowboarding
  in North America
Travel Online
Travel Health
Walks in London & SE
  England
Women Travel

Restaurant guides
French Hotels &
  Restaurants
London
New York
San Francisco

Maps
Algarve
Amsterdam
Andalucia & Costa del Sol
Argentina
Athens

Australia
Baja California
Barcelona
Boston
Brittany
Brussels
Chicago
Crete
Croatia
Cuba
Cyprus
Czech Republic
Dominican Republic
Dublin
Egypt
Florence & Siena
Frankfurt
Greece
Guatemala & Belize
Iceland
Ireland
Lisbon
London
Los Angeles
Mexico
Miami & Key West
Morocco
New York City
New Zealand
Northern Spain
Paris
Portugal
Prague
Rome
San Francisco
Sicily
South Africa
Sri Lanka
Tenerife
Thailand
Toronto
Trinidad & Tobago
Tuscany
Venice
Washington DC
Yucatán Peninsula

Dictionary Phrasebooks
Czech
Dutch
Egyptian Arabic
European
French
German
Greek
Hindi & Urdu
Hungarian
Indonesian
Italian
Japanese
Mandarin Chinese
Mexican Spanish
Polish
Portuguese
Russian
Spanish
Swahili
Thai
Turkish
Vietnamese

Music Guides
The Beatles
Cult Pop
Classical Music
Country Music
Cuban Music
Drum'n'bass
Elvis
House
Irish Music
Jazz
Music USA
Opera
Reggae
Rock
Techno
World Music (2 vols)

100 Essential CDs series
Country
Latin

Opera
Rock
Soul
World Music

History Guides
China
Egypt
England
France
Greece
India
Ireland
Islam
Italy
Spain
USA

Reference Guides
Books for Teenagers
Children's Books, 0–5
Children's Books, 5–11
Cult Football
Cult Movies
Cult TV
Digital Stuff
Formula 1
The Internet
Internet Radio
James Bond
Lord of the Rings
Man Utd
Personal Computers
Pregnancy & Birth
Shopping Online
Travel Health
Travel Online
Unexplained
  Phenomena
The Universe
Videogaming
Weather
Website Directory

Also! More than 120 Rough Guide music CDs are available from all good book and record stores. Listen in at www.worldmusic.net

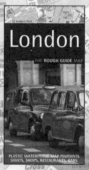

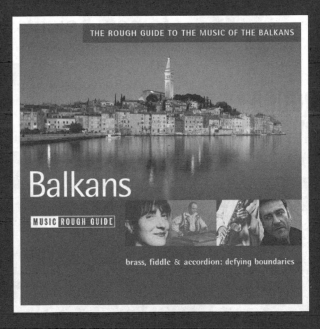

Baltic Holidays

Since starting out as Lithuanianholidays.com in 2000, we have branched out to become Baltic Holidays, a specialist tour operator to the Baltic States of Lithuania, Latvia & Estonia.

Specialists in:
- City breaks to Vilnius, Riga & Tallinn
- Baltic tours and country tours
- Tailor-made travel throughout the Baltics
- Family holidays
- City & Spa breaks
- City & Coast breaks
- Family research

Why use us ..?
- We are the only specialist UK travel company to deal solely with the Baltic States
- We visit Lithuania, Latvia & Estonia regularly
- Regular updates with our hotels and suppliers
- Up to date information on the best places to go
- We are fully ATOL bonded, ABTA bonded and members of AITO.

"Our travel through the Baltic States with your company went without a hitch and your wealth of local knowledge ensured we saw most of what there was to see and gain a rewarding insight to these wonderful countries."

Mr & Mrs South, tailor-made Baltic trip, May 03

Go with the leaders not the followers. You won't be disappointed.

Contact details:

Baltic Holidays
40 Princess Street
Manchester
M1 6DE

Tel: 0870 757 9233
Fax: 0870 120 2973
www.balticholidays.com
Email: info@balticholidays.com